THE ARAKAN OPERATIONS
1942 - 1945

Lieut-Colonel N. N. Madan

Published by

The Naval & Military Press Ltd
Unit 5 Riverside, Brambleside
Bellbrook Industrial Estate
Uckfield, East Sussex
TN22 1QQ England

Tel: +44 (0)1825 749494

www.naval-military-press.com
www.nmarchive.com

In reprinting in facsimile from the original, any imperfections are inevitably reproduced and the quality may fall short of modern type and cartographic standards.

OFFICIAL HISTORY OF THE INDIAN ARMED FORCES
IN THE SECOND WORLD WAR
1939-45

Campaigns in the Eastern Theatre

THE ARAKAN OPERATIONS
1942-45

The Naval & Military Press Ltd

TO ALL WHO SERVED

ADVISORY COMMITTEE

Chairman
SECRETARY, MINISTRY OF DEFENCE, INDIA

Members
Dr Tara Chand
Mr K. Zachariah
Dr S. N. Sen
Prof K. A. Nilakanta Sastri
Prof Mohammad Habib
Dr R. C. Majumdar
Lieut.-Gen. Sir Dudley Russell
Lieutenant-General K. S. Thimayya
Major-General S. P. P. Thorat
Military Adviser to the High Commissioner for Pakistan in India

Secretary
Dr Bisheshwar Prasad

CAMPAIGNS IN THE EASTERN THEATRE

CAMPAIGNS IN SOUTH-EAST ASIA 1941-42:
    (i) Hong Kong Campaign
    (ii) Sarawak and Dutch West Borneo
    (iii) Campaign in Malaya

THE RETREAT FROM BURMA 1941-42

ARAKAN OPERATIONS 1942-45

RECONQUEST OF BURMA 1942-45

POST-WAR OCCUPATION FORCES:
    Japan and South-East Asia

PREFACE

Wars have not been without their influence on the political, economic and social development of the human community. Hence it is not surprising that they have engaged the attention of the historians, who have examined the forces which have prompted them and reviewed the course of operations, the trends of strategy and tactics and the reactions on the defence organisation of states. The two World Wars of the present century have merited unprecedented attention which has led to the preparation and production of numerous accounts, some sponsored by governments, of the part played by the participating nations. The Government of India had also decided, long before the close of the Second World War, to produce a history of the operations in which Indian armed forces had participated. Consequently, an organisation was set up with the Chief of the General Staff for collecting and collating records. Beginning with one officer, this cell had, before the conclusion of the war, expanded into the War Department Historical Section. Subsequent to the partition of India, it was agreed upon by the Dominions of India and Pakistan that the project of recording the glorious achievements of the Indian armed forces in the Second World War should continue as a joint venture of the two states; that this combined organisation should function under a civilian historian and that it should be named the Combined Inter-Services Historical Section, India and Pakistan. This joint body was chartered to produce the official history of the part played by the pre-partition India and its armed forces in the World War of 1939-1945. The narratives were to deal with military operations and organisational activities, and were to provide a truthful, analysed record of the operations carried out by our armed forces, so as to be an authoritative reference work for the future leaders, a field of study and guidance for the military student, and a written monument to the achievements of the forces who served.

Keeping in view the fundamental objects, a history in about twenty volumes has been planned; it is divided into three series, viz. the campaigns in the theatre east of India, the campaigns in the theatre west of India, and the activities pertaining to organisation and administration for the conduct of war. The campaign volumes pre-eminently narrate the part played by the Indian armed forces in Africa, the Middle East, Burma, South-east Asia, Greece and Italy, but in doing so the achievements of the forces of the Allied nations fighting alongside them have been sufficiently highlighted as the operations have been studied as a whole in their geographical setting. The volumes relating to the campaigns in the eastern theatre narrate the story of the war in South-east Asia beginning from the Japanese conquest of Hong Kong, Malaya, Borneo and Burma to the recovery of these lands by the Allied nations. Two volumes in this series describe the reverses in South-east Asia and Burma, while the remaining volumes narrate the story of the reconquest of Burma including Arakan. Another volume relates to the activities of the Occupation Forces in Japan. The other series dealing with the campaigns in the western theatre covers the operations in North and East Africa, the Middle East, Greece and Italy. The volumes in the third series relate to the policy and planning of defence of India, expansion of India's armed forces and the organisation for war control, the development of technical services and supply organisation, and the war economy. There will be a separate history of the two infant services, the Royal Indian Navy and the Royal Indian Air Force, though all operations have been studied from the inter-service aspect.

India's rôle in the war was one of subordinate co-operation, for she was not the architect of policy either in determining the influences which heralded the war or in steering its course. Her line of action was laid down by His Majesty's Government in the United Kingdom, and later, with the integration of Allied command, higher strategy was planned by the Combined Chiefs of Staffs who disposed the available supplies and war equipment among the various theatres of war. In these narratives, therefore, 'higher direction' or 'Grand Strategy' finds no place as this was the concern of Washington or London. The Government of India, under the direction of Whitehall, was however responsible for devising measures for the territorial defence, and such plans as were then formulated have been discussed in one volume. Yet, the narratives of campaigns have necessarily to be prefaced by an analysis of the general strategic plan as also the strategic appreciations and plans of the local authorities who regulated the course of the campaigns. But the treatment of strategic problems has seldom exceeded the level of the theatre or army commander, and it is from his point of view generally that this history has been written. For the spheres beyond, the reader will have inevitably to depend on the volumes on 'Grand Strategy' planned by the United Kingdom Cabinet Historical Section or those in Washington.

We have been allowed full access to the official records of the Government of India, and the Historical Section has almost a complete set of War Diaries and despatches and reports of the commanders in the field. But, unfortunately, a large mass of high level records was destroyed at the time of transfer of power to the two Dominions, which has handicapped us in finding many important documents relating to policy and decisions. We were unable to make good this deficiency by drawing upon the resources of Whitehall, as the agreement with the War Office precluded reference to any papers beyond the army level. Within these limitations, however, we were able to derive considerable information from the War Office, the Admiralty, and the Air Ministry, where our Liaison Officers worked for some years, as well as from the Cabinet Historical Section. Their co-operation, on a reciprocal basis, has been of considerable benefit in enriching our sources of knowledge. We have also received documents from the archives of Canada, Australia and New Zealand under arrangements for mutual information on subjects of common interest. The exchange of drafts of narratives between the Commonwealth countries has been of great advantage in reducing points of controversy and eliminating wide divergences as to fact. Yet, on the whole, this history is based on the records in our possession of which free and full use has been made.

History, at best, is a narrative; to present an accurate narrative of events has been our endeavour. Yet, it is not a mere chronicle of events, for we have analysed the factors and influences which have produced them and thereby interpreted facts in their correct perspective. Our viewpoint has been one of objectivity, but in the sifting of material subjectivity cannot altogether be eliminated; in relating the exploits of our own troops we may have been at times led to emphasise their glorious achievements. But a panegyric is not our object and we have not hesitated to record reverses or recount inconvenient situations in which the troops were placed. However, as a civilian organisation, we have refrained from speculating on what a commander in a particular position should have done or passing judgement on his appreciation of the situation. We have marshalled facts to reconstruct the situations as we view them, and lessons as emerging from them have been deduced.

The present volume is the second to be published in the series of Campaigns in the Eastern Theatre, and describes the operations in the coastal belt of Arakan in Burma, from the close of 1942 to the end of the war against Japan. After the first reverses in Burma and the retreat of the Indian forces from there, which has been described in an earlier volume, the Indian military authorities were hard put to devising schemes for stemming the tide of Japanese advance against India and retrieving the situation in Burma. At that stage two sectors were selected for the operations of the Indian Army, Arakan and the Chindwin area. For some time little progress was made in the northern sector, and Arakan was the only theatre where, in spite of the general weakness of the Indian armed strength, strenuous endeavours were made not only to contain the Japanese might, but also to push it back and acquire a foothold on the soil of Burma for future operations. An important objective of the fighting in Arakan was the island of Akyab, which was to act as a base for attack on Lower Burma. In the earlier campaigns, however, Akyab remained a distant goal and the operations were mainly defensive in character so as to prevent the Japanese forces from launching an invasion against India in the Chittagong region. It was only after the establishment of the South-East Asia Command, that a comprehensive plan for the capture of Burma was adopted, and the mounting support in men and equipment made a dual move, both in Arakan and Upper Burma, possible. The 1944 winter operations in Arakan were aimed at the capture of its coastline for bases to supply the Fourteenth Army's advance into Central Burma. The Arakan campaigns were thus largely subsidiary to the main operations in Upper and Central Burma. As such a separate treatment of these campaigns requires explanation. It is true that the Arakan operations were subsidiary in nature but they formed a separate phase in the progress of war in Burma and have a peculiar unity about them. Hence it would not be proper to include them in a general account of the campaigns in Upper and Central Burma, which form the subject matter of another volume.

In these campaigns, Indian, British and African troops fought side by side or in different but contiguous sectors. In the later stages the operations were largely combined in which the units of the Royal Navy, Royal Indian Navy, Royal Air Force and the Royal Indian Air Force co-operated with the units of the Indian and British Army to capture the island bases or bottle up the Japanese forces on the coastline. The story, therefore, has been planned to present the strategical picture as a whole, and the fighting in different zones has been brought into full review in its inter-service aspect. The operations of the African divisions have been fully treated as their part was an important one. But, in the main, it is a record of the fighting of the Indian divisions who struggled to stem the tide of Japanese advance in the early stages, and successfully rolled it back in the later phases of the campaigns. The account is largely from the standpoint of the division or corps, but in the narrative of individual engagements, the actions of battalions, and sometimes even companies, have received fuller treatment. Acts of gallantry have been also mentioned. The story, however, aims at an analysis of the strategy employed, and tactics displayed, in a region interspersed with rivers, creeks, hills and forest.

This narrative is based largely on the War Diaries, reports and despatches of the commanders and the records of the Government of India which have been, where necessary, mentioned in the footnotes. The nature of basic material has been indicated in the bibliographical note at the end. Some of the important documents have also been given in the appendices, where also will be found location statements of the forces and the orders of battle on several dates. Maps and sketches have been interspersed in the text to illustrate the strategy of the campaign, or the tactics in a particular engagement. The spelling of place-names conforms generally to the system approved at the informal conference of British and American experts in October 1947, a report of which was communicated to us. In the maps conventional symbols have been used to represent the Allied and Axis troops, though coloured maps have been kept to a minimum as a measure of economy. In the text, the Japanese units have been mentioned in italics to distinguish them from the Indian, British or Chinese forces. We have also eschewed the use of the word 'enemy' to indicate the Japanese. Military abbreviations have, as far as practicable, been avoided. Nonetheless, some of these have been used and a glossary has been included.

Initially, the material for this narrative was collated by Lt.-Col. W. E. Teal, Major P. S. Mehta, and Mr Satpal Singh. But the present narrative is mainly the work of Lt.-Col. N. N. Madan, M.A., who was posted to the Historical Section as one of the Editors. To these officers I must express my indebtedness. I am also grateful to Mr P. N. Khera for revising the proofs and assisting me in editing the volume. I must also acknowledge the assistance rendered by Mr T. D. Sharma, the Cartographer, in preparing the maps.

The narrative has been shown to some of the commanding officers who were responsible for the campaigns in Arakan. I am particularly greatful to Lt.-General Sir Philip Christison, Maj.-General C. E. N. Lomax and Maj.-General G. M. Wood, Lt.-General K. S. Thimayya and Maj.-General S. P. P. Thorat, for their comments which have been extremely helpful in clearing many obscure points.

The Government of India have set up an Advisory Committee consisting of some leading historians and senior Service officers, under the chairmanship of the Defence Secretary, for professional guidance and to scrutinise the narratives and authorise their publication. There is a representative of the Pakistan Government on it, which Government has also appointed a committee of its own to examine the narratives before they are authorised for publication. The members of the Advisory Committee have given me the benefit of their experience and judgement in planning the history and reading the draft of the volume. To them I am indebted for their advice which has greatly compensated for the handicaps of a civilian editor responsible for the production of military history. But, for statement of facts and expression of views, I accept full responsibility.

In conclusion, I must acknowledge the encouragement and support which I have received from the Ministries of Defence of India and Pakistan, without whose constant guidance and co-operation this project would not have been possible. I am specially grateful to Mr H. M. Patel and Mr M. K. Vellodi, Secretaries, and Mr B. B. Ghosh, Joint Secretary, Ministry of Defence, India, for their interest in the work and constant support which they have given to the Historical Section.

BISHESHWAR PRASAD

June, 1954.

CONTENTS

		Page
INTRODUCTION		xxi

CHAPTER

I.	THE LAND AND ITS PEOPLE	1
II.	PLANNING FOR THE OFFENSIVE	11
III.	THE START OF THE OFFENSIVE	23
IV.	THE JAPANESE COUNTER MEASURES	51
V.	THE JAPANESE ADVANCE NORTHWARDS	56
VI.	THE THIRD PHASE	65
VII.	THE FOURTH PHASE	72
VIII.	THE MONSOON OPERATIONS—1943	89
IX.	PLANS FOR THE COLD WEATHER OFFENSIVE	98
X.	THE JAPANESE COUNTER-OFFENSIVE	110
XI.	THE ALLIES RESUME THE OFFENSIVE	138
XII.	THE MONSOON PERIOD—1944	164
XIII.	ALLIED PLANNING FOR THE POST-MONSOON OPERATIONS—1944	179
XIV.	OPERATION 'ROMULUS'	195
XV.	THE ADVANCE BEGINS	203
XVI.	OPERATION 'TALON'	213
XVII.	BLOCKADE OPERATIONS	222
XVIII.	THE MYEBON LANDING	230
XIX.	THE KANGAW BATTLE	243
XX.	THE INVASION OF RAMREE ISLAND	263
XXI.	THE FINAL PHASES IN ARAKAN	282
APPENDICES		308
BIBLIOGRAPHY		363
INDEX		367

LIST OF MAPS

		Page
1.	Topography of Arakan	7
2.	Rainfall in Burma. Mid-May to mid-October	9
3.	Japanese dispositions facing 47 Ind Inf Bde. 17 January, 1943	37
4.	Dispositions of forward troops of 55 Ind Inf Bde and Japanese troops. 31 January, 1943	42
5.	Japanese defences in Akyab Island. January, 1943	49
6.	Arakan. Situation first week in November, 1943	97
7.	Sketch of 7 Ind Div Admin Box after arrival of 89 Ind Inf Bde. February, 1944	127
8.	Arakan. Situation third week in February, 1944	136
9.	Arakan. Situation third week in June, 1944	163
10.	Myebon Peninsula	233
11.	Myebon Operations. January, 1945	239
12.	Kangaw area	244

		Facing Page
13.	General Map of Burma	1
14.	123 Ind Inf Bde attack—North of Rathedaung. 3 February, 1943	43
15.	Japanese dispositions in Burma in December, 1942 and movement of 55 Div to Arakan	51
16.	Japanese dispositions—end of Phase 1 and development of Phase 2. February, 1943	53
17.	Japanese dispositions—end of Phase 2 and development in Phase 3. March, 1943	57
18.	Japanese dispositions—end of Phase 3 and development in Phase 4. March-May, 1943	71
19.	Japanese counter-offensive. February, 1944	119
20.	Battle for Hill 551	151
21.	Myebon and adjacent area	231
22.	Kangaw Blockade	245
23.	Invasion of Ramree Island. January-March, 1945	263
24.	Capture of Akyab-Myebon-Kangaw-Myohaung-Ruywa and operations towards AN. January-March, 1945	283
25.	Arakan	372

LIST OF ILLUSTRATIONS

Admiral the Lord Louis Mountbatten of Burma	*Facing page*	10
General Sir George J. Giffard	,, ,,	10
General Sir Archibald P. Wavell	*Following page*	10
General Sir Claude J. E. Auchinleck	,, ,,	10
Lieutenant-General Sir Philip Christison	,, ,,	10
Lieutenant-General N. M. S. Irwin	,, ,,	10
Major-General H. R. Briggs	*Facing page*	11
Major-General Sir Frank Messervy	,, ,,	11
Major-General C. E. N. Lomax	,, ,,	88
Major-General G. C. Evans	,, ,,	88
Major-General D. F. W. Warren	*Following page*	88
Major-General E. C. R. Mansergh	,, ,,	88
Major-General H. M. Chambers	,, ,,	88
Major-General W. L. Lloyd	,, ,,	88
Major-General F. W. Festing	*Facing page*	89
Major-General H. L. Davies	,, ,,	89
A part of Ngakyedauk Pass	,, ,,	108
Road-sign on the Ngakyedauk Pass	*Following page*	108
Major-General H. R. Briggs arriving in the forward area	,, ,,	108
Tanks of the 5th Indian Division moving into the battle	,, ,,	108
Crossing a chaung at full speed—5th Indian carrier charges into action	,, ,,	108
Tank plays havoc with the camouflaged Japanese on Hill 1070 (Ngakyedauk Pass)	*Facing page*	109
Brigadier R. A. Hutton, Lieut.-Colonels K. S. Thimayya, S. P. P. Thorat and L. P. Sen	,, ,,	160
Rajputs rest by a cool stream after capturing Hill 551	*Following page*	160
Shell-blasted summit of Hill 551	,, ,,	160
Rajputs of the 26th Indian Division hew a path from the burnt hill-side	*Facing page*	161
Troops of the 25th Indian Division wading to the beach at Akyab	,, ,,	220
The ruins of Akyab after the Japanese deserted it	*Following page*	220
Havildar Gaje Ghale, V.C.	,, ,,	220
Havildar Prakash Singh, V.C.	,, ,,	220

Naik Nand Singh, V. C.	*Following page*	220
Jemadar Abdul Hafiz, V.C.	,, ,,	220
Jemadar (Actg Subedar) Ram Sarup Singh, V.C.	*Facing page*	221
Sepoy Bhandari Ram, V.C.	,, ,,	221
Havildar Umrao Singh, V.C.	,, ,,	221
Rifleman Bhanbhagta Gurung V.C.	,, ,,	221
Hill 170 held by the 25th Indian Division	,, ,,	262
Garhwali soldier by the side of a Japanese dummy tank made of bamboo (Ruywa)	,, ,,	306
Wire mesh and cocoanut matting used as road over mangrove swamp	,, ,,	307

Abbreviations

A.A.	Anti-aircraft.
AFVs.	Armoured Fighting Vehicles.
ALFSEA	Allied Land Forces South-East Asia.
ASSU	Air Support Signal Unit.
A.T.	Animal Transport.
A.W.D.	Advanced Workshop Detachment.
C.P.	Command Post.
C.R.A.	Commanding Royal Artillery.
D.M.I.	Director of Military Intelligence.
F.D.L.	Foremost Defended Locality.
F.F.R.	Frontier Force Rifles.
F.M.A.	Forward Maintenance Area.
F.O.O.	Forward Observation Officer.
F.S.D.	Field Supply Depot.
F.U.Ps.	Forming Up Places.
G.O.C.	General Officer Commanding.
G.P.T. Company.	General Purpose Transport Company.
G.R.	Gurkha Rifles.
G.S.O.	General Staff Officer.
H.Q.	Headquarters.
I.A.C.	Indian Armoured Corps.
I.C.P.	Inland Coastal Patrol.
I.W.T.	Inland Water Transport.
J.P.S.	Joint Planning Staff.
K.O.S.B.	King's Own Scottish Borderers.
K.A.R.	King's African Rifles.
L.A.D.	Light Aid Detachment.
L.C.A.	Landing Craft Assault.
L.C.M.	Landing Craft Mechanized.
L.C.S.	Landing Craft Support.
M.G.	Machine Gun.
M.M.G.	Medium Machine Gun.
M.L.I.	Mahratta Light Infantry.
M.T.	Mechanical Transport.
N.O.I.C.	Naval Officer-in-Charge.
O.C.	Officer Commanding.
O.P.	Observation Post.
OXF BUCKS	Oxfordshire and Buckinghamshire Light Infantry.
Q.F.	Quick Firing.
R.A.	Royal Artillery.
R.A.C.	Royal Armoured Corps.
R.A.F.	Royal Air Force.
R.A.M.O.	Rear Airfield Maintenance Organisation.
R.A.N.	Royal Australian Navy.
R.I.A.	Royal Indian Artillery.
R.I.N.	Royal Indian Navy.
R.N.	Royal Navy.
S.E.A.C.	South-East Asia Command.

Tac. R.	Tactical Reconnaissance.
W.A.	West African.
W/T	Wireless Telegraphy.
Y & L	York & Lancaster Regiment.

INTRODUCTION

The war had entered the fourth year when the initiative was wrested from the Axis Powers and the process had started by which eventually their defeat became possible. It was in the autumn of 1942 that the German armour had met with a setback in Russia, and insurgent movements had begun in the Balkan lands groaning under the heel of Nazism. By that time, the Italian empire in eastern Africa was shattered and her army as a fighting machine had been considerably disorganised. In the plains of Libya and Cyrennaica was being fought the grim battle between Field Marshal Rommel's forces and the British Eighth Army for the possession of North Africa, an important strategic base for the invasion of Europe. To Great Britain the importance of Egypt and the Libya desert was great for once they were lost to Hitler, the prospect of boring a hole into the Nazi fortress of Europe would be gone, and Germany might find an easy route to strike at Russia through Armenia and Georgia. The Caucasus, the largest source of Russian oil supply would then have become a hostile possession, and the mounting Russian resistance to Nazi aggression might have collapsed. But the repulse of Rommel's thrust so close to Alexandria had turned the tide and, henceforth, British advance westward developed into a war of attrition against the Afrika Korps, and the vision of controlling the Mediterranean and conquering Italy opened out before the United Nations. The war in the west was entering a new phase in which the United States was able to hurl her vast resources in men and material.

In the east also, the autumn of 1942 had seen the end of one cycle and the beginning of another. Impelled by economic considerations and desire for a prompt termination of the Chinese 'incident', Japan had been led earlier into the adventure of establishing the great 'Co-Prosperity Sphere' while the British Empire was involved in a deadly struggle with the Axis Powers. In this process the Japanese Government invoked the hostility of the United States whose entry in the war was facilitated by the attack on Pearl Harbour, evidently a short-sighted action. The crippling of the American Pacific Fleet for the time being led to its elimination; and the interval was employed by the Japanese war-lords to conquer Hong Kong, Malaya, Burma, Borneo, Java, Philippines, Carolines, Gilbert and Marshall Islands, Solomon Islands, Bismark Archipelago and New Britain. This sweeping victory in the south-west Pacific brought danger nearer to Australia whose line of approach to the United States was threatened. The only gap in the wide Japanese 'protective screen' in the South Pacific was the Papuan peninsula of New Guinea, wherein the seizure of Port Moresby would have completely cut the "line of supply from Hawaii and Panama to Australia". But at this point "the tide of victory suddenly began to ebb", for the United States, recovering slowly from the stunning blow of Pearl Harbour, started a series of raids with the object of securing "the island stepping-stones between Hawaii and Australia". Beginning with the raids on Marshall and Gilbert Islands the first offensive action was taken against Guadalcanal in the Solomon group of islands in the Coral Sea. The first set-back which Japan faced, however, was when her forces failed to exploit the Midway Island, the occupation of which would have led to the domination of the Central Pacific and the complete isolation of Australia. The battle was momentous as it greatly weakened the naval air arm of Japan and demonstrated the air-superiority of the United States, whose pace in constructing aircraft was not reached by Japan. The balance of naval power in the Pacific had definitely shifted to the United States, and the Japanese predominance in the South Pacific was in danger of crumbling.

By the end of 1942, in the west, the Battle of Britain was practically over and her production was increasing; the campaign for the control of the Mediterranean and the North African route to the Middle East had turned against Germany and Italy; the attempt to close the Red Sea and Indian Ocean route by expanding the Italian empire in East Africa had been frustrated; and the Axis diplomacy in the Middle East, in Iraq, Iran and Syria, had been defeated. Axis strategy to penetrate the Persian Gulf region, for snapping the fast mounting aid to Russia and threatening the western defences of India, had been successfully pierced. The British hold on Iraq and Syria had been fortified, Turkey had succeeded in maintaining her benevolent neutrality, Anglo-Russian control was imposed over Iran and the overland route from India to Egypt had been made secure. Russia was assured of growing supplies under Lease-Lend and her resistance to German attack was fast strengthening. The United States had not only entered the war but had become the grand arsenal for equipping the rapidly expanding armies of her allies. The supreme value of air power had been fully demonstrated by the initial successes of the Axis Powers. The United States and the United Kingdom had converted their industrial potential to produce more and more aircraft which were being sent to Russia, the Middle East, China and India to acquire air superiority. The United States was also assembling forces and equipment in Great Britain for mounting an offensive in Western Europe. The tempo of Allied war effort was thus increasing and the combination of the United States, United Kingdom and Soviet Russia, with all their vast resources, was recouping its strength to roll back the Axis aggression. The tide of reverses, it appeared, had receded and the time had come to plan offensive operations to recover the lost ground both in the west and the east.

In the east, Japan had gained phenomenal success in the first half of 1942 when British dominion over Malaya and Burma had been eliminated. From Burma the Indo-British forces had managed to withdraw, though not without considerable loss, to India, at the beginning of the monsoon. The whole of Burma, including the Arakan coastal area, was in Japanese occupation. The Japanese navy was supreme in the Bay of Bengal and the islands of Andamans and Nicobars had been turned into an important naval base. The loss of these eastern bastions of India's defence had heightened the danger of invasion to the Indian mainland, though immediately owing to the onset of the monsoon and their long tenuous line of communication, the Japanese were not in a position to cross the Indian frontier. There was no doubt that they intended to keep on to Burma, which was a valuable post in the perimeter of their defensive screen and an important jumping-off ground for any future plans against India. But, above all, their hold over Burma enabled them to strangle China as she could not get supplies from the United States easily, and without them her resistance would peter out. The only alternative was the air-lift which had to be flown across the Himalayas, which by its very nature was not considerable. The supreme need of supplying China demanded that Burma should be reconquered by the Allies. This was an important consideration with the United States, but for the British to this motive were also added the objects of recovering their Imperial possession and of forcing back the focus of danger from India. Hence, during the monsoon months of 1942, when, on the one hand, plans for the defence of eastern India and its coast line were being hammered out, planning had also started for the reconquest of Burma.

The problem was not an easy one. There was no British force left on the Burmese soil and there was little possibility of any resistance movement developing there which might collaborate with the British to stage their come-back. In India alone, therefore, could an offensive operation be organised, but there were insuperable difficulties in mounting it successfully at that stage. The Indian Army had been expanded and further programmes of expansion were laid out. But till 1942, such expansion had been conditioned by the overseas demands, particularly of the Middle East, and the North-West Frontier defence. An important limiting factor was the supply of equipment from the United Kingdom, whose resources were then at their lowest ebb. India was also at the bottom in the list of priorities. The political movement in the country had also considerably affected the full utilisation of her resources to fight the Japanese, and a settlement which might enthuse the people of India and evoke their zealous co-operation in war-effort was not in sight. Therefore, despite the sympathy for China and unequivocal repudiation of all forms of totalitarianism by the Indian political leaders, the India Command was in no position to organise an all-out effort to drive back the Japanese forces and open the Burma Road. Enormous resources were required for this purpose. The opening of the supply route to China was possible either when Rangoon and the entire Irrawaddy Valley had been cleared of the Japanese, or by constructing a diversionary road from eastern India to connect with the Burma Road in China. The first demanded the complete reoccupation of Burma and would necessitate not only an overland advance across the Assam-Burma border, where communications did not exist, but also amphibious operations on the southern coast to recapture Rangoon and from the base there to clear up the Irrawaddy Valley. Not till 1944 were the requisite land, air and naval forces assembled to execute this stupendous task. In 1942, so soon after the disastrous defeats in Burma and Malaya, and at a time when priority was given to the defeat of Germany by the Combined Chiefs of Staff, all that was feasible was to utilise the available resources in India for launching limited offensive operations to rehabilitate the morale and hold the Japanese forces in Burma to prevent their being used in other theatres.

The operations in Arakan had their origin at this moment of the progress of war. General Wavell had planned a limited offensive for the dry season of 1942-43, into Upper Burma directed towards the line Kalewa-Katha-Myitkyina and the River Irrawaddy, if possible. At the same time he "instructed the Eastern Army to push troops south from Chittagong towards the Burma border, and to improve communications with a view to an advance into Arakan later on". But his main objective in the south was Akyab which was to be recaptured by a sea-borne expedition. However, the means for an amphibious operation were lacking, and the Commander-in-Chief was by force of circumstances driven to undertake a land "advance from Chittagong down the Arakan coast to secure the Mayu Peninsula, whence an attack could be launched from short range"[1]. The attack on Akyab was to be a phase of the contemplated sea-borne expedition against Lower Burma as a complement to the land-thrust into Upper Burma. The operations in Arakan by themselves had only a limited objective, the capture of the airfields on Akyab island, and had been launched only when the sea-borne expedition proved to be impracticable. General Wavell, in his own words, "took the risk, sooner than keep my troops standing idle, of trying to reach Akyab by an overland

---

[1] Wavell's Despatch, March to December 1942, para 31.

advance"[2]. And this operation was to synchronise with the advance of the Chinese Armies from Yunnan and the IV Indian Corps from Assam into Upper Burma, which did not materialise. Initially, the object was a limited one and at no stage the Arakan operations had any character other than being of a diversionary nature or as auxiliary to the main operations proceeding southward from Upper Burma against Rangoon, which was the ultimate objective. At various stages, amphibious operations were planned for landings on the southern coast of Burma, for which Akyab and the Andamans were the necessary bases. And as air power was an essential element of victory, the occupation of the Arakan coast line, Akyab and Ramree islands and the construction or utilisation of airfields there, were important to render air-support to the land forces advancing south down the Irrawaddy Valley or to the amphibious expeditions probing into the accessible beaches.

In planning the defeat of Japan it was fully realised that her surrender would be possible not by beating her on the periphery but by invading the homeland and there destroying the will to fight. The reconquest of the landmass bordering the south-west Pacific or the step by step occupation of strategic islands in the South or Central Pacific, had their value in giving near air and naval bases for striking on the mainland of Japan. At the same time, the importance of a direct assault on the central parts of the wide perimeter which would open the sea-route and enable the naval and air forces to operate from a closer radius was not ignored. Operation 'Culvereen' was discussed, having as its objectives the capture of Northern Sumatra by amphibious operations. The reoccupation of the south-west Pacific simultaneously with the conquest of islands in the Central or Southern Pacific, and the reentry into the Philippines had the merit of taking the war to the very core of the Japanese empire. Thereby, the flanks of their extended periphery in Burma and Malaya would have fallen and China might have become a base for the strategic bombing of Japan. But for an amphibious operation of that magnitude, resources were not then available. Hence the strategy of the British High Command was necessarily limited to the reoccupation of Burma and then Malaya by land advance and limited amphibious operations, if practicable.

Strategy in Burma remained in its essentials constant and, depending on the practicability of means, was continuously in operation. There were three well-defined sectors, the northern from the Chinese border down the Hukawng Valley to the Myitkyina-Mogaung area, the central across the Chindwin to the Irrawaddy and the third, the coastal area of Arakan down to the Delta. The northern front was the responsibility of the Chinese forces while the

---

[2] Wavell's Despatch, January to June 1943, para 15.

other two were the commitments of the India Command or the South East Asia Command, established later. The inter-dependence of these operations has been very clearly emphasised by Lord Louis Mountbatten, thus[3] "Northern Burma could not be permanently secured unless Burma was occupied as far down as Rangoon; and this in turn could not be done without a comprehensive system of air supply to the troops engaged in the overland advance; while a sea-borne and air-borne assault from the south would greatly help the advance from the north—and indeed, at the time seemed an essential part of the campaign". In all plannings this factor was taken into account, and while greater importance was attached to the operations in the central sector, every endeavour was made to synchronise these with operations both in the north and south as obviously the lack of such synchronisation would adversely affect the chances of their success. Initially when in 1942 an advance down the Arakan coast was planned, it was conceived in conjunction with the move from Assam towards the Chindwin. It did not materialise and failed to divert the weight of Japanese counter offensive from the 14th Indian Division whose offensive therefore ended in a fiasco. It was dangerous to lose sight of this principle. Later operations were therefore planned to distract the attention and resources of the Japanese and by dividing them to weaken their capacity to resist the invading forces from India. The Arakan operations in 1944 and 1945 were aimed at containing the Japanese troops in the coastal regions and preventing their concentration against the advance of the Fourteenth Army. Later successes in Arakan also were possible because of the simultaneous pressure in three directions.

December 1942 saw the first operation in Arakan begun by the 14th Indian Division, whose objective after capturing the strategic Donbaik-Buthidaung area was to force its way down to Akyab. This overland offensive action proved to be abortive as the Indian troops failed to pierce the Japanese defensive positions. They were ultimately forced back to their starting points by a skilful Japanese counter-attack which disorganised the Indian lines of communication. This set-back demonstrated the grievous weakness in training for jungle warfare against an adversary who had gained by experience a mastery over the jungle and whose movements were not governed by an elaborate supply line. The monsoon months were, therefore, employed by the Indian forces in an intensive training for jungle warfare. Meanwhile, Burma and South-East Asia were separated from the operational responsibility of the India Command, and a new South-East Asia Command was established to harness the growing manpower in India and the fast producing equipment in the United States and the United Kingdom, to

---

[3] Mountbatten's Despatch, para 33,

clear Burma and Malaya of the Japanese and to render increasing aid to China.

The earlier campaigns in Arakan had a defensive aspect, for, though at every stage the capture of Akyab was an important object, the operations were directed mainly to the holding of the Maungdaw-Buthidaung line so as to prevent the Japanese forces from launching an invasion into the Chittagong area. And as long as an advance in the central sector had not fully developed, the operations in Arakan could not attain a definite strategic direction. The second stage began early in 1944 when the XV Indian Corps initiated the drive down the Mayu peninsula. It was part of a comprehensive plan for the conquest of Burma by the Fourteenth Army from the Assam frontier. These operations in the winter of 1944 were essentially aimed at speedily capturing the Arakan coastline and its bases to enable the Fourteenth Army's advance to be supplied from these areas.

The Japanese Imperial General Headquarters had contemplated an invasion of India which "was to be achieved by splitting open the British front, sealing off the eastern from the western half, and cutting the lines of communication of both. Each sector was then to be destroyed separately, and the roads through Chittagong and Dimapur laid open to the Japanese Army".[4] The operation was planned in two phases, the first in Arakan from where the port of Chittagong was to be seized and the reserves from the central sector were to be drawn off and kept fully committed in Arakan. This invasion came about at a time when the South-East Asia Command had itself planned a limited offensive to contain the major part of the Japanese forces and to bring them to battle wherever possible with advantage. Lord Mountbatten therefore felt happy that "the Japanese High Command played into our hands, at this point, by staging an all-out offensive. This had the double advantage of drawing the enemy forces in the direction we wished, at an earlier stage than an advance by IV Corps could have done, and of drawing them away from the N.C.A.C. front in far greater number than IV Corps would have managed to do. It was most fortunate that at this stage the enemy should choose to fight us on our own ground near our own bases, in the only areas where our existing lines of communication could adequately support us in a large-scale campaign, and where our air bases were sufficiently near the front to enable our supply to be undertaken......"[5] Yet the course of operations neutralised this optimism and "the situation was at times to prove extremely dangerous". The Japanese made full use of the elements of surprise and envelopment in their strategy

[4] Mountbatten's Despatch, para 62.
[5] *Ibid*, para 61.

and had almost succeeded in encircling the 7th Indian Division and isolating the 5th Indian Division nearer the coast.

Faced with danger and with their communications threatened, the South-East Asia Command developed the technique of forming defensive blocks or "Admin Boxes" "organised to resist interference" and withstand attack by a force up to one battalion in strength. The forces in such 'Boxes' were to be supplied by air for which all preparations had been made. In Sinzweya area the Japanese had succeeded in cooping up the corps troops and the brigades of the 7th Indian Division, which all had dug themselves in defensive 'Boxes'. The battle raged furiously, the Japanese trying to annihilate the encircled Indian forces, and the defenders trying to beat off the attacks to be able to launch a counter-offensive against their invaders. These tactics of "stay-put" were made possible by the full development of air-lift of supplies which enabled the defenders to exist independently of the land lines of communication. It was an innovation for Burma and clearly demonstrated the potentialities of air-supply in making the forces invulnerable in their most sensitive part, the line of supply. The battle of the 'Boxes' was fiercely fought and revealed the superiority of training and morale of the Indian forces. The Japanese failed to break the spirit of the XV Indian Corps and when the momentum of their attack had slackened and the vigour of their offensive had waned, more particularly owing to the breakdown of their administrative system, the Indian forces not only emerged successful from the fight but also adopted the counter-offensive and set in motion the process of clearing Arakan of the Japanese. "The defence of the Sinzweya Admin Box" was thus a turning point in the campaign and by its success enabled the South-East Asia Command to plan out the future strategy in Burma. And when in the spring of 1944, the Japanese invasion of Imphal and Kohima had also petered out, the plans for pushing the Japanese back from Burma and reconquering South-East Asia were developed fully.

In the strategy then adopted, greater weight was given to the overland advance into Upper and Central Burma (operation 'Capital'), but for facilitating it operations in Arakan ('Romulus' and 'Talon') and an amphibious drive down south up to Rangoon (operation 'Dracula') were also to be conducted simultaneously. The main operation, therefore, was that in Central Burma by the Fourteenth Army. Arakan was to be used mainly for providing air bases to maintain the rapidly moving force in the Chindwin or Irrawaddy valleys by freeing it from the necessity of depending on the tenuous land lines of communication. The other utility of Arakan was to contain a large Japanese force there and prevent it from switching over to the Central Burma front. This object called for the capture of Akyab, and the denial of the two main roads which connected the Arakan coast with the Irrawaddy valley. The Arakan operations, in this last stage of the Burma campaign, were, therefore, planned in phases. The first phase related to the clearing of the Mayu peninsula and the capture of the Akyab-Minbya line. The next phase was concerned with the occupation of Myebon-Kyakpyu region so as to bottle up the Japanese force in the north and prevent their use of the An-Minbu road which the Japanese had then constructed. The third phase was to drive down the Myebon-Taungup road and occupy the head of the Taungup-Prome road which was the most important line of Japanese supply. The last phase was the move down to Gwa, and thus eliminate Japanese forces from the west of the Arakan Yoma. The strategy was well planned and included land and amphibious operations, all made possible by the air supremacy of the Allies and their superiority in the matter of forces and their equipment. The Japanese were unable to concentrate larger forces in the Arakan area owing to their simultaneously being faced with a major attack in Central and Northern Burma.

Arakan operations had thus the character of an auxiliary campaign whose object was to contain the Japanese forces in this narrow coastal region and prevent their being used against the main attack of the Fourteenth Army. And as success came, the other object of clearing the coastal area of the Japanese forces and using it as a base for air-supply of the South-East Asia Command forces operating in Burma emerged more prominently. In the early stages, therefore, while the strength of the forces employed was not great, in later campaigns, no less than four divisions, a commando brigade, and an appropriate percentage of air and naval units were involved in the fight. The responsibility for these operations in Arakan lay on the XV Indian Corps which later came under the command of the Allied Land Forces South-East Asia. The troops involved were not all Indian, but included African and British troops besides some elements of the American Air Force. The Indian forces comprised the 5th, 7th, 14th, 25th and 26th Indian Divisions which were enagaged in Arakan at one time or another. Indian naval units and units of the Royal Indian Air Force also took active part in the operations. There were two West African Divisions, the 81st and the 82nd, as also an East African Brigade Group, the 22nd. The 3rd British Commando Brigade also played a major and important role in the reconquest of Arakan territory.

Arakan operations provided an important illustration of the effectiveness of combined operations and more particularly of the value of air-support in fighting in a terrain where lines of communication are either lacking or are extremely primitive. In the thick jungles or the coastal strips intersected by deep chaungs and in the mountainous regions where a small hostile force occupying a hill side could defy even a large force, the air power was invaluable as a means of supply or as an instrument of fire power for rendering close support to the ground forces. Another important lesson which was then learnt was the necessity of co-ordinated command wherein the three services would co-operate to integrate the employment of their units to the best advantage. The importance of air-lift of supplies cannot be minimised, for without it the trend of events in Arakan might have been the reverse of what happened.

The tactics of envelopment and cutting the hostile forces in their rear were adopted with profit by the Indo-British forces and by that means the Japanese were prevented from exploiting longer their initial advantage. The latter had frequently used the tactics of road-blocks to make the position of Indian and British forces uncomfortable. A leaf had been ultimately taken out of their book by the commanders in the XV Indian Corps when they staged a grand road-block at Kangaw and, as a result of the fierce fighting there, were able to destroy considerable Japanese forces and disrupt their line of retreat. The Kangaw operations were no less important than the 'Admin Box' fighting in their effect on the ultimate defeat of the Japanese. The terrain made the fighting difficult and therefore sanguinary. Yet the co-operation which was rendered by the naval and air forces to the units of the army was a remarkable achievement of combined operations and signifies the progress which had been made in developing the technique of this warfare.

Finally, although the Arakan campaigns brought unestimated success to the South-East Asia Command and contributed, though not decisively, to the reconquest of Burma, it will be correct to say that in the overall effort, for the defeat of Japan, the value of these operations was not very great. In importance, these cannot be compared with the operations of Guadalcanal or Okinawa, Philippines or New Guinea, or even with the operations by the XXXIII or IV Indian Corps in Central Burma. At best the Arakan campaigns helped to provide a base for supplying the main forces in Burma during their drive on Rangoon and preventing the Japanese from using a naval base from which they could have harassed the flanks of the Fourteenth Army. Nevertheless, the victories in Arakan had the effect of sealing off an exposed frontier of India which at one time had become vulnerable. But above all the fighting in this area in 1944-45 had the supreme importance of heightening the morale of the Allied forces and giving them hopes of final victory in the east.

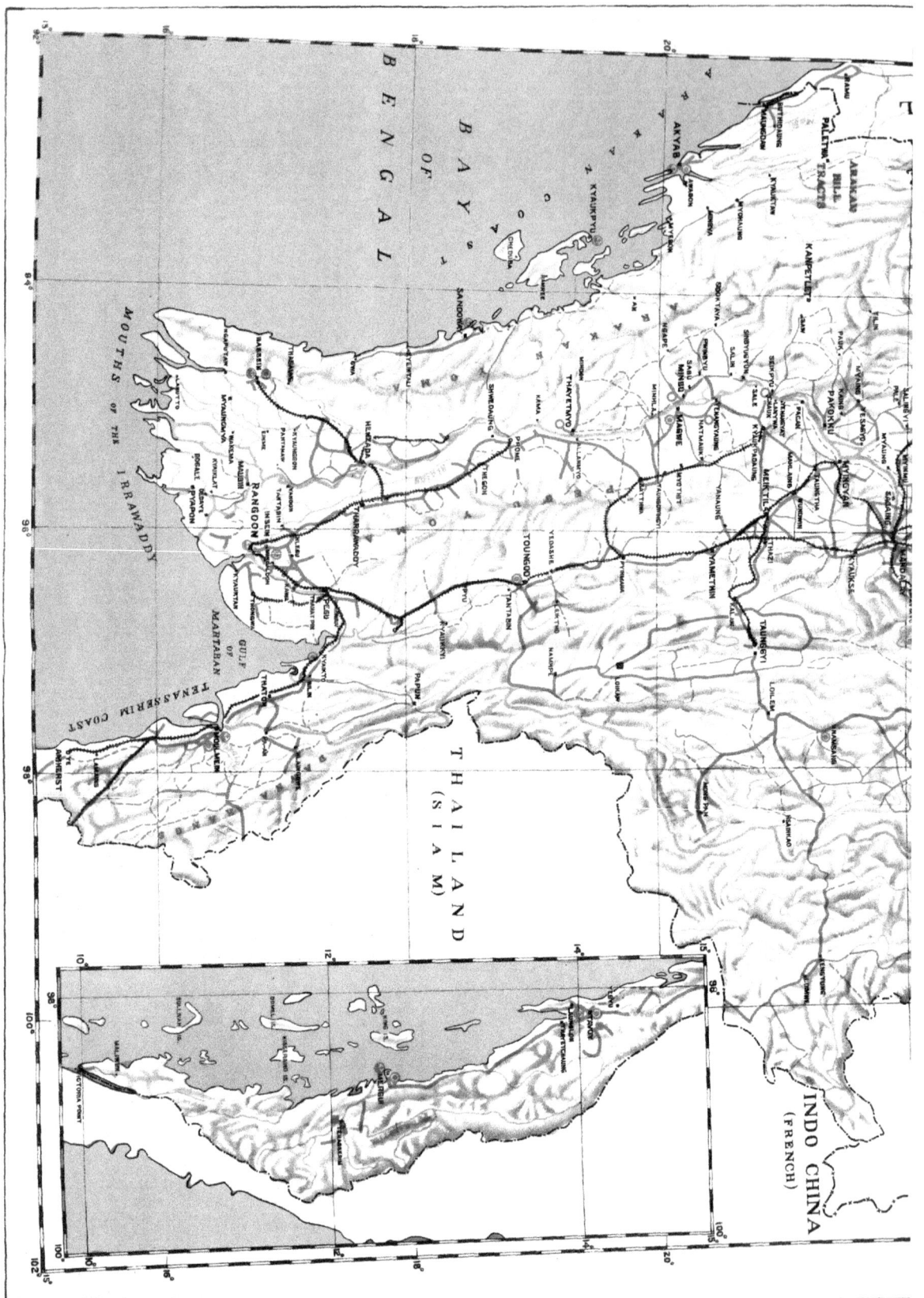

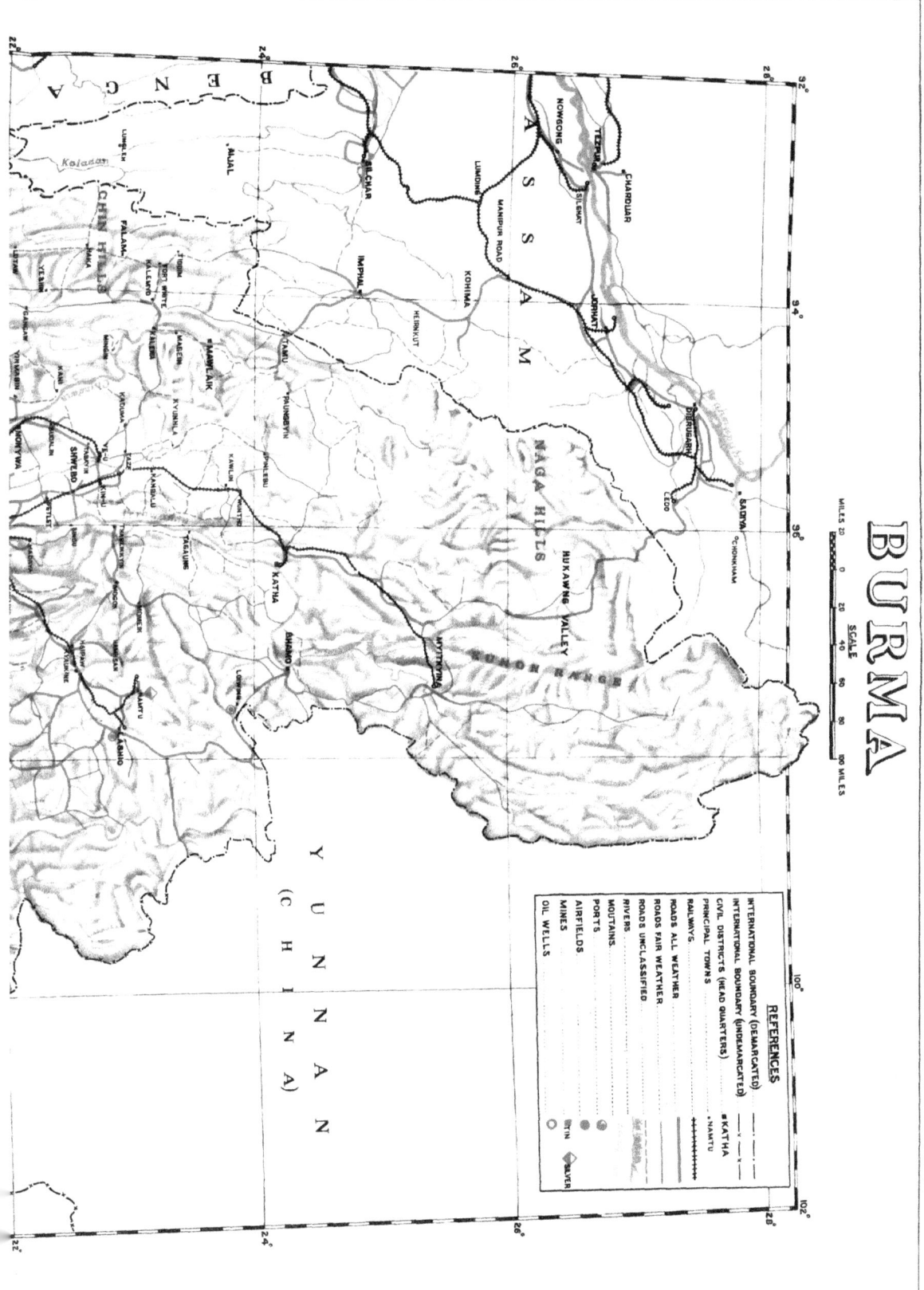

CHAPTER I

The Land and its People

History of Arakan

The country of Arakan was in ancient times known as Rakhaingpyi, or the land of Rakhaing. This term appears to have been applied by Indian Aryans to the people of Dravidian and Mongolian races. The country named Argyre by Ptolemy has been identified as Arakan and the name is supposed to be derived from silver mines existing there.[1] It is quite probable that this name is a corruption of the indigenous name Rakhaing, from which the modern European form—Arakan, may be derived. Although there is no record of silver having ever been found in Arakan, silver ore was plentiful in the neighbourhood of Martaban and Moulmein.[2]

The people of Arakan belong to the Mongoloid stock, and have kinship with the Burmese of the upper Irrawaddy. At one time there was a marked similarity between the language of the Arakanese and that of their neighbours, except for a few dialectal differences. But in the course of centuries, the Arakanese dialect acquired a large number of words of Indian origin also, while the race itself, to some extent, has become modified by an admixture of Indian blood.

The first known king of Arakan is mentioned as having reigned in a city called Ramawadi, which was the ancient name of the island known as Rambyi—corrupted in modern times by Indians and Europeans to Ramree. These early legends, however, lack historical basis, and it is not till the eighth century that the history of this land begins to assume a definite shape. In the year 788, a king named Maha Taing Chandra set up his capital at a place called Wethali. At this city a succession of nine kings, bearing the surname of Chandra, ruled for a period of one hundred and sixty-nine years. From the existing coins attributed to this dynasty, coupled with certain obscure references found in the chronicles of Arakan, one gets the impression that the Arakanese probably held Brahmanical doctrines. No clue, however, is found in these chronicles as to where this dynasty originally came from. During the tenth century, the Akyab district was exposed to the incursions of hill tribes when the Shans temporarily overran it. Throughout this

---

[1] *Progs. R. G. S.* for November 1882.
[2] Theobald's Geological Report quoted in the *Gazetteer of British Burmah*, Volume I, page 64.

period, settled government was the exception and the country suffered chronically from raids. A change of religion is also noticeable, as at the end of this century the Arakanese were professedly Buddhists, and Islam had also begun to spread.

From 1044 to 1287, the Pagan dynasty of Burma established its suzerainty over north Arakan but was unsuccessful in the south. But even in the north, the local rulers continued to be hereditary kings and sent merely propitiatory tribute to Ava. Gradually however, even the pretence of Burmese over-lordship disappeared.

In 1389, Arakan had unfortunately sided with Pegu when the latter was at war with Burma. As a result, Min Khaung, the king of Burma, invaded Arakan in 1404 and again in 1406 and during the latter year the Arakanese king, Min Saw Mun, was forced to take shelter in Bengal where he remained for nearly twenty-four years. In the interval, the unhappy land of Arakan became a battle ground for the armies of Pegu and Burma until 1430 when Min Saw Mun was restored to his throne. A new capital was thereafter founded at Myauku—now Myohaung—which continued to be the seat of government for the next four hundred years. The restoration of Min Saw Mun had been made possible with the help of Nazir Shah, the king of Bengal, whose vassal the ruler of Arakan became, but this relationship did not last very long.

Min Saw Mun's brother and successor, Ali Khan, did not long submit to the authority of Bengal. He took possession of the country as far as Ramu, and throughout a reign of twenty-five years, kept his lands free from attacks by his dangerous eastern neighbours. In 1459, his son Kahima Shah (1459-1482) occupied Chittagong which remained an Arakanese territory till the year 1666. In 1531, a young king of great ability named Minbin (1531-1553) came to the throne, and foreseeing trouble from the neighbouring king of Pegu, immediately commenced extensive preparations to defend his capital, Myohaung. A deep moat which could be filled with tidal water was dug and as he had planned, when the invaders did penetrate the eastern outworks of the city, he opened the sluice gates of his great reservoirs and flooded them out. He also managed to maintain his hold over Ramu and Chittagong in spite of heavy raids on these towns by the Tippera tribes. During his reign, coins were struck at Chittagong which bear his name and style him Sultan.

For many years after this, Arakan was left entirely undisturbed. Situated between Bengal and Burma, and far inferior to either in extent and resources, Arakan was not easily vulnerable. Its strength lay mainly in its jungles and swamps. These natural barriers helped in opposing the intrusion of enemies and thereby offered a reasonably safe refuge for its people. Trusting to these natural defences, the kings of Arakan might long have remained secure against foreign aggression ; unfortunately, they were not content for long to keep on existing in obscure independence and be satisfied with a calm atmosphere at home. They started encroaching on the domains of either their northern or eastern neighbours, depending on how the opportunity arose, and this eventually led them into trouble.

The Arakanese maintained sea-going craft, and Chittagong helped them by breeding a race of capable seamen. For centuries they were the terror of the Ganga Delta and at times they even dared to hamper Portuguese shipping. Finally, they united with the Portuguese freebooters who became their allies and settled in Arakan. The Portuguese were soon expelled owing to their piratical activities in 1605, and settled in the island of Sandwip, near the mouth of the Ganga. But soon after they obtained assistance from Goa, and attacked Arakan. This attack was successfully repulsed and the Arakanese, flushed with their victory, began to harass the lowlands of Bengal. The power of Arakan was then at its zenith, but it was soon to crumble and fall.

The capture of Chittagong in 1666 by Shaista Khan, the Mughal Viceroy of Bengal, ended Arakan's century of greatness which was soon followed by a century of chaos. The state of the country may be judged by the fact that in the next hundred years there were twenty-five kings of whom eight were usurpers. The last Arakanese king, Thamada (1782-1785), had less authority than ever, and was completely helpless when certain lords of his kingdom went to Ava asking for intervention. Their request was granted by the Burmese king Bodawpaya who invaded Arakan and captured its capital in 1784. Later, the Arakanese, oppressed by their conquerors, fled in thousands to take refuge into the British territories in India.

By this time British authority had been extended up to Chittagong. At about this time, the arrogant aggressiveness of the Burmese officers, prompted by orders from the capital, led to collision between the Burmese and the British authorities of the district. To demand the return of three important chiefs who had fled into British territory from Arakan, the Burmese General Nandakyoazo crossed the Naf river and entrenched his force on the opposite shore. A detachment of troops under Major-General Erskine was sent from Calcutta to oppose this violation of British territory. The Burmese were forced to withdraw and in course of time the three chiefs were handed over as fugitive criminals. Again in 1797 a similar incident occurred when thousands of Arakanese emigrated to the district of Chittagong, and once more a Burmese force crossed into British territory to compel the fugitives to return. The invaders entrenched themselves and repulsed an attack made on their positions by the local police battalion of the district, but king Bodawpaya, occupied at this time with designs on Assam and unwilling to commit himself too far, withdrew his troops. He then sent an agent to Calcutta to negotiate with Marquis Wellesley, the Governor General, for the restoration of the fugitives, at the same time threatening an invasion if his demand was not complied with. No action, however, appears to have been taken by the British.

In 1815 again, king Bodawpaya is reported to have sent agents to Bengal ostensibly for the purpose of demanding extradition of the refugees, but probably to concert measures for entering into a league with some of the princes of upper India against the British. The plan, however, did not materialise. Eight years later, the frontier of Chittagong again became the scene of aggression by the Burmese authorities in Arakan. At the mouth of the Naf river lies the island of Shahpuri which, due to its proximity to Chittagong, was considered to be a part of British territory. But the Burmese officers captured it in September 1823 and drove away a guard of twelve men of the provincial battalion of Chittagong, stationed on the island to protect British subjects residing there. This episode resulted in a formal declaration of war against Burma in the following year. The Company's government in Calcutta planned to occupy Arakan and then to strike at the capital of Burma through that province. Consequently, an army numbering eleven thousand men was assembled at Chittagong under the Command of General Morrison, and was directed against the city of Myauku or Myohaung which was surrounded by low hills affording excellent means of defence. The first assault by the British at a narrow defile was repulsed but the position changed on the following day. A frontal attack was made under cover of a brisk cannonade and the Burmaese fled precipitately. The whole Burmese garrison eventually retired east across the range of mountains to their own country. Thus, the southern districts of Arakan were occupied by the British without much opposition and the troops were distributed in cantonments along the sea coast on the site now known as Akyab. In spite of the difficulties of terrain and climate, the British had, by the end of the spring of 1824, driven the Burmese from the whole of their conquests in Assam, Manipur and Arakan, and had occupied Martaban and the whole coast of Tenasserim as far south as Mergui.

It now remained for the army in Rangoon under the command of Sir Archibald Campbell to carry on the war by advancing up the Irrawaddy river. This force of about twelve thousand men, consisting mostly of Madras sepoys, and some ships under the command of Captain Marryat, occupied Rangoon on 11 May 1824. The British had expected the Talaings to rise in their favour but the Burmese had deported the population, leaving the delta a waste whence the invader could get no information about supplies or transport. Nevertheless, it was round Rangoon that the Burmese armies were eventually broken. On 24 February 1826, General Campbell dictated the Treaty of Yandabo to the Burmese King Ba-gyi-daw whereby he yielded Arakan, Assam, Tenasserim and Manipur to the British.

Not long after, however, King Ba-gyi-daw was deposed by his brother Tharawadi who had a hatred for the British, a hatred which was taken up as a tradition by his successors. This resulted in many an act of violence towards the British subjects and led ultimately to the Second Burma War in 1852. This time the British force advanced to Prome and King Pegu, the then ruler of Burma, was informed that Prome was British territory; during this action it was not considered worth while even to sign a treaty.

King Pegu was later deposed by his brother Mindon who took care to avoid unnecessary conflicts with the British. But such was not the policy in 1878 when one of his younger sons, Thibaw, succeeded to the throne. During his time relations once again became strained with the result that the British Resident had to be withdrawn culminating in British subjects being exposed to violence. Thibaw also started sending ambassadors to Italy and France with the object of contracting alliances and thereby threatening British interests in Burma. The climax was reached when the Burmese Government imposed a fine of £230,000 on the Bombay-Burma Trading Corporation, which held certain forest concessions in Burma. The Indian Government's suggestion of arbitration was also rejected by Thibaw who apparently was in urgent need of money. As a result of this, once again the British Government declared war against Burma in 1885 and on 28 November Thibaw was taken prisoner; and by 1 January 1886, Upper Burma had been completely annexed by the British.

From 1825, the year in which Arakan had been annexed following the First Burmese War, British Burma had been made the administrative responsibility of the Governor General of India; in 1862, however, British Burma was made a province of India. Consequently, from that date till 1897, it was administered by a Chief Commissioner and thereafter by a Lieutenant Governor assisted by a Legislature of nine nominated members, five of whom were officials. This administrative set-up continued to be in existence till the year 1923.

In 1923, Burma became a Governor's Province with the result that the Government of India Act of 1919 became operative in that country. This change enabled the people of Burma to have a say in the affairs of their Government. But it also resulted in a change in the political outlook of the people, as well as in great political upheavals. Due to economic reasons as well as other factors, the anti-Indian feeling became pronounced and culminated in the demand for the separation of Burma from Indian administration. Later, this demand met with support from the Simon Commission. In 1930, due to a deterioration in the economic conditions in Burma, the anti-Indian feeling was further accentuated with the result that towards the end of the year the racial differences erupted in the form of the Burma Rebellion.

In 1935, the British Parliament passed the Government of Burma Act. This Act came into force in 1937 which finally effected the separation of Burma from India and conferred on the Burmese a very large measure of autonomy. Although the defence of Burma and the control of the armed forces as well as foreign affairs were still under the direct charge of the Governor, the subjects of law and order and finance were placed in charge of ministers, who were chosen from among the members of the Legislature. Nevertheless, stability was still lacking in the country and petty intrigues and selfish motives influenced the actions of some Burmese politicians. But although jealousies were uppermost and no settled line of policy was pursued, the politicians were always united in their demand for the complete independence of their country.

The Burmese were at first indifferent to the declaration of war in 1939. In fact, the Thakin party took advantage of this situation and fortified its resolve to secure the freedom of Burma by force while the British were carrying on the war in the West. In furtherance of this policy young Burmans were sent to Japan in 1941 to get training in fifth-column and sabotage activities. Although the Burmese had no love for Japan yet they were ready to take Japanese aid in order to free Burma from alien rule. In December 1941 the Burmese premier U. Saw, suspected of being in league with Japan, was put behind the bars by the British authorities. At the same time ex-premier Dr. Ba Maw, resigning his seat in the House of Representatives, delivered a speech in which he declared that there could be no help to Britain in the war unless complete independence was promised to Burma. For this declaration he too was imprisoned. On 14 April 1942, however, he managed to escape, and when the Japanese invasion of Burma was complete, he was appointed Chief Administrator of his country by the Japanese occupation forces.

Topography of Arakan

The land of Arakan consists of a strip of country running along the eastern seaboard of the Bay of Bengal. It stretches from the Naf estuary on the southern borders of Chittagong, to within ninety miles of Cape Negrais. On the east, it is bounded by the

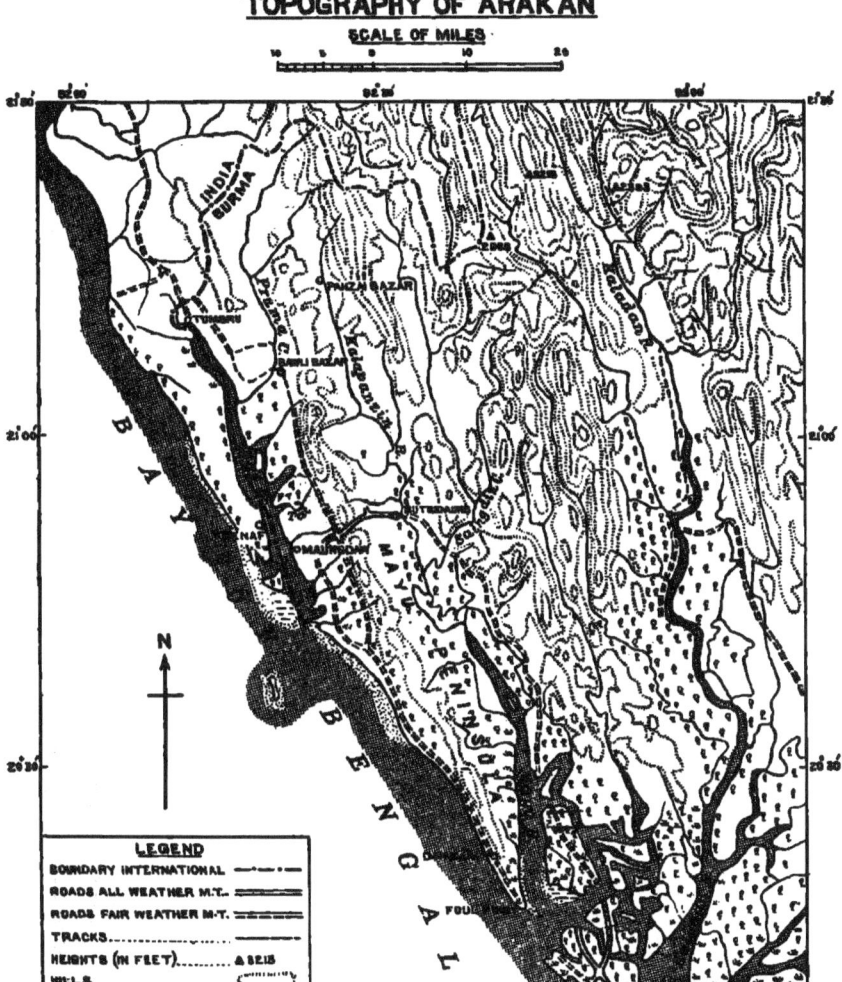

Arakan Yoma which separates it from the Irrawaddy valley. Along its northern border, its greatest breadth is about a hundred miles, gradually diminishing towards the south as it is hemmed in by the Arakan Yoma until in the extreme south it tapers into a narrow strip, not more than fifteen miles wide.

In general, Arakan consists of tangled, jungle-covered hills, which run down to a narrow coastal strip of paddy-fields and mangrove swamps, a highly malarial region infested with the most virulent type of mosquito. The hills and the coastal strip are heavily intersected by hundreds of streams (chaungs) and tidal creeks often many miles long, mostly unfordable and offering few landing points. In 1942, such landing points as existed were strongly defended by the Japanese, and since there was not a single beach along the hundred miles stretch of the coast from Akyab to Taungup, these chaungs constituted the only means of access to the hinterland.

The terrain of Arakan may be divided into four sectors:

(a) THE COASTAL SECTOR which lies between the Bay of Bengal and the foothills of the Mayu Range. It is upto two miles wide in the northern part of the Mayu peninsula, but narrows to a few hundred yards between Donbaik and Foul Point. Intersected as it is by innumerable tidal chaungs and swamps, it makes the deployment of forces in this area very difficult.

(b) THE MAYU RANGE with foothills on either side, rises to slightly under 2000 feet and forms the spine of the Mayu peninsula. Its jungle-covered slopes are particularly steep and rocky, constituting a formidable barrier to movement in any direction.

(c) THE MAYU VALLEY consisting mainly of flat paddy fields and swampy areas, is intersected by tidal chaungs and is completely dominated by the hills of the Mayu range.

(d) THE KALADAN VALLEY resembles the Mayu valley and lies some thirty air miles to the east of it.

Arakan is a part of Burma and lies between the Arakan Yoma and the Bay of Bengal. The grain of the country lies from north to south, and the main hill ranges are the Mayu range and the Arakan Yoma. Some of the peaks of the latter rise to over 10,000 feet and the highest is believed to be Mount Victoria. Both these ranges are steep and are covered with bamboo forest, a difficult physical obstacle to traverse. The three important rivers of Arakan are the Naf, the Mayu and the Kaladan. The Naf river originates at Tumbru and enters the Bay of Bengal just south of the village of Teknaf. Many chaungs flow into this river from the east, the more notable of which are the Tat chaung on which lies the village of Maungdaw, and the Pruma chaung which flows by Bawli

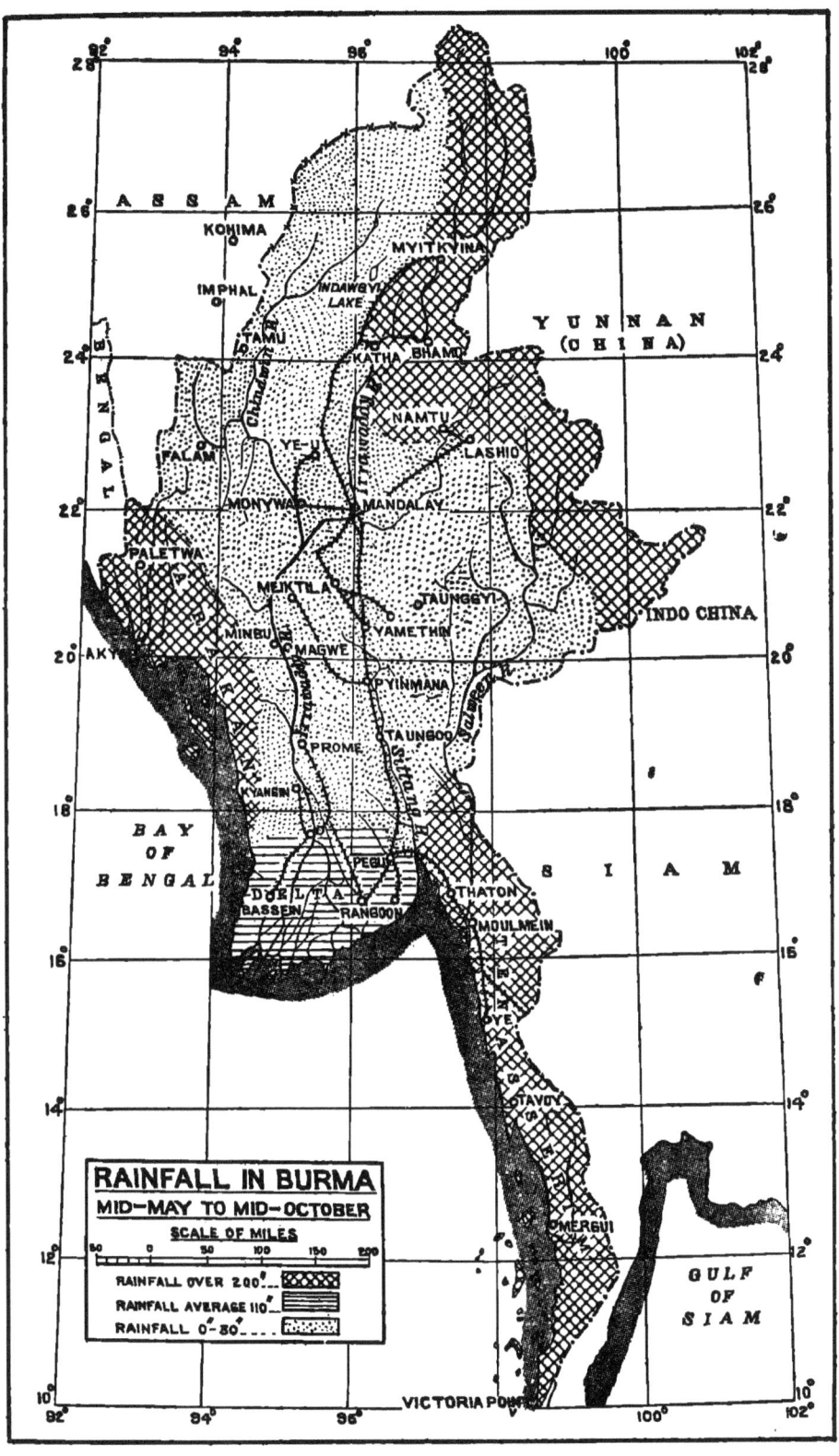

Bazar. The Mayu river rises near Panzai Bazar and before merging in the Bay of Bengal flows between Foul Point and Akyab island. This river changes its name to Kalapanzin north of the Shambank chaung, some ten miles south of Buthidaung. Numberless chaungs drain into the main stream from the west as well as the east; the most important of these is the Saingding chaung which joins the Kalapanzin river from the north east, five miles south of Buthidaung. The Kaladan river, has its source north west of Fort White and flows into the Bay of Bengal just south of Akyab island.

These rivers flow from north to south, and along with many of their chaungs were navigable for very considerable distances by shallow draught vessels of all types, including motor launches. Country boats and 'kishtis' could operate everywhere and so the waterways formed an important link in the British and Japanese lines of communication. But since the rivers and their tributary chaungs are mostly tidal and subject to excessive floods during the monsoon, they proved considerable obstacles to movement at times.

Arakan is cold in winter and hot in spring and early autumn. During the monsoon months (May to September) malaria is generally rife, and the average rainfall being 200 inches, vast areas become impassable to foot or wheeled traffic.

Admiral the
Lord Louis Mountbatten
of Burma,
Supreme Allied Commander
South-East Asia Command
(16 Nov. 1943—31 May 1946)

General Sir George J. Giffard,
Commander-in-Chief,
11th Army Group (later ALFSEA)
(October 1943—November 1944)

General Sir Archibald Wavell,
Commander-in-Chief, India
(11 July 1941—16 January 1942)
(7 March 1942—19 June 1943)

General Sir Claude Auchinleck,
Commander-in-Chief, India
(27 January 1941—4 July 1941)
(20 June 1943—14 August 1947)

Lieutenant-General
Sir Philip Christison,
Commander XV Corps.
(16 Nov. 1943—30 Sep. 1945)

Lieutenant-General
N. M. S. Irwin,
Commander Eastern Army
of India Command.

Major-General H. R. Briggs,
Commander 5th Indian Division
(May 1942—July 1944)

Major-General F. W. Messervy,
Commander 7th Indian Division
(30 July 1943—7 December 1944)

CHAPTER II

Planning for the Offensive

India is threatened

The fall of Rangoon in March 1942, and the subsequent occupation of Burma by the Japanese, were a great blow to the Allies. This strategically valuable area was now at the disposal of the Japanese forces so that the threat to the security of India and Ceylon became imminent and a grim reality. It was also obvious that the North-East Frontier of India had now to be well guarded, but the troops to deal with the situation were "dangerously weak". There were only one British and six Indian divisions available for the defence of the whole of India and Ceylon. These figures excluded the small number of troops set aside for the defence of the North-West Frontier and for internal security. Both the forces, however, were well below the estimated strength necessary for these commitments and none of the divisions was complete in equipment, training or ancillary troops.

The Eastern Fleet, which at that time could make available only one modernised battleship, was in no position to dispute with the Japanese fleet the command of the Bay of Bengal or the waters around Ceylon. Consequently, the Japanese had virtual control of the seas around India and an amphibious invasion of Ceylon or the east coast of India became a strong probability.

The condition of the Air Force was also quite alarming as it was much below the required strength for either a protective role or for direct support of the ground forces. There was only one fighter squadron available for the defence of Calcutta along with eight serviceable Mohawks, while the three fighter squadrons allotted for the protection of Ceylon were still in the process of being equipped to scale. In view of the raids on Ceylon by the Japanese in early April, it was fortunate that the equipping of these squadrons was completed by the end of March, while an extra fifty Hurricanes were also given to the island in the same month. The remainder of the Air Force (two fighter squadrons and one light-bomber squadron) which was allotted for Upper Burma had been practically wiped out by the Japanese attack at Magwe on 21 and 22 March 1942. The remnants were thereafter withdrawn to India to re-form.

The month of March 1942 was one of great anxiety for General Wavell, the then Commander-in-Chief in India. Just before the fall of Rangoon he had intimated to the Chiefs of Staff in London his inability to hold Burma with the meagre forces at his disposal. In his appreciation of the situation, he had anticipated an attack by the Japanese on the North-East Frontier of India and was consequently not in favour of the bulk of his forces being employed for the protection of Ceylon. At this stage he had also put up his immediate requirements to enlarge his forces, but the tense situation in the Middle East did not allow his demands to be met adequately. He was, however, promised the 5th and 2nd British Divisions along with a fair number of fighter and bomber aircraft, as soon as possible. But in spite of these promised reinforcements which were on their way to India, the operational strength did not materially increase before the middle of April. At the same time the heavy American bombers present in India could not be utilised as they were intended for use in China and could not be counted upon for any plan of defence, as they did not come under General Wavell's command.

Throughout this period, Ceylon was defended by two Indian brigades and two brigades of local troops. Two Australian brigades were also being lent for the defence of the island, along with an East African brigade that was already on its way. The ordering of the 16th Brigade of the 70th British Division, the only British division in India, to Ceylon by the British War Cabinet, was not in keeping with General Wavell's appreciation of the situation. In his cable to the Chiefs of Staff in London, he showed grave concern over this move as he considered that "at this time an undue proportion of our very inadequate land and air resources in the east were being allocated to the defence of Ceylon." Nonetheless, the move was carried out as the British War Cabinet ruled that the defence of the naval bases in Ceylon must have priority. It will thus be seen that the military situation in India at the end of March 1942 was indeed precarious.

On 5 April, 1942, the Japanese made a naval raid into Indian waters and attacked Colombo by carrier-borne aircraft; on the 9th of the same month Trincomalee suffered an air raid. Though considerable damage was inflicted by the defending fighters on the Japanese aircraft, the Blenheim bomber squadron that was sent to attack the Japanese aircraft-carriers was practically destroyed without accomplishing its object. The *Dorsetshire* and *Cornwall,* both 8 inch cruisers of the British Navy, along with the aircraft-carrier *Hermes* and a few small naval vessels, were sunk in the waters around Ceylon as a result of the Japanese raid. In the Bay of Bengal, the damage to the merchant shipping by the Japanese light forces and aircraft was near about 100,000 tons; and the dropping of a few bombs on Vizagapatam—the first on Indian soil—created a panic throughout the country. To quote a passage from General Wavell's despatch to the British War Cabinet, "This was India's most dangerous hour; our eastern fleet was powerless to protect Ceylon or eastern India; our air strength was negligible; and it was becoming increasingly obvious that our small tired force in Burma was unlikely to be able to hold the enemy, while the absence of communications between Assam and Upper Burma made it impossible to reinforce it".

Fortunately, the attack by the Japanese naval force on Colombo and Trincomalee did not develop into a major operation. This fact saved a nasty situation for the India Command and also gave rise to various conjectures. General Wavell thought it probable that this raid by the Japanese was made with the object of securing Indian rejection of the Cripps Mission's proposals, which were then under discussion in Delhi. Roy McKelvie, on the other hand, puts it down to the surprisingly antagonistic relationship that existed between the Japanese Army and Navy. He writes in his book[1] that, "Thus it is possible that the army, its hands full with conquests in South-East Asia, was not immediately prepared to back the navy in any new ventures, considering them nothing more than glamour-gathering escapades. And the navy, not burdened with the necessity of landing troops in Ceylon, preferred to sink merchant ships rather than come to any trial of strength with that unknown quantity, the British fleet."

Although the Japanese naval force withdrew, the days of anxiety for India were not over. When Lashio fell into Japanese hands, the Chinese troops operating under General Stilwell in Burma were placed in a precarious position. As a force they were cut off from return to China, and only one division, the 38th, was able to reach Imphal in any reasonable order or condition. A small portion of the rest of the force reached India by the Ledo route; this was accomplished only after considerable losses from starvation and disease, and General Stilwell himself had to make his way on foot to Assam. The remainder of the force had to fight its way to China through Kachin country. Meanwhile, the troops in Burma under the command of General Sir Harold Alexander were also being pushed northwards by the Japanese. When the latter broke through to Lashio in the second part of April, and the Chinese resistance in north-east Burma came to an end, it necessitated the ordering of the Burma army to withdraw across the Indian frontier into Assam. This was carried out and was completed by 20 May 1942.

The months of May and June again continued to be critical for India. Much to the annoyance of the India Command the Eastern

---

[1] *The War in Burma*, p. 52.

Fleet was further depleted, and the 5th British Division, which was on its way to reinforce India, was ordered to send two of its brigades to Madagascar. This place was being further reinforced by the East African brigade which was earmarked for Ceylon, while at the same time the two Australian brigades already in Ceylon had to be returned due to political reasons. The High Command's appreciation of the situation obviously differed from that of General Wavell and these changes were carried out in spite of protests from the latter. As things turned out the threat to India never developed.

During the summer, continuous efforts were made to build up the Air Force, and the arrival of the 2nd and 5th British Divisions also eased the situation to some extent. Thus, when the monsoon broke in July the critical period for India had passed.

Allied offensive planning

Meanwhile, as the Indian and British forces were being pushed out of Burma by the advancing Japanese army, elaborate and detailed plans were under review by the Allied commanders for the recapture of the lost land. From the very beginning of the Japanese offensive in Burma, various appreciations were being considered with a view to handling the situation which was getting beyond the control of the Allies; and accordingly as the military situation changed, the planning and its objects had also to be revised and re-adjusted.

As early as March 1942, the India Command's planning team had visualised and appreciated the possibility that the Japanese might get the upper hand in Burma by the end of the year. In view of this eventuality, the Director of Military Operations in General Headquarters, India, wrote an appreciation on 28 March 1942 in which he made the following assumptions:

(a) That by September 1942, the Japanese would have occupied Burma upto the general line Lashio—Shwebo—Paletwa.

(b) That the Allied forces would have withdrawn towards China and that the Chinese would still be in the war. Their morale, however, would be low and they would not be fighting hard.

Based on the above assumptions, the appreciation aimed at the destruction of the Japanese in Burma. The decision was thereupon taken that detailed planning, based on this appreciation, should be carried out. But the occasion for this did not materialise; later events dictated planning for Burma on a different basis altogether. By May 1942, not only had the Japanese occupied the whole of

Burma but had also cut the road to China, which was not at all in keeping with the Allied overall strategy in the Far East.

The British and Indian troops under pressure of Japanese air activity and the impending threat of a land attack, evacuated Akyab in the early hours of 4 May 1942. As will be remembered, the whole of Burma also fell soon after and the loss of Akyab as well as the Burma coast left the command of the Bay of Bengal to the Japanese. It was this situation that directly threatened the 1200 mile long eastern coast of India with a Japanese invasion.

On withdrawing from Akyab the most forward troops of the India Command were mostly in East Bengal, except for a small garrison at Chittagong; and the nearest reserves for these forward troops were at Ranchi (Bihar). The air force also was inadequate and poorly equipped. Because of the Japanese raid on Ceylon there were no reinforcements received in the Bengal Area with the result that the air defence of north-east India was totally inadequate. It was, however, fortunate that apart from making a few sporadic air raids on Chittagong and a small advance up the Kaladan valley towards Kyauktaw, the Japanese made no attempt to advance into India itself. The Eastern Command, which later became the Eastern Army, with its Headquarters at Ranchi, was responsible for all operations in this area.

From the point of view of defending India, the military situation of the defenders was desparately low. During May and June of 1942 it was appreciated that the Japanese might make a landing by way of the Brahmaputra river in order to sever Indian communications with Burma and China. It was also considered that a landing might take place either south of Calcutta, with the Calcutta area as its immediate objective, or to its south-west in an attempt to seize the industrial areas of Asansol and Tatanagar.

In order to meet this threat to the northern part of the east coast and the vital industrial centres of eastern India, the defences in the Eastern Army area were re-adjusted. The XV Indian Corps with its headquarters at Barrackpore, was given the task of contesting and delaying any Japanese attempt at landing on the Bengal-Orissa coast; the 14th and 26th Indian Divisions were allotted to the Corps for this purpose. No. 3 Inland Water Transport (Sunderbans) Flotilla, consisting of 100 launches, was also placed under the operational control of the XV Indian Corps; the Flotilla had the dual role of gaining information as well as taking offensive action against any hostile invasion fleet.

On 11 May 1942, the Joint Planning Staff of the India Command in their paper No. 15 examined the possibility of the re-capture of Burma by means of large scale offensive operations. Detailed planning was not attempted in this paper as it was considered that before a large scale offensive action could be staged against Burma, the strategic situation might be completely altered by American action in the Western Pacific, or by the course of events in Australasia, China, the Middle East or Russia. The broad aspects of the problem were, however, gone into and certain conclusions drawn. The general recommendations then made and the conclusions drawn by the planning team were as follows:—

I. "The resumption of the offensive in Burma is dependent on many factors beyond the control of the Indian Command. Primarily, it depends on strategic developments in the other war theatres, and their effect on the combined plans of the Allied Powers. It has been shown that the re-conquest of Burma may require a considerable effort and make heavy demands on our naval, army and air resources. But this is only one of the ways by which we can strike back at the Japanese, and it may not be the most economical method of doing so.

II. "We must know well in advance the part which India is expected to play in the defeat of the Japanese. For example, we must know whether our object is to be the re-occupation of Upper Burma to re-establish the supply routes to China, or whether India is to be the base for a major sea expedition by Allied forces, or whether India's role is merely to be ancillary to other major operations conducted from bases further east. In each case also we must have an indication of the dates by which we must be ready for such operations. On factors such as these will depend the whole course of our preparations. Only the chiefs of Staff in London and Washington are in a position to judge the relative importance of the efforts in the European, Middle East, Indian, Australian and Pacific theatres. Our first step, therefore, is to put the question to the Chiefs of Staff and ask for their directions.

III. "Whatever part we are called on to play, we consider that the following points are established:
 (a) Burma as a whole cannot be captured until we have taken Rangoon. This cannot be done without a sea-borne expedition.
 (b) For this, air and sea dominance must be achieved. The gaining of the former must be carried out either before or during the first stages of an operation.
 (c) The capture of the Andamans and the aerodromes on the Arakan coast is essential, as a preliminary.
 (d) The number of troops and air forces needed will be in the neighbourhood of eight divisions and five

hundred aircraft, unless the Japanese garrison of Burma can be reduced by diversions elsewhere, or by preliminary operations.

(e) It is too early to form an opinion on the necessity or otherwise of including operations against northern Sumatra as part of the plan for the re-capture of Burma."

General Wavell, the then Commander-in-Chief in India, was not in the least satisfied with this paper. His comments, made to the Chief of the General Staff were as follows: "The plan of the J.P.S. (Joint Planning Staff) for offensive action in upper Burma is disappointing. It has taken far too much account of our own difficulties, and has not considered those of the enemy, and is therefore planned on too conservative and defensive a spirit. If we are to make a successful come-back in Upper Burma, we must fight the battle more on the Japanese methods than on normal operational methods." After explaining in detail his views on this paper, he went on to say that, "We should issue a directive to the Eastern Army accordingly. The following is my general idea of what the directive might be:

I. It is at present impossible to tell whether the enemy will remain on the defensive or make an attack, what forces he will deploy on the Burmese frontier, or what the position on the Chinese side will be. But certain factors will obviously be in favour—

(a) Our Lines of Communication, if we work hard at their improvement, are likely to be better than the enemy's, after taking into account the comparative smallness of his requirements.

(b) We are likely to have air superiority over the enemy.

(c) The enemy's Lines of Communications will run parallel to his front and should therefore be vulnerable. We should make our plans to take the fullest possible advantage of these factors.

II. The objects of any offensive action taken by us should be to take advantage of the enemy's difficulties as outlined above; to try and get into touch with the Chinese; to raise the morale of our troops and in India generally by offensive action."

Based on the above lines the General Headquarters, India, issued Operation Instruction No. 4, dated 14 June 1942, to the General Officer Commanding-in-Chief, Eastern Army. It laid down that planning was to be carried out for a limited offensive in the autumn of 1942 into Upper Burma and that operations would be carried out by the Commander of the IV Indian Corps with such troops as might be placed at his disposal. The planning was to be directed in such a way that operations might be started on 1 October 1942. In the meanwhile, on 1 July 1942, the India Command Joint Planning Staff, in their paper No. 18, had presented another plan for an offensive operation into Burma. Its object was also to study the problems and ascertain whether an offensive could be launched on 1 October 1942. But once again the conclusions were neither encouraging nor helpful. The Joint Planning Staff remarked that, "In the early stages of study it became clear that the operation would only be possible on the date given if conditions were favourable in two main fields—maintenance and air. But the most detailed study has gradually and conclusively shown that it is impossible during the monsoon to bring about a maintenance situation which would allow the operation to be staged on 1 October, or indeed until some months after the rains are over. We have been most reluctant to come to this conclusion, but having done so we think it right to state it clearly at the outset." These conclusions were arrived at by the Joint Planning Staff after an examination of the problems of supply and transport and the availability of essential material. General Wavell, however, did not think much of their approach to the problem; in his note to the Chief of the General Staff he commented as before: "This paper is disappointing. The J.P.S. has considered our own difficulties almost exclusively and not those of the enemy, with the result that their plans have far more defensive than offensive spirit. I think I will now draft a directive for IV Corps who will in any event have to do the detailed planning. If the Japanese had planned on these lines we should still be holding lower Burma and Rangoon."

No one particular plan, however, could be adhered to as the overall military position of the Allies was changing from day to day. As one plan was being worked out in detail it had to be abandoned for another on account of either the paucity of men or materials. On 24 June 1942, therefore, when the Joint Planning Staff in their paper No. 19 planned an operation known as 'Probation,' the Chiefs of Staff again did not quite agree to it in its original form. The Joint Planning Staff had planned this operation on the following basis:

    I. "Our ultimate object is the re-capture of Burma. We cannot land the number of troops and equipment which will eventually be required without a port. There are three ports—Rangoon, Bassein and Moulmein.

    II. Bassein and Moulmein are small, difficult of access (it takes two days to reach Bassein from the sea if the draught is over 20 feet) and communications away from them are poor.

III. Our object therefore is: The capture of Rangoon with a view to further operations leading to the re-capture of Burma."

As this plan did not take full cognizance of the necessity of strategical surprise or of deceiving the Japanese into believing that it was not the intention to attack Burma, great stress was laid on a diversionary move which was recommended to be carried out along with this operation. Hence the Joint Planning Staff suggested that, "It is of great importance that the enemy should be led to suppose that we intend to make a powerful thrust from Assam so that he will be forced to keep a large proportion of his forces to cover such a move. Any advance which we are able to make from that direction will be of great value and we should be ready to exploit to the full any success we achieve there. It is especially important during our preliminary advances southwards along the coast that we make the enemy think that our intention is to thrust on a large scale into central Burma." They considered that Akyab should be captured as soon as sufficient fighters were available to operate from that aerodrome and ensure its safety, and that this operation might be carried out in August or September. The Chief of Staff's comment on this paper, addressed to the Commander-in-Chief, was that "We consider this a valuable document . . . . . we propose, if your Excellency agrees, to direct the Joint Planning Staff to re-write this paper in the light of the following remarks:

'The re-capture of Burma is not the ultimate object. It is to re-establish communications with China and to form a base for offensive operations against the Japanese, and that the object of the planning should be *The capture of the Rangoon— Moulmein area with a view to further operations.*'"

This operation was therefore re-written and at a meeting of the Chiefs of Staff Committee, held on 10 July 1942, the 2nd Division, 20th Independent Brigade Group, 10th Division and the 5th or 70th Division were allocated for this operation.

When the detailed planning was undertaken, the Joint Planning Staff came to the conclusion that due to various maintenance difficulties the offensive from Assam could not begin before December and that even that date was rather doubtful. But before any steps could be taken in pursuance of this plan it had once again to be changed in view of the telegram that was received on 10 July from Mr. Churchill, the Prime Minister of England. He suggested a combined operation in which an expedition of forty or fifty thousand British troops with suitable armour was to be launched across the Bay of Bengal. The difficulties inherent in such a plan were envisaged by the Planning Staff of the India Command and were put forward by them before the Commander-in-Chief. This venture, it was pointed out, would first of all require air superiority over the Bay of Bengal and secondly involve a considerable number of naval craft, which at that time was not available. Lastly, this operation could not possibly be carried out in the limited time that was given to them. All these factors were again responsible for a change in the plans and for a more realistic approach to the problem.

Till the end of June 1942 the general policy of the India Command for Arakan was to evacuate Chittagong, if attacked in force. With this object in view, demolition squads had been formed and a denial policy formulated. Denial Boards were constituted and given the task of making plans for certain essential demolitions and advising civil departments and commercial firms as to their course of action in an emergency. The XV Indian Corps continued to be responsible for the defence of Bengal and Orissa. The 14th Indian Division was deployed in Eastern Bengal while the 26th Indian Division was extended over the Calcutta area. The gap between the two Divisions was filled by the Sunderbans Flotilla, operating in the waters of the Meghna and Ganga rivers and in the Sunderbans. At the same time, two RAF Squadrons were re-equipped with more modern types of aircraft, and airfields at Chittagong, Comilla and Agartala were ordered to be hurriedly constructed.

The coming of the monsoon, however, brought about a change in the policy of the India Command. It was appreciated that the immediate danger of a Japanese attack on Chittagong had receded. In the first week of July, therefore, strict instructions were issued by the Commander of the 14th Indian Division to the Chittagong Area Commander, that Chittagong was to be retained as a land and air base against all attacks by sea, land and air. That an offensive—defensive policy had been adopted was further evident when, in the middle of September, the 14th Indian Division was ordered to move south of Chittagong and make contact with the Japanese.

Throughout this period, the morale of the Allied nations was at a very low ebb and the need for some successful action was considered essential to counteract this defeatist attitude. In view of this, General Wavell issued Operation Instruction No. 11 to the General Officer Commanding-in-Chief, Eastern Army, on 17 September 1942. The object of this instruction was:

    (a) "To develop communications and establish ourselves in a favourable position for re-conquering Burma and re-opening the Burma Road at the first opportunity.

    (b) To bring the Japanese to battle with the purpose of using up their strength particularly in the air."

The intention of the Commander-in-Chief was:

    I. "To capture Akyab and to re-occupy upper Arakan.
    II. To strengthen our position in the Chin Hills.

III. To occupy Kalewa and Sittaung and thence to raid the Japanses Line of Communication.

IV. To make such administrative preparations as will allow of the rapid advance of a force towards upper or lower Burma, should opportunity offer during the campaigning season of 1942-43."

"The capture of Akyab," this operation instruction goes on to say, "will form part of a separate instruction."

The plans under consideration envisaged an attack on Burma from two directions, one from Assam into Upper Burma and the other into Arakan. The initial inability to launch an offensive operation from Assam led to greater emphasis being placed on the operations in Arakan. In September 1942, General Wavell set on foot preparations for a seaborne expedition to re-capture Akyab. It was at first intended to be carried out at the beginning of December 1942, but neither shipping nor troops nor the necessary air force was available for various reasons, chief of them being the prolongation of operations in Madagascar. By the middle of November, however, all hopes of mounting a seaborne expedition against Akyab had to be abandoned; it was accordingly decided by the Commander-in-Chief, India, that the only chance of capturing it was by an advance on land from Chittagong down the Arakan coast to secure the Mayu peninsula, whence an attack on Akyab could be launched from short range. This plan had the disadvantage that it made surprise most unlikely, but General Wavell hoped that if the advance in Arakan could proceed rapidly it would be difficult for the Japanese to re-inforce Akyab in time. It had become quite obvious that Akyab was an important feature to hold, both for the British as well as the Japanese forces. To the former, it was important as an advanced air-base as well as a first step in pushing down the coast of Burma. To the latter, it was important mainly as an air-base. The range of Japanese aircraft, particularly fighters, was such that Akyab had less value to them as an air-base than to the British. It seemed, therefore, that the holding of it by the Japanese was more important to them from the negative aspect of denying it to the British, than from the positive one of using it themselves.

On 17 October 1942, the Eastern Army had issued an Operation Instruction which defined the tasks for the cold weather of 1942-43 as follows:

(a) "To develop communications and establish British forces in a favourable position for re-conquering Burma and re-opening the Burma road at the first opportunity.

(b) To bring the Japanese to battle with the purpose of forcing them to use their strength, particularly in the air."

The immediate intention of the General Officer Commanding-in-Chief, Eastern Army, Lieut-General N.M.S. Irwin, CB, DSO, MC was:—

    I. To capture Akyab and re-establish contact in Upper Burma.

    II. To carry out such administrative arrangements as would allow a rapid advance towards lower Burma, should opportunity offer.

The original plan for the re-capture of Akyab had envisaged a sea-borne assault on the island by a force to be prepared and embarked by the General Headquarters, India, co-ordinated with a land advance southwards down the Mayu peninsula.[1] This assault landing was to be carried out by the 6th British Brigade Group which, as part of the 2nd British Division, had been trained in, and equipped for, combined operations, while the advance down the Mayu peninsula was to be entrusted to the 14th Indian Division.

---

[1] Operations "CANNY" and "NIBBLE". File 139/10 and F.25.

CHAPTER III

The Start of the Offensive

Although the entire system of communications in the whole of the Arakan area was much too undeveloped and inadequate for the maintenance of a large modernised fighting force, the area under Japanese control was comparatively better in this respect.

The Indian Lines of Communication

Throughout the year 1942, the Japanese had considerable air and naval superiority in the Bay of Bengal; the Allies were therefore deprived of direct sea-borne communications from Calcutta to the port of Chittagong. Consequently, they were compelled to use the more difficult and only partially developed land communications between the bases in India and the eastern extremities of Bengal. Reinforcements in man-power, stores and equipment were, therefore, directed by one or the other of the two main routes of entry into eastern Bengal.

These routes were:

I. Calcutta-Goalundo Ghat (Broad Gauge Railway)
    Goalundo Ghat-Chandpur (River Steamer)
    Chandpur-Laksam-Chittagong-Dohazari (Metre Gauge Railway)
II. Calcutta-Santahar (Broad Gauge Railway)
    Santahar-Tistamukh Ghat (Metre Gauge Railway)
    Tistamukh Ghat-Bahadurabad (Ferry)
    Bahadurabad-Comilla-Chittagong-Dohazari (Metre Gauge Ry.)

Both these routes involved three and four transhipments respectively before stores could reach the road/railhead at Dohazari; and neither the rail nor the steamer service, available on these routes, was designed or equipped to handle heavy stores.

The only ports of any use or importance on the eastern Bengal or Arakan coast were Chittagong and Akyab. The former, a comparatively modern and well-equipped port, came into use during the later part of the First Arakan Campaign; by 1943 and 1944, it was gradually developed into a first class base port. Akyab, on the other hand, remained under Japanese control throughout this campaign. However, steamer services operated all the year round between Chittagong, Cox's Bazaar and Maungdaw; and on the Naf river between Maungdaw, Teknaf and Tumbru Ghat. But during the opening stages of the operations in Arakan, no steamer services operated south of Cox's Bazaar. Throughout the campaign the most extensive use was made of all waterways, and subsidiary steamer services were also considerably developed.

The road communications also were entirely inadequate. There were no roads fit for wheeled transport to the north of Comilla and until the Arakan highway was completed in the autumn of 1943, there was no continuous road leading southwards into the area of operations. A fair weather road existed from Comilla to Chittagong and it extended to the northern bank of the Karnaphuli river. A pack-track linked this river with the railhead at Dohazari from where a metalled road ran for some ten miles to the south, and then petered out. Another metalled mechanical-transport road connected Maungdaw to Buthidaung; it followed the pattern of a disused railway and passed through two tunnels near the summit of the Mayu range.

Apart from the Maungdaw-Buthidaung road, other communications across the Mayu range were:
- (a) The Goppe pass which linked Goppe Bazaar with Bawli Bazaar.
- (b) The Ngakyedauk pass which linked Wabyin with Sinzweya.
- (c) A track leading from Indin to Sinoh.

All the above routes were nothing more than tracks and were fit only for pack mules. Nevertheless, many a dry weather track was made fit for mechanical transport, as it was easy to do so over the paddy fields. They were extensively used but were exceedingly dusty in fair weather, while in the monsoon they became quite impassable.

A pre-war all-weather airfield existed at Chittagong. This was progressively developed to meet the requirements of modern aircraft, while in other areas fair weather airstrips were constructed as needed—which again were mainly on paddy fields. These also were completely useless during the monsoon period, though reasonably adequate in the dry months.

The Mayu river was the main line of communication for the troops operating east of the Mayu Range; an inferior track between Buthidaung and Rathedaung also existed, but it could be used only when the weather permitted.

The Japanese Lines of Communication

The Japanese forces in Burma and Arakan were largely based on Rangoon. Their line of communication to the Mayu peninsula and the Kaladan valley was by rail and/or river to Prome from where a mechanical-transport road crossed the mountains westward to Taungup. A fair weather road ran northward from Taungup, and after a certain number of intersections by various chaungs, it reached Kyauktaw on the Kaladan river. From Taungup, a coastal road also extended southward to Sandoway and Gwa.

In addition to the mouth of every river and chaung from Taungup to Akyab in which inland water transport (IWT) could operate, the Japanese also controlled the two land lines of communication (partly road and partly track) into the Kalapanzin valley. One of these ran northward from Akyab involving ferry crossings over the various chaungs through the Kudaung island; the other started from Kyauktaw in the Kaladan valley and going westward across the mountains of Kanzauk, came down into the Kalapanzin valley at Htizwe. An indifferent road also ran northward from Myebon to Kyauktaw after passing through Minbya and Myohaung (involving ferry crossings over the various chaungs); and in Myebon itself, the Japanese possessed a small but very valuable anchorage through which they could pass a good amount of traffic from the sea to the hinterland.

The Japanese inland water transport system which was based at Tamandu, was easy to maintain and reasonably sound. The traffic to Akyab was taken via Myebon and the Min chaung, while from Akyab onwards the Mayu and the Kaladan rivers were used.

Throughout the period of their occupation of this area, the Japanese had made very extensive use of impressed local labour. Country carts and boats were also lavishly used to carry stores and equipment to their forward defended localities. Much of their movement, however, was carried out at night on account of the action of the Royal Navy (RN) and the Royal Indian Navy (RIN) vessels, which were operating in the chaungs and rivers round Akyab and to its south. The overall operations of the Royal Air Force also had a bearing on forcing the Japanese to avoid large scale movements by day.

It will thus appear that the organisation of the Japanese lines of communication was simple in the extreme, though judged by the British and American standards, it was entirely inadequate. Nevertheless, it worked quite smoothly and enabled the men and material to reach the forward areas.

Initial advance to Maungdaw and Buthidaung

Throughout the monsoon period in 1942, conflicting reports had kept coming in about the activities of Japanese troops in the Burma area. Information was also not lacking about the Japanese-trained Mughs in north and east Arakan, and by the middle of September 1942, it was estimated that there were approximately 3,000 Japanese troops positioned in that area. It had been found through Allied intelligence sources that the majority of these Japanese troops belonged to the *213th Infantry Regiment* of the *33rd Japanese Division*. This formation had been made responsible for the defence of Akyab and Arakan and the India Command had been informed that this Regiment's dispositions in the Arakan area were as follows:

2nd Battalion was in the area of Rathedaung,
3rd Battalion was in occupation of Donbaik and the surrounding country,
the rest of the troops were stationed in the Akyab area.

During the period from March 1942 to the end of July 1942, the 14th Indian Division was stationed in East Bengal and comprised the 47th and 49th Indian Infantry Brigades. The 47th Indian Infantry Brigade was more or less responsible for the defence of the Feni area while the 49th Indian Infantry Brigade was responsible for three separate battalion areas spread over Noakhali, Chandpur and Laksam. At the beginning of May 1942, however, the 49th Indian Infantry Brigade along with a proportion of divisional troops was ordered to proceed to Imphal. The 14th Indian Division was thus left with the 47th Indian Infantry Brigade only and this state of affairs continued until the end of August.

By then, however, in view of the change in policy which assumed a defensive role by the end of the monsoon period, the tasks of the 14th Indian Division had to be revised. Consequently, in August, the role of this Division in regard to Chittagong had altered; it was decided that this place would be defended at all costs as opposed to the original policy when it was intended to evacuate it in the event of an offensive action by the Japanese. The 123rd Indian Infantry Brigade was, therefore, sent to Chittagong from Imphal for the defence of this area. This Brigade had not had an easy time in north Assam and apart from its not being fully equipped, it had also suffered badly from sickness before its arrival.

In the middle of September 1942, as a result of the adoption of an offensive policy by the India Command, the 14th Indian Division was ordered to move south of Chittagong with the object of gaining contact with the Japanese. Consequently, the 55th Indian Infantry Brigade, which formed part of the 7th Indian Division and was located in the Attock area, was sent to join the 14th Indian Division. It took over the role of the defence of Chittagong from the 123rd Indian Infantry Brigade, thereby freeing the latter for the southward advance.

According to the Eastern Army Operation Instruction No. 15, dated 17 October 1942, the 14th Indian Division, reinforced by three battalions under the Headquarters, 88th Indian Infantry Brigade for line of communication protection, was to advance southwards and by 1 December 1942 was to be in position as follows:

I. One Brigade Group in the area Rathedaung-Buthidaung-Maungdaw.
II. One Brigade Group in the area Tumbru-Cox's Bazaar, in support of the leading brigade.
III. One Brigade Group in the Chittagong area.

The "V" Force in the area was also placed under the command of the 14th Indian Division while a number of river-craft and country boats, known as 2000-Flotilla, were organised into an Operational Headquarter and two squadrons of twelve patrol craft each; its tasks were operational patrols and escort duties in the Naf and Mayu rivers.

The first move in the occupation of Arakan in accordance with the Eastern Army instructions was the despatch of a company of 1/15th Punjab Regiment to Maungdaw which "V" Force had reported clear of the Japanese. This detachment which formed part of the 123rd Brigade moved by sea to Cox's Bazaar, thence by track to Tumbru Ghat and thereafter by country boats. A bigger detachment could not be sent as it would have been impossible to support it until the communications between Cox's Bazaar and Tumbru Ghat had been properly established. By 17 October 1942, however, Maungdaw and Buthidaung had both been occupied by the troops of the 1/15th Punjab Regiment without opposition and it was hoped to retain these two villages as a base for operations further south as far as Foul Point. As Maungdaw possessed jetties, it could also be used by river steamers sailing direct from Tumbru which was at the head of the Naf river, some twenty miles north of Maungdaw. At the same time Buthidaung provided an essential base and spring-board for the operations in the Mayu valley. The 14th Indian Division had also obtained control of the only mechanical-transport road across the Mayu Range.

By the evening of 18 October 1942, the Headquarters of the 14th Indian Division had moved from Maynamati to Chittagong and for the next two days there was not much activity on this division's front. On the night of 20 October, however, a message was received from the 123rd Indian Infantry Brigade saying that the Japanese were intending to attack Buthidaung and Maungdaw in full force. Air action was asked for by the forward troops with the result that Rathedaung was bombed by the Royal Air Force planes on 23 October.

It would appear that the Japanese reaction to the southward advance by this Indian division was very quick and determined. On the morning of 24 October, the 1/15th Punjab Regiment flashed a message, reporting heavy fighting at Buthidaung. By mid-morning of the same day it was known that the Japanese had advanced against Maungdaw in fairly large numbers; simultaneously, they had also attacked Buthidaung by landing troops, some 8 miles south of it via the Mayu river. The Japanese detachment which was moving against Buthidaung was very bravely tackled by the Indian force and one of the launches was sunk on the way to its objective. In view of the numerical superiority of the attackers, the 1/15th Punjab Regiment detachment had perforce to withdraw via Teknaf to the area of Bawli Bazaar. This detachment, at the time of its being landed at Maungdaw had been ordered not to become heavily engaged with the opposite force, and its role was purely one of gaining information and imposing as much delay on the hostile force as possible.

In view of the withdrawal of troops from Maungdaw and Buthidaung and the occupation of these places by the Japanese, the commander of the 14th Indian Division had to make a quick appreciation of the new situation. In the first instance he ordered the 123rd Indian Infantry Brigade to reinforce Bawli Bazaar by the rest of the 1/15th Punjab Regiment which was to be sent there immediately by an overland route. The brigade was, at the same time, warned to first make certain whether a force of a battalion strength could be maintained in that area. Meanwhile, as mentioned earlier, the detachments of this battalion which had to retreat from Maungdaw and Buthidaung were already making their way via Teknaf to Bawli Bazaar.

On 26 October, after having held various consulations with his staff officers, the Divisional Commander ordered that Bawli Bazaar would be held at all costs and that the road Bawli Bazaar-Taung Bazaar was to be carefully protected and watched. At this stage information had also reached confirming that Maungdaw had been occupied by the Japanese patrols at 2200 hours on 24 October. In the morning of the same day Buthidaung and Maungdaw were both bombed, each by six bombers of the Royal Air Force.

Early in the morning of 27 October, news was received that the 1/15th Punjab Regiment detachments from Maungdaw had arrived at Bawli Bazaar. The same report went on to say that the Japanese were in occupation of Taung Bazaar and that their next objective was possibly Bawli Bazaar. The 123rd Indian Infantry Brigade had all this while been moving the bulk of its personnel to Cox's Bazaar by the sea and river routes. This had been a very slow movement as there were only two small ships available on this run, and their total carrying capacity was about 200-350 personnel and 250-300 tons. The normal turnround of the ships was two days but as all personnel and stores had to be disembarked in small boats about two miles from the landing stage, the turnround was often much longer. During the last week of October the commander of this brigade had commenced his advance to Ramu and Ukhia with the troops he had collected at Cox's Bazaar. Although there was no hostile opposition during this move, the brigade had to overcome tremendous physical difficulties. The means of transport between Cox's Bazaar and the forward troops were practically on a porter basis; the monsoon was not over and very frequently the troops were cut off for days at a time and the men had very often to be put on half rations.

Late in the evening of 30 October, the 123rd Indian Infantry Brigade opened its Advanced Headquarters at Ukhia and immediately positioned a platoon of the 1/15th Punjab Regiment at Goppe Bazaar. By that time, the brigade had been ordered by the Divisional Commander that no withdrawals would be allowed from the positions then in occupation by its troops. The threat to Bawli Bazaar continued but so far an attack had not materialised.

Such was the situation at the end of October 1942 on the Arakan front and for nearly a month and a half after this no further operations were undertaken by either side. The lack of an organized line of communication or of through communications south of Dohazari had severely handicapped the Indian forces. A limited number of men and only a certain quantity of material could be maintained in the forward areas, but exceptionally bad weather added to the difficulties of administration. All these factors imposed delay and prevented an immediate resumption of the operations.

Even now, it was not quite certain as to what the Japanese strategic plan was, but to the India Command it appeared that the Japanese intention was to deny them the general line, Maungdaw-Buthidaung. Information was also lacking as to the Japanese strength and dispositions, south of this line. To a very large extent, however, this lack and uncertainty of information had been alleviated by the creation of "V" Force and the excellent work which it was carrying out. This Force was commanded by Lieut.-Colonel Donald who was formerly an Inspector of the Burma police in the Shwebo Division and consisted mainly of locals led by British officers who continually succeeded in penetrating behind the Japanese positions in quest of information. In addition to this, reliable contacts had also been established in most villages of the Mayu peninsula and as far afield as the Kaladan valley. This resulted in a fairly reliable and regular flow of information to reach back to the British local commanders who make the utmost use of it.

The Second advance through Maungdaw and Buthidaung

Throughout the stalemate period, vigorous patrolling had been carried out by the 14th Indian Division, southwards from Bawli

Bazaar. But their main advance was delayed due to bad weather, administrative difficulties, and unusually heavy rains for the time of the year. This situation continued till about the middle of November 1942 and it was also at this time that it became apparent to the Eastern Army that the necessary resources for a landing operation at Akyab could not be made available during the winter of 1942-43; plans for a sea assault had therefore to be abandoned. General Wavell, the Commander-in-Chief in India, states in his second despatch from India Command, "Early in autumn I set on foot preparations for a sea-borne expedition to recapture Akyab. It was at first intended to be carried out at the beginning of December, but neither the shipping, troops or necessary air force could be made available for various reasons, principally the prolongation of operations in Madagascar. By the middle of November I was forced to abandon hope of being able to mount the sea-borne expedition against Akyab, and decided that the only chance of capturing it was by an advance from Chittagong down the Arakan coast to secure Mayu peninsula, whence an attack on Akyab could be launched from short range. This plan had the disadvantage that it made surprise most unlikely, and Arakan was a most unfavourable theatre, into which I should certainly not have made a deep land advance on any scale, had sea transport been available. I also realised that the troops available had had little opportunity of training in jungle warfare. I hoped, however, that if the advance in Arakan could proceed rapidly, it would be difficult for the Japanese to reinforce in time; and considered it was better to take the risks involved than to remain inactive on this front during the winter."

On 19 November 1942, instructions were accordingly issued to the Eastern Army; and the 123rd Indian Infantry Brigade with the addition of the 1/7th Rajput Regiment, were in position, ready to make the final advance on Maungdaw and Buthidaung, early in December 1942. These troops were in contact with the Japanese north of Maungdaw, but not to the north of Buthidaung; in the latter place the foremost Indian and British troops were established in Taung Bazaar.

The plan for the recapture of Maungdaw and Buthidaung was an attack by one battalion on Buthidaung, from positions east of the Mayu hills while two battalions were to assault Maungdaw. The fourth battalion of the brigade was then to cross the Mayu river south of the road Maungdaw-Buthidaung and thereby assist in the capture of Buthidaung by an advance from the south of that place. The bulk of the maintenance for this force was to be brought in through Maungdaw, soon after its capture; a track, later known as the Goppe Pass, had to be made over the hills, east of Bawli Bazaar, to enable the battalion to enter the Kalapanzin river valley for an attack on Buthidaung.

The commander of the 14th Indian Division wanted to carry out the attack on Maungdaw and Buthidaung when the above dispositions had been completed. Intelligence sources had indicated that the Japanese did not have more than one battalion between Maungdaw and Buthidaung and it appeared that the chief centre of resistance would be the area of the Razabil village. The Eastern Army Commander, however, decided to halt the advance of the 14th Indian Division until such time as the remainder of the 47th Indian Infantry Brigade could also be brought up and concentrated, the tracks to Goppe Bazaar and Taung Bazaar made fit for mules and one extra battalion placed at Taung Bazaar for the attack on Buthidaung. The Army Commander's reasons for halting the 14th Indian Division's advance at this stage, as mentioned in "Brigadier Creffield's report" were as follows:—

(i) "Our advance from the position we had reached was about to meet the first Japanese prepared positions and it was essential that our first action should be a successful one.

(ii) The Goppe Pass should be made fit for mules to enable that flank to be reinforced with another battalion and given additional fire support to that part of the attack.

(iii) It would give time to build up bigger reserves and improving communications between Cox's Bazaar and the foremost troops."

The dispositions of the troops which were either in Arakan or earmarked for that area, by the end of November 1942, were:

123rd Indian Infantry Brigade On battalion of the 47th Indian Infantry Brigade	Tumbru—Bawli Bazaar—Taung Bazaar with a detachment at Teknaf.
47th Indian Infantry Brigade less one battalion	Moving up from Chittagong to Cox's Bazaar. Detachments in Ramu and Ukhia.
55th Indian Infantry Brigade	At Chittagong.
88th Indian Infantry Brigade	At Comilla with a battalion at Feni.

The line of communication for the forward troops was very tricky, difficult and inadequate. Its various stages were:

Chittagong to Cox's Bazaar	By sea.
Cox's Bazaar to Nawpara-Tumbru	Animal transport, pack and draught. A few 15 cwt. vehicles were also being used.

Tumbru-Nawapara to Bawli Bazaar and Teknaf	By means of Sampans.
Bawli Bazaar to forward troops which were to the west of Mayu hills.	Pack transport.
Bawli to Goppe and Taung-Bazaars	Pack transport upto the foot hills, and then porter; a limited amount of sampan lifts on the Kalapanzin river was also being utilised between Goppe and Taung Bazaar.

A sea line of communication between Chittagong and Maungdaw was at this stage envisaged and a sea convoy of small ships belonging to 2000-Flotilla was planned to land supplies and stores at Maungdaw, within 24 hours of its capture. It is worth mentioning that when the occasion arose, prodigious feats in transferring stores by sea from Chittagong to Cox's Bazaar and Maungdaw, in worn-out river craft and under the most adverse conditions were performed by the Naval Officer In Charge (N.O.I.C.) at Chittagong.

In view of the subsequent experience of Japanese tenacity in defence, the Eastern Army Commander's decision to strengthen the 14th Indian Division's spearhead before allowing it to advance was probably the right one. Nevertheless, this decision delayed the advance by about 14 days, and just before it commenced, the Japanese had withdrawn from Maungdaw and Buthidaung. On 16 and 17 December 1942, the forward patrols of the 14th Indian Division found to their surprise that Maungdaw and Buthidaung were both clear of Japanese troops. It is not quite certain as to why these places were evacuated and information through Japanese sources is also not forthcoming in explanation of this fact. Consequently, these places were immediately occupied and consolidated. This reoccupation of Maungdaw and Buthidaung enabled the 14th Indian Division to undertake a planned and co-ordinated advance to the south, down the Mayu peninsula.

After the occupation of Maungdaw and Buthidaung, the 14th Indian Division's next objective was Foul Point and Rathedaung. At this stage the arrival of the 6th British Infantry Brigade, which had commenced to concentrate in Chittagong, had an important influence on the operations of the 14th Indian Division. This brigade was destined for attack on Akyab and was not under the command of the Divisional Commander, except for administration. As has been already mentioned, it had been planned to carry the bulk of the maintenance stores through Maungdaw when that place was captured. It was, therefore, unfortunate that a few days before the occupation of Maungdaw, in spite of strong protests by the Commander of the 14th Indian Division, six small vessels which were to be used for the carriage of stores between Chittagong and Maungdaw were allotted to the 6th British Infantry Brigade for their training in Chittagong and subsequent operations. This considerably increased the maintenance difficulties of the 14th Indian Division.

After the occupation of Maungdaw and Buthidaung the advance by the 14th Indian Division continued on a two-brigade front. The 47th Indian Infantry Brigade advanced down the coastal sector to the west of the Mayu range while the 123rd Indian Infantry Brigade advanced down the east bank of the Mayu river. Their objectives were Foul Point and Rathedaung respectively. Only the 55th Indian Infantry Brigade remained as reinforcement in the hands of the Divisional Commander. Two factors, however, prevented him from having this brigade close to the front as a reserve. He was still responsible for the defence of the line of communication up to the Meghna river, and apart from the 55th Indian Infantry Brigade, which was responsible for the defence of Chittagong, he had only two battalions to assist him in this task. These were the 14/12th Frontier Force Regiment and the 5/9th Jat Regiment, both belonging to the 88th Indian Infantry Brigade. The Divisional Commander was not quite certain as to how secure his right flank was from attack; during this period the Japanese Navy had command of the sea in the Bay of Bengal and a Japanese naval force had been reported in this area. The other factor was his maintenance difficulty. Prior to the capture of Maungdaw, the maximum of troops which could be maintained by the line of communication from Cox's Bazar-Tumbru-Bawli Bazaar and Taung Bazaar, was already being maintained; and although the road Dohazari-Tumbru was being improved, it could still be used only by light mechanical transport, not exceeding 15 Cwt. As it was, there was very little of this type of mechanical transport available. The decision, therefore, to take six small ships from the planned sea line of communication from Chittagong to Maungdaw, increased the maintenance difficulties of the 14th Indian Division. Consequently, it became still more difficult to bring the 55th Indian Infantry Brigade forward even after the capture of Maungdaw.

The two brigades continued their advance and made good progress in the early stages without encountering any opposition. The 47th Indian Infantry Brigade advanced with two battalions forward for the capture of Foul Point. Practically no opposition was met north of Indin while intelligence reports indicated that the Japanese strength south of this point was not very considerable. The 5/8th Punjab Regiment and 1 Inniskillings were the forward battalions and were supported by the carriers of the former. By the end of December, therefore, Indin to the west and Sinoh to the east of the Mayu range were occupied by the patrols of the 5/8th Punjab Regiment; later, these positions were consolidated by 1/7 Rajput. On 31 December 1942, 1/7 Rajput repulsed a series of Japanese attacks throughout the day which were made on their positions in Sinoh. On 1 January 1943, some carriers of the 5/8th Punjab Regiment, one of the leading battalions of the 47th Indian Infantry Brigade, made a successful reconnaissance down the west beach of the Mayu peninsula and actually reached Foul Point, without making any contact with the Japanese troops.

In the meanwhile, east of the Mayu river, the advance of the 123rd Indian Infantry Brigade had also proceeded unhindered until the force had moved south of Htizwe. It appeared that the Japanese did not anticipate any Allied advance along this flank and had actually moved few troops from the Mayu peninsula to defend this flank. At this stage the Eastern Army had ordered the 14th Indian Division to move a battalion into the Kaladan valley, as the appreciation was that if the Kaladan river was left undisputed in the hands of the Japanese it would provide the latter with an important artery of communication, whence infiltration could be undertaken against the left flank and the line of communication of the Indian forces, advancing southwards. Consequently, as a result of this appreciation, wireless telegraphy (W/T) observation units were established in the Kaladan valley. This necessitated the establishment of forces in this area for the purpose of observing and reporting Japanese movements and restricting the use of the river by them.

To carry out this task, though a large numercial strength could not be deployed, two forces were sent into the Kaladan valley. One of these, the 8/10th Baluch was detailed by the 14th Indian Division thus leaving the 123rd Indian Infantry Brigade only with two battalions for the advance on Rathedaung. The two Forces were called:

    (a) Tripforce—Consisting of the Tripura State Force led by Indian and British officers. It commenced its advance from Dohazari and developing the Sangu river as a line of communication, occupied Paletwa and Kaladan without opposition at the end of December 1942.

    (b) Soutcol—Consisting of the 8/10th Baluch and engineer and medical detachments. It advanced from Taung Bazaar on the Kalapanzin river and developing a mule track reached the Kaladan river at Apaukwa, some ten miles south of Kyauktaw.

The physical difficulties encountered by the 123rd Indian Infantry Brigade in its advance on Rathedaung were very considerable. There was no practicable land communication, hence the bulk of this brigade was transported and maintained by sampans, collected in the Mayu and Kalapanzin rivers after the capture of Buthidaung. This had consequently not only slowed up their advance but had also limited the front to one battalion. On 27 December 1942, two days after the 10th Lancashire Fusiliers' patrols had entered Rathedaung the troops of this Brigade were also in occupation of Alethangyaw and Lambaguna.

From the positions that the 47th and 123rd Indian Infantry Brigades had reached by the end of the year, no immediate follow-up was practicable and a delay of some ten days ensued. To a large extent, the reasons for this delay were the restrictions imposed by administrative and maintenance difficulties. It will be seen that these brigades of the 14th Indian Division were operating nearly 150 miles forward of their railhead, and the line of communication, incompletely developed and comparatively unorganised, was tenuous in the extreme. Moreover, the weather conditions were such that all wheeled movement had been restricted. These factors would naturally limit any further advance. However, whatever may have been the causes of the delay, there can be no doubt of the serious and unfortunate results that ensued. The Japanese were quick to take the fullest advantage of this unexpected opportunity given to them. They re-occupied Rathedaung and at the same time despatched companies to Laung Chaung and Donbaik, and thereby gave evidence of their determination to resist the attempts of the Indian Division to penetrate into Arakan.

The hardening of Japanese resistance in the Mayu Peninsula and in the Mayu valley suggests that the Japanese had appreciated the intention of the Eastern Army to capture Akyab, and had rightly estimated its importance. They had decided, therefore, to stand and fight at Donbaik and in the neighbourhood of Rathedaung, as these places were of great natural strength and easy to defend. They also held that it would compel the Indian troops to fight at the end of a long and very thin line of communication while the Japanese forces would fight comparatively close to their base at Akyab. In addition, the Japanese were enabled by this means to stabilise their immediate front whereby they could prepare for their favourite manoeuvre—a hook round one or the other of the flanks of the opposite force.

Fighting at Donbaik

After this initial advance, although no major developments followed, the Eastern Army kept planning and manoeuvring to attack the Japanese forces in the Donbaik and Rathedaung areas. Active patrolling was carried out with a view to gaining information about Japanese strength and disposition, and the early part of January 1943 was spent in the tactical deployment of troops. On 11 January, 1/7 Rajput, less one company, concentrated in the Sangan chaung area, and the next day, the 47th Indian Infantry Brigade headquarters moved to the new location at Kodingauk. The same day, headquarters of the 130th Field Regiment along with the advance party of a Medium Machine Gun Company of 9 Jat arrived at Shinkhali. On 16 January, the commander of the 47th Indian Infantry Brigade held a conference to determine the attack on Japanese positions north of Donbaik, and Operation Order No. 9 was issued to all concerned. The positions of the units were reshuffled and orders given that the Inniskillings and 1/7 Rajput would take over the right and left forward areas respectively; the take over was to be completed by 0600 hours on 17 January. In the meantime, the company of 1/7 Rajput which was at Thikado was ordered to move and join its battalion in the Donbaik area, and the brigade headquarters Command Post (CP) was established at 640860. (see Map on next page)

On 18 January 1943, 1 Inniskillings and 1/7 Rajput, supported by two batteries of field artillery, one mountain battery and four carriers began the attack on the Japanese positions, which were manned by about a company of troops with mortars and medium machine guns (MMGs) all along the chaungs to the north of Donbaik, as well as in the foothills, north-east of Donbaik village. The attack was preceded by a successful effort on the part of the carriers to draw the Japanese fire. Fire was drawn from three mortars, one medium machine gun and three light machine guns which disclosed their location as being in the area of the "chaung FDL" (foremost defended locality), and in the foothills to the east. As a result, shortly before the attack went in, these Japanese positions were subjected to intense artillery bombardment.

The attack went in according to plan and 1/7 Rajput, advancing from the hills under cover of smoke, succeeded in making its way through dense scrub and jungle to within a mile of Donbaik. But owing to the nature of the country, they were unable to clear the foothills of Japanese machine guns and snipers, who continued to sweep with automatic fire the open ground between the foothills and the sea shore. The Inniskillings, however, were held up in front of Japanese FDLs on the beach in the "Village Area". It appeared that Japanese were well dug in and had mortars and light machine guns covering the beach sector and hence the leading company of the Inniskillings suffered a large number of casualties. Consequently, A company of the Inniskillings was sent round to

THE START OF THE OFFENSIVE

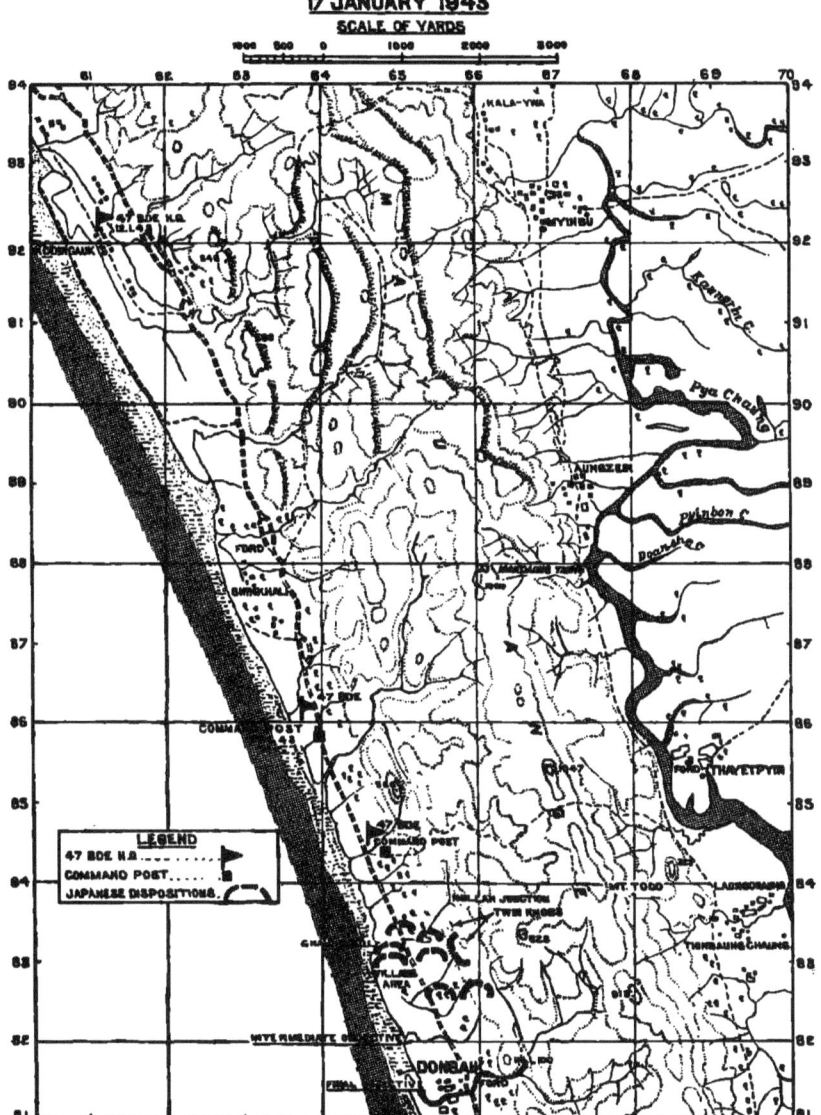

attack the Japanese from the left flank, but owing to the thick jungle country very little progress was made. Orders were therefore given to the battalions to consolidate the ground gained while plans were made to continue the attack on the next day. In the meantime, D and B Companies of 1/7 Rajput had kept on advancing and had lost touch with their battalion headquarters. Intense fire had been kept up the whole day by both sides but owing to the nature of the country the Japanese had not suffered much as they had the advantage of perfect camouflage and concealment. Their exact positions, therefore, were extremely difficult to locate, and by continuously using their large number of alternative posts they were at an advantage against the brigade artillery fire.

The position on the morning of 19 January was that the Japanese had been driven back on the east flank, but they were still in occupation of the "Village Area". The brigade headquarters therefore decided to capture this locality and then continue the advance to Donbaik. The attack was to be made by A company of the Inniskillings, which was to get covering fire by the rest of the battalion, along with a company of 1/7 Rajput. Artillery concentrations were laid down on the eastern and western face of the "Village Area" as well as on the Wadi Junction while the carriers of 5/8 Punjab operated along the beach under command of the Inniskillings.

A company of the Inniskillings, while attacking the Japanese flank, was suddenly fired upon from behind by medium machine guns. Due to this, the attack could not be carried out according to plan, while two platoons were immediately detailed to clear the medium gun posts. All this time, A company of 1/7 Rajput had kept the Japanese busy in the "Village Area", while the carriers which were advancing along the beach came under heavy anti-tank gun fire. One carrier was set on fire and two more were put out of action; the remainder became unserviceable owing to mechanical defects caused by the salt water. In spite of their great courage and gallantry in their supporting role they could not help the plan of attack any more. It was in this action that Havildar Parkash Singh of 5/8 Punjab earned the award of the Victoria Cross. He was recommended by the commander of 1 Inniskillings and his recommendation read as follows:

> ".......... On 19 January 1943 in the Donbaik area, three carriers were put out of action by an enemy Anti-tank gun and lay on the open beach covered by enemy Anti-tank and light machine guns. One of those carriers was carrying the survivors of another carrier in addition to its own crew. Havildar Parkash Singh seeing what had happened, went out, from a safe harbour in his own carrier and with complete disregard for his own personal safety, rescued the combined crews from one disabled carrier. He also brought back

the weapons from the carrier. Having brought the crews to safety, the Havildar again went out on the open beach in his carrier still under very heavy Anti-tank gun and machine gun fire and with the utmost disregard to his personal safety, dismounted and connected a towing chain on to a disabled carrier containing 2 wounded men. Still under fire, he directed the towing of the disabled carrier from under enemy fire to a place of safety. The Havildar's very gallant actions, entirely on his own initiative, were an inspiration to all ranks, both British and Indian."

At 1100 hours on 19 January, A company of the Rajputs was pinned to the ground in front of Japanese positions at 650834 while A company of the Inniskillings was in touch with the Japanese posts in the dense jungle at 655834. The brigade thereupon ordered C company of the Rajputs, which was in reserve, to clear those posts and exploit as far as the "chaung FDL". This attack was put in at 1530 hours across open ground but C company was practically decimated before it reached the objective. One result of this attack, however, was that the Japanese could advance no further, and later in the evening, A company of 1/7 Rajput was able to withdraw slightly to a more secure position, with the Japanese in front of it rather than to its right rear. This company of 1/7 Rajput also went in to clear the Japanese from the feature known as TWIN KNOBS and put in an attack with great dash, but immediately came under withering fire from a previously unlocated machine gun. A few men only of this company reached their objective and only twelve men eventually returned to tell the tale. In the meantime, some Japanese troops had succeeded in infiltrating into the area along the northern slopes of TWIN KNOBS and were preventing the supply of ammunition and rations to the Rajput companies along the top of the feature. Consequently, as these companies had by this time exhausted both rations and ammunition, they were ordered to withdraw with the remainder of the battalion.

On the 20th, it was discovered that the Japanese had used either some form of flame thrower or some substance in their mortar shells which caused a few of the Indian troops to be burnt. A conference was held at the brigade headquarters and since the attack had not succeeded according to plan, orders were issued to all concerned to re-organise the battalions and consolidate the ground gained. D and B companies of 1/7 Rajput had in the meantime returned after being away from their headquarters for nearly 24 hours without rations or ammunition. They had apparently been hiding in the hills and jungles and had indulged in a little sniping with the Japanese.

Warning orders for the relief of the 47th Indian Infantry Brigade were received on the 21st and for the next few days minor artillery engagements and sporadic bombing attacks were carried out by the opposing forces. Troops of the 55th Indian Infantry Brigade, the relieving unit, started arriving in the Donbaik area, and by 1200 hours on the 24th the outgoing brigade had moved to Kodingauk and by evening tide had gone on to Waybin. The next day, the 47th Indian Infantry Brigade reached Ukhia where it was told to stay and enjoy a much needed rest.

The 55th Indian Infantry Brigade began preparations for another attack on the Japanese positions in front of Donbaik. This attack, supported by as much artillery and air craft as possible, along with half a squadron of the 146th Royal Armoured Corps Regiment, was the first fully co-ordinated attack to be delivered in Arakan. It was planned and carried out on much more ambitious lines than any delivered previously.

According to the plan of fighting outlined in Operation Instruction No. 1 of the 55th Indian Infantry Brigade, 2/1 Punjab occupied TWIN KNOBS at 11-30 hours on 30 January 1943. The same day, the plan of attack which was to be put in on 1 February was circulated to all concerned. The zero hour was 1130 hours and the attack was to be carried out in three phases:

Phase I—The capture by 1/17 Dogra, supported by the tank detachment, of Japanese FDLs in the area of the Chaung running westwards from 652832, and the capture of the wooded area at 647830.

Phase II—Thereafter 1/17 Dogra supported by the tank detachment to capture the Chaung running westwards from 634831 up to the Wadi junction.

Phase III—Exploitation to Donbaik.

The disposition of the forward troops of the 55th Indian Infantry Brigade on 31 January 1943 was as shown in Map on page 42.

Japanese positions previous to 1 February 1943

The information gained later from the captured Japanese prisoners of war indicated that *No. 3 Battalion, 213 Infantry Regiment of 33rd Division* was positioned along the west of the Mayu Range, possibly with elements of *No. 2 Battalion* up to a company in strength, most of them in the Laungchaung area. The Japanese battalion was disposed as follows:

No. 9 Company was in the "chaung FDL" and also held positions immediately north of it.

No. 10 Company was in reserve and on 3 February was detailed to attack Hill 566, which was the Indian Observation Post (never actually attacked).

No. 11 Company was in Donbaik village and chaung.

No. 12 Company was in the area between the south Knob and Hill 100 along with the battalion headquarters.

Two 75 mm Regimental guns and at least three anti-tank guns with one captured British 2-pounder were in the "chaung FDL". The others were probably 37 mm guns. In this area there was a much greater allotment of light machine guns than is normal in a company. Thus there was a considerable amount of fire power, most of which consisted of automatic weapons. Five 90 mm mortars with several smaller ones were evenly distributed among the companies along with a fair number of medium machine guns.

There were 2 or 3 light machine guns and at least one medium gun at S5 which was a small, circular fortified position dug in under a clump of tree. This position had, in addition, a crawl trench connecting it with the jungle to the east and to S4 to the west.

At various times, mortar, medium machine gun and anti-tank fire were reported from S4 also. This was a position similar to S5, and was dug into the sides of a subsidiary nullah, leading out of the main chaung. Two of the three British tanks which were ditched on 1 February got stuck in this area.

Mortars and medium machine guns were also sited in the area of M16, a small nullah to the west of S4. Further to the west along the chaung there were a series of fox-holes on the north bank which led into such completely protected dug-outs as even the British 25 pounder guns could not penetrate. The "Village Area", however, had no prepared positions.

Zero Hour on 1 February 1943

Supported by eight armoured fighting vehicles (AFVs) the 55th Indian Infantry Brigade attacked the Japanese positions according to plan. Owing to the unexpected resistance, however, the 1/17th Dogra Regiment was unable to reach the start line in time and hence the tactical surprise in the sudden use of AFVs was lost. Consequently, when the eight Valentine tanks approached the "chaung FDL" three tanks got stuck and the leading tank's wireless faded out. The remaining tanks had therefore to follow their leader out of action. Nevertheless, by the evening, the tanks had made a second sortie reaching almost to the mouth of the "chaung FDL" and were shooting at the "Village Area" whilst at about 1640 hours, 2/1 Punjab had occupied the "Wadi Junction" without opposition. By darkness, 1/17 Dogra was consolidated from the edge of the jungle at 652837 to the north Knob and 2/1 Punjab from the "Wadi Junction" to the south Knob.

Throughout this day British artillery activity was most extensive. Support was given to 2/1 Punjab during the preliminary

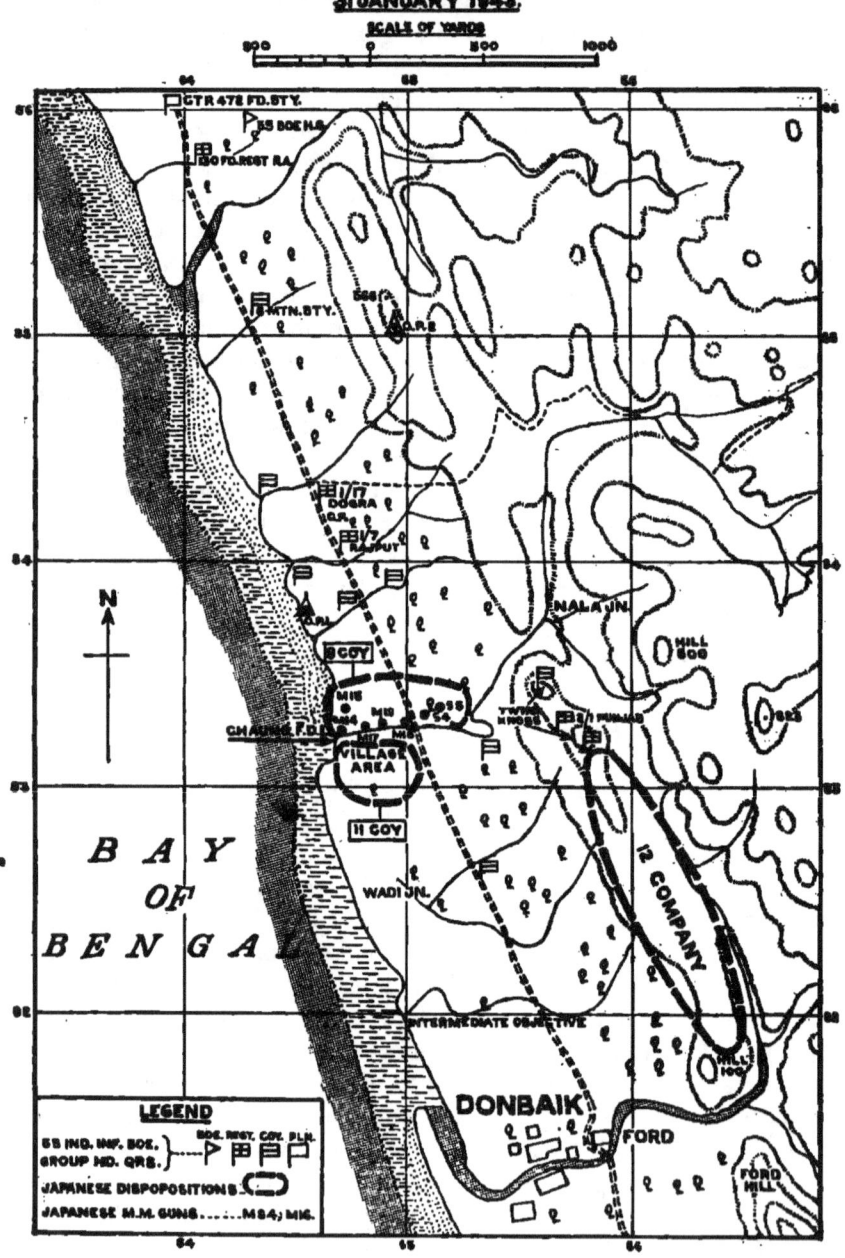

advance to establish themselves in the jungle, west of the TWIN KNOBS. The support for the attack timed at 1130 hours consisted of a smoke screen at the mouth of the Creek to behind the north-east edge of the wooded "Village Area" towards "Wadi Junction" in order to defilade the left flank of the attacking forces. The night of 1/2 February was quiet. Preceded by artillery concentrations on the "Nullah FDLs" and wooded village strong point, the offensive was once again renewed by 1/17 Dogra and 2/1 Punjab at 0900 hours on 2 February. As a result of the artillery concentration a fierce conflagration was seen in the "Village Area", which was taken to be the result of some ammunition having blown up. By 0930 hours, 2/1 Punjab attacking from "Wadi Junction" (651825) had gained the wooded area under the cover of a most effective smoke screen. This area was overrun except for a strong point in the north-east corner, which continued to hold out for the rest of the day, despite shelling by mortars and artillery. Meanwhile, one company of 1/17 Dogra was progressing west along the nullah from the edge of the jungle; another company dominated the jungle itself while a third was encircling a strong point to the south of the nullah.

By 1130 hours the further advance of 2/1 Punjab was still held up by the resistance from the north-east corner of the "Village Area" and a strongly held point at 646833 in the nullah. At the same time, a company of Dogras was attempting to deal with a strong point at 648834, about 60 yards north of the nullah and nearly 400 yards from the edge of the jungle, while another company was finding opposition in the wooded promontory at 652832.

In the early afternoon, 2/1 Punjab withdrew a little from its positions to allow the artillery to fire, and heavy concentrations were thereupon put down on the areas of resistance, confronting both 2/1 Punjab and 1/17 Dogra. At the same time the carriers went in with great dash in an effort to clear up the situation at the mouth of the Creek, then link up with 2/1 Punjab and finally carry out a reconnaissance as far as Donbaik. But intense machine-gun fire was encountered by them from the northern edge of the Japanese FDLs; and after a strenuous fight, the engagement had to be broken off. Artillery concentrations had also not reduced the Japanese resistance and by the evening of the 2nd the situation was substantially the same as after the initial attack in the morning. As darkness fell, the Japanese put in a counter-attack on the "Twin Knobs", particularly the South Knob, but the attack was driven off and the position was maintained.

The second attack, however, also proved unsuccessful due mainly to the cleverly sited Japanese light machine gun posts and their use of "fox holes" with trap-door covers which could not be discovered until the attack had begun.

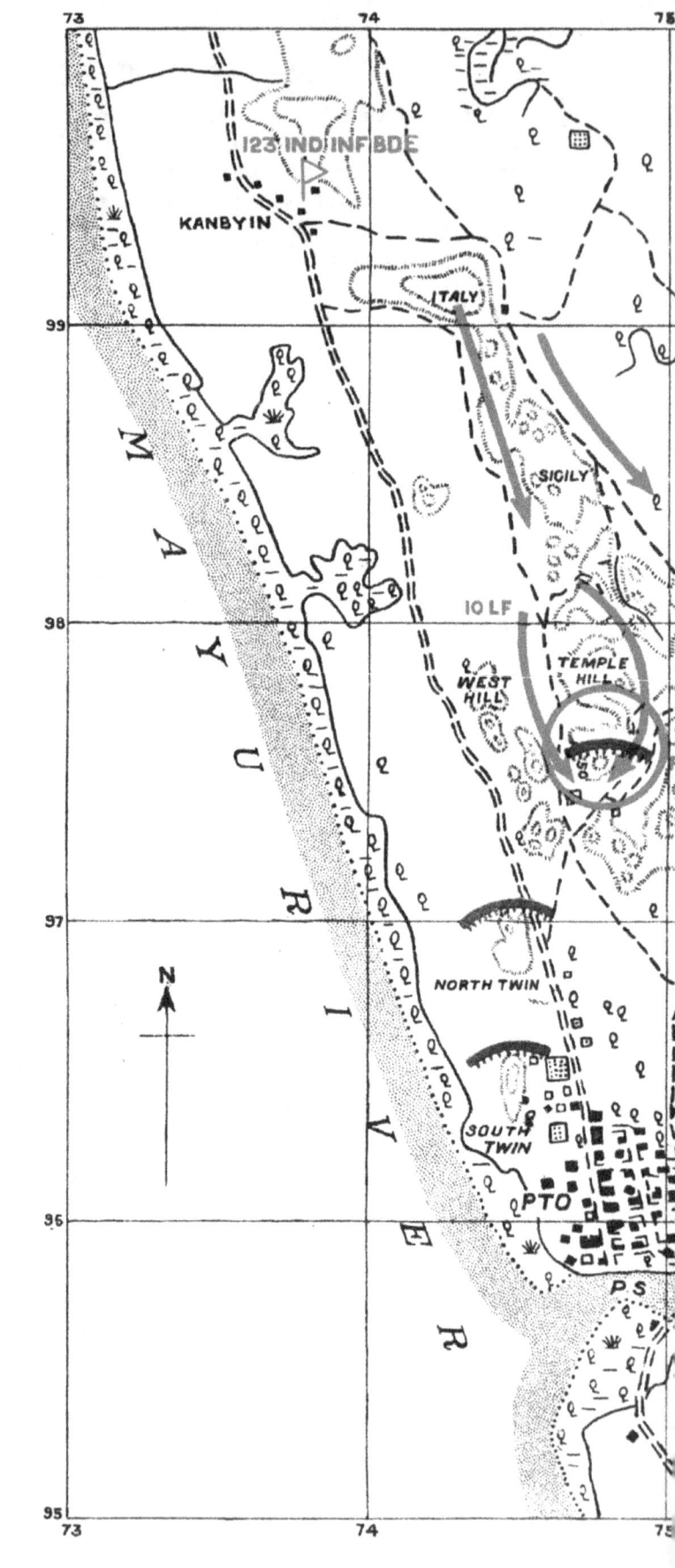

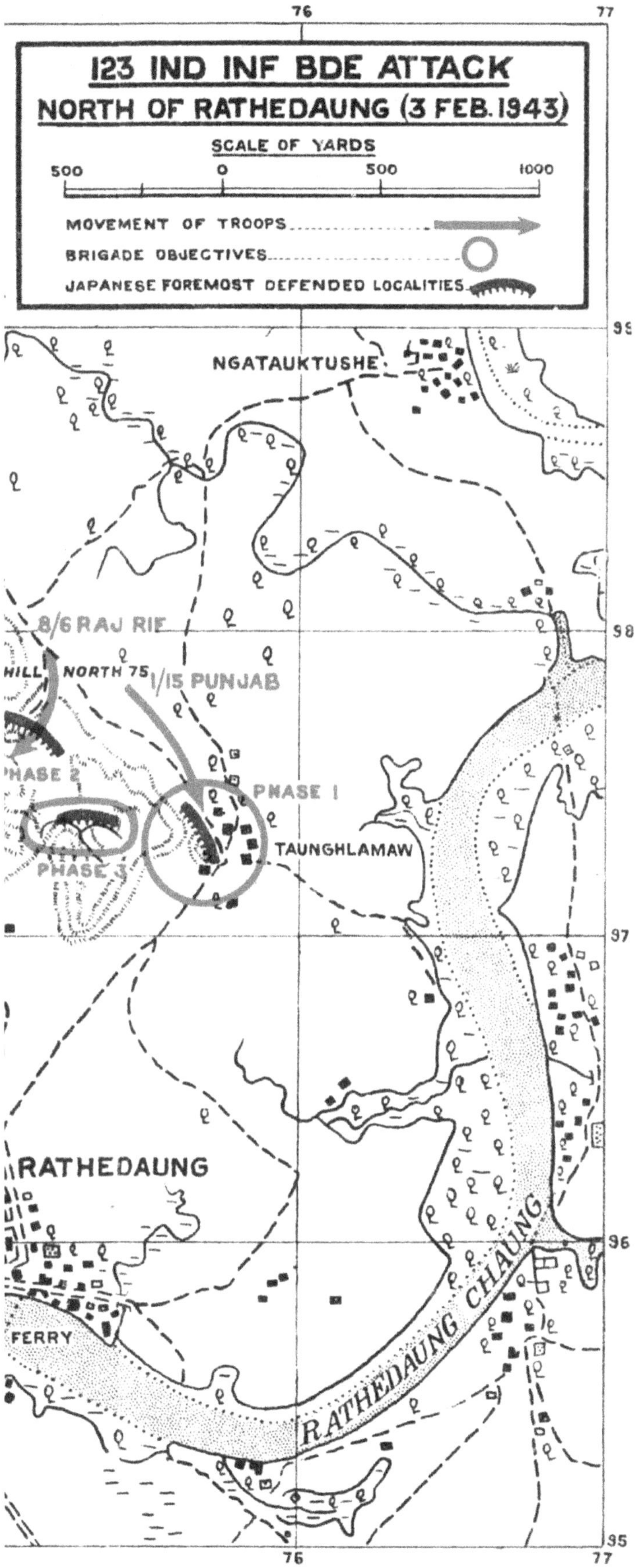

123 IND INF BDE ATTACK
NORTH OF RATHEDAUNG (3 FEB. 1943)
SCALE OF YARDS
500
0
500
1000
MOVEMENT OF TROOPS
BRIGADE OBJECTIVES
JAPANESE FOREMOST DEFENDED LOCALITIES
76
77
99
98
97
96
95
NGATAUKTUSHE
8/6 RAJ RIF
HILL
NORTH 75
1/15 PUNJAB
PHASE 2
PHASE 1
PHASE 3
TAUNGHLAMAW
RATHEDAUNG
FERRY
RATHEDAUNG CHAUNG

Subsequent full-scale operations in the Donbaik area were delayed until 18 February 1943, due to the difficulties of communication. Reinforcements of men and material were very slow in reaching the forward areas and the long stretch of hastily constructed road was subject to continual interruption by rain. At the same time, the supply by sea was also hampered by lack of vessels which might suitably use the anchorages at Cox's Bazaar and Maungdaw. In consequence, and to the great disadvantage of the Indian force, the Japanese were afforded a breathing time of which they took the fullest advantage. They strengthened their positions and laid mine fields against the future use of tanks, which had already been handicapped by the terrain and the difficulty of deployment and manoeuvre. It is therefore not surprising that the attack on 18 February was no more successful than the previous ones. Very heavy opposition was encountered by the Indian and British forces, and although Japanese counter-attacks failed, they gained local successes by infiltration. The Inniskillings and the Dogras and the 2/1st Punjab Regiment came under heavy fire from the Japanese strong points suffering considerable casualties.

123rd Indian Infantry Brigade attack on Rathedaung

Meanwhile, on 3 February 1943, the 123rd Indian Infantry Brigade had renewed its attacks in the Rathedaung area, but without any success. This period is also notable for increased Japanese air activity and the constant attacks by day and night on the brigade headquarters, administrative areas and forward positions.

The attack by the 123rd Indian Infantry Brigade on 3 February 1943 was divided into three main phases.

First Phase—At 0700 hours, 1/15 Punjab was to capture Taunghlamaw village and ring contour 757972. The village was known to have been unoccupied.

Second Phase—10 Lancashire Fusiliers was to capture West Hill.

Third Phase—1/15 Punjab was to capture ring contour feature 754973 ; 8/6 Raj Rif to exert pressure on hill 75 North and occupy it if opportunity was offered.

At 0700 hours on 3 February the first phase of the 123rd Indian Infantry Brigade attack started when 1/15 Punjab put in the attack with three companies, on an objective positioned south of Taunghlamaw village, north-west of Hill 75. By 0920 hours they were half way up this Hill with one company on the east side of the feature centred at 757972, and were engaged in heavy hand-to-hand fighting with the defenders. Eventually, the unoccupied village of Taunghlamaw was secured by this battalion but two of its companies on Hill 75 were encountering small-arms fire from the top. Thereafter, they were pinned down by the Japanese machine gun fire which caused 75 casualties to these two companies.

The second phase, an attack on West Hill by 10 Lancashire Fusiliers, started at 0900 hours. The battalion advanced slowly to carry out its task but came under grenade discharger fire while still about 600 yards from the objective. By 1445 hours it had advanced about three-quarters of the way along West Hill when it suddenly encountered opposition from Hill 75 and from West Hill itself. Meanwhile, 8/6 Raj Rif, advancing on Hill 75 from the north got closely involved with the Japanese on the top of the feature. At 0730 hours, C company of 8/6 Raj Rif, supported by two platoons of B company put in an attack on Hill 75. When within about 50 yards of this feature, they came under heavy machine gun fire which caused 118 casualties; nevertheless, the objective was gained.

By the evening, the position was as follows: 10 Lancashire Fusiliers was consolidating the gains on West Hill with one company on the feature at 742983. 1/15 Punjab was disposed with two companies held up by three medium machine guns on the spur, running south-east of Hill 75, while one company was in Taunghlamaw village. 8/6 Raj Rif, having suffered heavy casualties, had returned to the areas north-east of Hill 75.

The next day, also, no progress could be made by the 123rd Indian Infantry Brigade due to stiff Japanese resistance. It was therefore mostly spent in consolidating gains that had been achieved after the attack on 3 February, and on the following days also no further planned offensive was undertaken. Patrol activity, however, was maintained by both the sides and occasional artillery duels were the only offensive action on this front.

From the night of 5/6 February, however, the Japanese began to increase their activity and showed an offensive tendency. Their harassing fire, aimed at the forward troops of the 123rd Indian Infantry Brigade was more frequent while their patrolling became more active and belligerent. The overall situation, nevertheless, remained the same and in view of the stalemate it became apparent that this attack had also failed to achieve its object.

Further attack on Donbaik—18 February 1943

While the attack on Rathedaung was put in by the 123rd Indian Infantry Brigade on 3 February 1943, the position on the Donbaik front was not very hopeful from the point of view of the 55th Indian Infantry Brigade. After the attack on Donbaik on 1 February 1943 the troops of this brigade had met with stubborn and vigorous resistance. The Japanese defensive positions had proved to be much too strong for British artillery and could not be assailed due to their being cleverly sited and concealed.

After the fighting which took place on 1 and 2 February this front had remained comparatively quiet. Sporadic artillery and mortar fire was indulged in by both the sides but otherwise there was not much offensive activity. From 7 February onwards, however, this front became a little more lively. The Japanese increased their raids and patrol activity but were paid back in the same coin with equal vigour by the troops of the 55th Indian Infantry Brigade, though for the next four or five days the Rajput company in its positions on SOUTH KNOB had a very uneasy time.

On 12 February 1943, the Brigade Commander made an outline plan to put in a further attack on the Donbaik front and the 55th Indian Infantry Brigade Operation Order No. 2, dated 16 February 1943, was issued to all concerned. The intention of this order was stated to be that "55 Indian Infantry Brigade Group will destroy all Japs and Jap Posts in the Chaung and Village Areas." The attack was to be put in at night, immediately preceded by artillery concentration on the area of Japanese FDLs, and the zero hour was to be 0430 hours on 18 February 1943.

During the night of 16/17 February, pre-arranged machine-gun concentrations were fired by the 9 Jat (machine gun battalion) on Point 832 and harassing fire by artillery was maintained along the line of Japanese FDLs, continuing until 0500 hours on the morning of 17 February. In return, a Japanese patrol during the same night attempted a raid on the 5/8 Punjab positions but the attempt proved to be unsuccessful. At the same time, the Rathedaung area was also witnessing some very intensive patrolling by both sides.

On the night of 17/18 February, a small scale commando raid was carried out by a force about 20 strong, comprising infantrymen and engineers, in an area approximately 6 miles south of Rathedaung. The raiding party was carried up the Mayu river in motor launches which stood on the west bank; from this position onwards the assault boats were used. A couple of bridges were sucessfully blown and a few mines were also laid by this party.

At 0400 hours on 18 February, 1943, the 55th Indian Infantry Brigade began a planned attack on the Japanese positions along the Chaung. The attack was put in with 1 Inniskillings on the right and 2/1 Punjab on the left, attacking the left and centre of the Japanese FDLs. The Inniskillings captured the western end of the Chaung and from this point thereafter they attacked south into the wooded village as well as east along the lines of the Chaung. By 0800 hours they had reached the village where fighting was in progress and had advanced along the Chaung to Point 647832. On the other hand, 2/1 Punjab had met with heavy opposition from the beginning of the advance, and had also encountered mines; having encountered such heavy opposition and having suffered many casualties the battalion was held up along a line 648833-648834-649834, by two main centres of Japanese resistance. These centres of resistance were S4 and S5, on which, consequently, a prolonged bombardment was brought down.

South of the TWIN KNOBS, the 1/17th Dogra Regiment began its advance at 0610 hours but came up against a Japanese Post further down the spur. While in this position, the Japanese brought down heavy machine gun fire on the Dogras from the area of Point 823. Owing to heavy casualties which were sustained by this battalion, the advance was later suspended and effort was thereafter concentrated on clearing the Chaung area.

By mid-day of 18 February the position in the Chaung area was that the Inniskillings held the Chaung from the sea to about point 647832 and the northern "Village Area"; continued strong resistance was still coming from S4 and S5. 1/7 Rajput, which was to the left of 2/1 Punjab, thereupon began to advance west along the Chaung, supported by fire from 3.7" Howitzers, in order to contact 1 Inniskillings and to attempt to isolate the Japanese at S4 and S5. But this move was met by strong Japanese mortar fire and the attack was halted.

The Inniskillings could not hold their position in the Chaung as they were pinned down by Japanese machine guns and snipers and the situation by the nightfall of 18 February in this area had become most obscure. Although the Divisional Commander had expressed the wish that the Inniskillings should "hold present gains at all costs and try to improve their position by local action directed towards South and East," the battalion had to be withdrawn in the early morning of 19 February. Heavy artillery fire was then put down on the Chaung from 0315 hours to 0430 hours. The rest of that day was spent in artillery duels and patrolling by both sides.

During this period the 71st Indian Infantry Brigade had been ordered to concentrate at Indin and since the brigades of the 14th Indian Division employed on the Donbaik and Rathedaung fronts, were worn out and tired, it was decided to re-adjust the divisional forces. On 20 February, therefore, the 14th Indian Division Operation Instruction No. 16 was issued. The 71st Indian Infantry Brigade was given the task of operating on the Donbaik front; the 123rd Indian Infantry Brigade was to continue operations in the Rathedaung area until relieved by the 55th Indian Infantry Brigade. The 47th Indian Infantry Brigade's tasks were (*i*) operations in the area between the summit of Mayu hill and Mayu river and (*ii*) the selection and preparation of defensive position for one battalion in the Indin area. The 55th Indian Infantry Brigade was to be re-organised with a view to relieving the 123rd Indian Infantry Brigade. The relief of 2/1 Punjab and 1/7 Rajput by 7/15 Punjab in the chaung area took place on 21 February while the Inniskillings were relieved by 1 Lincoln the next day.

Henceforth the position on this front remained static but artillery fire and patrolling were kept up by both the sides. On 26 February another battalion, the 1/17th Dogra Regiment, was relieved by 9/15 Punjab without any incident and, thereafter, the rest of the month went by without any change in the positions of the opposing forces.

Lessons from the 123rd Indian Infantry Brigade attack north of Rathedaung

Some very important lessons were brought out from the action on 3 February 1943. On that day, the various attacks launched by 1/15 Punjab, 10 Lancashire Fusiliers and 8/6 Raj Rif, failed to accomplish their objectives. The story in each case was almost identical; the Japanese held their fire till these troops were within fifty to a hundred yards, thereby causing the latter enormous casualties, mainly through aimed fire at close range. Also, the brigade attacked in broad daylight (the country was considered too difficult for night attacks) and the Japanese had the additional advantage of having the sun behind them. There is also no record of the brigade ever using a smoke screen to help in the attacks, thereby minimising the "aimed fire" of the Japanese. Although the Mountain Battery in support of the 123rd Indian Infantry Brigade had no smoke shells, there would have been no difficulty in putting up a smoke screen with the help of the eighteen 3 inch mortars (six per battalion) in the possession of the brigade. It is admitted that "smoke" was inclined to pillar on a dry, warm day; but had the attack taken place at first light, the pillaring would have been correspondingly reduced. In any case, smoke shells could have been effectively dropped in the valleys between the small knolls (about fifty feet high) which were occupied by the Japanese; mutual support by aimed fire would then have been impossible for them.

The Japanese had been in their positions several days before the 123rd Brigade put in the attack. Their defensive positions were well dug in and were above those of the brigade. It might have been tactically sound to have treated such positions as "Strong Points".[1]

It is more than probable that had the Indian and British forces fully observed the principles of CONCENTRATION, that is, using maximum effort on one objective rather than mediocre efforts on three or four, the Japanese might have been driven from their strongly entrenched positions.

Infantry fire power was not developed to the maximum; in the

---

[1] *A.I.T.M.*, 18 December 1942, page 9.

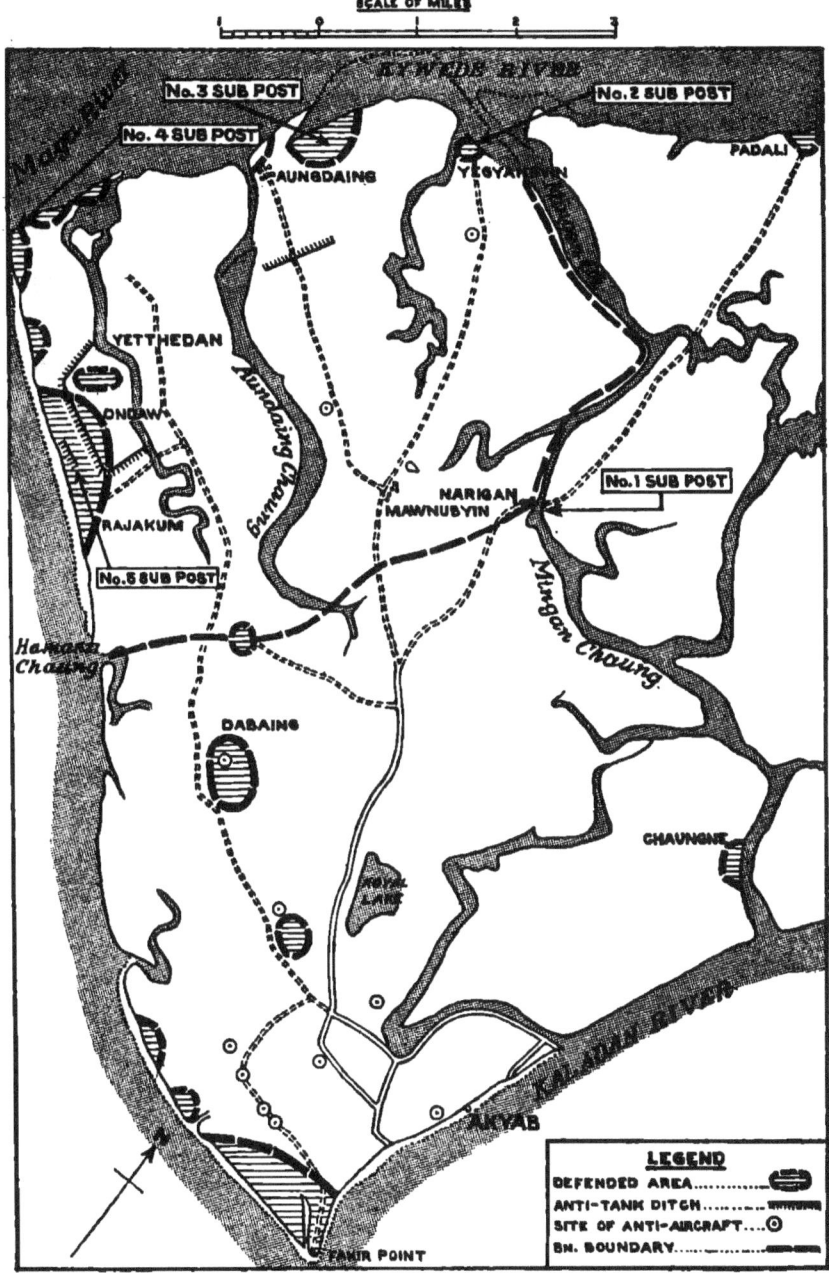

Rathedaung area which consisted mainly of small hills, rear companies might often have influenced the course of battle by light machine gun and mortar fire.

It will therefore be apparent that two infantry brigades of the 14th Indian Division had failed in their object at Donbaik. In spite of considerable casualties and much expenditure of material, their positions were virtually no further forward than at the beginning of the year. Their chances of reaching Foul Point and thence of assaulting Akyab were also receding.

Japanese resistance had hardened everywhere, and later events proved that the Indian troops had reached the most southernly limits of their advance.

CHAPTER IV

The Japanese Counter Measures

The Indian offensive and Japanese withdrawal

When the Indian attack was launched in Arakan in December 1942, the Japanese strength in that area was one regiment only[1]—*the 213th Regiment of the 33rd Division*. Certain captured documents that are available are much too incomplete to give a full account of the initial stages of the operations. It is, however, known that the *2nd Battalion* only was forward on the Maungdaw-Buthidaung line in early December, and some elements at least of the *3rd Battalion* were at Kyauktaw and Myohaung. This left the *1st Battalion* and the remainder of the *3rd Battalion* for the defence of Akyab. At this stage, the Japanese were faced with the problem of disposing their forces for the defence of Akyab island; they could not afford to place too much of their strength in the forward areas for what might only have been a diversionary move, pending a seaborne attack on the port of Akyab. Accordingly, the Japanese decided that no attempt should be made to hold Buthidaung and Maungdaw, and hence the *2nd Battalion* had evacuated its positions on the night of 15 December. The *5th and 6th companies* of this battalion withdrew to Rathedaung while the *7th* and *8th companies* took up their positions in the Laungchaung-Thitkado area on the Mayu peninsula.

Stabilisation of Japanese resistance at Rathedaung and the Mayu peninsula

The Indian advance therefore had started without opposition and Maungdaw and Buthidaung were occupied on 17 December, and the Japanese were not encountered in any strength until the beginning of January 1943. It was about this time that the Japanese postions were stabilised and the Indian troops met with opposition at Rathedaung and Laungchaung, and subsequently at Donbaik. Previous to this, the Indian patrols had pushed past Donbaik where no Japanese had been seen, on to Kondan and Foul Point. A patrol on 4 January had reported only a small number of Japanese troops at Donbaik, but two days later, the Japanese had reinforced their position there with elements of the *3rd Battalion, 213th Regiment,* and the Indian troops attempting to advance were repulsed with the

[1] *History of 33 Japanese Division,* File 7725. Also File 9100—p. 2.

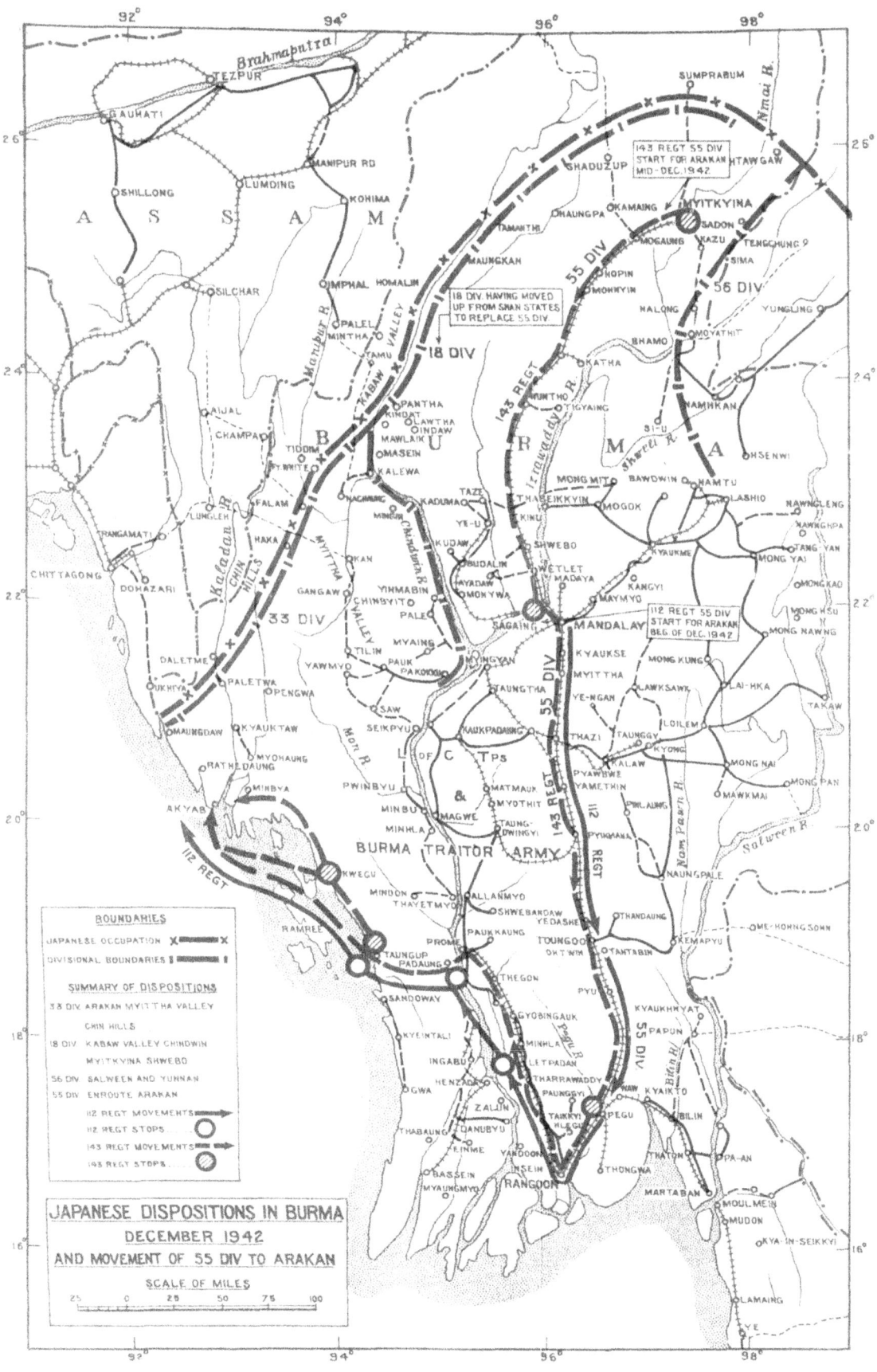

loss of three carriers. Later, the Japanese strength at Donbaik was gradually built up to approximately one battalion, and it was strong enough to withstand a formidable attack by the Indian forces on 18-19 January.

The Japanese dispositions in the end of December 1942 and early January 1943 were as follows:

Akyab	*1st Battalion, 213th Regiment* and the bulk of *3rd Battalion, 213th Regiment.*
Donbaik-Laungchaung	Elements of *3rd Battalion* and two companies of *2nd Battalion, 213th Regiment.*
Rathedaung	Two companies of *2nd Battalion* with machine guns and infantry artillery.
Myohaung-Kyauktaw	Remainder of *3rd Battalion, 213th Regiment.*

The selection of Rathedaung as a point of resistance by the Japanese was influenced by the natural strength of the place; wherever possible, they based their strong points on high ground with a flank naturally defended by a river or some similar obstacle. At Rathedaung, they had the Mayu river on their left flank and chaungs to their rear, with hill features in, and in front of, the town itself. This position was naturally favourable to a defence carried out with the minimum of troops, and it is of interest to note that at no time, apparently, did the garrison of this town exceed two rifle companies of infantry along with a few medium machine guns (MMG's) and some infantry artillery.

Rathedaung was in fact a key position, and in view of the 14th Indian Division's advance down the Kaladan river, the Japanese had realised the danger of their right flank at Rathedaung being by-passed, and had therefore taken steps to counteract it. While the first reinforcements received in the form of the *2nd Battalion, 112th Regiment* were put in at Myohaung to hold the lower Kaladan, later ones were disposed in the Batarai-Kamai area in order to close the gap between Myohaung and Rathedaung. This re-inforcement was carried out in the second half of January 1943, by which time the position had been more or less stabilised. In the meantime, Indian troops had occupied Kyauktaw on 17 January after a short engagement with the *6th Company, 2nd Battalion of the 112th Regiment* which had taken over from the elements of the *3rd Battalion, 213th Regiment.*

Japanese re-inforcement of Arakan

The launching of the Indian offensive on 17 December 1942 did not take the Japanese by surprise. The latter had already considered the question of re-inforcements and as early as 4 December 1942, orders were issued to the *112th Regiment of the 55th Division*, which at the time was training at Sagaing in the Mandalay area, to proceed at short notice to Arakan.² About the same time, the second Regiment of the *55th Division*—the *143rd Regiment*, which was in the Myitkyina area, was relieved and ordered to proceed to lower Burma. This move was taken as a precautionary measure. It enabled the troops to be concentrated in lower Burma in case an invasion there was attempted by the Allies; they could also be moved forward, ready to follow up the *112th Regiment* to Arakan, if necessary. Most of the *143rd Regiment* and other *55th Division* units were at Pegu for nearly three weeks—from the middle of December 1942, to early January 1943.

The move of the *112th Regiment* to Prome was started on 8 December 1942 and after the Irrawaddy river had been crossed, the journey to Rangoon was carried out by rail. From there, the *1st* and *2nd Battalion* proceeded to Prome while the *3rd Battalion* went as far as Letpadan. Two companies of the *2nd Battalion* were the first to leave Prome on their onward journey and on 6 January they were followed by battalion headquarters. As previously stated, this battalion moved to the Kaladan river and contacted Indian troops at Kyauktaw on 17 January 1943. The *1st Battalion* was the first to follow the *2nd Battalion*, reaching Akyab towards the end of January. A portion of the *3rd Battalion* then moved into Prome and the regimental headquarters left for Taungup on 26 January 1943. Transport difficulties appear to have held up their onward transit from Taungup; a severe shortage of craft was experienced and navigation difficulties also proved serious. The situation was somewhat eased by the arrival of five craft from Bassein. They took five days, travelling day and night to accomplish the journey, but two out of a total of seven were sunk by RAF action.³

The move of the *112th Regiment* to Akyab may be considered to have been completed by the beginning of February 1943, when the regimental headquarters arrived. It is of interest to note that due to the traffic bottle-neck at Taungup the regiment could not move forward by complete units; small composite parties, therefore, continued to arrive at intervals until the end of February 1943.

The move of the *143rd Regiment* was also being carried out at the same time and over-lapped, at least in part, with that of the *112th Regiment* at Taungup, at the end of January. By the end of this phase, however, the *143rd Regiment* had not managed to move further north than the Taungup-Prome area.

¹ *A Short History of Japanese 55 Div.*, page 2, file 7247.
² *Outline of No. 31 Operation*, p. 3, file 7247.

JAPANESE D
END OF PHASE I AND DEV
FEBRUAR

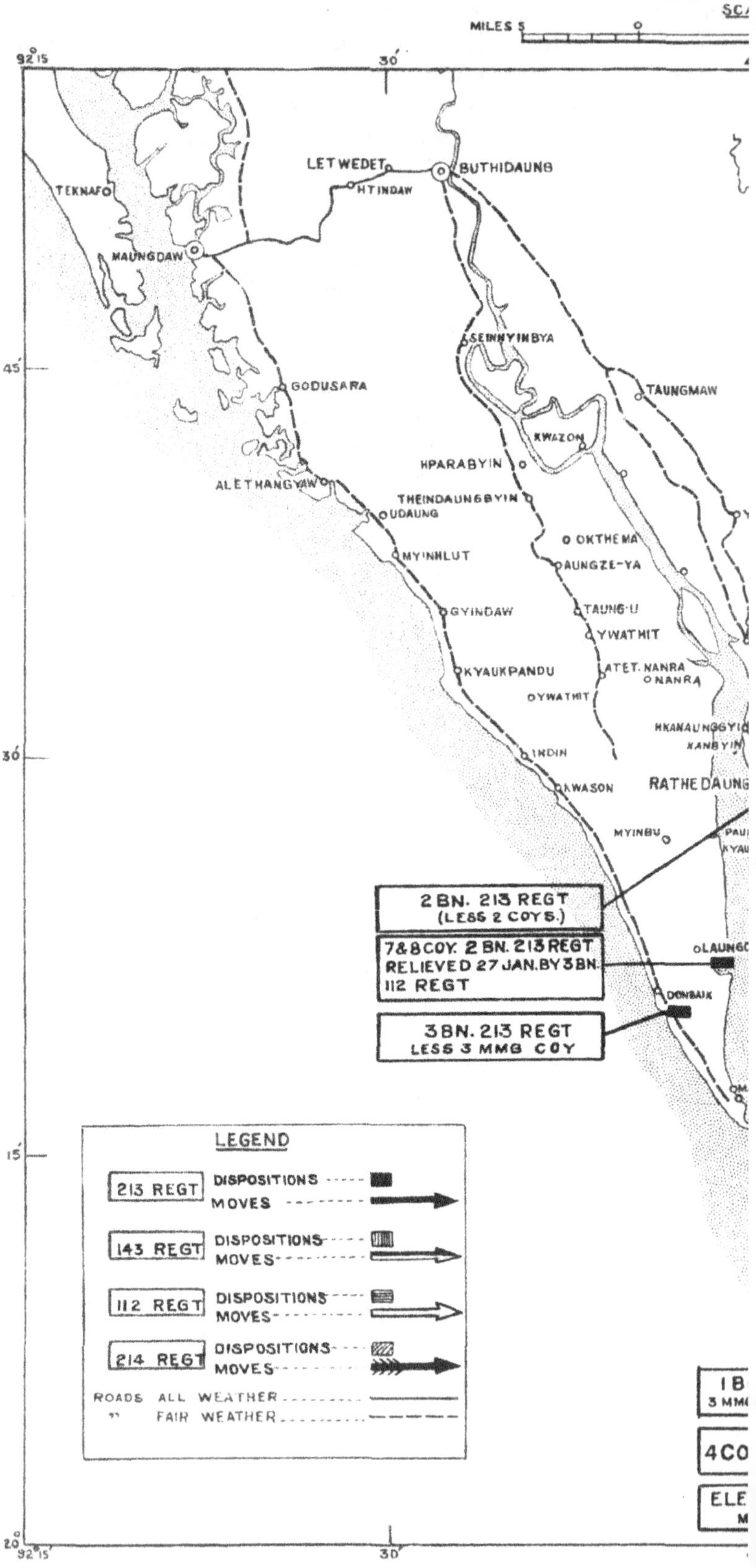

DISPOSITIONS
DEVELOPMENT OF PHASE 2
RY 1843

SCALE: 5 — 10 — 15 MILES

- KYAUKTAW
- THAYETTABIN
- TAWEYA CHAUNG
- YO CHAUNG
- APAUKWA
- OKANZAUK
- OGRITCHAUNG
- YEZOGYAUNG
- OMRAWCHAUNG
- KYAUKTAN
- NTIZWE
- THAUNGDAFA
- OLEKKWASON
- NYAUKCHAUNG
- GALE YWA
- BIDA
- KTAW
- CHAUNG
- OKUDAUNG
- MAYU RIVER
- PO-RHR-BYIN
- MYOHAUNG
- KALADAN RIVER
- ABYI CHAUNG
- PADALI
- PONNAGYUN
- AKYAB
- BARONGA ISLANDS

1 BN. 112 REGT (LESS 2 COYS)

2 BN. 112 REGT (LESS 4 AND 5 COY)

5 COY. 2 BN. 112 REGT

N. 213 REGT.
COY. 3 BN. 213 REGT.

Y. 2 BN. 112 REGT

MENTS 112 REGT MOVING FORWARD

143 REGT. AT PROME & TAUNGUP MOVING UP

Japanese dispositions at the end of January and at the beginning of February 1943 were, therefore, as follows:

Akyab	*1st Battalion 213th Regiment, 5th Company 2nd Battalion 112th Regiment, 4th Company 2nd Battalion 112th Regiment.*
Donbaik	*3rd Battalion 213th Regiment.*
Laungchaung	*7th and 8th Companies of 2nd Battalion 213th Regiment.*
Rathedaung	*5th and 6th Companies and MG Company of 2nd Battalion 213th Regiment.*
Batarai-Kamai	*1st Battalion 112th Regiment* less two companies.
Taungup-Prome	Elements of *143rd Regiment, 3rd Battalion 112th Regiment* and portions of other battalions of the *112th Regiment*, all *en route* northwards.

The timing of the Japanese moves is worth noting. Apparently, it had become obvious to them that the Allies were planning some offensive and that certain phases of it would inevitably involve land operations in Arakan. But they could not be sure that a sea-borne invasion of Akyab or landings further south of it might not also be attempted.

By the beginning of December 1942, the Japanese had become fairly confident that something was afoot, hence the southward move of the *55th Division* which enabled them to have troops at hand, both for re-inforcing Akyab and for the defence of lower Burma, if necessary. At the same time, their occupation of the advanced Buthidaung-Maungdaw line by as weak a force as one battalion (reported by British agents as two), enabled them to gain valuable time, as it forced the Allies to concentrate their troops further back thereby delaying their ultimate advance. Later on, the evacuation of this forward line by the Japanese was also timed exceedingly well and was completely successful.

Another factor in timing on which the Japanese relied with complete justification was the resistance of their troops when they reached the prearranged positions at Rathedaung and in the Mayu peninsula. In spite of the slow rate of the re-inforcements reaching Taungup (one infantry regiment plus ancillary troops per month) the issue at stake was not much affected; the forward troops held on to their positions as expected and, despite superiority, the Indian division made no progress.

As time went on, it became clearer to the Japanese that the sea threat, if any, would be directed against Akyab. The troops retained there were therefore mainly engaged in making and improving beach defences so that by the end of this phase, they had made Akyab formidable against attack.

CHAPTER V

The Japanese Advance Northwards
Phase Two

The dispositions of the Indian forces at the end of February and the beginning of March 1943 were as follows:—

The 26th Indian Division had been ordered to the Arakan area and on 24 February, the 71st Indian Infantry Brigade had relieved the 55th Indian Infantry Brigade in the Donbaik area.

The 47th Indian Infantry Brigade had been called forward from rest at Ukhia and assigned to the area astride the Mayu range, to protect the immediate line of communication of the 71st Indian Infantry Brigade.

The 55th Indian Infantry Brigade had moved to Buthidaung for re-organisation prior to relieving the 123rd Indian Infantry Brigade, in the area north of Rathedaung; the latter then moved out of Arakan on being relieved.

At the beginning of March 1943, the 14th Indian Division had under command the 71st Indian Infantry Brigade, the 47th Indian Infantry Brigade and the 6th British Infantry Brigade on the Donbaik Front, and the 55th and 123rd Indian Infantry Brigades on the Rathedaung Front. At the same time the Kaladan Detachment was also directly under its operational control, and the 4th Indian Infantry Brigade from the 26th Indian Division was *en route* to this area. This division was also responsible for the line of communication from Dohazari to Donbaik and Rathedaung a distance of nearly 150 miles. But, by that time, the Japanese had begun showing signs of activity in the Rathedaung area, as well as in the Kaladan valley. It was, therefore, decided that the commander of the 14th Indian Division should be given a subordinate commander to control the operations east of the line, inclusive Mayu river—Buthidaung—Taung Bazaar—Panzai Bazaar. The forces in this area were thereafter called "Mayforce" and Brigadier A. C. Curtis DSO, MC, was appointed to be its commander.[1] He assumed command from the mid-night of 14/15 March, using originally the machinery of the Headquarters, 123rd Indian Infantry Brigade at Buthidaung, pending the arrival of a separate force headquarters and signal section. The tasks given to the commander of this Force were:—

    (a) Protection of the left flank of the 14th Indian Division against attack or infiltration from the east by tracks

[1] File 8294—p. 12.

leading into the Mayu and Kalapanzin valleys from the direction of the Kaladan river.

(b) To prepare for an offensive southward with the object of securing the general line Rathedaung Chaung from the junction of the Mayu river to about Batarai (0191). The offensive, however, was not to be attempted until the arrival of the 4th and 71st Indian Infantry Brigades in this area.

(c) Pending the above offensive, the 55th Indian Infantry Brigade was to oppose any Japanese advance in their positions south of Htziwe, and in the event of any deterioration of the situation in this area, the commander was at liberty to withdraw this brigade to the general line Remyet Chaung-Maraw Chaung, subject to the prior sanction of the Divisional Headquarters. The overall responsibility of all operations in Arakan, however, was still that of the Commander of the 14th Indian Division.

Activities in the Kaladan valley

Early in March 1943, three Japanese battalions (*1st and 2nd Battalions of the 112th Regiment* and *the 2nd Battalion of the 213th Regiment*) with artillery support, moved into the Kaladan valley from Akyab. Simultaneously, an additional force infiltrated through the hills from Pakokku on the Irrawaddy and threatened "Tripforce" which was in the area of Paletwa on the Kaladan river. This necessitated the withdrawal of both "Tripforce" and "Soutcol". The former retired to new positions at, Mowdok on the Sangu river, Labawa on the Picahung and Satpaung on the Kaladan river. The Japanese then crossed into the hills to the west of the Kaladan valley but did not follow up the pursuit. A part of "Soutcol" was cut off but the remainder succeeded in retiring to Adengri and Kudeir.

These Japanese successes presented an immediate threat to the Indian forces in the Mayu peninsula, the Mayu valley and also to their line of communication.

Japanese defence of Rathedaung

By February 1943, fighting on the peninsula had stabilised at Donbaik, Laungchaung, and across the Mayu river at Rathedaung. During the latter half of January 1943, the *2nd Battalion of the 112th Regiment* had taken up positions in the Myohaung area, and at the beginning of February, elements of the *1st Battalion of the 112th Regiment* had moved to Batarai and Kamai. The divisional headquarters of the *55th Division* under Lieutenant-General Koga was at that time in Akyab where Colonel Tanahashi paid a visit on 4 February 1943. As a result of this visit, Colonel Tanahashi, the Commander of the *112th Regiment*, held a conference of his officers

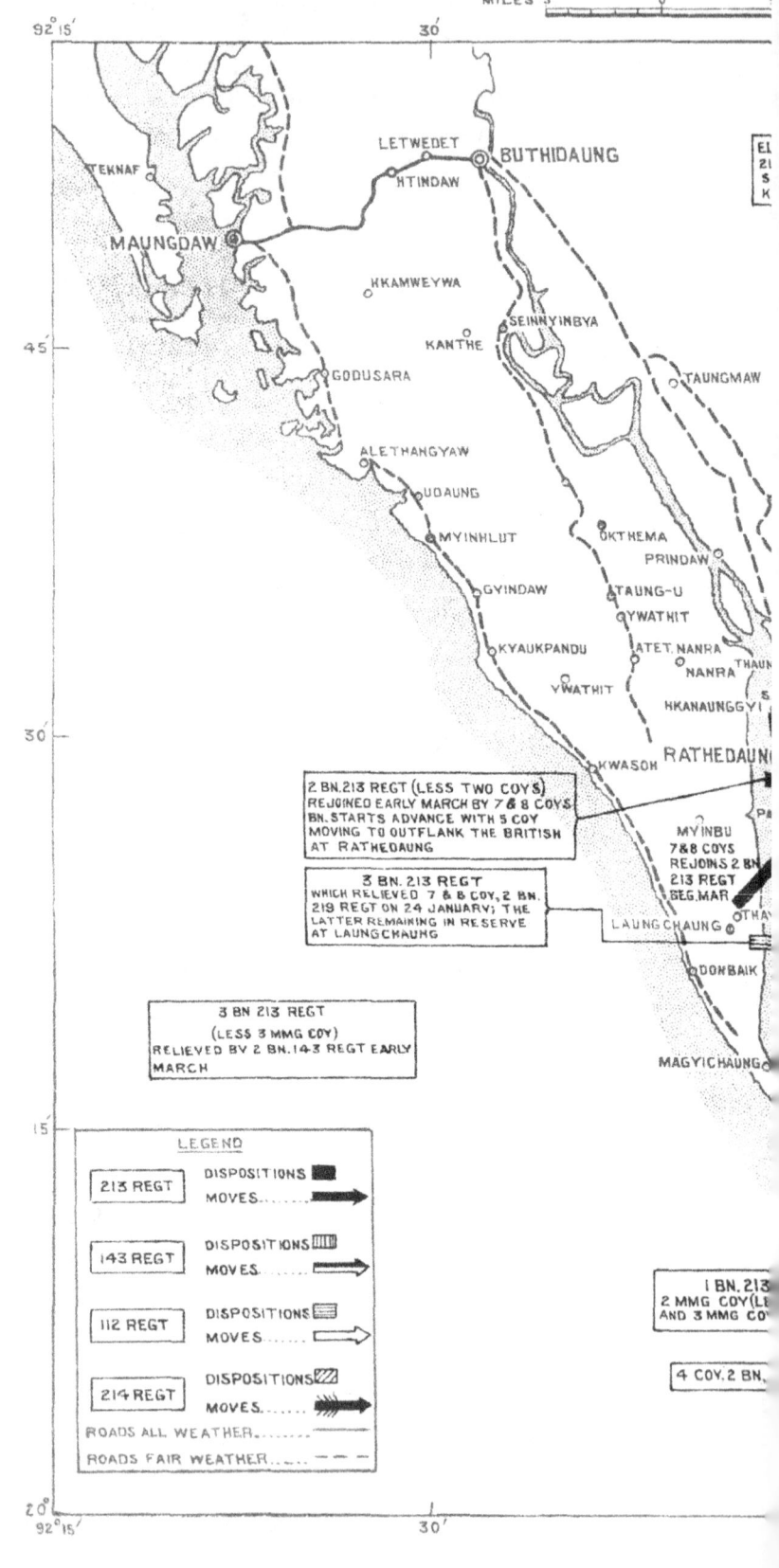

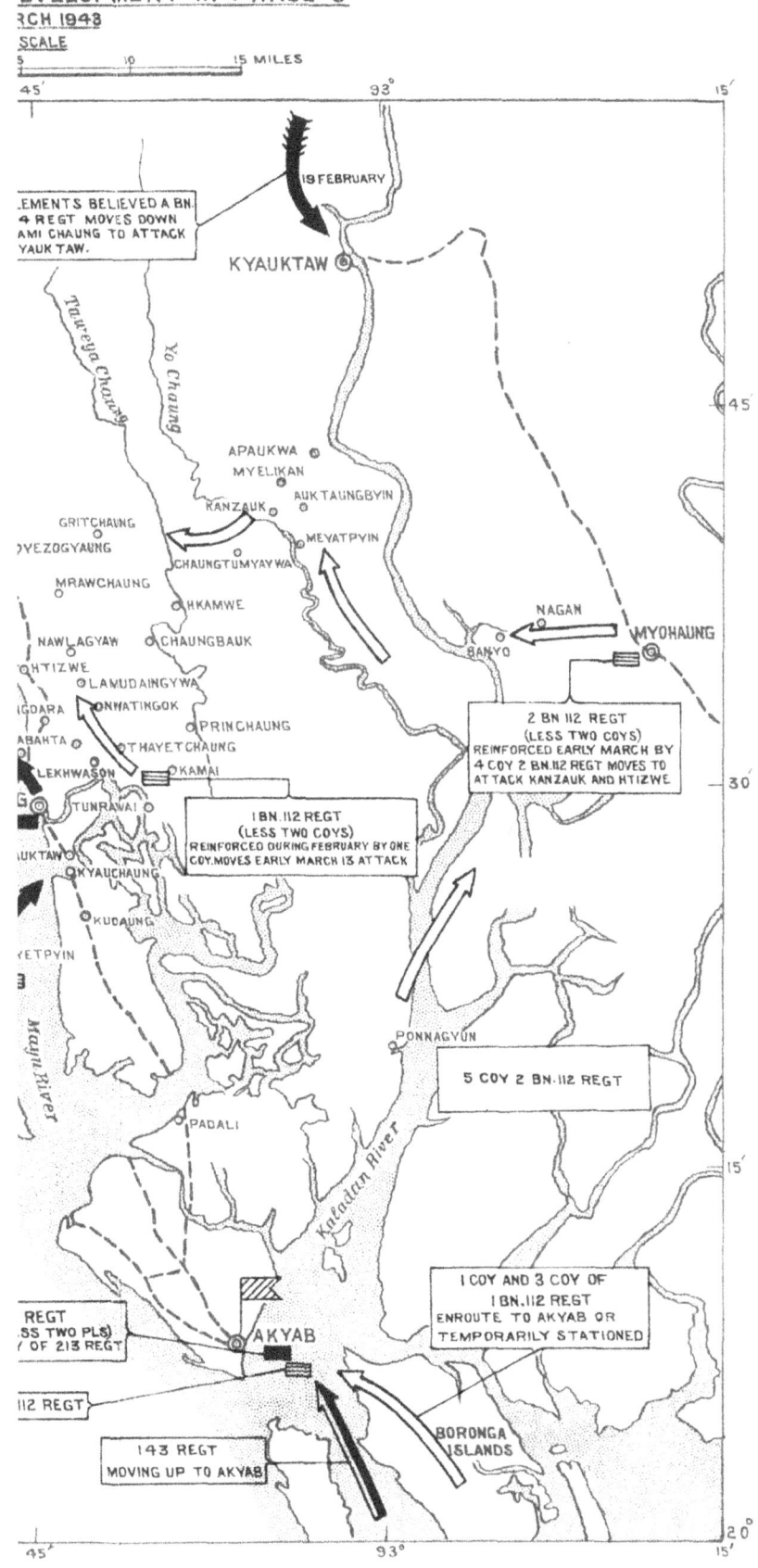

in order to give out his plan of attack; and it was decided to attack by an outflanking movement to the east of Rathedaung towards Htizwe, and then push southwards to Rathedaung.

During the next two days, plans to this end were formulated and submitted to the headquarters of the *55th Division*; the decision, however, was to postpone the attack until greater strength was available. It is of interest to note that the subsequent Japanese offensive followed very closely the original plan—namely, a flanking and encircling movement while the weight of the Indian forces was still contained by the *2nd Battalion* (less two companies) of the *213th Regiment* in Rathedaung. The encircling movement was to be carried out by two columns; the first (*1st Battalion 112th Regiment*) was to proceed via Kamai and Thayetchaung to Mrawchaung where it would join with the second column (*2nd Battalion 112th Regiment*), coming up via Taungbin and Awrama; the latter move was subsequently modified to a move via Kanzauk. From Mrawchaung, both columns were to attack Htizwe and then continue southwards to attack the Indian force in the rear at Rathedaung.

Tanahashi detachment

The forces, under the command of Colonel Tanahashi, consisted at this time of the following units:

112th Regiment	No. *4 Company;* No. *2 Company* less one platoon.
	One Platoon of No. *1 MG Company;* No. *2 MG Company* less two platoons.
	Signal Company.
Engineers	One platoon of *55th Regiment;* one section of *55th Division* Engineers.
Munition Artillery	*4th Company, 33rd Munition Artillery Regiment.*
	Part of *Miyawaki Regiment* (*213th Regiment*).
Troops in occupation of Rathedaung	*2nd Battalion* of *213th Regiment* less *7th and 8th companies.*
	One platoon of *2nd company 112th Regiment.*
	One *MG platoon.*

After a detailed appreciation of the situation, Tanahashi came to the conclusion that it was essential to occupy Kamai. Consequently, a reconnaissance was carried out and on finding that the place was free of Indian troops, it was occupied by a platoon of the *4th Company, 112th Regiment.*

Tanahashi continued to examine the possibility of an early offensive and therefore on 11 February, 1943, he paid a visit to

Rathedaung. A captured document shows that the strength of his troops concentrated at this time north of Pauktaw, was under 1000. These were made up of the following units:

HQ *112th Infantry*, Artillery and Signal Detachments.

1 Battalion *112th Infantry* less two companies.

One platoon of *4th Company* of *2nd Battalion, 112 Regiment*.

MG Company less two platoons of *2nd Battalion, 112th Regiment*.

2nd Battalion less two companies of *213th Infantry*.

4th Company of *55th Munition Artillery* (4 guns), Detachment *55th Division Signals* and other details.

All these units were under strength through sickness or casualties and due to some of the personnel being still *en route*.

Japanese dispositions in February 1943

The remainder of the Japanese troops in Arakan at this period were disposed as follows:—

Donbaik	*3rd Battalion, 213th Regiment* less *3rd MMG Company*.	
Laungchaung	*7th* and *8th Companies* of *2nd Battalion, 213th Regiment*.	
Akyab	Division Operations HQs *1st Battalion, 213th Regiment*; *3rd Battalion, 112th Regiment* (under command of Kawashima).	Miyawaki Detachment O.C. *213th Infantry Regiment*.
	4th Company less one platoon of *2nd Battalion, 112th Regiment*.	
	Two platoons *2nd MMG Company* of *213th Regiment*.	
	3rd MMG Company of *213th Regiment*.	
En route to Akyab or temporarily stationed .	*1st* and *3rd Companies* of *1st Battalion, 112th Regiment*.	
Myohaung	*2nd Battalion* less two companies of *112th Regiment* and two platoons *MMG Company*.	Hoshi Detachment O.C. *112th Infantry Regiment*.
Unlocated	*5th Company, 2nd Battalion* of *112th Regiment* (Perhaps at Ponnagyun).	

It will thus be evident that a total of six infantry battalions was in Arakan; the *143rd Regiment* was still in the process of movement from Taungup—some of them by the land route which took twenty-four days in the process.

In spite of the small number of troops at his disposal, Tanahashi was determined to make the most of his opportunities. He therefore issued orders on 16 February 1943, for vigorous reconnaissance and maximum endeavour to capture prisoners; a detailed report and an appreciation of the situation was sent the same day to the *55th Division HQ*. Tanahashi's orders were put into effect without delay and at Rathedaung patrolling was started with renewed vigour. The platoon at Tunrawai was ordered to make a surprise attack on Batarai, two miles north of Kamai; it was also to reconnoitre Lekhwason on the opposite side of the river.

When this platoon entered Batarai, the place was found to be completely empty. Patrols were also sent five miles north of Kamai; they made no contact, however, and local inhabitants reported that there were no Indian or British troops even five miles further north of that place. This lack of opposition gave Tanahashi the impression that the Indo-British forces were withdrawing; he therefore contemplated an immediate advance. The lull in the proceedings which was interpreted as a sign of impending Allied withdrawal, was later reconsidered as possibly betokening preparations for an attack. The Japanese Commander, therefore, kept his troops in the area and made preparations for the forthcoming operations.

Policy of defence

On 19 February 1943, details were received of an engagement which had taken place the previous day at Donbaik. Though the Japanese forces there had withstood the attack and had inflicted heavy losses on the 14th Indian Division, their own losses were apparently not inconsiderable. Information was also received that it had been decided to re-inforce the *213th Regiment* detachment at Donbaik with the *3rd Company, 1st Battalion of the 112th Regiment* from Akyab, and later it was decided to send in addition the *3rd Battalion of the 112th Regiment* from Akyab to the Mayu peninsula, as the *143rd Regiment* had not yet arrived. Colonel Tanahashi was also told that the *1st Company of the 1st Battalion* would not be under his command; the detachment was therefore reduced to—

> HQ *1st Battalion, 112th Regiment* and *2nd Company*.
> HQ *2nd Battalion, 213th Regiment*.
> *5th* and *6th Field Companies*.
> *MMG Company*.
> Some Infantry Artillery, Munition Artillery and ancillary troops.

The necessity for re-inforcing Donbaik made it plain to Tanahashi that the *55th Division* would have difficulty in re-inforcing his command in the near future. As his force was weak in infantry, he decided on a policy of defence, using his heavy weapons to their greatest advantage. Accordingly, steps were taken to construct strong points in the Batarai-Kamai area, though at the same time, plans for a future offensive action still went ahead.

On 23 February 1943, the Japanese received information from the locals of the intention of the 14th Indian Division to advance down the Tawbya Chaung; a platoon (which was later re-inforced) was therefore ordered to go to Princhaung and Porhibyin, east-south-east of Kamai. The possibility of this move on the part of the Indian Division made the Japanese regimental commander move a battalion artillery platoon (two 70 mm guns) and one quick firing (QF) gun to Kamai. Also, the platoon at Tunrawai and Batarai was recalled to the *4th Company, 112th Regiment* in Akyab and its place was taken by some engineer platoons.

Further preparations for an offensive

Towards the end of February, a number of guns, ammunition and some re-inforcements arrived at Rathedaung, and further preparations for an offensive were put in hand; but at the same time, training for "operational defence" was not forgotten. As it was still considered that there was an appreciable threat down the Tawbya chaung, a battalion was detailed to gain information about the British battalion which was thought to be at Awrama; it was also to see that the Indo-British forces did not use their main strength against Kamai by diverting their main effort towards Rathedaung.

Preparations for the Japanese offensive were almost complete at the end of February; and by the beginning of March, elements of Tanahashi's force were pushed forward along the line Nwatingok-Ywathit. On 3 March, Tanahashi went forward to a place near Kamai to hold a Commanders' conference in order to discuss future operations, which was joined by the Chief of Staff the following day. Latest reports had again shown that there were no hostile troops in Lekhwason or Kanbyin, and a Japanese patrol had brought back information that Nwathingok was also clear of Indo-British troops. Accordingly, on 7 March, headquarters Tanahasi Force crossed to Lekhwason; the same day, the Indo-British forces were reported (incorrectly, as it turned out) to be withdrawing to Ttizwe and Thaungdara. The attack on these two places were therefore decided upon.

Events on the Kaladan River

During the time that the Japanese offensive from Rathedaung was being prepared, other events were taking place on the Kaladan river. Reports of a Japanese force which had moved by the Kanpetlet route to Arakan, became current from 19 February onwards when they were said to be moving down the Semi chaung. This force eventually occupied Kaladan on 24 February 1943. Subsequent reports stated that this force was moving down the Pichaung—and in early March, Kyauktaw was attacked by a force from the north. There is reason to believe that this force was all or part of a battalion of the *214th Infantry Regiment* which is now known to have moved in from the Pakokku area across the lower Chin hills. Another force which used this route later was identified as a squadron of the *55th Cavalry Regiment*.

About the same time, other developments were also taking place on the lower Kaladan river ; the *2nd Battalion of the 112th Infantry Regiment* (less 5th Company) had left Myohaung in early March and by the 6th of that month had concentrated due west of the Banyo-Nagan area. Their task was to eliminate opposition on the Kaladan river and to secure and exploit the Japanese position on the right (eastern) flank.

Japanese defence of Donbaik

By the middle of January, the Japanese had taken up positions in the Chaung about half a mile north of Donbaik and also in the hills which were two miles north of the Chaung. With their left flank firmly resting on the sea, they held the nullah till the end of the operations ; some changes, however, did take place in the hill positions, where, by the end of January, they had been pushed back to, and then off, the feature known as TWIN KNOBS—just east of the nullah.

The beginning of February saw the Japanese still on the defensive in these positions, and all the while, they were busy preparing defensive works, which were strong enough to repulse an attack, although the Indian troops managed to penetrate to within a mile of the village. It was in this attack that two irreducible "strong points" were first encountered by the attacking force. Bearing out the dictum of aggressiveness even in static defence, the Japanese carried out several local attacks between 6 and 16 February—although their maximum strength was one battalion as opposed to a whole brigade on the other side (the 55th Indian Infantry Brigade).

On 18 February, the Indian troops launched a major attack to evict the Japanese from the nullah, but though they were able to occupy the west side of it and a wood to its south, progress to the east down the chaung was held up by many "strong points" that the defenders had constructed. Eventually, even the ground that had been captured by them with great difficulty, had to be yielded by them as a result of a strong Japanese counter-attack again the next day. The position remained quiet until 23 February, when a period of artillery exchanges was entered upon. By 27 February, the Japanese had started patrolling well forward of the hills with a view to keeping the Indian division engaged while the offensive to the east of the Mayu river was being rapidly prepared and was about ready for launching.

Throughout this period, the *3rd Battalion of the 213th Infantry Regiment* had held the Donbaik front; it was relieved by the *2nd Battalion of the 143rd Infantry Regiment* early in March when the operations from Rathedaung were started. In support was the *3rd Battalion of the 112th Infantry Regiment* which arrived in Laungchaung on 24 January 1943.

The dominant note in this phase was the offensive attitude adopted by the Japanese. Colonel Tanahashi was prepared to visualise an offensive as early as 10 February 1943 and the final offensive, launched nearly a month later, was undertaken by a force of only three battalions; these were the *1st* and *2nd Battalion of the 112th Infantry Regiment* and the *2nd Battalion of the 213th Infantry Regiment* with artillery and other support, while containing forces operated in the Kaladan valley and on the Mayu peninsula. In the Japanese sub-units also, the offensive spirit was inculcated at all times as may be seen from the active patrolling in the Batarai area, the results of which were undoubtedly satisfactory.

The Japanese were also able to dominate the no-man's land according to their wishes and their encounter with the Indo-British forces heightened their own morale and probably led the latter to believe that a stronger force was opposing them than was actually the case. This heightened morale, and the knowledge of the stubbornness of his troops in a defensive role, enabled Colonel Tanahashi to keep isolated detachments at Tunrawai, Kamai and elsewhere; the Indian forces on the other hand were much concentrated in and around Rathedaung. As a result, the stage was well set for the favourite Japanese enveloping move along the eastern flank of the Indian positions. This quest for a counter-offensive on the part of the Japanese, even when in a position of considerable numerical inferiority, was founded on the well-known maxim that "offence is the best defence", and in this connection, Von Clausewitz's views are strikingly appropriate.[2]

---

[2] "A fundamental principle is never to remain completely passive but to attack the enemy frontally and from the flanks, even while he is attacking us. We should therefore defend ourselves on a given front merely to induce the enemy to deploy his forces in an attack on his front. Then we in turn attack with those of our troops which we have kept back. The art of entrenchment shall serve the defender not to defend himself more securely behind a rampart, but to attack the enemy more successfully. This idea should be applied to any passive defence. Such defence is nothing more than a means by which to attack the enemy most advantageously, in a terrain chosen in advance, where we have drawn up our troops and have arranged things to our advantage." *On War*, Vol. III, p. 186.

Another feature worth noticing is the splitting up of the Japanese units and sub-units. This was not such a serious matter with the Japanese as compared with the other armies. The whole of the 55th *Division* came from the island of Japan—about two-thirds the size of Sicily, while an infantry regiment had an even more circumscribed area. There were thus no "personal" difficulties in different sub-units. Even the mixing up of the sub-units of the 33rd and *55th Divisions* did not create any undue problems owing to the very marked homogeneity of the Japanese race—in language and in customs. Furthermore, this practice was so widely adopted in training that it was accepted automatically in war.

In view of the possibility of such an organisational set up, it is well to remember that the presence of a platoon did not guarantee the presence of its company—and the presence of a company did not guarantee the presence of its battalion. The inevitable tendency to exaggerate the number of enemy seen, or believed to have been seen, and the casualties inflicted on them must therefore be guarded against. In most of the campaigns against the Japanese—whether in southwest Pacific, Malaya, Burma or elsewhere, the number of Japanese was nearly always considerably exaggerated.

CHAPTER VI

The Third Phase

(From early March 1943 to end of March 1943)

Allied operations in the Mayu valley

The Japanese were quick to react to the withdrawal of the Indo-British forces from the Kaladan valley and on 13 March 1943, five days after the evacuation of Kanzauk, heavy fighting broke out south and east of Htizwe.

The foremost defensive positions of the 14th Indian Division were in the Htizwe area, as the troops had been unable to maintain their more southernly positions near Rathedaung. The Japanese launched repeated attacks on the positions manned by the 55th Indian Infantry Brigade and the fighting was intense and bitter, in which 2/1 Punjab particularly distinguished itself. On the night of 16/17 March, the 55th Indian Infantry Brigade disengaged itself under orders and crossed the Mayu river by the Htizwe ferry; a large quantity of stores, equipment and a number of mules were either lost or abandoned. The Japanese, however, failed to follow up this advantage. About the same time, Japanese parties infiltrated through the hills to the east of the Mayu valley, to the Taungmaw area approximately 15 miles south of Buthidaung, and to an important defensive area on the road south of Rathedaung.

Final attack at Donbaik

The previous failures of the 14th Indian Division in front of Donbaik and its withdrawal from Htizwe, made it abundantly clear that it had little or no chance of reaching Foul Point; there was also an indication that a Japanese counter-offensive was in the offing. The Navy had stated that the assault on Akyab island must take place before 15 March 1943, because after that date, it might not be possible to use landing craft for the assault. It was therefore considered that at least a fortnight was required at Foul Point, after its capture, to concentrate stores and personnel for the assault on Akyab. However, in view of the situation that existed at the end of February, the commander of the 14th Indian Division gave it as his opinion that Foul Point and Rathedaung could not then be captured in time to carry out the assault on Akyab. Consequently, he advocated a defensive policy and issued orders to his brigade commanders to prepare monsoon defensive positions.

This reasoning of the Divisional Commander was apparently sound. He had tried, without success, for two months to break down the Japanese resistance with the result that the troops under his command were tired and sadly depleted due to battle casualties and sickness. At the same time there were indications that the Japanese were reinforcing their positions and were also making preparations for an offensive. Even if Foul Point and Rathedaung were to be captured at this stage it would be too late to carry out the assault on Akyab. The Division would be forced to evacuate these areas for administrative reasons prior to the monsoon, as there were no all-weather communications forward of Maungdaw and Buthidaung. The Mayu river was too exposed to be a suitable line of communication and there was not sufficient country-craft on this river for maintaining the divisional force at Foul Point and Rathedaung. The divisional commander, therefore, appreciated that even if further attacks were successful they would result only in the temporary occupation of a piece of ground at the expense of valuable lives; also, if the operation was to prove unsuccessful the Division would not be in a good position to oppose the Japanese offensive, particularly when the Japanese would be able to denude Akyab of troops, after it had become apparent that a landing would be impossible because of sea conditions. But in spite of all these reasons the Higher Command decided to stage one more and final attack against the Japanese positions north of Donbaik.

Till then, all infantry brigades had been engaged except the 6th (British) Infantry Brigade Group which had been held at Chittagong; it was to have put in an assault on Akyab island after the 14th Indian Division had secured Foul Point. However, this brigade was now brought forward from Chittagong, and supported by all available artillery and tanks of a Squadron of the 146th Regiment RAC, it went into the attack on 18 March 1943. But although it fought with great determination and gallantry, it was no more successful in its attempts on the Donbaik front than its predecessors. Renewed attacks on 20 March also proved a failure.

Japanese offensive from Rathedaung and Kaladan

In the beginning of March 1943, the 55th Indian Infantry Brigade had commenced to relieve the 123rd Indian Infantry Brigade in the Htizwe area. The former brigade commanded by Brigadier Hunt had under its command in the Htziwe area the 10th Lancashire Fusiliers, 2/1st Punjab Regiment, 8/6th Rajputana Rifles and a company of the 1/15th Punjab Regiment. A small detachment from this brigade had been placed on the line of communication, half-way between Kyauktan and Kanzauk, in the Kaladan area. But before the change-over had been finally completed the Japanese had begun their offensive.

The Japanese advance from Rathedaung had started in the early morning of 7 March when the troops of the *5th Company, 2nd Battalion of 213th Regiment* infiltrated into positions on the hill south east of Kanbyin, immediately in the rear of the Indian right flank positions on the high ground, north of Rathedaung. In these positions, they resisted Indian attacks throughout the morning and afternoon, receiving support from the *Munition Artillery Battalion* which was moved up to positions near Sabatha for that purpose. This had considerably reduced the strength of the Rathedaung garrison and it was not until the following day that the replacements arrived from the *8th Company, 2nd Battalion, 213th Regiment*, which had recently been relieved at Laungchaung. On the 8th, the *5th Company, Munition Artillery* failed to knock out some bren-gun carriers which were operating in front of its positions; quick firing guns were therefore sent to help and the *3rd Company 1st Battalion, 112th Regiment* was also put under the command of the *2nd Battalion, 213th Regiment*.

On the right flank, a composite force was placed under the command of Lieutenant Yamaguchi. Its composition was as follows:

Horiuchi Platoon (from *3rd Company, 1st Battalion, 112th Regiment*).
Osumi Platoon (from *6th Company, 2nd Battalion, 213th Regiment*).
A section of Engineers.
One quick-firing gun.
A mortar platoon.

They were to attack westwards on 8 March to capture the feature overlooking Thaungdara from the north-east. At the same time, the *1st Battalion, 112th Regiment* (less *1st* and *3rd Companies*) was to seize the high ground (point 220) north-west of Nwatingok. They were to secure this feature with minimum force, and then, as far as possible, to reinforce the Rathedaung front where the intention was to retain certain vital and important positions.

Yamaguchi's attack failed completely and his detachment was disbanded the following day, but point 220, however, was taken. This compelled the Indian forces to re-orientate their line from a general east-west direction to one running through Sabathe, then north-north-west along the Sabathe Chaung, to east-north-east of Htizwe. On 8 March 1943, Japanese air reconnaissance reported that about eight hundred Indian troops were moving south along the foothills near Mrawchaung—some four miles north of Point 220. Movement of troops including artillery was also reported between Mrawchaung and Buthidaung.

Hoshi Detachment

Meanwhile, the *Hoshi Detachment* of the *2nd Battalion, 112th Regiment* in the Kaladan which had concentrated in the Banyo-Nagan area, moved from there on the night of 6/7 March 1943. Travelling along the Kaladan river, the main body landed on the west bank in two parties—one at the mouth of the Kinzwang Chaung and the other at Bomein, then both moved north-west to the Apaukwa-Kanzauk area; other small parties continued up the Kaladan to land near Apaukwa.

It will be remembered that the Kaladan Detachment was located mostly at Apaukwa and Kanzauk and was under the direct control of the 14th Indian Division. Before the Japanese commenced their offensive the divisional commander had considered withdrawing this force from the Kaladan area. A shorter line of communication had been constructed to the Kaladan from Kyauktau near Htizwe to Kanzauk and Apaukwa. The divisional commander, therefore, had decided that he would accept the risk of keeping the 8/10th Baluch Regiment in the Kaladan as it was still required to prevent Japanese infiltration via the Kanzauk-Kyauktau track. Furthermore, it was thought that even if the situation deteriorated completely, this force would be able to fight its way out either via the Kanzauk line of communication or the original line of communication. The Taung Bazaar track could be defended with a very small force at its exit in the Kaladan valley. Had this line of communication remained open and the commander of the Kaladan Detachment made plans to withdraw via this route, if and when threatened, an orderly withdrawal by the Detachment with all its equipment and animals would have been possible.

By 8 March, Japanese troops were already in the Kanzauk area and approaching via Pyaungseik and Auktaungbyin. One column veered south-west to fight a successful engagement on the 8th at Panpechaung which forced the Kaladan Detachment there to withdraw across the hills to the Mayu valley. Their withdrawal via the Taung Bazaar track was cut off. The troops had therefore to withdraw through unreconnoitred jungle tracks on to the Buthidaung-Htizwe track, and were forced to abandon practically all their equipment and animals. Their casualties, however, were not very heavy. The whole of the lower Kaladan was now in Japanese hands and their right flank had thus been made secure.

On 11 March 1943, Colonel Tanahashi and the Chief of Staff of the *55th Japanese Division* decided to bring the *2nd Battalion, 112th Regiment* across the hills via Awrama, to assist in the attack on Mrawchaung. In the meantime, thorough offensive reconnaissance of that area was ordered with the object of threatening the Indo-British line of retreat, and on the 12th, *Munition Artillery Battalion* was pushed up to Lamudaingywa which was about three miles from Mrawchaung and Htizwe. On the 13th, an attack was put in on the feature, Point 199, east-north-east of Htizwe; fierce fighting followed in which an Indian company was surrounded but later extricated itself. The Japanese suffered many killed and wounded but succeeded in gaining the highest points—though not in clearing the feature itself. Their hold on these was strengthened the next day.

Attempt on Mrawchaung

In the meantime, the *2nd Battalion of 112th Regiment less 5th Company* moved across from Kanzauk and was reinforced by the cavalry elements of the 55th *Cavalry Regiment* which had crossed over the Myittha valley. The battalion moved through Awrama to debouch from the hills at Lainggwinshe, due west of Point 199 and about two miles south of Mrawchaung. This move took place on 13 March and its object was to occupy Mrawchaung and break through to Htizwe. To accomplish this, the *6th Company* was sent ahead on 14 March and it seized the high ground (Point 74) overlooking Mrawchaung, while the rest of the battalion attacked the high ground one mile further south. The latter attack, however, failed completely and heavy losses in men and material were sustained. The Japanese were surprised at the unexpected opposition and generally lost their heads and panicked. The force had, therefore, to be withdrawn and was re-organised south of Mrawchaung.

During this time, a detachment of the *2nd Battalion, 213th Regiment* (the identity has not been established but it was possibly the *8th Company*) was sent into the hills well east of Mrawchaung and ordered to proceed through Gritchaung (which it reached on the morning of the 13th) to emerge at Yezogyaung some four miles north of Mrawchaung, and to exploit towards Kwazon. It not only reached Yezogyaung but by the 17th, was reported in the foothills at Taungmaw, which was over six miles further north.

The battle further west had been going rather more according to plan. In front of Rathedaung, the *2nd Battalion, 213th Regiment* had maintained its positions on the hill between Kanbyin and Hkanaunggyi (though Indian troops were in possession of those places) and, further north, it had entered Ywathit, four miles north of Rathedaung. From there it crossed the Thaungdara Chaung and broke into the western extremity of Thaungdara village on the morning of 15 March; like the *112th Regiment*, it had suffered heavily in casualties.

Attack on Kyauktau and Htizwe

The withdrawal of the Kaladan Detachment had exposed the flank of the 55th Indian Infantry Brigade in the Htizwe area.

Although there was a small detachment of troops half-way between Kyauktau and Kanzauk, it was fully realised that the former place was a very important point in the defences, south of Htizwe. The occupation of this area, therefore, by the Japanese would mean that all traffic to and from the 55th Indian Infantry Brigade area would have to cross the Ngasanbaw chaung which was over 200 yards wide, and across which a ferry operated from Htizwe to the bank immediately opposite that place.

In conformity with the appreciation, 16 March was spent by all forward units of the Japanese force in making preparations for further attacks. Zero hour for the attack on Kyauktau-Htziwe was mid-night of 16/17 March. The main weight of the Japanese attack, with its flank guarded by the *6th Company* holding the narrow gap between the hills and the Chaung at Mrawchaung, was swung left, and the high ground west of Thaungdara was captured at 0400 hours. The *1st Battalion of 112th Regiment* attacked Htizwe an hour later and was in occupation by 0530 hours while the *2nd Battalion of 213th Regiment* completed the occupation of Thaungdara. But this thrust was unsuccessful in cutting off the 55th Indian Infantry Brigade troops.

The Japanese made further determined attacks in an endeavour to occupy the Kyauktau area. Heroic actions were fought by the 8/6th Rajputana Rifles and later by the 2/1st Punjab Regiment. In one of these engagements, the commanding officer of the Rajputana Rifles was killed and in view of the critical stage of the operations his loss had certainly an adverse effect on the morale of his men.

Subsequent operations eventually led to the withdrawal of the 55th Indian Infantry Brigade to Buthidaung. The commander of this brigade was hindered in the conduct of his operations by the number of animal units in his area when his positions were attacked by the Japanese. He was, of course, entirely dependent on animal transport for his mobility and mule leaders being unarmed could not be expected to put up much of a show when attacked. The brigade was, therefore, compelled to retire hurriedly after abandoning much equipment and animals. The 1st Dogra Regiment was of great help while acting as a rearguard to the 55th Indian Infantry Brigade, during its withdrawal.

The Japanese were somewhat taken aback by the success of their manoeuvre and were, therefore, slow in their pursuit. The *2nd Battalion, 112th Regiment* centered at Kyauktauo, and the *1st Battalion, 112th Regiment* centered at Htziwe, were ordered to send reconnaissance parties forward, and the *2nd Battalion of 213th Regiment* reverted to the divisional command. In the general advance that followed, the right flank was quickly pushed forward to Taungmaw where the 55th Indian Infantry Brigade troops were making a final stand, while the left flank advanced across to the

Mayu river to dig in at Remetchaung, about three miles north of Htziwe. Operation Headquarters then moved to Kyauktau.

Having repeatedly failed to take the Donbaik position (which put the assault on Akyab quite definitely out of the question) the 14th Indian Division commander considered that the loss of the Htziwe area severely threatened his positions on the Mayu peninsula. The whole of the 47th Indian Infantry Brigade less the 5/8th Punjab Regiment was east of the Mayu ridge, and prior to the loss of Htziwe, was being maintained across the Mayu river from a Field Supply Depot situated at Htziwe. This Field Supply Depot had, however, been withdrawn before Htziwe was captured and troops of the 47th Indian Infantry Brigade were being maintained via a track from Indin to Atet Nanra. But with Htziwe in Japanese hands this line of communication also became vulnerable and Japanese movements across the Mayu river were reported soon after. The Divisional Commander, therefore, again recommended that further attacks in the Donbaik area should cease and that the troops should withdraw to a defensive position in the Kyaukpandu area. This was the most forward position, which he decided, he could hold during the monsoon. He had, therefore, taken steps to prepare for its defence.

But the Divisional Commander was not allowed to carry out his withdrawal plan, and was again ordered to make another attempt on Donbaik. The 6th British Infantry Brigade, therefore, put in another attack on Donbaik on 20 March and once again failed to dislodge the Japanese from their positions. By now the Japanese had crossed the Mayu river in strength and had commenced their advance on Atet Nanra, and parties had begun to infiltrate on to the Atet Nanra—Indin track. The 47th Indian Infantry Brigade and the 6th British Infantry Brigade consequently found themselves badly disposed to meet this Japanese threat. The bulk of the 47th Indian Infantry Brigade was 10 to 12 miles south of Atet Nanra taking part in the fruitless offensive in the Donbaik area. The whole of the 6th British Infantry Brigade along with a proportion of the divisional troops were then about 12 miles south of Indin, dependent on a line of communication which was threatened by the Japanese. Such was the position when the Japanese once again started their planned offensive which later was to prove very costly to the Indo-British forces.

JAPANESE DI
END OF PHASE 3 AND DEVE
MARCH–MA

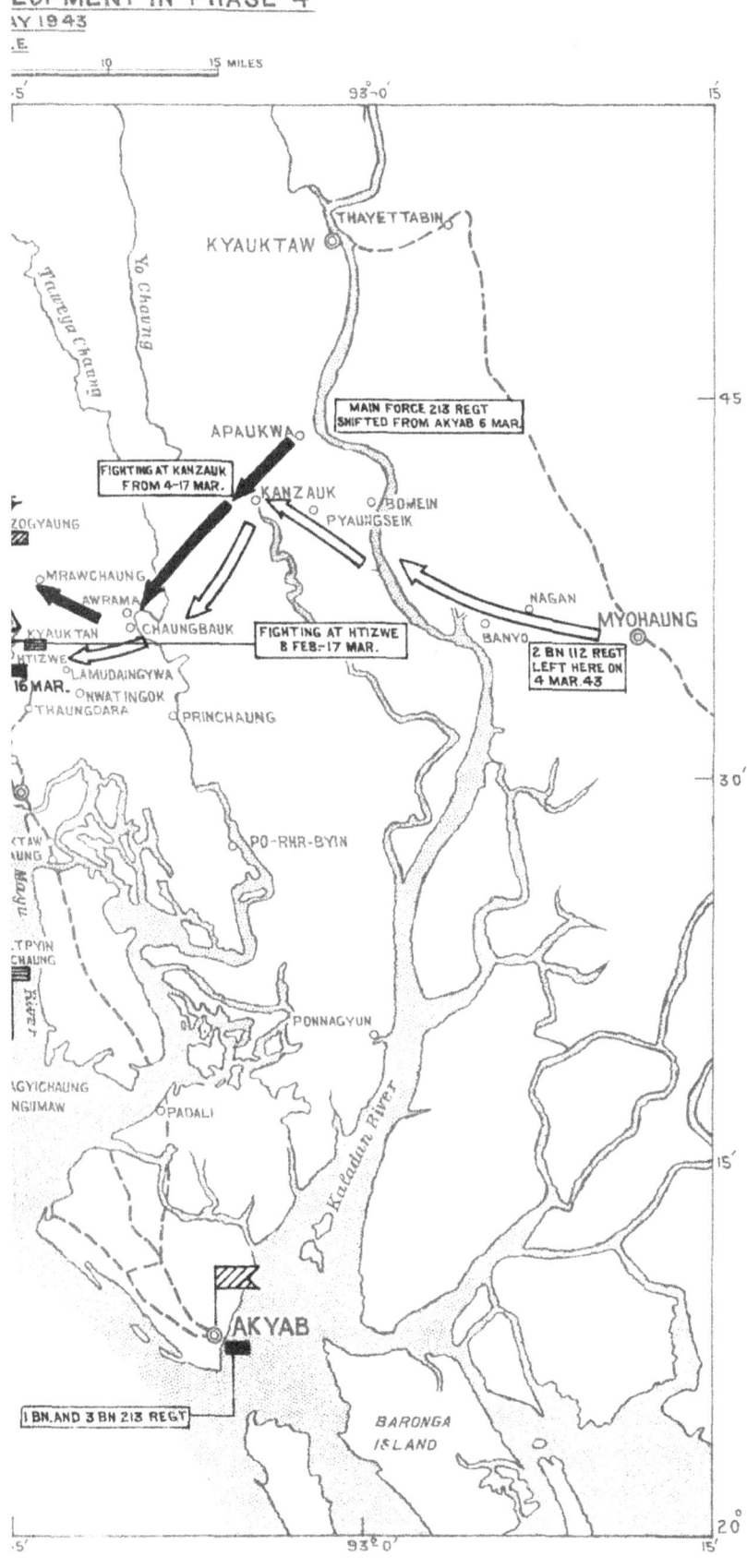

CHAPTER VII

The Fourth Phase

(From the end of March 1943 to mid-May 1943)

Operations on the Mayu Range

From about the end of March 1943, the Japanese developed their plan known as "Operation No. 31" and moved to the offensive in all sectors. Their ground troops were well supported by their air force and the *55th Japanese Division* was reinforced by a battalion of the *33rd Division*, and this whole force was concentrated in Arakan.

Having captured Htziwe and threatened Buthidaung at Taungmaw, the Japanese crossed the Mayu range and advanced on Atet Nanra, from where a track crossed the Mayu range to Indin on the west side. This track was important because it provided the line of communication to the 47th Indian Infantry Brigade which was positioned astride the Mayu range and was just north of the more southerly position of the 6th British Infantry Brigade, facing Donbaik.

In view of this situation, General Lloyd, commanding the 14th Indian Division, held a conference with the Commanders of the 47th Indian and 6th British Infantry Brigades at Kyaukpandu, and once again gave out his plan for withdrawal to the Kyaukpandu position; but at this stage he could issue orders only for the *preparations* for such a withdrawal as he was still very doubtful if the Eastern Army Headquarters would give permission for an actual withdrawal. The permission was never given.

During this somewhat precarious situation, there was a sudden change in the command of the 14th Indian Division. The Army Commander, Lieutenant-General N. M. S. Irwin, CBE, DSO, MC, took over personal command of this division from Major-General W. L. Lloyd, CBE, DSO, MC, on 3 April, and on 4 April handed over the command to Major-General C. E. N. Lomax, OBE, DSO, MC, the Commander of the 26th Indian Division, two of whose brigades, the 4th and the 71st, were already in action.

Meanwhile, on 1 April 1943, the 47th Indian Infantry Brigade had been withdrawn from its position to cover Sinoh, from where a fresh track to Indin had been constructed, as soon as it had become clear that the original track from Atet Nanra was threatened. But, on the night following General Lloyd's departure, when his withdrawal plan had perforce to be carried out, both the brigades were cut off and because of the delay, it was proving impossible to organise and hold the Kyaukpandu position.

When the Japanese threat to Atet Nanra developed, the Field Supply Depot at Indin had been withdrawn and a small dump placed behind the Kyaukpandu position, about two miles south of Gyindaw. Also, because of the threat to the 47th Indian Infantry Brigade's line of communication to Atet Nanra, 1st Royal Berks from the 6th British Infantry Brigade was brought back to protect it against Japanese infiltration. But on 3 April, 1943, before either the 6th British or 47th Indian Brigades had commenced their withdrawal, two companies of this battalion were cut off at Point 191 between Indin and Atet Nanra, and immediately after, the Japanese had placed a road-block at Indin. These companies had, therefore, to be supplied by air drop, and apart from the 14th Indian Division's improvised air dropping from Lysanders in the Kaladan area, this was the first and last occasion on which supply by air was carried out during this campaign. The line of communication to the 47th Indian Infantry Brigade was then closed; but fortunately, they had about four to five days' reserve of supplies and ammunition.

When the Atet Nanra—Indin line of communication was first blocked by the Japanese, one serious aspect of the isolation of the 47th Indian Infantry Brigade was the fact that they had over a thousand mules that were also cut off; and although it was possible for the personnel to withdraw over the ridge through the jungle, the mules could not be evacuated in a similar manner. Attention, therefore, turned to an unused track between Sinoh and Indin, approximately two miles south of the Atet Nanra track. This unused track had previously been reconnoitred and photographed from the air and due to the steep exits at the Sinoh end, had been pronounced difficult for personnel and impassable for animals. Nevertheless, the mules had to be got out immediately; therefore, the 47th Indian Infantry Brigade was ordered to commence work on this track from its end while every available man was set to work from the Indin side. It is to the credit of the engineers and the services, and to all those who were employed on this task, that the track was completed within 48 hours. Nearly all the mules were thereafter withdrawn and a limited amount of maintenance was also despatched to the 47th Indian Infantry Brigade. But it was obvious that owing to this new track being too close to the Atet Nanra track, its being used would very soon come to the knowledge of the Japanese.

During this period while the threat to Atet Nanra was developing, the 4th Indian Infantry Brigade from the 26th Indian Division had completed its concentration in the Maungdaw area. Earlier, it could have been used to relieve a tired brigade but by now it had been decided to open up a new line of communication for the 47th Indian Infantry Brigade via the east flank of the Mayu ridge from Buthidaung. With this object in view the brigade was ordered to concentrate at Hyparabyin on the west bank of the Mayu river, prior to an advance to the Atet Nanra area. Unfortunately, the long mule columns which constituted this brigade's First and Second Line Transport were much too cumbersome for it to have concentrated its maximum strength in the Atet Nanra area. The Japanese had, therefore, gained time to consolidate their position round Atet Nanra, and secure the Atet Nanra—Indin line of communication. The brigade had therefore to be withdrawn before it could achieve its object, which was to meet the Japanese threat, west of the Mayu ridge.

Fighting in the Indin-Sinoh area

When the Japanese crossed the Mayu range on the Atet Nanra track and put down a very strong road-block at Indin, astride the line of communication of the 6th British Infantry Brigade Group, the latter was still occupying the positions facing Donbaik. It comprised four infantry battalions. The 1st Battalion Royal Berks, which was located near Indin and had assigned to it the task of protecting the brigade administrative area, came early into contact with the Japanese.

The plan of the Divisional Commander of the *55th Japanese Division* was apparently not only to make a thrust to drive back the Indian and British forces from Rathedaung, but also to push them back to where they had started, and to restore the situation whereby a deep defence of Akyab could be obtained. Preparations had therefore been made for the operations on the Mayu peninsula, both from Donbaik-Laungchaung and from across the Mayu river, and nearly six battalions of infantry appear to have been involved apart from the forces holding elsewhere. As regards the troops already on the peninsula, the *1st Battalion of 143rd Regiment* relieved the *3rd Battalion of 112th Regiment* in the Laungchaung area and the *2nd Battalion, 143rd Regiment* had previously relieved the *3rd Battalion, 213th Infantry Regiment* at Donbaik. Both Japanese battalions in this sector were, therefore, fresh.

Of the relieved battalions, that of the *112th Regiment* moved to join its regiment north of Rathedaung on or about 24 March 1943, while that of the *213th Regiment* would seem to have returned to Akyab; its casualties had undoubtedly been severe. Troops which crossed the Mayu river to participate in the operation comprised all the three battalions of the *112th Regiment* and the *2nd Battalion of 213th Regiment.*

On the Mayu river a conference between Tanahashi, commanding the *112th Regiment*, and the Chief of Staff, *55th Division*, on 20 March 1943, had settled the details of the crossing. The main crossing was carried out on the night of 24/25 March, 1943, at Prindaw, about 4 miles north of Htizwe, and no opposition was encountered. There were, however, natural obstacles to overcome in the shape of unexpected creeks, between the landing point and the hills. This caused considerable difficulty and folding boats (carrying 15-20 men each) had to be used.

It was not till the afternoon of 25 March that the Allied Intelligence received reports that some Japanese had crossed the Mayu river. Nearly 300 of them were reported to have been engaged north of Atet Nanra and a comparatively smaller force was reported to be in the hills further west. In actual fact, the situation was becoming considerably more serious for the 14th Indian Division, for by the next day the *1st Battalion, 112th Regiment* had seized the high ground north-west of Atet Nanra overlooking the entrance to the pass there. The *2nd Battalion, 112th Regiment* was near Aungzeya, five miles further north, and the *3rd Battalion, 112th Regiment*, which was relieved in Laungchaung between 18 and 23 March, had also arrived in the area. At Taung-U, two miles south of Aungzeya, was the *2nd Battalion of 213th Regiment* (less one company) and some artillery.

The next stage in the Japanese manoeuvre was the cutting off of the 6th British and 47th Indian Infantry Brigades to the south, by the seizure of Indin. Little time was wasted in developing the move on Indin and troops were pushed steadily westward across the hills. Japanese supply arrangements at this time gave some cause for anxiety as unit rations were very short and the *divisional headquarters* was approached with a view to dropping supplies by air. Whether this was carried out or not is not known, but one report was received at this time of parachutes being dropped. The attack on Indin was to be co-ordinated with a drive from the south of the peninsula and the *143rd Regiment* in the south had received orders on 24 March to press forward at dawn on 1 April.

By 1 April, therefore, the headquarters *112th Regiment* had advanced across the watershed of the Mayu range to Point 184, four miles north-north-east of Indin ; the Indo-British opposition at the eastern entrance of the pass from Atet Nanra had been driven south to Sinoh and the nearest opposing troops were at the western exit at Ywathit. Tanahashi, therefore, was able to move his troops north of Indin. The *1st Battalion* occupied the hills round and west of Ywathit, the *2nd Battalion* occupied the knoll 1½ miles south-west of Point 208 and the *3rd Battalion* occupied the high ground a little further to the north. In doing so the *3rd Battalion* suffered 85 casualties according to a casualty return.

A captured Japanese diary has the following entry for 2 April[1]: "There is a lot of enemy MT activity. The troops opposing us are British and have no will to fight and are just knocked down in the stride of our attack." Encouraged by the progress he had made, Colonel Tanahashi decided on an immediate attempt to cut off the British withdrawal through the narrow coastal gap at Indin and for that purpose ordered all battalions to carry out attacks on Indin. These attacks started at an early hour on 3 April, 1943 when the *3rd Battalion* (the strongest) engaged the *1st Battalion Royal Berks* on the road near the road-bridge, a mile to the north of Indin. Later, the same force captured the bridge and thus cut off communications with Indin from the north. The Japanese then went on to capture the horseshoe-shaped high ground just north of Indin. Fierce counter-attacks were put in by the British defenders under cover of heavy artillery fire and these inflicted very heavy casualties upon the *3rd Battalion*.

By late evening of 3 April the *1st Battalion* was in position north of Indin and the *2nd Battalion* had pushed forward towards Point 127, overlooking Indin from the south-east. The same evening, the 1st Royal Scots, from the 6th British Brigade, was ordered to clear Indin and the rest of the brigade was ordered to withdraw to the Kyaukpandu area. The battalion attacked from the south on 4 April and suffered 200 to 250 casualties, but failed to dislodge the Japanese. Things, however, had not gone according to plan with the Japanese either, as the late arrival forward of a company of the *1st Battalion* necessitated the postponement of a night attack on 3/4 April. By the next morning, the opportunity was lost for the Japanese, and the British force cleared the positions to the north held by the *1st* and *3rd Battalions*. The same night the 6th British Infantry Brigade Group broke contact in the Donbaik area and regrouped just south of the Japanese road-block at Indin. On 5 April the brigade attacked hostile positions dominating the road-block, but, in the meanwhile, the Japanese *2nd Battalion* had occupied Point 127 and was infiltrating into the village from the south. During the course of these operations the Brigade Headquarters, established in the brigade administrative area, was overrun. The brigade commander (Brigadier Cavendish) and some of the staff were captured. The former was later reported by the Japanese to have been killed by shell fire[2] and most of the brigade records were lost.

Thereafter, the fighting in the Indin area became very confused. The Japanese were in fact never cleared from this area in spite of the repeated attacks by the British troops, and the 6th British Infantry

---

[1] *D.M.I.* File 9100, page 7.
[2] Japanese "*Operation No. 31*", page 10, file 9100. See also file 7552, part IV, page 30 and Part I, page 76.

Brigade Group's withdrawal was eventually carried out mostly along the beach area. Under cover of all available artillery and in conjunction with the maximum available air support, this British brigade was withdrawn northwards to the area of Kyaukpandu. It was impossible to use the road, which was blocked and dominated by the Japanese; the brigade had therefore to withdraw along the seashore and by-pass the Japanese positions. The 130th Field Regiment put up a magnificent effort while helping in this withdrawal. It was situated to the south of Indin when the withdrawal was ordered, and it carried out its task with smokescreens and firing with open sites at the Japanese positions, the personnel themselves finally making a dash for these positions across the breach, in full view of the Japanese.

In the meanwhile the threat to the area west of the Mayu range had also developed. This area contained many administrative units placed to support and maintain the 6th British and the 47th Indian Infantry Brigades. As there were no troops and no prepared positions north of the Kyaukpandu area, the whole of the coastal sector including Maungdaw was vulnerable to a Japanese encircling movement, based on the Mayu range. To meet this threat, the danger of which was very apparent to the Commander of the 14th Indian Division, the 4th Indian Infantry Brigade was withdrawn from Hparabyin and moved down to Gyindaw, while 2/8 Punjab Regiment was brought to protect the Headquarters of the 14th Indian Division.

It will thus be seen that the Japanese had again forced a retirement by an out-flanking movement, but had suffered heavy casualties in doing so and had failed to annihilate the forward Indian and British brigades, which was their intention. Nevertheless, they had converged on Indin and had occupied it by the evening of 6 April.

In the south of the peninsula also, Japanese hopes had been running high since the news had been received on 24 March that the *143rd Regiment* was to attack in conjunction with the advance of the *112th Regiment,* further north. Morale was high but the fact that the Indian and British troops did not start withdrawing the next day occasioned surprise, as did the heavy artillery fire they put down in the days that followed. On 21 March, the Japanese had been told that the forces opposing them showed signs of an early retirement and that they were to press home their pursuit.

On 1 April, 1943, the Japanese attack commenced according to plan; at this stage the *2nd Battalion* held the left flank and *1st Battalion* the right. The units of the *1st Battalion* started to advance through the hills on the right flank. This advance was supported by heavy Munition Artillery fire and was successful in effecting the withdrawal of the Indian and British troops in the plains from

Thayetpyin opposite Laungchaung, to Myinbu five miles further north. On the second day again the attack was continued up the Mayu range to "Hill 1000", two miles north-west of Thayetpyin, and the feature was occupied without difficulty. Pushing on through the hills the next Japanese objective was Conical Hill, four miles to the north-west; but a stiff fight was necessary before two platoons could gain control of the Conical Hill itself. In doing so, however, they had again got behind the Indian positions on the plains at Myinbu; and a further withdrawal to Sinoh, due east of Indin on the opposite side of the Mayu range, was made inevitable for the Indian and British forces when Myinbu itself was attacked on 4 April.

This manoeuvre on the left flank naturally endangered the positions of the 14th Indian Division at Donbaik, and the 6th British Infantry Brigade had, therefore, started to withdraw on 3 April, the date on which Tanahashi began his attacks on Indin with the object of cutting off their retreat. For unknown reasons, the *2nd Battalion's* follow-up from Donbaik was slow and the British rearguard experienced no difficulty till Indin was reached. There, as stated before, it met the main Japanese enveloping attack and had to fight its way out. The objective of the *1st Battalion, 143rd Regiment* at this time was also to join in the battle of Indin. But it failed to achieve this, due perhaps partly to natural obstacles but probably also to the inability to make satisfactory progress against the resistance offered.

While the *55th Division (112th Regiment* and *143rd Regiment)* was engaged on this push towards Indin, elements of *2nd Battalion, 213th Regiment* had moved four miles north from Aungzeya to Theindaungbyin where they had a minor encounter with the Indian troops on 31 March, but the main strength remained in the Aungzeya-Okthema area in a protective role.

It had now become obvious that the Japanese offensive was planned to concentrate their main effort on clearing the Mayu peninsula. The situation on 7 April in regard to the Indian and British troops may briefly be summed up by as follows:—

The 6th British Infantry Brigade—This brigade had suffered heavy casualties. It was occupying a defensive position in the Kyaukpandu area to cover the withdrawal of the 47th Indian Infantry Brigade.

The 47th Indian Infantry Brigade—At this stage the Japanese were on the Sinoh track and the brigade was infiltrating across the ridge as best as it could and had been ordered to concentrate in the Lambaguna area. It had been forced to abandon most of its equipment and its ranks were severely depleted. Under the existing circumstances it could no longer be regarded as having any immediate fighting value.

The 4th Indian Infantry Brigade had been ordered to take up

a "lay back" position in the Gyindaw area, north of the 6th British Brigade, leaving a detachment in the Hyparabyin area.

The 55th Indian Infantry Brigade (along with 8/10 Baluch from the Kaladan)—These troops were located in the Buthidaung area and were more or less in the same condition as the 47th Indian Infantry Brigade. They had been ordered to relieve the 4th Indian Infantry Brigade at Hyparabyin.

The 71st Indian Infantry Brigade was placed in the Thaungmaw-Kwason area ready to oppose any Japanese advance in that locality.

The 123rd Indian Infantry Brigade was also in the Buthidaung area disposed to protect the area from Japanese infiltration from the Kaladan and via the west bank of the Mayu river. Its ranks were badly depleted and its fighting value was not much better than that of the 55th Indian Infantry Brigade.

The 36th Indian Infantry Brigade was commencing to concentrate in Cox's Bazaar.

On 7 April, when the 6th British Infantry Brigade was in the Kyaukpandu area and the 4th Indian Infantry Brigade was concentrating in the Gyindaw area, small parties of Japanese troops were beginning to infiltrate along the ridge and attempting to come in on the road. It was therefore decided that Headquarters 6th British Infantry Brigade should withdraw all transport and heavy equipment. This was successfully achieved on the night of 10/11 April. But before the 6th British Brigade Commander had time to organise the defence of the Kyaukpandu area, the Japanese were already in front of, and on the flank of this area, while Allied intelligence reports further indicated that the Japanese were also advancing along the top of the Mayu ridge. Consequently, on 9 April, General Lomax, Commander of the 26th Indian Division, decided to bring the 6th British Infantry Brigade back to the Lambaguna area, leaving the 4th Indian Infantry Brigade with 2 Durham Light Infantry under command, in the Gyindaw area.

At this stage it was decided that there would be a gradual take over by the 26th Indian Division (Major-General Lomax) from the Headquarters 14th Indian Division and that the 47th, 55th and 123rd Indian Infantry Brigades would be withdrawn together with the majority of the divisional troops. The 23rd Infantry Brigade (70th British Div.) was to be brought forward and the Headquarters XV Corps was to take over operational control in the area; the administrative control of the operations was to be retained by the 14th Indian Division until the 26th Indian Division had taken over, after which XV Corps was to assume full control.

By 11 April nearly three quarters of the 47th Indian Infantry Brigade had arrived at Lambaguna. It is difficult to give an accurate picture of how the majority of troops were able to withdraw from the 47th Indian Infantry Brigade area. A large number did come down the Sinoh track although others definitely found this track to be blocked by the Japanese. They therefore made their way through the jungle, south of this track. Thereafter they made for the beach and walked through the 6th British Infantry Brigade area. While these moves were taking place the divisional headquarters received information that the Japanese were using boats on the coast at night time. With a view to stopping this, the Royal Air Force was asked to drop flares on the beaches in the Kyaukpandu area. But this proved unfortunate, because elements of the 47th Indian Infantry Brigade imagined that these flares were being dropped by the Japanese in order to discover their escape route. The troops of this brigade therefore waded out to sea in order to keep clear of the beaches and by doing so lost a lot of equipment which they were carrying.

The 6th British Infantry Brigade also, by 11 April, was successfully withdrawn to an area about six miles south of the Razabil road junction. All battalions of this brigade were then very much under strength and had suffered heavy casualties. Hence on 12 April, General Lomax decided that he must have the 36th Indian Infantry Brigade forward, and orders for this brigade to concentrate in the Maungdaw area were issued soon after. At the same time he also decided to withdraw the 71st Indian Infantry Brigade from the Taungmaw area in order to create a reserve, and to bring the 4th Indian Infantry Brigade back to the Lambaguna area. On 14 April, the 4th Indian Infantry Brigade withdrew to the Lambaguna area meeting with very little opposition. Meanwhile patrols from the 55th Indian Infantry Brigade at Hyparabyin on the east and from the 4th Indian and 6th British Brigades on the west, were patrolling the ridge, but very few contacts were made. On the same day the Commander of the XV Indian Corps, Lieut-General W. J. Slim, CB, CBE, DSO, MC, assumed general operational control of the troops in Arakan and Chittagong, and the commander of the 26th Indian Division took over immediate command of the operations.

During the initially successful advance southwards, the higher command had depended greatly on 'V' Force for information, but during the static period in front of Donbaik they relinquished many contacts and in consequence suffered from the lack of 'V' Force information during their withdrawal northwards. This was a very serious factor. Since the standard of patrolling of the Indian and British troops was not high, it became difficult to follow the movements of the many small parties of Japanese who were operating against the forward troops and on their flank.

The situation to the east of the Mayu range had also deteriorated, and simultaneously with the fighting at Indin, the Japanese had infiltrated into the Indian forward positions in the Mayu valley, and developed an advance along the spine of the Mayu range.

Throughout this very trying period, the work of the Royal Air Force over forward areas was invaluable, in particular of the 28th Squadron who carried on continuous Tactical Reconnaissance (Tac R) duties and worked unceasingly to provide information and photographs of Japanese movements.

Defence of the Tunnels area

By now it had become clear to General Slim that the Japanese advance was directed against the Maungdaw-Buthidaung road which carried the maintenance of all troops in the Mayu valley, and provided the only means of switching forces across the Mayu range by motor transport.

The Indian brigades, many of whom had been engaged for long and continuous periods, were tired. Battle casualties had not been very severe but malaria and fever had exacted a very heavy toll amongst the troops who had been given practically no anti-malarial training, and for whom very few protective measures were then available. Reinforcements were also arriving untrained and completely unfit to play their part in the current operations. It was therefore all the more essential for the XV Corps to secure the road from Maungdaw to Buthidaung. There was a considerable Indian force in the Mayu valley and extensive dumps of supplies had been established at Buthidaung. The loss of control of the road virtually involved the impossibility of maintaining adequate forces in the whole of the Mayu valley. Japanese occupation of Buthidaung and the Mayu valley would enable them to mount operations against the Indian line of communication to the west of this range, as well as against the area in which lay the greatest weight of the Allied administrative installations. Consequently, it was decided to secure the road and its terminals at Maungdaw and Buthidaung.

A critical area of defence lay in the neighbourhood of the Tunnels where the road crossed the summit of the range. The 71st Indian Infantry Brigade was therefore withdrawn from its forward positions in the area of Kwazon and Taungmaw and was concentrated in the Tunnels area, and made responsible for its defence.

On 15 April, the troops of the XV Indian Corps were disposed as follows:—

West Mayu Ridge
    4th Indian Infantry Brigade
    3/9 Gurkha Rifles
    8/8 Punjab
    2 Durhams Light Infantry
    Battery 130 Field Regiment Royal Artillery

6th British Infantry Brigade
1 Royal Scots
1 Royal Berkshire Regiment
1 Royal Welch Fusiliers
13 Field Regiment less
  two Batteries

Astride Indin road, approximately 6 miles south of Razabil road junction.

Maungdaw
2/8 Punjab

Tunnel Area, Road Maungdaw-Buthidaung
Company 10 Lancashire Fusiliers
1/15 Punjab
One Mountain Battery

East Mayu Ridge

71 Indian Infantry Brigade   Buthidaung
1 Lincolnshire Regiment less two Companies
7/15 Punjab (under orders of move to Maungdaw)
9/15 Punjab (in process of moving from Kindaung area)
Two Companies 1 Lincolnshire Regiment—South of river at
  Kindaung
10 Lancashire Fusiliers less one Company—North of river at
  Kindaung

55 Indian Infantry Brigade
6/11 Sikhs   Hyparabyin less one coy
2/1 Punjab   2/1 Punjab at Kwason
Two Mountain Batteries
1 Dogras   Taung Bazaar.

By this time, the 47th and 123rd Indian Infantry Brigades along with attached units had left the area; and from now on till the end of the month no big change in the disposition of Indian and British troops took place, but several minor moves were carried out. On 16 April, 7/15 Punjab moved into the hills between the 4th Indian and 6th British Brigade areas with the object of blocking the Japanese advance along the top of the Mayu ridge. The Lancashire Fusiliers moved over to Maungdaw but later went back to the Tunnels area. The 55th Indian Infantry Brigade at Seninbiya was joined by the 1/15th Punjab Regiment while Headquarters Mayforce moved to the west side of the Mayu ridge in the Tunnels area. In the meantime, the 36th Indian Infantry Brigade which had been concentrating in the Maungdaw area completed the process by 24 April.

During this period it had become increasingly difficult to maintain the unprotected line of communication to the 6th British

Infantry Brigade Group and the 4th Indian Infantry Brigade, at Kyaukpandu and Gyindaw respectively. The British brigade was therefore brought back to occupy a defensive area near Dilpara and the Indian brigade to the Alethangyaw-Lambaguna area. These new dispositions shortened the line of communication west of the Mayu range, and afforded a certain degree of protection to Maungdaw. But in spite of this the Japanese had continued their drive along the spine of the Mayu range, using an existing track thought to have been made by elephants. Efforts were made to oppose them on this track but they proved to be unsuccessful owing to the impossibility of maintaining troops in the vital areas. The almost insuperable difficulty was the provision of water which had to be carried up by pack mules and by hand. Also, available unit strengths did not permit of sufficiently frequent relief of troops on the spine of the range; it was proving a physical impossibility for most of them to remain there for more than very short periods. Air bombing was continuously undertaken but its effect was minimized by the extreme narrowness of the target area and by the difficulty of pin-pointing the Japanese who moved in very small and well-dispersed parties.

It was therefore decided to concentrate on the defence of the Tunnels area. The positions there were placed in the form of a horseshoe with the open end to the south, and it was confidently expected that the Japanese would advance into it and would thereafter be halted and destroyed there. The Japanese fulfilled these expectations but unfortunately the "sides" of the horseshoe were not maintained.

On 4 May, the Japanese occupied Point 551. This feature dominated the road from Maungdaw to Buthidaung, just east of the Tunnels. The 36th Indian Infantry Brigade made several brave attempts to recover this area and 8/13 Frontier Force Rifles played a gallant and major part in these attempts. But the Indian brigade failed to dislodge the Japanese and by 5 May, the latter had managed to cut the road between the 3rd and 4th milestones, west of Buthidaung.

Final withdrawal and evacuation of Maungdaw

The situation at the beginning of May 1943 was that all the troops east of the Tunnels, in the Mayu valley and at Buthidaung, were cut off from their main base at Maungdaw, hence reinforcement and maintenance had become impossible with the resources available. In consequence, a withdrawal became inevitable and was immediately ordered. The 55th Indian Infantry Brigade and all the troops east of the Mayu range withdrew across the Nagakyedauk Pass. Field

Artillery was successfully driven out through the Japanese positions along the Maungdaw-Buthidaung road while mechanical-transport vehicles were driven across country as far north as possible on the west bank of the Kalapanzin valley, and were parked near Taung Bazaar.

The 6th British Infantry Brigade Group and the 4th Indian Infantry Brigade remained in their positions at Dilpara and Lambaguna respectively. Headquarters 26th Indian Division moved back to Maungnama on the road from Maungdaw to Bawli Bazaar. Taung Bazaar and the western end of the Soutcol route to the Kaladan remained firmly in Indo-British hands.

The loss of Buthidaung and of the control of the road Maungdaw-Buthidaung uncovered the left flank of all Indo-British positions west of the Mayu range. Constant reports were received of Japanese movements up the Kaladan valley which had been laid open to the Japanese when Indian and British forces had to withdraw from their positions there in early March 1943.

It was then decided by the Corps Commander to secure Maungdaw and also the ground necessary for its retention throughout the coming monsoon, and the 26th Indian Division was disposed to this effect. At the same time, the possibility of a wider encircling movement by the Japanese ultimately directed against the railhead at Dohazari was also taken into consideration. For this purpose the 23rd Infantry Brigade of 70th British Division which had been brought into Arakan and placed under the command of the 26th Indian Division, was positioned in the valley of the Pruma Chaung, north of Bawli Bazaar; it was however not engaged by the Japanese. The 14th Infantry Brigade of the same division had also been brought in and located at Cox's Bazaar.

But the changed tactical situation influenced General Slim in deciding to abandon the plan for securing Maungdaw. The chief reasons for his decision were:—

- (a) The east flank of any position taken up must be exceedingly vulnerable and the whole area of defence in danger of being cut off by the Japanese operating from the Mayu range.
- (b) Available resources were inadequate to extend the area of defence sufficiently to prevent hostile interference with maintenance by the Naf river. There could be no maintenance by land which in any event would be impossible during the monsoon.
- (c) All units were very seriously under-strength due to battle and, above all, sickness casualties.
- (d) Reinforcements were inadequately trained and very often unfit to take their place in battle.

(e) The Japanese continued to infiltrate into the forward positions.

(f) Constant reports were being received of an hostile build-up in the Kaladan valley against his eastern flank.

The commander of the 26th Indian Division was therefore given a new set of tasks in the following order of priority[3]:—

(a) To withdraw all his forces with minimum loss to the line Barden—Nhila—Pruma Chaung—Goppe Bazaar. This line was to be held until the break of the monsoon (15 June).

(b) To evacuate maximum possible of all stores and equipment from Maungdaw.

The evacuation of Maungdaw was then commenced and a priority was allotted to ammunition, ordnance stores, engineer stores and supplies. The withdrawal was successfully carried out and Maungdaw was abandoned on 12 May 1943; but it had not been possible, with the river craft and mechanical transport available, to clear all the stores and equipment.

The Japanese plan

It is well to consider the moves and counter-moves which the Japanese carried out, enabling them to push the Indo-British forces back from where they had started. Documents are now available which throw some light on this subject although in some cases full information is not yet available.

As was to be expected, there was a pause in operations after the battle of Indin and, apart from two small attacks on the road, 6 miles north of Indin on the morning of 8 April, and shelling of the road, conditions remained comparatively quiet. Small elements of Japanese troops were, however, pushed ahead through the hills and, by 11 April, were on the high ground just east of Gyindaw and Myinhlut. But the battalions of the *112th Regiment* were very considerably under strength as a result of casualties suffered, and hence were not in a position to stage an effective offensive. They were for that reason unable to exploit to their advantage a further Indo-British withdrawal to Alethangyaw on 13 April. Meanwhile, on 10 April, the *143rd Regiment*, whose casualties had been comparatively light, had started to move north from Indin. It kept mostly to the hills, and crossing the summit, west of Okthema, turned north-west up the main ridge, passing Points 701 and 1006, west of Hyparabyin, on 17 and 18 April. This advance remained unopposed until the night of 18 April, when the Japanese advanced guard exchanged shots with the forward Indian troops. The following day the advance was continued along the high

---

[3] See file 7552, Pt. II, pages 107-108.

ground through Point 860 toward Point 613. At the same time, the detachment of the *2nd Battalion, 213th Regiment* had been advancing slowly with little opposition in the plains, to the east of the *143rd Regiment*.

On 23 April, Gudabyin on the Mayu river was occupied by the troops of the *2nd Battalion, 143rd Regiment* and at the same time the *1st Battalion* was outflanking the Indian and British positions at Kanthe and Seinnyinba. The Japanese Commander's plan at this stage of the proceedings was to clear the area south of the Kanthe Chaung and to advance to the line of the Kin Chaung, about two miles further north, and there prepare for an attack on Buthidaung. The *1st Battalion* was to carry out mopping up operations south of Seinnyinba and then advance to the Kin Chaung, preparatory to an attack on Buthidaung.

An attack was put in on the Seinnyinba area on the evening of 25 April after artillery concentration had been put down on the hostile positions, west of the village. This was followed by an attack in close formation which cost the Japanese dearly in casualties; but, at the same time, it forced the outposts of the 55th Indian Infantry Brigade to withdraw to the Kanthe Chaung, and to its north.

By 27 April, *Headquarter 1st Battalion, 143rd Regiment* was on the hill feature 578, just over a mile west of Kanthe. The following day attacks were again made on Indian troops on the ridge to the north-west of Kanthe, but these were not successful and the Japanese were forced to retire, under cover of darkness, to their previous positions.

While the *1st Battalion* had been working up the eastern foothills, other troops had been proceeding up the main ridge to the west of them, and had come in contact with the Indian troops due west of Kanthe. The identity of this Japanese force is not known but it is believed to have comprised of troops drawn from the *112th Regiment*. The contact was maintained in the vicinity of Kingyaungtaung till 6 May when events further north necessitated a withdrawal of the Indian detachment; the rest of the *112th Regiment* remained west of the Mayu range where they engaged in small scale patrolling, sniping and foraging operations as far north as Alethangyaw. There was also some exchange of artillery fire but no advance or encirclement was attempted.

In the meanwhile, the *143rd Regiment's* direct assaults in the Kanthe area had been costly and largely ineffective up to the end of April. But in May, different tactics were adopted—tactics of infiltration. On 30 April, small Japanese parties reached Wahkaung Chaung, 2½ miles north of Kanthe, which put them well behind the Indian forward position, and the following day similar parties were sighted two miles further to the north-west. By 2 May, those at

Wahkaung Chaung had been reinforced sufficiently to put in successful attacks on the Indian posts there, and others, again in small numbers, had pushed forward to within half a mile of the Maungdaw-Buthidaung road. By 3 May, this party had been reinforced till it was in sufficient strength to stop all but essential traffic from using the road. This successful penetration opened up the way for the *1st Battalion, 143rd Regiment* to follow up via Pt. 557, Pt. 388 and Pt. 429 to its objective which was the high ground north of Milestone 2 on the Maungdaw road. The *2nd Battalion* advanced to the Kin Chaung according to plan and on the night of 4/5 May fought a successful engagement near Letpangaing, 3 miles north-west of Seinnyinba, causing Indian forces to withdraw. They withdrew to the north of the Maungdaw-Buthidaung road on 7 May and with them went the small detachment that had been positioned at Kindaung, north of Taungmaw and west of the Kalapanzin. This sector had remained entirely quiet since the centre of interest had shifted to the Mayu peninsula. The road to Buthidaung was now open to the Japanese.

Fighting for the road to Maungdaw had been going on ever since the first Japanese appearance on Pt. 551 near the Tunnel at the highest part of the road, on 2 May. They exploited their position to the full and while they made no progress near Pt. 551 they had effectively cut the road at Milestone 2½ and had established themselves firmly across it and had also destroyed a bridge in that vicinity.

It was evident to the Japanese that with Buthidaung in their hands and a good water line-of-communication behind them, they would be in a good position to concentrate a considerable force against Maungdaw, or threaten it from the north in the same way as the Indo-British positions at Donbaik had been threatened from Atet Nanra a month before. In view of this eventuality, the XV Corps decided to evacuate Maungdaw on the night of 12/13 May 1943 and *No. 1 Company, 1st Battalion, 143 Regiment* was therefore able to enter the town the following day. Thus the first phase in the battle for Arakan ended much where it had started, and both the opposing forces were back in the positions they had occupied about six months ago. The Japanese did not press their advance right home and at no time did they cross the India-Burma frontier.

Comments

The dispositions of the Japanese for the capture of Indin and the advance to Buthidaung and Maungdaw are, unfortunately, not known in greater detail. But it is tolerably certain that the Japanese attacking force at Atet Nanra—Indin amounted to three battalions, that the containing force protecting the Japanese line of communication from the north was one weak battalion, and that the follow-up force from Donbaik—Laungchaung was two battalions, more or less up to strength. These two follow-up battalions, gradually suffering increasing losses, carried on the pursuit that ended with the recapture of Buthidaung and Maungdaw. At the same time another battalion of the *214th Regiment* and possibly some other units were holding passive positions east of the Mayu river and in the upper Kaladan valley.

It is unnecessary to point out how the usual Japanese tactics of envelopment were again successfully employed; but a point of interest is their use of surprise. The Japanese training for war has always laid stress on the element of surprise and they have always practised the use, among other means, of all physical difficulties of ground to obtain it. In this case the move of the *1st Battalion, 143rd Regiment* was almost entirely through wooded, mountainous country with a considerable scarcity of water. Captured diaries refer to the extremely difficult physical conditions obtaining, but the result was success; the Japanese appeared unexpectedly, grew in strength unexpectedly, and finally forced the Indo-British withdrawal.

Again it may be noted how much the Japanese owed to manoeuvre; in any "action" as such, they lost heavily and often failed to achieve their object, but their surprise approach and the demoralizing effect of their unexpected arrival eventually won them the day.

Finally, it should be observed how near the Japanese were to defeat at the moment of their success. All reports show that they were exhausted to a degree, short of water, food and ammunition—literally at the very end of their effort. But they succeeded because of their tenacity and their refusal to give in.

Major General C. E. N. Lomax,
Commander 26th Indian Division
(April 1943—March 1945)

Major-General G. C. Evans,
Commander 5th Indian Division
(July 1944—September 1944)

Major-General D. F. W. Warren,
Commander 5th Indian Division
(September 1944—February 1945)

Major-General E. C. Mansergh,
Commander 5th Indian Division
(22 Feb. 1945—19 April 1946)

Major-General H. M. Chambers,
Commander 26th Indian Division
(25 March 1945—30 Jan. 1946)

Major-General W. L. Lloyd,
Commander 14th Indian Division

Major-General F. W. Festing,
Commander
36th British Division
(28 Nov. 1942—28 August 1945)

Major-General H. L. Davies,
Commander 25th Indian Division
(August 1942—August 1944)

CHAPTER VIII

The Monsoon Operations—1943

Disposition of the Indian forces

The end of the First Arakan Campaign coincided with the approach of the monsoon in May 1943, when the forward troops of the 26th Indian Division were found facing the Japanese forces on the Maungdaw-Buthidaung line. On 9 May 1943, the 26th Indian Division issued Operation Order No. 2 to the effect that "26 Indian Division will secure a line Barden—Nhila—Pruma chaung—Bawli Bazaar—Goppe Bazaar—Taung Bazaar. This line will be held until at least the break of the monsoon." The code word for the move of units to their new positions was "Arakan". The first stage of this operation was the clearance of Maungdaw and until that was completed, the rest of the units were to hold fast to their respective positions. "May Force", which had done some excellent work, ceased to exist on 9 May 1943, and the 71st, 36th and 55th Infantry Brigades which were parts of this force, reverted to the control of the 26th Indian Division. The withdrawal of the troops to their new positions started at 0800 on 11 May when the code word "Arakan" was sent out to all the units concerned.

On 13 May 1943, the 26th Indian Division Operation Instruction No. 15 was issued which cancelled Operation Instruction No. 14 and defined the brigade areas and their roles, as indicated below:—

I. *71st Indian Infantry Brigade—based on Nhila.*
   (a) To watch the sea-coast of Teknaf peninsula as far north as Elephant Point, with at least one company located at Bardeit.
   (b) To prevent Japanese penetration northwards up the Tek Naf peninsula.
   (c) To secure the Pruma chaung.
   (d) To secure road exclusive Bawli Bazaar—Godura.

II. *36th Indian Infantry Brigade— based on Bawli Bazaar.*
   (a) To secure the line of communication of the 4th Indian Infantry Brigade from inclusive Bawli Bazaar to exclusive Goppe Bazaar.
   (b) To prevent Japanese penetration northwards up the road Maungdaw-Bawli Bazaar across country between inclu-

sive Bawli Bazaar and exclusive Goppe Bazaar. For this purpose, one battalion would be located in the Mai Daung area, *i.e.*, at the summit of the pass between Bawli Bazaar and Goppe Bazaar.

III. *4th Indian Infantry Brigade— based on Goppe Bazaar.*
   (a) To prevent Japanese penetration from the east of Taung Bazaar.
   (b) To prevent hostile penetration from the direction of Kyaungdaung Bazaar.
   (c) To secure the line of communication from Taung Bazaar to Goppe Bazaar, both inclusive.

IV. *55th Indian Infantry Brigade—based on Wetkyein.*
   (a) To prevent Japanese penetration from the east across river Kalapanzin between inclusive Kyaungdaung Bazaar and exclusive Panzai Bazaar.
   (b) To act as immediate support to the 4th Indian Infantry Brigade.

V. *23rd Brigade—based on Shabe Bazaar.*
   (a) To prevent Japanese penetration from the direction of both Panzai Bazaar and Faqira Bazaar.
   (b) To act as immediate support to the 55th Indian Infantry Brigade.

VI. *6th British Brigade—based on Taungbro.*
   (a) To secure area Taungbro—Tumbru Ghat—Nawapara.
   (b) To act as immediate support to either the 36th or 71st Brigade.

VII. *14th Brigade—based on Cox's Bazaar.*
   To act as divisional reserve anywhere within the divisional area.

By this time either the momentum of the Japanese offensive had spent itself when they had reached the outskirts of Maungdaw, or it may be that they had attained their objective. The fact remains that they made no effort to harass or obstruct the withdrawal of the Indian and British troops from Buthidaung and Maungdaw. The Japanese themselves did not occupy Maungdaw in strength until two days after its evacuation by the other party.

Subsequent to this withdrawal from Maungdaw on 12 May 1943, two major attempts were made by the 26th Indian Division to destroy the stores and equipment left behind. The Royal Air Force carried out a heavy raid on the town a day after the withdrawal, while the second attempt was made on the night of 16/17 May when a small patrol was sent down the Naf river. It came under heavy Japanese light machine-gun and mortar fire which sank the boat, and the party had to swim over to the Teknaf shore. The same night, another patrol clashed with a Japanese raiding party in which one of the latter was killed and three captured.

At this stage of the campaign, when the monsoon was about to begin in all its intensity, it was realised by the XV Indian Corps that the maintenance of a numerically large force would not be possible in the area then under occupation. The withdrawal of extra brigade groups was therefore planned to take place in six stages and the 26th Indian Division Operation Instruction No. 16 laid down the programme as follows:—

1st stage	23rd Brigade group relieves 55th Brigade group;
2nd stage	55th Brigade group moves out of area for Ranchi;
3rd stage	6th Brigade group moves out of area for Chittagong;
4th stage	23rd Brigade group moves out of area for Chittagong;
5th stage	14th Brigade group moves out of area for Chittagong.

Depending on the tactical situation, it was laid down that the sixth stage would deal with the 26th Indian Division Headquarters along with the 4th Brigade Group moving to Cox's Bazaar.

The above-mentioned Operation Instruction only laid down the details for the first and second stages and D day for these moves was 17 May 1943. In accordance with the 26th Indian Division Operation Instruction No. 17, dated 17 May 1943, detailed orders were issued for "stage three" which was to be carried out on 23 May 1943, while "stage four" was to begin on the 25th of the month.

On 22 May 1943, the 26th Indian Division Operation Instruction No. 21 laid down a skeleton plan for the monsoon defences. It was decided to put one infantry brigade in the area Tumbru-Nhila-Prume chaung, with two medium-machine-gun companies in support. The role of this brigade was to be as follows:—

(i) Prevention of Japanese penetration in Teknaf peninsula and up the Naf river.
(ii) Security of Pruma chaung.
(iii) Security of the Tumbru ghat area and of the installations located in it.

Another brigade was to concentrate in the area of Bawli Bazaar, Goppe Bazaar and Taung Bazaar. It was to be given support by two mountain batteries and two medium-machine-gun companies and its role was:—

   (i) To maintain mastery over the area south of Bawli Bazaar as far as inclusive road Maungdaw-Buthidaung by vigorous patrolling.
   (ii) Prevention of Japanese penetration from the north-east and south into the area south and west of the general line Faqira Bazaar—Bawli Bazaar.
   (iii) Security of Bawli Bazaar area and of the installations located in it.

The third brigade was to be at Cox's Bazaar and its role was to act as divisional reserve, and to prepare and man the defensive layout at Cox's Bazaar.

It was appreciated that even if the Japanese undertook no large scale operations during the monsoon they would undoubtedly carry out harassing operations with the probable object of winkling the Indian and British troops out of their positions. The positions of the brigades were therefore laid out with the object of defeating such Japanese tactics. The principles which guided the dispositions were:—

   (i) "All positions will be capable of all round defence and special attention will be paid to defence against enemy mortar fire.
   (ii) All positions will be mutually supporting.
   (iii) Where allotted, medium machine guns will be dovetailed into the general layout.
   (iv) Tactical rather than close defence wire will be erected.
   (v) All positions down to and including section posts will be stocked with ammunition, supplies for garrison for 5 days, and with water."

By the middle of June, the various units had taken up their respective positions and a definite policy for the monsoon period had been laid down. On 14 June 1943, General Slim, commander of the XV Indian Corps, issued the following Operation Instruction:—

   (i) "Until weather conditions permit the resumption of the offensive, the policy of formations in contact with the enemy will be aggressive defence.
   (ii) Contact with the enemy will be maintained continuously and the monsoon period will be used for gaining the upper hand of the Japanese in patrol work and minor enterprises."

Owing to the difficulties of transportation in the rainy season, it was only possible to maintain two brigades of the 26th Indian Division in forward areas. These two were the 36th Indian Infantry Brigade and the 71st Indian Infantry Brigade. The 4th Indian Infantry

Brigade was held as divisional reserve at Cox's Bazaar while the other brigades, as has been mentioned, were withdrawn to Chittagong.

Monsoon operations and after—1943

While the troops in the forward areas were busy patrolling their respective sectors, the Japanese directed their energies towards the construction of strong defences on tactical features and vantage points; they began to draw in their outlying detachments to form them into larger and more compact bodies. But the Indian patrols allowed them no respite; harassing raids by day and night into the Japanese held territory, even in the foulest weather, kept their hands full. In this way the month of June went by with the Indian troops doing intensive patrolling in accordance with the Eastern Army's directive.

On 8 July, a company of 1 Lincolns of the 71st Indian Infantry Brigade carried out a raid on Maungdaw and remained in occupation of the town for five hours. As a result of this raid the Japanese reinforced and strengthened their defences in the coastal sector; this was revealed when subsequent British patrols met with stiffer resistance about a thousand yards north of the Maungdaw-Buthidaung road. The Japanese further utilised the monsoon period in constructing a strong line of defence astride the Maungdaw-Buthidaung road, which they hoped would prove to be impregnable. During the early monsoon period, Japanese patrolling and other offensive activities were conspicuous by their absence. At the beginning of the dry weather, however, deep and intensive patrolling by the Indian troops disclosed that the Japanese main defensive line stretched and extended from Point 124, north of Razabil, west of the Bawli road, on to Point 1301 on the spine—Letwedet, Sinohbyin villages and east of the Kalapanzin-Pyinshkala positions in the hills, to the east of Sannynweywa. The Japanese had built strong bunkers, roofed dug-outs and communication trenches which rendered their positions impervious to mortar and light artillery fire. At this stage, it was estimated that four Japanese battalions manned these front-line positions and that three more battalions were behind their main defences.

The beginning of August saw a marked increase in Japanese activity in the western foothills and on the spine of the Mayu range, north of the Maungdaw-Buthidaung road. At this time was also revealed the necessity of relieving the 26th Indian Division, which, having arrived in April, had fought strenuously and continuously throughout under the most exacting conditions of the monsoon in Arakan. The relief of this division was, therefore, decided upon and the 7th Indian Division was earmarked to take its place. In August, the 114th Indian Infantry Brigade (7th Indian Division) took over from the 4th Indian Infantry Brigade the whole area in Arakan, excluding the Naf river and the peninsula. The 4/5th Gurkha Rifles thereupon moved over the Mayu ridge to Taung Bazaar. At the same time the Somerset Light Infantry, less two companies, moved to Bawli South in the role of brigade reserve; the other two companies were sent to hold the summit and western entrance of the Ngakyedauk Pass and to probe south towards the Maungdaw-Tunnels road. The 4/14th Punjab Regiment less two companies was put in reserve at Bawli North. One company took over Goppe Bazaar while another held the summit of the Goppe Pass and commenced to patrol in force along the spine of the Mayu ridge.

The change-over between these two divisions had been planned to take place in even stages. Consequently from June onwards, two platoons from each battalion of the 114th Indian Infantry Brigade had been attached to the units of the 26th Indian Division for periods of about three weeks at a time, in order to gain operational experience; and during this period of attachment the platoons had taken part in several patrol actions, in one of which a platoon of the 4/14th Punjab fought a very successful all-night action near the waterfall on the Ngakyedauk Pass.

These various patrol activities by the Indian and British troops were not at first taken serious notice of by the Japanese, but by the beginning of September, a significant change was noticeable in their attitude, east of the Mayu range. The Japanese added active patrolling to their role of static defence and their patrols penetrated further north reaching villages up to two miles south of Taung Bazaar, on both sides of the Kalapanzin river. In the first week of September, therefore, Indian patrols came under brisk light-machine-gun and mortar fire from the area between Ngakyedauk and Awlanbyin villages on the Ngakyedauk Chaung. Casualties were suffered by both sides, and during the same period contact was also made by the two opposing forces in Upper Kaladan valley. The month of September, thus, was mostly spent in active patrolling of the forward Japanese positions by the Indian and British troops, and some of these positions, north-east of Maungdaw and north-west of Buthidaung, were pinpointed. By means of this vigorous and effective patrolling, the Indian divisions were able to retain the initiative in Arakan throughout the monsoon, and were determined not to allow it to pass to the Japanese when the dry weather came.

In the meanwhile the move of the remainder of the 7th Indian Division was well in hand. The 89th Indian Infantry Brigade had begun to relieve the 114th Indian Infantry Brigade on the coastal plain to the west of the Mayu range. The 114th Indian Infantry Brigade thereupon started moving to the east side of the Mayu range. Because of the scarcity of transport the move of this brigade was carried out with great difficulty. The mule companies in Arakan had suffered considerably from the monsoon and, therefore, the number of mules available had grown less and less everyday, so that eventually local coolies on prohibitive rates of wages had to be employed. Nevertheless, by the end of September, the 114th Indian Infantry Brigade was completely on the east side of the Mayu range while the 89th Indian Infantry Brigade had established itself on the coastal plain to the west. Of the latter brigade the 2nd King's Own Scottish Borderers (KOSB) was positioned in the Wabyin area, the 4/8th Gurkha Rifles in an area nearly 10 miles south of Bawli, while the 7/2nd Punjab Regiment was in the Bawli area and on the summit of the Goppe Pass.

On 5 October 1943, General Slim issued instructions as commander, XV Indian Corps, (then in Ranchi), laying down the policy that was to be followed when the Corps re-assumed control of operations in Arakan in November 1943. The main purpose of these was:—

(a) "To ensure that, when the Japanese attack, the line at present held is maintained.

(b) To make preparations to attack the Japanese positions in the areas Maungdaw-Buthidaung-Kyauktaw, in conjunction with a sea assault on the Arakan coast with the eventual object of driving the Japanese out of Arakan and Akyab.

(c) If the sea assault is not made, to capture and hold a line sufficiently forward to allow us the use of lateral road Maungdaw-Buthidaung, the mouth of the Naf river and the air strips in Maungdaw, Buthidaung and Kyauktaw."

It had by then been fully realised that the key to further progress, both on the coastal plain and in the Kalapanzin area to the east of the Mayu Range, lay in obtaining command of the heights of the Mayu range; these varied in altitude between 1,000 feet and 2,500 feet, and more or less completely dominated the whole area. Plans were therefore put into operation for the dual purpose of obtaining a secure footing on the Mayu range and moving into closer contact with the Japanese Foremost Defended Localities (FDLs) than had hitherto been possible.

On 14 October, the 2nd King's Own Scottish Borderers moved south from Wabyin and occupied some low wooded hills in the area of Zeganbyin; at the same time a company of the 4/8th Gurkha Rifles claimed the main ridge and took possession of two dominating features. As a result of these moves the Indian and British troops were brought into closer contact with the Japanese forward positions. From this time onwards till the end of the month, the 7th Indian

Division kept putting slow, increasing pressure upon what then appeared to be a relatively docile opponent.

South-East Asia Command comes into being

On 1 November 1943, the XV Indian Corps under Lieut-General A. F. P. Christison C.B., M.C., assumed the operational control of the Arakan area, south of Chittagong; it was allotted two Indian divisions, the 5th and the 7th, as well as the 81st West African Division for the coming cold weather operations. It started moving from positions covering Cox's Bazaar against the forward positions of the Japanese *55th Division*. The beginning of November, therefore, saw troops of the 5th Indian Division arriving in Arakan. By the 9th of the month they had assumed responsibility for the coastal plain, the western slopes and the crest of the Mayu range.

The month of November was also notable for various engineering activities which the XV Indian Corps had carried out to improve their lines of communication. With the arrival of the 5th Indian Division, the 89th Indian Infantry Brigade moved over the Ngakyedauk Pass to the east side of the Mayu range in order to link up with the 33rd and 114th Indian Infantry Brigades which were advancing south from Taung Bazaar. Since a whole division was then on the east side of the Mayu range it was essential to have a lateral road across this range in order to supply this division. The divisional engineers had, therefore, started work on the largest project so far—which was the construction of a road over the Ngakyedauk pass from the Bawli-Maungdaw road to the east side of the Mayu range. The first object was to make it fit for mules and then later to open it to jeeps. With the aid of thousands of coolies and tons of explosives the road across the 5 mile pass was constructed in about ten days and thrown open to mule traffic. In another ten days the Jeeps were also using it!

From the midnight of 15/16 November, the command of all operations against the Japanese in South-East Asia passed into the hands of the Supreme Allied Commander, South-East Asia, Admiral Lord Louis Mountbatten. The Fourteenth Army, commanded by Lieut-General W. J. Slim, CB, CBE, DSO, MC, which was to conduct future operations in Burma, came under his command.

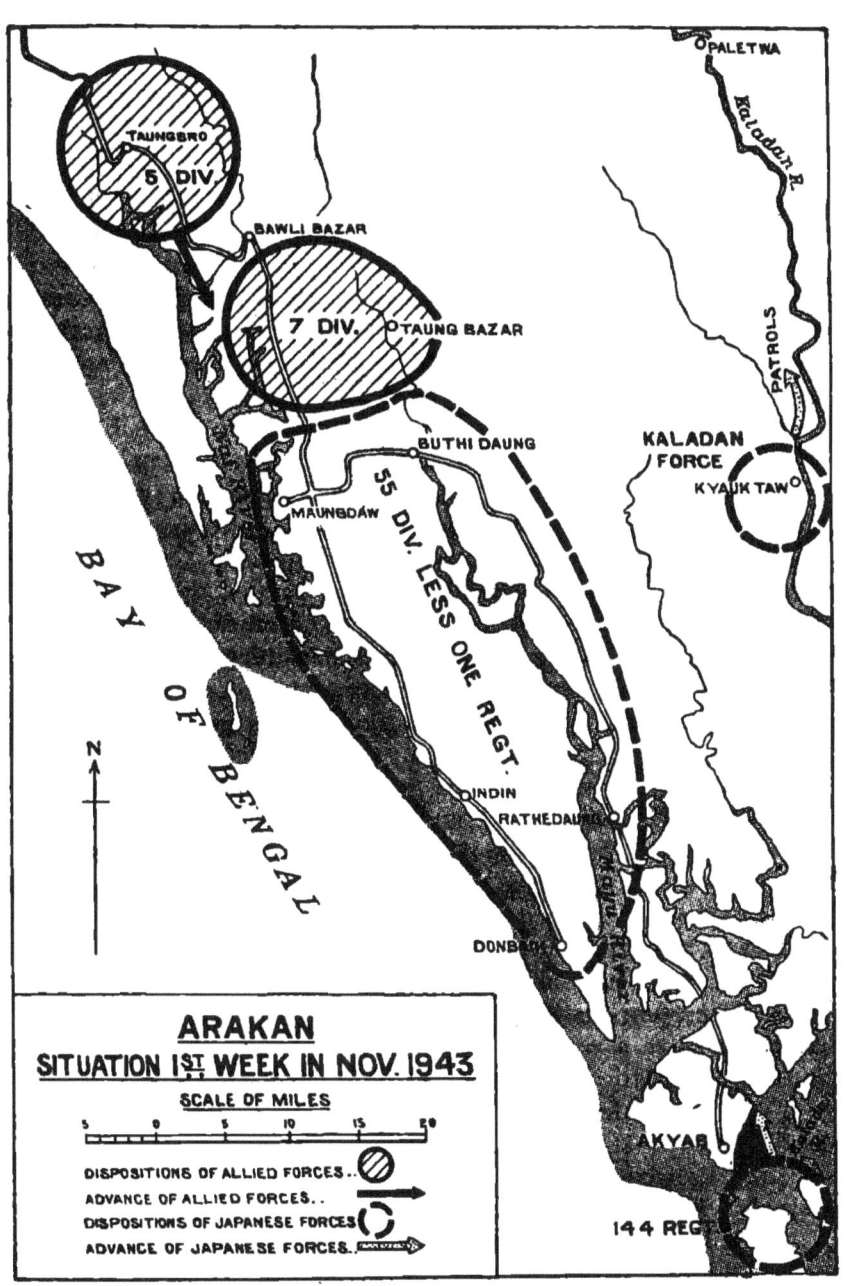

CHAPTER IX

Plans For The Cold Weather Offensive

The lessons of the First Arakan Campaign were too fresh to be disregarded by the planning staff of the South-East Asia Command. In this campaign it had been conclusively proved that a small force, deployed on a broad front in the jungle-clad hilly country of Arakan, served no useful purpose whatsoever and that piecemeal attacks at lengthy intervals against the Japanese were a waste of human effort and lives. In this first major conflict with the Japanese, the Indian and British troops had held both sides of the Mayu range, but there were no troops on the range itself. Consequently, the Japanese were able to exploit the tactical advantage by advancing along the summit of the range and splitting the opposing forces. Since the same tactics could again be employed, Lieut.-General Christison, Commander of the XV Indian Corps, was ordered to capture the Maungdaw-Buthidaung road, which was a lateral communication of considerable strategic value. For otherwise, its possession by the Japanese would enable them to switch their troops from one side of the range to the other, and thereby outflank the XV Indian Corps positions quite easily.

About the end of November 1943, the 5th Indian Division was deployed on the Mayu range, and along the west of it to the sea. This had relieved the whole of the 7th Indian Division of its commitments west of the Mayu range. The 7th Indian Division had, therefore, concentrated east of the range holding the Ngakyedauk Pass as well as a lateral jeep track on the range which connected the two divisions. It had taken over both the banks of the Kalapanzin river. To prevent his left flank being overrun, General Christison decided to place a complete division in the Kaladan Valley; and the 81st West African Division, which arrived in India in August 1943, was chosen for this role. The task assigned to this division was three-fold:—

   (a) Protection of the flank of the main force—the 5th and 7th Indian Divisions;
   (b) To act as a diversion to the main thrust and draw off as many Japanese troops as possible;
   (c) To threaten the Japanese flank in the Mayu Valley.

For this purpose, the African Division began concentrating in Chiringa, south of Dohazari, in the early part of December 1943.

In the meanwhile the 7th Indian Division was ready for a limited thrust forward—limited, because large-scale operations could not be undertaken until all the three divisions in Arakan were in position and ready to go forward according to a co-ordinated plan. The Fourteenth Army had ruled that "the immediate operational policy in Arakan is to retain the initiative in minor operations only and not to get committed to any major operations until the concentration is completed and we are ready to fight with our full naval, army and air forces in co-operation." It was anticipated that this would not be accomplished before the middle of December. At the time of laying down this policy only the two leading brigades of the 5th Indian Division, the 123rd and 161st Indian Infantry Brigades, were in position, west of the Mayu range; but the third brigade, the 9th Indian Infantry Brigade of this division, was still on its way to Arakan.

One of the main causes of failure in the First Arakan Campaign was the paucity of good means of communication; this factor was therefore given full consideration when plans for future operations were being prepared. The entire programme of laying new tracks and improving the existing ones, constructing fair weather roads and bridges and improving the existing ones, and constructing new airstrips, was taken in hand. It was decided to bring the Bawli-Maungdaw and the Maungdaw-Buthidaung roads to an all-weather standard. As has been mentioned earlier, the mule track on the Ngakyedauk Pass was, in a very short time, converted into a road fit for mechanised transport before serious operations began in January 1944; this difficult piece of construction was one of the brilliant achievements of the engineers of the 7th Indian Division. At the same time the engineers of the XV Indian Corps completed the construction of a low level bridge over Pruma Chaung at Bawli Bazaar; and General Christison, Commander of the XV Indian Corps, made sure that whatever else might happen, faulty communications were not to be allowed to stand in the way of successful prosecution of the campaign.

7th Indian Division's advance begins

On the night of 30 November/1 December, troops of the 7th Indian Division began a two-pronged advance southwards, east of the Mayu range. One column advanced without opposition across the Ngakyedauk Chaung occupying an area extending from the village of Ngakyedauk to the ridge about $1\frac{1}{2}$ miles north-west of Sinohbyin village. The other column crossed the Ngakyedauk Chaung to the west of Awlanbyin and near its junction with the Kalapanzin river. Only slight opposition was encountered but this was rapidly overcome because, before the commencement of the advance, the area had been kept under close observation for quite a long time. In the face of this advance, the Japanese were forced to thin out from these positions but they re-formed again at Ngakyedauk Chaung, a distance of about two miles to the south. During the night of 1/2 December, the Japanese suddenly attacked the Indian troops who in their turn were forming up for an attack on the hill feature at Point 206, three quarter of a mile north of the Ngakyedauk Chaung; the attack, however, was beaten back after close fighting. In the fighting that took place during these two days the Indian division got the better of the Japanese and inflicted many casualties.

The month of December was uneventful as far as major developments were concerned. This was due to the fact that the commanders of the 5th and 7th Indian Divisions had received instructions from the commander of the XV Indian Corps, in the beginning of the month, to the effect that their sole aim was to be the maintenance of close contact with the Japanese positions on the general line Maungdaw-Razabil-Letwedet-Letwedet Chaung and thence east to the mountains, three miles east of the Kalapanzin. These instructions were to be effective up to 31 December 1943 and the object was to be achieved by infiltration and local action.

In conformity with these instructions there was no major attack launched by the Indian forces and the Japanese too continued to be on the defensive. Nevertheless, infiltration and local actions were executed by all the three brigades of the 7th Indian Division. The 33rd Indian Infantry Brigade less 4/15th Punjab Regiment having concentrated in the Linbabi area, and the 89th Indian Brigade having moved across the Ngakyedauk Pass, the stage was set for the mopping up operations of the Japanese outpost line. The 89th Indian Infantry Brigade, whose leading troops crossed the Mayu range on 14 November, had made slow progress in the extremely dangerous jungle of the foothills in which they were operating. The first troops over the pass had been of 7/2 Punjab who were soon followed by the remainder of the brigade on the night of 15/16 November. During this advance a company of the 4/8th Gurkha Rifles occupied a high feature up on the slopes of the Mayu range, known as Cliff Ridge. It later proved to be an ideal observation post from which the entire panorama of the Kalapanzin valley and the town of Buthidaung seemed spread like a map at the feet of an observer. Brigade Headquarters had then established itself within the area of 7/2 Punjab at Sinzweya while 4/8 Gurkha Rifles had swung round and taken up positions at the foothills, about a mile to the south. The 2nd King's Own Scottish Borderers took up positions to the east of 4/8 Gurkha Rifles while 7/2 Punjab sealed the rear of the brigade area in the Sinzweya area. Thereafter, this brigade settled down to continuous patrolling, and shortly before the Christmas of 1943, 7/2

Punjab managed to capture two large prominent hill features in front of the KOSB's positions.

In the meanwhile the 114th Indian Infantry Brigade had also advanced considerably and Christmas Day saw the brigade disposed in depth with its forward battalion, 4/5 Gurkha Rifles, on the Mayu Chaung in contact with the Japanese at Kyaukit and Pyinshe Kala. The 4/14th Punjab was echeloned in the rear and further east, covering the Taragu Chaung, while the Somerset Light Infantry was in reserve in Taung Bazaar. At the same time, the 33rd Indian Infantry Brigade was disposed on a line which ran from the river Kalapanzin at Maungyithaung where it tied in with the forward battalion of the 114th Indian Infantry Brigade on the Mayu Chaung, and then westwards to positions overlooking the Letwedet Chaung. This was done in conformity with the policy that there was to be no slackening off at Christmas; the Allies feared that the Japanese might take advantage of any signs of idleness to regain some of their lost ground.

At the end of December, the 5th Indian Division held the area from the sea to the crest of the Mayu range while the 7th Indian Division had moved into the Kalapanzin valley. The latter was laid out in positions in a rough line stretching from the summit of the Mayu Ridge in the west to the Arakan Yoma in the east. According to General Giffard, "the stage was set for an attack on the main enemy positions." On 1 January 1944, General Giffard issued an Operation Instruction, based on the Directive of the Supreme Allied Commander, directing the Fourteenth Army "to secure the mouth of the Naf River—Maungdaw—Buthidaung, and exploit success to the maximum." The main object at this time was "to improve the general situation in Arakan" and to contain and destroy the maximum of Japanese forces. On this basis, operations were undertaken and the immediate objective was to secure "the necessary jumping off places for our offensive." Operations in January thus had the aspect of being preliminary to the main offensive which was being prepared, but these met with stubborn Japanese resistance.

Offensive operations in January 1944

A serious effort to harass the Japanese and capture their forward positions west of the Mayu range began on the night of 30/31 December 1943, when troops of the 161st Indian Infantry Brigade moved to positions on the high ground immediately northeast of Bakkagona and in the rear of the Japanese positions. The next morning, the 161st Indian Infantry Brigade put in an attack on Point 124, a Japanese "strong point" about two miles north of Razabil; but this attack did not succeed. Major-General H. R. Briggs, DSO, Commander of the 5th Indian Division, thereupon appreciated that frontal and direct assaults on the Japanese strongpoints might prove very costly. Therefore he sent his troops round the position and, by 8 January 1944, had completely surrounded Point 124. At the same time, on the main range and on its western slopes, the other brigades of this Indian division had also wrested some ground after a series of attacks.

Having completed the encirclement of the Japanese posts on Points 124 and 141, north of Razabil, troops of the 5th Indian Division pushed on towards Maungdaw. On 8 January, the 2nd West Yorks, the leading battalion, advanced south-west, and in the night, one of its companies was in occupation of Maungdaw. Thereafter, this force continued its advance across the Magui Chaung until eventually the West Yorks were in possession of Bagona, Thazegon and Nalpannya ; during this advance two companies of this battalion had swung north in the foothills and moved towards the Razabil cross-roads. Later, owing to Japanese infiltration and difficulties of supplies, the battalion had to take up new positions at Nyaunggyaung, Nalpannya and Pandawbyin. During this advance the opposition from the Japanese was negligible and no major operation had been undertaken by either side. However, the Japanese had deserted their well-prepared positions and had fled into the eastern hills before the advancing Indian forces. In the meantime the Japanese, north of Razabil, finding themselves completely isolated had also left their positions under cover of darkness and thick jungle, and had withdrawn further to the south. While this advance was taking place, the 81st (WA) Divisional Recce Regiment had come under the command of the 5th Indian Division on 19 January 1944 ; the regiment had moved south and had concentrated in the area of Maungdaw. At the same time, 3/2 Punjab which was the Divisional Defence Battalion had taken up an operational role under the command of the 123rd Indian Infantry Brigade and had taken over the positions of the Mayu range from 2/1 Punjab.

The Japanese had perhaps anticipated the Indian advance and had therefore taken steps to check it on the ground of their own choosing. They had turned the area around the "Tunnels", through which the main road passed, into a strong fortress with two strong buttresses—Razabil on the west and Letwedet on the east. It was a very strong position which had to be tackled by the Indian force before the Maungdaw-Buthidaung line could be breached. It consisted of a series of strong points honeycombed with bunker-type positions in the nature of a fortress, and sited most adeptly on strategic points. Thirty feet deep dugouts connected with underground passages in the hills, rendered these defensive positions impervious to any amount of shelling.

At this stage, therefore, the general plan of operation of the XV Indian Corps was to attack and capture the two buttresses in turn and thus surround the garrison of the "Tunnels" fortress. The 5th Indian Division was assigned the task of taking Razabil, while the 7th Indian Division was detailed for the capture of Buthidaung, to cut in behind the Letwedet "fortress". In conjunction with these two tasks the 81st West African Division was to advance down the Kaladan river to capture Kyauktaw, thereby cutting the Kanzauk-Htizwe road, which was the lateral line of communication for the Japanese. Based on this plan the main offensive was launched by the XV Indian Corps on 19 January 1944. This land offensive had originally been planned to synchronise with a sea landing by the 2nd British Division further south down the Mayu peninsula ; but the landing did not eventually materialise and thus the "right hook" of this Allied offensive could not materialise.

The capture of Maungdaw and the advance of the XV Indian Corps troops to Dilapara south-east of Maungdaw, led them to the rear of the Razabil fortress, manned by the Japanese. But this did not seem to have perturbed the latter who continued to hold the strong line of defence, extending from the Razabil fortress to Point 731 on the Mayu range. The command of the main features along this defence line gave the Japanese mastery over the entire country which they overlooked, and thus frustrated all attempts by the Allied forces to reach the Maungdaw-Buthidaung road. On the front held by the 5th Indian Division, the 123rd Indian Infantry Brigade continued to operate on the western foothills and the spine of the Mayu range, carrying out a number of raids on the Japanese positions, but nothing of material value was achieved. On the other hand, a Japanese counter-attack on 10 January on the Indian positions, half a mile east of Point 1301 on the spine, forced the latter to carry out a restricted withdrawal. But although this lost ground was recaptured a few days later, a condition of stalemate appears to have been established on this front.

In the meanwhile, west of the Kalapanzin river, the 7th Indian Division had also been carrying out its tasks as laid down by the Corps commander. On the front occupied by the 33rd Indian Infantry Brigade, the 4/15th Punjab Regiment had, in the middle of January, captured a feature known as Point 121. This was achieved by a series of successful operations and in the face of considerable opposition. At the same time 1 Queens, then patrolling the features surrounding Point 162, attempted to occupy the point itself. Two of its companies which were entrusted with this task while cutting their way through the jungle on to the feature came under very heavy fire and were forced to withdraw.

On the front held by the 114th Indian Infantry Brigade also a good deal of activity was taking place. The task of this brigade was to destroy by infiltration tactics the Japanese garrisons then holding

Kyaukit, Pyinshe Kala and Zadedaung, and then to continue the advance to the south by outflanking Buthidaung. This operation was known as Operation 'Hook' and the horsed wing of the Gwalior Lancers was put under the command of this brigade for the purpose. The 25th Mountain Regiment which had crossed the river was also to help in this operation. On 16 January, the first phase of Operation 'Hook' was put into action. 4/14 Punjab met with stiff opposition on the Taungdaungywa feature, its objective, but captured it and held it against strong counter-attacks and heavy mortar and automatic fire. At the same time 4/5 Gurkha Rifles, side-stepping these features to the east, pressed on towards the first objective which was the high ground, some 2½ miles south of Taungdaungywa. Avoiding tracks, nearly all of which were known to be picquetted, the battalion cut its way through the jungle on a compass bearing and the advanced guard company surprised a considerable force of Japanese, digging in astride the Thayet Kin Manu track. The Gurkhas went straight into the attack and the Japanese fleeing in disorder left behind a rich haul in documents, maps and artillery equipment. The Japanese also left behind three dead bodies which included that of an officer of the *112th Regiment*. This was most significant and was the first indication of the Japanese concentration in the Kalapanzin Valley. But the Gurkhas were not left alone for long. The Japanese after having put in a few counter-attacks had also managed to place a road-block on the supply route of this battalion. A quick reconnaissance showed that the block was covered by at least two platoons of Japanese in mutually supporting positions. The Gurkhas nevertheless put in an attack and although they suffered thirty casualties, the Japanese again had to flee leaving a number of dead behind. Thereafter, the 'Hook' line of communication was left severely alone.

In the centre of the 114th Indian Infantry Brigade positions, the Somerset Light Infantry attempted to capture the Pyinshe Kala redoubt. It put in the main attack from the rear which at first achieved partial success, but harassing fire and a counter-attack by the Japanese led to the capture of a key-point by them which overlooked the rest of the Somerset positions. Thereafter, heavy casualties began to occur and the ground gained had to be surrendered. On the front occupied by the 89th Indian Infantry Brigade, 7/2 Punjab and 4/8 Gurkha Rifles made some advance in the foothills against stubborn Japanese resistance and the brigade was within a mile of the Maungdaw-Buthidaung road. Although the brigade had suffered some casualties it had still been in a position to push in the screen of outer defences and patrol bases which the Japanese had maintained in advance of their main defensive line, north of the road.

Thus, by the middle of January 1944, the stage was very nearly set for an attack on Buthidaung and the elimination of all Japanese forces, resisting north of the Maungdaw-Buthidaung road. On the left of the 89th Indian Infantry Brigade, the 33rd Indian Infantry Brigade was facing Point 162, the feature MASSIF, while on the right flank, the 5th Indian Division had captured Maungdaw and was then heavily engaged in the Razabil fortress area; but Point 1301 and the "Tunnels" area, which was the key to what one Japanese "Operation Order" aptly described as "The Golden Fortress of the Mayu Mountains", were still holding out.

It is worth mentioning that this period also saw a marked increase in the air activity of both the opposing forces. Dive bombing and strafing of Japanese positions by British and Indian aircraft became a common occurrence in Arakan. The troops were provided with a real thrill when they watched a dog-fight in the air on 15 January. Soon after dawn on that day, a force of Japanese fighters visited the scene of battle over Maungdaw and Buthidaung. But the spitfires of the Third Tactical Air Force also appeared about the same time and a combat between the two air forces followed. This air battle continued for two to three hours over the land and sea. In this engagement, the Third Tactical Air Force Fighter Squadron destroyed fifteen Japanese aircraft and damaged many others with the loss of only two of its own planes.

At this stage of its offensive, when the troops were facing a stiff and stubborn opposition, the XV Indian Corps decided that a certain feature known as ABLE, which formed the bastion of the Japanese defence line north of the road, and also completely dominated the entire plain, must be attacked and occupied. The commander of the 89th Indian Infantry Brigade, who was mainly responsible for initiating this decision, was asked to detail a battalion of his brigade to carry out this task. Thereupon, the 2nd King's Own Scottish Borderers who were at this time in reserve, were appointed for this operation and the 7th Indian Division artillery along with the 6th Medium Regiment was given in support.

When the plan to capture ABLE was receiving the final touches, it was realised that as a preliminary to this operation it was imperative to clear another feature known as PIMPLES, which was situated in an open paddy field, some distance to the north-east of ABLE itself. The final plan thus was to capture PIMPLES by mid-night of 18/19 January while the attack on ABLE was to follow immediately. From the information brought by patrols, the impression had been gathered that the feature PIMPLES was unoccupied; but when the leading company of the 2nd King's Own Scottish Borderers tried to get a footing on PIMPLES, it was discovered that the feature was far from being unoccupied. This company was therefore unable to clear the Japanese from their position but shortly after mid-night another company of this battalion managed to establish itself on the north-east corner of ABLE against considerable opposition, and by the early morning of 19 January, the battalion had established itself on the eastern half of the feature. For the next two days small local advances were made but since the feature had not been captured, it seriously threatened the line of communication of the King's Own Scottish Borderers. Consequently, on the night of 21/22 January two companies of the 7/2nd Punjab Regiment were sent forward with orders to attack and capture PIMPLES. This feature was eventually taken in spite of severe opposition which was offered throughout this night. A counter-attack by the Japanese on the night of 23/24 January was driven off by the Punjab Regiment; nevertheless during this period, casualties in both the King's Own Scottish Borderers and the Punjab Regiment were fairly heavy.

Thereafter, activity was limited to patrolling but on 27 January, 4/1 Gurkha Rifles was sent forward from the 33rd Indian Infantry Brigade to assist the King's Own Scottish Borderers in their task. The first attack of the Gurkhas was put in on the night of 27/28 January, and, although it was pressed home throughout the night, little headway was made and heavy casualties were sustained from the Japanese bunker positions at the top of every little ridge. However, two days later, the Japanese having withdrawn from the feature, the Gurkhas occupied ABLE and relieved the King's Own Scottish Borderers who had had a most gruelling time in this action. Having occupied the ABLE feature, 4/1 Gurkha Rifles moved south and cut the Maungdaw-Buthidaung road by seizing a feature known as CAIN, which lay to the south of the road.

On the night of 2/3 February, the 89th Indian Infantry Brigade was relieved of its commitments by the 9th Indian Infantry Brigade of the 5th Indian Division. The latter had come over to the east side of the Mayu range and therefore the 89th Indian Infantry Brigade was ordered to proceed to a reserve area to the rear of the 33rd Indian Infantry Brigade, with the intention of using it in an attack on Buthidaung.

5th Indian Division operations in the Razabil area

During the period that the 7th Indian Division was battling for the possession of the features ABLE and PIMPLES, the Corps Commander was considering and revising the appreciation of the general situation and had come to realise the importance of the Razabil cross-roads, both to the Japanese as well as to the Indian forces. By the third week of January, therefore, General Christison finally decided to reduce the Razabil fortress by an "all-out" attack. Having finally decided on an operation to carry out this task a number of additional supporting troops were then placed under the command of the 5th Indian Division. These additional troops comprised the 25th Dragoons Regimental Group (Tanks), 6th Medium Regiment RA and the 7th Indian Field Regiment RIA; the Strategic Air Force was also given in support of this operation. A few minor moves had also taken place during this period. On 20 January, the 81st West African Recce Regiment, which had earlier been placed under the command of the 5th Indian Division, relieved a company of 2 West Yorks, south of Maungdaw, and 290 Inland Water Transport (SP) Company, which also came under the command of the 5th Indian Division, was to support the West Africans in their raids against the Japanese rear positions in the coastal sector.

Early on 26 January 1944, an operation was started by the 5th Indian Division to dislodge the Japanese from the line Razabil cross-roads—Point 731—Point 1301; and the troops that carried out this task were the 123rd and 161st Indian Infantry Brigades. In conformity with the plans for this operation the frontline troops facing the Razabil fortress were withdrawn a thousand yards to enable the heavy bombers of the Strategic Air Command to drop their loads on the Japanese positions. The attack opened with an air strike on the area of the "cross-roads" by 24 "Vengeance" dive bombers, 16 B24s and 12 B25s so that a total of about 90 tons of explosives including some 2,000 lb. bombs was released.

Immediately after this bombing, 4/7 Rajput launched an attack by creeping forward under a heavy barrage supported by mortars, medium and light machine-guns and concentrated fire from its artillery. The battalion was also supported by 25 Dragoons which went into action for the first time. As the infantry troops advanced, the tanks hidden in the gardens of plantain trees rolled forward, taking up strategic positions on the right flank of the fortress; from there they fired round after round into the Japanese bunker defences which were already denuded of all foliage by the constant pounding by artillery.

Nonetheless, heavy and concentrated machine gun and grenade fire from the well dug-in and carefully prepared Japanese positions prevented the attacking troops from reaching the top of the hill; but they did succeed in establishing themselves on the lower slopes; the attack therefore met with limited success only. Although some progress was made, the attack was not pressed home as the main thrust was due to come further east. As night fell, the Japanese tried all methods, including infiltration and counter-attacks, to dislodge the Rajputs from the foothold they had gained on the feature, but failed to do so.

The next day saw the renewal of effort against these positions but no further headway could be made. Meanwhile, as the Rajputs were busy attacking the Razabil fortress, 1/1 Punjab, 2 Suffolks and 1 Dogra were sweeping the area between Bawli road and Point 731, but only a little progress was made against determined Japanese opposition, whose bunkers were successfully engaged by medium artillery and many were smashed by direct hits.

Eventually it became clear that the Japanese were holding a "fortress" covering the "Tunnels Area"; it was therefore decided that the main Corps thrust should be switched over to the 7th Indian Division front. In view of this, 25 Dragoons was withdrawn and readjustments were made in the positions of the 5th Indian Division so as to give its troops some rest after several days of hard fighting. Consequently, as has been mentioned before, on 29 January, the 9th Indian Infantry Brigade was ordered to move over the Mayu Range and take over the front of the right brigade of the 7th Indian Division.

In the meanwhile, the 81st West African Regiment had not been idle while operating along the Mayu coast. On the night of 27/28 January, patrols from this unit landed near Kanyindan, south of Maungdaw. During this landing one of the patrols while approaching the village was fired upon by the Japanese; the western end of the village was thereupon engaged with light machine-guns and grenades and about six casualties were inflicted on the Japanese. Another patrol landed at Alethangyaw, but the state of the tide did not permit the men to penetrate very far. A village in this area was visited and found clear of the hostile elements, while yet another patrol landing at Thabyebaw also reported no Japanese troops in the vicinity.

Axis of Allied Advance shifts from West to East of the Mayu Range

By the end of January, good progress had been made on both sides of the Mayu Range and the 5th Indian Division had captured the whole area except the main positions in the "fortress" in the Tunnels area. General Christison, therefore, decided to shift the axis of advance from the west to the east of the Mayu Range. Nevertheless, throughout the course of his offensive operations, the XV Indian Corps Commander had always kept in mind the possibility of a Japanese counter-move. His suspicions were all the more heightened and confirmed when certain documents captured by the 114th Indian Infantry Brigade, east of the Kalapanzin river, showed that an intelligence squad from the *118th Regiment* of the *55th Division* was engaged in reconnaissance, east of the Kalapanzin. Elements of a new regiment were also detected and a detachment of the Indian National Army was learnt to have been ordered to concentrate east of the Mayu Range. Therefore, when the actual counter-attack came, the Corps Commander was not taken completely unawares. However, it could not be predicted exactly as to where the blow would

Part of Ngakyedauk Pass.

Road-sign the Ngakyedauk Pass erected by men of the 7th Indian Division.

Major General H. R. Briggs Commander, 5th Indian Division arrives on a tank in the forward area.

Tanks of the 5th Indian Division moving into battle.

Crossing a chaung at full speed as 5th Indian Division carrier charges into action.

With its 75 mm. guns blazing from the top of the Ngakyedauk Pass, this tank plays havoc with the camouflaged Japanese on Hill 1070.

fall. But this possibility of a Japanese counter-offensive had not deterred General Christison from going ahead with his plans for offensive operations. He had, however, been careful to conceal the fact that the main offensive action of the Corps was to be launched on the front held by the 7th Indian Division. He had detailed 290 Inland Water Transport (IWT) (SP) Company to carry out dummy reconnaissances giving the impression of landing operations being actually planned between Alethangyaw and Indin between 12 and 25 January. This was with the object of making the Japanese pay more attention to their vulnerable and exposed left flank and in the hope of leading them to deploy extra troops for the defence of this area. The other deception plan which was undertaken was that the 5th Indian Division should carry out harassing and "Bunker busting" tasks. A reserve squadron of tanks and a battery of medium artillery were therefore left in the area to assist in these tasks. As will be seen, the object of the newly planned operation was to encircle and destroy the elements of the *143rd Regiment* holding the line Letwedet-Buthidaung.

CHAPTER X

The Japanese Counter-offensive

By the end of January 1944, the stage was set for an all-out attack on the Japanese, east of the Mayu range but, at that moment, the Japanese staged a counter-stroke. This blow, however, was not unexpected and fortunately it followed exactly the same pattern as before. But though bold in design and speedy in execution, it lacked originality, flexibility and foresight in conception; the whole plan was based on the assumption that the XV Indian Corps would retire if its rear was threatened. A captured directive by the Commander of the Japanese *55th Divisional Infantry Group* ended with the significant phrase: "as they have previously suffered defeat, should a portion of the enemy waver, the whole of their unit at once will get confused and victory is thus certain." They were working on a fixed time table and refused to believe that the British-Indian forces had experienced their outflanking tactics too often to be ensnared in them again. Their situation maps indicated the 7th Indian Division as completely annihilated, and the routed 5th Indian Division, trying to escape via the Teknaf peninsula, being ruthlessly chased and hammered by the Japanese victorious forces.

At the beginning of February, the situation was that the XV Indian Corps was holding the Mayu peninsula as far south as the Maungdaw-Buthidaung road. The 5th Indian Division was disposed west of the Mayu range holding Maungdaw and part of Razabil at the western end of the Tunnels, while the 7th Indian Division was east of the Range, the two being in contact through the Ngakyedauk Pass. The *55th Japanese Division* with elements of one other division and the Indian National Army was disposed with the object of checking the advance of the XV Indian Corps southward, and diverting its attention from the central front. The *54th Japanese Division* was in reserve in south Arakan.

The Japanese Plan

Before narrating the bitter fighting that ensued, a brief outline of the Japanese plan may appropriately be given here. This account of Japanese operations from the beginning of December 1943 to the end of February 1944 is based mainly on captured diaries and various other documents, as well as on the statements made by certain senior ranking Japanese prisoners-of-war. The evidence available has shown that the Japanese once again attempted to defeat superior forces by a boldly conceived and initially well-executed plan, depending largely on bluff and determination and aided by small deceptive operations.

At the end of November 1943 the Japanese Order of Battle in Arakan (Akyab and to the north) was as follows:—

Headquarters *55th Division*
55 Cavalry Regiment
55 Mountain Artillery Regiment (less 2 Battery)
3 Medium Artillery Regiment (2 Troops only)
112 Infantry Regiment
143 Infantry Regiment
1 Battalion, *213 Regiment*
Ancillary troops.

During December 1943, there was very little activity except for slight pressure by the Indian and British forces in the Maungdaw area. The *143rd Regiment* was holding the Maungdaw-Buthidaung front with the *1st Battalion* to the west of the Mayu range up to the Kalapanzin river inclusive Buthidaung, and the *2nd Battalion* to the east of the Kalapanzin in the Dabrugyaung area. The Kaladan valley was covered by the *Kubo force*, consisting of the *1st Battalion of 213th Regiment* in the Labawa-Daletme area. Detailed preparations for the attack which began on 4 February 1944 and which was known to the Japanese themselves as "Operation C", "were initiated as early as December 1943; the planning for this, however, must have been made at a still earlier stage."

The over-all intention of the Japanese Command was to annihilate the Indian and British forces in the Maungdaw and Buthidaung areas. The general plan was to re-group their *55th Division* with an outflanking force of four battalions south-east of Buthidaung, and a "holding force" of two battalions on the line Maungdaw-Buthidaung, by 10 February 1944. The "holding force" was then to pin down the opposing forces along the whole line while a thrust was made round the left of east flank to a depth of about fifteen miles. Following this the outflanking force would cut the Indian and British lines of communication and at the same time crush these forces by pushing them to the south against the defensive positions of the "holding force". The maximum air support available was to be applied over a period of about seven days during this operation.

The *55th Division* was to be re-inforced for this offensive by the addition of its third regiment (*144th Regiment*) and also by the *111th Regiment less 3rd Battalion* from the *54th Division*. The *144th Regiment* was *en route* to Arakan from Rangoon on 4 November 1943 and eventually arrived in Akyab towards the end of December; the *111th Regiment* less *3rd Battalion* arrived in Akyab during the latter half of January 1944.[1]

[1] 3 *Battalion 111 Regiment* was employed in the Kaladan valley.

Preparations and re-grouping

Major General Sakurai, commanding the *55th Division Infantry Group*, was to be in charge of these offensive preparations. His responsibilities as Akyab garrison commander were to be taken over by Colonel Kawashima of the *55th Division Cavalry Regiment*. As a cover for the move of the Divisional Infantry Group forward to Seinnyabya, Colonel Kawashima was ordered to deal with locals "on behalf of General Officer Commanding *Sakurai Division Infantry Group*".

The first step towards the preparation for the offensive was to reorganise the *55th Mountain Artillery Regiment* of which *1 Battery* had not yet arrived in Arakan. On 9 December, eight captured mortars along with some ammunition were allotted to the *Regiment* which was then reorganised with *2* and *3 Batteries*; each battery consisted of one troop of four mortars and two troops of four guns each. In each gun troop, however, one section (two guns) was dismounted, as were the four guns for which mortars had been substituted. These eight guns were formed into dismounted sections of one or two guns each, which were to be given static roles during the offensive.

By 14 December 1943, 53 other ranks drawn from the division had arrived in Akyab for a 45-day mechanical transport training course, which was scheduled to finish on 31 January 1944. These drivers were initially trained by the *55th Cavalry Regiment* in Akyab. At that time, the Japanese may have visualised keeping this Cavalry Regiment in Akyab as a "mobile reserve"; later, however, it was sent up the Kaladan valley.

About this time, also an anti-aircraft artillery unit under the command of a Captain, with a total strength of 105 all ranks and armed with 12 medium machine guns, was formed, and its training was undertaken immediately. This unit was organised in accordance with a more vigorous Ack-Ack policy, which the division intended to follow.[2]

The next change in the organisation of the division was the formation of a *"Sakurai Volunteer Platoon"* of 110 other ranks; this was divided into six sections, each under a Japanese non-commissioned officer. Only 10 other ranks of this platoon were to be Japanese while the remainder were to be found by local enlistment from amongst those who had completed their training at the Akyab "Youth Training Centre". The employment of this unit, however, was not to be authorised until it was ready for action.

During the first half of December 1943, the *112th Regiment* less *1st Battalion* in Akyab occupied defensive positions on the Mayu

---

[2] It is quite probable that the Machine guns were captured from the British in Malaya or Burma during the withdrawal.

peninsula, with the headquarters and reserves in Hparabyin. The *112th Regiment* had two tasks; firstly, to train for Operation 'C' and secondly to be prepared to prevent any landings on the coast. For up to the time of taking the offensive, the Japanese never relaxed their readiness to resist a sea-borne attack by the opposing force. Therefore, when in the latter half of December, the *144th Regiment* arrived, it left *3rd Battalion* on Baronga Island, the rest moving to the Kyauktau area to carry out "toughening up" training.

From 6 January 1944, the *Divisional Infantry Group* had begun to concentrate in the Dabrugyaung area and by the middle of the month had started taking up its planned strategic positions; these moves were intended to be completed by 10 February 1944. The moves were carried out by the different units as follows:—

The *144th Regiment*, less *2nd Battalion* in *Kyauktau* and *3rd Battalion* in Baronga Island, took over the defences of the Mayu peninsula; it concentrated behind *1st Battalion of 143rd Regiment* positioning one of its companies on the tip of the peninsula. *2nd Battalion* remained in reserve while *3rd Battalion* made ready to move to Sinoh on relief by the *111th Regiment*.

The *112th Regiment*, less *1st Battalion* stationed in Akyab, moved to Dabrugyaung, having handed over the defence of the Mayu peninsula to the *144th Regiment*. The *1st Battalion* of the *112th Regiment* was to follow its parent unit later on after being relieved by a battalion of the *111th Regiment*.

"Kubo Force", which comprised *1st Battalion 213th Regiment* less *3 Company*, moved to the Kyaungdaung area, south-west of Buthidaung; its route lay via Kyaktaw-Apaukwa and Kyauktau. *3 Company*, with *No. 1 Platoon Machine-Gun Company* remained as a "right wing detached force", based on Paletwa; its role was the prevention of British and Indian infiltration down the Kaladan Valley.

Allied pressure increases

While the Japanese moves were in progress, the activity of the XV Indian Corps in the Maungdaw area had also increased, although, east of the Kalapanzin river, the situation was fairly quiet. On 11 January 1944, the troops captured Bangona and their drive eastwards to the hills threatened the rear of *1st Battalion 143rd Regiment*. This situation compelled the Japanese to stage a counter-attack in order to restore the situation. *2nd Battalion, 112th Regiment* was therefore sent west across the Mayu Range and consequently came under the command of the *143rd Regiment*.

By 16 January 1944, the Indian force had captured the coastal plain as far south as Chiradan, having come against only a slight opposition. In the direction of the hills to the east, however, it met with greater resistance as the Japanese had disposed their forces for the counter-attack; they had *1st Battalion, 143rd Regiment* in the hills running south from Razabil to inclusive Hill 90, and *2nd Battalion, 112th Regiment* was in position from exclusive Hill 90 to about east of Chiradan.

Japanese counter-attack

On the evening of 16 January 1944, the Japanese assaulted and captured the Indian positions in the vicinity of Hill 90. Having struck at the centre of their east flank, the Japanese, on the following night again attacked from both the south as well as the north extremity of the flank; *2nd Battalion, 112th Regiment* was directed north-west through Chiradan and Tatu Gyaung while *1st Battalion, 143rd Regiment* was directed south-west through Maunglakata and Nyaunggyaung. Both these attacks converged on Bangona which in turn was frontally attacked by a fresh unit—the "Kanetoshi" unit of about 100 other ranks. The attack was put in on the rising of the moon at about 0200 hours on 18 January 1944 and was preceded by a five minute intense artillery bombardment of Maungdaw and Keinchakata, north of the objectives; this was probably with a view to preventing the opposing forces from re-inforcing themselves by the only two roads available, and also possibly as a deceptive measure.

Allied withdrawal

As will be remembered, by first light of 18 January 1944, the Allied forces had started withdrawing—the main force falling back northwards, but a few detachments also moving westwards into Pandawbyin and Paingsapadi. This continued on the 19th and 20th. On 21 January, *1st Battalion, 143rd Regiment* faced about and started advancing northwards on to the bridge at Milestone 21. *2nd Battalion, 112th Regiment*, still moving in a northernly direction, attacked Pandawbyin with its main strength, and in conjunction with the attack of *1st Battalion, 143rd Regiment*, advanced on the bridge at Milestone 21. No large scale attack, however, was made; instead, patrols were sent forward and contact with the opposing forces was made, without any decision being arrived at. Minor clashes continued, and after this date, the situation was more or less stabilised on the general line Myaunggyaung-Razabil-Rekhat Chaung. Towards the end of January several further attempts made by the Japanese to infiltrate west from the Razabil area were also not successful.

By about the end of January 1944, the Japanese had realised that the troops of the XV Indian Corps were concentrating in strength, north of Buthidaung. Several minor actions had taken place during which Sinohbyin had been occupied by the 7th Indian Division on the night of January 20/21 and other Japanese forward positions had also been captured on both sides of the Kalapanzin river. At this time, the commander of the *55th Division* had estimated the Indian strength at two divisions, amounting approximately to 20,000 troops and about forty or more guns. To counteract this estimated strength of the Indian divisions, the Japanese were preparing to attack with seven or eight battalions and since the date of this Japanese offensive was brought forward from the middle to the beginning of February 1944, the movement of units to their forming-up areas was accelerated accordingly.

Further concentration of the Infantry Group

On 24 January, *2nd Battalion of the 112th Regiment* was taken away from the Commander of *Doi Force* and was ordered to rejoin *112th Regiment*, east of the Mayu Range. During this period, *111th Regiment* had also started arriving in Akyab and by the end of January, *1st Battalion, 112th Regiment* had moved forward on being relieved; *112th Regiment* was therefore now complete. Eventually, *111th Regiment* took over Baronga island from the *3rd Battalion, 144th Regiment*, thereby enabling the latter to move forward to the Sinoh area. At the same time, *55th Cavalry Regiment* had also moved north to Kyauktau on the Kaladan river where the "right wing detached force" in the upper Kaladan came under the command of this unit to form what was known as the *Kawashima Force*.

By 27 January, the Allied forces had made considerable infiltrations on the east bank of the Kalapanzin river; the officer commanding the *112th Regiment* was therefore ordered to prepare and be ready to assault, and was told to hand over the defence of the plain from the Kalapanzin eastward, to *Doi Force*. The *Divisional Infantry Group* moved forward from Seinnyinbya to the south of Buthidaung on the night of 31 January/1 February and Advance *Divisional Headquarters* moved from Rathedaung to Seinnyinbya during the same period. *2nd Battalion, 143rd Regiment*, already in the area, came under the command of the *112th Regiment*, thereby completing this force according to plan. Kubo Force in the area of Kindaung also prepared to move forward so that the weight of the *Divisional Infantry Group* was distributed east of the Kalapanzin river, in the general area of Dabrugyaung-Kindaung, well poised to advance. A "booty transport unit" was also organised, consisting of a company of *55th Transport Regiment* and attached troops, to collect and classify into separate groups all captured equipment, arms and ammunition. Buthidaung was to be the supply base with the line of communication running north, along both the banks of the Kalapanzin river.

Organisation of the 55th Division

The organisation of the *55th Division*, commanded by Major-

General Sakurai, after regrouping and just before the offensive was launched, is set out below:—

Headquarters Divisional Infantry Group
    Kanetoshi Unit (Defence).
    55 Division Infantry Group wireless Section.
    Ancillary troops.

Tanahashi Force (Commanded by Colonel Tanahashi)
    112 Infantry Regiment.
    2 Battalion of 143 Infantry Regiment.
    Two Mountain guns and four Mortars from 55 Mountain Artillery Regiment.
    55 Engineer Regiment (less one company and platoons).
    No. 10 River Crossing Materials Company.
    1 Section Division Wireless Unit.
    Ancillary troops.

Kubo Force
    1 Battalion 213 Regiment (less one company and one Machine-gun Platoon).

DOI Force
    143 Infantry Regiment (less two Battalions).
    Two Mountain guns from 55 Mountain Artillery Regiment.
    Two Troops 3 Medium Artillery Regiment.

Yoshida Force, under direct Command of 55th Division comprising:—
    144 Regiment (less 2 and 3 Battalions).
    14 Independent Anti-Tank Battalion (less one company and one platoon).
    Tank Company, 55 Cavalry Regiment.
    Nine Mountain guns, 55 Mountain Artillery Regiment.
    Ancillary troops.

Kawashima Force (Colonel Kawashima) consisting of:—
    55 Cavalry Regiment (less Tank Company).

Divisional Units
    Artillery Unit (Lieut.-Colonel Kobayashi) consisted of eleven Mountain guns and four mortars of 55 Mountain Artillery Regiment.

Divisional Signal Unit. (less one wireless Section)
Transport Unit:—Consisted of various Mechanical Transport units, River Crossing Units and Water Transport unit.
Reserves: 2 and 3 Battalions of 144 Regiment.
Medical Unit.
Ordnance Unit.
Veterinary Unit.
Other Ancillary Troops.

The Japanese plan of attack

While the South-East Asia Command had been planning for seven separate but related operations in Burma, the Japanese High Command had also planned for an all-out offensive, first in Arakan and subsequently on the central front. But for many reasons Lord Mountbatten's offensive plans did not materialise and in his words "the frame-work of our seven related operations had been destroyed piecemeal". However, his offensive came on a very small scale during the winter months and, both in Arakan and on the Chindwin, could have no other object but that of containing the major part of the Japanese forces. But it was impracticable for the new command to destroy the hostile forces by a major operation, until the occasion was offered by the Japanese plan of offensive in early 1944. Their invasion plan, known as Operation 'C', was a "Grand Design" and had been considered long by the Japanese High Command. Detailed planning was ordered by the *Imperial General Headquarters* to proceed in January 1944. This plan had for its object the invasion of India "by splitting open the British-Indian front, sealing off the eastern from the western half, and cutting the lines of communication of both. Each sector was then to be destroyed separately; and the roads through Chittagong and Dimapur laid open to the Japanese army at which stage the Japanese hoped to incite a general uprising in Bengal".[3]

The plan was to be carried out in two phases, Phase I being concerned with Arakan. In this sector the Japanese plan, which was captured early in the battle, was mainly one of encirclement and destruction of the isolated divisions of the XV Indian Corps. The main spearhead of this bold design was the *Tanahashi Force* whose role was to move up between the flanks of the 7th Indian Division and the 81st West African Division, take Taung Bazaar from the rear, and after sweeping round it, to cut the Ngakyedauk Pass, thereby trapping the 7th Indian Division to the east of the Mayu Range.

On the completion of this manoeuvre, the *Tanahashi Force* would capture and hold the line of the Ngakyedauk Chaung between Sinzweya and the Kalapanzin river. The *Kubo Force* was to follow a parallel route as far as Goppe Bazaar, push over the Goppe or Chota Maunghnama Pass and cross the range in order to cut the Bawli road in the vicinity of Maunghnama. *Doi Force*, a holding force, was to attack from the Maungdaw-Buthidaung line.

The Japanese appraisal was that this manoeuvre through Sinohbyin from the south and combined with air attacks, would result in dividing the 7th and 5th Indian Divisions and cutting them off from the Corps Headquarters, thus breaking their line of supply.

[3] *Report to the Combined Chiefs of Staff* by the Supreme Allied Commander South-East Asia, p. 39.

This would compel the 7th Indian Division to escape across the Mayu Range where it might be cut to pieces and completely disintegrated. The Japanese Task Forces would then combine to crush the 5th Indian Division, cut it off from the north by the road-block at Maunghnama, and destroy it when moving west across the Naf river.

Intensive air support was to be given during this offensive which was worked out in great detail. It was to be provided by 7 *Flying Brigade*, from February 4th to 10th. The details were:—

4 February	From 0810 to 0910 hours. Approximately 70 fighters were to maintain air supremacy over Buthidaung. 12 of these fighters were to strafe and bomb the British artillery, north-west of Buthidaung. This was probably because the Tanahashi Force would be crossing the Kalapanzin river about this time and would consequently be most vulnerable to artillery bombardment.
5 February	At 0830 hours, five medium bombers would fly in from the west to bomb the British artillery, north-west of Buthidaung; 40 fighters were to give protection to these medium bombers.[4]
6 February	From 1230 to 1330 hours. About 40 fighters were again to maintain air supremacy over Buthidaung. The reason for this air cover at this time and during this stage of the operation is not quite clear. It may have been to cover Japanese troops and supplies, moving into Buthidaung and Sinohbyin, which they presumed would be completely in their hands on this day. As time was of the main importance to them, they probably intended to move large quantities of supplies forward, and establish dumps for the

[4] The Japanese had always respected the British superiority in artillery and had tried on most occasions to counter-balance this by either using covered approaches or resorting to night marches. In this particular operation, they apparently could not do so; it throws some light on how seriously they considered the effect of the British artillery on their large columns, moving in fairly open country by daylight. It is also probable that the Japanese wanted to delay, as long as possible, the use of their own artillery for counter-battery purposes, and also perhaps to gain surprise.

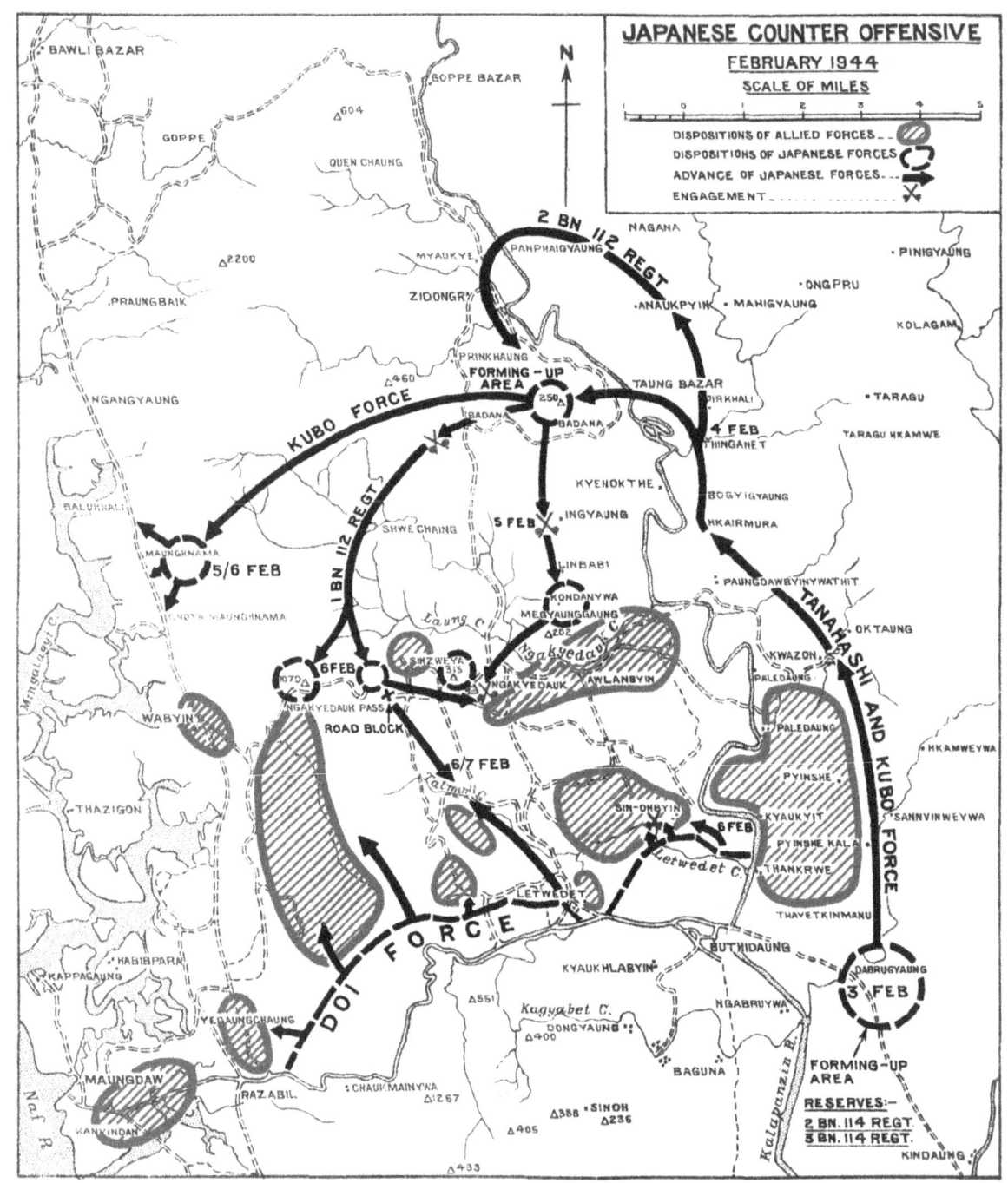

	continuation of their onward drive during daylight.
7 and 8 February	No programme for any sorties.
9 and 10 February	Air supremacy to be maintained over Maungdaw and shipping to be attacked in the Naf river. By 10 February, Tanahashi Force was to have crossed the Mayu Range and commenced the attack on the rear of the Indian positions in the Maungdaw area; the air attacks on the shipping in the Naf river were probably based on the assumption that by this date the opposing forces would try to withdraw by water.

The indications of a Japanese counter-offensive were much too apparent at the end of January; consequently, General Giffard and Lieut.-Generals Slim and Christison made adequate preparations to meet it. Their forecast was that the attack was imminent and that it would be launched, on the model of earlier attacks, along the east side of the Kalapanzin Valley with the object of cutting off their main forces in that area and outflanking the XV Indian Corps. In the words of General Giffard it was their view that "if the 5th and 7th Divisions held their positions against a frontal attack, while at the same time preparing an all round defence to meet attacks from the flank or rear, it would be possible to destroy any Japanese outflanking detachment with the reserves". Accordingly, one brigade of the 36th Indian Division and another of the 26th Indian Division were moved south. General Slim ordered all formations in the forward areas to hold their ground, and they were told that if they were cut off by the Japanese they would be supplied by air. Arrangements were therefore taken in hand with all speed for the air lift of supplies. These preparations had a vital effect on the issue of the battle and proved the value of air transport, without which the troops could not have been supplied nor morale sustained.

There were some changes in the dispositions of troops also. This was with a view to strengthen the forces to the east of the Mayu range. To free the 7th Indian Division for operations against Buthidaung, the 9th Indian Infantry Brigade of the 5th Indian Division was moved east, so also were a tank regiment and a regiment of medium artillery from before the Razabil position to the 7th Indian Division area. Also, to stem the counter-offensive, the 89th Indian Infantry Brigade of the 7th Indian Division and the tank regiment were moved northwards to be in mobile reserve, while the 5th Indian

Division was ordered to occupy part of the Mayu range. By this means the XV Indian Corps had in reserve one infantry brigade and a tank regiment east of the Mayu range to meet the Japanese threat.

The Japanese Offensive

During the night of 3/4 February 1944, *Tanahashi Force* moved north, thus starting an offensive operation which had an important bearing on the Arakan Operations. The first indication that Japanese forces were on the move was received from the 114th Indian Infantry Brigade area. It appeared that a Japanese column virtually passed within a few hundred yards of the Brigade Headquarters and Somerset Light Infantry positions. In the initial stages this movement was not detached as coming from a hostile element, since the Indian brigade itself was accustomed to carry out most of its moves under cover of darkness, particularly the moves of the batteries of the 25th Mountain Regiment which was still being deployed to maintain the 'Hook' operation. It was not till a mule column of 53 Animal Transport Company, which, while taking up supplies to 4/14 Punjab and 4/5 Gurkha Rifles, was shot up that the hostile nature of this unidentified activity at night was discovered. This fact was confirmed at 0500 hours on 4 February when the Somerset Light Infantry reported to the Brigade Headquarters that its patrols had seen three parties of Japanese troops moving north between the forward companies of the battalion. On the same day, an unusually large number of Japanese bombers and fighters swept over both the Indian division areas in Arakan. But since the anti-aircraft fire from the Allied guns kept these bombers at a safe distance from their ground installations, the hostile aircraft had to drop bombs from a great height causing very little damage. The fighters straffed from low altitude the Headquarters of the XV Indian Corps and Bawli Bazaar but caused no casualties.

As the sun came up and the mist gradually cleared, the infiltration by Japanese forces through the 114th Indian Infantry Brigade area was made more visible. Consequently, the few Japanese parties that were spotted were subjected to heavy fire by the batteries of 25 Mountain Regiment. Nevertheless, the brigade was at this time placed in a very precarious position. The Brigade Headquarters which was on the Pyinsha Kala ridge had only one section of 421 Field Company defending its area, while the nearest mobile reserve was a very tired company of 4/14 Punjab which had suffered heavily in the recent 'Hook' operation. However, this company was called in soon after mid-day to Kwazon and so were the two weak platoons of the Somerset Light Infantry. In order to ease the situation in Kwazon where the Brigade Administrative Area was established the company of 4/14 Punjab launched an attack that afternoon and succeeded in capturing the knoll overlooking the Kwazon bridge. News was also received that a 7th Indian Division reconnaissance party had been ambushed at the junction of Tatmin Chaung and Letwedet, and that the Commander Royal Engineers of the 7th Indian Division and the Officer Commanding Field Park Company were killed, while another sapper officer had been wounded. During the skirmish a dead Japanese had been identified as belonging to the *112th Regiment*. Another message from the 7th Indian Division had passed on the information that the Japanese had over-run Taung Bazaar and were moving west and south-west in great strength. Obviously the march of the Japanese *55th Division* on Chittagong had begun.

Before the Japanese offensive had started, the tanks, the medium artillery regiment, the Indian Field Regiment and the 9th Indian Infantry Brigade (5th Indian Division) had crossed to the 7th Indian Division area via the Ngakyedauk Pass, to support the 7th Division's impending operations. As will be seen, these reinforcements, originally meant to support the advance of the 7th Indian Division, proved of great value at the time when this division became encircled.

It has now come to light that the *Tanahashi* and *Kubo Forces* left the Dabrugyaung-Kindaung area on the evening of 3 February 1944. They moved north, keeping to the east of the 114th Indian Infantry Brigade positions in the Paledaung area, and, on the morning of the 4th, arrived in the vicinity of Taung Bazaar without making any appreciable contact with the opposing forces. The *2nd Battalion, 143rd Regiment,* which was the leading unit of the Tanahashi Force, attacked Taung Bazaar from the east and after encountering very little resistance, captured the area round the Kalapanzin river. The rest of the force then crossed the river and formed up in an area about three miles west of Taung Bazaar. At the same time, the *2nd Battalion, 112th Regiment,* which had been detached from the main force before the latter reached Taung Bazaar, had continued north, and having by-passed the 7th Indian Division positions, had crossed the Kalapanzin at Panpaigyaung, about five miles north-west of Taung Bazaar. Meanwhile, Kubo Force had continued west to cut the Bawli Bazaar road according to plan.

While the Japanese force had gone through the Indian positions and made its way to the north, the situation in the 114th Indian Infantry Brigade area was still chaotic and uncertain. Though some units of this brigade had been badly mauled and overrun by the Japanese troops, the 4/5th Gurkha Rifles was still carrying out its part in the 'Hook' operation. By midday on 4 February, the Gurkhas had captured the hill over-looking Dabrugyaung. But by late afternoon, the situation in the Brigade Administrative Area had become very critical. The Gurkhas were therefore ordered to withdraw and send at least two companies, if possible, by forced march, back to Kwazon. The 4/14th Punjab formed a corridor for this withdrawal and by nightfall two companies of Gurkhas had arrived to strengthen the Brigade Administrative Area. On the morning of the 5th, these two companies attacked and cleared the Kwazon ridge against slight opposition.

While the Japanese attack was being put in with full vigour on 4 February, the 89th Indian Infantry Brigade was enjoying its first day's rest in a period of over three months. It will be remembered that this brigade had been relieved of its positions in the eastern foothills and had been moved to the rear of the 33rd Indian Infantry Brigade. But once the seriousness of the situation had been appreciated, this brigade was ordered to move northwards in order to establish itself on a line approximately five miles north of the Divisional Headquarters, which was at this time in the Laung Chaung valley. The brigade with one squadron of tanks was further ordered to conduct a sweep as it advanced and to deny to the Japanese all likely lines of approach, leading southwards. The 4/8th Gurkha Rifles was given the left side of the line and was ordered to move up the Laung Chaung valley into the area of Badana West. The 7/2nd Punjab was to be in the centre with its objective as Badana East, while the Brigade Headquarters and the King's Own Scottish Borderers were to move up into the Linbabi area.

The first contact made by 7/2 Punjab with the Japanese was in the area of Ingyaung on the evening of the 4th. The Japanese had obviously not expected to meet any resistance in this area and were therefore temporarily caught unprepared. By late evening of the same day, however, 7/2 Punjab took up positions in the area of Ingyaung while the King's Own Scottish Borderers and Brigade Headquarters positioned themselves for the night in the Linbabi area.

On 5 February, the Japanese force was again split up. The *1st Battalion, 112th Regiment* advanced south-west towards the hills in the direction of Shwechaing; the rest of the force (which was less *1st* and *2nd Battalions of 112th Regiment*) moved south with the intention of taking up positions on the hills, about a mile north of the Ngakyedauk Chaung—somewhere between Hill 202 and Hill 165. According to the Japanese plan, the next objective of the Tanahashi Force was the village of Ngakyedauk; the intention being for *1st Battalion, 112th Regiment* to send a large detachment south of Sinzweya for attacking Ngakyedauk from the west, simultaneously with an attack from the north by the *2nd Battalion, 143rd Regiment* and the *2nd Battalion, 112th Regiment*.

Up to midday on 5 February, the Japanese moves had gone according to plan. At Buthidaung, the *2nd Battalion, 144th Regiment* had been brought forward and put under the command of the *Doi Force*; this had been considered essential because the pressure of the 7th Indian Division on the main front had not yet diminished. The Japanese, however, were still confident of not only holding the attacks of this division, but as a result of putting this extra battalion into the battle, they hoped to seize the opposite positions in the Sinohbyin area—simultaneously with their attack on Ngakyedauk.

At midday on 5 February, the Japanese, much to their surprise, met with stiff resistance at Ingyaung, which prevented the advance of the main body of the Tanahashi Force to its forming-up position. Repeated attacks on the afternoon of 5 February failed to dislodge the 7/2nd Punjab Regiment and the King's Own Scottish Borderers from their positions. Throughout the 5th and the 6th, these positions were maintained and were instrumental in preventing a large portion of Tanahashi Force from pushing rapidly southwards towards Sinzweya. Time and again, the Japanese hurled themselves in successive attacks had wasted much of their precious strength which necessitated their falling back after suffering considerable casualties. During this battle, the Indian and British battalions fought a series of bitter and prolonged engagements against a determined force vastly superior in numbers. There is no doubt that in these two days of fighting the 89th Indian Infantry Brigade fulfilled its task as a defensive screen to the rear of the 7th Indian Division area. Although powerless to deny all approaches to the attackers, it bore the brunt of the Japanese advance and made its real contribution to the eventual defeat of the Japanese. It will also not be out of place to mention here the brave and courageous tasks which the Advanced Dressing Station of 66 Field Ambulance performed while attached to this brigade during these two days of fighting. They were successful in evacuating all the wounded without loss and worked continuously under the most arduous conditions possible. By the evening of the 6th, the 89th Indian Infantry Brigade less 4/8 Gurkha Rifles was ordered to withdraw southwards and take up positions north and south of the Ngakyedauk Chaung, west of Awlanbyin; this was successfully accomplished on the night of 6/7 February, but a great deal of unnecessary stores and equipment had to be abandoned.

In the meanwhile, 4/8 Gurkha Rifles which had moved up the Laung Chaung Valley had come in contact with the Japanese on 5 February. While moving up, the battalion which had under command a troop of tanks of 25 Dragoons was badly shot up by medium machine-guns situated on the hills, east of the valley. Fairly heavy casualties were sustained but an immediate counter-attack supported by tanks drove off the hostile party. Since the tanks had to return to their base in the Divisional Administrative Area, it was decided that the battalion would harbour in its present positions for the night and that patrolling to the south would be carried out till the next day.

Headquarters 7th Indian Division overrun

It will be remembered that the Tanahashi Task Force, after capturing Taung Bazaar had begun to advance southwards. In view of this development, Commander, XV Indian Corps agreed to release the 25th Dragoon Regiment which, prior to the Japanese attack, was on the west side of the Mayu Range. 1 Squadron, consequently, moved over the Ngakyedauk Pass to the 7th Indian Division area on the afternoon of 3 February, while the rest of the Regiment crossed over during the early hours of 4 February.

By 0400 hours on 6 February, a major portion of *1st Battalion, 112th Regiment,* which formed part of Tanahashi Task Force had managed to arrive at the eastern end of the Ngakyedauk Pass. This battalion had, while moving to Shwechaing, met with some resistance in the Badana area, suffering heavy casualties which prevented its further movement until nightfall. Later, however, in the hours of darkness it had managed to continue infiltrating southwards. At 0500 hours, before the morning mist had completely lifted and in spite of its being on the move since 3 February, with little or no rest, this column put in an attack on the Headquarters 7th Indian Division, which happened to be in its line of advance. The Divisional Headquarters situated on the Laung-chaung Chaung was attacked severely and overrun. A frontal attack was first made by the Japanese on the signal lines which were nearest to the entrance of the Headquarters area, but this attack was repulsed. They then put in further attacks and succeeded in infiltrating through the thick jungle into the Divisional Headquarters area and managed to establish a machine-gun post on the hill behind it. At about 0830 hours a squadron of 25 Dragoons also joined in the confused fighting and started shooting blindly into the jungle; but no sooner had the mist cleared than it began to rain heavily which only added to confusion.

The whole position in the Divisional Headquarters area had by then become untenable and it had become clear that the Headquarters area could not be held for long by the small number of officers, clerks, orderlies and other personnel who were acting as the defenders. At 1030 hours the signals had withdrawn into the Royal Artillery Headquarters lines and, thereafter, the whole of the Divisional Headquarters made independently for the combined XV Corps Troops and 7th Indian Division administrative base by splitting into small parties. General Messervy, Commander of the 7th Indian Division, along with his staff fought his way out and slipped through the Japanese screen trying to make his way towards the Corps Troops and Divisional Administrative "Box" Area at

Sinzweya. Hour after hour the game of hide-and-seek went on until this party reached the administrative base where the General reorganised his Headquarters. A few of those constituting this party were ambushed, but on the whole casualties were not as severe as might have been expected; on the other hand, the divisional signal personnel was responsible for inflicting sufficient damage against the attacking Japanese. In re-forming, the Divisional Headquarters Signals and other equipment was loaned by the Regimental Headquarters, 24 Anti-Tank Regiment and the 9th Indian Infantry Brigade Headquarters, while 25 Dragoons lent a wireless set as well as an armoured car. By such means wireless communication was eventually re-established.

While Divisional Headquarters was surrounded and overrun, the 33rd Indian Infantry Brigade which was till then completely in the dark about the situation had sent a strong reconnaissance party composed of 1 Queens to investigate the firing that was coming from the Divisional Headquarters area; this party had eventually returned with the report that they had been fired upon by the Japanese in British uniforms from the trenches around the Divisional Headquarters.

During this period it is worth mentioning that the only defence of the 7th Indian Division Headquarters was 24 Engineer Battalion Headquarters with one of its companies. The signallers had a fair number of casualties while the rest of the Divisional Headquarters hardly suffered any. Most of these casualties were caused by hostile mortar fire and by the escaping parties being ambushed on the way to the Administrative Base at Sinzweya, in which the Staff Officers and clerks had joined with the infantry in confused hand-to-hand fighting. Also, by this time, the situation on the 114th Indian Infantry Brigade front had become more stabilised. The brigade had thereafter been concentrated and regrouped in the area of Kwazon at the confluence of the Myaw Chaung and Kalapanzin river. From this position it was ordered to maintain a "strongpoint" and to operate offensively and prevent any Japanese parties, no matter how small, from getting back to their own line.

While these events were taking place, *Kubo Force*, which had crossed the Mayu range to cut the Maungdaw—Bawli Bazaar Road on the night of 5/6 February succeeded in damaging three bridges; but soon after it was attacked by the Indian and British forces and driven back to the hills where it was contained.

Activities of Doi Force

While the adventurous push of the *Tanahashi Task Force* was being carried out with great speed and boldness, the 33rd Indian

Infantry Brigade had been attacked in full force on the night of 4/5 February. *Doi Force* which was responsible for this attack managed to infiltrate to the rear of this brigade's positions whereby the latter lost all contact with its Divisional Headquarters, and the situation had become confused. By 7 February, however, the brigade had adopted a defensive "Box", the south and east sides of which were defended by 1 Queens. Point 182, which was at the north-west corner of the "box" and was of vital importance, was garrisoned by a company of 4/1 Gurkha Rifles. The 4/15th Punjab Regiment was at this time holding Point 121, a prominent feature which overlooked the Kalapanzin. Many an attempt made by the Japanese to capture this area was foiled by the defenders. Brigade Headquarters itself was stoutly defended by a company of 1/11 Sikh and by 63 Mule Company, whose personnel established the fact that leading mules was by no means their only accomplishment.

Reorganisation of the 7th Indian Division

By 7 February, the 7th Indian Division whose positions had been infiltrated into by the Japanese troops was forced to form itself into a series of "boxes". These were located as follows:—

1. Divisional and Corps Troops Administrative Box at Sinzweya.
2. 114th Indian Infantry Brigade Box at Kwazon.
3. 33rd Indian Infantry Brigade Box located, north-west of Buthidaung. This brigade was spread over a large area. 4/1 Gurkha Rifles was on feature ABLE with a connecting link to the rest of the brigade centred on Gun Valley, formed by 284 Anti-Tank Battery and a Pioneer Company in Tatminyaungywa. 136 Field Regiment was also in this "box"; and 4/15 Punjab with 503 (Jungle) Battery were in the BULGE.
4. Awlanbyin Box consisted of 7 Indian Field Regiment, one troop 86 Light Anti-Aircraft Battery, one company of 1/11 Sikh, one company 7/2 Punjab, 1 Pioneer Company and rear wagon lines of 25 Indian Mountain Regiment.

General Messervy, after extricating himself and his staff from the Japanese, had arrived at the eastern end of the Ngakyedauk Pass near Sinzweya. This was originally the Corps Administrative Base for their offensive operations, west of the Mayu range but later on it came to be known as the 7th Indian Division "Administrative Box" because all this division's administrative troops were brought into it to strengthen the defences. It was an open area of paddy fields surrounded by high hills; and in their first rush the Japanese were already occupying some of these hills. This Administrative Base originally contained not more than a few hundreds of Corps

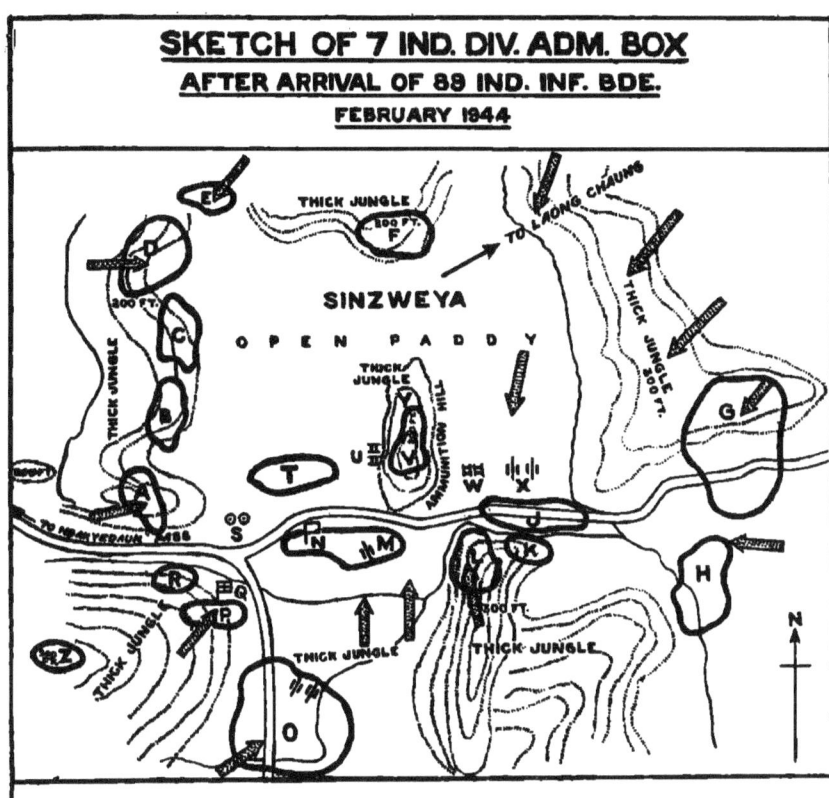

SKETCH OF 7 IND. DIV. ADM. BOX AFTER ARRIVAL OF 89 IND. INF. BDE. FEBRUARY 1944

KEY

- A ONE COY. 2 W YORKS.
- B SUPPLY DEPOT.
- C TWO SUPPLY ISSUE SECTIONS.
- D ONE MULE COY.
- E 89 BDE. B ECHELON.
- F 33 BDE. B ECHELON.
- G 4/8 GURKHA RIFLES. (89 BDE.)
- H 89 BDE. H.Q. & 2 K.O.S.B.
- J DIV. SIGS. ONE SEC. M.T. OFFS. SHOP.
- K 136 FD. REGT. B ECHELON.
- L ONE BTY. 24 L.A.A. REGT. LATER ONE COY. 7/2 PUNJAB (89 BDE)
- M 7 DIV. H.Q. & 9 BDE. H.Q. & 2 GUNS. 24 MOUNTAIN REGT.
- N GARRISON H.Q.
- O 9 BDE. B ECHELON & 1 BTY. 24 MOUNTAIN REGT.
- P 40 REINFORCEMENTS QUEENS, LINCOLNS & K.O.S.B.
- Q M.D.S.
- R REAR 7 DIV. H.Q.
- S TWO HY. A.A. GUNS.
- T MOB. RES. OF TWO COYS. 2 W. YORKS, LATER TWO COYS. 2 K.O.S.B.
- U ONE SQN. 25 DRAGOONS.
- V 1/2 BTY. 24 L.A.A. REGT.
- W ONE SQN. 25 DRAGOONS.
- X ONE BTY. 6 MEDIUM REGT.
- Y AMMUNITION DUMP.
- Z PART OF 'V' FORCE.
- ⇒ JAPANESE ATTACKS

and Divisional administrative troops who are a necessary adjunct of a fighting force. But later on when the 7th Indian Division Headquarters and further divisional administrative troops collected round it, the numbers swelled to a few thousands comprising all varieties of men of a modern army; the doctor, the tankman, the gunner, the mule driver, the sapper, the clerk and the cook, were all fairly well represented. The infantryman, however, was still absent. It was from this Base that orders had gone out to the other brigade "boxes" to remain where they were. The Divisional Commander issued orders to all the brigades and their troops that there would be no withdrawal but that the troops would dig in wherever they were and allow the Japanese to attack and get killed.

As the Japanese offensive developed, more and more troops kept filtering into the "Box". These included 491 Light Anti-Aircraft Battery, 9 Battery 6 Medium Regiment, 205 Anti-Tank Battery, tanks of 25 Dragoons, 9 Brigade Headquarters B Echelon, two batteries of 24 Mountain Regiment from the 5th Indian Division and 2 West Yorkshire Regiment less one company of the 9th Indian Brigade. The organisation of the defences of this "Box" was simple to the extreme. Each separate unit or in some cases each group of small units was responsible for its own defence, which was co-ordinated with that of its next-door neighbour, the Headquarters, 124 Light Anti-Aircraft Regiment being used for this purpose.

The Japanese Divisional Infantry Group attack Sinohbyin

While the Allied troops were hastily building up their "defence boxes", the plans of the Japanese offensive were not moving smoothly. Major-General Sakurai was getting impatient in having to wait for Colonel Tanahashi to force his way through to the Ngakyedauk area in order to take part in the combined drive, from north and south. General Sakurai thought that valuable time was being lost by this unfortunate delay and consequently the element of surprise that they had achieved in their first thrust through Taung Bazaar was also lessening.

On 6 February, therefore, heavy frontal attacks were made towards Sinohbyin in which the newly brought forward unit—the *2nd Battalion, 144th Regiment*, also took part. Further attacks were made on 7 February, but all of them were repulsed by the 33rd Indian Infantry Brigade. All this while contact was still not made with the Tanahashi Force, which had by now begun to feel the difficulties of maintenance and supply. As has been mentioned before, the 89th Indian Infantry Brigade was doing its job extremely well. The Japanese expenditure of ammunition had been considerable and their long and vulnerable line of communication, running through Taung Bazaar and then south to the *Tanahashi Force*, was neither convenient nor sufficient.

During the night of 6/7 February, however, the right wing of *Tanahashi Force* which comprised *1st Battalion, 112th Regiment*, had continued to infiltrate south and reached the Tatmin Chaung, south of Kreingyaung; and here, for the first time, contact was made to the south with small parties of *Doi Force* which had managed to infiltrate behind the 33rd Indian Infantry Brigade positions. Thereafter, ration trains of coolies moved up through the Tatmin Chaung from the Letwedet area on 7 February but numbers of these were captured by the Indian troops, in and around the Tatmingyaungywa area. Eventually, *1st Battalion, 112th Regiment* established a road-block on the Ngakyedauk Pass and established its Force Headquarters on Hill 315, immediately north of Sinzweya. Thus the 7th Indian Division Administrative "Box" was surrounded and the siege was begun.

Battle of the "Box"

The siege of the 7th Indian Division Administrative "Box" turned out to be a series of large and small battles in which it is difficult to mention everyone deserving praise. On the night of 7/8 February, a party of Japanese succeeded in infiltrating into the Administrative "Box" and occupied the Main Dressing Station. The Japanese showed great brutality and remained in occupation of this hospital for nearly twenty-four hours. This period of occupation was one of horror for the staff and patients of the Main Dressing Station. A doctor, Captain S. N. Basu, who managed to escape through nothing short of a miracle, told the following most gruesome story:—

> "All the doctors and the medical staff were lined up in a row. A middle-aged Japanese officer, whom the Japanese addressed as "General", with a long sword hanging by his side, was escorted in. The "General" after waving his long ornamented sword most ceremoniously over the heads of the unfortunate captives, retired. This was the signal for the massacre of the medical staff who, one after another, were all shot through the head. The sick and the wounded lying in the hospital became terrified and those with sufficient physical energy ran away into the nearby jungle, where they fell victims to the Japanese who lay there waiting to annihilate them."

This episode, however, ended when a company of 2 West Yorks assisted by tanks drove the Japanese out of the Main Dressing Station area after a battle which lasted nearly twenty-four hours.

Soon a change in Japanese plans had to be made. Colonel Tanahashi, in view of the existing deployment of his force, was not quite satisfied with its tactical usefulness towards achieving the ultimate object. The situation was far from conforming to the plan that was originally laid down. Consequently, he directed part of his force to infiltrate through the 89th Indian Infantry Brigade positions to reinforce the road-block which he had established and which was held by *1st Battalion, 112th Regiment*. The situation in the Ingyaung area had also by now become very confused. Small parties of troops of the 89th Indian Infantry Brigade and Japanese forces had become inextricably mixed so that to arrange a concerted attack was almost impossible. Numerous small actions, therefore, which were fought on 7 and 8 February, resulted in no decision. Colonel Tanahashi, however, continued to push from Ingyaung, through the hills, that part of his force which was still concentrated southwards. By 9 February, the main body of *Tanahashi Force* was spread out from the Badana Chaung and south through the hills, to the east of Awlanbyin, while another strong detachment was assembled to the south of it. Simultaneously on 8 and 9 February, the *Doi Force* had also launched further diversionary attacks on the 33rd Indian Infantry Brigade positions and extended this activity along the west to Maungdaw, where also some small attacks were put in.

By 9 February, Major General Sakurai had abandoned all hopes of destroying the 5th Indian Division which was to the west of the Mayu Range; he, therefore, ordered *Tanahashi Force,* which according to the original plan should have been west of the Range, to concentrate instead in the Sinzweya area. Its task was to make every effort to destroy the 7th Indian Division troops in that area which the Japanese estimated at three battalions of infantry and about eight guns.

Japanese offensive reaches its climax

During the course of 9 and 10 February, the Japanese, as ordered, had been heavily attacking in the Sinzweya-Ngakyedauk area, from the north as well as from the south. The bulk of *Tanahashi Task Force* was in the area of Hill 315 and *2nd Battalion, 144th Regiment* had been moved from the Sinohbyin area to carry out these assaults. But in spite of all their efforts the Japanese were not achieving any appreciable success. On the night of 9/10 February, the West Yorks in the Divisional Administrative Base were once again subjected to heavy attacks but this only resulted in more Japanese casualties. On the same night a second attack was put in by the Japanese with the object of destroying the tanks of 25 Dragoons, as they realized that the tanks were proving a continual source of worry; but once again their attempt was unsuccessful. They even went so far as to put in a suicidal bayonet charge across open paddy fields in a desperate attempt to reach the tanks and destroy them with gun cotton charges. But this resulted in a complete annihilation of the attackers.

It is true that the Japanese by 10 February, according to their planned programme, had succeeded in completely encircling the 7th Indian Division. They had occupied positions on hills overlooking the Divisional Administrative "Box" and were frantically assaulting and harassing the troops in the "Box" itself. Their artillery was keeping up a constant shelling of the Indian positions and yet they were no where near attaining the final object of the push which began on 4 February 1944. Many times during the fighting which took place on the 10th, 11th and 12th the Japanese did manage to fight their way on to vital hills features at the edge of the "Box" but every time they were blasted off by the combined fire of medium tanks, and artillery guns of various calibre firing over open sights at point-blank range.

The "Box" area had by now taken on a new appearance. The dense jungle-clad hills were clear of all foliage and in its place, bare leafless tree stumps were all that remained of the battle-swept hills. Countless Japanese bodies littered the area and many a burnt out vehicle standing in the open paddy bore mute testimony to the fierceness of the battle. Nevertheless, perhaps as a last desperate venture, the Japanese at first light on 12 February put in an attack on "Artillery Hill"—a small feature garrisoned by a mixture of gunners from various regiments—and succeeded in infiltrating on to it. But this only enraged the Dragoons who blasted this feature with their 75 mm guns thereby enabling a company of 2 West Yorks to occupy it without any opposition.

Meanwhile, the *Kubo Force* was also not finding things going according to plan. On the morning of 11 February they had made further attacks on the Bawli Road in an attempt to block it effectively. But these were again driven back by the troops of the 5th Indian Division. Again a party of approximately a hundred Japanese and Indian National Army personnel crossed the Mayu Range by the Chhota Maunghnama Pass with the object of cutting the Bawli Road, which was the main line of communication for the 5th Indian Division. This party managed to cause considerable damage to the mechanical transport of 25 Dragoon Regimental Group and was also instrumental in setting fire to the tentage of a Casualty Clearing Station. But on the arrival of the troops of the 5th Indian Division this Japanese party disappeared into the hills, only to reappear in small groups as nuisance parties.

Another Japanese column that proceeded towards Goppe Pass, was also accorded a hot reception by the 18th Indian Mule Company which was established there. Grand work was done by the personnel of this mule company who were encamped among the hills.

Whenever a possible threat developed, they at once put out patrols to watch for any Japanese attempt to use the pass, westwards across the hills. This had given the Japanese the impression that the pass was strongly defended and had compelled them to turn toward the unfrequented Chhota Maunghnama Pass.

Although the "Boxes" during this period of fighting were hard-pressed and surrounded and were literally besieged by the Japanese forces, the morale of the 'garrison' had been kept up and their fighting efficiency maintained by ensuring a constant supply of food and ammunition. This was made possible by means of "supply drops" by Dakotas which commenced on 11 February and continued daily until the siege was lifted.

History was made by the Troops Carrier Command operating over the Arakan area during this period. For three weeks the aircraft of this command supplied and maintained the Indian and British troops, with their tanks and artillery, in keeping up their fight. Flying in daylight with escorts of Spitfires and Hurricanes, supply dropping Dakotas defied the reinforced Japanese fighter strength over the battle zone. During the twenty-one days of the main action, 1,626 tons of vital supplies were dropped to the besieged troops. When the divisions of the XV Indian Corps had been cut off, every available transport aircraft was mustered to maintain supplies without which the various defensive "Boxes" would not have been able to continue the fight. But for this air supply, the outcome of this action might have been far different. To quote the Supreme Allied Commander, South-East Asia "in spite of severe ground and air opposition, our pilots continued with great courage and skill to maintain this supply, losing only one Dakota (C-47) in the process. Not only basic supplies were dropped, but also the new 'SEAC' newspaper, cigarettes, and mail from home; and it was afterwards found that by sending these amenities we had been able to make the troops realize that though temporarily encircled they were at no time isolated."[5]

While these supplies were being dropped, the Japanese artillery kept up constant shelling and their mortars used to open up with smoke and incendiary bombs to destroy these supplies. On 15 February their gun fire managed to hit the ammunition dumps on "Ammunition Hill", causing several to go up in flames.

The initiative passes to the Indian Army

During 12 and 13 February, the general situation in both the opposing forces remained fairly static; but thereafter the Japanese began to lose the initiative. They were far behind their schedule

---

[5] *Report to the Combined Chiefs of staff* by the Supreme Allied Commander South-East Asia 1943-45, page 43, paragraph 84.

and in spite of repeated attacks on the Ngakyedauk "Box", no signs of large scale collapse of the XV Indian Corps troops had become apparent. On the other hand, the Japanese had suffered very heavy casualties and had failed to capture the Indian stocks of supplies and stores on which they were relying. All these factors, combined with the shortage of supplies and the constant and continuous attacks by the besieged forces in the area of the road-block in the "Pass", made the Japanese realize that their offensive, as originally planned and later amended, must be abandoned.

Kubo Force, more isolated than the rest of the Japanese troops north of the Maungdaw-Buthidaung road, was feeling the shortage of supplies rather acutely. To some extent this was also true in the case of troops further to the south; but supplies in small quantities were still being brought up north along the eastern slopes of the Mayu Range, together with reinforcements from *3rd Battalion, 143rd Regiment*, to the main force of Colonel Tanahashi, immediately east of Sinzweya. As related earlier, the Japanese had run short of supplies owing to their exaggerated and false assumptions. Starting their large-scale offensive on 4 February they had assumed that they would require at the most ten days to complete their object, which was to annihilate the 7th Indian Division and to put the 5th Indian Division to rout, and for that reason their forces had carried only ten days' rations. Although they had successfully completed the first phase of their operation, they had soon begun to realise that they had underrated the capacity of resources of the Indian divisions.

The middle of February, however, saw a change in the situation so far as the XV Indian Corps was concerned; the tables had turned in its favour. Instead of the Japanese encircling the Indian and British forces, the former were themselves encircled between the 5th and 7th Indian Divisions in the northern sector of the battle zone. Shortly after the Japanese offensive had begun on 4 February the seriousness of the situation had been well appreciated by the Allied Higher Command. Consequently, reinforcements had been arranged for from India and the 26th Indian Division then under training in Eastern India was ordered to move post-haste to Arakan. Two of its brigades were quickly moved to Bawli Bazaar where they were ordered to form the left pincer of the movement to crush *Tanahashi Force* against the 7th Indian Division. The 26th Indian Division had thereafter moved over the Goppe Pass into the head of the Kalapanzin Valley and by 10 February had captured Taung Bazaar.

By 14 February, the relative situation of the opposing forces had again altered considerably. The troops of the 7th Indian Division had adopted an aggressive defence and were inflicting casualties on the Japanese by hundreds every day. Two brigades of the 26th Indian Division were steadily pushing down southwards; the 71st Indian

Infantry Brigade advanced to secure the Taung area with the object of establishing contact with the 114th Indian Infantry Brigade (7th Indian Division) which was east of the Kalapanzin, and the 4th Indian Infantry Brigade advanced along the eastern foothills of the Mayu range in order to destroy the Japanese who were entrenched in that area and to re-establish contact with the 7th Indian Division Administrative Box. The 36th Indian Infantry Brigade then began devoting its entire attention to attacking and destroying the Japanese in the foothills, west of the Mayu range. Meanwhile, troops of the 5th Indian Division with the help of the 123rd Indian Infantry Brigade were attacking the Pass from the west. The 36th Indian Infantry Brigade, (26th Indian Division) detached from the main division, was assigned the task of mopping up the Japanese who had crossed the Range by the Chhota Maunghnama Pass and were carrying out raids on the Bawli Road. But owing to the extremely difficult nature of the country and also to the need for ensuring safety of the line of communication, all these operations were proceeding rather slowly.

A final and desperate effort by the *Tanahashi Force* at this stage also did not succeed. On the night of 14/15 February, Colonel Tanahashi made another attempt by attacking south from Hill 315 across the Ngakyedauk Chaung. It was only partially successful but counter-attacks put in by the 7th Indian Division compelled the Japanese to withdraw north of the chaung. 15 and 16 February saw a lot of confused fighting; nevertheless the Japanese still held on to their main positions on Hill 315 in the Pass, as well as at Maunghnama.

By 16 February, however, twelve days after the capture of Taung Bazaar by the Japanese, the *Tanahashi Force* had begun to lose its offensive power, though it still continued to make daily attacks in various directions in a last effort to break the 7th Indian Division positions in the Sinzweya-Ngakyedauk area. Meanwhile, *Kubo Force*, which had been forced to split up into small parties, had already begun to retreat east across the Mayu ridge.

But the Japanese, in spite of their heavy losses, were still putting up a brave fight. On the evening of 14 February they succeeded in occupying Point 1070, a commanding feature on the Ngakyedauk Pass. But the troops of the 5th Indian Division decided to by-pass this point via the north and continue to press on towards the 7th Indian Division Administrative "Box". In the meanwhile the 4th Indian Infantry Brigade which was approaching the Sinzweya area from the north, had arrived near Point 315. This high feature north of and overlooking the Administrative "Box" was held by the Japanese and had proved a constant source of trouble. On the 16th 1 Lincolns, a battalion of the 4th Indian Infantry Brigade, made desperate efforts to capture this feature; but the attack was un-successful and the battalion suffered heavy casualties, though a few men under Major Hoey who was posthumously awarded the Victoria Cross did reach the summit and make their way through into the "Box". The sight of these men and the knowledge that they belonged to the 26th Indian Division greatly improved morale, as it was a sign that relief was near.

While these operations were taking place for the relief of the besieged troops in the Administrative "Box", other aggressive and harassing tactics were also being kept up on the Mayu coast. During the night of 16/17 February, a small number of Indian troops made a water-borne raid on the Mayu coast, attacked a village two miles north-west of Alethangyaw and killed six Japanese; in this raid two badly wounded Japanese were also captured and brought back.

By 19 February, small parties from *Tanahashi Force* had begun to withdraw to the east and south, and *Doi Force* made a gallant attempt to assist in this withdrawal. On the night of 18/19 February they put in an attack north towards Ngakyedauk in order to distract the attention of the Indian force but this attack was broken up by the latter.

For the next twenty-four hours, operations on all sectors continued slowly; the Japanese nevertheless were trying to put up a desperate resistance wherever they were. On the night of 19 February another raid was carried out on the Mayu coast, this time on Indin. On 20 February troops of the 5th Indian Division recaptured Point 1070 on the Ngakyedauk Pass and strong fighting patrols were thereafter pushed through to the 7th Indian Division Administrative "Box". Meanwhile the 4th Indian Infantry Brigade was gradually concentrating around Point 315 area in order to liquidate this feature at the earliest opportunity.

The Collapse of the Japanese Counter-offensive

Thus, by about the beginning of the third week of February, due to the display of superior tactical ability by the local commanders, the farsightedness of the Allied Higher Command and the magnificent fighting spirit and efficiency of the troops, better trained and more adequately equipped than ever before, and due mostly to the "all-out" co-operation of the air force, the first major defeat on the Japanese arms in Burma had been inflicted. The infantryman, the gunner, the signaller, the sapper, the tankman, and the Services had all joined hands to beat back the Japanese onslaught. The Indian muleteers of mule companies, who had never been taken seriously as fighters, had the first Japanese prisoner of the "Box" to their credit. The new technique of "staying put" when surrounded by the Japanese and relying upon air supply until relieved, had been tested and proved

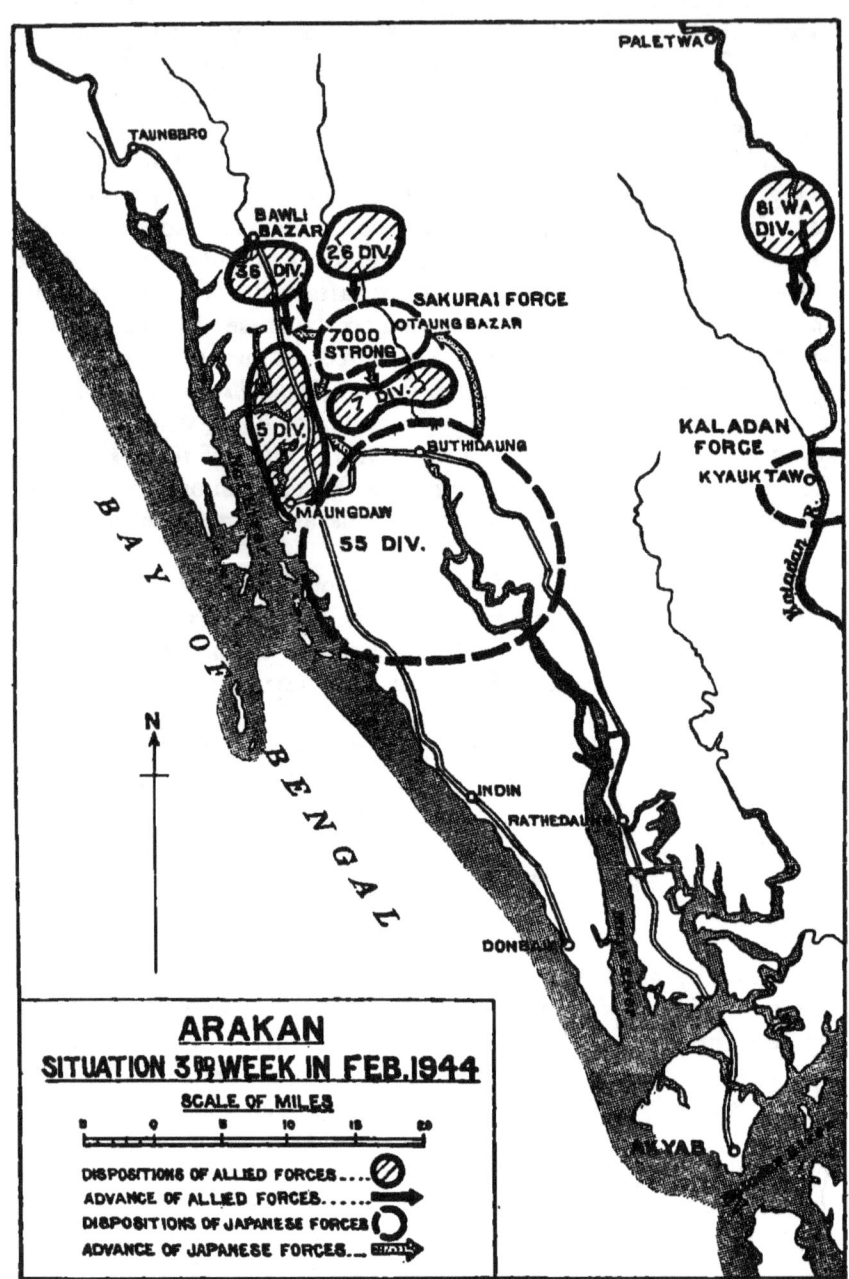

feasible. It was to be used successfully to a far greater extent a few months later at Imphal.

Reports had now begun to come in from the 33rd and 114th Indian Infantry Brigades to the effect that large parties of Japanese troops were moving southwards. On 23 February, operations to clear the Pass continued and at about midday after severe fighting a British officer of the 5th Indian Division who had led Punjabi and Rajput troops in a two-day jungle march to the rear of the Japanese hill bunkers and had stormed and cleared them, came out of the jungle to greet a Scottish soldier of the 2nd King's Own Scottish Borderers. After nearly three weeks of fierce and continuous fighting the siege had been raised and the pass had been re-opened. Thereafter, the isolated pockets of Japanese resistance were at once liquidated. On 26 February, Point 315 also fell to the Indian divisions and heavy casualties were inflicted on the now depleted and retreating Japanese who, smarting under their first serious failure, turned eastward. *Tanahashi Force*, now split into small parties, was withdrawing in haste, leaving behind many hundreds of dead.

While the Divisional Administrative "Box" battle had been taking place, the 33rd Indian Infantry Brigade had stayed put in its original positions. Shortly after the Japanese offensive began, the brigade had been reinforced by a squadron of tanks from 25 Dragoon. It had also put up a magnificent show in which 4/15 Punjab, 1 Queens and 1/11 Sikhs had played a full and useful part. On the 114th Indian Infantry Brigade front also, many casualties had been inflicted on the Japanese by offensive action. A light airstrip had also been constructed within the "Box" of this brigade and seriously wounded personnel had been flown out by small American planes. This had gone on all day and every day and the American Pilots had shown extreme bravery in this dangerous and arduous task.

By 29 February the battle of the "Boxes" could be safely claimed to have been won by the Indian and British forces. Of all the large-scale operations that the Japanese had conducted in Burma, this had proved the costliest, both in human lives as well as in prestige. Out of a total number of approximately 8,000 Japanese soldiers, hardly 2,000 escaped unscathed. A total of about 4,500 dead was actually counted which increased to over 6,000 in the later part of the operations, which ended when the monsoon broke out in June 1944. The Japanese casualties were nearly three to every one of the Indian or British. In the words of General Sir William Slim, Commander of the Fourteenth Army, "The Battle of Arakan was the first occasion in this war on which a British Force had withstood the full weight of a major Japanese offensive.—held it, broken it, smashed it into little pieces and pursued it, and anybody in 7 and 5 Indian Divisions who was there has something of which they can be very proud indeed."

CHAPTER XI

The Allies Resume the Offensive

The Kaladan Valley

While events were moving fast to the east and west of the Mayu range, developments were also occurring elsewhere in Arakan—developments which had an indirect but nevertheless important bearing on the main operations.

By the middle of December 1943, the 81st West African Division which consisted of only two brigades was concentrated in the Daletme-Satpaung area in the upper reaches of Kaladan. The division was reinforced by two Indian battalions—7/16 Punjab and 5 Mahrattas—as well as an East African battalion. The role assigned to the two Indian battalions was the protection of the rear of the division during its advance; the East African battalion was to operate on its left flank. The West African Division was expected to reach Kyauktaw about the middle of January 1944 but its advance was delayed by the loss in the Bay of Bengal of the ship that was carrying all its anti-aircraft and anti-tank guns, together with a workshop and some of the signal equipment.

It will be remembered that General Christison was fully alive to the danger of possible Japanese diversion across the apparently impassable Kaladan ranges to cut his main Line of Communication for Arakan. He was also fully aware that a small force of a brigade or equivalent strength would only give a false sense of security, as had happened during the previous Arakan campaign. But, at the same time, the deployment of a big force in a country without the semblance of a reasonable Line of Communication, also presented its own set of difficult problems. The only solution, therefore, appeared to be to maintain the whole force by air. Because of commitments in other theatres, however, the chance of securing a sufficient number of "supply dropping" aircraft did not seem fabourable at first but, after careful consideration of the requirements of this theatre, it was agreed to supply the entire Kaladan force by air.

Besides the difficulties of supply and maintenance, the problem of the evacuation of casualties was no less serious. To overcome this difficulty, the troops operating in the Kaladan valley undertook to construct suitable landing strips for Moths and Dakotas. Because of the nature of the country, the selection and construction of airstrips, reasonably safe from Japanese attacks, was by no means easy;

but the West Africans overcame this difficulty. Even places for "supply dropping" were not easy to find and the distribution of supplies amongst the troops was a lengthy and time consuming process. Difficulties of transport were partly met by the construction of rafts, and porters had to be used for evacuating casualties on some parts of the route.

Activities of the 81st West African Division

Before the middle of February, the advanced troops of the 81st West African Division had reached the outskirts of Kaladan village. On 10 and 12 February, two serious attacks were launched against Japanese strong points around the village but both the attacks failed. Meanwhile, the Japanese had launched their offensive on the main Arakan front. It was at this stage that the commander of the 81st West African Division received instructions from the XV Indian Corps asking him not to be held up by Japanese strong points but to by-pass them, if necessary. The division was ordered to push down the Kaladan Valley, and not to be delayed by small dug-in Japanese parties, and reach Kanzauk Pass, as fast as possible. There were two intentions behind this move; firstly, to cut the Japanese line of communication by which they brought reinforcements from the Kaladan into the Kalapanzin valley, and secondly, to threaten the Japanese right flank and distract their attention from the main offensive.

In consequence, the Japanese positions around Kaladan village were by-passed, and these tactics succeeded to such an extent that the Japanese evacuated the village without much delay. This manoeuvre further forced the Japanese troops to begin their general withdrawal southwards, fighting isolated actions. On 25 February, the Allied troops crossed the Pi Chaung just short of its confluence with the Kaladan river and overcoming slight opposition occupied Kyauktaw, which was their first main objective; later, Apaukwa also fell without much opposition. Thereafter, the division's main effort was directed towards the capture of Kanzauk with a view to threatening the Japanese line of communication.

Japanese counter-offensive in Kaladan

The Japanese, while fighting a delaying action down the west bank of the Kaladan river and holding the opposing forces frontally on the Myohaung road, had been building up a force of approximately three weak battalions, in order to carry out a counter-stroke in the Kaladan Valley. During the night of 1/2 March, this force moved round a small Allied detachment, south of Thayettabin and seizing that place, captured Pagoda Hill opposite Kyauktaw by 3

March. They then crossed the Kaladan river and occupied the area between the Pi Chaung and the Kaladan river, in some strength. This counter-attack by the Japanese had been possible with the help of elements of the Japanese *54th Division*. These had been brought up with the object of liquidating the 81st West African Division and thereby threatening the left flank of the rest of the XV Indian Corps. Due to the success of this counter-attack the 81st West African Division had perforce to take up new positions in the area, west of the Pi Chaung, where it resumed its role of flank protection for the main force of the XV Indian Corps. Unfortunately, this reverse had a bad effect on the West African troops and for the rest of the month this division could not be used for serious offensive action.

Consequently, the rest of the month of March was not notable for any major or serious action. But in the first week of April, the West African Division cleared the Japanese from the area of the Kaladan village; following this, again only small scale engagements took place in the Kaladan and Pi Chaung valley, north of the Kaladan village.

81st West African Division leaves Kaladan

On 10 April, to fill the hole, east of the Kalapanzin river in the main theatre of operations, left wide open by the sudden withdrawal by air of 7 Division to the Imphal front, the West African Division, less one West African battalion and 7/16 Punjab, marched straight through the Japanese lines across the Kaladan ranges along a single-file track and, arriving in the Kalapanzin valley south of Taung Bazaar, started offensive operations against the Japanese in the new area. The two battalions left behind were to contain and harass the hostile force to the best of their capacity and were also intended to give to the opponent the impression that the main force was still operating in the Kaladan Valley.

Mopping up operations

Meanwhile in the western sector, the last part of February was taken up by large mopping up operations. During the night of 24/25 February and 25/26 February, the main body of the Japanese *Sakurai Force*, which was then in the general area of Point 315, east of Sinzweya, split up into two columns of varying size in an endeavour to return to their own lines. Some of the units did succeed in the attempt by slipping through the jungle under cover of darkness, but this was achieved at a very heavy cost. By March 2, the area had been largely cleared with the exception of stragglers, though one large party of about 300 Japanese was still reported to be on a hill, east of Ngakyedauk village. By the end of the week, however, the *Bawli Raid Column* had been virtually eliminated and mopping up of the remnants of the *Sakurai Force* had been almost completed.

West of the Mayu range, on the night of 5/6 March, a strong party belonging to the *1st Battalion, 112th Regiment*, which had seen heavy fighting with the *Sakurai Force*, carried out a daring raid on the Headquarters of the 29th Indian Infantry Brigade (36th Indian Division) in the western foothills, north-east of Zeganbyin, but was eventually driven off with many casualties. The same night, another Japanese party of about the same strength raided the gun positions of a British medium artillery regiment in the Mwelabinga area, about two miles north of Razabil, causing serious damage to a gun. Casualties were sustained by both sides.

Resumption of Offensive against the Japanese

The petering out of the Japanese counter-offensive enabled the Indian Army to resume the suspended offensive. Though the Ngakyedauk Pass had been opened on 29 February and the Japanese columns had been thrown back, it was not before 5 March that the XV Indian Corps could begin its general offensive. Plans for this had been formulated earlier, and the first objective was to capture the Maungdaw-Buthidaung road and the mouth of the Naf river, so that supplies could be brought by sea at Maungdaw and Teknaf, and moved to the troops along the road. This would facilitate the problem of transport and enable the advance southward. The moment for the commencement of the offensive operations was most favourable and psychological, for the Japanese offensive had crumbled, raising the morale of the Allied forces.

The Japanese were still in occupation of their main defensive line and had strengthened their position between Htendaw and Letwedet, and had moved troops into positions east of the Kalapanzin. They had also brought up strong reinforcements and were prepared to resist fiercely. Besides, there were other serious limiting factors to rapid advance. Both air-supply and land lines of communication were severely strained and the condition of roads in Arakan was none too satisfactory while their improvement was also difficult owing to the lack of local stone and other material. Coastal shipping and inland water transport also could not much relieve the situation for the ports of Cox's Bazaar, Ultakhali and Maungdaw were both inadequate and undeveloped.

In early March 1944, the XV Indian Corps had five divisions in Arakan, four of which were poised for an attack on the Japanese defence line along Maungdaw-Buthidaung. The 5th Indian Division to the west of the Mayu Range was allotted the task of capturing

Razabil area, while the 7th Indian Division, east of the Range, was to reduce Buthidaung and the other Japanese strong points in its neighbourhood. Two divisions, the 36th Indian Division of two brigades only, and the detachments of the 26th Indian Division, were in the centre on the spine of the Mayu range, with Goppe Bazaar and Bawli Bazaar respectively as their bases; they were charged with the work of liquidating Japanese columns in the rear and clearing the Ngakyedauk Pass and the Tunnels area. The last division, the 81st West African Division, still less one brigade, was in the Kaladan valley, in position to defend the eastern flank of the main force and to stage a flanking attack, when necessary, against the Japanese forces.

Offensive operations by the 7th Indian Division—Capture of Buthidaung

The ball was set rolling by the 7th Indian Division which had for its objective the capture of Buthidaung and liquidation of the Japanese in that area. An offensive plan had been prepared early in February, before the Japanese counter-offensive, in which this division was commissioned to capture the features POLAND, Point 142, WEST FINGERS and the ASTRIDE position in one night, and then Buthidaung the next morning. This plan was modified and the operation, known as operation 'Stag Hound' was the responsibility of the 33rd Indian Infantry Brigade and the 89th Indian Infantry Brigade which formed part of the 7th Indian Division. The former supported by Corps artillery was to attack and capture Japanese held features and positions called CAIN, RABBIT, POLAND, Point 142 and WEST FINGERS. This phase was to be completed by 7 March, and subsequently the 89th Indian Infantry Brigade was to exploit eastwards and attack and capture Buthidaung. Fullest use was to be made of the tanks, and for that reason the sappers took to the work of making roads tankable.

For this operation the 33rd Indian Infantry Brigade was relieved by the 89th Indian Infantry Brigade of its commitments north of Point 162 and had the support of 136 and 139 Field Regiments, 7 Indian Field Regiment and 6 Medium Regiment from the east side of the Range, and 130 Field Regiment and 1 Medium Regiment from the west. In artillery this made a total of seventy-two 25 pounders, sixteen 3.7" howitzers and thirty-two 5.5" guns, a considerable array of fire concentration. The approach march for the operation was made on the night of 6/7 March, and the first phase was to be the capture of the features POLAND and RABBIT by 1/11 Sikhs. This initial operation was successful and was greatly helped by fire concentration by the Corps artillery. The next move was made by 4/15 Punjab, preceded by a "terrific concentration of fire", against Point 142. The weight of the fire can be estimated by the number of shells fired, which was 15,000, carrying a total of 225 tons of high explosives, into a target area approximately 500 by 300 yards. This point was also captured and the battalion exploited its success in the morning of 7 March by seizing three spurs to the east of the point which completely dominated the Maungdaw-Buthidaung road. Immediately after, CAIN was captured by 1 Queens and thereby the first phase of securing a position astride the Maungdaw-Buthidaung road was completed.

The next phase was the capture of ASTRIDE position with the object of opening the road to Buthidaung. For this purpose 1/11 Sikhs was placed under the command of the 89th Indian Infantry Brigade on 10 March. Success in this action was to be exploited by 4/8 Gurkha Rifles and 25 Dragoons by passing through and capturing Buthidaung. The attack by the Sikhs was a frontal assault preceded by a heavy concentration of fire, almost 7000 shells being put down on a front of approximately 500 yards. In the din and smoke of this barrage, the tanks could move undetected, and 1/11 Sikhs advanced with great rapidity and captured this most strongly held position without stiff resistance on 11 March. By 1400 hours, the Sikhs, having no contact with the Japanese, sent out two platoons riding on a troops of tanks of 25 Dragoons, who carried out a wide flanking move and entered Buthidaung which had been evacuated by the Japanese. Thus the town was captured without resistance one day before the schedule, and was occupied by 4/8 Gurkha Rifles on 11 and 12 March.

However, on the night of 12 March, the Japanese tried to infiltrate into their former positions covering the road. These attempts were beaten off by the Sikhs, but in the morning it was discovered that a platoon of the Japanese had succeeded in holding a spur called INDIA HILL. As the feature overlooked the main road, it was imperative to liquidate the Japanese force there immediately. It was not possible for the artillery to be active owing to the vicinity of the Sikh positions, but one Lee tank was available for the support of the platoon which was detailed for this task. The feature was a knife-edged ridge with steep jungle-clad slopes, and the Japanese had constructed deep well-concealed trenches and fox-holes during the night. In this action Naik Nand Singh, who led a section, showed extreme gallantry and won the Victoria Cross, the first in the 7th Indian Division. He led his section along a narrow track, the only approach on to the hill, to the crest where it came under heavy machine-gun and rifle fire. Every man went down, either killed or wounded. But unmindful of the danger Naik Nand Singh dashed forward alone under intense fire at point blank range, and while approaching a trench, was wounded by a grenade. Ignoring the injury, he captured the trench killing both its occupants with his bayonet. Such bravery was repeated twice and in spite of the second wound he rushed and captured two other trenches bayonetting their occupants also. This brought to an end all hostile fire and the remaining platoon was able to capture the remainder of the position, in which thirty-seven out of the forty Japanese were killed. It was Naik Nand Singh's gallantry and devotion to duty in face of danger that brought victory to the Indian Army and made the capture of Buthidaung possible.

The occupation of Buthidaung was followed by mopping up operations for the next few days, consisting of clearing the Japanese from the nearby features. In these actions, the most strenuous was the fight for Point 162 which was attempted by 1 Queens with artillery support, but it was difficult to dislodge the Japanese from there, and all attempts were unsuccessful. Later however 2 K.O.S.B. was able to take it with tank support. One of the fiercest action of the campaign was fought by 7/2 Punjab on a feature known as BULGE, on the west bank of the Kalapanzin river, almost at the same time as the operations undertaken against Buthidaung. This battalion was ordered to occupy and hold this feature which consisted of many small hills covered with thick undergrowth, and the battalion was in position there on 8 March. This position had been previously evacuated by the Japanese, but on the night of 10/11 March they infiltrated on to a ridge immediately over-looking the battalion headquarters. It was part of a Japanese suicide squad which had been charged to hold the position until completely annihilated. The Punjabis made continuous attacks with the aid of tanks for two days, and ultimately succeeded in clearing it of the Japanese, but the loss on both sides was great. The Japanese lost 179 men in killed out of a force of 180 while the Punjabis lost over 150 in killed and wounded, including their commanding officer, who was also killed in this gallant action.

Another battle was fought in the area of Zadidaung and Kyaukit where the Japanese had occupied small hill features; the 114th Indian Brigade was ordered to clear these positions. The Japanese abandoned Pyinshe Kala as a result of a fortnight's day and night action by snipers, mortars and artillery. The Zadidaung feature, however, had to be attacked by 4/14 Punjab who cleared it without any artillery or tank support. By 5 April 4/5 Gurkhas dominated the Kyaukit area after having been occupied in continuous assaults on a series of features which were held by the Japanese. Another action in the same period was fought by 1/11 Sikhs and 4/15 Punjab who were engaged in clearing a Japanese infiltration in the rear of the 7th Indian Division, on a ridge to the east of the old administrative "Box".

5th Indian Division resumes the offensive

It has already been stated that the efforts of the 5th Indian Division to reduce the Japanese strong point at Razabil had proved costly and were almost fruitless. It was therefore evident that if these positions were to be captured, a change of tactics was needed, and General Briggs, the Commander, was not slow in thinking out new ways of dealing with a determined foe. He decided to cut him off from the rear, a manoeuvre so often employed by the Japanese themselves. It had also become apparent that the Japanese, having failed in achieving the object of their offensive plan, were intending to hold their former line of defence. The XV Indian Corps therefore thought it imperative that the hostile force should be destroyed in the Razabil—Tunnels area before further operations could proceed.

The 7th Indian Division was, in the meanwhile, carrying out an operation to capture the area immediately east of the eastern entrance to the Tunnels road. According to the plan laid down, after the 7th Indian Division had accomplished its task, the 26th Indian Division was to carry out an operation to capture the Tunnels road which fell within its boundary. It was further decided that alongside these two operations, the 5th Indian Division should be given the task of capturing the Razabil "fortress". According to the Divisional Operation Order No. 21, dated 6 March 1944, the 161st Brigade was to attack the fortress from the east and the south, while the 123rd Brigade was to infiltrate from the north; the 9th Brigade was to co-operate from the west. D day for this operation was 10 March 1944 and the code name for it was 'Markhur'.

At 1900 hours on 9 March, operations to reduce the Razabil fortress were commenced. 1/1 Punjab crossed over the coastal plain and entered the hills to the east of the Razabil-Indin Road via the Thazegon track. By 0700 hours on the morning of the 10th, they had succeeded in cutting the Maungdaw-Buthidaung road. Meanwhile, 4/7 Rajput had quickly followed up and having secured a base, enabled the Royal West Kents to pass through and proceed north-west toward the eastern perimeter of the Razabil "fortress".

3 Jat then moving north of the hills east of the road, encountered a little opposition from the Japanese. A small party was therefore left to contain them whilst the remainder of the battalion pushed on. By nightfall, the 5th Indian Division battle front extended along the line from road Razabil—Indin at 370379 to the road Maungdaw—Buthidaung at 385398.

South of the road, 1/11 Sikh had reached a high feature just north of Dongyaung and had encountered only slight opposition; the attack by 4/1 Gurkha Rifles had also been successful.

Throughout the 10th and 11th of March the fighting continued but with very little Japanese opposition. To the east and the southeast of the "fortress", there was no appreciable change in the situation, nor was there any engagement between the opposing forces. To the south, however, 3 Jat had continued its advance northwards and by the evening of the 11th had reached the line of the Magui Chaung, south of Point 110.

Throughout the 11th, the area of the Razabil fortress was subjected to artillery and air bombardment, which produced little reaction on the part of the Japanese. By 12 March 1944, the operations against the Razabil fortress had been successfully concluded and the troops of the 5th Indian Division were moving eastwards without meeting much Japanese opposition. By the evening of the same day Buthidaung had also been captured by the 7th Indian Division.

Thus, by the middle of March, the Japanese troops had been evicted from the Razabil fortress and other strong points in that vicinity. The advance of the XV Indian Corps thereafter continued along the Maungdaw-Buthidaung road and the heights dominating the western tunnel were captured, although with great difficulty. Troops of the 36th Indian Division, advancing along the main Range captured Point 731, but the Japanese garrison on Point 1301 on the main ridge, vigorously opposed all efforts to dislodge them.

Whilst withdrawing some of their troops southwards in the face of heavy and sustained pressure, the Japanese maintained three "blocks" or series of strong points manned by troops who were probably ordered to fight to the last man. These three "blocks" were (*i*) in the area of the Tunnels (*ii*) in the positions on Point 162, north of Letwedet, and (*iii*) at Kyaukit, east of the Kalapanzin. Indian troops east of the Mayu Range carried out a successful encircling movement round Buthidaung and captured all the high ground west and south-west of the village, thus enabling the detachments to enter the town itself.

5th Indian Division transported to Assam by air

While the 5th Indian Division's push was successfully proceeding, news was received that it was to be transported by air immediately to the IV Corps battle front in Assam, to assist in dealing with the latest Japanese threat to the Imphal plain. This was the first time that a formation of the size of a division, complete with artillery and mules, was flown "in toto" from one theatre to another.

25th Indian Division relieves the 5th Indian Division

The relief of the 5th Indian Division by the 25th Indian Division began in the middle of March and was completed before the end of the month. The newly arrived troops, though remarkably efficient and determined, were unacquainted with the country and, in addition, found themselves in the midst of a large-scale operation which, fortunately, was proceeding according to plan. However, they did not lose much time in settling down and adapting themselves to their new, unhealthy environment.

It had been the intention of the Allied High Command to move the 25th Indian Division to Ranchi (India) in February 1944 and to place it there as Army reserve, but the events in Arakan changed its destination. The 5th Indian Division had been in action for nearly two years, having fought in the desert earlier; the 7th Indian Division had borne the brunt of the battle in Arakan and its losses in men and equipment had been fairly heavy; the 26th Indian Division had also been robbed of rest by the same turn of events. All these divisions were therefore due for relief. At this stage, a new factor further influenced the situation. For some time past there had been indications that the Japanese were preparing a major offensive across the river Chindwin against the IV Corps troops, and reinforcements were badly needed for that front. The fact that the 25th Indian Division was a high scale mechanised division, prevented its being sent to that theatre. The Army Commander (Lieut.-General W. J. Slim, C.B.E., D.S.O., M.C.) required an animal transport (A.T.) division from Arakan; the choice therefore fell upon the 5th Indian Division since from its position on the road, it could most quickly and easily be withdrawn from contact. As the new Japanese offensive developed, the urgency for relief increased. The 5th Indian Division was thereupon flown to Imphal, and the 25th Indian Division's first object was to get into action as quickly as possible to secure the former's release. Thus, the hope of the Corps Commander of giving this new division a leisurely take-over, was rudely shaken, and the units of the 25th Indian Division found themselves literally buttoning up their coats as they hurried down the road from their concentration area at Chiringa, to carry out their new role. Green battle-dress had been issued, without buckles, and at every halt the tailors were busy trying to fit these suits to the wearers.

A further trial for this division, and one which was aggravated by the haste imposed upon it, was occasioned by the loss of, and damage to, its equipment on the journey from India. The 51st Indian Brigade went first into action and this was the only brigade to be involved in heavy fighting at the outset; it was therefore fortunate that its entry into Arakan was less hurried with the consequence that its losses on the journey were the lightest.

When the 25th Indian Division appeared on the scene, the other divisions in the Mayu peninsula were located as follows:—

The 5th Indian Division was in Maungdaw and in the foothills for five miles to the south of it; the capture of the important Razabil "fortress" at the western end of the Tunnels road had formed a suitable climax to its part in the campaign.

The 36th Indian Division was disposed on the "spine" of the peninsula and was fighting for the possession of the Tunnels area.

The 26th Indian Division was in Taung Bazaar and in the country to the south of it. It was moving forward to relieve the 7th Indian Division in the Sinzweya "box" and the line of Buthidaung road.

The original plan had been for the brigades of the 25th Indian Division to take over successively from those of the 5th Indian Division. In pursuance of this plan, the 51st Brigade (Brigadier T. H. Angus, D.S.O.) moved south from Chiringa on 18 March and relieved the 123rd Indian Infantry Brigade in the foothills, north of the Tunnels road, and at the same time came under the command of the 5th Indian Division. So far all went well; but it was at this stage that the Corps Commander received orders to release the whole of the 5th Indian Division at once. Consequently, on 20 March, the 51st Brigade was replaced in its new positions by a brigade of the 36th Indian Division under whose command it passed and was itself moved south of the Maungdaw-Buthidaung road to relieve another brigade of the 5th Indian Division. Thus it came into a new country with a new task and under a new division. The battalions it relieved were in the middle of an operation and hence their positions were fluid. It is therefore not surprising that the Japanese seized this opportunity offered to them, to inflict what damage they could to the untried troops. In particular, 16/10, Baluch who took over widely dispersed company localities in the difficult country west of Hill 1440, received a rude initiation into the art of battle before it could be concentrated in a strong position at Hill 109.

Meanwhile, the 74th Brigade (Brigadier J.E. Hirst D.S.O.) had landed at Chittagong and was making its best speed forward. 6 Oxf Bucks was motored straight through to Bawli with the temporary role of defending the Corps Headquarters and the adjacent medical installations. The remainder of the brigade, after a very brief halt at Chiringa in order to pick up their baggage, moved into the Kanyindan-Razabil area. Throughout this period, the Divisional Headquarters had been on the move, and, on 27 March, two days after his arrival at Maungdaw, Major-General Davies took over command of his two brigades which were then in action.

At the beginning of April, the 53rd Brigade (Brigadier G.A.P. Coldstream) began to come forward. 9 York and Lancaster was the first to arrive and relieved 6 Oxf Bucks at Bawli. The latter battalion rejoined its brigade and took up positions in the foothills, west and north of Hill 731.

During the night of 24/25 March, a Japanese force of approximately one battalion moved through the foothills east of the Kalapanzin and, crossing the river, appeared south of the eastern exit of the Ngakyedauk Pass early on March 25, laying a number of anti-tank mines on the tracks. The Indian troops in that locality immediately took up positions in the old 7th Indian Division administrative "Box" area, and operations to deal with the infiltrating force commenced without delay. Within the next two days, more than 100 of the raiders were killed. The Japanese were later forced to surrender many features which they had seized.

Battle for the "Tunnels" area

The capture of Point 1301 on the main ridge was a pre-requisite to the achievement of mastery over the Tunnels on the Maungdaw-Buthidaung road. Previous attacks on this Japanese stronghold had not met with any success. On 19 March, however, this feature was captured after a dummy dive bombing attack and the pressure was increased on the western Tunnel, although the Japanese held on tenaciously to the Tunnel area as a whole, and put in a series of counter-attacks which were all beaten off.

In the meanwhile, the Japanese had reinforced their positions and stiffened their resistance in the foothills, south of the Maungdaw-Buthidaung road. Although the western end of the Tunnel fell to the Allies on 28 March, the Japanese still held on to its eastern end.

At this time in early April 1944, the XV Indian Corps had five divisions less two brigades under its command for operations in Arakan—the 25th, 36th, 26th and 7th Indian Divisions and the 81st West African Division. The Corps Commander's plan, at this stage, was briefly to establish a monsoon line along the axis of the Maungdaw-Buthidaung road to be held by the 25th Indian Division. In order to achieve this object, it was necessary to evict the Japanese from their strong positions, in and around the Tunnels area. The 36th Indian Division was, therefore, allotted this particular task while the 26th Indian Division was directed on objectives further east, including the difficult feature, known as Point 551.

The role allotted to the 25th Indian Division was as follows:—

(1) To hold a firm base with a mobile reserve in the Maungdaw-Razabil area.

(2) To take over and hold successively positions captured by the 26th and 36th Indian Divisions on the spine of the Mayu peninsula.

(3) To assist the actions of the other two divisions by vigorous

patrolling and offensive action in the foothills, south of the Tunnels road.

The Corps plan also indicated that the capture of Hill 1433 was highly desirable for the security of the ultimate monsoon defences. In general, therefore, each of these three objects was a brigade task. The defence of the Maungdaw base fell to the 74th Indian Infantry Brigade; the arrival of the 53rd Indian Infantry Brigade was well timed for it to take over in the Tunnels area while the 51st Indian Infantry Brigade, which already held positions in that area could best undertake the third task of diversionary patrols.

In view of its role, it is not altogether surprising that the heaviest fighting at first fell to the lot of the 51st Indian Infantry Brigade. Immediately west of the "Spine" were two features which were of tactical importance as stepping-stones to the main ridge. These had been occupied by 17 Mahrattas on their first take over from the 5th Indian Division. On 5 April, the Japanese attacked these features. The ground favoured them as they had perfect observation of the Mahratta positions from the dominating heights of Hill 1433 and Hill 1440. Their assault on Hill 904, the more northernly of the two features in question, was successful; the Indian troops had to withdraw to the positions on the slopes of the features. The Mahratta company on the other feature also withstood some savage attacks for some time, but in the end it was also forced to give ground. Keen fighting continued for several days until the Divisional Commander placed 8 Hyderbad less two companies under the 51st Indian Infantry Brigade to reinforce the Mahrattas in their battle. 8 Hyderabad was up till then the divisional headquarters battalion.

On 9 April, while this action was still in progress, the Japanese launched a fresh attack against 16/10 Baluch in their position on Hill 109. In this attack the former employed a new battalion which had recently arrived from Akyab. The assault was put in at first light on the 9th, but since the Japanese had been, surprisingly enough, very noisy in their forming up, the Indian troops were not taken by surprise. In close support of 16/10 Baluch was a mortar battery of 27 (Jungle) Field Regiment. Sixteen mortars of this battery, together with six mortars of the infantry battalion, opposed the Japanese with a devastating defensive fire and caused heavy casualties among them. Though the Japanese gained an intermediate objective, they could get no further and subsequently had to withdraw, leaving behind their dead and wounded. 16/10 Baluch had two killed and four wounded, but it had more than avenged the rough handling it had received in the first few days of action and was the first battalion of the 25th Indian Division to win the envied trophy of a Japanese officer's sword.

Meanwhile, fighting had continued in the area of Hill 109. A company of 8/19 Hyderabad had recaptured this feature by a silent night attack on 11 April. But on account of this feature being clear of jungle and bushy growths, it was under 'observation' of Japanese artillery fire. Consequently, activity by day was impossible, while by night, Japanese patrols round the perimeter prevented freedom of movement. As a result of continued and heavy fighting, many dead bodies of both the opposing forces were lying unburied on the ground and efforts to procure lime or to dispose them had proved unsuccessful. Eventually, the stench became so unbearable that the Divisional Commander had no alternative but to order the withdrawal of 8 Hyderabad from the feature. Furthermore, he appreciated that these features had no tactical significance in themselves but only as part of the dominating height of Hill 1433. Hence he decided to abandon aggressive operations in this area in favour of an attack on Hill 1433 itself from the north.

During this period, 17 Mahrattas relieved 8/19 Hyderabad as divisional headquarters battalion in order that their men might be rested; but the two companies which were not required for the defence of divisional and brigade headquarters, remained at Kanbyin under the command of the Hyderabad battalion.

The battle on the "Spine"

While these operations were in progress, the 36th Indian Division had been winning successes in the task of capturing the Tunnels area and the surrounding heights, although stubborn resistance had to be overcome before most of the objectives were captured. The 53rd Indian Infantry Brigade, (25th Indian Division) which was to take over the newly won ground, had now concentrated at Bawli, and from there its battalions were called forward at appropriate intervals. The taking over and relief followed smoothly and without much Japanese interference, but for some weeks the brigade passed quite a few uneasy nights as the Japanese "jitter parties" were very active.

By the middle of April 1944, the Tunnels area was very largely occupied by the XV Indian Corps; fighting, however, was still in progress, further to the east. Hill 1267 was the most southernly locality held by the Indian troops on the "Spine", but Hill 1433, which was over a mile to the south, was still a Japanese stronghold. This farther and higher position gave the Japanese an excellent Observation Post (O.P.) and a base for operations, either northwards along the ridge, or down into the western foothills where the 51st Indian Infantry Brigade was in position.

To implement the plan of the 25th Indian Division to take by assault Hill 1433 from a new angle, 14/10 Baluch was moved from

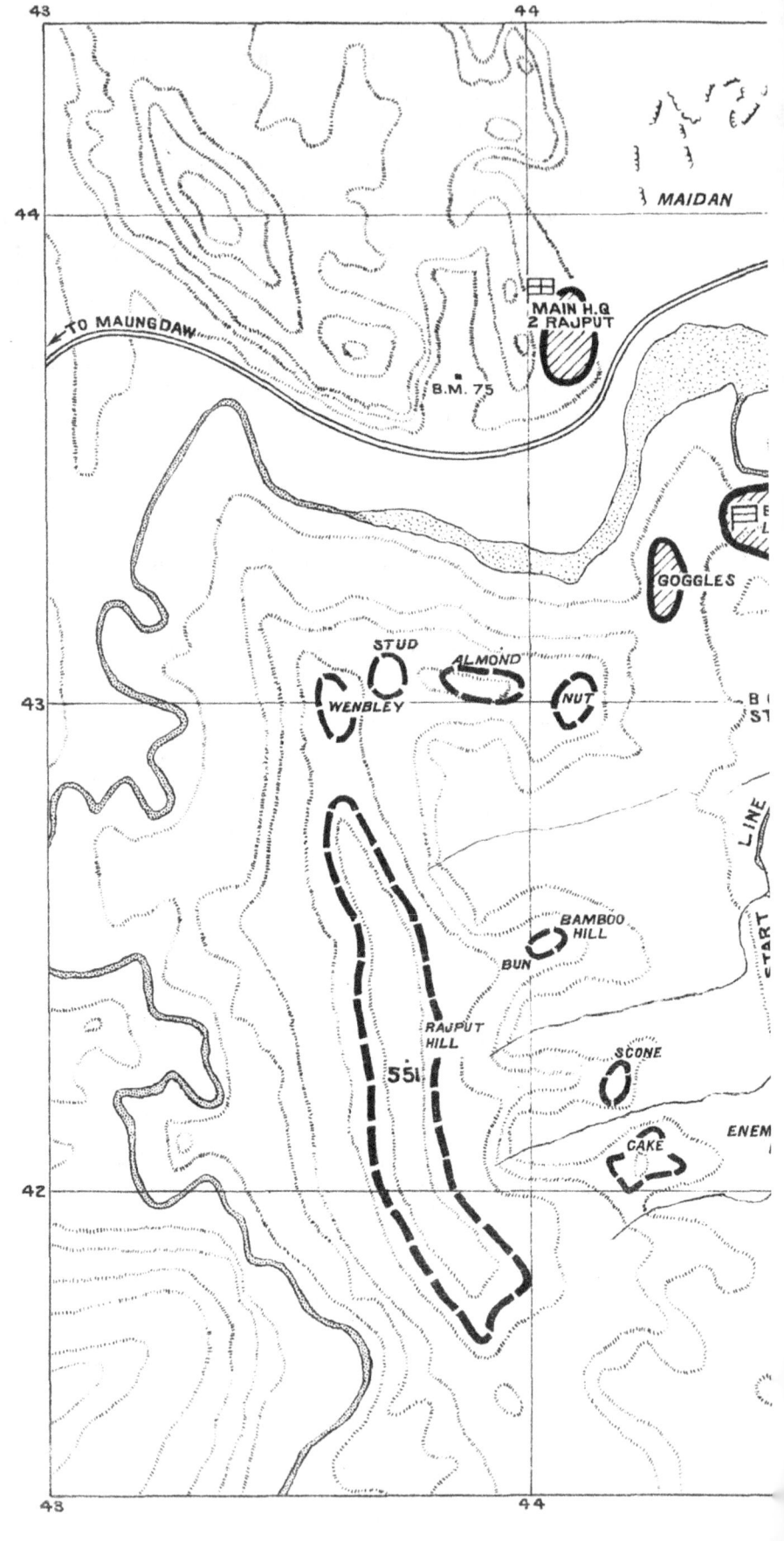

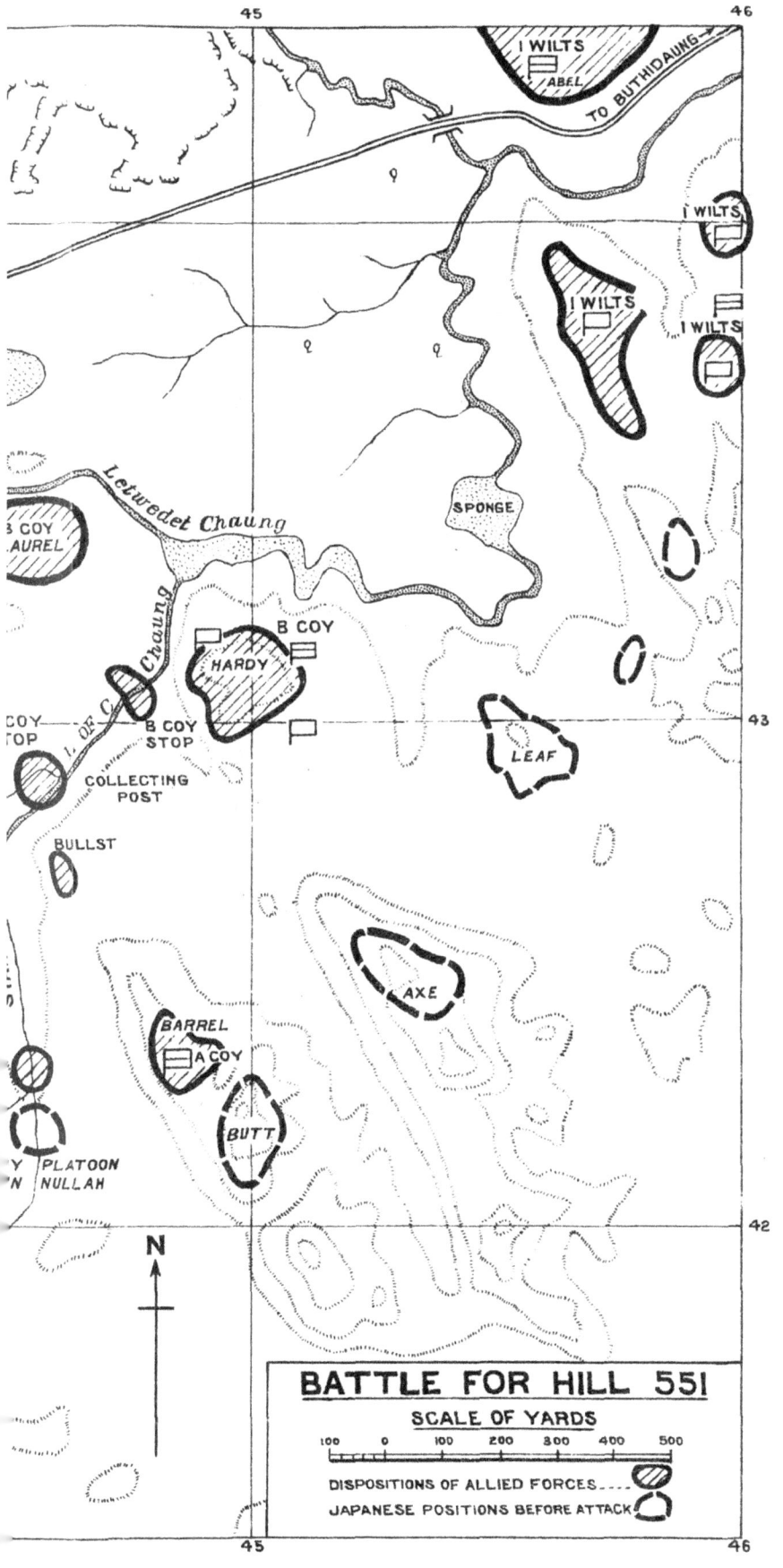

Kanyindan, where it had been in reserve, to Hill 1267, and placed under the command of the 53rd Indian Infantry Brigade; 6 Oxf Bucks moved down to Kanyindan and took over its former role.

In his new position, the 14 Baluch commander was faced with a difficult problem. Between his base on Hill 1267 and his final objective lay a series of smaller features, connected by a narrow knife-edged ridge which precluded deployment on other than section frontage, for on either side were precipitous slopes covered with thick jungle. One of these intermediate features, which had been named COCK, was approached from the north by a steep scarp, and on its reverse slope the Japanese had built themselves a strong defensive position, supported by medium machine-guns.

On 17 April, 14/10 Baluch put in an attack, but though they overran an outpost, the main position could not be taken. Every time the Indian troops approached the crest, they were met with a hail of grenades; while those who managed to reach the top fell victims to the Japanese machine-guns. The attack had therefore to be called off and, although it was renewed on subsequent days with every manner of new stratagem, no better success could attend these efforts. Soon it became clear that the position could only be carried at heavier cost than its importance justified and so the attempt was reluctantly abandoned.

The fight on Hill 551 (later known as Rajput Hill)

Further to the east, the 26th Indian Division was engaged in a stiff struggle for Hill 551. This feature, which was later known as Rajput Hill, guarded the entrance of the Maungdaw-Buthidaung road into the hills. It was a formidable looking feature, a knife-edged ridge over 1,000 yards long with a sheer drop, on the west, from the crest of the ridge to the floor of the valley below. This ridge was a veritable fortress, the ridge itself and its foothills being dotted with Japanese strongpoints and bunkers, especially on the main ridge and north of the feature. From these points the Japanese could dominate the Maungdaw-Buthidaung road, particularly at the eastern end of the Tunnels pass. This feature was therefore of considerable tactical importance for either side, and the Japanese were defending it in strength. Operations continued throughout the latter part of April, but although troops of the 26th Indian Division secured intermediate objectives on the northern slopes, the Japanese contested every yard of the advance and by several counter-attacks recovered most of the ground they had lost.

At the beginning of April 1944, the 4th Indian Infantry Brigade, having fought its way down from Taung Bazaar, had secured all the features overlooking the eastern end of the Maungdaw-Buthidaung road, except Point 551. The 2/7th Rajput Regiment at this time held positions astride the road on CAIN and ABEL and from these positions kept patrolling vigorously, probing the hostile positions and beating off many attempts by the Japanese to recover the ground they had lost. Meanwhile, the 13th Frontier Force Rifles had occupied all the ground on the right flank of the 4th Indian Infantry Brigade, aided by the Wiltshire Regiment, but was unable to cross the road because immediately to the south, completely dominating the road, was Point 551.

It was, however, the task of the 4th Indian Infantry Brigade to take this formidable feature and plans were put into operation for its capture. Twice during April, attacks were put in by the Wiltshire Regiment and 13 Frontier Force Rifles, both by daylight, and supported by air, tanks and artillery; extremely heavy concentrations having been put down in support of the infantry attacks. The success of both these attacks was however limited and by the end of April, only BARREL, LAUREL, HARDY and GOGGLES features had been occupied. Point 551 still remained to be taken, though it had been battered almost out of recognition by the terrific weight of shell and bomb. A new plan was then put into operation, and 2/7 Rajput and 1/8 Gurkha, who had been brought in to relieve the Wiltshire Regiment and 13 Frontier Force Regiment respectively, took up positions on BARREL, BULLET, LAUREL and HARDY features, on the foothills and eastern approaches to Point 551.

The plan for the attack was very simple. The D day was fixed for the night of 2/3 May 1944. It was to be a night attack, unheralded by heavy artillery concentration, as had been the case in the previous attacks. The objective of 1/8 Gurkha was the large feature to the north of Point 551 known as WEMBLEY, ALMOND and NUT (later known as Gurkha Ridge). The objectives of 2/7 Rajput were first of all the three strongly defended Japanese positions on hills known as BUN, CAKE and SCONE, which guarded the eastern approaches to Point 551.

Action of 1/8 Gurkha Rifles on Gurkha Ridge

Gurkha Ridge, consisting of the features WEMBLEY-STUD-ALMOND-NUT was a steep ridge running east and west and just south of the road Maungdaw-Buthidaung. Owing to previous artillery bombardment the ridge was completely bare of vegetation or any kind of cover. The 1/8th Gurkha Rifles had taken over positions occupied by 2/13 Frontier Force Rifles with the result that one of its companies on the GOGGLES feature was in close contact with the Japanese. This relief took place on the night of 28/29 April and during the process a certain amount of noise was made by the outgoing unit. The Japanese, taking advantage of this, crept near the position and fifteen minutes after the completion of the relief, put in a determined attack supported by mortars, machine-guns, rifles and hand-grenades. The forward platoon bore the brunt of the attack and fierce hand-to-hand fighting took place. The successful breaking off of this platoon from a determined and forceful Japanese attack was largely due to the cool, calm leadership of the junior commanders. Since the combined attack of 2/7 Rajput and 1/8 Gurkha Rifles was scheduled to take place on the night of 2/3 May, the intervening days and nights were spent in reconnoitring the lines of advance by 1/8 Gurkha Rifles.

The general plan of attack was that seven separate columns would advance silently by night; the reserves being ready to exploit immediately. The advance of 2/7 Rajput and B company (less one platoon) of 1/8 Gurkha Rifles was to start at 2200 hours. 1/8 Gurkha Rifles would start at 0230 hours. The reasons for staggering the timings of start were:

(a) The Rajputs had much further to advance and their line of advance was covered;
(b) 1/8 Gurkha Rifles had a bare ridge without cover to advance; therefore it was essential for this battalion to move when the moon was down.

The plan of 1/8 Gurkha Rifles was to infiltrate into the Japanese positions during the hours of darkness in four separate columns.

The companies moved to their assembly areas and crossed their respective start points at 0230 hours without incident. At first light, A company was seen moving on the feature known as WEMBLEY. The Japanese were in strength in a bunker position on this feature. It was a narrow, bare, knife-edged ridge and any advance along this ridge came under heavy fire from a Japanese bunker position on STUD. By putting down artillery fire on to STUD a few daring men managed to rush along the narrow knife-edged ridge and get into the Japanese bunker position, killing all the occupants by means of grenades, kukris and the bayonet.

As daylight broke, the platoons from B and C companies, whose objectives were ALMOND and STUD, crawled forward thirty yards from the crest of the ridge and the Japanese position. As daylight grew, they were unfortunately spotted by the Japanese who opened withering fire with medium machine-guns and light machine-guns from ALMOND and NUT. Finding it impossible to get forward and suffering many casualties, the platoons were forced to withdraw. The leading section did reach the crest and remained in a disused Japanese trench for a considerable time. However, when the Allied artillery began to shell ALMOND, the section made a dash for it down the hill and got back to safety with only two casualties.

B company (two platoons) had started with 2/7 Rajput at 2230 hours but was held up by a strong Japanese position, south of NUT.

Thus at first light of 3 May, the situation was as follows:—

A company had captured WEMBLEY.

Platoons of B and C companies had failed to take STUD and ALMOND.

B company less one platoon had failed to take NUT and was held up south of the NUT feature.

About 0700 hours, after consultation with A company commander on WEMBLEY, it was decided to attempt the capture of STUD from WEMBLEY. Artillery fire was therefore brought down on ALMOND and NUT and D company from GOGGLES was also giving covering fire. One platoon of A company rushed across the open ground and stormed the bunker position on STUD, killing all the occupants. Two medium and four light machine-guns were captured in these attacks on WEMBLEY and STUD. By 1000 hours, all objectives except ALMOND and NUT had been captured by the brigade.

On 5 May, it was decided to make another attempt at capturing ALMOND and NUT. One platoon of B company, one platoon of D company and D company headquarters were detailed to carry out this attack. The plan was to attack from the west from the direction of WEMBLEY preceded by an artillery bombardment. B company's platoon was to pass through and take NUT and consolidate. The essence of the plan was to get into the Japanese positions as soon as possible after the artillery concentration. Unfortunately, the Allied artillery programme broke down at the start, hence the leading platoon, hearing and seeing no artillery fire, did not advance. However, the Forward Observation Officer with the battalion headquarters then managed to bring down some fire on the east end of ALMOND and NUT, at the same time as the company commander ordered the advance. The two platoons, therefore, did get artillery support and some excellent shooting by the battery concerned had a marked effect on the course of the battle. The B company platoon led by the platoon commander charged down from STUD, yelling and shouting and was soon amongst the Japanese on ALMOND. Soon after, the situation was brought under control and the platoon began to consolidate.

The second platoon of D company was then immediately passed through on to NUT. The Japanese showed signs of clearing out, but the platoon went quickly and fiercely over very difficult ground and stormed the hostile trenches.

Another platoon of D company which had occupied the portion immediately north of NUT and had withdrawn for the artillery concentration, had by that time reorganised in its old position. Straightaway, a fighting patrol was sent from this platoon which mopped up and probed on farther, while the attacking platoon consolidated. This patrol found the Japanese bunker position, which had held up B company earlier, to be empty. Thus the task of 1/8 Gurkha Rifles was accomplished and a part of the phase for the battle of Point 551 was completed.

Operations by 2/7 Rajput against Point 551

When the actual plan for the attack had been evolved, 2/7 Rajput had carried out careful practice and rehearsals on the ground, under conditions similar to those expected during the real attack. The battalion was reminded by the brigade commander that it was essential for this attack to be successful as the capture of Point 551 was vital for the security of all Allied forces in the surrounding area.

The task of taking BUN, CAKE and SCONE was allotted to D company while C company was to take advantage of the success on any one of D company's objectives and push through to Point 551. The starting line was a nullah running along the east of Point 551, about 1,000 yards from the ridge itself. This starting line had been secured several days before and had been held, against many Japanese attempts to take it, by the valiant work of A company positioned on BARREL and BULLET, and B company on LAUREL and HARDY. The stage was therefore all set for the attack.

On 2 May 1944 at about 2200 hours, C and D companies reached the main headquarters, having marched down from the rear headquarters on OCTOPUS, where they had been resting and preparing for the attack. From the main headquarters they moved forward with the tactical headquarters, followed by the carrying platoon, composed of newly arrived recruits. It had been appreciated that to enable the troops to hold on to Point 551 after its capture, it would be necessary for water, ammunition and supplies to be rushed up to C and D companies, immediately after consolidation. These stores were therefore dumped at the Gateway which was between B company positions in LAUREL and HARDY, ready to be sent up as soon as required. The carrying party remained in the Gateway while D company, C company and tactical headquarters moved towards the starting line, which was reached without incident. Any noise made by this party was covered by a light harassing fire, which was being brought down on BUN, CAKE and SCONE; this harassing fire had been directed on this area since the early hours of the morning. This fire was to continue on BUN, CAKE and SCONE until half an hour after the zero hour, when it was estimated that the attacking platoons would be drawing closer to their objectives. The fire was then to lift to the top of the ridge of Point 551, again with the purpose of drowning the noise of the approach of C company.

Zero hour was 2200 hours and right on time, D company moved off through the thick jungle on the banks of the chaung towards its objectives; 14 platoon to BUN, 15 platoon to CAKE and 16 platoon to SCONE. Leading each platoon was a detachment of unit Pioneers, cutting the way through the dense jungle with dahs and armed with wire cutters, should Japanese wire be encountered. Once the last man of D company had left the chaung, no more was heard of the company for three hours as it made hardly a sound and the wireless sets which had been allotted to each platoon, were silent. It therefore appeared to the commanding officer of 2/7 Rajput, who was in his tactical headquarters on the Starting Line, that D company had failed to reach its objective, especially when light machine-gun and rifle fire was heard from the direction of BUN, followed by complete silence. The commanding officer, therefore, decided to commit C company, as the route to Point 551 was a long one and there were but a few hours of darkness left. C company, thereupon, started along the track made by 14 platoon toward BUN. Hardly had the last man left the nullah when from BUN came a sudden fusilade of automatic and rifle fire, followed by D company's war cry of "*Ya Ali*"—a cry that could be heard a mile away at the rear headquarters. For several minutes there was heavy firing and sounds of bursting grenades, then all was quiet again. Soon after, however, from the tactical headquarters which had moved to HARDY, was seen the welcome sight of tracer fire from a light machine-gun from BUN; this was the success signal. 15 and 16 platoons, having taken their objectives with negligible opposition, success signals followed in quick succession from CAKE and SCONE also.

When the radio sets of D company platoons opened up, the story of how BUN was taken became known. 14 platoons had reached the lower slopes of Bamboo Hill, east of BUN, when it was fired upon by a light machine-gun from a Japanese bunker, halfway up the slope. It was impossible for the platoon to advance without suffering heavy losses; volunteers were therefore asked for to knock out this light-machine-gun post. The bunker having been successfully dealt with, the platoon had then advanced towards the Japanese positions on the upper slopes of Bamboo Hill and BUN. So strongly did they press in their attack that the Japanese fled from their positions. D company commander, having secured BUN, closed the rest of the company onto BUN and placed his men in positions as protection for the line of communication from the chaung, through BUN, to the top of Point 551.

C company, which had reached BUN just as D company's attack was going on, pushed forward as soon as the success signal had been given. The jungle beyond was found to be too thick to penetrate quickly. As cutting was a lengthy procedure and daylight was not far off, the C company commander took his company up one of the chaungs, running up to Point 551. No news was received from the company as the radio could not be used on the move in the jungle, but just as first light was dawning, tactical headquarters on HARDY could see the men moving on the ridge of Point 551. It was uncertain as to who they were but as light grew it was almost certain that they were the men of C company, especially as they appeared to be waving their arms. A few minutes later a message was received over the radio from C company to say that one platoon was in position on Point 551 while the others were moving up.

Although Point 551 was captured by the Indian troops after much difficulty there were many Japanese counter-attacks which they had to face throughout that day. To commemorate the way in which this battalion of Rajputs seized and held this famous ridge, the battalion was congratulated by the 26th Indian Division Commander and a Divisional Order was issued that Point 551 would in future be known as Rajput Ridge.

While the 5th Indian Infantry Brigade of the 26th Division was battling for the hill of Point 551, the 25th Indian Division was naturally eager to do what it could to help the sister division. 14/10 Baluch was therefore ordered to operate in the thick jungle country, south of Hill 551, with the object of harassing the Japanese rear and, if possible, finding and cutting their line of communication. 14 Baluch carried out this task with great vigour and cunning and killed a large number of Japanese at negligible cost to itself.

During the morning of 4 May the original two platoons of C company of 2/7 Rajput which had attacked and taken the hill were relieved by the carrier platoon and one platoon of C company; this garrison on Rajput Ridge was christened Craiforce. In accordance with the pre-arranged programme, this force withdrew after completing the task and the new ground was taken over by the 53rd Indian Infantry Brigade of the 25th Indian Division. On the morning of 6 May, the position was handed over to 2/2 Punjab; the feature BUN was also handed over to this battalion, D company having defended this hill bravely in spite of heavy shelling and counter-attacks throughout the day and night. Their work finished, both companies returned to the rear headquarters for a well-earned rest. The Japanese in the meantime had withdrawn to the southern crest of Hill 551 and for the next few weeks 2/2 Punjab shared the feature with them. Life was not comfortable for Indian troops for, as the fighting season waned and the Indian divisions withdrew, the Japanese found fewer targets for their guns, and, therefore, 2/2 Punjab received their more concentrated attention. Hardly a day passed without 2/2 Punjab suffering casualties from the Japanese shells, and since the whole feature was under hostile observation, maintenance could only be conducted by night.

On 20 May in the early hours of the morning the Japanese

launched a counter-attack on the 2/2 Punjab position. Unfortunately the assault coincided with an inter-company relief which was in progress. The Punjabis were caught at a disadvantage and were driven back to the extreme north of the ridge; here, however, the Japanese were halted. Soon after day-break, 2/2 Punjab was attacking again; its thrust carried it beyond the original forward positions but it was prevented from seizing the whole feature on account of accurate fire from the Japanese medium machine-guns. In this action the Sikh company greatly distinguished itself.

At about the same time, the Japanese attacked the 25th Indian Division positions on the Spine, both north and south of the Tunnels area. 4 Royal Garhwal Rifles soon broke up the northern attack, while 14/10 Baluch made short work of the southernly party, driving the Japanese back down the hillside at the point of the bayonet and capturing a mass of equipment. Japanese documents show that this attack and the one on Hill 551 were part of the same operation in which the Japanese plan had been to recapture the "west" Tunnel by a three-pronged thrust.

The situation on Hill 551, however, remained unchanged until the first rains fell at the end of May, when the Japanese withdrew.

The West of the Range

The 51st Indian Infantry Brigade (25th Indian Division) meanwhile had not escaped the Japanese attention. Since the operations against the Spine had been discontinued, the role of this brigade had been mainly defensive. The divisional commander felt that the most dangerous move which the Japanese could make was an attack from the south on the Tunnels road, with the object of cutting his line of communication with the 53rd Indian Infantry Brigade. To guard against this, all possible avenues of approach had to be firmly held. One of these lay through the deserted village of Kanbyin, where 8/19 Hyderabad, with two companies of 17 Mahrattas under command, was in position. The Japanese apparently took exception to its presence and subjected it to regular artillery bombardment. On 18 May, this unit's "Command Post" received a direct hit and the battalion commander was wounded. Major K.S. Thimayya, G.S.O. II of the division, who had recently been posted as second-in-command of this battalion but had not yet taken over, at once went forward and assumed command. He was the first Indian officer to command a battalion in the 25th Indian Division.

The 74th Indian Infantry Brigade had been in divisional reserve (25th Indian Division) throughout the campaign and except for 14/10 Baluch its battalions had experienced little action. When the division had first entered Arakan, commando troops of 3 Special Service Brigade were operating in the coastal plain, several miles south of the divisional area. When these commandos were withdrawn in the middle of April, the Japanese had reoccupied the country they had vacated. The villagers of this area were friendly to the Allies and had often helped by giving information about the Japanese. This attitude of the villagers was resented by the Japanese who took their revenge by a number of brutal executions. This situation called for action and a clear chance was offered of disposing of these Japanese, who had dared to leave the shelter of the hills. The task fell to 6 Oxf Bucks who, on 6 May, carried out a raid in strength on the village of Thayegonbaung. The operation was supported by a troop of Grant tanks of 25 Dragoon Guards, while companies from 3/2 Gurkha Rifles and 16/10 Baluch covered the flanks. Unfortunately, owing to inaccurate information regarding the behaviour of the tide, the tanks were unable to ford the Godusara chaung. The raid nevertheless proceeded and achieved a large measure of success.

Monsoon dispositions—1944

The monsoon rains were soon due. Hence further actions were planned and considered with an eye to the future monsoon dispositions. It may be noted that the original task of the XV Indian Corps was briefly to establish a monsoon line along the axis of the Maungdaw-Buthidaung road, which was eventually to be held by the 25th Indian Division. From the very beginning, therefore planning had been in progress for the occupation of monsoon dispositions, keeping fully in view the difficulties which would be encountered in maintaining the division during the rains.

The topography of the area played a large part in finally deciding the actual positions to be occupied during the monsoon as well as the necessity of further operations, which were considered essential in achieving the overall object. There was only one pass over the Mayu range through which passed an all weather road: this was the Tunnels road, the fight for which has already been described. Its alignment had originally been made for a railway, but long before the Arakan campaign had started, this had been replaced by a road, partly of brick and partly of stone construction. Although it was narrow and in disrepair, it was capable of sufficient improvement to carry the traffic which was required for a division's maintenance. The Tunnels pass had therefore two great and important factors to recommend it; firstly, it was the only really worth while tactical objective between Bawli and Foul Point, and secondly, it was the only area the terrain of which was capable of maintaining a large force. Since the Arakan road ceased to be an all weather road, south of Bawli, maintenance behind Maungdaw had to be carried by water. This, however, presented no great difficulty as the Naf river offered a sheltered waterway between Tumbru and

GROUP OF FOUR OFFICERS

Lieut.-Colonel S. P. P. Thorat, Commanding 2/2 Punjab Regiment.

Lieut.-Colonel L. P. Sen, Commanding 16/10 Baluch Regiment.

Brigadier R. A. Hutton, Commander 51 Indian Brigade.

Lieut.-Colonel K. S. Thimayya, Commanding 1/19 Hyderabad Battalion.

Rajputs rest by a cool stream after capturing Hill 551.

Shell-blasted summit of Hill 551.

After capturing Hill 551 in the Mayu Range, Rajputs of the 26th Indian Division hew a path from the burnt hill side.

North Island—the little island just north of Maungdaw. The XV Indian Corps had, in this area, established the necessary administrative installations and suitable craft were available, though their number was limited.

The 25th Indian Division was, therefore, to occupy a position, similar to a bridgehead in hostile territory, with the object of holding firmly the valuable "Tunnels" defile and protecting the line of communication to it from the immediate beachhead area. The division's front looked inland or eastwards, as much as it did to the south, and the northern flank appeared at least as vulnerable as the other because it could be approached by the Ngakyedauk Pass, which had always been a favourite route of the Japanese.

The withdrawal of the other divisions in the XV Indian Corps was also taking place in easy stages. In April, the 7th Indian Division had been withdrawn for a brief but well earned rest before finally moving north to take a gallant part in the battle of Imphal. The 36th Indian Division had followed some weeks later while the 81st West African Division, having completed its task in the Kaladan Valley, marched straight through the Japanese lines and up the banks of the Kalapanzin river in its journey back to Chiringa. Finally, at the end of May 1944, the task on Hill 551 having been accomplished, the 26th Indian Division evacuated Buthidaung and marched north to the monsoon quarters in Taung Bazaar including the areas of Bawli, Tumbru and Cox's Bazaar.

With the departure of these forces the regrouping of the 25th Indian Division became essential. Firstly, the 51st Indian Infantry Brigade evacuated the localities south of the road and took up positions covering the northern flank at Nawrondaung and Waybin. The 74th Indian Infantry Brigade, on the other hand, was entrusted with the Maungdaw "Keep"; 14/10 Baluch was reverted to its own brigade and came down off the "Spine" to a position on the road between the Tunnels and Razabil, where it could cover the south flank, which had become exposed by the withdrawal of the 51st Indian Infantry Brigade. In the 53rd Indian Infantry Brigade, 2/2 Punjab had experienced an expensive and arduous time on Hill 551; hence it was withdrawn as the divisional headquarters battalion and its place was taken by 17 Mahrattas. Thus the battalions of the 53rd Brigade were so disposed that 4 Royal Garhwal Rifles was on the "Spine", astride the Tunnels, while 9 York and Lancaster and 17 Mahrattas were covering the eastern approaches to the north and south of the Tunnels road respectively. As for the artillery, 8 Field Regiment R.A. came into the Maungdaw "Keep" and 5 Indian Field Regiment was positioned in the 51st Indian Infantry Brigade area at Nawrondaung. The 27th (jungle) Field Regiment R.A., whose support to the infantry had been of the highest value and which had

had a tough time, was withdrawn to Chiringa to rest and reorganise on a 25-pounder basis.

The monsoon broke later than was expected and although there were showers from the end of May, the heavy rains did not come until 15 June. Now for the first time, the Allied troops were going to remain in Maungdaw, which was almost the limit of their exploitation during this campaign. The Japanese, on the other hand, did not see it fit to hold their ground and had therefore withdrawn to more distant monsoon quarters leaving the 25th Indian Division in undisputed possession of the country it had elected to hold.

Conclusion

A study of this campaign shows once again that the Japanese tried to out-manoeuvre and defeat superior forces by a boldly conceived and initially well-executed plan. They relied largely on bluff and determination and utilised to the full their numerous small deceptive operations. But this time the Japanese had failed and had been decisively defeated. Their attack had collapsed and all they had achieved was to disorganise the Allied arrangements for an advance; and at a cost of 6000 killed, all they had managed was to capture large quantities of British equipment, most of which could not be evacuated.

The Imperial forces did not react in the way that the Japanese expected and thus the latter were prevented from exploiting the considerable degree of tactical surprise which had been gained in the initial stages of the operation. That this was possible, was due principally to the better training of British and Indian troops and above all to the Allied ability, when necessary, to keep the troops supplied by air. Another plausible reason may have been that the Japanese had under-estimated their opponents from the beginning. It was perhaps this mistake that was chiefly responsible for the failure of their effort.

The skill and endurance of the Japanese commanders and their troops during this operation was shown to be of a very high order. Having succeeded in pushing the whole of the *Tanahashi Force* right through the XV Indian Corps left flank without contact, they had the advantage of more or less complete surprise in their initial attack; and once they got to grips with the opposing forces, they continued fighting without respite for sixteen days and nights. Their supplies were always low and on many an occasion, most of their units lived on yam and water only. Severe losses due to hard fighting appear to have had not much effect on the offensive spirit of the Japanese units; and at the end, the bulk of their forces, although completely exhausted and split into small bodies, managed to withdraw into their own lines, farther to the south.

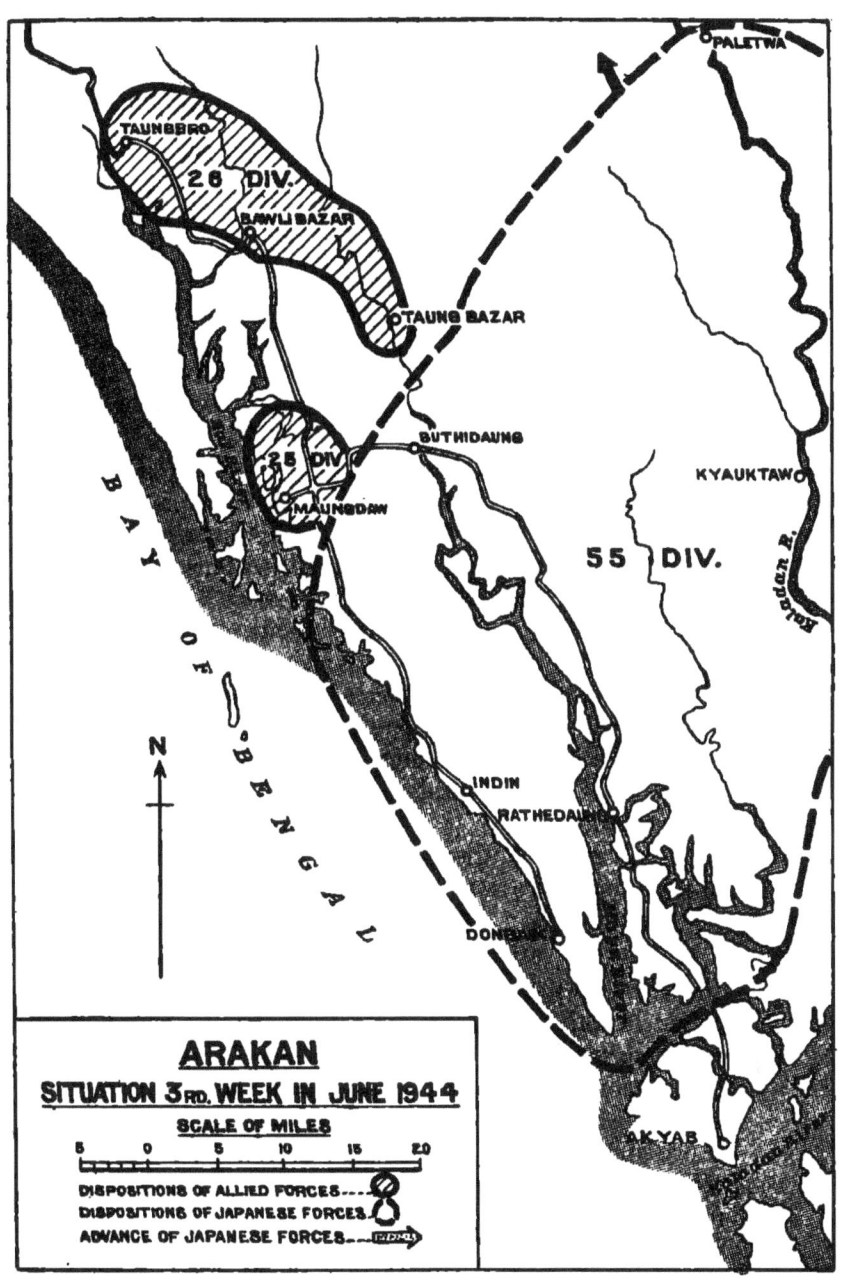

CHAPTER XII

The Monsoon Period—1944

About the middle of June 1944, the monsoon set in with full force making large scale operations in Arakan generally impracticable. As will be remembered, the climatic conditions during the monsoon and the topography of the country are such that human life can just about exist without indulging in the intricate and difficult art of warfare. The chaungs become flooded and the paddy fields and the so-called roads turn into an expanse of mud and water. There is hardly any month during this period which can safely boast of more than half a dozen dry days.

With the advent of the monsoon, the XV Indian Corps soon discovered that the Japanese had withdrawn the bulk of their troops and all their artillery, further to the south. Permanent garrisons, however, were left behind by them on certain features, such as Hill 1433. The rest of their forward troops seemed to be living a nomadic existence—digging a series of positions in various places and occupying them in turns. The Japanese patrol activity also appeared to have been mainly concerned with defensive missions for they rarely approached close to the Indian lines and seldom attempted to penetrate them. The initiative, therefore, lay with the troops of the 25th Indian Division, who were able to have just as much or as little fighting as they chose.

By the middle of June, the 25th Indian Division had occupied its monsoon positions and was the forward division of the XV Indian Corps in the Arakan area. The divisional Headquarters was in the Maungdaw area along with the divisional services while the three brigades were positioned as follows:—

51st Indian Infantry Brigade:
The Headquarters with the Brigade Signal Section and one platoon of Divisional Headquarter Battalion in the Kwelabinga area, north of the Maungdaw-Buthidaung road. 8 York and Lancaster in Waybin. 16 Baluch at 348451 and 8 Hyderabad at 354437.

53rd Indian Infantry Brigade:
The Headquarters with the Brigade Signal Section and one platoon of Divisional Headquarter Battalion at 41684015. 9 York and Lancaster at 429437. 2/2 Punjab at 430433 and 4 Royal Garhwal Rifles at 417417.

74th Indian Infantry Brigade :
Headquarters with Brigade Signal Section and one platoon Divisional Headquarter Battalion at Kanyindan. 6 Oxf Bucks also at Kanyindan. 3/2 Gurkha Rifles was in the area of "Razabil fortress" and 14/10 Baluch at 393496. 17 Mahrattas (the Divisional Headquarter Battalion) less three platoons was at Kaungdaw while most of the divisional artillery was in the area of North Island and Kayugyaung. The divisional engineers were mostly in Kayugyaung, Tunnels Road, Kanyindan, and Kwelabinga.

Although it was not known at the time, one of the main reasons for the reduced activity on the part of the Japanese was that the main body of the Japanese *55th Division*, which had been operating in Arakan since the beginning of 1943, had begun to withdraw to the Delta area in south-west Burma. It was to relieve the Japanese *2nd Division*, which in turn was being despatched to north-west Burma to re-inforce the Japanese forces which were not making much headway against the Fourteenth Army in the Assam operations. A detached force consisting of three infantry battalions, a cavalry regiment and some artillery under the command of Major-General Sakurai was left behind in Arakan to attempt to deceive the XV Indian Corps into believing that the whole division was still fighting. To give the impression of a big force, this detachment of Japanese troops—better known as *"Sakurai Detached Force"*—kept moving from one place to another, digging a series of positions at different places. In the Upper Kaladan Valley and across the Indian frontier at Mowdok and Singpa was a mixed force of *55th Cavalry* and *143rd Regiment* and the *1st Battalion* of Bose Brigade of the Indian National Army. Down south, the *54th Japanese Division* was spread over Akyab, Ramree and Cheduba islands.

Bolster Force

The XV Indian Corps in the meantime was breaking all the accepted rules of the campaign by continuing to fight during the rainy season. Patrol activity was increased and, irrespective of weather conditions, Indian and British soldiers were going out of their way to seek the Japanese and do as much damage as was possible.

At the end of June 1944, reports were received that the Japanese were raiding villages in the coastal plain in search of food and that atrocities were being committed if the food was not forthcoming. The Japanese were also reported to be carrying out reprisals on the villagers concerned whom they suspected of giving information to the Allies. On an appeal by one of the village headmen, the 25th Indian Division sent a platoon of 3/2 Gurkha Rifles to their aid, and

such immediate success attended this platoon's arrival that the divisional commander decided to maintain a force permanently in this area. This was done with the following two objects in view:—
- (a) to establish a base from which patrolling of the coastal plain could be carried out;
- (b) to protect the local population from Japanese raiding parties.

To achieve the above objects a task force from the 74th Indian Infantry Brigade was despatched to this area. It consisted of one company from 6 Oxf Bucks and one from 3/2 Gurkha Rifles with machine-gun and mortar detachments along with an artillery Observation Post. This force, under a single commander, was known as Bolster Force and, on 3 July, it took up permanent residence in the little village of Ponra. It had an administrative base a mile further to the west on the banks of the Naaf river, which was maintained as a miniature beach-head of its own. From this base, the Force was to prevent infiltration of Japanese patrols, north of the Ton Chaung into the general area, all inclusive Godusara, Lambaguna and Ponra, as well as to patrol the coastal plain with a view to protecting the local population from Japanese raiding parties. Although the sphere of its operations was limited by the range of artillery support from the Maungdaw base, the employment of a battery of heavy Ack-Ack guns in a ground role, with a reach of 19000 yards, gave this force all the elbow room it normally required to carry out its task. Within the first few days of its arrival it succeeded in killing some Japanese troops and capturing a few members of the Bose Brigade. Thereafter it dominated the whole area and lived amicably with the villagers.

Monsoon tasks

Except for patrol activity and a daily average of about three inches of rain, nothing of importance occurred during the month of July. However, the 25th Indian Division had to cope with two major landslides on the Maungdaw-Buthidaung road. Till the state of the ground permitted active operations, they were carrying out the following tasks as laid down by the XV Indian Corps:—
- (a) "hold present defensive areas
- (b) patrol vigorously
- (c) maintain and improve the 'Tunnels' road."

Although on a diminished scale due to heavy rains, offensive patrolling to dominate the coastal sector was also continued throughout this period.

The tasks of the 26th Indian Division during this normally inactive season were to:—
- (a) "hold present defensive areas

(b) patrol vigorously
(c) maintain and improve Goppe Pass road
(d) be prepared to re-inforce area Goppe-Gaung quickly by upto one battalion
(e) hold one brigade group in Corps reserve."

The 4th Indian Infantry Brigade was made the Corps reserve while the 71st Indian Infantry Brigade was ordered to hold one battalion at 12 hours' notice to move from Bawli Bazaar in order to carry out task (c).

The 81st West African Division, then resting at Chiringa, was told to:—

(a) "be prepared to re-inforce 1 Tripura Rifles with upto one battalion.
(b) watch approaches from the east within divisional area."

On 7 July, a small party of Japanese troops, probably a long range patrol, carried out a raid on a forward post on the 26th Indian Division front at Panzai Bazaar, to the north of Taung Bazaar. By immediate action, however, the party was chased out soon after it had raided the Indian post.

Activity in the Kaladan Valley

Throughout the monsoon period, activity in the Kaladan Valley was confined to deep patrolling by the Indian and British troops and in trying to arrest any penetration by the Japanese from that flank. During July, increased Japanese activity was noticed in the upper Kaladan and Sangu river valleys; a Japanese party was ambushed in the Mowdok area and heavy casualties were inflicted. During the last week of July, a Japanese patrol proceeded along the upper Kaladan valley upto a place about 35 miles north of Daletme, but soon after returned to its base. Again, on the night of 29/30 July, Indian patrols reported that a party of Japanese had arrived at Singpa, about 4 miles west-north-west of Mowdok.

This increased Japanese activity along the Kaladan and Sangu rivers was perhaps an attempt to cover their preparation of a forward base in the general area of Daletme, from where they hoped to attempt a raid on the area of the main Allied Arakan line of communication, during the early part of the next dry weather.

The month of August was spent in active patrolling of the Japanese forward positions by the Indian and British troops, but in the Kaladan valley, no further change took place and the Japanese continued to maintain their forward detachments in the Mowdok area. During this month, although the rains had begun to slacken, it was not before the middle of September that military operations on a large scale could be undertaken by either side.

Meanwhile, during the third week of August, Bolster Force, which had consisted of the units of the 74th Indian Infantry Brigade, was relieved by units of the 51st Indian Infantry Brigade, and the new composition was to work under the orders of the former brigade. One company each from 8 York and Lancaster and 8 Hyderabad with two 3" mortar detachments along with artillery support, formed the bulk of this Task Force. The 25th Indian Division Operation Instruction No. 21, dated 6 August 1944, laid down that this Force "will act offensively with strong fighting patrols against any Japanese parties located in the area. It will not operate into the hills East of the area, nor will it operate South of the Ton Chaung with the one exception that recce patrols when necessary may proceed to Hinthaya."

Operations against Hill 1433

When the monsoon had broken in full intensity, both the sides had to leave a part of the territory which they had previously held. Nevertheless, the XV Indian Corps commander had all the time kept in view the fact that on the approach of better weather conditions, a race between the two opposing forces might develop to re-occupy certain features of major tactical importance; he was therefore determined that his own troops would not be outwitted in this race. He also wished to enlarge the Maungdaw-Tunnels base so as to have room and security for the concentration and subsequent deployment of the large force which he intended to employ for the forthcoming offensive.

To this end, an operation was planned to take place in the middle of September. The objects of this operation were:—
    (1) to seize certain features on the "Spine", between the Ngakyedauk Pass and the Tunnels,
    (2) to capture Hill 1433, and
    (3) subsequently to re-occupy the positions in the western foothills, which had been vacated by the 51st Indian Infantry Brigade at the start of the monsoon.

In carrying out the first task, no opposition was expected, nor, in fact, was any encountered. The area involved was the responsibility of the 51st Indian Infantry Brigade, which, using 16/10 Baluch, completed the operation without any incident.

The story of Hill 1433 was, however, very different. The Japanese had continued to maintain a considerable force on this very vital feature (which had been named LION) and had also built a strong covering position on a feature called TIGER, which was some five hundred yards to the north of LION. In these positions, the Japanese were expected to put up a strong stand, for from these heights they had complete observation of Allied activity in the

Maungdaw plain to the west, as well as of Hill 551 and the surrounding country, east of the Mayu range.

In view of the stiff fight that the Japanese were expected and likely to put up, the 25th Indian Division commander made a deception plan to distract the former's attention from the "vital objective" and, if possible, to cause the Japanese to misplace their reserves. Bolster Force, which at this period was composed of troops from 6 Oxf Bucks and 2/2 Punjab, was still in occupation of the village of Ponra. The Divisional commander's plan, therefore, was to simulate the build-up of a brigade group in this area in order to mislead the Japanese into thinking that an advance south towards Myinhlut was intended. To create the right atmosphere, fresh camp sites were chosen and prepared and large administrative dumps (mainly of sand) were developed. River traffic was increased to suggest the maintenance of a bigger force than was already there, while the Divisional Signals were responsible for instituting wireless deception on a suitable scale.

Plan and capture of Hill 1433

On 26 August 1944, a warning order was received by 3/2 Gurkha Rifles to be prepared to carry out a special operation: it later proved to be the capture of the feature 1433 on the main spine of the Mayu Range. By 1 September, therefore, A company complete had been brought back from Bolster Force and D Company had relieved a company of 4 Royal Garhwal Rifles on Point 1267, which was about 2500 yards north of feature 1433. Also, from that date on, reconnaissance of the routes to the objective had started.

It was appreciated that the main spine of the Ranges dropped steeply down to ravines which were 1200 feet deep or more, and the sides of the Range were covered with dense jungle; movement through them, which was difficult enough under normal conditions, was further restricted on account of deep gorges, scoured out by incessant rain. The monsoon had made the whole area extremely slippery and constant mists restricted observation.

The difficulty experienced by 14/10 Baluch in the attempt to advance down the ridge had not been forgotten, and so when 3/2 Gurkha Rifles was entrusted with this task, the commanding officer of this battalion had different ideas for its execution. The hillsides were a little less steep on the east than on the west of Hill 1433, and reconnaissance patrols eventually confirmed the fact that it would not be possible to scale the cliffs from the west of this feature. The commanding officer's plan was, therefore, to form a "firm base" on a low jungle ridge, east of the feature, and from there launch company attacks up the eastern and southern slopes, while at the same time exerting pressure from the north, along the crest of the ridge itself. By this means he hoped to achieve surprise, attack the Japanese from an angle at which their fire power would be least effective and, infiltrating inside their position, be able to defeat their forces in detail. To add weight to this attack, a company of 17 Mahrattas was also placed under command, to be used for the protection of the east flank as well as the "firm base" thereby releasing more Gurkhas for the main attack.

By 5 September, the relief of 3/2 Gurkha Rifles in the Razabil area by 8/19 Hyderabad had been completed, and the former had established themselves in Point 1267 area. A reconnaissance was carried out and the "base area" was selected at 438374 : thereafter final orders for this operation were issued in the evening to all concerend.

On 6 September, an Advanced Dressing Station was opened in Point 1267 area and two Field Companies and the whole of the divisional artillery were placed in support of the battalion. Royal Air Force support was also arranged and porters from a pioneer company were provided for carrying stores. In the afternoon of the same day, the B company patrol which daily moved to HORSE, a feature about 200 yards north of TIGER, remained in occupation of that feature; at the same time, D company (less one platoon which was occupying NUTS) moved in fading light, on man-pack with an Observation Post and the battalion signal party to secure the "base area".

On 8 September, before day-light, A and C companies, each of which had an artillery Observation Post party, a small headquarter Regimental Aid Post, Assault Sections of the Indian Engineers and some battalion pioneers, moved on man-pack and concentrated in the "base area", without incident. Tactical battalion headquarters, Royal Artillery team and an additional Regimental Aid Post provided by the Advanced Dressing Station, moved to HORSE at dusk. B company, with one section of battalion 3" mortars under command, leaving one platoon behind on HORSE, moved to its "forming up" positions on the eastern slopes below TIGER. On the same day, one company (less one platoon) of 17 Mahrattas having been placed under command, moved to the "base area".

The attack was put in before dawn on 8 September 1944. It was raining and the hill tops were blanketed in low cloud. It was only because of the careful reconnaissance of the preceding days that the troops were able to scale the precipitous slopes and hit the proper objectives at the right time.

At 0200 hours A company advanced from the "base" followed by C company at 0230 hours; both the companies were lightly equipped in order to facilitate the scaling of the hillside in darkness. At 0500 hours the divisional artillery opened up on targets to the west of 1433; at the same time B company assaulted TIGER from the east, C company assaulted 1433 from the south, while A company attacked the same feature from the south-east. All these assault companies reached the crest of the "Spine" at the fixed time and occupied the allotted places.

A platoon of B company managed to enter the TIGER area but was driven out by heavy grenade and small arms fire just as its second platoon was entering, which in turn was also driven out. The Japanese were in far greater strength and in far better prepared positions on TIGER than had been expected. Consequently, the B company assault platoons suffered considerable casualties and the dead and wounded were brought back to the Regimental Aid Post on HORSE.

The two leading platoons of C company reached the crest of the "Spine" without incident and from there they assaulted towards Point 1433 at 0500 hours. Overcoming some bunker positions they were eventually pinned to the ground about 80 yards from the actual "Point" by heavy automatic fire; a number of casualties were suffered. At the same time the reserve platoon of C company with company headquarters encountered small arms and grenade fire from 1433 and was consequently checked for a while. As a result, this platoon could not reach the crest of the "Spine" until about 0600 hours. On reaching the crest, the company commander found his two assault platoons pinned just north of 1433, hence he decided that no further progress in that direction was possible. It appears that he decided to make a reconnaissance northwards towards TIGER where he thought that B company might have arrived, but while doing so he unfortunately lost his life. Within a few more hours C company lost all its officers and there was no news of it except of the small company headquarters party which remained in communication with the base area. On the assumption that C company had probably reached the crest, D company was moved during the morning from the "base" to C company headquarters in order to consolidate the positions already gained. The D company commander gradually located most of C company and relieved it in the forward positions, just north of Point 1433.

'A' company reached its assault position about 0430 hours. One platoon was immediately put into position to the south of 1433 as a "firm base". At 0500 hours the leading assault platoon attacked the hostile position on 1433 from the south. It overran the forward Japanese positions and later pressed on towards the summit of 1433; one section actually reached the summit but was driven back by heavy fire. The remainder of the platoon was held up about 50 yards from the top by medium machine-gun fire and grenades. The platoon then tried to work round to the west but the slope was precipitous and the Japanese were able to throw grenades on to it;

the second assault platoon trying to exploit to the east was also held up about 60 yards from the summit on its eastern side. The 1433 feature, like TIGER, proved to be far stronger than information had indicated; consequently, the company commander finding that he could make no further progress and having suffered a number of casualties, gradually withdrew his company into the "firm base", leaving one section in position about 50 yards from the summit on the southern side.

The distance between the positions held by 3/2 Gurkha Rifles on the north of 1433 was only 130 yards from the positions held to the south of it, and the Japanese on the crest of the feature were nearly encircled. At this stage A company commander reported that he had lost 40 to 50 men and asked for reinforcements and medical assistance. Later, however, on reviewing the situation he reported that he could hold on until the following morning.

It had been hoped that TIGER, assaulted by two companies from different directions, would fall and that a line of communication could be opened along the "Spine" towards 1433. As soon as it was realised that the assaults had failed, 93 and 425 Field Companies Indian Engineers, which had just completed a stretcher track to HORSE, were instructed to build a porter track to the "base area" and later develop it into a mule track.

At first light on 8 September 1944, the 17 Mahratta company (less one platoon) also had moved south-east from the "base" to secure the flank of the route of A company. The situation by the afternoon was therefore as follows:—

    B company was in HORSE area and pressing towards TIGER.
    The Japanese were holding TIGER.
    D company (less one platoon) and C company were just north of 1433.
    Japanese were on 1433.
    A company was just south of 1433.
    Base area was held by battalion details.
    17 Mahratta company (less one platoon) was south-east of the base area.

After reviewing the situation, the brigade commander ordered that the positions already secured would be held. The divisional commander in consultation with the brigade commander now made the following decisions: first, an additional company of 14/10 Baluch was allocated for the stiffening of the most southernly Gurkha company which had suffered many casualties and had a wide front to cover. Secondly, another company of 17 Mahrattas with the missing platoon of the first company was put in support, maintaining its original role. At this stage when elements of the three battalions were involved, the troops committed were formed into a composite force under the commanding officer of 3/2 Gurkhas and the force was called Bison Force. Also at this stage, since direct assaults on bunkers had proved costly, the divisional commander ordered that these should be discontinued in favour of a policy of encirclement and siege.

At first light on 9 September, the Baluch company advanced from the "base" to A company's position south of 1433 and A company (less one platoon) came back to the "base area". Throughout the day the "base area" was intermittently but ineffectively shelled by the Japanese while active patrolling was carried out in all directions by the sub-units of Bison Force. Thereupon it was decided to adopt a policy of softening the Japanese power of resistance, and arrangements were made to bring a 3.7″ Howitzer on to the "Spine" to strafe TIGER over open sites and to concentrate a 25 pounder battery on the same target. Meanwhile, battalion 3″ mortars continued regular fire on this feature and for the next two days active patrolling and the softening of TIGER continued.

On the morning of 12 September at 0500 hours, a feint attack on TIGER by parties of B company from the north and east, and D company from the south, was launched. It succeeded in drawing heavy small arms fire from the Japanese position which enabled the attacker to pin point the Japanese defensive positions more accurately. The clearing of the jungle by artillery and mortar fire had by then facilitated general observation on to TIGER. The feint attack later withdrew without incident.

Later at 0900 hours, patrols from the Baluch company just south of 1433, found the top of the feature unoccupied; thereupon the company immediately started consolidating on the main position. In the meantime D company sent two strong fighting patrols to discover whether the Japanese were still in position on TIGER. Some hostile fire was opened on them but it became clear that opposition had become very weak. The Japanese then withdrew from TIGER and could be seen moving rapidly westwards. On 12 September, therefore, five days after the beginning of this operation, the whole ridge was held by the 25th Indian Division. Thus ended the most difficult operation that this division had as yet been called upon to perform. Casualties had inevitably been heavy but a valuable prize was won because the Japanese had lost their best observation post and the closest patrol base to the Indian positions.

Bolster Force withdrawn

With the fall of Hill 1433, its satellite Hill 904 also fell into Indian hands. Meanwhile, the deception plan had also been achieving its object as the Japanese were showing increasing interest in the activities of Bolster Force, because no attempt to succour their troops on Hill 1433 had been made. They had once more brought their guns forward and on 13 September, the "administrative base" was heavily shelled, causing casualties as well as damage. Again, two days later, the Japanese launched a determined assault by night on the village of Ponra but the fire of artillery and infantry weapons of the defenders broke up their attack and they had to withdraw, leaving behind their dead and wounded. The following night they renewed their onslaught but with no better results.

While the Japanese were attacking the Ponra area, the 74th Indian Infantry Brigade was pushing southward in fulfilment of the third object of the plan of the XV Indian Corps. It was realised that the next vital feature to be taken was Point 109, on the Bawli-Indin road, south of Maungdaw. This hill had proved a valuable outpost when 16/10 Baluch had held it before the rains. It was situated north-east of Godusara village at the western entrance to a pass from Godusara to Sennyinbya. The ground lent itself to strong defence, as the Japanese had learnt to their cost in their ill-fated attack during the preceding April. Furthermore, with this feature as a "base", Indian patrols could keep a wary eye on Japanese activities in the western foothills and the garrison would be well placed to meet any Japanese offensive, directed to Maungdaw from the south-east. After having appreciated the situation, the operation to seize this feature began on 14 September and 6 Oxf Bucks was detailed to carry out this task. No serious opposition was encountered from the Japanese, but several pockets of resistance had to be liquidated by a series of minor, but none the less dangerous, operations and, by 16 September, Point 179 had fallen to the British troops.

By this move of 6 Oxf Bucks to Point 109, a much larger force was brought within the patrol range of the country in which Bolster Force was operating. Since this Force in the position then occupied by it had fully served its original purpose, the divisional commander decided to withdraw it; it was therefore sent back on 17 September 1944.

At about the same time, 14/10 Baluch sent out one of its companies on a special mission to the Kanbyin area. This small force was given the name of Bastion. Its task was to prevent Japanese infiltration northwards on to the road, or westwards towards the coastal plain and to discover by means of active patrol activity Japanese strength and intentions. This Force took up a permanent position on the feature, formerly known as GREEN TREE HILL of pre-monsoon fame.

Since the middle of August, the Allies had been receiving

reports from their intelligence sources that the Japanese *55th Division* was withdrawing from northern Arakan, leaving behind only a task force of all arms to cover the retreat. In order to gauge the true state of affairs, the Corps commander ordered the 25th Indian Division to undertake a comprehensive patrol programme to discover in detail the dispositions and strength of the Japanese forces and, if possible, to get identifications and prisoners. The commander further indicated that in view of the known Japanese situation, the troops participating in this operation should not hesitate to take considered risks.

Consequently, an operation called 'spread' was planned and the brigades of the 25th Indian Division were given definite tasks and areas. The 51st Indian Infantry Brigade was to search the country east of the positions as far as the Kalapanzin river; 16/10 Baluch was chiefly responsible for this duty. Further south, on the 53rd Indian Infantry Brigade front, 9 York and Lancaster was ordered to carry out a battalion sweep in the direction of Buthidaung. The 74th Indian Infantry Brigade was made responsible for the western foothills and the coastal plain, south of the Godusara chaung.

The result of all this patrolling, however, was, on the whole, disappointing. No prisoners were taken and although the information gained confirmed earlier reports, it also showed that wherever the Japanese were stationed, they were in reasonable strength and had put up strong defences. Identifications also showed that at least one battalion from each of the three regiments of the *55th Division* was still on the immediate front.

Situation in the Kalapanzin and Kaladan valleys

East of the Kalapanzin river, on the 26th Indian Division front, Japanese activity consisted of motor patrolling in the area, south-east of Taung Bazaar. And in the Kaladan Valley, information received at the end of September showed that the Japanese were still in occupation of the Mowdok area.

Until the first week of October, nothing of importance took place. The Indian force kept up its programme of deep patrolling of the entire front while a few patrol clashes took place, east of the Kalapanzin and on the coastal sector. In the first week of October, however, the Japanese put in a few half-hearted attacks on the 74th Indian Infantry Brigade positions, in the western foothills, south of the Maungdaw-Buthidaung road. But east of the Mayu Range, on the 53rd Indian Infantry Brigade front, patrols of 9 York and Lancaster penetrated as far south as Baguna, without encountering any Japanese; the latter, however, continued to hold their positions in the area Point 162—Sinohbyin "bulge". During the same period, two platoons from 14/10 Baluch, supported by artillery fire, launched an attack against a Japanese strong point in the western foothills, about two and a half miles north east of Godusara. They met with such heavy rifle and automatic fire that eventually they had to withdraw.

About this period, the Japanese made a daring attempt to capture Goppe Bazaar. The attack was launched in their customary manner of making a wide swoop round the flank to surprise the 26th Indian Division's forward posts in the rear. On 5 October, a Japanese force estimated at 600 strong, assembled in the area, north-east of Taung Bazaar. Having thus assembled on the left flank of the 26th Indian Division the force split up into two columns, one moving to the Goppe Bazaar area while the other, consisting of about 50 men, moved further north to the Panzai Bazaar area. During the nights of 5/6 and 6/7 October, the Japanese put in probing attacks on the 4th Indian Infantry Brigade positions at Panzai Bazaar. A company of 5/9 Jat was attacked but without success. During 6 October the column attempted to cross to the west bank of the Kalapanzin river at Goppe Bazaar, but was driven back. The Indian forces used mortar and artillery with devastating effect on such Japanese groups as were spotted by the patrols. This brisk patrolling on the part of 2/7 Rajput, 5 Jats and 1 Royal Garhwal Rifles foiled the plan of Japanese attack.

The Japanese plan which, to a large extent, was discovered through captured documents and marked maps and was pieced together, was based on very inaccurate information regarding the strengths and dispositions of the troops of the XV Indian Corps and was ambitious in the extreme. The plan showed that Major General Sakurai was in personal command of this "Task Force" and his intention was to destroy the Goppe and Panzai Bazaar garrisons before moving southwards in order to destroy the Indian troops, stationed at Taung Bazaar. In conjunction with this southward movement, small detachments from this "Task Force" were to operate across the Goppe Pass and harass the lines of communication, south of Bawli Bazaar.

It is interesting to note, from the information available, that the composition of this "Task Force" suffered from a lack of artillery, mortars and coolies and that only seven days' rations were carried by the troops. The plan having failed, an unusual feature of the operation was the speed with which the decision to withdraw was put into effect. This decision was, no doubt, caused by the unexpected strength of the Indian force and the heavy casualties sustained by the troops of the "Task Force", due to the use of artillery and mortar fire which the Japanese, without their own artillery and mortars, could not retaliate.

The withdrawing elements of the Japanese "Task Force" were

chased by the troops of the 4th Indian Infantry Brigade and a party of about 200 Japanese was located three miles north-east of Taung Bazaar. It was attacked by a company of 1 Royal Garhwal Rifles with artillery support. During the course of this skirmish, a portion of the Garhwal company got surrounded. These encircled troops, however, fought with great dash and courage and forced their way out at the point of the bayonet. Eventually, the Japanese after suffering heavy casualties, dispersed into the hills, further to the east.

While this brief action in the Kalapanzin valley was in progress, the 81st West African Division, which was deficient by a brigade throughout the campaign, had begun its advance into the Kaladan valley and had made the first move in the XV Indian Corps drive through Arakan. The first task of this division was to capture Singpa and Mowdok, which two places the Japanese had taken on 12 June 1944 and had thereby been in occupation of a bit of the Indian soil. On 1 October, the West African Division, which was concentrated in the area of Tukpui, three miles west of Mowdok, prepared to advance down the Kaladan valley. During the following days, the Japanese fell back from Singpa on to Mowdok; the latter was captured by the 1st Sierra Leone Regiment of the 6th African Brigade on 8 October. The opposition was very slight and immediately after this operation, the West Africans continued their southward drive to regain contact with the Japanese forces. By 18 October 1944, the last of the Japanese had been driven from the Indian soil.

The West African advance was thereafter resumed in three columns; the first moved along the Pi Chaung, the second along the Kaladan valley while the third took the route of an old jeep track, which was constructed during 1943 along the axis of the Palet Chaung. Good progress was made by all the columns and until 31 October very little opposition was met; only delaying positions were encountered which were all overcome. Eventually, these Allied troops reached the Japanese positions which were constructed as "stops" and were covering the main approaches to Paletwa. Though these "stops" in the upper Kaladan valley were pushed back to within three miles of Paletwa, the Japanese continued to offer stiff resistance in this sector.

Meanwhile, the column operating along the Pi Chaung was progressing well. It had continued its advance and by the first week of December, the forward troops of the west African Division had reached an area, 22 miles south of Paletwa, though a few Japanese pockets of resistance were still holding out further to the north.

Allied patrol activity

The main Allied front remained comparatively quiet except for artillery duels and intense patrol activity, throughout the second half of October and nearly the whole of November. Aggressive patrolling was mostly being done by which means it was learnt that the Japanese were thinning out and were generally withdrawing from their forward areas. Subsequently, it was reported that the information about their thinning out was in actual fact a move on the part of the Japanese to re-organise their positions. It was later comfirmed that the main body of the Japanese force had moved out of Arakan and the small force left behind was manoeuvring and doing its best to obscure that fact.

During the last week of October the Japanese evacuated their troops from Long Ridge, which ran north-south in the area, south-east of Taung Bazaar, and also withdrew from their positions along the Myaw Chaung, which they had held throughout the monsoon.

CHAPTER XIII

Allied Planning for the Post-Monsoon Operations—1944

While the XV Indian Corps was carrying out limited operations in Arakan, the Supreme Allied Commander, South-East Asia Command, had been attending a conference (Tolstoy II) held by the British Prime Minister in Cairo. After attending this meeting, Lord Louis Mountbatten came to Delhi on his way to Ceylon and held a meeting at 1130 hours on Sunday, 22 October 1944, at the Supreme Allied Commander's Rear Headquarters in Delhi. At this meeting he said that "he had returned through Delhi especially to meet the Commanders-in-Chief and the C-in-C, India in order to tell them of his conversations in Cairo." At this meeting he informed all those assembled that "in the course of the general discussion which ensued, everyone agreed that the first step must be to release military formations in Burma, to produce the necessary military force for an amphibious operation."

Back at his Headquarters in Ceylon the Supreme Allied Commander, at a meeting held on 28 October 1944, outlined the form in which proposals for the future strategy should be presented to the Chiefs of Staff. He said that "in the light of the discussions held on the various proposed operations, the overall long term objective for South East Asia was the capture of Singapore. Working backwards, it would therefore be necessary to obtain an advanced naval and air base which when developed could be used for further operations to the south, or, if necessary, to the north. For an amphibious operation to seize such bases, it would be necessary to release forces from Burma. This was best achieved by the early clearance of Arakan, culminating in the capture of Akyab."

On 4 November 1944, Headquarters South East Asia Command Operational Directive No. 22 was circulated for final consideration at the Supreme Allied Commander's meeting. This directive dealt with operations in Arakan and its object was as follows:—

To clear Arakan down to the line inclusive Akyab—Minbya as early as possible with a view to releasing
  (a) two divisions to replace reserves; and
  (b) certain administrative and engineer units for pre-monsoon operations, 1945.

On 15 November 1944, the XV Indian Corps ceased to form part of the Fourteenth Army and became an independent Corps, operating directly under the command of the newly formed Headquarters Allied Land Forces South-East Asia, which had replaced the Eleventh Army Group in the conduct of all land operations in the Burma theatre. On this date a new directive was issued, and the task of the XV Indian Corps was defined as that of clearing the Japanese from Arakan.

At this stage the XV Indian Corps Order of Battle included two Indian divisions, the 25th and the 26th, and two West African Divisions, the 81st (which consisted of two brigades only) and the 82nd which was still in India. Of these divisions, the 25th Indian Division was deployed in contact with the Japanese in their monsoon dispositions, in the general area of Maungdaw and the Tunnels on the Maungdaw—Buthidaung Road. The 26th Indian Division had been disposed throughout the monsoon with one brigade at the head of the Kalapanzin river in the area of Bawli, Taung and Goppe Bazaars, one brigade resting on the line of communication at Tumbru, and one brigade resting at Cox's Bazaar. It was to be withdrawn for rest during the first week of November, before undergoing intensive training to prepare it for a seaborne assault role, later in the campaign. Its place in the Kalapanzin valley and at the head of the Goppe Pass, was to be taken over by the 82nd West African Division, which had started arriving to join the Corps from India, and was concentrating at Chiringa.

In addition to these four divisions, there was also under the command of the XV Indian Corps the 3rd Special Service Brigade (later designated the 3rd Commando Brigade). This formation was concentrated at Teknaf and was responsible for the security of the Naaf peninsula, though at the same time it was gaining experience and assisting the 25th Indian Division by sending units across to the mainland, where they took their turn in the line and in patrolling the Maungdaw area, prior to the opening of the campaign. Also earmarked for the Corps were the 50th Indian Tank Brigade and the 22nd East African Brigade Group, neither of which was made available before December 1944.

The XV Indian Corps Plan

In broad outline the tasks which the Corps had to perform, were as follows:—

    (1) To clear the Japanese out of Arakan.
    (2) To capture Akyab and Kyaukpyu in time to provide adequate bases from which to supply the Fourteenth Army in its advance on Rangoon.
    (3) To kill as many Japanese as possible in the process.

The operation to carry out these tasks was given the code name of 'Romulus' and was planned with a geographical division of operations into two sectors: the Mayu sector and the Kaladan sector. The operations in each sector were planned in phases and were to begin in the Kaladan sector, where the 81st West African Division was to secure the general line of Bidonegyaungwa—Kaladan village by 1 December.

The first phase in the Mayu sector could not start until 11 December, but by that date, the area of operations was expected to have dried out sufficiently for armour and guns to move across country, and air support to be given from fair weather fields. The 25th Indian Division and the 82nd West African Division (which was to take over the Taung-Goppe area from the 26th Indian Division, prior to D Day) were therefore ordered to begin their advance on 11 December with the object of securing the general line Indin-Sinoh-Htizwe by 31 December.

The second phase in both sectors was to be completed by 14 January 1945. In the Mayu area, the 25th Indian and the 82nd West African Divisions were to secure the area of Foul Point-Kudaung Island and also the line of the road from Htizwe to Apaukwa. In the Kaladan sector, the 81st West African Division had the task of securing the area of Kyauktaw-Thayettabyin-Teinnyo-Apaukwa.

In the Kaladan sector, the third phase was the relief of the 81st West African Division by the 82nd West African Division which was to move over the Htizwe-Apaukwa road and release the 81st West African Division to proceed into Corps reserve, as soon as Myohaung was captured.

The third phase in the Mayu sector was to be the mounting of Operation 'Talon'—a name given to the seaborne assault of Akyab island. This operation was to be carried out by the 26th Indian Division with the 3rd Special Service Brigade under command. D Day for this operation was originally fixed for 18 February but was later advanced to 20 January. The island was to be completely occupied by 31 January 1945.

The most detailed planning and intensive training of the Royal Navy, Army and Royal Air Force formations involved was to precede the operations, and every effort was made to ensure success for this first major amphibious operation carried out in the Burma theatre. As it eventually turned out, the initial successes of Operation 'Romulus' were so far in advance of expectations that Operation 'Talon' ultimately proved to be unnecessary and the available resources were thus freed for employment elsewhere.

The fourth phase of this operation, as originally planned, had the same objective in both sectors of the operation, namely, exploitation by the 26th Indian Division and the 82nd West African Division to the line Minbya-Myebon, by 28 February 1945.

The units, participating in this operation, were ordered to carry out the following tasks:—

81st West African Division: It was to continue its drive down the Kaladan valley by advancing from Paletwa to Myohaung.

82nd West African Division: It was to capture Buthidaung first, then cross the Kalapanzin river and advance south to Htizwe. On arrival at Htizwe, the division was to move east over the Kanzauk Pass into the Kaladan valley where it would relieve the 81st West African Division, which had the task of clearing this valley as far as Myohaung, after which it was to come into the Corps reserve at Chiringa, for eventual shipment to India. The 82nd West African Division, on the other hand, would take over the advance from Myohaung, southwards to Myebon.

25th Indian Division: It was to clear the Mayu peninsula and Mayu valley with the 82nd West African Division acting as left flank guard along the general axis of the Mayu river as far as Htizwe, with the object of seizing Foul Point and Kudaung Island as soon as possible.

26th Indian Division: With the 3rd Commando Brigade under command, it was to make a seaborne assault to capture Akyab and consolidate the whole of the island. It was then to advance north-east through the chaung country and exploit to the line Minbya-Myebon, where it would link up with the 82nd West African Division.

22nd East African Brigade: On arrival, it was to come under the direct command of the XV Indian Corps and was to be placed initially in Corps reserve at Chiringa. Here it was to be readily available to secure any part of the line of communication against a counterhook or outflanking movement by the Japanese, which might interfere with the operations of the forward divisions, or prejudice the security of airfields.

81st West African Division Plan

Having occupied Mowdok on 9 October 1944, the two brigades of the 81st West African Division were faced with an advance south down the river valley of more than 60 miles through very difficult, mountainous and thickly jungle-clad country, in order to reach their first objective, the line Bitonegyaungwa-Kaladan by 1 December, a period of only seven weeks.

The Japanese strength opposing this African Division was known to consist of the *55th Cavalry Regiment*, one company of the *143rd Regiment* and the 1st Battalion of the Bose Brigade of the Indian

National Army. Provided that there was simultaneous pressure on the Mayu front, it was considered that this would be the maximum infantry force that the Japanese would deploy against the African Division in the Kaladan, north of Kyauktaw. Were this the case, then the 81st West African Division would have a numerical superiority of two to one. It was also to have two batteries of mountain artillery under command which would give it, at least in the first phase of the advance, a two to one superiority over the Japanese artillery. However, the offensive employment of both air and artillery was unlikely to be fully developed until this division, having cleared the very thick country through which it would pass in the early stages, had reached the more open terrain of the Lower valley. There was also no possibility of tanks joining this division in the early stages, nor in fact until it had secured the eastern end of the Htizwe-Kenzauk pass, nor was the support of fighting rivercraft yet forthcoming. The Japanese were in a position to employ such craft, but in view of past experience it was considered unlikely that they would attempt to do so until the low ground had been reached.

The line of the 81st West African Division's advance was to follow the grain of the country which facilitated forward movement but hampered any lateral movement. The Axis of the advance followed two main valleys, namely those of the Kaladan river and the Pi Chaung. North of a line from Wabyin along the Pi Chaung to Khabaw on the Kaladan, valleys are narrow and thickly wooded; the country was therefore favourable for the Japanese to adopt delaying tactics. South of this line the valleys widen and the hills become gradually lower until they unite some miles north of Kyauktaw and become one wide valley, largely open and cultivated. In this lower portion of the valley, therefore, the country was less suitable for delaying tactics and favoured the construction of air strips to assist the African Division in its advance.

In the matter of communications the Japanese had a heavy advantage in holding the mouth of the river, as they also had in their possession the road south from Kyauktaw to Myohaung. It was, therefore, practicable for them to carry out rapid concentration from the south, if they were prepared to weaken their forces in the Mayu sector. The Htizwe-Kanzauk track, still wholly in Japanese territory, was reported as being fit for jeeps with a little work on it. Nevertheless, against these Japanese advantages in communications, the fact that the 81st West African Division was to be wholly maintained by air, placed the latter in a very flexible and advantageous position which more than counter-balanced the lack of good ground communications.

In making his plan, the Divisional Commander of the 81st West

African Division had a number of courses open to him. The possibility of making a simultaneous advance down the two main valleys had all the normal advantages of a wide frontal advance; but with only two brigades under command there would be an inevitable lack of depth and a danger of defeat in detail, which caused this course to be discarded. An advance down both the valleys but not simultaneously, with the non-advancing brigade maintaining a firm base including a bridgehead into the valley of the advancing brigade, had the advantage of largely obviating the disadvantages of the simultaneous advance of both brigades and, it was presumed, would also keep the Japanese in a state of perpetual uncertainty. But this would have involved the covering of a great deal of additional ground and the possibility of splitting up the "back stop" brigade, in the event of its having to move to the assistance of the leading brigade in the other valley. This plan, although feasible, was far from simple. There was also to be considered the possibility of using only one of the two valleys as the axis of advance (selecting the Pi Chaung, as this presented the most direct and the quickest route to Kyingri, where the first Dakota strip was to be opened), and of leap-frogging the two brigades down this route, leaving only detachments in the Kaladan valley to safeguard the eastern flank. This course was believed to provide depth and freedom of movement and would have given a periodical rest to each brigade in turn, which was not possible in a parallel advance down both the valleys. This course, however, had the disadvantage of lacking in surprise as it was one which the Japanese would probably expect the 81st African Division to select in order to secure Kyingri. It was also thought that a very considerable detachment would have to be left in the Kaladan valley. For these reasons this course was also not adopted. Another course open to the Divisional Commander was of leap-frogging both brigades down the Kaladan valley and leaving a protective detachment in the valley of Pi Chaung. This plan had all the advantages of the previous one except that it was not the most direct route to Kyingri. It had the added advantage in that a greater force than in Pi Chaung could be developed as smaller protective detachments would be adequate to protect the west flank. At the same time there was more scope for the construction of air strips which would ease the problem of casualty evacuation. This plan was consequently adopted as the most feasible and advantageous under the circumstances.

25th Indian Division Plan

As will be remembered, the operations in the Mayu sector were the responsibility of two divisions; the 25th Indian Division was to clear the Mayu peninsula upto Foul Point and occupy Kudaung island while the 82nd West African Division was to make a parallel advance east of the Mayu Range and down the axis of the Kalapanzin-Mayu rivers, thereby fulfilling the task of protecting the left flank of the 25th Indian Division, in addition to clearing the Japanese from the Kalapanzin valley and opening up the Pass from Htizwe to Kanzauk, in the Kaladan valley. In the phased programme, planned for operation 'Romulus', the advance of the 81st West African Division in the Kaladan valley began considerably before D Day in the Mayu sector; it can be said to have begun on 9 October, the date on which the division captured Mowdok. On the other hand, D Day for the Mayu advance was planned for 14 December. It will be seen that in effect the beginning of phase one in the Mayu sector was coincident with the completion of the first phase in the Kaladan area.

When the 81st West African Division began its advance early in October, there was much preparation to be carried out in the Mayu peninsula, before any operations could be undertaken. The 82nd West African Division had still not completely arrived from India while the 25th Indian Division was in a state of reshuffling and re-grouping. Moreover, the 25th division suffered a heavy blow in the breakdown of the health of its Commander. Major General H. L. Davies, CB, CBE, DSO, MC (late Royal Garhwal Rifles) had till now, formed and trained the division, and guided it in its critical battles to date; and in spite of failing health, had brought it through the trying conditions of the monsoon with its morale unimpared. But now, a change was considered necessary. On 14 October, therefore Major-General G. N. Wood, OBE, MC, arrived in Maungdaw and took over the command of the 25th Indian Division, and one of his first tasks was to make certain readjustments in the divisional layout. The 53rd Indian Infantry Brigade had spent the whole of the monsoon in the Tunnels area where conditions had been very unpleasant, and the patrolling programme heaviest. The advent of mobile operations demanded that each brigade should be one hundred per cent fit. A few days before the new commander's arrival, 9 York and Lancaster had been withdrawn to Nhila for a period of rest on the suggestion of the Corps commander. In order to give the remainder of the brigade as far as possible the same facility, a relief was carried out between the 53rd and 51st Indian Infantry Brigades and the change over was completed on 22 October.

As the Corps commander had planned to move an increased number of administrative installations in the Maungdaw "Keep", to be ready for the forthcoming operations, all troops of the 25th Indian Division which were in Maungdaw, Kanyindan and Kwelabinga, were ordered to quit before the end of the month. Divisional headquarters therefore moved to Razabil and the 74th Indian Infantry Brigade started to spread further south in the coastal plain.

The 51st Indian Infantry Brigade at this time consisted of three Indian battalions, each under an Indian commanding officer and had the distinction of being the first brigade of the Indian Army to be so constituted.

The Divisional commander's object, that of clearing the whole of the Mayu peninsula and securing Kudaung Island, had many implications. The most important of these was that the vital area of Maungdaw and the Tunnels Road to Buthidaung and the Kalapanzin river to the east, once secured, must at all times be firmly protected against any possibility of Japanese interference. The second was that as many Japanese in the Mayu peninsula as possible must be brought to action and destroyed and as few as possible allowed to escape to reinforce the Japanese formations, south of the peninsula. Since any land lines of communication which the Indian Division might use near the Mayu spine would be insecure, the division's supply system would have to be based partly on the sea and partly on the Kalapanzin waterway from Buthidaung; any deficiency thereafter would have to be met by air supply. Finally, it was appreciated that a speedy advance down the Kalapanzin river and the country to the east of the Mayu Range would disrupt the Japanese communications and cut their line of retreat in that direction.

The general topographical considerations which governed the plan of operations were, first, the existence of the secure water lines of communication provided by the western seaboard, where chaung mouths made excellent harbours for Inland Water Transport craft and where the open beaches, which could be supplied from a Forward Maintenance Area on St. Martin's Island, were well suited for discharging these craft. On the eastern side of the spine, the Mayu river made an excellent line of communication, once Buthidaung had been secured as a roadhead, and the necessary craft and boats introduced. This entailed moving some 700 boats in lorries or on transporters through the Tunnels. The western coastal plain which was flat and considerably intersected by tidal chaungs, extended as far south as Myinhlut where it narrowed to a defile lending itself to defence by the Japanese who were known to have prepared strong positions at Indin and Donbaik.

The Mayu spine itself had to be excepted as being eminently a Japanese country in which it would probably take a considerable amount of time to destroy them. It was also considered that in the event of the 25th Indian Division attempting to pass a force down each side of the spine, the hills would present a particular difficulty by acting as a screen against wireless communication between the two lines of advance. They would also provide the Japanese with most valuable observation posts from which they could overlook any day movement made by the troops of the 25th Indian Division. Then, again, there had to be considered the all-important security of the Base Area comprising Maungdaw, the Tunnels Road to Buthidaung and the northern passes, Ngakyedauk, the Maunghnamas and Goppe.

Since, in the past, the Japanese had proved very sensitive to any attempt at an advance made by Allied troops down the coastal plain, it was now planned to implement a deception by carrying out small seaborne raids on the coast prior to D Day and to carry out reconnaissances in force into the Alethangyaw area.

To advance on the whole front from the sea to the Kalapanzin would have removed the threat to the Base area and lines of communication, but would have involved slow and laborious operations in the centre of the peninsula where the "Spine" area added to the difficulties by being an ideal "natural defence" from the point of view of the defenders. Further, such an advance would have given no chance of destroying the Japanese, but would have merely forced them back on to a shorter line, and eventually into Akyab. The alternative of only advancing down the sea coast and the "Spine" would have had substantially the same result as any advance over the whole front, and would have constituted no threat to the Kalapanzin line of communication. The third course, of taking no offensive action in the "Spine" or coastal belt but heavily defending the Base Area while thrusting strongly down the Kalapanzin alone, was attractive, but impolitic from considerations of supply and communications.

The course finally selected was to move simultaneously one brigade group down the coast, supplied by sea, and one brigade group down the Kalapanzin. The Kalapanzin Force was to use rafts and river craft for its first line transport. At the same time a strong covering force was to be maintained to protect the Base Area from which mobile columns could be found, first for very active patrolling and later for mopping up the "Spine" area. This course would also ensure the employment in an offensive role of the maximum force which could be administratively maintained. At the same time it would allow the 25th Indian Division to fight on the ground of its own selection and suitable for its superior armament and mobility. The tactics employed would aim at by-passing any concentration in strength by the Japanese, after which the brigade group left in defence of the Base Area could be ordered to press south and mop up isolated Japanese troops in detail.

This plan had every advantage from the administrative angle

also since the brigade advancing down the west side of the "Spine' could be fully maintained from the sea and need leave no road line of communication behind it which would be open to attack by the Japanese, overlooking it from the hills inland. An essential element of this selected course of action was the rear and eastern flank protection and support to be given by the 82nd West African Division on the axis of the Kalapanzin river, since there were still some Japanese forces in the Taung Bazaar area. This would also entail the closest co-operation between the two divisions.

The appreciation of Japanese opposition was as follows: Through intelligence reports, it was gathered that the Japanese forces were divided into two groups. The *Matsu Force* was operating in the Kaladan valley under the command of Major-General Koba, the General Officer Commanding of the *54th Division Infantry Group*. It consisted of one regiment of cavalry, one battalion of infantry, one battalion of the Indian National Army, a company of engineers and two companies of artillery—in all about 2500 men. On the other hand, the force on the Mayu front was commanded by Major General Sakurai, the General Officer commanding of the *55th Division Infantry Group*. As a result of losses suffered at the battles of Taung and Goppe Bazaar, Hill 1433 and air offensive sweeps in the coastal belt, it was considered that this force comprised some 1800 men only. At this stage the Allies also expected that both these Japanese forces were intent on delaying their advance as long as possible and that eventually the latter would fall back on Akyab which was garrisoned by part of the *54th Division*. It was appreciated that though the Japanese had little use for this port themselves, they would put up a stiff fight to deny its use to the Allies as a forward base. As far as could be ascertained the island's garrision at this time comprised a Regiment of infantry less detachments and a company of artillery, with some air defence troops.

The plan of the 25th Indian Division, therefore, was for the 74th Indian Infantry Brigade to advance down the coastal plain on the west of the Mayu peninsula, cutting its tail as it went and being supplied by Inland Water Transport Craft from the sea; simultaneously, the 53rd Indian Infantry Brigade was to advance down the Mayu valley, being supplied by air until such time as the Kalapanzin river could be opened for maintenance through Inland Water Transport. The 51st Indian Infantry Brigade was to follow up later and mop up the Japanese pockets in the Mayu hills which had been by-passed by the other two brigades. The essence of the plan lay in the refusal to present General Sakurai with his favourite target of a vital maintenance road and in the fact that each brigade group was strong enough to deal with any concentration of force which may be brought against it.

Plan of the 74th Indian Infantry Brigade—The Order of Battle as finally selected for this brigade was:—

Headquarters, Signals and LAD Comd—Brigadier J.E. Hirst D.S.O. 74 Indian Infantry Brigade
6 Oxf and Bucks
14/10 Baluch
3/2 Gurkha Rifles
One platoon 7/16 Punjab Regiment
8 Field Regiment R.A.
One battery less one troop—6 Medium Regiment R.A.
93 Indian Field Company
35 I.C.P. R.I.A.S.C.
39 Animal Transport Company less detachment
Detachment 68 G.P.T. Company R.I.A.S.C.
One company 61 Indian Field Ambulance
A.W.D. 76 Indian Infantry Workshop Company
One section 25 Indian Division Recovery Company
Detachment 25 Indian Division Provost Unit
Detachment 606 Field Security Section
Detachment V Force.

It was known that down the west of the Mayu peninsula there was a rough fair-weather motor-road leading as far south as the Mayu Chaung and that beyond this the beach was suitable for mechanised transport. The Brigade Commander's plan, therefore, was to form a compact brigade group on a mechanised transport basis which could advance along the existing routes. As speed was a vital factor since Foul Point had to be captured by 15 January 1945, the Brigade commander decided to move his force as close to the sea as possible, thereby skirting the Japanese positions which were known to be sited in the foothills. But this could not be easily managed south of Gyindaw as beyond that point the coastal plain was very narrow, and the Japanese might well be expected to make a fight for the Kyaukpandu defile. East of Kyaukpandu was a pass which crossed the Mayu Range about which the engineer intelligence suggested that it would be possible to make a road fit for 15-cwt trucks at this point. Hence the Brigade commander came to the conclusion that he must force the Kyaukpandu defile, whatever the cost, and that even if the Japanese were to prove stubborn farther south, he could still maintain the mobility and momentum of his advance by transferring part of his force to the east of the Range.

Although the allotment of artillery to this brigade was generous, the commander readily accepted the offer of two destroyers for bombardment support; he considered that these would be invaluable for shelling such Japanese positions in the hills as were defiladed from his own guns. The destroyers allotted were the *"Napier"* and *"Nepal"* of the Royal Australian Navy under command of Captain Buchanan R.A.N.

Plan of the 53rd Indian Infantry Brigade—The order of Battle as finally selected was as follows:—

    Comd—Brigadier A.G. O'Carroll Scott, OBE
    H.Q., Signals and L.A.D. 53 Ind Inf Bde
    9 Y & L
    17 Mahrattas
    4 Royal Garhwal Rifles
    One Company and one platoon 7/16 Punjab Regiment
    One battery of 27 Field Regiment R.A. (less one troop)
    34 Indian Mountain Regiment (19 and 33 Batteries)
    Mortar battery of 7 Indian Anti-Tank Regiment
    4/25 Indian Field Company
    58 Indian Field Ambulance (less one company) with 6 Mobile Surgical Unit
    34 I.C.P. R.I.A.S.C.
    18 Animal Transport Company R.I.A.S.C.
    Detachment 25 Indian Division Provost Unit
    A.W.D. 76 Indian Infantry Workshop Company
    Detachment Field Security Section
    Detachment 'V' Force.

This brigade was faced with a harder problem than fell to the lot of the 74th Brigade. No road existed down the east of the Mayu Range and such tracks as did exist, ran along the foothills where the Japanese had sited their defences. As speed was equally important, it involved by-passing a lot of opposition. The brigade commander, therefore, was ordered to forge the use of mechanised transport and to make the Kalapanzin river the axis of his advance and boats his main means of transportation.

These craft had to be assembled on the west coast and launched at Buthidaung which was still in Japanese hands. Instead of waiting for the fall of Buthidaung, which was the first objective of the 82nd West African Division, the Brigade Commander decided to start on a mule-borne basis with Seinnyinbya as his objective. He thought that the opposition which he would meet would occupy his time until his boats reached him. After this, he proposed to send back the bulk of the mules but to retain a sufficient number to enable him to operate at a distance from the river, should the need arise. His boats were to carry the entire stores of the brigade group and also the 25-pounder guns ; as a secondary role they could be used to transport infantry from the west to the east bank of the Kalapanzin river, as and when the tactical situation so demanded. The infantry was to advance by bounds along the banks of the river and the flotilla was to follow behind, closing up as successive bounds were made good.

His ultimate objective was Foul Point and he expected to make Myinbu his last bound before his final attack.

The chief task during the planning period was therefore to procure sufficient number of boats and to arrange for their transportation to Buthidaung. In all, nearly 650 craft of various types and load capacities were required; large rafts for mules, guns and other heavy baggage, assault boats, life-boats, "Sampans" and canoes. 400 country craft were purchased from local civil sources and about 100 lorries and transporters were used to convey the fleet to Buthidaung, a two-way road was cut for the purpose and special traffic control was set up. Finally, local caulkers were brought forward to assist the Sappers in making the boats sea-worthy after the inevitable damage in the road transit. This last aspect of the operation was primarily an engineer concern and was well executed.

Since the administrative plan was based on air supply, the brigade commander decided to take an air drop every third day, because he felt that this would least impede the rate of his advance. He also had it in mind that at a later stage when the Japanese had been driven south and were no longer a threat to the Kalapanzin river, the Maintenance would revert to inland water transport channels from a Field Supply Depot (F.S.D.) at Buthidaung.

Plan of the 51st Indian Infantry Brigade.—The final Order of Battle was as follows:—

    Comd.—Brigadier R.A. Hutton, O.B.E., D.S.O.
    H.Q., Signals and L.A.D. 51 Ind. Inf. Bde.
    2/2 Punjab
    16/10 Baluch
    8/19 Hyderabad
    One platoon 7/16 Punjab Regiment
    One battery 27 Field Regiment R.A.
    7 Indian Anti-Tank Regiment (less two batteries).
    63 Indian Field Company
    33 I.C.P. R.I.A.S.C.
    One company 56 Indian Field Ambulance
    A.W.D. 77 Indian Infantry Workshop Company.

In addition to the above the support of the corps Artillery Group and of one squadron of 19 Lancers was also promised to the brigade. It was, however, difficult for the commander to make his plans in advance for they depended entirely on the Japanese reaction to the progress of the other two brigades. Until he was relieved by the 22nd East African Brigade, his hands were tied, but the Japanese on Hill 1440 were within hitting range and so he proposed to do them harm. After his relief, he intended to follow the 74th Indian Infantry Brigade down the west of the "spine", carrying out such sweeps eastwards as occasion demanded.

The Role and Plan of the 82nd West African Division

The third division to take part in the general advance at the beginning of operation 'Romulus' was the 82nd West African Division. Unlike the 81st West African and the 25th Indian Divisions, it was new to the XV Indian Corps and unfamiliar with the country in which it was to operate. Furthermore, it was as yet untried in battle.

The first brigade of the division to arrive in the operation zone was the 2nd West African Brigade which began to concentrate in Taung Bazaar on the Kalapanzin, on 8 November. By the 11th, the concentration was complete and the brigade assumed responsibility for the Kalapanzin area. The 36th Indian Infantry Brigade of the 26th Indian Division was thereby released, and was able to rejoin its parent unit at Rejukhal, south of Cox's Bazaar, where it concentrated for training and rest.

On 29 November, the 4th West African Brigade arrived, together with divisional headquarters, which was established at Razabil in the 25th Indian Division base area. The 4th West African Brigade proceeded at once to Taung Bazaar and relieved the 2nd West African Brigade, which in turn came down to concentrate near the divisional headquarters at Razabil. By 8 December, the 1st West African Brigade had also arrived in the Razabil area.

It was intended that this African Division should form up to carry out its tasks with two brigades in the Tunnels area on the Maungdaw-Buthidaung road from where they would start their offensive on D Day, assisted initially by the 25th Indian Division. The third brigade was to be used for the defence of Taung Bazaar and the upper Kalapanzin until the threat of a right hook by the Japanese had been dispelled by the advance of the 81st West African Division. The date of the release of this third brigade was to depend on the Corps Commander's personal decision.

The nature of the country and the topographical and communication problems which this division had to face, had made it apparent that its most serious concern was the possibility of a right hook by the Japanese between its own eastern flank and the 81st West African Division in the Kaladan—a form of tactics in which the *55th Japanese Division* had particularly specialized. The road as well as the river lines of communication were, throughout their links, vulnerable to infiltration from the east, and it was impossible to deny the Japanese observation over either of them. It was, therefore, essential to plan a course of action by which this division's advance would progressively hold firm bases and "stops" at the more important vulnerable points along its axis of advance.

The 1st and 2nd West African Brigades were to form up in the Tunnels area along with the headquarters of the division. As this forming up line was within the 25th Indian Division's area, the close proximity of the two divisional headquarters made possible the close liaison which was necessary for the success of the coming operation. The third brigade of the division—the 4th West African Brigade—was already in the Taung-Goppe area and was to remain there until released.

Prior to D Day, the 51st Indian Infantry Brigade of the 25th Indian Division was to assault and occupy the features known as "POLAND" and Point 142. The capture of these features would then enable the 2nd West African Brigade to advance down the road to Buthidaung while the 1st West African Briagde would advance further south upon Baguna. The latter brigade was then to cross the Kalapanzin river and make for "VITAL CORNER" as one of its first objectives on the east bank. The capture of this feature was of special interest to the 25th Indian Division as it dominated the river and the 53rd Indian Infantry Brigade "flotilla" could not sail while it was still in Japanese hands. The plan was that when the 1st West African Brigade had been firmly established, the 4th West African Brigade would drive down upon it from its position, south of Taung-Goppe area—acting like a hammer on the 1st West African Brigade anvil. Subsequently, the 1st Brigade would be left at Buthidaung for its protection while the remainder of the division would advance along the road (through Kindaung) towards Htizwe. The rate of advance of this division was to be closely co-ordinated with that of the 53rd Indian Infantry Brigade in order that this division's task of protecting the left flank of the Indian brigade could be effective. Eventually, the 82nd West African Division was to cross the intervening hills into the Kaladan valley and there link up and relieve the 81st West African Division.

Role of the 50th Indian Tank Brigade

The XV Indian Corps had been allotted the 50th Indian Tank Brigade for the season's operations. The brigade arrived in the forward area during the first week of December 1944 and was concentrated initially at Wabyin, north of Maungdaw. The Brigade Order of Battle comprised:

- 146 Regiment R.A.C. (The Duke of Wellington's Regiment with Lee/Grant tanks)
- 19 Lancers I.A.C. (with Sherman tanks)
- 45 Cavalry I.A.C. (with Stuart tanks)
- The 2nd Battalion of the 4th Bombay Grenadiers (Motor Battalion).

The Arakan terrain over which the XV Indian Corps was to operate was not suited for even small-scale armoured manoeuvre, principally on account of the great number of impassable natural tank obstacles. The tanks had, however, previously been of great use in very close support of infantry assaults and had excelled themselves in "bunker busting" roles. In view of these considerations, it was decided that though the topography of the area would not make it possible to operate tanks east of the Kalapanzin river, they would be useful in supporting roles in the Mayu sector, to which only they were allocated.

One squadron of Stuart tanks of 45 Cavalry was placed in support of the 51st Indian Infantry Brigade (25th Indian Division) to protect the Maungdaw-Tunnels base area. 19 Lancers less one squadron was held in corps reserve, to be asked for by the 25th Indian Division as additional tank support. On this reserve, one squadron was earmarked to operate if required in support of the 74th Indian Infantry Brigade in its coastal advance.

The 82nd West African Division was initially allotted the remaining squadron of 19 Lancers, to operate in support of the 2nd West African Brigade, while the two remaining Stuart squadrons of 45 Cavalry were allocated, one to the 4th West African Brigade at Taung Bazaar and the other to the 1st West African Brigade.

The British Regiment, 146 Regiment R.A.C., was allocated to the support of the 26th Indian Division at a later date in its projected assault on Akyab island.

CHAPTER XIV

Operation 'Romulus'

Phase One in the Kaladan Sector

It will be rememberd that the 81st West African Division had occupied Mowdok on 9 October 1944. Its two brigades were then faced with an advance south down the river valley of more than 60 miles through difficult terrain, in order to reach their first objective, the line Bidonegyaungwa-Kaladan, by 1 December 1944. After the capture of Mowdok the next necessary step for this division was to drive the Japanese from Mowdok Taung to open the way for an advance down the Pi Chaung. Hence, on 10 October, the 1st Sierra Leone Regiment assembled at the north end of Mowdok to attack this feature, while the 5th West African Brigade moved south in the area of Topui, some four miles south-south-east of Mowdok. On 11 October, the 4th Nigeria Regiment attacked Mowdok Taung after getting supporting air strike, but it was held up by the Japanese light and medium machine-gun fire; the following day, the 1st Sierra Leone Regiment attempted to by-pass the Japanese on the track of Sahak but this attempt also proved unsuccessful.

On 13 October, the 5th West African Brigade was making good progress in the Pi Chaung area and meeting practically no opposition on the way east, in order to concentrate at Hnonbo, situated on the west bank of the Kaladan river. On 14 October again another air strike was put down on Mowdok Taung; immediately after, the 4th Nigeria Regiment followed up and, capturing this feature, began to exploit north-east towards Sahak. It enabled the 1st Sierra Leone Regiment to firmly establish itself on this feature by 17 October and capture Labawa on 18 October. By that time the 5th West African Brigade had also concentrated on a general line facing south, running from Sepeo on the Pi Chaung to Hnonbo on the Kaladan.

On 23 October, the divisional headquarters established itself at Labawa with the 5th African Brigade concentrating at Sepeo and to its north on the Pi Chaung, while the 6th West African Brigade began concentrating at Hnonbo. These concentrations were completed by 30 October, enabling the division to begin its advance down to the south. A day before this, the first Moth aircraft air strip had also been opened at Ngasha and the first casualties evacuated by air.

In the beginning of November 1944, it had become apparent to the commander of the XV Indian Corps that the Japanese had withdrawn south and east to Paletwa. It was believed that the Japanese troops had concentrated behind forward screens in three main localities for the protection of Paletwa. The first locality was Kru Chaung, nine miles west of Paletwa; the second was in the area of Yowang and Auklo, three miles west of Paletwa, while the third was in the Mila and Palet Chaungs. Hence, on 2 November, the 81st West African Division advanced behind a reconnaissance screen of the Divisional Reconnaissance Regiment and moving south down the Pi Chaung, the Mila and Palet Chaungs and the west bank of the Kaladan river, contacted the Japanese forward screen, some six miles north of Paletwa. To the west, however, leading West African patrols had reached Langlodaung, 12 miles west of Paletwa, without meeting any opposition, and on the same day the 6th West African Brigade had secured Bongyo, which was nearly five miles due south of Sepeo.

For the next few weeks the southward advance of the division continued without incident; the 4th Nigeria Regiment and the 22nd Anti Tank Regiment, however, had been left behind as a "back stop" in the Mowdok Taung area. On 13 November a captured map indicated the threat of a possible left hook by the Japanese from the Satwei area on the Pi Chaung. To meet this the 5th West African Brigade was ordered to concentrate at Auklo, two miles due west of Paletwa, and the 6th West African Brigade was ordered to stand by, to move to the same area if required. The concentration at Auklo was completed on the 14th, and on 16 November, the 5th West African Brigade was told to continue its advance to the line Mizewa-Mwondaung, four miles to the south. The 6th West African Brigade at the same time was concentrated at Auklo with the 81st Reconnaissance Regiment watching Satwei. On 19 November, the 5th West African Brigade by-passed the Japanese in the Satwei area and by 20 November the troops left behind at Mowdok Taung had arrived at Teimagyaung Pya, which was five miles north-west of Paletwa. On this day another Moth aircraft air strip had been opened at Auklo. By 21 November the 4th Nigeria Regiment and the 30th Mountain Regiment had also joined the 6th West African Brigade at Auklo.

By 23 November, the 5th West African Brigade had also concentrated at Mizawa and on the 25th of the month the 6th West African Brigade had started on its advance to Ridaung. The Japanese were reported to be still holding out in Paletwa and had continued to occupy Point 175 on the west bank of the Kaladan river, despite acrid air bombing by the Allies. It had now become apparent that the Japanese had not intended to hold this African Division, north of

Paletwa, but had merely tried to delay the advance as much as possible with a series of quickly broken off actions.

Having arrived at Mizawa the 5th West African Brigade began the last lap of its advance to the Bidonegyaungwa-Kaladan line, and by 29 November the brigade was at Bidonegyaungwa, having met very slight opposition. The following day the Divisional Reconnaissance Regiment, which had been moving some miles ahead of the leading brigade, reported its arrival at Kyingri on the Pi Chaung. This place lay in a flat, cultivated area, surrounded on three sides by a loop in the Pi Chaung; consequently, it had always been regarded as an objective of the very first magnitude as it provided facilities for an air strip from which the division, having secured its first bound, could re-equip before continuing the second phase of its advance. Eventually the first Dakota air strip was built at Kyingri.

On 1 December, the 5th West African Brigade was on its way to consolidate the Kyingri area, meeting slight Japanese interference, and by 3 December 1944, the division had firmly established itself on the line Kyingri-Kwangyaung-Orama, thus completing the first phase of its advance.

Operations in the Mayu Sector

In the area of the 25th Indian Division there were three main objects to be achieved, prior to the advance on D Day. Firstly, there were the deception operations on the coast and in the Alethangyaw area; secondly, the 74th Indian Infantry Brigade (the coastal brigade) had to begin its advance to Myinhlut, thereby saving time and assisting the deception plan; lastly, the 51st Indian Infantry Brigade, which was to remain in defence of the base area, had to open the way for the 82nd West African Division by seizing certain important and vital features.

A good deal of special training was required by the 53rd and 74th Indian Infantry Brigades. This aspect presented no difficulty to the former as it was in a rear area but it was not so easy for the 74th Brigade on account of its operational commitments in the coastal plain. The 3rd Commando Brigade, which by 24 October had concentrated at Teknaf, offered to take over some of the forward positions of the 74th Indian Infantry Brigade. The 25th Indian Division commander welcomed this offer and for a period of about three weeks during November, Commando Brigade troops held the "patrol base" at West Chiradan. Under the command of the 74th Indian Infantry Brigade the Commandos did some extremely good patrolling and had to their credit the first Japanese prisoner of war taken by the 25th Indian Division. Thus the 74th Indian Infantry Brigade was made free to a large extent to prepare and train itself for the battle ahead. But the training of the 53rd Indian Infantry

Brigade was of a very specialised nature. It had to learn how to operate on a "boat basis", to study the number and type of craft which were required by each of its sub-units, to experiment in embarking awkward equipment, and to teach both men and mules how to swim. The craft of watermenship was entirely new to the majority of officers and men.

With the approach of D Day it became increasingly important for the 25th Indian Division to obtain Japanese identifications; a most intensive programme of offensive patrolling in strength was, therefore, organised and carried out along the whole front. Consequently, by the middle of November, Corps Intelligence had a fairly clear picture of Japanese strengths and dispositions in the Mayu peninsula. It was known that the Japanese had built up a screen facing the Allied forward positions, but there was still some doubt as to what lay behind the screen itself. Therefore, the divisional commander, ordered a series of co-ordinated and wide-spread patrols to obtain this information and the most intensive patrol period began on 19 November, after which the whole divisional front was the object of continual probing upto D Day. The units of the 3rd Special Service Brigade (Commando Brigade) had, however, returned to Teknaf on 1 December, where this brigade again concentrated and was placed under the command of the 26th Indian Division, for the proposed assault on Akyab.

In the patrolling programme, the 74th Indian Infantry Brigade was allotted the area west of the Mayu range; the 51st Indian Infantry Brigade, with 9 York and Lancaster under command, took the 'spine' and the country east of it, towards Seinnyinbya and Buthidaung. At the same time the latter brigade also planned a series of raids on known Japanese localities with the object of securing identifications.

Preliminary Operations in the Mayu Sector

On 20 November 1944, the 51st Indian Infantry Brigade Warning Order No. 18 was issued dealing with four special "Ghast" Operations to be started on 21 November 1944. These different operations were as follows:—

Operation A

8/19 Hyderabad with a detachment of brigade signals, artillery team and an engineer reconnaissance party was given the following tasks:—
   (a) Hold TICKER (434442).
   (b) Ascertain strength and identity of the Japanese on POLAND (473444) and Point 142 (4744).
   (c) Later, as a separate operation, ascertain the strength and indentity of the hostile force in Punkori (4847).

Operation B

9 Y & L, with a detachment of brigade signals, artillery team, 63 Indian Field Company and a detachment of 59 A.T. (Mule) Company, was:—

    (*a*) To hold ADAM feature (464035).
    (*b*) Establish a base in area Square 4842.
    (*c*) Ascertain the strength, location and indentity of any hostile troops between Buthidaung and Baguna.

Operation C

16/10 Baluch with a detachment of brigade signals, an artillery team and an assault section Royal Engineers (if available) were detailed to:—

    (*a*) Take over and hold WEMBLY (436430), Point 551, CRAB, Point 126 and Point 1433.
    (*b*) Patrol the "Spine" northwards to including EASY.
    (*c*) Ascertain the strength and indentity of the hostile troops on OFFICE (456407) and, if possible, destroy the garrison.
    (*d*) Assist Operation D.

Operation D

2/2 Punjab with a detachment of brigade signals, artillery team, a Field Company and some porters, was:—

    (*a*) To hold the feature known as OYSTERS (4039).
    (*b*) Establish base in the area Square 4835.
    (*c*) Ascertain whether the Japanese were holding the pass, west of Kanthe (5031) and whether there were any hostile troops between Point 302 (4932) and Kanthe.
    (*d*) Ascertain whether the hills in the Square 5035 and Point 151 (5135) were under hostile occupation, and if so, in what strength.

On 21 November at 1300 hours, the tactical headquarters and headquarters company of 8/19 Hyderabad had established themselves on feature ADAM (460440) and, a few minutes later, were joined by C company. At the end of the day by 1800 hours, A company was firmly entrenched on TICKER (434442) while B and C companies had established firm bases on the feature known as EVE (4544).

At 0935 hours, unit 3" mortars and the artillery in support started putting down a high explosive and smoke concentration on POLAND and, by 0940 hours, the leading platoons of C and D companies, under cover of smoke alone, had started their advance on to the objectives on POLAND itself and, within twenty minutes of this attack being put in, the feature had been taken. Only D company had met with a little resistance from a bunker, situated on the north spur of the feature; the opposition against C company had been very slight indeed. In view of its tactical importance, POLAND was consolidated and held.

While this raid was being carried out, B Company, which had established a firm base at 472453, seized and consolidated Point 142 on 23 November. By the end of the month, having carried out its tasks, the battalion was pulled in and stationed at BM 75 for rest and re-organisation.

Alongside Operation A, 16/10 Baluch was also busy carrying out its allotted tasks. The battalion did not find much difficulty in the first two tasks but very heavy opposition had to be faced in carrying out the third, that of capturing the feature known as OFFICE (456407). This hill feature, about a mile east of Hill 1267, was subjected to heavy artillery concentration. Immediately after, a company of 16 Baluch commanded by Major M. Usman made a brilliant dash to capture it. The attempt was successful, and in this assault the outstanding courage displayed by Sepoy Bhandari Ram, earned for the 25th Indian Division its first award of the Victoria Cross.

The information gained by the patrol activities of 2/2 Punjab and 9 Y & L was also of great help to the 25th Indian Division in the forthcoming operations. A large number of identifications were made and Japanese locations and strengths were reported. By 25 November it was apparent that the Japanese were intending to make a stand on a general line along the feature OFFICE—Kagyabet Chaung-Kyaukhlabyin. On 27 November "V" Force reports again indicated a general thinning out by the Japanese in the Mayu Range and in the area east of the Kalapanzin. This thinning out was reported to be mainly in the direction of Thaungdara, south of Htizwe, on the east bank of the Mayu river, but it was not clear whether the Japanese were going to remain in this area or were just passing through. The 74th Indian Infantry Brigade, in the meantime, was also patrolling in the Mayu range, south and east of Maungdaw, to a depth of 6 to 9 miles, but found little to report. Though incidental to the object of gaining intelligence, these patrol operations resulted in over thirty Japanese being picked up dead, and many more casualties were inflicted by artillery concentration, called down by the patrols, on hostile positions.

On 28 November 1944 the headquarters of the 25th Indian Division opened at Razabil and by 29 November, the headquarters of the 82nd West African Division had also arrived and opened up, one mile east of this area. The latter also resumed command of the 2nd West African Brigade in the Upper Kalapanzin and proceeded to relieve that brigade by the 4th West African Brigade ; the 2nd West African Brigade also began to concentrate at Razabil. Meanwhile, Corps engineers were completing the extensive task of constructing an alternative route through the Tunnels defile, to afford one-way traffic running simultaneously in each direction, though it was quite impossible to by-pass the two tunnels themselves, which always remained a bottleneck. The "Htindaw Bowl" had been reconnoitred and a key plan made for the concentration of infantry, artillery, tanks and administrative installations in this limited area, and the important task of covering the concentration fell to the 51st Indian Infantry Brigade.

On 1 December, the troops of the Commando Brigade had all returned to the Teknaf peninsula from the mainland and were relieved in forward positions by the units of the 74th Indian Infantry Brigade. The 50th Tank Brigade had also arrived and concentrated at Wabyin ; two companies of the Bombay Grenadiers forming part of this formation were placed temporarily under the command of the 51st Indian Infantry Brigade to assume responsibility for the flank protection of the Base Area, along the 'Spine' astride the Ngakyedauk Pass and for the protection of the airfield at Maunghnama. By this date, the 74th Indian Infantry Brigade had also established a patrol force, based as far south as the village of Lambaguna, some 8 miles due south of Razabil.

It was now appreciated that the Japanese held hill-feature of Inbauk dominated the route which, for the first few miles of the advance, both the 53rd Indian Infantry Brigade and the 1st West African Brigade had to follow. It was, therefore, essential that this feature should be captured in time to allow the 25th Indian Divisional Sappers to develop the track for the use of the two brigades. On 3 December, therefore, 9 Y & L under the command of the 51st Indian Infantry Brigade, successfully carried out the task of securing this village. At this stage also, the 7th Indian Anti-Tank Regiment had rejoined the 25th Indian Division ; it had been left behind in India when the division had sailed for Arakan. It returned, consisting of three batteries equipped with 3" mortars, with 6-pounder anti-tank guns as a secondary armament ; the batteries were also capable of taking over a defensive position in an infantry role. One battery was allotted to the 53rd Indian Infantry Brigade, the second was detailed for the defence of divisional headquarters, while the rest of the regiment was placed under the command of the 51st Indian Infantry Brigade for the defence of the Maungdaw 'Keep'.

In the final week, prior to D Day, the 51st Indian Infantry Brigade did all in its power to assist the 82nd West African Division in the task ahead of it. The former's knowledge of the country was by this time intimate and it had the full measure of the Japanese forces which confronted it. The brigade readily seized the chance offered to it of capturing certain intermediate objectives on the road to Buthidaung, by doing which it could now fairly claim that it had opened the way for the advance of the 82nd West African Division.

During this forming-up period, the Allied forward troops had been frequently subjected to shell fire in their new positions, and on 7 December, the Japanese at last showed signs of actually taking some initiative on the ground. During that night, a party of unknown strength, supported by artillery, mortars, and light-machine-gun fire, made a very "determined" attack on a feature, in the area of Point 162. This feature was in the 51st Indian Infantry Brigade's sphere of activity, but was not occupied by its troops, nor had it been occupied for a considerable time. This attack was perhaps an ingenious method of sustaining morale, for documents captured later showed that the Japanese claimed to have driven away the Allies easily from this position. On 11 December the Japanese bombed the divisional headquarters area of the 25th Indian Division at Razabil.

The same day a reshuffling in the command of the brigades of the 25th Indian Division had taken place. The commander of the 53rd Indian Infantry Brigade (Brigadier Scott) had fallen ill. This was a serious blow as Brigadier Scott had conceived and planned in fullest detail the intricate water-borne advance down the Kalapanzin. His place was temporarily taken by Brigadier Hutton of the 51st Indian Infantry Brigade who handed over the command of his own brigade to Lieutenant-Colonel Thimmayya of the 8/19th Hyderabad Regiment. In the same brigade Lieutenant-Colonel S. P. P. Thorat was commanding the 2/2nd Punjab Regiment, while Lieutenant-Colonel L. P. Sen was commanding the 16/10 Baluch Regiment.

The preliminary operations and preparations were now complete and the stage was set for the long-awaited offensive. Although 14 December had been fixed as D Day, Brigadier Hirst of the 74th Indian Infantry Brigade had sought and obtained permission to start two days before this date and had already edged his way south, down the coastal plain. On 11 December, 6 Oxf Bucks, leading the brigade advance, had occupied the village of Udaung, some 14 miles from Maungdaw, without any resistance from the Japanese.

CHAPTER XV

The Advance Begins

74th Indian Infantry Brigade Operations

On 12 December 1944, the 74th Indian Infantry Brigade was along the line of the Taungbo Chaung. The Brigade Commander selected Myinhlut as the first objective of his advance and planned to reach it by 15 December. The advance was made by short bounds, with battalions leapfrogging past each other, and the pace was determined by the speed at which the Indian Sappers could repair or construct a road for the long attendant column of vehicles. According to the original plan, the foothills were avoided in order to by-pass any Japanese positions they might be harbouring, and the troops kept close to the sea. These by-passed positions, however, were shelled by Allied artillery as well as by the supporting destroyers. The latter were at call on 14 December when they carried out a bombardment of Point 230, a prominent isolated feature, overlooking the coastal plain where it begins to narrow on entering the Gyindaw defile, a distance of four miles south of Udaung and only two miles north of Gyindaw itself.

The brigade reached Myinhlut within the appointed time with very little opposition during its advance. A minor clash with the Japanese patrols *en route* had occurred and Indian troops in the village of Tattobyin were engaged by Japanese artillery, but casualties were very slight. At this stage it became apparent that the brigade would have to force the Kyaukpandu defile, which lent itself to defence. Nevertheless, this was accomplished rather easily and two days later the brigade had slipped through the defile unopposed and was in occupation of Indin. The divisional commander, who had come up to visit the brigade, attributed the general lack of opposition by the Japanese to the fact that they were holding the Spine and were planning to come down and neutralize the brigade's advance by cutting its (non-existent) line of communications. Therefore, he ordered the brigade, while maintaining its present position south of Kyaukpandu, to immediately detach a battalion to seize Donbaik with all speed, before this place could be reinforced by the Japanese. 6 Oxf Bucks was appointed to carry out this task, and, early on the morning of 22 December, the battalion reached its objective unopposed after a night's march of over twenty miles. Thus fell the Donbaik position of sinister memory which the Indo-British offensive of 1943 had failed to take after attacks of unsurpassed gallantry.

With the taking of Donbaik with such negligible opposition, it became apparent that the Japanese were not preparing to defend Foul Point; the Kyaukpandu base and the pass over the Spine, therefore, began to lose their significance for the XV Indian Corps. Accordingly, the brigade was closed in upon Donbaik. By 27 December, the whole of the south of the peninsula was reported clear of the Japanese; thereupon the brigade concentrated near Magyi Chaung, where it was poised for the assault on Akyab Island.

The essence of the plans of this brigade was to avoid all unnecessary contact with the Japanese and to make the best speed possible towards the final objective. Its task was to seize Foul Point by 15 January, a task, which was in fact accomplished by 29 December, within a period of 17 days after commencing the advance.

Co-ordinated action by the 53rd Indian Infantry Brigade and 82nd West African Division

Before 14 December 1944, the 53rd Indian Infantry Brigade had left its temporary harbour behind Hill 551 and was concentrated in the Inbauk area, where the mule track from the Htindaw Bowl debouches into open country. In the meantime, 17 Mahrattas had been sent ahead to occupy the high ground, north of Mrosara Khal, to cover the start of the advance. As has already been mentioned, the track to Inbauk had to be shared with the 1st West African Brigade, which meant that the two brigades could not be deployed simultaneously. Priority, however, had to be given to the 1st West African Brigade, since its task of crossing the Kalapanzin and seizing "VITAL CORNER" was an immediate pre-requisite to the launching of the 53rd Indian Infantry Brigade's flotilla. Furthermore, the 1st West African Brigade could only cover the left flank of the 53rd Brigade if it took the lead at this stage. Consequently no move could be made by the 53rd Indian Infantry Brigade before the afternoon of 15 December.

Meanwhile, the 2nd West African Brigade had commenced operations against Buthidaung. Pushing forward in the grey light of dawn on 14 December, the brigade passed through the 51st Indian Infantry Brigade and rapidly occupied the hills around Buthidaung, meeting very slight opposition. Delay, however, was caused by a number of aerial bombs with which the retreating Japanese had mined the road. These were quickly and efficiently removed by the sappers of 425 Indian Field Company and the African Engineers. Buthidaung was finally entered on 15 December and the only opposition encountered was a bunker position in the hills a little to the south. Here, tanks of the 19th Lancers came into action and destroyed the bunkers, rapidly killing the occupants.

While these little pockets of resistance were being eliminated, 425 Indian Field Company, whose task it was to prepare jetty areas and traffic circuits to receive the convoy of boats, was already hard at work. The main launching site was within 400 yards of a Japanese bunker position, but the Indian Sappers set about their tasks, finding their own local protection. Starting from 16 December and lasting approximately four days, the immense task of transporting and launching the flotilla of some 700 boats of the 53rd Indian Infantry Brigade, was concluded. The 2nd West African Brigade had by that time established a bridge-head on the east bank of the Kalapanzin river. Meanwhile 1st West African Brigade also had moved up for its assault-crossing of the Kalapanzin which it carried through without incident. The 82nd West African Division had thus secured both its first objectives and the advance of the XV Indian Corps was safely launched on all divisional fronts.

While these events were going on in Buthidaung, the advance of the 53rd Indian Infantry Brigade had also begun. By 18 December, 4 Royal Garhwal Rifles had occupied Seinnyinbya unopposed and the rest of the brigade was disposed in the area to the north. "VITAL CORNER" had fallen to the 1st West African Brigade and the river was opened for the comparatively safe passage of boats. In due course the boats began to arrive but not in the orderly convoys which had been expected. This was partly because the boats were desptached as soon as repairs were effected and partly because the vagaries of the tide were little understood.

It would be anything but fair to dismiss this operation lightly. In a campaign that was noted for endless and unusual problem of maintenance and supply, for the solution of which there was no precedent, the transportation of the craft to Buthidaung stood out as a very great achievement. Some of the boats carried in the immense convoy of over 600 vehicles were so large that they could clear the "Tunnels" with only inches to spare. Several miles of rope was used for securing the boats to the vehicles; the "sampans" and "dug-outs" were to form the first line transport of the 53rd Indian Infantry Bridgade while the larger boats were to provide a second line echelon, both for the Indian Brigade and for the 82nd West African Division.

The 53rd Indian Infantry Brigade, however, worked furiously to overcome its problems and in due course concentrated in Seinnyinbya, less 9 Y & L, which crossed an arm of the river under shell fire to occupy the northern of the two large islands (Christened "York" and "Lancaster"), which are embraced by its waters. The occupation of these islands took place on 20 December; there was no opposition on the islands themselves but on their way to land, the boats were shelled from the foothills to the east of the river, and casualties were suffered both in personnel and craft. On the following day, the advance over land was continued and the large village of Kwazon was occupied without much difficulty.

While the 53rd Indian Infantry Brigade was making rapid advance down the axis of the river, the 82nd West African Division, to the east, was meeting determined opposition on the road from Buthidaung. On 19 December, the 1st West African Brigade took a great stride when it occupied Kindaung village and forced the crossing of the Saingdin Chaung. On the same evening, African patrols were reported to be four miles south of the village and also to be proceeding up the chaung itself.

During the third week of December the 4th West African Brigade had been released from its holding role at Taung Bazaar and had begun its move south to round up the remaining Japanese north of Buthidaung. The brigade suffered an initial set-back in having to leave behind its supporting squadron of tanks and artillery, for it was found impossible to maintain any speed in face of the difficulty of ferrying the heavy equipment across the numerous tidal chaungs. These guns and tanks were, therefore, returned to Taung but not before a squadron of 45 Cavalry had driven the Japanese from one strongly held bunker position. The brigade, thus made light, thereafter made swift progress, rejoining the division in the Buthidaung area.

Having secured Kindaung, the 82nd West African Division soon came up against a very strong delaying position on the general line of the villages of Dodan, Kringyaungywa and Hponnyoleik, and on the two features known as Point 200 and Point 268, to the east. This line was held with great determination by a strong Japanese company, supported by additional medium machine-guns and light machine-guns. The two features to the east were particularly troublesome and a number of attacks against them were all unsuccessful. On the morning of 22 December, however, troops of the 1st West African Brigade moved down a subsidiary loop of the river in boats and seized the high ground at Point 101 and Point 154, north of the village of Zadidaung, on the west bank of the Saingdinbwe chaung. Although this assault was strongly opposed by the Japanese, they were eventually driven off. It could now safely be claimed that the Kalapanzin plain, north of the Saingdin chaung, was cleared of the Japanese.

Meanwhile, the 53rd Indian Infantry Brigade was also advancing according to plan; 4 Royal Garhwal Rifles was probing the defences of the Japanese but the latter were clinging to them tenaciously. For some days this pressure was continued supported by artillery and aircraft. At the same time, 9 Y & L having occupied Kwazon was trying to contact the Japanese forces on the east bank of the river. It soon became apparent that the route followed by 9 Y & L was the obvious one in view of the continued resistance met by 4 Royal Garhwal Rifles. The brigade commander, therefore, selected the island route of advance. The next few days saw no appreciable change in the situation. 9 Yorks and Lancasters continued to gain success on the east bank of the Kalapanzin but 4 Royal Garhwal Rifles was still opposed by the Japanese in great strength. It was not until 27th December, when patrols of the 74th Indian Infantry Brigade were already at Foul Point, that the 53rd Brigade was again able to move.

The move forward of the 53rd Indian Infantry Brigade towards its last bound entailed the crossing of the Mayu river, the capture of Rathedaung and finally the occupation of Kudaung island. To the west, the Japanese still held out in the hills and even by 27 December, Hparabyin had not been captured. It was reported that elements of the Japanese *143rd Regiment* had arrived in this village on 20 December, having withdrawn from Kindaung and crossed the Mayu river to the south.

On 29 December, 17/5 Mahratta Light Infantry passed through 9 Y & L at Kwazon, moved down the river in boats and occupied the village of Prinshe. On the same day, 4 Royal Garhwal Rifles entered Hparabyin, after a long march through the foothills to the west of the river. Also by that date, the 82nd West African Division had reported that Taungmaw and Yezogyaung were both clear of Japanese troops. The leading troops of this division, were now within eight miles of Htizwe. At this stage the 4th West African Brigade was leading the divisional advance while the 2nd West African Brigade secured the Forward Maintenance Area at Buthidaung.

Having occupied Prinshe, 17/5 Mahratta Light Infantry sent fighting patrols across the river to Htizwe who reported it unoccupied. These patrols remained on the far side and again exploited towards Rathedaung. This place was also found to be deserted and was at once occupied by the Mahrattas. By now it had become apparent that the Japanese plan was to escape over the Kanzauk Pass. By 31 December, 9 Y & L, after a long and arduous journey down the river, landed on Kudaung island and occupied it, thus fulfilling the brigade task.

The Japanese resistance in the Mayu valley was now completely fading away; they had withdrawn east to Kanzauk and a large column was known to have moved from there to Myohaung. It thus seemed unlikely that the 82nd West African Division would encounter any determined resistance on its way into the Kaladan. While the 53rd Indian Infantry Brigade had advanced southwards,

4 Royal Garhwal Rifles had stayed behind to liquidate Japanese opposition in the Hparabyin area. After this place had fallen on 29 December the Garhwalis had continued their advance and when their work was accomplished they were transported to Kudaung island.

The situation by the end of 1944 was, therefore, as follows:—
The 74th Indian Infantry Brigade had reached Foul Point on 26 December; the 53rd Indian Infantry Brigade had secured Kudaung island by 31 December. Thus, in the Mayu sector, Operation 'Romulus' was a fortnight ahead of schedule. It had taken the 25th Indian Division less than three weeks to secure its final objectives on either side of the "Spine"; but mopping up operations in the hills, however, were not quite at an end.

Mopping up operations by the 51st Indian Infantry Brigade

While the two brigades were moving down on either side of the Mayu spine, the 51st Indian Infantry Brigade was still entangled round the Tunnels area. The task allotted to this brigade yet remained to be carried out. Therefore, on 17 December 1944, when the 22nd East African Brigade began to take over the defence of the "Spine" and "Tunnels", the 51st Indian Infantry Brigade was made ready to carry out its mopping up tasks in conformity with the 25th Indian Division's plans. The brigade this time was under the temporary command of Lieut-Colonel Thimmayya.

The advance of the 74th Indian Infantry Brigade along the coastal sector and of the 53rd Indian Infantry Brigade down the Mayu river, had left behind a number of rather bewildered Japanese detachments who were garrisoning strongholds on the "Spine". Amongst these Japanese garrisons, the most northernly was on Hill 1440, a long jungle-covered feature on which, it was estimated, were about two platoons of the Japanese. In order to liquidate this feature, the hill was subjected to two heavy air-strikes and was later accurately shelled by a 7.2" howitzer. As a result of this bombardment the Japanese had to withdraw; consequently, on 19 December, troops of 8/19 Hyderabad, whose patrols were already familiar with this feature, destroyed the remaining defences. These were found to be exceedingly strong although they had been very much damaged by Allied bombing and gun fire. While Hill 1440 was being eliminated, 2/2 Punjab was carrying out extensive patrolling in the western foothills of the Mayu range.

On 22 December, the 51st Indian Infantry Brigade began to spread southwards, down the coastal plain, with 2/2 Punjab leading the advance. For the next two days the advance was entirely unopposed with no sign of any Japanese troops, and it was not until 25 December that 2/2 Punjab reported fresh contact with the

Japanese. One of its patrols had located a Japanese strong point in the "Spine" on Hill 1296, situated south-west of Seinnyinbya. On getting this report the patrol was withdrawn; the hill was then subjected to heavy artillery fire which forced the Japanese garrison to vacate the feature.

It will be remembered that during this period 4 Royal Garhwal Rifles (53rd Indian Infantry Brigade) had, for some days, been holding up north of Hparabyin. Allied intelligence reports had placed the Japanese strength to be approximately 500 which was concentrated in this area, but the intention of this force could not be predicted with certainty. The 51st Indian Infantry Brigade was, therefore, ordered to concentrate in the Myinhlut area by 27 December with the object of attacking eastwards over the Mayu range in order to destroy this Japanese force and thus prevent its escape towards Akyab. This operation was carried out according to plan but no opposition was met; it was discovered that the Japanese had already slipped away. On 30 December, a company of 16/10 Baluch made contact with 17/5 Mahrattas near Atet Nanra and, as subsequent patrolling showed, the Mayu peninsula was now clear of the Japanese.

During this period 8/19 Hyderabad was detached from the 51st Indian Infantry Brigade and, together with 7/16 Punjab, was marching to Foul Point in order to take part in the landing on Akyab. In the meanwhile, the 51st Indian Infantry Brigade concentrated at Indin where it remained till it rejoined the 25th Indian Division after Operation 'Talon' had been completed.

Phase Two in the Kaladan Sector

On 3 December 1944, the 81st West African Division was established on the line Kyingri-Kwangyaung-Orama, thereby completing the first phase of its advance according to plan. The division was then ready to start the second phase of the advance to the area of Thayattabyin, in the open valley to the south.

Prior to this advance the appraisal was that the Kaladan river would have to be crossed at a point which might enable the division to outflank Kyauktaw to the east. This place had been heavily fortified by the Japanese in the previous season's fighting against this division. Thus, as soon as the Kyingri air strip was opened and effectively secured, the 6th West African Brigade prepared to cross the Kaladan, at the village of Tinma on the east bank, a point slightly south of Kyingri on the Pi Chaung. At the same time a "holding" force was to be left on the west bank, both to keep up the deception for as long as possible, and to prevent any counter-thrust by the Japanese up the Pi Chaung or along the west bank of the Kaladan.

During the night of 4 December, the divisional troops made a scramble crossing of the river and were not opposed on landing.

The bridge-head was therefore rapidly enlarged and the ferrying of troops continued for several days. The 6th West African Brigade made a "firm base" about two miles east of the river while the 5th West African Brigade and the divisional headquarters formed a separate "box" on the river bank in the area of Tinma village. It was not till 9 December that the Japanese guns opened up on the crossing area; African casualties from this shelling were about three killed and nine wounded.

In the meantime, the force known as "Hold Force", left behind at Kyingri, consisting of the Divisional Anti-Tank Regiment (operating in an infantry role) and the Divisional Reconnaissance Regiment, was patrolling vigorously to give the impression that an advance down both the banks of the river was intended. This deception was most successful for it appeared to tie down at least 500 Japanese troops on the far bank. These Japanese troops kept up a very energetic patrolling towards the "Hold Force" base on the Kyingri air strip and were thus effectively kept out of the battle. The 81st Divisional Reconnaissance Regiment, in fact, consisted of only two squadrons; the third squadron was under the command of the 4th West African brigade of the 82nd West African Division in Taung Bazaar, where it was engaged in patrolling the "Soutcol" route. This route ran from Taung Bazaar in the Kalapanzin through the hills to the east to Kaladan village and was a likely route for a right hook by the Japanese, should they pass a force north of the advancing 81st West African Division. "Hold Force", therefore, sent fighting patrols to link up with this squadron on the "Soutcol" route, but no Japanese opposition was encountered.

Throughout this action so far, the Japanese were slow to react to the crossing of the river by the 81st West African Division. On 15 December, however, they launched an attack supported by the fire of 75 mm and 105 mm guns. The attack was directed on the 6th West African Brigade front, and after much heavy fighting was eventually driven off. In this action 30 Mountain Regiment, Indian Artillery, played a very gallant part and Havildar Umrao Singh of this unit won the Victoria Cross.

While concentrating at Tinma village, the appraisal of the divisional commander was that the period of Allied superiority in artillery fire power had come to an end and that henceforth the division would be both outnumbered and outranged in this respect by the Japanese. Although air superiority offset this disadvantage to a great extent, it had become evident that more counter-battery assistance would be required by the 81st West African Division to operate successfully in the open country that lay before it. Various plans of bringing in more artillery were considered but were discarded due to the inadequacy of the means. Since no further artillery was to be placed in support, it was decided that the line of advance of this division would take the form of a wide hook, through the hills to the east. By this means it was intended, having by-passed Thayattabyin, to descend on the Japanese lines of communication, once a firm base had been established north of Myohaung.

With a view to carrying out the second phase of the operation according to the new plan, patrolling was carried out into the hills along the line of advance, while the division rested and re-equipped at Tinma, where a new Dakota air strip was opened. On the Pi Chaung, "Hold Force" continued to patrol south with great vigour to tie down the Japanese preparing for the supposed advance down the west bank. This deception undoubtedly succeeded for the Japanese were never quite certain down which bank of the Kaladan the main thrust was intended to be delivered.

On 19 December 1944, the West African Division began its move for the second phase of the operation. By the following day its leading troops were already eight miles south-east of Tinma and a major left hook was developing. The 6th West African Brigade led the advance while the 5th West African Brigade followed by the same route on to the Yan Chaung, and thence due south. Moreover, as part of the deception plan, the 5th West African Brigade left a small party in the Tinma area for several days. This had the effect of very ingeniously diverting the attention of the Japanese from the main outflanking movement, which was very successfully carried out, and the bulk of the division had arrived at Thandada village, six miles south-east of Thayattabyin, by 22 December. By this move the Japanese had been completely outwitted, for the major part of their force was still north of Thayattabyin, preparing for an action which could not now take place on the ground of their choosing.

From 24 December onwards the 81st West African Division remained in its new "firm base" in the hills, south-east of Thayattabyin, where it was subjected to persistent probing by the Japanese to its west. The Japanese were at the time undoubtedly concentrating along the west side of the isolated feature known as Point 317, which ran beside the Thayattabyin-Myohaung road, and which it directly overlooked from the east. This feature, known throughout the operation as WEST DOWN, was about three-and-a half miles across at its widest part. Being thickly wooded and with many defiles in its sides, it made an admirable forming-up position for an attack by the Japanese from the west on the 1st West African Division's concentration area.

The moment this threat became apparent, the XV Indian Corps decided that all available air support should be given to the African Division for a minimum period of three days. With this support it was intended to carry out a saturation bombing on West Down in order to knock out the Japanese guns and to smash the impending attack then in preparation against the 81st West African Division. It was hoped that these measures would more than compensate for the lack of artillery fire power of this division.

The saturation attack, was therefore, carried out from 29 December to 31 December, during which period waves of bombers were continuously over the target, throughout the hours of daylight. During these three days no less than 240 fighter-bomber sorties were flown, dropping an overall bomb weight of 90,000 lbs of explosives, while light bombers, mainly of the United States Army Air Force, flew 213 sorties, dropping 428,030 lbs of bombs and 1,230 gallons of Napalm incendiary oil. This bombing experiment proved completely successful. The persistent probing of the 81st West African Division's concentration area from the west ceased abruptly and the Japanese thereafter appeared to be concentrating more on preventing any southward movement by this division than to attack it themselves.

On 4 January 1945, the Divisional Reconnaissance Regiment left "Hold Force" at Kyingri and began to move south on the west side of the Kaladan river, towards Apaukwa and Kanzauk. Here it was to meet the 4th West African Brigade, the first brigade of the 81st West African Division to cross the pass from Htizwe. The latter reached Kanzauk on 7 January, 1945, whence, having met 81 Reconnaissance Regiment, it proceeded east to Apaukwa, arriving there on 9 January. On 10 January, the 4th West African Brigade came under the command of 81st West African Division for the operation to capture the city of Myohaung.

CHAPTER XVI

Operation 'Talon'

Recapture of Akyab Island

Ever since the withdrawal from Burma and the Arakan coast in May 1942, India Command had been intent on the recapture of Akyab. Various plans for an amphibious assault on this island were made but were repeatedly cancelled owing to the lack of essential resources. The naval and air forces available were never adequate, nor was the Allied military situation on the mainland very encouraging. Ultimately the situation at the end of the monsoon in 1944 was such that new plans were again thought of for capturing certain vital features. By this time the Allies had secured complete command of the sea and the air and were thus, for the first time, able to plan to use the mobility conferred by the possession of sea power and air power to seize and retain the initiative and force the Japanese to fight on the ground not of their own choosing.

On 8 November 1944, the Supreme Allied Commander, South East Asia, had issued a directive[1] to his Commanders-in-Chief to clear Arakan (Operation 'Romulus) and ultimately to capture Akyab (Operation 'Talon') by an amphibious assault not later than the end of January 1945. This task was allotted to the XV Indian Corps which had passed out of the Fourteenth Army and was directly under the command of the Allied Land Forces South-East Asia (General Sir Oliver Leese, Bt., K.C.B., C.B.E., D.S.O).

By 27 November 1944 the plans for 'Romulus' and 'Talon' had been completed. The campaign was to be a continuous series of combined operations, controlled by a Combined Headquarters, consisting of the Headquarters of the Naval Force (Rear Admiral B.C.S. Martin), XV Indian Corps (Lieut-General Sir A.F.P. Christison) and 224 Group R.A.F. (Air Commodore, later Air Vice-Marshal, the Earl of Bandon).

Strategic importance of Akyab

Akyab island is low-lying and flat and is separated from Foul Point by the four-mile wide estuary of the Mayu river. Between the island and the mainland to the east, flows the six-mile wide estuary of the Kaladan, the mouth of which, sheltered on the south side by the Baronga islands, formed Akyab harbour. To the north, Akyab

---
[1] SEAC Despatch.

is separated from Kudaung island by the mouth of the Kwede river where it joins the Mayu estuary and by the broad Mingan Chaung, which, running east and west, links up the junction of the Mayu and Kwede rivers with the northern end of Akyab harbour in the Kaladan. The island is nearly nine miles long and ten miles wide at its widest parts and consists in the main of paddy fields. It is wooded but has practically no prominent features other than numerous tidal chaungs and creeks, the banks of which are mostly fringed with mangrove swamp. The general direction of these chaungs is west and east and hence they formed considerable obstacles to progress into the interior.

The value of the Akyab island to the XV Indian Corps, in particular, and to the South-East Asia Command, in general, was very great. Its situation as a port and town, set between the mouth of the two main rivers of Arakan, was of considerable administrative importance, particularly for giving assistance to the troops who were still driving south down the Kaladan river. Its political position in the administration of the liberated areas was also believed to be considerable; hence the moral effect of its capture was likely to be far reaching. But more important than either of these considerations was the fact that the need for a "base" for the future Allied drive down Arakan was becoming paramount. Cox's Bazaar was at the time a hundred miles in the rear of the forward troops, and Chittagong, the nearest railhead, was over 170 miles away. The capture of Akyab to serve as the future base became, therefore, most necessary. Apart from its importance as a valuable harbour, the island also offered great scope for the establishment of an air base. It already possessed a civil airport, capable of conversion into an all-weather airfield and, in addition, apart from the existence of several disused fair-weather landing grounds, the flat nature of the terrain made airfield construction and development comparatively easy. Furthermore, the harbour and dock installations, combined with the good road system, were most useful adjuncts. It was therefore believed that the opening up of such a base would not only assist the subsequent operations of the XV Indian Corps in Arakan, but would also provide the Fourteenth Army with a Rear Airfield Maintenance Organisation, which would be invaluable during the latter's advance down the valley of the Irrawaddy.

To the Japanese, however, this island was not vital to their land strategy at this stage of operations, but, because of its importance to the Allies, it was of great strategical value to them in the over-all picture.

The original plan

The original plan for the assault on Akyab island was an

amphibious assault to be carried out by the 26th Indian Division with the help of the 3rd Commando Brigade. D Day was fixed tentatively as 18 February 1945. The naval support for the operation was to be provided by a Naval Bombardment Force consisting of one battleship of eight 15" guns, three cruisers of twelve 6" guns, one cruiser of eight 5.25" guns and five destroyers of four 4.7" guns. The air support which would be made available, comprised ten heavy bomber squadrons (Liberators), four medium bomber squadrons (B. 25s), five light bomber squadrons (Mosquitoes), eleven long-range fighter squadrons (Thunderbolts), one twin-engined fighter squadron (P. 38s), four ground attack squadrons (Hurricanes) and five single-engined fighter squadrons (Spitfires).

The shipping available was sufficient to lift the 3rd Commando Brigade, two other brigade groups, the Beach Group, a proportion of the divisional troops and certain Royal Air Force assault units, in the assault convoy. It was calculated that the build-up convoy would arrive on D+5, if four personnel ships and three M.T. ships were released from the assault convoy by first light on D+1. The landing craft available were capable of unloading all personnel by 2359 hours on D Day.

The main landing was planned to be made on the east coast. The assault was to be carried out by the 71st Indian Infantry Brigade Group, supported by a Field Regiment, an Artillery Regiment armed with 3" mortars and a jeep-drawn mountain battery. A fourth infantry battalion, temporarily withdrawn from the build-up brigade, was also to be allotted. 146 Regiment R.A.C., less one squadron, was to furnish tank support.

A subsidiary landing was planned to take place at H hour with the object of capturing the Fakir Point defences. This landing was to be complementary to the main landing and was to be carried out by the 3rd Special Service Brigade, less one Commando unit. The remaining Commando unit was to be given the task of making landings on Savage island and on all the three of the Baronga islands. This was to be carried out during the night preceding D Day with the object of securing the channel approaches to the main beaches and thus preventing the Japanese from interfering with the main assault by gun-fire.

The essence of the whole plan was the speed of advance inland and consequently the deployment of maximum hitting power at the earlist possible moment. Both, the landing of the 71st Indian Infantry Brigade and the subsidiary landing by the 3rd Special Service Brigade to the south, were to be preceded by "saturation bombing" of selected target areas and were to be supported by naval and air bombardment of considerable intensity. Having established itself ashore the 71st Indian Infanrty Brigade was to press on with all speed and to consolidate by nightfall on D Day along the general line Akyab town—Royal Lake—Ondawgyi, situated south-west of Royal Lake.

The 36th Indian Infantry Brigade was detailed as the follow-up brigade. This formation was scheduled to land on the main beaches between H+5 hours and H+11 hours on D Day. It would thus have been available for further exploitation inland or such other employment as might be ordered by the commander of the 26th Indian Division, in accordance with the existing tactical situation.

Change in the plans

The appreciation and plan, outlined above were the result of a long period of continuous planning on a corps and divisional level, carried out while the first stages of Operation 'Romulus' were in progress. D Day for Operation 'Talon' could, therefore, only be provisionally fixed, which, as has already been mentioned, was 18 February 1945.

But the progress of Operation 'Romulus' was exceptionally fast. By the end of the year, phases one and two of this operation in the Mayu sector had been completed, two weeks ahead of schedule. The 25th Indian Division had made much more rapid progress than had been expected and, as has been mentioned before, the 74th Indian Infantry Brigade and the 53rd Indian Infantry Brigade were established at Foul Point and on Kudaung island, by the beginning of January. Thus, these two brigades of the 25th Indian Division were already facing the northern shore of the island of Akyab. On the other hand, in the Kaladan sector, the second divisional objective had also been reached and the time programme maintained to a day. In view of these factors, D Day for Operation 'Talon' was advanced to 20 January 1945.

The operations in the Mayu peninsula were, however, still incomplete and there remained the possibility of remnants of the Japanese garrison of the peninsula arriving in Akyab before D Day. It was therefore thought possible that the Japanese would be able to produce in this island a maximum garrison of approximately 4,000 men at the time of the Allied assault.

While these appreciations were taking place, intelligence reports, at the end of December 1944 continued to be received by the Allies indicating that there were now very few Japanese troops left in Akyab island. But most of these reports were not of a high grading and it was considered doubtful whether they formed a reliable guide, particularly as it was known that the major portion of Akyab island was a prohibited area for the locals. Of the original garrison of *11th Regiment* (Japanese), *3rd Battalion* and *3rd Company* of *1st*

Battalion had been identified in the Kaladan valley, but there had been no trace of the *2nd Battalion* or of the *1st Battalion* (less *3rd Company*); there was, therefore, a possibility that both these battalions were still in Akyab. At the end of December, therefore, it was estimated that the Akyab garrison would be about one battalion group, including airfield defence and divisional troops.

All these reports at this period confirmed the fact that the Akyab garrison had been considerably weakened. At the beginning of January, therefore, it appeared that a rapid change of plans by the Allies had become essential. The 25th Indian Division had reached its adjacent objective earlier and in a much less weary state than had been expected. Furthermore, in the Kaladan sector, the *"Matsu Force"* was being hard pressed by the 81st West African Division and it was imperative, therefore, that the XV Indian Corps should move a force to the line Myebon-Minbya, in order to block the Japanese lines of communication and escape route as early as possible.

The new plan

In spite of the latest appreciation of the situation which demanded swift action by the XV Indian Corps, the date of Operation 'Talon' could not be advanced earlier than 20 January owing to the shipping difficulties. But if the Allies were to take advantage of the situation as it existed at the end of December, a new plan was necessary to achieve the same object as was laid down for Operation 'Talon.' A new plan was, therefore, quickly prepared for an assault landing, to be made on the north-west beach of the island, followed by the capture of Akyab from the landward side. The initial landing was to be made by the 3rd Commando Brigade and the operation was to be mounted in the Naf river, supported by all available air and naval bombardment. Simultaneously, the 53rd Indian Infantry Brigade was to cross the two miles wide mouth of the Kwede river in country craft, from Kudaung island. The 74th Indian Infantry Brigade was to be ferried across the four mile wide Mayu estuary from Foul Point, to follow up the 3rd Commando Brigade.

Since speed was essential if contact was to be regained with the Japanese, D Day was fixed for 3 January 1945 and H hour was 1230 hours. Although the 25th Indian Division, expecting very slight opposition, was eager to take over the task of seizing Akyab island forthwith, this was not agreed to, for at this stage an unopposed landing could not be guaranteed. Hence it was that the 3rd Commando Brigade made the first landing in assault craft. The Commander of the 25th Indian Division suggested, and the Corps Commander agreed that the 25th Indian Division should take over the task.

As time was short and combined planning could only satisfactorily be done at the XV Corps headquarters, the task of planning was delegated to the commander of the Assault Brigade, who was helped by the C.R.A. 25th Indian Division to co-ordinate the fire support of the Royal Navy, the R.A.F. and the Divisional artillery. General Wood subsequently held a quick co-ordinating conference, and was able to accept this ready made plan as his own with little modification.

The assault Brigade (3rd Commando Brigade) was to complete loading in the Naf river by 0800 hours on D—1 (2 January 1945) and was to sail that afternoon for the lowering positions, west of the assault beaches. The assault brigade was then to be taken ashore in landing craft consisting of two waves, after which, the craft were to come back to Foul Point in order to ferry-in the follow-up brigade (74th Indian Infantry Brigade). The embarkation and landing of the follow-up brigade were to proceed as fast as possible and were to continue night and day, until completed. To help the assault the Naval Bombardment Force was to fire pre-arranged concentrations on selected targets in the area of the beaches, from H−30 to H+15 hours. Thereafter, the fire was to be at call through Forward Observation Officers (FOOs). While this firing was at call, an attacking force consisting of HMAS *"Napier"*, HMIS *"Nepal"* and HMS *"Shoreham"* was to be available for bombardment duties, once it could be released from the Naval Assault Force. The 25th Indian Division was to exploit success by seizing all commanding ground on the Baronga island and on the Pauktaw peninsula to the north. It was then to advance by way of the rivers and establish a base, south-east of Minbya, prior to attacking Myebon.

Air and Naval support—Despite the shortage of time for preparing this new plan, both the Royal Navy and the Royal Air Force were able to provide considerable supporting forces. The Naval Bombardment Force consisted of—

HMS *"Newcastle"*
HMS *"Nigeria"*
HMS *"Phoebe"*
HMS *"Pathfinder"*
HMS *"Rapid"*
HMS *"Roebuck"*.

These ships were under the command of Rear Adimiral A.A. Read, C.B., who was Flag Officer of Force 61.

The Allied air forces which were made available included seven squadrons of P-47s (six of the Royal Air Force, one of the United States Army Air Corps), three squadrons of Hurri Bombers, three squadrons of Spitfires, one squadron of P-38s (United States Army Air Corps), four squadrons of B-25s (United States Army Air Corps), two squadrons of Beaufighters and one squadron of Hurricanes (for tactical reconnaissance). Out of a total of 180 aircraft made available for this operation for close support, 128 Mitchells, Hurricanes and Thunderbolts were to engage pre-selected targets from H−210 to H+20. Thereafter they were to return to base and remain at call, together with the planes of 52 Aircrafts, which were to be at call from H hour. The latter included counter-battery patrols and smoke-laying aircraft.

The Assault on Akyab

On 1 January 1945, Allied reconnaissance aircraft reported that local inhabitants were working on the main Akyab airfield and had showed no anxiety at the appearance of the aircraft. Consequently, on 2 January 1945, messages written in Urdu and Burmese were dropped on the island asking the locals to sit on the ground if the island was occupied by Japanese troops but if it was not occupied, the locals were instructed to stand up with their hands above their heads. When, having dropped these instructions, the aircraft reappeared some ten minutes later over that area it received the signal to say that there were no Japanese on the island. On the same day, therefore, an Air Observation Post pilot discovered that a strip, north of the Royal Lake, had apparently been prepared for him to land his craft and he did so. On landing, he was given a rousing reception and was informed by the locals that the Japanese had left Akyab the preceding day and that there were then left only a few Japanese troops in the north-east corner of the island. After returning to report, he again flew back to the island and leaving his "orderly" as hostage, brought back a former Government official for interrogation by the Corps commander. On being questioned this civilian officer confirmed the news that the Japanese had relinquished Akyab island.

Although it was confirmed that the Japanese had abandoned Akyab, yet the doubt did not cease to be entertained that the landing would be entirely unopposed. Since the assault was to take place the next day and the troops were by that time at sea, a quick decision had to be taken regarding the immediate course to be followed. As a precautionary measure it was decided to carry out the entire operation, as planned, but without the sea and air bombardment, unless these were specially called for. The entire navy, air force, and artillery were, therefore, to be at their respective stations and at immediate call, while the assault was to continue without firing. Once this decision was taken, these orders were conveyed to all concerned in time.

The detailed plan to be followed was that the 3rd Cammando Brigade would capture the Akyab beach from 7767 to 755641 and exploit to about the village at 816592. Thereafter, 8/19 Hyderabad would take over close protection of the beach. The 74th Indian Infantry Brigade would then pass through the beach and the harbour, preparatory to its move on Akyab town on D+1.

On the morning of 3 January 1945, the commander of the XV Indian Corps took his seat on a high point, overlooking the narrow waters. With him were the General Officer Commanding, 25th Indian Division and a group of senior naval, military and air force officers. Out at sea to the west could be seen a host of landing craft of two types approaching the landing beaches in neat formation; and far out on their flank lay the escorting cruisers and destroyers. As the landing craft approached the Akyab beaches, the naval vessels swung south and took up the positions from which they would have made their bombardment, had the landing been contested by the Japanese. But the landing was quiet and the commandos quickly established their beach-head and, along with the Beach Group, set about their tasks. The tanks of the 19th Lancers had followed close behind the infantry. As soon as they had unloaded their cargo of men, the assault craft turned north to the ferry terminal at Foul Point, where troops of the 74th Indian Infantry Brigade and 8/19 Hyderabad were waiting.

8/19 Hyderabad marched down to the beach and embarking into LCMs, landed unopposed on the north-west beach of Akyab island. From there they moved into the area of Kalawga (7663) covering the beach-head. By nightfall of 3 January 1945, in much less time than had been expected, the whole of the 74th Indian Infantry Brigade Group, along with its essential vehicles and mules, was also ashore and in harbour on Akyab island, behind the leading Commando elements.

It is worth mentioning here that the first troops to land on Akyab island were the men of 4 Royal Garhwal Rifles. They landed near Padali before dawn on 3 January 1945, to intercept any Japanese troops who might try to escape through this village. This battalion had made an unopposed scramble landing from Kudaung island at the north-west beaches of Kwede village of Akyab island at 0330 hours.[2]

Early on the morning of 4 January 1945, in accordance with the pre-arranged plan, the three battalions of the 74th Indian Infantry Brigade advanced on a wide front through the Commandos and entered and occupied Akyab town and its harbour. Their orders were to seize and place guards on all important buildings and installations, but such plans were unnecessary, for they found nothing but abandoned streets and ruined houses. Barounga island and the

---

[2] War Diaries of 74 Indian Infantry Brigade, 8/19 Hyderabad Regiment and 4 Royal Garhwal Rifles.

Troops of the 25th Indian Division wading to the beach at Akyab.

The ruins of Akyab as it was found after the Japanese had deserted.

Havildar Gaje Ghale, V.C.,
2/5th Royal Gurkha Rifles, Chin hills
(May, 1943)

Havildar Prakash Singh, V.C.,
5/8th Punjab Regiment, at Donbaik
in the Mayu Peninsula (January, 1944)

Naik Nand Singh, V.C.,
1/11th Sikh Regiment, Kalapanzin
Valley (March, 1944)

Jemadar Abdul Hafiz, V.C.,
3/9th Jat Regiment, Near Imphal
(April, 1944)

Jemadar (Actg. Subedar) Ram Sarup Singh, V.C., 2/1st Punjab Regiment, Near Tiddim (October, 1944)

Sepoy (now L. Naik) Bhandari Ram, V.C., 16/10 Baluch Regiment, East Mayu (November, 1944)

Havildar Umrao Singh, V.C., Indian Artillery, Kaladan Valley (December, 1944)

Rifleman Bhanbhagta Gurung, V.C., 3/2 Gurkha Rifles, "Snowden hills" near Tamandu (March, 1945)

Pauktaw peninsula were also found to be clear of the Japanese and were occupied by this brigade.

The local inhabitants gave a rousing reception to the Allied troops. Civil administration of the island was immediately resumed by Wing Commander Brasdley, Chief Civil Affairs Officer for Arakan; he had been the last civil administrator in Akyab before its evacuation by the British.

In Akyab no booby-traps were encountered except in the neighbourhood of the Japanese headquarters near Royal Lake. From the military aspect, however, the situation was very depressing. All the harbour facilities were out of commission and appeared to be damaged beyond repair, and two ships had been sunk at the harbour entrance itself. The airfields had been made unusable and one, the main strip on the island, had been mined by the Japanese. But the work on the strip was begun immediately. The divisional engineer resources were supplemented by 6 Oxf Bucks and, as a result, a squadron of Spitfires was able to fly just in time to deal with the first Japanese air attack on Allied shipping in the port on 7 January 1945, and to shoot down five "Oscars" with no loss to themselves.

Thus the first task allotted to the XV Indian Corps was concluded. The base, so badly needed for the supply of the Fourteenth Army requirements, had been secured and already work for its development was in hand.

CHAPTER XVII

Blockade Operations

The capture of Akyab which had been effected earlier than had been expected in the estimated progress of Operation 'Romulus', called for a reconsideration of the whole situation in Arakan. It had become apparent to the South-East Asia Command that the Japanese had started a gradual withdrawal of their troops from Akyab at the end of the monsoon in 1944, and most of them were withdrawing to join the *"Matsu Force"* in the Kaladan area. The last Japanese elements, which seemed to have consisted of the *1st Battalion, 111th Regiment (less 3 Company)* and some anti-tank and air defence troops, were reported to have left Akyab on 31 December 1944. Their destination appeared to be Ponnagyun, some twelve miles to the north on the west bank of the Kaladan river, and they had left behind only patrols in the north-east portion of Akyab island. Further intelligence reports had also confirmed that in northern Arakan the Japanese were attempting a co-ordinated withdrawal; and since there was no sign of any big counter-attack by the Japanese in Arakan, the main object of the Allies now was that of annihilating as many Japanese troops as possible before the latter could withdraw across the Yomas into the Irrawaddy valley.

Hence, in the first few days after the occupation of Akyab, the Corps did some quick thinking and quick planning. In order to take full advantage of the situation created by rapid success, the Corps commander decided to strike as early as possible at the Japanese line of retreat. Consequently, as a first step towards this plan, the 53rd Indian Infantry Brigade was ordered to despatch a force of two battalions across the island and engage the Japanese at Ponnagyun and then on towards Minbya; the object being to keep in contact with the Japanese and oblige them to keep their troops facing west. For this task the divisional battalion, 7/16 Punjab, was put under the command of the 53rd Indian Infantry Brigade; and the 51st Indian Infantry Brigade, which had been left behind at Indin, was ordered to concentrate on Akyab as soon as possible.

Action by the 53rd Indian Infantry Brigade

In view of the urgency to cut off the Japanese line of retreat, the 53rd Indian Infantry Brigade, now under the command of

Brigadier B.C. Hgerty, D.S.O., started "mopping up" and "blockade" operations in the area of Yo river and Minbya. The plan was for 9 Y & L to move on 6 January 1945 from Kudaung island via Tawbya river, Mingan and Kin chaungs to Ponnagyun (0376). From here, the battalion had to transfer to the Royal Navy landing craft and then proceeding north up the Kaladan river was to establish a "block" in the area of the Yo river.

The next battalion to be used for this plan was the 4th Royal Garhwal Rifles. This battalion was to move down to Akyab island from Padali, and then to embark and land at Ponnagyun.

At the time of the planning of this blockade, 7/16 Punjab was at a place called Thanthama, north-west of Akyab. The battalion was ordered to secure a beach-head at Pauktaw, and having done so, to hold it so that the troops might follow through with the intention of cutting the Japanese Line of Communication to the Kaladan.

Disruption of the Japanese line of retreat

On 6 January 1945, at 0700 hours, 9 Y & L commenced its move under a heavy downpour of rain. The battalion embarked, with the tactical headquarters leading the way, in the naval launch and the remainder in fleming-boats. Unfortunately, the fleming-boats which were obsolete proved entirely unsuitable, with the result that B company of this battalion had to be left behind and could not rejoin the battalion until late in the afternoon.

At 1230 hours, B company arrived at the village of Modinbyin (9683) and was told by the local inhabitant that the Japanese were still in great strength at Ponnagyun. At the Chaung junction (975805) the battalion was fired upon by Japanese light machine-guns. The fire was returned and it appeared that the Japanese had withdrawn to Diparon (9880). The battalion then heavily bombarded the Japanese position and made an unopposed landing in the area 971807.

In view of the fact that the Japanese were in strength at Ponnagyun, 9 Y & L changed its plans into an outflanking movement. The main object now was not to capture Ponnagyun but to advance further up the Kaladan river and establish a block at Yo river. The risk, therefore, of attempting to force a passage through Mingan and Kin chaungs, in very vulnerable and extremely unsuitable craft, did not appear justified. Hence the battalion decided to withdraw after dark and make a detour via the Mikyun chaung, Myinwa river and Mingyaung chaung to the Kaladan at the north-east tip of Akyab island.

While these activities of 9 Y & L were going on, 4 Royal Garhwal Rifles was also on the move to carry out the tasks allotted to it. At 0938 hours on 8 January 1945, it set sail from the Akyab jetty and by 1130 hours had commenced landing in the Ponnagyun area. But the landing was unopposed and by 1700 hours the entire battalion was concentrated in its new positions. Meanwhile 9 Y & L had concentrated in the area of Modinbyin (9683). On learning that 4 Royal Garhwal Rifles had occupied Ponnagyun without any opposition, it advanced to Ponnagyun via the Mingan and Kin chaungs. Having arrived at Ponnagyun, 9 Y & L was then ordered to advance further in order to establish a block on the Yo river, thereby cutting the escape line of any Japanese troops who might still be left west of the Kaladan river. The disposition of this battalion on 9 January was as follows:—

Battalion less two companies was at Ponnagyun.
C company and Tactical Headquarters in area 046878.
D company with two sections of mortars in area 045900.

During the night, while the situation remained normal on the 9 Y & L sector, a strong Japanese force covered by armed motor launches attempted a landing at Ponnagyun jetty, at about 2230 hours. C company of 4 Royal Garhwal Rifles engaged them with heavy fire; nevertheless, one boat-load of Japanese was successful in landing and a confused, close-quarter fighting between C company and the raiders ensued in which the Japanese were driven off with substantial losses and the fighting ended at 0115 hours on 10 January. It was realized that small arms fire was ineffective against the armoured boats that the Japanese had used in this raid; with anti-tank rifles, however, the boats would have been undoubtedly sunk.

For the next two days 4 Royal Garhwal Rifles did routine patrolling and also operated east up the Kaladan river. This was to deceive the Japanese in believing that Allied main thrust would come from the east, whereas in actual fact it was to be launched from the south, *i.e.* from Myebon.

On 10 January however, 9 Y & L had established a block on the Yo river. On the night of 11/12 January 1945, the Japanese attempted to withdraw from the hills to the west through Yongon village where the 9 Y & L was positioned, and crossed the Kaladan river by landing craft. This attempt proved very costly to them and at first light on 12 January twenty-four Japanese bodies were counted and a quantity of equipment captured. British casualties in this action were 12 killed and 19 wounded. As a result, Yongon village was strengthened by concentrating more troops in that area.

On 13 January, B company of 9 Y & L while patrolling to Panila (030955) and Kinpala (9895) without seeing any Japanese troops made contact with the patrols of the 81st West African Division Reconnaissance Regiment. The latter were operating south from the area of Pyinyashe (015085). By 18 January 1945, 9 Y & L was completely relieved in its positions by the 81st West African Division, and thereafter moved back to Akyab island.

The Kyeyebyin battle

It is now necessary to recount the activities of 7/16 Punjab. This battalion on 4 January 1945 had concentrated at Thanthama, near the coast to the north-west of Akyab. On 6 January, it had come under the command of the 74th Indian Infantry Brigade and had secured a beach-head at Pauktaw on 10 January, supported in its task by the cruiser H.M.S. *"Phoebe"*. The battalion having concentrated in Pauktaw was informed by the local inhabitants that the Japanese had withdrawn from that area in the north-east direction, about ten days earlier. Further information gained showed that the Japanese were in very bad health and had very little ammunition at their disposal.

On 12 January 1945, 7/16 Punjab was put under the command of the 53rd Indian Infantry Brigade. For the next two days it carried out patrol duties in landing craft, across the Kywegu river without encountering any Japanese troops and by 14 January had concentrated in the area of Pulibauk (026700).

On the same day Allied intelligence reports further revealed that the Japanese *54th Division* was pulling out south to Taungup, leaving strong rearguard forces in the Kaladan area; the locals helped in giving some further valuable information.

During the course of its patrol activities, C company of 7/16 Punjab, while trying to land at Kyeyebyin, was fired at by light machine-guns and snipers. Again, when one of the LCSs proceeded upstream, it was engaged by a 37 mm gun and badly damaged. On 16 January, a patrol of A company sailed to Kyabaikke (331713) and Palaungbyin (345726) but did not encounter any Japanese. On the same day, a company of 7/16 Punjab reported that Thazi (293722) was also clear of the Japanese but once again the patrol to Kyeyebyin had to engage in a little skirmish; about twenty Japanese had put up some resistance but had eventually run away.

On 18 January 1945, a platoon of D company was ordered to take up a permanent position in Kyeyebyin village. This platoon, in addition to its normal establishment of equipment and arms, was given a wireless set and a detachment of 3" mortars. This platoon took up its new positions in the village after meeting with a little opposition from about two sections of Japanese troops. The village of Kyeyebyin is bounded on the immediate south by a deep, unbridged chaung; 100 yards to the east is a large tidal river and 50 yards to its west is another deep chaung, flanked by a marsh. At the northern end of this village was built up a fresh water tank, about 15 yards square. It was on the banks of this tank that the platoon was sited so that any approach by the Japanese had to be made over open fields, from the north.

At about 1900 hours on 19 January, in the light of the rising moon, about 50 Japanese approached this platoon's positions, from the north-east and north-west. As the Japanese closed in, they were greeted with a volley of mortar, grenade and automatic weapon fire. Nevertheless, some of them succeeded in infiltrating round the east flank of the platoon and thereby constituted a threat to the 3" mortar detachment, which was situated about 15 yards behind the rear section of the D company platoon. Hearing of this situation, the D company commander at Pulibauk set off to take charge of the position accompanied by another platoon. With courage and initiative he managed to retrieve the situation and, clearing the village, secured the east flank of the forward platoon. The second platoon which he had brought with him was held in reserve for any future counter-attack that might have to be delivered.

At about 2300 hours the Japanese again opened up on these two D company platoons with 75 mm guns, 4" mortars and MMGs. This time the Japanese attacking force proved to be about 150 strong. They attacked three times between 2400 hours and 0600 hours, first from the north-west, then from the north-east and finally from the north. The two D company platoons, however, fought very bravely and a high standard of courage and initiative was shown by all concerned. Hand-to-hand fighting took place and the Japanese assault was broken up time and again.

On the morning of 19 January 1945, the D company platoons discovered that the Japanese commander of the attacking party had been killed along with his wireless set so that none of the attacking party had any orders to withdraw. The Indian platoons thereafter opened up with everything they had. Forming batteries of their grenade dischargers and 2" mortars, and aided by the long range hitting power of their 3" mortars, they took a terrible toll of the already defeated Japanese, who were trying to escape back towards Minbya. About 100 Japanese bodies were later counted. Indian casualties in this action were only two killed and four wounded. It was in this battle during the night of 18/19 January that one of the killed, No 14922 Lance/Naik Sher Shah, was awarded the Victoria Cross (posthumous) for his bravery.

By midday of 19 January the villagers of Kyeyebyin brought information about Japanese concentrations in certain areas to the north-east of the village. The Allied air attack was therefore arranged to take place at 0800 hours on 20 January which was carried out with accuracy and did a lot of damage to the Japanese.

For the next few days, 7/16 Punjab further patrolled up to a depth of six to ten miles north of Pulibauk without meeting any opposition, or seeing any Japanese. On 22 January 1945, it was relieved by 4 Royal Garhwal Rifles, which arrived from Ponnagyun to Pulibauk on 25 January and completed the taking over by the evening of the same day. On 26 January, 7/16 Punjab had left for Myebon.

On 23 January 1945, latest aerial photographs of the Mingye area had been dropped on the forward Indian positions, by means of Hurricanes. These photographs showed that the Minbya area was strongly defended by a system of trenches along with medium machine-guns and some higher calibre gun positions. It also proved the fact that these Japanese positions dominated the whole of the area below Minbya itself. At the same time, the brigade headquarter intelligence report had also confirmed that the Japanese *111th Regiment* less one battalion, about a company of the *154th Regiment*, one battery of the *54th Division Field Artillery*, some engineers and a few mules were moving up from Yongon and Ponnagyun area towards Minbya.

Fall of Myohaung

At this stage it would not be out of place to refer to the activities of the 82nd West African Division as this force was eventually to meet 4 Royal Garhwal Rifles in the Minbya area. It will be remembered that the 82nd West African Division was to take over from the 81st West African Division in the Kaladan valley, after the latter had captured Myohaung, and was to continue operations down the waterways, south-east from Myohaung. The 82nd West African Division completed the crossing of the hills from the Kalapanzin to the Kaladan and its 4th Brigade, which was leading ahead, pushed on faster to join the 81st African Division in the capture of Myohaung. Contact with the Japanese in the Kalapanzin valley had by this time been lost and the two remaining brigades of the 82nd West African Division carried out a normal move through a country notable for its grandeur and beauty. This period, however, marked the closing of their road supply system and the commencement of a long period of air supply, which was proving so important a factor in the Burma campaign.

On 25 January, the 81st West African Division entered Myohaung in which some brisk fighting was experienced by both the 1st and the 4th Brigades. Thereafter, the 82nd West African Division concentrated in Myohaung for a short rest prior to taking on further tasks. The 1st West African Brigade, however, was meanwhile pushing on without a pause to exploit the capture of Myohaung and secure the crossing of the Lemro river, east and south-west of Myohaung; this was achieved without incident. It also continued to advance against light opposition down the west

Occupation of Minbya

4 Royal Garhwal Rifles, having arrived at Pulibauk on 25 January, took over the task of pinning down nearly 2,000 Japanese who were believed to be in the Minbya area. In view of the proximity of the 1st West African Brigade that was probing down the Lemro river, the role of 4 Royal Garhwal Rifles was confined to active patrolling only. Apart from occasional patrol clashes, south of Minbya, and the despatch of two companies to operate ten miles away on another of the Japanese escape routes, the stay of this battalion at Pulibauk was without incident.

In the meantime, Hpontha, about 16 miles south-east of Myohaung, fell to the 1st West African Brigade on 29 January, and, on 1 February 1945, Minbya was occupied by 22 Anti-Tank Regiment.

On 28 January, 4 Royal Garhwal Rifles had come under the direct command of the XV Corps Tactical Headquarters. Although Minbya was out of this battalion's patrolling area, it was granted permission to do so after being informed by the locals that the Japanese had cleared out of that area. Accordingly, on 2 February 1945, B company patrolled to Minbya and found that it really had been evacuated by the Japanese; at the same time it contacted the West Africans in their southward drive. Minbya was finally cleared of the Japanese on 3 February 1945.

The final stages

Before closing the chapter on the blockade operations, subsequent to the assault on Akyab, mention may be made of the movements and activities of 17/5 Mahratta Light Infantry. This battalion left Rathedaung in heavy rainfall and by crossing several chaungs on the way, in unit "sampans", reached Padali on 6 January 1945. By 15 January, it had completed concentration at Akyab and from there moved on to Ponnagyun on 20 January 1945. From Ponnagyun the battalion was ordered to proceed towards Minbya. The route it followed was along the north-east via Hinkaya (145815), Pyinkala (210805) and Kula (240835). On 26 January, the headquarter company and C company reached Mingan (277840), on the west bank of the Yede river, and on the same day A company concentrated at Damagya (274818). On 27 January, C company which was stationed at Mingan opened fire on a Japanese vessel in the Yede river. Thereafter, Mingan was subjected to heavy fire by the Japanese from the direction of Minbya. Some Japanese fire also came from the east bank of the Yede river opposite Mingan but this was soon stopped by A company which opened up medium machine gun fire in this area of the east bank. It appeared that the Japanese fire from the opposite bank came from some naval craft which soon after turned and fled eastwards along the Sadaing chaung.

No more Japanese forces were encountered by this battalion which eventually concentrated at Kywenazwe (247856) with the exception of A company which was stationed at Kula. Later on, the battalion was transported to Myebon in steamers on 2 February 1945.

CHAPTER XVIII

The Myebon Landing

The new appreciation

Soon after the capture of Akyab island the Allied appreciation of Japanese dispositions was summed up as follows: Of the two main Japanese task forces, it had become clear that the *Sakurai Force*, having been obliged to withdraw from the Mayu peninsula into the Kaladan valley, had, some time in early January, passed through the *Matsu Force*, commanded by Major-General Koba, and that the former was on its way to join its division in south-west Burma. The role of the Japanese *55th Division* now appeared to be the defence of the Arakan Coast from Taungup to Pagoda Point, keeping its central reserve of troops in the area of Henzada-Prome. In the Kaladan and Lemro deltas, *Matsu Force* was believed to consist of two regimental groups. To the north of the area Mychaung-Minbya, there was the *111th Regiment* less the *2nd Battalion*; this was originally thought to be in the Tamandu area, under Colonel Yagi. The other regiment, the *154th* was in the area of Myebon and Kangaw. This regiment was believed to be short of the *2nd Battalion*, which was in central Burma, but had been reinforced by a draft from that battalion along with the *54th Reconnaissance Regiment* (less one tank squadron). At this time, Allied intelligence reports had also indicated that the headquarters of the *154th Regiment* and a battalion were in the area of Letpan while another battalion was in Myohaung. Of the 1st Battalion of *111th Regiment*, the remnants of the *2nd Company*, which had failed to get away from Akyab via Ponnagyun, were being mopped up on the west bank of the Kaladan. Headquarters of the Japanese *54th Division* was known to be at Kolan, near An.

At the time of this appreciation the Japanese had not attempted to contest the 82nd West African Division's crossing of the Htizwe-Kanzauk track into the Kaladan; this division was, therefore, now rapidly preparing to relieve the 81st West African Division as soon as Myohaung had been captured.

It had always been the Corps Commander's intention that as soon as Akyab was secured, they would exploit to Minbya and Myebon, but the Supreme Allied Commander had later directed that there was to be no further exploitation without his orders. But with Akyab in Allied hands and patrolling towards Minbya already in

MYEBON AND ADJACENT AREA

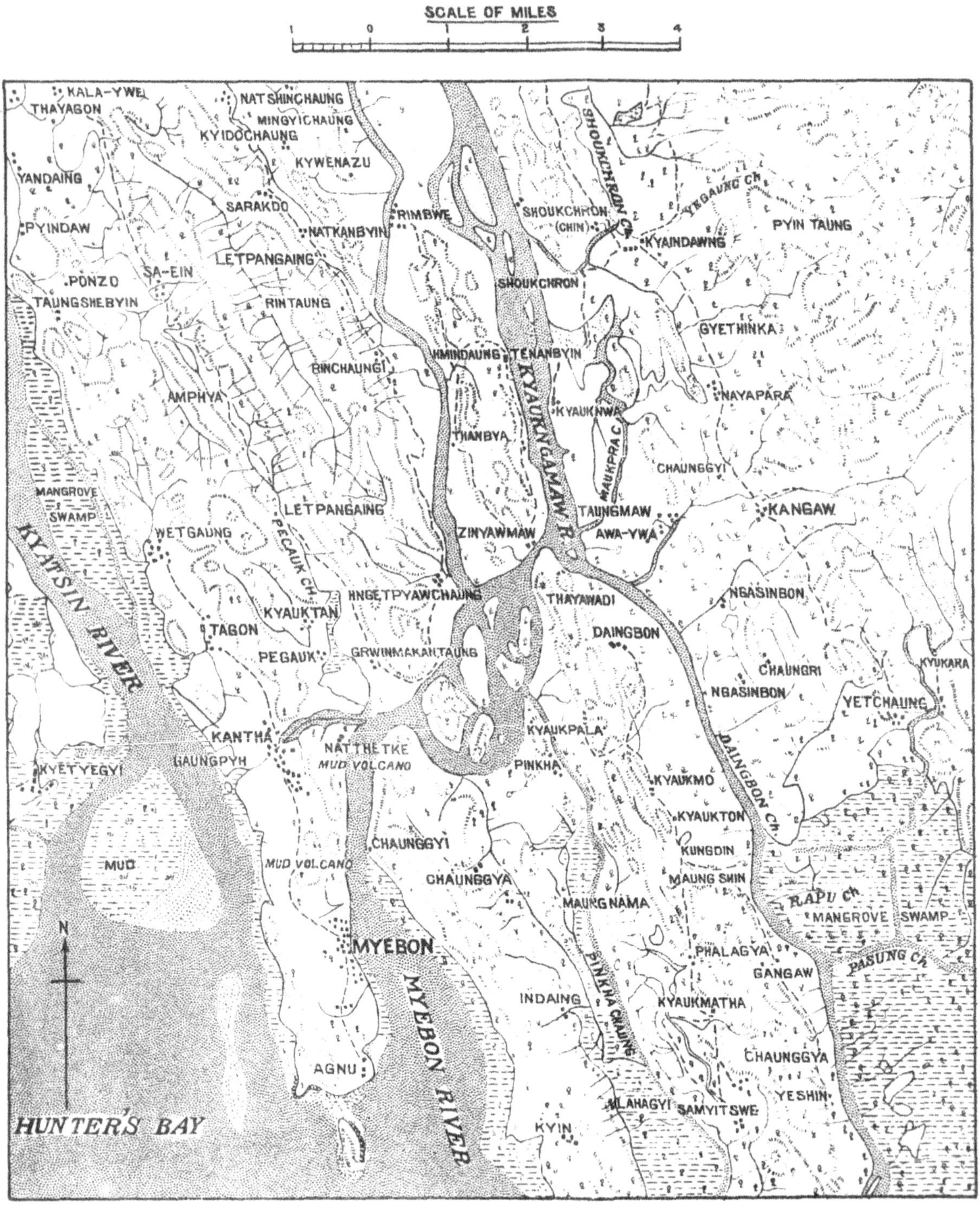

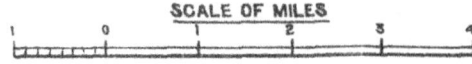

progress, there was a golden opportunity for the Allies to establish quickly a "block" on the Japanese Line of Communication, in order to catch the largest possible number of General Koba's troops. Effectively carried out with maximum speed, such an operation might lead to the destruction of the Japanese northern group.

To this end, the 26th Indian Division, which was originally intended to take Akyab, had been planning an advance along the chaungs towards Minbya, to link up with the West Africans in the Kaladan. But as the situation developed, it had become obvious that the 25th Indian Division could mount this operation more quickly than the 26th Indian Division which was then in Cox's Bazaar.

In addition to this thrust at Minbya, which was eventually undertaken by the 25th Indian Division, the Corps Commander had also been thinking in terms of capturing the Myebon peninsula, lying thirteen miles east-south-east of Akyab, which commanded the two main waterways used by the Japanese, *viz.* the Kyatsin river and Daingbon Chaung.

It was originally intended that the Myebon assault should be carried out by the 3rd Special Service Brigade (3 Commando Brigade) while the 36th Indian Infantry Brigade (26th Indian Division) was to be used as a follow-up brigade. The assault on Minbya was to be made by the 71st Indian Infantry Brigade while the 4th Indian Infantry Brigade (both of the 26th Indian Division) secured its line of communication towards Akyab.

But as events took shape, the 53rd Indian Infantry Brigade (25th Indian Division) along with 7/16 Punjab Regiment had been committed towards the Minbya front. There was also little doubt in the mind of the Corps Commander that only an assault landing on the Myebon peninsula and exploitation to the road where it ran in a defile close to the coast, would achieve the object of cutting the main Japanese line of communication. Although it was admitted that a landing at Myebon would not provide immediate distraction to the Japanese who were fighting in the Myohaung area, as would an assault further to the north, yet it was evident that a blow to the far south in the Japanese rear was likely to give a better chance of cutting off the maximum number of the latter, behind the "block". It had also the added advantage of requiring fewer troops to carry out the operation and of completely freeing the 26th Indian Division for other tasks.

The Supreme Allied Commander therefore concurred in the Commander XV Indian Corps' plan for the assault on Myebon peninsula, which employed only the 25th Indian Division and 3rd Commando Brigade for the purpose. At the same time, it was also decided to press on with the capture of the Ramree island with the help of the 26th Indian Division and, having cleared it of the

Japanese, to exploit in the direction of Cheduba and Sagukyun, while the construction of airfields in the north of Ramree could commence earlier than planned originally.

Once this decision had been taken and the various units allotted the tasks they were to perform, the Corps Commander relieved the 25th Indian Division of its responsibilities for the operation which the 53rd Indian Infantry Brigade was carrying on towards Minbya. Consequently, the 53rd Indian Infantry Brigade along with 7/16 Punjab came directly under the XV Indian Corps while the 25th Indian Division was left to plan the assault on Myebon.

Morale and disposition of the XV Indian Corps

Even after the capture of Akyab the troops of the XV Indian Corps were found to be fresh and unweary and their morale was very high due to repeated successes. The 81st West African Division, however, had been in action for over a year and it was to return to India after being relieved by the 82nd West African Division, soon after the capture of Myohaung. The 82nd West African Division had had to march a considerable distance; it had fought its way from Buthidaung to Htizwe against determined Japanese rearguard action, but its casualties had been light and it was in a fairly good condition for its future operations in the Kaladan valley. The 25th Indian Division had come a long way and at great speed. The only strong opposition experienced by it had been on the 53rd Indian Infantry Brigade front; while, on the other hand, the 74th and 51st Indian Infantry Brigades were quite fit and ready for further operations.

The 26th Indian Division had not taken any active part since the beginning of Operation 'Romulus.' Throughout this period it had undergone intensive training particularly in combined operations. This division, which had had very considerable expereince against the Japanese in Arakan, was now at Chittagong and was available for a seaborne assault along with the 3rd Commando Brigade, which had also not been committed to any large extent.

The 22nd East African Brigade had not been committed to any battle at all; it had been held as corps reserve on the general line of communications on the Mayu 'Spine'. Its main action had been to mop up all the Japanese garrisons that had been by-passed by the 25th Indian Division in the Mayu peninsula.

The Myebon peninsula

The Myebon peninsula lies about 35 miles east-south-east of Akyab. It projects from the mainland into Hunter's Bay and is a little less than a mile-and-a-half in width. From its southern beaches it is about four-and-a-half miles to the Kantha chaung, which

MYEBON PENINSULA

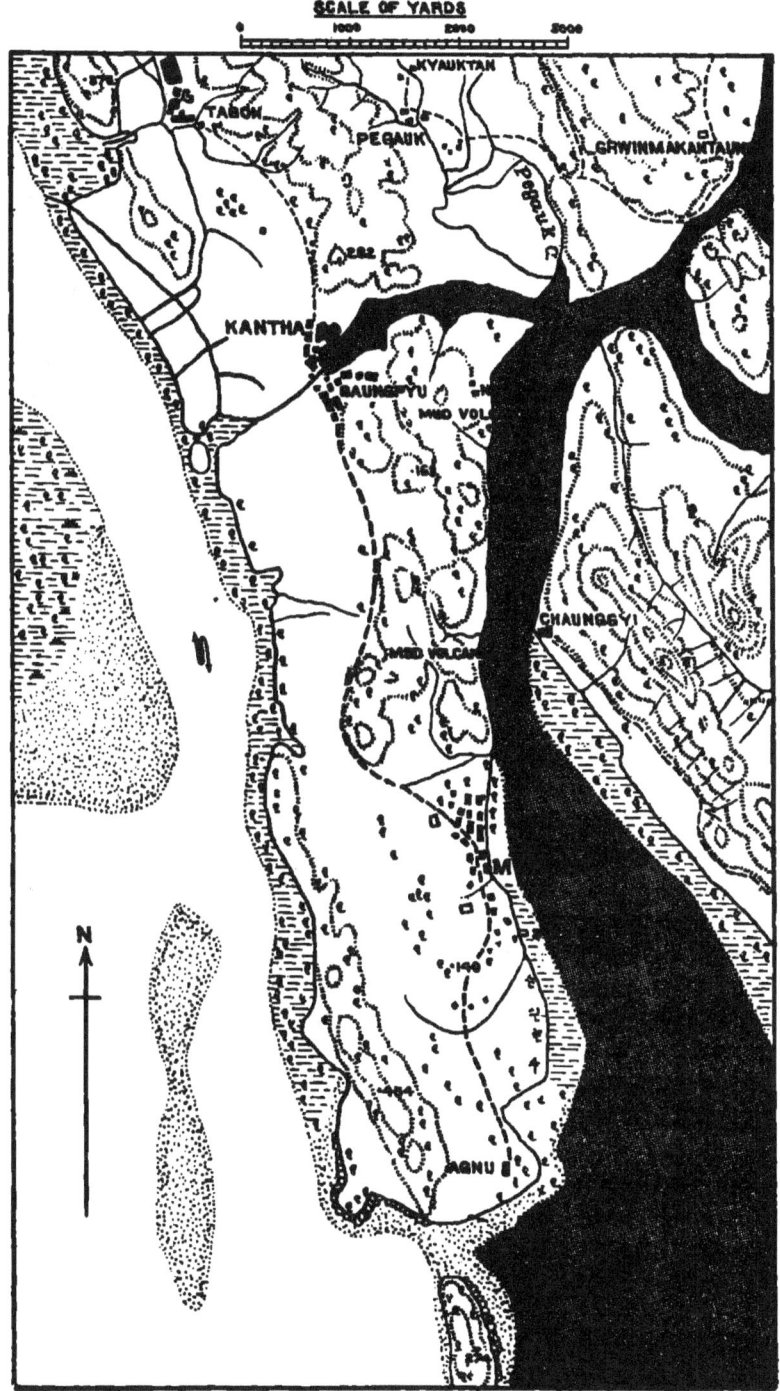

SPOT HEIGHTS SHOWN ARE IN FEET......-282

completely separates it from the mainland. The peninsula lies between the estuaries of the Kyastsin river to the west and the Myebon river to the east.

The village of Myebon is situated by the side of the Myebon river, about two miles from the southern end of the peninsula. South of the village on the east side of the peninsula, the terrain is clear of hill features; but to the north of the village there starts a range of high ground which runs due north to the Kantha chaung, overlooking both the river to the east as well as the half-mile-wide strip of flat ground that runs up the entire length of the centre of the peninsula. A string of connected features runs diagonally from the centre of the south beach to about midway up the western coast line of the peninsula; the highest of these features is Point 454. To the north of this again is about two miles of flat country which runs right up to Kantha Chaung, midway from one coast to the other. Thereafter, immediately north of the chaung, there is a belt of flat country but this and the chaung itself are dominated by the southern ends of three parallel mountain ranges, which continue due north up to about Minbya. A large part of the peninsula is heavily wooded.

The Assault Plan

On 11 January 1945, the 25th Indian Division received the following orders from the XV Indian Corps Commander:—

"You will carry out Operation "Passport' with a view to securing Myebon peninsula as a firm base. From this firm base you will operate south and south-east to cut the enemy's Line of Communications as far as the hills, east of Kangaw (5350)".

The Commando Brigade consisting of 1 and 5 Army Commandos and 42 and 44 Royal Marine Commandos, was placed under the command of the 25th Indian Division for this purpose. As has already been mentioned, in order to enable the General Officer Commanding of the 25th Indian Division to concentrate his division entirely on the Myebon operations, the XV Indian Corps had taken over the command of the 53rd Indian Infantry Brigade and 7/16 Punjab (less one company), which were operating towards Minbya. In addition, all the troops of the 25th Indian Division, not Directly taking part in moving to Myebon, also came under the command of the XV Indian Corps with effect from 2359 hours on 11 January 1945.

Operation 'Passport' was naturally mounted under an Inter-Service Command. The Joint Force Commanders were Major-General Wood (G.O.C. 25 Indian Division), Capt. D. Hill, D.S.O., R.N. and Wing-Commander Drake, D.F.C., R.A.F. The assault Commanders were Brigadier C.R. Hardy, D.S.O., (Commanding 3

Commando Brigade), Capt. M. H. St. L. Nott, R.I.N., and Squadron-Leader D.T. Lees, R.A.F.

The Force Commanders decided that the only beach suitable for the assault was CHARLIE Beach, at the south-east corner of the peninsula, alongside the village of Agnu. As there was an extensive mud-flat off this beach, it was necessary for the assault to be made at, or just before, high water. There was also a good sandy beach at the south-west corner of the peninsula, but it had no exits; a rocky promontory would have prevented vehicles from getting off this particular beach. The other beaches in the area had neither sufficient exits nor suitable terrain for establishing the requisite type of beach-heads.

The 3rd Commando Brigade was to assault and secure the southern portion of the peninsula, including Myebon village and its jetty. The 74th Indian Infantry Brigade was then to land on D+1, pass through the occupied beach-head to complete the occupation of the peninsula and then exploit north or east as the tactical situation might indicate. The whole assault was to be supported by a maximum effort of 224 Group R.A.F. and the guns of the two sloops, H. M. I. S. *"Narbada"* and H. M. I. S. *"Jumna"*. H. M. A. S. *"Napier"* (a destroyer with six 6″ guns) and the A.A. cruiser *"Phoebe"* were also available but were not expected to get close to the shore owing to their deeper draught and the shallowness of the water.

The composition of the land force was greatly limited by the shortage of naval craft, and for this reason it became even more necessary to choose between tanks and guns. The choice, however, fell on the tanks and, as it later turned out, the choice was a wise one. A remarkable situation, therefore, arose in which an assault landing likely to be opposed was launched without the inculsion of any field artillery whatsoever.

Reconnaissance

As D Day for Operation 'Passport' had been fixed for 12 January 1945, planning had to be made very hurriedly. Little, however, was known about the Myebon peninsula and its surrounding waters. Existing maps at the disposal of the planners were not very accurate and the available naval charts were so incomplete that they did not even show any soundings of Hunter's Bay. Extensive reconnaissance was, therefore, immediately undertaken and motor launches were continuously working at night, taking soundings and correcting existing charts. A personal reconnaissance of the approaches to the proposed landing beach was also made by Brigadier C.R. Hardy, D.S.O., and Captain Nott, R.I.N.

During the course of these reconnaissances it was found that the approach to the chosen beach on the south-east face of Myebon peninsula was blocked by a row of huge wooden stakes. These stakes had been driven into the sea-bed, individually. They had probably been lashed between two country craft at high water and then, due to the drop in tide, been forced down until they were now firmly embedded in the mud. These wooden stakes were about 10" in diameter and approximately 15 feet high; they were placed 8 to 10 feet apart and covered a distance of about 400 yards parallel to, and about 300 yards out from, the line of low water. The distance between the stakes did not allow the passage of LCAs and as there was no other beach for assault purposes the requisite gap between the stakes had to be made. It was thought that land mines dropped by aircraft might possibly do the necessary damage but the results could not be guaranteed; so the idea was given up. Consequently, on the night before D Day a Naval Combined Operations Pilotage Party crept up to the selected stakes at low water and attached "delay charges" to these anti-boat obstacles; these were timed to go off at first light on 12 January 1945.

Eventually, on the morning of the landing these charges did go off in time, creating gaps which were perfectly suitable for the passage of the landing craft and complete tactical surprise was thereby achieved.

The assault landing

Preceded by heavy air strikes and a preliminary naval bombardment, the 3rd Commando Brigade made the assault landing on the southern tip of the peninsula, under cover of a perfect smoke-screen laid down by Hurricanes. D Day was 12 January 1945, and H hour was 0830 hours. No difficulty was experienced in passing through the gap in the stakes and the Allied Bombing Squadron had caught the Japanese unawares.

The naval and air bombardment had prevented most of the Japanese from manning their posts and only light opposition was encountered by the first wave of the Commando Brigade. An early opposition, however, came from two 75 mm, two 37 mm and one British 2-pounder gun; but the weight and devastating effect of the preliminary Allied bombardments had very greatly reduced the effectiveness of this opposition. As a result, within a few moments of the Commando's first landing, the 37 mm and the British 2-pounder gun had both been overrun and captured.

The Japanese beach-head defences in that area consisted of a series of well-constructed bunkers, protected by an anti-tank ditch and a rather incomplete series of beach mines. Though within half an hour of the landing, the line from Pagoda Hill (437382) to about 427378 had been secured, yet, thereafter, the opposition stiffened considerably. The subsequent flight of the Commandos met with increasing difficulty owing to the falling tide, so much so that late-comers found themselves confronted with about 400 yards of waist-deep mud, and one tank was lost in it. Subsequently it was also discovered that although quite suitable for the original landing, this beach, nicknamed CHARLIE RED, was totally impracticable for the maintenance and landing of guns and tanks.

The only other alternative appeard to be the beach to the west. A quick sapper reconnaissance disclosed that, by heavy blasting, a track could be made through the ridge of the rock at the eastern end, which separated the western beach from CHARLIE RED. As a practicable maintenance beach was absolutely essential, the decision to go ahead with the new plan was made by the Joint Force Commanders in H.M.A.S. *"Napier"* during the afternoon of 12 January. Work was, therefore, undertaken and carried out by 63 Indian Field Company throughout that day and all night, and from early the next morning, until the conclusion of the operation. The new beach (known as "EASY BEACH") proved entirely satisfactory.

Meanwhile, the Commandos had pushed on ahead. Agnu village was quickly captured and after the Pagoda Hill feature had been cleared with the help of air support, their drive north towards Myebon village was resumed. During this period H.M.I.S. *"Narbada"* steamed up the Myebon river and shelled the village and its jetty area from almost point-blank range. Later the *"Narbada"* was taken as far as the Pier (437401) in support. It was a very anxious passage for this ship as the depth of the river for a considerable way was only 12 feet 10 inches while *Narbada's* draught was 12 feet 6 inches. She did eventually manage to creep along and, under cover of her fire, an attempt was made to land some tanks on the portion of the beach, immediately to the north of CHARLIE RED. Although one tank actually got ashore, the beach came under such heavy Japanese shell fire that the attempt had to be abandoned. This beach was subsequently found to be very heavily mined.

The remainder of the tanks were eventually landed on "EASY BEACH" and this task was accomplished by nightfall of 12 January, but as a result of the area being muddy and sandy as well as mined to some extent, these tanks could not be got into action. By the close of 12 January, however, except for two LCM (Landing Craft Mechanized) loads, the whole assault force had managed to land on the peninsula.

During the night of 12/13 January, Allied motor launches patrolled the Myebon river as far as Diangbon chaung; they met with fire from 75 mm and 37 mm guns as well as light machine-guns from both banks of the river. Naval casualties during 12 January were two killed while one LCA (Landing Craft Assault) was sunk by Japanese gun fire.

On the morning of 13 January, 8 to 10 Japanese aircraft (Oscars) failed in an attempt to bomb Allied shipping. Three of these planes were claimed to have been destroyed by the Royal Navy's Anti-aircraft guns and two by the Royal Air Force. The same day, with the help of heavy and close support from the Royal Air Force the Commandos cleared the defended hill features to the west of Myebon village. A major feature of these ground operations was the deployment of armour in close support of the Commando Brigade's exploitation, rapidly engaging Japanese bunkers in their defensive positions, which threatened to hold up the infantry advance. Fire was normally controlled by an officer from the Tank Regiment, who accompanied the leading infantry sub-unit on foot carrying a 38 set (wireless), netted on to the tank commander's frequency. This Forward Tank Officer called for fire support as required by the infantry, to either destroy or neutralise the Japanese defensive weapons, or to give covering fire, ordering the lifts as required. High explosive and anti-personnel shells and co-axial machine-guns were all used by the tanks. The infantry occasionally employed No. 77 smoke grenades as a means of indicating its positions. Tanks also undertook diverse other tasks including the clearance of jungle with high-explosive and indirect shoots under the Forward Tank Officer's control.

The follow-up landings had also continued according to plan, and by mid-day of 19 January, the first artillery was put ashore. This consisted of one medium gun and a troop of Bofors. The difficulties in landing artillery had proved even more severe than those of landing the tanks on the previous day. During the period when it was not yet possible to get the guns into action ashore, much valuable support was given by field guns mounted in Z craft and brought into action while still afloat. Each Z craft was capable of mounting a troop of 25 pounders. These craft were extremely manoeuvrable and could normally be brought into action within fifteen minutes. By means of this arrangement, guns could be fired from areas where no ground positions were available, although it was desireable to beach the craft on mud or sand before firing. One such craft manned by 27 Field Regiment was made available for the Myebon Operation, where it proved invaluable during the first three days of the battle.

Later in the day, the leading troops of the Commandos had entered the outskirts of Myebon village. Stiff opposition on the feature 428402, west of Myebon, and later at Pagoda Hill 434419, north of the town, had failed to hold up the advance and both positions were in their hands by nightfall. By this time also tactical

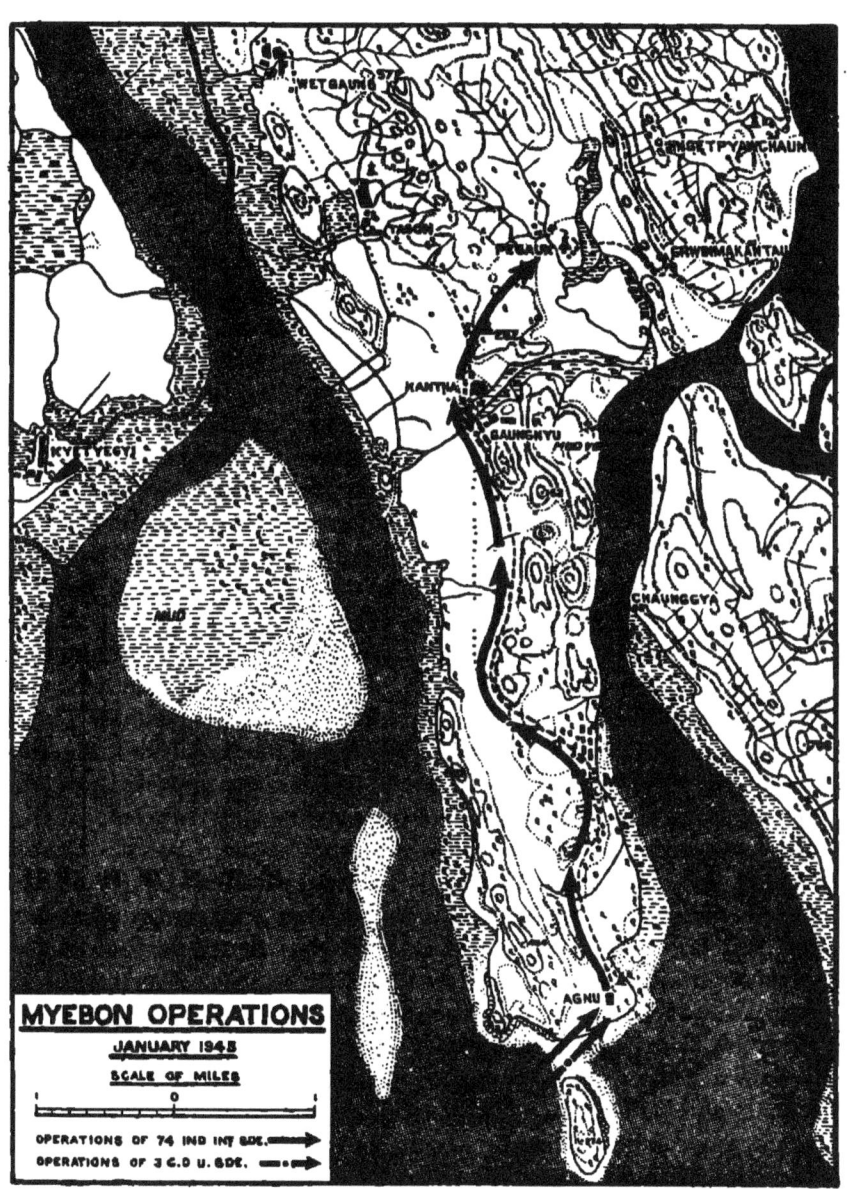

headquarters of the 25th Indian Division had been established at "EASY BEACH", on the south end of the Peninsula.

Activities of the 74th Indian Infantry Brigade

The 74th Indian Brigade had been organising and preparing to carry out its tasks as a follow-through brigade and was in readiness to land on the peninsula the moment a beach-head had been established by the Commandos. But shortage of shipping made it impossible to bring the whole brigade in one wave; it was therefore decided that the first flight would consist of Oxf Bucks in Landing Craft, 3/2 G.R. to be ferried in HMS 'Phoebe', while 14/10 Baluch was to follow later, as and when more naval craft became available. Certain vessels were earmarked for the carriage of stores; battalion stores were to be carried in one LCM while the rest of the craft were to transport 19 mules, 6 trucks and 3 water-carriers.

At 1200 hours on 12 January 1945, 6 Oxf Bucks embarked at Akyab. On 13 January, they had landed on EASY BEACH in the area between 422374 and 429373 without meeting any Japanese opposition. Immediately after landing they took over the beach-head positions that had been secured by the Commando Brigade.

On the same day, 3/2 G.R. sailed in HMS "Phoebe" at dusk. But owing to shallow water, she could only get to within 14 miles of the Myebon beaches by the early hours of 13 January. At 0800 hours, the battalion was transhipped in mine-sweepers which took them to within a mile of the beach, whence they were put ashore in LCAs. During the last phase of their Journey, the Japanese put in an air attack which resulted in two of their planes being shot down.

By the night of 13/14 January, it had become apparent that the Japanese were trying to delay the advance beyond Myebon so that they could withdraw the maximum number of their troops. During the day time, Allied motor launches had patrolled nearly all the chaungs and rivers, south of chaung junction 4849, but no Japanese craft had been seen or encountered. During the night, however, a Japanese powered country craft, loaded with stores and men was seen attempting to escape and was successfully sunk with all hands.

By 14 January, all the units of the 74th Indian Infantry Brigade had been landed ashore. The 3/2 Gurkha Rifles had moved forward and concentrated in the area at 434394, ready to follow up the Commando Brigade which had been meeting with heavy opposition in the Myebon village area and its surrounding hills. On 15 January, a plan was envisaged whereby the Commandos were to capture the hill feature in the area 4244; 3/2 Gurkha Rifles was then to exploit through to Kantha and push on to occupy the hill feature, Point 262.

The Commandos commenced their advance assisted by tanks of

19th Lancers, against very heavy Japanese opposition. They put in an attack on Point 200, a feature about two and a quarter miles to the north of Myebon village, but were held up near the crest of the hill. Later, a 19th Lancers' tank climbed the hill to within 40 yards of the crest and knocked out a few bunkers and three light machine-guns, before toppling over backwards owing to the steepness of the slope. Thus Point 200 fell to the Commandos who, pushing on ahead, also secured Point 163, a feature lying two miles north-west of Myebon village.

On 16 January, the village of Gaungpyu was reported to be clear of the Japanese. Consequently 3/2 G.R., along with tactical headquarters and a mortar section on mules, moved through the forward Commando troops and occupied the area. Their further advance was delayed due to the naval bombardment which the Allies were putting down on Point 262. The safety line was the line of the chaung which could not be crossed till the bombardment was over.

Immediately after the bombardment had been called off, a patrol was despatched to the village of Kantha. On its return it revealed that the place was deserted. D company of 3/2 G.R. thereupon crossed the line of the chaung and occupying the village, started reconnoitring Point 262. It was later discovered that this feature was defended by a garrison, about a company in strength, with 90 mm mortars, two 75 mm guns and medium machine-guns; the remnant of the *54th Reconnaissance Regiment* formed the garrison. The Japanese had dug themselves well in round the brick stump of a Pagoda situated on the top of Point 262 with the result that the D company patrol lost one man and suffered eleven wounded. Consequently, further attempts to reconnoitre this feature were abandoned.

The decision to capture the feature, Point 262, was taken on the morning of January 17. It was appreciated that this jungle-clad and knife-edged feature, would prove a difficult proposition if a normal attack were put on it. A very heavy supporting fire plan was therefore laid down, comprising an air strike, naval gun fire, and all available ground weapons. The air strike was delayed according to the plan laid down but finally went in at 1200 hours and bombing and strafing was accurately carried out on the objective. The assault went in but was strongly opposed; D company, however, managed to obtain a footing on the southern edge of the hill but could not advance any further owing to heavy automatic and mortar fire. An outflanking movement to the east was then put in, closely supported by the tanks, and in spite of heavy opposition, one of the platoons captured the Pagoda stump. Having obtained this foothold the whole of D company dug in and prepared themselves for any counter-offensive that may be put in by the Japanese. The whole operation was fought in the face of stiff and determined opposition and was carried through with the utmost gallantry. The Japanese put in four counter-attacks that night but the D company perimeter was not penetrated. The Gurkhas found 60 Japanese dead, and secured some Japanese guns and mortars for a cost of 1 Gurkha killed and 30 wounded.

Thereafter the 74th Indian Infantry Brigade kept up some very active patrolling in the north of the peninsula and by 21 January, there remained no signs of any Japanese troops in the Myebon peninsula. In the drive up this peninsula, steady progress had been made by the Indian and British forces against a very stubborn and tenacious opponent. Every hillock of any size had to be attacked, and the support of tanks had proved invaluable. During the early stages of this particular campaign, much effective direct support was also obtained from the air force, but after 14 January their main effort had been switched over to the Myohaung area.

From the very beginning of these operations, coastal forces of the navy had rendered most valuable support. Motor launches had established a series of blocks which had denied to the Japanese the passage of Pyunshe and Daingbon chaungs. In addition to the sinking of several armed Japanese craft which had attempted to run the blockade, the navy had also taken a lot of prisoners through whom some very useful information had been obtained.

CHAPTER XIX

The Kangaw Battle

The Blockade

The whole of the Myebon peninsula was now held by the XV Indian Corps. 14/10 Baluch had exploited deeply, having several clashes with the Japanese stragglers. An ordnance store, a small hospital and a company headquarters were all found later in the Pegauk area, about a mile to the north-east of Hill 262. 6 Oxf Bucks had also swept north-east and eventually secured Zinyawmaw, from which position anti-tank artillery was able to dominate any movement on Daingbon chaung. The Japanese had lost a considerable portion of their force and their water line of communication and the *Matsu Force* was now firmly blocked. Their water route of exit to the south towards Tamandu and Taungup had also been cut by the Royal Navy and Royal Indian Navy motor launches which had started operating day and night in the main chaungs. In the course of their patrols Allied naval craft had sunk fourteen Japanese launches, six of which were carrying an armament of 75 mm regimental guns and two 37 mm anti-tank guns. This decisive naval success was the first fruit of the Myebon battle.

At this stage of the operation, the Commander of the 25th Indian Division decided to make the 74th Indian Infantry Brigade responsible for the defence of the peninsula and the 3rd Commando Brigade was relieved of operational commitments for a brief but well earned rest. By this time, the Forward Maintenance Area (FMA) had been opened on EASY BEACH and transport and supplies had begun to come in on every tide. By 18 January the main divisional headquarters of the 25th Indian Division had opened just outside Myebon village and news had also come through that the 51st Indian Infantry Brigade's concentration was now complete on Akyab Island.

With the closing of their water line of retreat, it became apparent that the Japanese *Matsu Force*, whose fighting strength had been reduced considerably, in its withdrawal from the Myohaung-Minbya area, would have to retreat down the remaining escape route, which was the Myohaung-Tamandu road. Although the XV Indian Corps had no intention to assault the Minbya hill features, it was considered that the Japanese would not stay there much longer, as they were in grave danger of being cut off by an encircling movement by the 53rd Indian Infantry Brigade and by the 82nd West African Division,

KANGAW AREA

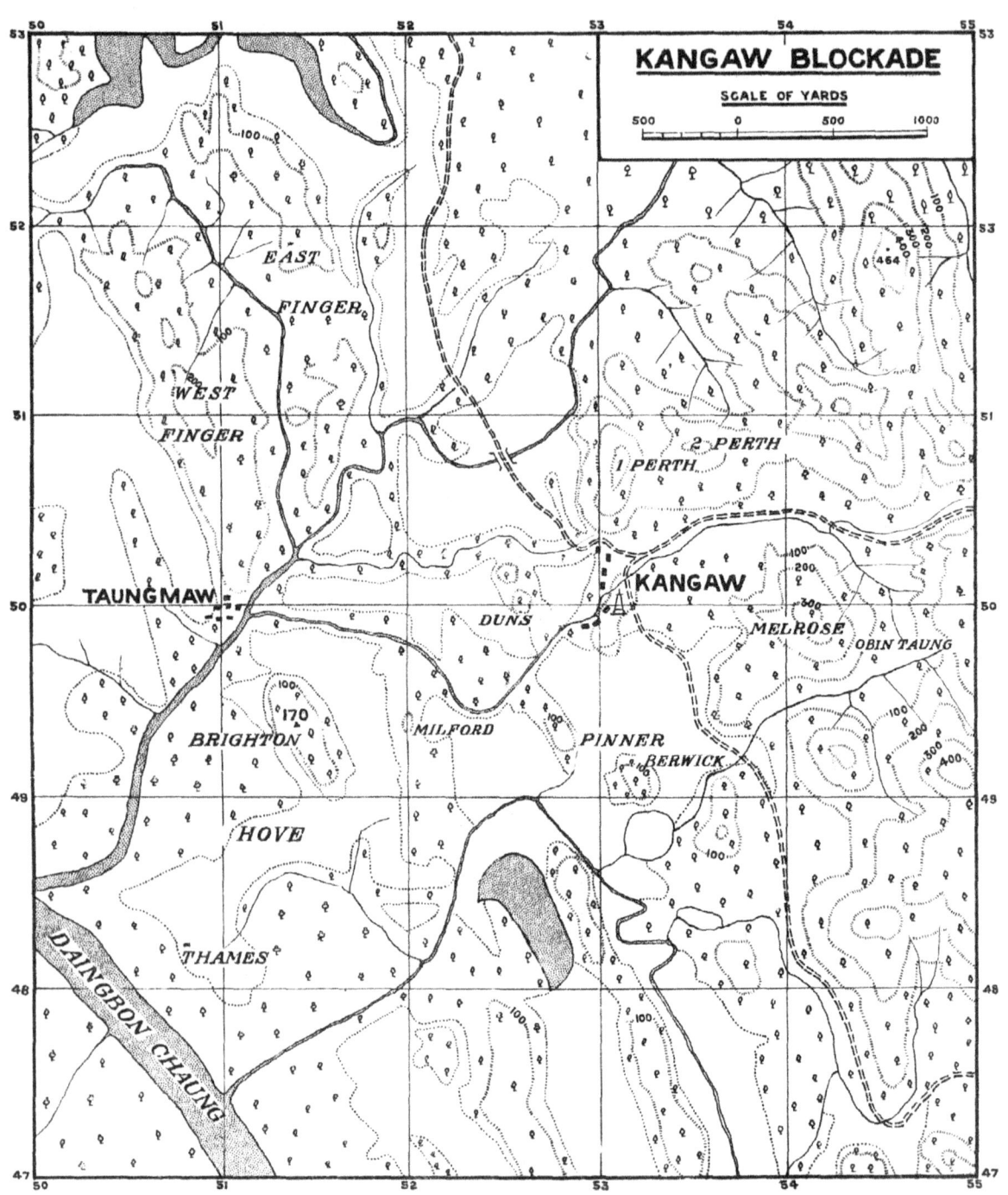

when exerting pressure from the north. The XV Indian Corps Commander, therefore, thought it to be a good opportunity to extend the operations from Myebon, across the Daingbon chaung, in order to intercept the Japanese withdrawal by cutting the Myohaung-Tamandu road. It was obvious that this operation would have to be mounted quickly in order to catch the Japanese, but the main considerations were, once again, unknown territory, lack of readily available forces and perhaps a long maintenance route, as all the shorter routes already were under fire from the Japanese artillery.

It was further appreciated that the most suitable place to impose such a block in order to cut off the maximum number of Japanese troops would be the bend in the road at Kangaw, where it leaves the plain and swings east into the hills. This block was to provide the anvil on which to smash the *Matsu Force* by the hammer of the 82nd West African Division.

Planning

Shortly after the troops of the 74th Indian Infantry Brigade had crossed to the north of Kantha chaung, air reconnaissance and captured documents had shown that a series of very strong defensive positions existed on the line from Kangaw village, on the main road north-east of Myebon, to the opposite bank of the river to the Myebon peninsula. This defensive position of the Japanese effectively blocked the approach of the Indian forces to Kangaw and the road from the west. This road appeared to be sufficiently difficult in itself and presented a problem which had to be overcome. In the meantime the 74th Indian Infantry Brigade was already finding the mountains, north of the peninsula, difficult of passage and the speed of its advance was, therefore, slowing down.

The success of the Kangaw landing depended largely upon the advantage to be obtained by initial surprise. The objective—the main road, where it skirted the foothills just north of Kangaw village—was by no means easily accessible and was known to be very heavily defended. The other courses which were open to the Joint Force Commanders were as follows:—

    (*a*) A land advance, north-east from Kantha, which involved the crossing of three major chaung obstacles under Japanese observation.

    (*b*) A water-borne advance by the most direct route from the Myebon river and through the Zinwamaw narrows; and lastly,

    (*c*) An indirect water-borne advance south-east from Myebon into the lower Daingbon chaung, thence northwards up the chaung to the objective, a distance of about eighteen miles.

The last course was chosen chiefly for its element of surprise, and it was also decided that the operation was to be mounted from the Myebon peninsula. The craft would then have to put out into Hunter's Bay, travel south and east through the narrows of the Thegyan river and then turn north and make their approach up the Daingbon chaung to the selected beach, two miles south-west of Kangaw village. This course had the advantage of putting troops ashore on the flank of the Kangaw defence. The Japanese defences appeared to be sited, facing north and north-west. After the landing a bold advance was to be made in order to cut the road.

The actual area selected for the landing and for the subsequent beach-head lay between two unnamed chaungs that flowed with the Daigbon about a mile and a half, south-west of Kangaw. Two beaches were selected; one was on the east bank of the Daingbon between the two smaller chaungs, the other on the northern bank of the lower subsidiary chaung. They were known as "THAMES" and "HOVE" respectively. The high spring tides which coincided with the landing were taken into account but it was not expected that they would swamp the whole beach-head area, as in fact happened with very serious results.

This beach-head was virtually an island. It was bounded on three sides by chaungs and closed at the eastern end by a knife-edged feature known as PINNER. In the middle, running north to south between the subsidiary chaungs, was a large feature known as Hill 170, whilst between the two was a third and smaller ridge named Milford. Except for these three ridges, the country was flat paddy land and the whole area was under constant Japanese observation, both from the Fingers, north of Taungmaw, and from the two massive features just east of Kangaw village, dominating the road running between them; these two massive features were known as PERTH and MELROSE respectively. Between the bridge-head island and the main road there were two smaller features called DUNS and BERWICK, which, with Kangaw village itself, dominated all movement on the road from the western side.

The plan was for the 3rd Commando Brigade, which had had only four days' rest after the Myebon battles, to land on the chosen beaches and secure the bridge-head, inclusive of Hill 170, and features Milford and Pinner. The 51st Indian Infantry Brigade was then to come forward from Akyab and, passing through the Commando bridge-head, was to capture the features known as DUNS, BERWICK, PERTH, and MELROSE. The securing of these features in the manner described would then have provided a complete blockade of the Kangaw area.

Landing and subsequent operations

On the evening of 21 January 1945, only nine days after the assault on the Myebon beaches, the 3rd Commando Brigade once again embarked on naval craft and set sail for its launching positions about six miles south of Kangaw. For the initial landing, artillery support was one troop of 25 pounders of 27 Field Regiment R.A. mounted on a "Z" craft anchored in the Daingbon chaung, and the guns of H.M.I.S. *'Narbada'*, lying off Myebon. In addition to this, the bulk of the remainder of the 25th Indian Divisional artillery had been deployed in the northern sector of the Myebon peninsula along with one troop of guns from 6 Medium Regiment, Royal Artillery, and a 7.2" howitzer, back from its travels with the 53rd Indian Infantry Brigade. Although this additional support was not used for the assault landing, it did great damage to the Japanese in the subsequent battle.

On 22 January, at 0600 hours, the 3rd Commando Brigade proceeded up the Thegyan river in order to be in time in their release positions; behind their vessels followed H.M.I.S. *'Nardaba'*. At 1000 hours, the troops were disembarked into landing craft, which then proceeded towards the assault beaches.

The approach of the first wave of landing craft up the chaungs, winding inland through miles of thick mangrove swamp, was made in broad daylight with no preliminary bombing, no naval or artillery bombardment and no fighter cover.

The landing itself was covered by an air strike on Hill 170. Just before the landing craft touched down, two squadrons of Mitchels bombed this hill which dominated the landing point, while Hurricanes laid a smokescreen for the assault troops. At the same time Thunderbolts attacked the Daingbon village. No other strikes were laid on for D Day as sufficiently good targets had not yet come to light.

The landing was made on both beaches simultaneously on the flood tide at 1300 hours on 22 January 1945. The move was entirely successful and complete tactical surprise was obtained. In order to mislead the Japanese, a few sloops and motor launches had made diversionary attacks in the Myebon river and the fact that the Allies had not taken the obvious chaung route, northwards from Myebon, helped in providing additional deception.

The Commandos quickly advanced eastward and without meeting any opposition, secured the southern end of Hill 170 (Brighton). The northern end was found to be held by about one platoon of Japanese but due to insufficient time before darkness, they could not be shifted by the forward Commando troops. This Japanese party after launching small but determined counter-attacks during the night, was finally driven off by the Commandos on the morning of 23 January. This success was quickly followed by occupying MILFORD and PINNER.

The feature PINNER contained well sited defensive positions and artillery bunkers. But these had been designed to meet a threat from the north and were, therefore, not defended by the Japanese. The position therefore was that the Indian division was in occupation of a narrow strip of flat, open country largely flooded, which the Japanese overlooked from positions, situated on jungle-clad features, on which accurate Allied artillery fire could not easily be brought to bear. The Commandos had secured their objective, which, together with the beach-head, was as much as they could hold safely against Japanese counter-attacks.

The Japanese had by now realised the urgency of keeping their escape route open and, therefore, reacted quickly to this vital thrust, made by the XV Indian Corps. They had become aware of the fact that the capture of Kangaw would cut their last escape route for vehicles and guns from northern Arakan. This made them launch a series of strong and determined counter-attacks. The Commandos were therefore subjected to heavy shell fire and counter-attacks continuously throughout the night, but in spite of heavy casualties, they did not yield any ground. The Commando casualties during this period were 25 killed and 81 wounded.

By 1300 hours on 23 January, 8/19 Hyderabad had arrived at the Kangaw beaches without meeting any Japanese opposition or shelling on the way. This was the first battalion of the 51st Indian Infantry Brigade to come forward, and immediately on landing, it took over the defence of the beaches. With much difficulty, for the beach was water-logged by the high spring tide, a troop of Sherman tanks (19th Lancers) was also put ashore. At 1530 hours the Japanese commenced shelling on Hill 170. They shelled the area above and below this feature where the battalion was going to take up its positions. D company and battalion headquarters started moving into this area at 1600 hours and every one started digging in at once. At 1830 hours the Japanese again started shelling with 75 and 105 mm guns and 3" mortars. This shelling continued the whole of the night but did not cause any casualties.

On 24 January, D company of 8/10 Hyderabad moved forward to PINNER and took over its defences from the Commando troops. The latter had been heavily shelled and mortared the previous night and had sustained heavy casualties. By 1700 hours of the same day, D company was firmly dug in and established in its new position.

On 25 January, 16/10 Baluch crossed the Myebon river in LCSs and harboured at HOVE for the night. On the 26th, the battalion moved to PINNER and relieved one of the Commando units. The Japanese took a heavy toll of this battalion by 75 mm gun fire on this feature throughout the day in which the battalion lost two killed and twenty-one wounded. On this day also battalion headquarters and headquarter company of 8/10 Hyderabad, moved into an area on the same feature.

The 51st Indian Infantry Brigade had by that time concentrated in the Commando bridge-head area and the Brigade commander Brigadier Hutton had assumed charge of all troops in the area. Thereafter, he and the 25 Indian Division Commander made a personal reconnaissance and formulated their plan for putting a "block" on the main road. By this time Japanese artillery, small arms fire and suicide parties were becoming increasingly active and it had become apparent that the Japanese were going to fight hard to defend their positions on PERTH and MELROSE, which dominated the road. A bid was, therefore, made for heavy strikes by the Strategic Air Force—the first was a most heartening sight when on 27 January, five squadrons of Liberators came over and made a most accurate bombing attack on these two major features, disclosing a number of previously unlocated positions. On the night of 26 January, 8/19 Hyderabad had sent out two reconnaissance patrols; one was sent to DUNS and the other to Kangaw. The DUNS feature, which dominated the road leading through Kangaw, was reported to be strongly defended while the report on Kangaw showed that the village was a mass of bomb craters and damaged bunkers.

By 27 January, 2/2 Punjab had also concentrated on the beach, west of Hill 170. About noon on the same day the Brigade commander issued the following orders for the future plan of operations:—

- (a) 8/19 Hyderabad to capture PERTH, using DUNS as a stepping-stone. 16/10 Baluch to capture MELROSE with their firm base at BERWICK.
- (b) 2/2 Punjab to concentrate at PINNER in bridge reserve with the probable task of either supporting the 8/19 Hyderabad attack on PERTH 1, or taking PERTH 2 after Hyderabad had captured PERTH 1.

At 0300 hours on 28 January, C and D companies of 8 Hyderabad attacked the feature DUNS. C company managed to capture the south portion of the feature but D company was held up by strong bunker positions towards the north. At first light on the same day the Japanese started reinforcing their positions on the north and west side of the feature. Heavy artillery, mortar and automatic fire was also brought down on the Hyderabad battalion from the direction of PERTH and the FINGERS. But due to the thickness of trees it was not possible to detect the direction of the fire, and consequently the Indian casualties were heavy. Fire support was then intensified and B company was sent to reinforce C and D companies;

but the whole feature was infiladed by Japanese fire, while the forming up positions were also under perfect observation. Ammunition became exhausted and eventually the battalion was withdrawn on the personal order of the Brigade Commander. The Hyderabads had shown great fortitude in this fierce encounter with a skilful and unexpectedly powerful defence. Casualties however, had mounted to 19 killed and 61 wounded and the help of A company was required in bringing back the wounded. By 1500 hours, 8/19 Hyderabad had withdrawn to MILFORD while PINNER was taken over by 2/2 Punjab.

Meanwhile, 16/10 Baluch was directed against the more southernly hill feature of MELROSE. This battalion had been more fortunate than the Hyderabad at the outset, for BERWICK, their intermediate objective, proved clear of hostile troops; it was therefore occupied by first light. Meanwhile, MELROSE feature had been systematically shelled, dive-bombed and strafed for four successive days prior to its being attacked on the morning of 28 January. The battalion plan was for B and D companies to move up to BERWICK in darkness at approximately 0200 hours on 27 January and to remain there till H hour. The plan of attack for the various companies was as follows:—

A company's objective was Kangaw hills
D company's objective was North MELROSE
B company—South MELROSE

C company was put in reserve with Battalion Headquarters. The start line for A company was the feature PINNER and for B and D companies BERWICK. The starting time was to be 1015 hours or the dropping of a smoke-screen on 28 January.

The attack was to be followed by a Thunderbolt strike on feature east of MELROSE, and then a Hurricane strike from 0945 hours to 1015 hours. A smoke-screen was also to be laid down in front of the attacking troops.

On 28 January, the attack went in as planned. A company met no opposition and having secured the Kangaw hills got down to digging and consolidating its positions. B and D companies, having concentrated unopposed at BERWICK, advanced to the foot of MELROSE, under heavy anti-tank, machine-gun and small-arms fire from bunkers and defensive positions, situated on its lower slopes. Nevertheless, they pushed on ahead and captured two Japanese bunkers in front of them. These two platoons then continued their advance up the spur of the feature, followed by company headquarters and the reserve platoon.

On the Baluch right flank, B company, during its advance, had come under fire from bunkers on the ridge, and cross fire from the nullah running east and west behind MELROSE, but it destroyed the opposition and moved towards the top of the ridge. The momentum of the attack carried the B and D companies to a false crest below the summit but here they were compelled to halt. Altogether, about eight bunkers of different sizes had been over-run on the lower slopes of the ridge, and some sixty Japanese killed; others were forced to run away to the higher part of the hill.

A substantial footing had been secured by 16/10 Baluch at the cost of heavy casualties; therefore C company was rushed up to consolidate the ground gained. As the only line of advance for this company was through open paddy fields, it came under heavy fire. Although suffering a number of casualties it managed to reach the forward companies in time to help them in driving off the first counter-attack which was put in by the Japanese at 1300 hours.

Before this counter-attack had been put in by the Japanese, the commanding officer of the Baluch Regiment had been given the option of either withdrawing his force from MELROSE, or holding to the ground that he had gained. The commanding officer decided on the latter course and ordered A company to vacate Kangaw and hold BERWICK, which he considered to be a vital feature as it controlled and overlooked the line of communication from the rear to MELROSE.

A company of 2/2 Punjab had also been placed under the command of the Baluch Regiment to support the attack on MELROSE. This company with three rifle companies of 16/10 Baluch, occupied a defended locality on MELROSE base position for the night of 28/29 January. During the course of the night, the Japanese put in about eight counter-attacks; their object appeared to be to remove the dead and wounded as well as to make an attempt to pierce the Indian perimeter. All these attacks were, however, repulsed successfully with heavy losses to the Japanese.

Brigadier Hutton then decided to postpone the attack on the higher feature until such time as it had been further softened by artillery fire. The two assaulting battalions had suffered about 150 killed and wounded in the day's fighting, and the casualties in the rear areas had also not been light owing to unremitting shell fire by the Japanese. Throughout the day of 28 January alone, the Japanese had fired over 800 shells on the very restricted area of the bridgehead which was considered to be the heaviest artillery concentration ever put against Allied forces in Burma. Guns of every description and size up to 150 mm had been in action.

Change of Plan

By the end of January it had become apparent that the Japanese defences protecting the Kangaw road were much stronger than had been assumed originally. The commander of the 51st Indian Infantry Brigade in consultation with the 25th Indian

Division Commander now decided to abandon any further attacks on PERTH and to concentrate his force on the right flank where, by securing MELROSE and Kangaw village, the main object of effectively blocking the road could be achieved. Hence, on 29 January at 1030 hours, 2/2 Punjab was ordered to capture the MELROSE feature. The battalion's plan was to attack MELROSE with two companies, with its axis of advance from the south to the north. The right hand company was to attack the feature from the south-east slopes and thus avoid hostile fire from PERTH. The left hand company was to attack up the south-west slope. The forward companies would thus be in a position to avoid the full force of Japanese small arms fire by being, to a large extent, defiladed from it. The artillery plan was laid on with concentrations on MELROSE. These concentrations were to be controlled by the Forward Company Commanders through their Forward Observation Officers (FOOs). The whole PERTH feature was to be kept under fire and screened from MELROSE by means of smoke, and air support was co-ordinated with the artillery support. A few dummy runs were also arranged to take over MELROSE ridge during the attack. Battalion 3" mortars were to be used for supporting the concentration of the attacking companies at their forming-up places (F.U.Ps) and later for close support and consolidation.

At the same time 16/10 Baluch was allotted the task of capturing the Kangaw village.

The Blockade

It was planned to attack MELROSE after it had been softened by an air attack; this air strafing had been timed to take place at 1030 hours on 29 January and was also to serve as a signal for the assaulting of the MELROSE feature. As things turned out the air strike did not materialize. Since it was considered that the attack could not be postponed much longer, as sufficient day-light was required to consolidate and dig trenches after capturing MELROSE, an improvised fire plan consisting of an artillery barrage was hastily planned in lieu of the air raid. But even this artillery attack could not be begun before 1200 hours.

The forward companies, B and C companies of 2/2 Punjab, reached their forming-up areas on the lower slopes of MELROSE. These companies had crawled under a smoke-screen which had been put down with the help of the Baluch Regiment along with the 3" mortars of 2/2 Punjab. On reaching the MELROSE slope, the companies suddenly came under heavy 4" mortar and small arms fire from the foremost Japanese defences. These positions were, however, tackled with such determination and under such effective mutual covering fire between the attacking companies that most of the Japanese in the area were destroyed. Once again the companies advanced and once again they were subjected to hostile fire which appeared to come from an intermediate position, some 50 feet below the crest of the feature. Although the casualties were mounting up the leading troops continued their advance while the Japanese continued to attack with small arm and grenade fire at a more or less point-blank range.

From now on what happened can best be described as a mad charge up the slope culminating in a bitter hand-to-hand fighting. The Japanese asked for no quarter and gave none, and in this desperate struggle it must be said to their credit that they fought most magnificently. On the part of the Indian troops there were many deeds of valour performed on this day, some recognised but many more passed unnoticed and unheeded. After a grim struggle the MELROSE feature was captured by the Punjab Regiment by 1400 hours. Over a 100 Japanese bodies were counted on the ground while the Indian battalion had suffered about 80 casualties, most of which were only wounded. Tactical headquarters moved to MELROSE at 1430 hours and by the same evening the Indian troops had taken up defensive positions on this feature and were determined to hold it to the last man.

But a little after midnight on 29/30 January the Japanese started counter-attacking the MELROSE position. The first two attacks were not heavy but the third was an all-out affair which was designed to dislodge the Punjab troops from the feature. After some very fierce fighting this attack was also beaten back with heavy casualties to the Japanese. Between 0530 hours and 0700 hours of 30 January, two more counter-attacks were put in by the Japanese. Previously, ammunition had been short and for this reason the situation had for a time become critical. But ammunition was rushed up to the leading companies from the MELROSE base and this enabled them to hang on and crush the last two Japanese counter-attacks. Daylight saw about 40 to 50 Japanese bodies on the ground, many of them to within five yards of the leading section posts of the defenders. The Japanese had managed to drag away many of their dead but even as late as 0715 hours they were making frantic attempts to remove the remainder.

About 1500 hours on the 30th the Japanese started a very heavy artillery bombardment on MELROSE and MELROSE Base, using 150 and 105 mm guns and some 25 pounders, simultaneously from the north and north-east. This heavy bombardment by the Japanese caused a slight disorganisation in the tactical position of 2/2 Punjab. The commanding officer of this battalion then requested the Brigade commander that the three companies of 16/10 Baluch, then situated at MELROSE BASE be placed under his command for operational purposes. This was agreed to and by reorganising his troops the commanding officer of 2/2 Punjab was able to coordinate the defences of MELROSE and MELROSE BASE positions. The co-operation of these Baluch companies was so advantageous that it enabled the troops involved on the MELROSE feature to repulse four Japanese counter-attacks on the night of 30/31 January. The capture and then holding on to this feature by the Indian troops marked the turning-point in the battle for Kangaw.

The next object which had to be taken in order to completely block the road was the village of Kangaw; and 8/19 Hyderabad was detailed to carry out this task. On 29 January at 1630 hours, A company of this battalion proceeded to PINNER with the intention of getting on to Kangaw hill. They occupied it without opposition. Till then it was believed that the Japanese were occupying PAGODA PIMPLE, situated at the furthest end of the Indian positions. But on 30 January, a patrol of A company reported that PAGODA was unoccupied and that they had pushed on to within a few miles of the road. The patrol had then met with light machine-gun fire from the PERTH feature which compelled it to withdraw. Air strafing was made throughout the day on PERTH while the Japanese on their part continued to shell the Indian positions intermittently.

B company moved to PINNER at 1300 hours, and battalion headquarters and headquarters company arrived by 1610 hours and took over their new positions from the Commando troops. C and D companies plus the mortar platoon, however, remained behind on MILFORD. From PINNER another patrol of A company sent to Kangaw village found it completely empty and unoccupied. This completed a great performance by the 51st Indian Infantry Brigade. The capture of MELROSE with the capture of Kangaw village finally cut the Japanese escape route. The main road itself was also discovered to be physically blocked by three enormous 1000-pound bomb craters.

The Japanese counter-attack

The 82nd West African Division in the meanwhile had taken over from the 81st West African Division in the Myohaung area. The former had even reached Hpontha and had begun their southward advance in order to drive the Japanese against the Kangaw block.

Faced with the possibility of being completely encircled and cut off by these Allied tactics, the Japanese were forced to think quickly in terms of withdrawing their remaining forces. The leading brigade of this West African Division had already made some rapid progress southward through Hpontha and so some very quick action was indicated on the part of the Japanese commanders in the Kangaw area.

Captured documents have revealed that the Kangaw defences consisted of a Japanese regiment less one battalion, supported by a battalion of field artillery and a company of field engineers—a probable total of about 2,600 men. The commander of this Japanese force was Colonel Murayama, who was evidently determined to keep the main escape route open to enable the *Matsu Force* to withdraw. About half of the *Matsu Force* was to move down this blockaded road from Minbya, accompanied by its guns and heavy baggage; the remainder had made way to the south-east from Hpontha, making use of the Taywe Chaung and the hill tracks. To ensure the safe withdrawal of the road party along with the valuable guns and heavy equipment, Colonel Murayama planned to capture BRIGHTON (Hill 170), thus splitting the Allied forces at the wasp-like waist of the beach-head, and thereby cutting off the 51st Indian Infantry Brigade troops and forcing them to release their grip on the road.

As a preliminary to carrying out their attack on Point 170, the Japanese started shelling MILFORD and BRIGHTON at 0430 hours on 31 January, 1945. They used 75 and 105 mm guns, and the climax of this bombardment was reached just before 0600 hours, thus covering the noise of this forming-up.

Just before dawn on 31 January, 1945 the Japanese moved forward from their concentration area on West Finger, waded quietly through the Taungmaw Chaung, and formed up in the 150 yards deep belt of mangrove trees between the chaung and Hill 170. This hill which was on the northern end of BRIGHTON and was opposite MILFORD, could not be subjected to fire by the Allies until daylight, as it was being held by the forward elements of the Commando units. At first light, the Japanese launched what was to prove their heaviest and most desperate counter-attack of the whole campaign. As the sun rose, a battalion of the *154th Japanese Regiment*, supported by a detachment of assault engineers, made an all-out assault on Point 170. The platoon of assault engineers with pole charges and anti-tank mines moved round the north-east slopes of the feature; this move was covered by a silent attack of a company of infantry against the most northern defences of this hill.

By this means the Japanese secured a certain measure of surprise, gained a foothold and pushed forward to capture about one-third of the extent of Hill 170, while their assault engineers broke into the tank harbour where one troop of three tanks of 19th Lancers was stationed. The tank crews were alert inside their tanks, but the Japanese succeeded in setting fire to one of the Shermans, from which the crew could not escape, and blew the tracks off of another. The third tank remained unharmed and, with the supporting platoon of the Bombay Grenadiers, maintained such a resistance as wiped out the engineer assault party.

While the leading Japanese infantry was fighting for the northern end of Hill 170, the remainder of the assault force—another two companies—crossed the chaung and concentrated in the mangrove area, in order to put in further assaults. It was obvious that the Japanese intended to establish themselves on Hill 170 without any regard for the casualties that it might cost them. By establishing themselves here they would cut off the British and Indian troops on the road from the beaches, thereby severing them from their source of supply. Had this action been successful it would probably have been impossible for the 51st Indian Infantry Brigade to maintain their stranglehold on the road at this critical time, and the whole of the Kangaw Operation would have been doomed to failure. There is no doubt that the Japanese had certainly made a sound appreciation of the situation. But this was as far as Colonel Murayama's plan managed to go. On the other hand, the target provided by over 300 Japanese in the mangrove swamp, in a space of 150×75 yards, was hit by the divisional artillery and all mortars within range; this created such havoc in this Japanese supporting force that it was unable to reach Hill 170 and exploit the initial gains of the leading attackers.

But the Japanese artillery similarly concentrated on neutralising Indian positions, which they still had under perfect observation, and troops could not be moved forward across the open for counter-attacks in daylight, without the certainty of undue losses. Therefore 1 and 5 Commandos on Hill 170 were left to fight their own local battle. In the confused situation a proper plan of fire support was not possible. The Commandos suffered heavy losses in making some very gallant local counter-offensives, but the Japanese could still not be evicted from the hill. It was during this crisis that Lieut. G.A. Knowland (Royal Norfolk Regiment) of 1 Commando won the Victoria Cross at the cost of his life; his was but one of many deeds of desperate gallantry seen on this day.

The coming of night, however, restored the possibility of regaining the initiative. The 7/16 Punjab, the Divisional Headquarters Battalion, had just reached Kangaw after its independent successful operations towards Minbya, and had undertaken the local defence of Hove beach. As soon as darkness fell, this battalion moved forward on to Hill 170, and with co-ordinated artillery and mortar support, passed through the Commandos and recaptured the northern end of the hill. They were heavily shelled, but the Japanese assault force was at its last gasp. Early next morning 7/16 Punjab swept onwards through the mangrove swamps and cleared the position to the Taungmaw Chaung.

The scene was one of massacre. Although the fiercest fighting took place on 31 January, the Japanese continued to put in determined and unfailing attacks on the fresh battalion over the two days that followed. Carnage in this action was incredible; there are stories of Indian, British and Japanese soldiers being extricated from beneath mounds of corpses, practically unhurt, but unable to move from the weight of the bodies pinning them to the ground. It was nearly three whole days of grenade and bayonet work at close quarters; and by 2 February, over 700 Japanese bodies had actually been counted on the ground on the small hill.

74th Indian Infantry Brigade joins the battle

After this costly counter-offensive by the Japanese on Hill 170, the Divisional Commander appreciated that although renewed counter-attacks could be expected in the forward areas, the Japanese were not in a position to launch any further major offensive on the original bridge-head. He therefore, decided to withdraw the Commando Brigade and ordered the 74th Indian Infantry Brigade which was then in the area, north-east of Myebon, to operate northwards along the axis of the Pyunshe and Kyaukgnamaw chaungs; the object being to harass from the flank that part of the *Matsu Force* which was withdrawing from Hpontha under pressure of the 2nd West African Brigade.

6 Oxf Bucks was detailed to carry out this task. This battalion operated strong patrols from firm bases, established north of Zinyamaw, during the period 1 February to 7 February. It carried out several raiding operations in LCAs across the Kyaukgnamaw river, visiting the villages of Melun, Smoukron and Kyaingdaung and killing some 18 Japanese troops. On the morning of 7 February, 6 Oxf Bucks supported the 14/10 Baluch operation on the east bank of Kyaukgnamaw river. Later, on 11 February the battalion established contact with the troops of the 82nd West African Division in the Shoukchron area. By 20 February, this battalion had concentrated near Point 163 on the Myebon peninsula, remaining in readiness to proceed to Ruywa.

From 9 February onwards, 14/10 Baluch carried out some very extensive patrolling, and on the 16th, it moved to Taungmaw and from there to Kangaw.

The Japanese attempts to escape

In spite of British artillery and air bombardment, the Japanese still remained in some strength on the FINGER and PERTH features and, almost every night, they were putting in small but desperate counter-attacks against the Baluch and Punjab positions on MELROSE. The occupation of Kangaw village by the Hyderabads had eventually cut the road and so the idea of capturing PERTH was given up, as both unnecessary and costly. To capture and hold the FINGER feature was also considered as overambitious; it would have taken more troops than could be spared by the 51st Indian Infantry Brigade. The Commando troops had been pulled out and the water shortage made the landing of further troops undesirable. Any major attack was, therefore, forbidden for the time being by the Divisional Commander who expected a Japanese reaction of repeated counter-attacks. The Japanese played up well and lost many men in abortive night attacks during the next three days.

The DUNS feature had also remained in Japanese hands since the failure of the Hyderabad Regiment's first attack, on 28 January. On 11 February at 0730 hours, D company of 8/19 Hyderabad supported by the tanks of 19th Lancers assaulted this feature. The attack was put in from the south while the tanks went into action aided by artillery and mortar fire, and quickly silenced the Japanese guns. The whole of DUNS was cleared of the Japanese by 1100 hours, and, soon after, the Sappers arrived to blow up all the bunkers and the dug-in tunnels. During this action the Japanese lost 20 killed including an officer while the Indian casualties were two killed and six wounded. The company thereafter withdrew from this feature with their booty of three light machine-guns.

In the meanwhile, Indian troops in Kangaw and on MELROSE were growing a little weary of killing the Japanese. But in case the Japanese should withdraw completely, a plan was evolved to form a "Jock" column, consisting of 7/16 Punjab with one troop from 19th Lancers and artillery support. This column was to be formed and held in readiness to pursue the fleeing Japanese down the road, from Kangaw to Kyweguseik.

In the meanwhile, considerable re-grouping was going on in the remainder of the 25th Indian Division. The commander of the XV Indian Corps had decided that the 53rd Indian Infantry Brigade had completed its task by sweeping the chaung country between Akyab and Minbya; and any Japanese left in that area were only stragglers in the process of withdrawing. The 53rd Indian Infantry Brigade was, therefore, ordred to concentrate in Myebon, and 9 Y & L which, after its operations at Ponnagyun had returned as garrison force to Akyab island, was immediately ferried across to this destination. The other two battalions, 4 Royal Garhwal Rifles and 17/5 Mahrattas, followed the same route as 7/16 Punjab and the brigade reverted to the divisional command on arrival. Meanwhile, north of Kangaw, patrol reports from 6 Oxf Bucks indicated the feasibility of operations by a larger force in that area. 14/10 Baluch was accordingly moved from Kantha where it was relieved by 9 Y & L and ferried across the Kyaukgnamaw chaung to Kyauknwa. One company of 6 Oxf Bucks supported the crossing while the remainder of the battalion was held in reserve at Tenanbyin. The object of this operation was firstly, to clear up the Japanese in the FINGERS, south of the proposed bridge-head, who had remained a menace to the 51st Indian Infantry Brigade, and secondly, to assist the 2nd West African Brigade by reconnaissance and aggressive action against the Japanese right flank.

The crossing was made on the night of 6/7 February, and 14/10 Baluch gained the first objectives without opposition; but during the night of 7/8 February a Japanese counter-attack, though repulsed, dislocated the Baluch plan to cross the chaung, which separated them from the FINGERS. This chaung proved a severe physical obstacle and although, later on, patrols got across on to the northern end of both FINGERS, it proved almost impossible to bring down the whole force. The Divisional Commander therefore issued orders not to press the assault on FINGERS and diverted the main efforts of this force to offensive action eastwards against the Kani-Kangaw road. The diversion was achieved without further fighting, and four days later, 7/16 Punjab cleared the WEST FINGER from the south. Later, after finding that the EAST FINGER had been abandoned by the Japanese, the battalion withdrew into the 51st Indian Infantry Brigade bridge-head.

Photographic reconnaissance during the last few days had revealed the presence of a new foot-path. It swung east into the hills, about a mile north of Kangaw, and west round the back of PERTH, rejoining the main road about two miles east of the Kangaw village. It had been realized that the Japanese might by-pass any road-block by going into the jungle, but in this case, it was certain that the track was impassable for wheels and guns. It was also realised that most of the *Matsu Force*, which had previously been hemmed in between the 51st Indian Infantry Brigade and the 82nd West African Division, had pulled out along this path.

But still some Japanese were stubbornly holding on to PERTH and to the hills, immediately to the east of it. Their object appeared to be to contain the Allied troops as long as possible, in order to ensure the safe withdrawal of their Kangaw artillery. As the 1st and 4th West African Brigades were driving south-east down the Taywe chaung towards Kyweguseik, the 25th Indian Division Commander decided to link up with these brigades as soon as possible by a drive south from Kangaw. But before the "Jock" column could get through to the road it was considered necessary to capture PERTH as well as the other feature known as Obintaung which dominated the road. As the 2nd West African Brigade, which was driving the rearguard of *Matsu Force* southwards from Hpontha, had reached the village of Kani, it was put under the command of the 25th Indian Division. General Wood thereupon ordered this brigade to sweep south-east through the hills behind PERTH while

14/10 Baluch was ordered to move south from the Kyauknwa bridge-head and then east through Kangaw village, to clear Obintaung. As hostile artillery activity had now practically ceased, it was assumed that the Japanese had thinned out in that area.

Meanwhile, on 12 February at 1300 hours A company of 8/19 Hyderabad put in an attack on PERTH and promptly cleared eight bunkers inflicting fourteen casualties on the Japanese. A counter-attack put in by the Japanese was beaten off which cost them another six casualties. The whole of the PERTH feature was cleared of Japanese troops and the bunkers were found to be full of Japanese equipment and ammunition. Although the Sappers would have done a quicker job in destroying the bunkers, the assaulting troops took full advantage of grenades by means of which most of the bunkers were destroyed. After clearing the feature the company withdrew back to its battalion.

However, the next four days proved most difficult as the spring tides had risen again and once more the whole Kangaw area was flooded, making movement impossible for five hours during every tide, while wheels could not move at all.

Consequently, the launching of the pursuit column was delayed and it was not until 17 February that 7/16 Punjab could start their dash for Kyweguseik, nearly twelve miles away. By this date, 8/19 Hyderabad had again seized PERTH and 14/10 Baluch had cleared Obintaung. The dominating feature of PERTH even now was not easily yielded. Three strongly defended bunker positions remained on the crest but the Hyderabad troops would not be denied in their last attack. They stormed the Japanese out of the bunkers, killing 25 men of the garrison. By 20 February the "Jock" column was on its way south towards Kyweguseik and Tamandu, but the delay caused by the floods prevented their regaining contact with the retreating Japanese.

The end of the Battle

This decisive battle of the Kangaw blockade which lasted for twentytwo days has been described as one of the heaviest battles fought in Burma. The Japanese positions behind PERTH and MELROSE were found to be fantastically strong, consisting of underground vaults from which tunnels led to infantry and artillery bunkers constructed of whole tree trunks and of a network of deep trenches and foxholes.

The Japanese counter-attack against Hill 170 was based on a very sound appreciation of the situation. But as things turned out, the Indians and Commandos hung on to this vital feature after indulging in the fiercest fighting of the whole campaign.

There was no doubt that the Japanese had been hit in an

extremely vulnerable quarter. Their defences had all faced north except where PERTH and MELROSE covered the road, as it swung east into the hills. They had spent many months in preparing to meet a threat from this direction and had built up extensive stocks of supplies and ammunition in the area. In their struggle to regain this vital area, the Japanese had thrown in three regiments as well as divisional and army troops.

During the whole period of this battle, the Japanese suffered at least two thousand killed and wounded, lost 15 large and 12 small armed motor-craft along with quantities of other equipment. Against this figure the Indian and British casualties were 210 killed and 750 wounded, while the morale of the Commando Brigade and the 51st Indian Infantry Brigade had risen all the higher. The toll of captured guns rose to 26 but the Japanese unable to get them past the Kangaw road-block threw all their remaining artillery into the chaungs; the gun muzzles protruding from the waters at low tide bore a silent witness to the magnitude of the Japanese disaster. But Allied artillery had not suffered lightly. The victorious infantry were full of enthusiasm for the constant and accurate support given by 8 Field Regiment and 27 Field Regiment R.A. and 7 Indian Anti-Tank Regiment RIA of 25 Divisional Artillery, both in attack and defence. The observation parties of artillery units had constantly been with the leading infantry and had suffered heavy casualties, while the gun positions on the beach-head were under observation by the Japanese, and were unable to dig in owing to the swampy nature of the ground. Never had any programme of fire been curtailed by such heavy counter-bombardment.

The administration of Allied Kangaw force had presented a number of difficulties. No source of water supply had been found in the original beach-head; consequently, some 4000 gallons of water a day had to be brought by LCMs from Myebon—a distance of 18 miles. Later, as the battle advanced, this want was partially supplied by utilising the seepage into two large bomb craters at the foot of Hill 170; the water was muddy and evil-smelling, but drinkable in default of a better supply. Wheels were useless in the beach-head and the majority of mules landed soon became casualties. Hence supply and the evacuation of wounded were matters of sheer man power. The porters of the Indian Pioneer Corps Companies were inadequate in numbers, and had to be supplemented by infantry. But the medical units, 58 and 61 Indian Field Ambulances, and No. 1 Indian Bearer Company never failed, and gained the admiration of the whole force.

Finally it must be remembered that the whole supply of the beach-head was maintained by the naval landing craft, working the long route from Myebon.

In the words of the General Officer Commanding the 25th Indian Division, expressed in a Special Order of the Day on the conclusion of this battle, "every man who landed on the Kangaw beaches can recall the fact with pride."

Hill 170, shelled and snipped persistently by the Japanese, continued to be held by the 25th Indian Division.

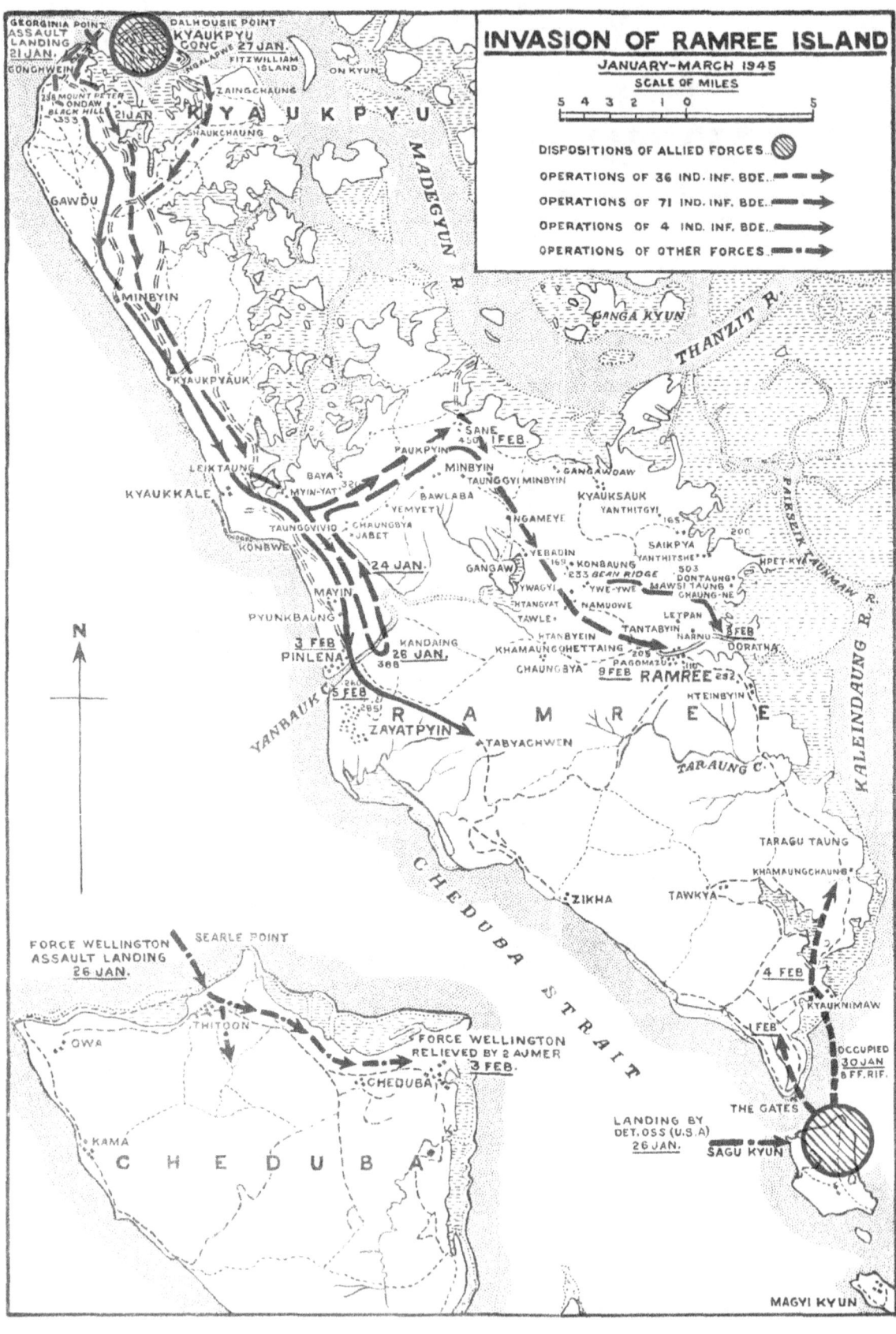

CHAPTER XX

The Invasion of Ramree Island

Preliminary

Immediately after the capture of Akyab on 3 January 1945, and while the 25th Indian Division was engaged in fighting on the Myebon peninsula, it was decided by the XV Indian Corps Commander to launch a sea-borne assault against Ramree Island.

Ramree, which is a large island lying off the coast of central Arakan, some 70 miles south-east of Akyab, is a little more than 50 miles in length from north to south and about 15 miles in breadth, at its widest part. It is separated from the mainland of Arakan by approximately 6 miles of water, mangrove swamp, mud-flats, bars and small low-lying islands, all of which are liable to inundation by the sea, according to the state of the tide and the season of the year. The main township is Kyaukpyu, on the extreme northern end of the island; it is a well developed trading station with some good, permanent buildings and local administrative services. It was previously an important port of call for coastal shipping and its harbour provided sheltered anchorage for large ships. Twelve miles off the south-west coast lies the smaller island of Cheduba and one mile from the southern tip of Ramree are situated the small islands of Sagu Kyun, Magyi and Platt.

It was decided to capture Ramree island first, then Cheduba and subsequently to clear the subsidiary islands, as a prelude to further landings on the Arakan coast. Apart from destroying the Japanese garrison there, the capture of Ramree island, it was believed, would deny to the Japanese a most valuable staging point in inland water communications on which they were largely dependent. The island would also provide a valuable jumping off place for the Allies for future water-borne attacks on the mainland between Kantaunggyi, which was the Japanese base, and Taungup. Its capture would also provide forward landing grounds for the air transport squadrons employed in the maintenance of the Fourteenth Army in its rapid advance towards Mandalay. The main objective in this operation was Kyakpyu which could not only be developed into a major air-supply base, but owing to its good anchorage, could also provide easy access for shipping from India bringing supplies direct for air transportation from this port. The strategic importance of Ramree, therefore, was in connection with the operations of the Fourteenth

Army in the heart of Burma. Its possession would, it was presumed, also help in the capture of Taungup and the exploitation of Taungup-Prome road. Apart from the destruction of the Japanese garrisons, the acquisition of Cheduba and Sagu Kyun had no strategic value other than of ensuring a free passage to the Allied craft operating off the west and south coasts of Ramree, through the Cheduba Strait and "The Gates"—the narrows between Ramree and Sagu Kyun.

The task of carrying out this operation was allotted to the 26th Indian Division, which at that period was concentrated south of Cox's Bazaar, where under the original plan, it had undergone training for the assault on Akyab.

The 71st Indian Infantry Brigade, supported by the 146th Regiment Royal Armoured Corps with Lee tanks, was commissioned to complete the capture of Ramree island, and 2/7 Rajput drawn from the 4th Indian Infantry Brigade was additionally allotted to this Brigade for the task. The balance of the 4th Indian Infantry Brigade was then made responsible for following up the assault brigade and securing the final divisional concentration area and Forward Maintenance Area at Kyaukpyu. This brigade was then to resume command of its battalion which had been loaned to the assault brigade and thereafter patrol the many small islands to the north-east of Kyaukpyu. It was ordered, subsequently, to launch raids on the Japanese lines of communication in the area of Anand Letpan.

The 36th Indian Infantry Brigades was allotted three main tasks for this operation:

(a) To capture the island of Sagu Kyun.
(b) To assault the southern end of Ramree island and occupy the area as far north as Kyaukinmaw.
(c) To provide the force to relieve Force Wellington[1] and continue its exploitation of the whole of Cheduba island, and finally to allow the Marine Force to withdraw, after capturing the island.
(d) Raid the Japanese lines of communication in Taungup and Sandoway areas.

Neither the assault on Sagu Kyun, to the south end of Ramree, nor on Cheduba, was to take place simultaneously with the main assult on Kyaukpyu, which was carried out on 21 January, 1945. These minor landings were to be put into operation at times, dictated by the progress made on the main front. It will be later seen that in point of fact, the early success of the 71st Indian Infantry Brigade was so much more than what was anticipated that some modifications

---

[1] A force of 500 Royal Marines known as Force Wellington had to carry out the initial operations against Cheduba island which was entirely a Royal Navy responsibility.

were eventually made to the task, originally allotted to the 36th Indian Infantry Brigade.

Appreciation of Japanese opposition

Before the assault on Ramree island was launched, considerable intelligence data had to be collected by the Allies. The assessment of the strength of the Japanese garrison on the island was particularly important at this stage in view of the constantly changing disposition which the Japanese were being forced to make throughout Arakan. In order to gather information regarding Japanese strength and dispositions, a number of reconnaissance raids were made, both on Ramree and Cheduba, during the ten days preceding the assault. These raids were mostly carried out by an American Army detachment of the Office of Strategical Services and by the British Special Boat Section, attached to the Commando Brigade.

These raids were successful and, from reports received, it was deduced that the Japanese garrison in the whole group of islands consisted of two battalions of the *121st Regiment*, belonging to the *54th Division*. Along with some artillery and their administrative staff it was estimated that their strength was approximately 1800 men. The majority of this force was naturally expected to be on Ramree and it was thought that at the most, a single company would be found on Cheduba. It was further considered that since the newly made An Pass road into the Irrawaddy valley was showing signs of becoming a passable route for the Japanese withdrawal from Arakan, their reasons for holding these islands were less strong now, and that it was likely that the Japanese had already begun to reduce the strength of their garrison. Nevertheless, considerable opposition was expected at Kyaukpyu where the Japanese had mounted strong gun positions in caves, immediately overlooking the landings. Consequently, a strong Naval Bombardment Force had been assembled at Chittagong and Akyab to support the landing of the 71st Indian Infantry Brigade.

Planning

The assault on Ramree island was known as Operation 'Matador' and the island itself was termed as 'ASSASSIN.' The area chosen for the landing was between Georgina Point (5666) and Dalhousie Point (6066) while the whole of this beach-head was known as FOX sector. This whole sector was further divided into three sub-sectors:

    (*i*) Georgina Point to south end of Bay (575653)—known as FOX GREEN.

    (*ii*) South end of Bay to Rocks (588662)—known as FOX WHITE.

    (*iii*) From Rocks to Dalhousie Point—known as FOX RED.

Owing to high embankment behind FOX RED, it was decided that all vehicles would be landed on FOX WHITE beach. There was to be no preliminary bombardment but eighteen Thunderbolts were to strafe the beach area from H−5 to the time of landing, irrespective of the fact whether there was opposition encountered or not; the direction of this strafing was to be from east to west.

The 71st Indian Infantry Brigade had to land on Kyaukpyu island with the intention of capturing the general line—Kyauktalon (5564), Point 195 (5764), Point 90 (5862), South end of island (5962), Jetty (603631) and east end of island (6264), on D day. The assault was to be launched in three phases:—

(i) Assault landing and capture of beach-covering positions.
(ii) Advance to and capture of brigade-covering positions.
(iii) Advance to and capture of divisional covering positions.

In the absence of any Japanese opposition the assault troops were to move straight on to their objectives for Phase II without further orders.

The brigade was to land at H hour on a two-battalion front; 1 Lincoln to the right on FOX WHITE, 5/1 Punjab to the left on FOX RED, while 1/18 Royal Garhwal Rifles was to act as a follow-up battalion. 5/1 Punjab was to assault and capture the general line of the brigade, covering position from all including Thabyacheing (5863), South end of island (5962), Jetty (603631) to East end of island (6264), on D day.

Method of Assault

Phase I

Responsibility of 1 Lincolns—This battalion was to land on a two-company front with hundred yards between the companies; A company to the right and B company to the left. The former's objective was the area including the road junction 577653 to excluding road junction 583649. B company's objective was including road junction 583649 to excluding road junction 591649. D company was to land at H+5 hours and mop up housed and wooded areas between the beach and A company's objective, and later, to establish company headquarters in the area of road junction 582651. Bangalore Torpedoes were to be carried by all the three companies and were to be used only when considered absolutely necessary.

Responsibility of 5/1 Punjab—This battalion was to assault the FOX RED beach, also on a two-company front with A company to the right and B company to the left, and secure the line of the beach-covering position. A company's objective was all including road junction 591649 to road junction 596651. B company's objective was School to road junction 607657.

In case of heavy opposition during Phase I no move was to be made forward until help was obtained from 1/18 Royal Garhwal Rifles.

Phase II

Responsibility of 1 Lincolns.—A company's objective was Georgina Point and Pyindaw. The company was to move to this objective as soon as possible via the coast road, with one or two platoons working along the ridge to the west of the road. In case of heavy opposition at this stage, no move was to be made till tank support became available. It was essential that Georgina Point was taken early, since it appeared to be the only exit for the Japanese from Kyaukpyu and was also a possible direction from which a Japanese counter-attack could be expected. D company's objective was the ridge from 577649 to 579647; from here it was to cover Point 195, with one troop of tanks at hand to support when ordered. B company's objective was bridge at 588638; on its capture the company was to secure all available local craft on the Indian side of the chaung. This attack was to be supported by tanks depending on the situation. C company was to land at H+30 and move to the area at 682651.

Responsibility of 5/1 Punjab

Stage 1—C company having landed on FOX RED beach at H+5 hours and having completed its mopping up operations was then to advance and capture Kanyindaw 6164. D company, landing at H+20 hours on FOX RED beach, was to advance and come into reserve at Amara Para.

Stage 2—A company was to advance and secure the line of excluding bridge 588638 to including Thabyacheing 5863 and link up with 1 Lincolns along this line. B company had to patrol through Kyaukpyu and clear any opposition that it might meet. D company had to advance and capture all including Ngalapwe to Jetty 6063. It had then to arrange to collect as many boats as possible for use in Phase III by 5/1 Punjab and 1/18 Royal Garhwal Rifles.

Phase III

A codeword was to be sent by wireless telegraphy for commencement of the third phase which was to take place in two stages. The responsibility of 1 Lincolns was as follows:—

> B company's objective was Point 195. It was to attack this hill from the south-west with the support of a troop of tanks.

C company was to move to the area of Georgina Point and north end of the ridge, by the coastal road. On the capture of Point 195, A and C companies were then to attack the final objective. With A company to the right and C company to the left, the former's objective was the beach 554651 to including road 559651; C company's objective was excluding area 559651 to including hill 565650. A troop of tanks was given in support of each company.

In the event of no opposition up to this stage, C company was to move direct to area Pyindaw and A company to Kyauktalon.

Responsibility of 5/1 Punjab—On orders from the battalion headquarters one platoon from either C or D company had to stand in patrol to the north end of the spur 619625.

Naval Support

There was to be no preliminary bombardment but certain selected targets were to be engaged by the Royal Navy if the 71st Indian Infantry Brigade commander should consider it necessary to do so. Two LCs (M) were to be positioned on the east flank of 5/1 Punjab. An officer of the rank of lieutenant with one No. 46 wireless set was to travel in one of these in order to assist in controlling their fire. Support was to be given by observed fire and the probable targets to be engaged were the foxhole positions to the west of the Jetty and certain bunker positions that had already been located. These LCs (M) were to operate along the coast from the Jetty to Kyaukpyu until the companies of 5/1 Punjab were established on the beach-covering positions. A destroyer was also to be ready at H hour for the support of 5/1 Punjab.

Air support

A continuous fighter patrol of Thunderbolts and Lightnings was to be maintained over the convoy, the sea approaches to the island and the beach area, from H – 150 until last light on D day.

Eighteen Thunderbolts were to strafe the landing beach areas from H – 5 to the time the landing craft touched down, irrespective of any opposition. Four squadrons of fighter bombers were also made available for engagement of targets through normal ASSU (Air Support Signal Unit) channels.

Landing and subsequent operations

On 21 January 1945 at 0700 hours, 1 Lincolns embarked into LCs and assaulted the northern tip of Kyaukpyu. The Royal Naval element of the Bombardment Force supporting the landing included the battleships HMS *Queen Elizabeth*[2], HMS *Phoebe*, HMS *Rapid*, HMS *Flamingo*, HMAS *Napier*, and HMIS *Kistna* and *Amir*. The second salvo from HMS *Queen Elizabeth* scored a direct hit on the Japanese ammunition depot. When the first wave of the assault craft which was escorted by armed motor launches was about a mile from the beaches, the naval bombardment opened up. The shore targets were bombarded by naval craft from 0900 hours onwards. Japanese guns returned the fire for some 20 minutes but their shooting was erratic and no ship or craft was hit. Twelve squadrons of Liberators also took part in the strafing of certain targets, especially Kyauktalon, Black Hill (555608) and Ondaw, while Thunderbolts swept the beach from H−5 to H hour.

The assault craft reached Kyaukpyu at 0933 hours, after one landing craft and one motor launch had been sunk by mines, and A and B companies of 1 Lincolns went ashore with very little opposition. B company pushed on to the airfield at 595645 while A company wheeled right to Georgina Point and secured it by 1100 hours. A company then moved on to capture Kyauktalon. The Japanese withdrew fairly rapidly and contact could not be made with them by the assaulting troops until the evening of that day. By 1800 hours, 1 Lincolns Battalion Headquarters was established at Kyauktalon. A company after some patrolling moved on to Gonchwen while C company advanced to Ondaw. Meanwhile B company, after a heavy air strafing by Thunderbolts on Point 195, captured this feature and remained in position until relieved by 2 Green Howards, at about 0700 hours on 22 January. By the evening of 21 January, A company had patrolled Black Hill and Mount Peter where some Japanese had been located.

1/18 Royal Garhwal Rifles and 5/1 Punjab had also landed simultaneously without opposition. B company of 5/1 Punjab landed to the left of Kyaukpyu town while A company landed to the right of it, at 0935 hours. Both companies pushed on to their objectives supported by tanks without any opposition, and by 1230 hours battalion headquarters had reached Pagoda Hill (608644). The battalion was informed by the local inhabitants that there were no Japanese at Kyaukpyu.

The chief difficulty of 1/18 Royal Garhwal Rifles was in getting across the mangrove chaung which separated the ridge at Point 90 from Kyaukpyu mainland. However, country boats were commandeered and use was made of Royal Engineers Assault Boats. The mud was waist deep and embarkation and disembarkation were, in consequence, very difficult. Nevertheless, by 2200 hours on D day, C company

---

[2] This was the first occasion since the Dardanelles Operations of 1915 that "*Queen Elizabeth*" was in action against the enemy.

was established on Point 90, B company was on the bank of the island to the north of this point, while D and A companies and battalion headquarters were established on the ridge to the north-east of Point 195, across the chaung.

On 21 January, 2/7 Rajput of the 4th Indian Infantry Brigade had also taken a share in the day's battle. The battalion had established its headquarters at 596658. This battalion was to hold the beach-covering positions after the 71st Indian Infantry Brigade had moved on to carry out Phase II of the assault. They had to hold the island of Kyaukpyu till the arrival of the rest of the 4th Indian Infantry Brigade.

On 22 January 1945, the defence of Kyaukpyu passed into the hands of the 4th Indian Infantry Brigade from the 71st Indian Infantry Brigade.

On the same day 1/18 Royal Garhwal Rifles had marched to the south-east end of Gonchwein to form up for the attack on Mount Peter. This attack was to be preceded by a naval and air bombardment while the Lincolns had also to put in a simultaneous attack on Black Hill. At about 1130 hours, it became apparent that Mount Peter and Black Hill were not held by the Japanese. Both the battalions, therefore, marched on towards Minbyin about eight miles to the south; the Lincolns marched by road while 1/18 Royal Garhwal Rifles went across country, to the west. Both the battalions met on the road at Yeandaung, a mile and a half to the north of Minbyin. Here, 1/18 Royal Garhwal Rifles formed a perimeter for the night and experienced a good amount of inconvenience due to the absence of blankets and rations which did not arrive until the early hours of 23 January.

In the meantime, B company of 1 Lincolns had been relieved by a company of Green Howard on Point 195 and had, therefore, rejoined its parent unit. The same night, A company of Lincolns raided Minbyin and the beach area. The Japanese were withdrawing with great speed and so the company was not able to establish contact with them; the battalion eventually harboured for the night at Minbya.

On 22 January, while 1/18 Royal Garhwal Rifles and the Lincolns were marching south towards Minbyin, C company of 5/1 Punjab moved across the Ngalpwe chaung in two LCMs to take Zaingchaung (640614) while by 0900 hours, A company had reached Shaukchaung (626590).

On 23 January the Lincolns searched Minbyin village at first light, and by 0700 hours had moved up to occupy the area at 5748; reconnaissance patrols had proceeded inland along the track to the east during the morning but had met no Japanese. Consequently, on the same day, 1/18 Royal Garhwal Rifles as well as 5/1 Punjab which had come down to Minbyin by road, moved through the Lincoln Battalion positions and spread out, south and east respectively.

By 1430 hours, 1/18 Royal Garhwal Rifles had marched to the village of Kyaukpyauk which was about 4½ miles to the south of Minbyin. From here the battalion advanced further south and reaching Wame-Aung continued its march towards Kyaukkale. This move was carried out at 1730 hours and, hence, when the leading company, the A company of 1/18 Royal Garhwal Rifles, approached Kyaukkale, darkness was approaching. The intelligence report collected by this company from the local inhabitants revealed that there were some Japanese in the village. A company was, therefore, directed to Point 285 (650344), which dominated the village from the south. This company by-passed the village and after meeting slight opposition from the Japanese secured Point 285 after some confused fighting.

Meanwhile, 5/1 Punjab on passing through 1 Lincolns had proceeded towards Wame-Aung. The battalion arrived at Kyaukpyauk at 1800 hours on 23 January after an extremely trying march and took up positions for the night in that village.

On the morning of 24 January, while 5/1 Punjab remained at Kyaukpyauk and 1/18 Royal Garhwal Rifles was poised a little to the north of Kyaukkale, with its A company positioned at Point 285 and B company at Leiktaung, about a mile to the north-east, 1 Lincolns advanced south by passing through the above two battalions. At 0800 hours it started advancing south down the beach with the object of securing Konbwe. It received the help of 160 Field Regiment R.A. as well as HMS *Pathfinder*, which moved along the coast in support. The Lincolns were moving with their C company as an advanced guard. Having arrived at Point 250 (679314), they by-passed this point and C company moved across to occupy the summit of the ridge, commanding the beach. The Japanese at this stage put down a severe mortar fire from reverse slopes of the ridge as well as from the village of Konbwe. The guns of 160 Field Regiment and HMS *Pathfinder* then opened up on the Japanese positions and a little while later the Japanese fire was silenced. Without much difficulty A company then moved through C company positions and occupied Konbwe, which was the objective of the battalion.

On 25 January, 5/1 Punjab, which had concentrated at Kyaukpyauk, moved along the beach to Kyaukkale. From here the battalion passed through 1/18 Royal Garhwal Rifle's positions and moved on to Konbwe, which was reached at 1230 hours. The road from Kyaukkale to Konbwe was found to be heavily mined. While at Konbwe, the battalion came under Japanese fire at about 1910 hours, but once again this hostile fire was silenced by the guns of HMS 'Pathfinder'.

On the same day, patrols from A and B companies of 1 Lincolns had also moved south from Konbwe to secure the high feature at 7028 and 7128, which overlooked the main road. When the patrols reconnoitred these features they were found to have been abandoned by the Japanese. A large quantity of kit, stores and ammunition was captured and it was found that the positions on these features were heavily dug with employments at the north and south ends.

At midday on 25 January, 5/1 Punjab continued its adavnce south to occupy the village of Kayin and probe further south to the line of Yanbauk chaung. The battalion moved south at 1600 hours, but, since the road was booby-trapped with 250-lb bombs and the bridges were found dangerous to cross, the unit's mechanised transport could not move forward on that night. Meanwhile, 1 Lincolns had positioned itself on the two high features, east and west of the road, and although the Japanese fired from close range on this area, there were no casualties suffered by the Indian or British troops. At the same time the Royal Engineers got down to build new bridges for mechanised transport.

At 0900 hours on 26 January, A company of 1 Lincolns moved forward to make a reconnaissance of Yanbauk chaung, in the area opposite the village of Kanyingauk (770260), it established a base at Pyunkhaung and from here a platoon was sent to reconnoitre the river bank at 756256. Later in the day assault boats were moved to the chaung, and 5/1 Punjab also joined the Lincolns in making the assault crossing.

C company of 5/1 Punjab moved forward over very bad track which was extremely muddy, so much so that the last 800 yards passed through deep mangrove swamp. Only six assault craft were available for the crossing and the troops went across the chaung under heavy machine-gun and mortar fire cover. When the assault boats were in mid-stream and battling hard against the strong tidal current, the Japanese opened up with medium and light machine-gun fire from the high ground to the east overlooking Kandaing chaung. Allied counterfire resulted in shaking the Japanese aim and one after another the assault craft were landed on the far side. The balance of C company which had not crossed with the first wave had also given help in providing strong close-supporting fire for the assault troops. Unfortunately, due to the strong tidal currents in the chaung and the determined defence put up by the Japanese the assault troops failed to establish any beach-heads on the opposite shore. It was, therefore, decided to withdraw the troops. The withdrawal operation, carried out under heavy fire cover, proved a success. One boat, however, got sunk with all its personnel.

While 5/1 Punjab and 1 Lincolns had successfully withdrawn on this day from Yanbauk chaung, 1/18 Royal Garhwal Rifles less B company had marched south on the coast road from Kyaukkale to Konbow. B company had swept round eastward to the village of Myinyat where Japanese concentrations had been reported. But no Japanese were found there. The company established itself on the high ground at 6933. The rest of the battalion, in the meanwhile, took up positions already vacated by the Japanese to the south and north of the village of Konbaung.

On 27 January, 5/1 Punjab once again made an unsuccessful attempt to cross the Yanbauk chaung. Its craft were destroyed but luckily it received help from the Royal Marines of HMS *Pathfinder* who proceeded to its rescue in LCPs (M). A small bridge-head which the troops of 5/1 Punjab had just then managed to establish was evacuated under cover of artillery, naval machine-gun and mortar fire.

On 28 January, intensified Japanese activity was noticed on Point 388 (760234) and Point 264 (741218). These points along with Point 285 (753198) were then subjected to fire, while B company of 5/1 Punjab had a skirmish with the Japanese patrol.

Operations on Cheduba Island

Before proceeding to discuss the change of plan which resulted from the strong Japanese defensive position at Yanbauk chaung, it is necessary to review the activities and achievement of the 36th Indian Infantry Brigade and Force Wellington.

While fighting continued on Ramree island, Force Wellington with its naval support, had made a successful landing on Cheduba island on 26 January 1945. On 3 February 1945, the 2nd Battalion of the Ajmer Regiment relieved the Marines in their bridge-head on this island. The territory up to the south-west end of Searlepoint had been cleared of all Japanese and civil administration of the island resumed. At the same time, Magyi and Platt islands which had been abandoned by the Japanese had also been occupied. On 30 January 1945, Martin Force[1] landed and occupied Sagu Kyun island without meeting any opposition. The responsibility for this island was taken over by two companies of 8/13 Frontier Force Rifles and 27 Mountain Battery along with other ancillary troops. On 1 February 1945, one of the companies of 8/13

[1] Martin Force comprised of A and B companies of 8/13 Frontier Rifles and half of Headquarter and Admin Company personnel, together with 27 Indian Mountain Battery, one company 12 F.F.R., M.G. Battalion detachment, 83 Field Company detachment, 36 Indian Infantry Brigade Signals detachments, 1 Field Ambulance.

Frontier Force Rifles from Sagu Kyun island moved across and made a landing on the southern tip of Ramree island, and by 4 February the remainder of the battalion had landed and cocentrated at Kyauknimaw.

Change of Plan in Ramree operations

In spite of heavy naval and air support, the 71st Indian Infantry Brigade was finding it difficult to cross the Yanbauk chaung which was heavily defended by the Japanese. The original plan of approaching Ramree town was, therefore, abandoned and new tasks were allotted to the brigades of the 26th Indian Division. These were as follows:—

(a) 71st Indian Infantry Brigade was to leave a holding force on the north end of Yanbauk chaung. The remaining force was then to advance to Sane village and approach Ramree town from that direction. This manoeuvre was expected to result in out-flanking and by-passing the Japanese at Yanbauk chaung.

(b) 36th Indian Infantry Brigade had to launch nuisance raids against the Japanese lines of communication on the mainland, after the former had established a bridgehead at Kyauknimaw. The brigade was then to make a thrust northwards with the object of attacking the Japanese at Yanbauk chaung from the rear. It had also to make a thrust to the east, in the direction of Ramree town and thus establish a link in that area with the 71st Indian Infantry Brigade.

(c) 22nd East African Brigade, which was then at Akyab, was to relieve the 4th Indian Infantry Brigade at Kyaukpyu.

(d) 4th Indian Infantry Brigade was to move south in order to reinforce the 71st Indian Infantry Brigade and help in thrusting towards Ramree town.

On 29 January 1945, it was reported that the Japanese were withdrawing via the path, to the north-east of Myinyat. 1/18 Royal Garhwal Rifles, therefore, sent A and D companies to establish patrol bases and dominate the area by guerrilla activities. A company was made responsible for the area covering Lebongyauk, Sane, Minbyin, Yemyet, Taunggvivin and Baya; B company was to establish a base at Point 320 (723343) and work along the areas of Minbyin, Baya, Taunggvivin and Konbwe.

On 30 January, A company guerrilla patrols reported contact with the Japanese in the Minbyin area. The latter escaped through the town and took up positions on the high ground to the south-east. They were also spotted on the oval feature to the north-west of Minbyin and, consequently, A company commander concentrated all his patrols in the area to the south of the Minbyin chaung; the object was to dominate the chaung and drive out the Japanese who were moving along it to the south-east. At the same time, D company was ordered to concentrate on Yemyet.

On 31 January, A company reported that the Japanese appeared to be concentrating in the area at 807360 from where the latter were subjecting the former to heavy mortar fire. This company, therefore, while maintaining contact with the Japanese, manoeuvred to get astride the Minbyin chaung, in order to cut the latter's escape route to the south-east. On the same day, an accurate air strafing of Points 260 and 388 was carried out by twentyfour Thunderbolts.

On 1 February after this preliminary bombardment B company of 5/1 Punjab went across the Yanbauk chaung and landed on the opposite shore. This move had been carried out in order to deceive the Japanese into believing that the brigade was to put in an attack from the south of Yanbauk chaung. In reality, the other battalions were carrying out their moves to the north and east in order to avoid the Yanbauk chaung line.

On 31 January, while 5/1 Punjab was busy preparing to carry out the deception plan, 1 Lincolns had moved through Konbwe and proceeded east-north-east via the track route. B and D companies had kept on advancing and gone through the villages of Tabet, Yemyet, Bawlaba and Paukpyin. During this move the advance patrols had a little skirmish with the Japanese. A hostile post was discovered in the hills in the area 800376; artillery fire from 160 Field Regiment was, accordingly put down in this area, as well as in a thick jungle which was situated opposite Point 450 (8138), and overlooked Sane. Soon after, a platoon of B company quickly occupied Point 450 without opposition and under its fire cover, D company proceeded to search the village of Sane.

The 1 Lincolns soon after occupied Sane and found the local inhabitants extremely helpful. Many booby-traps and mines were discovered, and information gained showed that the Japanese had withdrawn to the south. In the meanwhile, the Royal Engineers worked on the track to make it fit for tanks and mechanised transport. Patrols were immediately sent out to contact the Japanese and follow their lines of withdrawal, and by 1500 hours the battalion's wheeled transport had also reached Sane village.

1/18 Royal Garhwal Rifles had also been busy on 31 January. B company of this regiment left Konbwe on this day and joined the Battalion Headquarters at Yemyet. In the afternoon, the battalion less B company concentrated at Taunggyi Minbyin, while B company pushed on to Ngameye. On 2 February 1945, 1/18 Royal Garhwal Rifles less A company concentrated on the ridge overlooking the village of Yebadin; A company was situated on the pimple to the east of the village in area 863308. From its positions on the ridge, B company sent out patrols to reconnoitre Point 233 (886273) which met with heavy Japanese opposition and had to withdraw. By 2 February, 1 Lincolns had also moved to Minbyin and had relieved the rear parties of 1/18 Garhwal Rifles in the Taunggyi-Minbyin area. By the end of the day the Garhwal Rifles had moved south to Yebadin.

By nightfall of 2 February, D company of 1 Lincolns had moved south and taken up positions at Ngameye. On the morning of 3 February it was decided that the Lincolns should assault and take Point 233. Hence, the battalion moved up via the Minbyin track at 0800 hours on 3 February and on the way down to the forming-up positions picked up D company on passing through Ngameye. While crossing the Hengetpyo chaung (8830) the battalion was shelled by Japanese 75 mm guns and suffered some casualties. However, the hill features overlooking the Yanbauk chaung were occupied and patrols were then sent to reconnoitre the crossing of this chaung in order to reach Ywe-Ywe village.

From their positions A and B companies of 1 Lincolns supported by Spitfires and an artillery barrage, put in an attack on Point 233. The assault troops met with very heavy Japanese machine-gun fire from that point as well as from other hill features, due east and south-east of it. As a result, A company had to withdraw at about 1500 hours, but even during its withdrawal 75 mm gun fire was kept up on it by the Japanese.

At this stage 1/18 Royal Garhwal Rifles came into the picture again. Its C company was sent to Point 169 and the rest of the battalion took up defensive positions in the hill features to the north of Point 233 where it remained during the night of 3/4 February. The Japanese raiding parties were very active during the night with their grenades and sniping activities. Casualties were suffered as well as inflicted by this battalion.

On 4 February, 1/18 Royal Garhwal Rifles was ordered to take BANANA ridge (896295) and the BEAN feature (896274), as a preliminary to a second attack to be put in by 1 Lincolns on Point 233. For this purpose, 1/18 Royal Garhwal Rifles, supported by two troops of the tanks of 146 Regiment R.A.C., moved up along the east flank and, under cover of air bombardment and artillery fire, attacked these features to the east of Point 233. B and D companies advanced along the lower western slopes of BANANA ridge; they were to assault the BEAN ridge after a preliminary air and artillery bombardment and their objectives were the northern and southern halves of BEAN respectively. The battalion attack was supported by one battery of 160 Field Regiment and a squadron, less one troop, of tanks.

The battalion, less B and D companies, advanced to a

small feature east of Konbaung village. While moving up it came under heavy fire by 75 mm guns which caused a few casualties. At 1430 hours on 4 February, B and D companies put in their attack on BEAN and met with very heavy opposition from light machine-guns and mortars. D company got to positions on the north end of the feature having suffered thirty casualties, including one officer who was wounded; but B company was unable to get to the south end of the feature. Even when C company was sent to the help of B company the Japanese fire and determination proved too much for these troops. After some very hard hand-to-hand fighting they had to withdraw back to their battalion having suffered a considerable number of casualties.

The attack by 1/18 Royal Garhwal Rifles thus proved to be only a partial success. While this attack was going on, Point 233 was also being strafed with high-explosive bombs, and C and D companies of 1 Lincolns, under cover of this strafing and artillery fire, had moved forward to attack it. Their attack was successful and the companies infiltrated on to the feature and occupied the summit. There was, however, still one area which could not be overcome. Nevertheless, before the Japanese were able to recover from this surprise, B company had followed up the success of the C and D companies. The Japanese counter-attacked the feature with the help of mortar fire, but the Lincolns held on to their positions which they had consolidated before darkness set in. The southern slopes of the feature were, however, still in Japanese hands. By nightfall A company had also joined the battalion having moved up from the Yenbauk chaung.

On 5 February 1945, the Garhwal Battalion was again given the task of clearing the BEAN and BANANA features. In support it had one troop of the Royal Armoured Corps and a battery of 160 Field Regiment Royal Artillery. At 1200 hours, therefore, D company advanced and, passing through B company positions, established itself on the south end of BEAN. Here it was heavily counter-attacked and again pushed back. But the main Japanese counter-attack had been smashed owing to some very accurate fire on this ridge by the tanks. Hence by the evening, D company was again established in a position which dominated the south end of BEAN. Meanwhile, C company had proceeded carefully up the BANANA feature, the object being to clear the Japanese strongpoint that was known to be established at its south end. By 1800 hours this company had reached the crest of the BANANA ridge and only one Japanese strongpoint towards the north end had not been occupied. As the company moved forward to assault this Japanese strongpoint, intense light machine-gun fire from both the flanks opened up while volleys of grenade and small arms fire were also poured down on it from the front. In the absence of tank support and also due to the shortage of ammunition C company had eventually to withdraw back to its battalion positions.

While 1 Lincolns and 1/18 Royal Garhwal Rifles were thus busy with their operations against Point 233, 5/1 Punjab, after having been relieved on 3 February by 2/7 Rajput, had passed through Minbyin and marching along the road had arrived at Yebadin, and taken over from 1/18 Royal Garhwal Rifles. On 6 February again, 5/1 Punjab was relieved at Yebadin by 2/13 Frontier Force Rifles and on the same day this battalion was given the task of clearing BANANA ridge. The battalion less D company thereupon moved to Point 169 and established tactical headquarters a little forward of this feature. In the meantime the Japanese were reported to have moved away from BANANA ridge along the south-east slope; the battalion, thereupon, occupied the ridge without any opposition. 1/18 Royal Garhwal Rifles then took over the ridge from 5/1 Punjab and remained in position while the latter continued the advance towards Ramree town. On this day, 1 Lincolns also had occupied the hill of Point 233 feature as well as Namudwe village. They had then pushed on, having crossed the road, towards Htangyat and Tawle. 5/1 Punjab had then moved due east towards Point 320 (898257) on its way to Ramree. The road was found to be heavily mined and booby-trapped with a few bridges destroyed. But C company had reported after reconnaissance that there were no Japanese troops on Point 320 (898257). The battalion had, therefore, continued its advance along the road towards Ramree town accompanied by its D company. During this advance they found the country to be extremely dense with forests and although the road was good, it was heavily mined. The Royal Engineers were doing their best to clear the road and the night of 6/7 February was spent by 5/1 Punjab in area 914254.

In the meanwhile, the 4th Indian Infantry Brigade had also been active and doing its bit for the Ramree operations. Having taken over the defence of Kyaukpyu on 22 January, it had carried out reconnaissance of the islands to the north-east and had cleared them of the Japanese. Soon after, the brigade had handed over the defence of Kyaukpyu to the 22nd East African Brigade and had moved further south. On 3 February, 2/7 Rajput of this brigade had taken over the defence of Maybin from 5/1 Punjab. On 4 February patrols from this brigade had crossed the Yanbauk chaung and had brought back the information that Point 260 (741218), Point 285 (754198) and Ywahaung village were clear of the Japanese. Apparently, the Japanese had withdrawn from these areas because of the move of the 71st Indian Infantry Brigade towards Ramree town from Sane village, and also because of the landing of the 36th Indian Infantry

Brigade at Kyauknimaw on the southern end of Ramree island. On 6 February, therefore, 2/7 Rajput crossed the Yanbauk chaung and followed the withdrawing Japanese up the Ledaung chaung.

On the 71st Indian Infantry Brigade front, at 0800 hours on 7 February, the Lincolns continued their advance east along the road towards Ramree town. When this battalion approached the crossroads at 928239, the advanced guard was heavily engaged by the Japanese from the flanks. This hostile fire was eliminated with the help of the supporting tanks. The battalion's A company thereafter advanced to attack and occupy Point 205 (934238). The attack was heavily opposed by the Japanese stationed to the west and south of this high feature. C company then moved up into positions in order to cover the withdrawal of A company.

The Japanese held out all day on Point 205 and on the high features which were on either side of the road to Ramree town. Obviously, their object was to prevent the Allied troops from entering the town by means of dominating the features that surrounded it. By nightfall of 7 February, however, 1 Lincolns had occupied positions that overlooked the road to Ramree from the north and had also blocked the road that led into the town from the south-west.

On the same day, 5/1 Punjab had also continued its advance by leap-frogging the companies. A company and battalion headquarters, moving through B company positions, pushed on to Tantabyin while D company also followed through to arrive at Doratha. At the end of the day the battalion harboured in the area at 948248. By then, B and C companies had also arrived at Tantabyin.

At dawn on 8 February, patrols from 1 Lincolns discovered that the Japanese were still in bunker positions in the surrounding hills that covered the approaches to Ramree. At that time the tracks were being put right by the Sappers to be used by tanks and heavy mechanised transport. D company of this battalion was, therefore, sent towards the road leading into Ramree town from the north, with the object of covering the activity of the Sappers.

At 1100 hours, Point 205 after a slight opposition fell to C company. Immediately after, D company split up into small parties to locate and pin-point such Japanese troops as might still be on the hill feature covering the road, due west of Point 205. While carrying out this task with the help of tanks, D company suffered a few casualties. Nevertheless, one bunker was destroyed by direct hits from the supporting tanks and gradually the Japanese were forced to withdraw from these positions. B company then pushed through D company and cleared the road as far as the features SADDLE at 935244. 5/1 Punjab had also made good progress on its own front and was now dominating Ramree town from the north.

On the morning of 9 February, patrols from the Lincoln battalion were able to penetrate the road up to Ramree. B and C companies of this battalion thereupon entered Ramree town at about 0900 hours. At 1100 hours the whole battalion less A company moved forward to occupy the area of southern Ramree. B company occupied Point 292 (961228), C company occupied Point 110 (952226) and D company was made responsible for the whole of the south-west area; battalion headquarters was positioned just below Point 110. A company continued to remain in the area of the cross-roads in order to clear up such Japanese snipers as were proving a nuisance to the traffic on the road to Ramree. 5/1 Punjab also entered Ramree town from the west and 1/18 Royal Garhwal Rifles too, arrived in that area.

In the meantime, the 36th Indian Infantry Brigade had commenced picketing the Kalaindaung river and the chaungs to the south-east of Ramree town, thus preventing the Japanese from escaping to the mainland.

On 10 February, 5/1 Punjab increased its activities to clear the Japanese from around the town. Although the areas immediately surrounding Ramree were clear of the Japanese, some snipers were still found to be very active, while small parties were spotted to be fleeing towards the north. Battalion headquarters thereupon moved to Pagomazu leaving C company on the Tantabyin feature where, situated in caves, large dumps of Japanese ammunition were located. A company then chased the Japanese in the areas of Naramu, Chaung-ne, Dontaung and Hpet-kya to wipe them out. B company with the same intention moved along the areas of Letpan, Point 300 (974275) and Yanthitshe. The object of both these companies was to scour the countryside and to kill and drive as many Japanese as possible into the marshes and chaungs, the entrances of which were covered by Allied naval craft.

Clearing of the island

Though Ramree town was captured, yet the island could not be cleared completely of the Japanese for quite a few days. During the mopping up period the Japanese were driven to the mangrove swamps where they had to encounter hunger, starvation and thirst, while several are known to have been devoured by crocodiles. On 11 February intelligence reports indicated that the Japanese were concentrated in some strength on the Mawsi Taung feature (Point 503). Their strength was estimated to be between 400 to 800 men. The 71st Indian Infantry Brigade thereupon decided to drive them north-east by advancing against them in a series of lines. The plan was as follows:—

Line 1—The route of advance to be followed was from

Yanthitgyi, then along the chaung to east of Thitakhauk Taung, Myinkhon chaung, Point 273 (924268) then along the Letpan Chaung to Letpan and on to Awadaung.

Line 2—Starting from Saikpya towards Point 334 (9430) and then to Hngetkywe Chaung and on to a little south of Point 300 (973275).

Line 3—The route was similar to Line 2 with the exception that below Mawsi Taung feature, the line was to move north of the hill running east of Dontaung.

Line 4—Was to manoeuvre in such a way as to make a circle covering the areas of Yanthitshe and Point 200 (984310).

These mopping up operations to be carried out in a series of lines were to be undertaken by three battalions—5/1 Punjab, 1/18 Royal Garhwal Rifles and 2/13 Frontier Force Rifles which had been put under the command of the 71st Indian Infantry Brigade for these operations. Each battalion proceeded along the various routes described by keeping two companies forward.

On 11 February 1945, the Japanese decided to abandon further organised resistance in these areas. By the evening of that day, however, they had made a last effort to rescue the remnants of their hard-pressed garrison in the area of Ramree. Under cover of light bombers, forty powered-craft set out from Taungup to help to ferry across to the mainland the hard-pressed Japanese soldiers who were then fighting for their lives. Thirty-six of these craft were sunk on their way to Ramree while the remainder were sunk on their return trip with all personnel on board. No casualties whatsoever were suffered by Indo-British naval personnel. HMS *'Pathfinder'* and *Paladin* were attacked from the area; the former was slightly damaged and had to retire for inspection and repair.

These mopping up operations continued till about the end of the month and most of the Japanese were either starved or destroyed by those that had put a blockade round their escape routes. By 22 February, the invasion of Ramree island had successfully ended and Allied ships were thereafter withdrawn from this area.

While the island was being cleared, the Allies were, at the same time, making rapid progress towards setting up of the base at Kyaukpyu. The security of this town had ceased to be the responsibility of the 26th Indian Division, and had been taken over by the 22nd East African Brigade immediately after its arrival. A Sub-Area Headquarters was also set up and work on the construction of the all-weather airstrip and other base installations immediately taken in hand.

CHAPTER XXI

The Final Phases in Arakan

The New Situation

One of the severest handicaps in the conduct of the Allied advance, not only in Arakan but throughout the whole of the campaign in Burma, was the problem of maintenance and supply. In its drive down south, along the Irrawaddy corridor towards Mandalay, the Fourteenth Army had found itself in a country without any lateral communications; in the XV Indian Corps area this problem had largely been solved by the use of shipping and local river-craft to supply its divisions on the coast, during their advance. Most often it was necessary to maintain the West African Divisions only by air as they were operating inland, beyond the reach of waterborne communications.

By the beginning of February 1945, the Fourteenth Army's advance was progressing much beyond the normal expectations of the South-East Asia Command. This force was rapidly outstripping its bases in Assam and Manipur and the possibility of its capturing Mandalay and advancing sufficiently rapidly to capture Rangoon itself, before the beginning of the monsoon, was being entertained. Consequently, in order to ease the supply situation, large all-weather airstrips were being hastily constructed on Akyab island and at Kyaukpyu on Ramree island so that Rear Airfield Maintenance Organisations (RAMOs) could be set up and bases stocked with supplies. Thereby the Fourteenth Army could be supplied from the south by a shorter route than the one that was being used by its own transport squadrons.

Shortage of shipping had always been a source of some embarrassment to the XV Indian Corps during its advance. During this period it became all the more necessary to use all possible shipping for stocking the Akyab and Ramree air bases for the Fourteenth army; this still further limited the shipping that was at the disposal of the Corps.

In order to conserve as much supplies as were being brought into Arakan for the maintenance of the Fourteenth Army, the Allied High Command decided to withdraw further formations of the XV Indian Corps from the battle area and send them back to India as soon as they could possibly be spared. The 81st West African Division had already reached India and it was decided that the 25th Indian

Division, which had continuously been in action for about twelve months, should be the next to be withdrawn. The 82nd West African Division, it was realised, had marched many a mile in difficult country and the 1st and 4th West African Brigades were still fighting inland; but on the whole this division had met with less resistance than the others and it was, therefore, earmarked to remain in the field upto the last. Although the 26th Indian Division had taken part only in the Ramree operations, and although it was still required to make more landings on the mainland, it was decided that this division should be the next to withdraw after the 25th Indian Division, because of the length of service it had put in the Arakan area.

As for the 3rd Commando Brigade, it had by now been the spearhead of three assaults, hence it needed complete rest, particularly after the strenuous fighting at Kangaw. The 50th Indian Tank Brigade which was widely scattered in support of various divisions, could not be given enough suitable employment because of the nature of the country; hence it was also to be withdrawn as early as possible.

By this time the whole of the XV Indian Corps headquarters had moved down to Akyab island. The advanced headquarters of the supporting 224 Group, Royal Air Force, and a Combined Headquarters along with the Headquarters Naval Force had also been established on this island.

Appreciation and plan

The principal task of the XV Indian Corps at this stage was to help and assist the Fourteenth Army in its advance towards Mandalay and the subsequent drive on Rangoon; this task could be accomplished by holding the attention of the Japanese Higher Command to the coastal sector. Further territorial conquest in itself was now of small consideration; the supply bases which had been the objective of the campaign were now in Allied hands and there was no other major strategical prize in the Arakan area. It was, however, appreciated that aggressive action along the coastal sector would hold the Japanese to their seaward defences and thus induce them to retain their strategic reserve in readiness to meet the probable threat of further Allied amphibious operations.

At the end of December 1944, when the 25th Indian Division was concentrating at Foul Point for the crossing to Akyab and the 82nd West African Division was turning its face towards the Kaladan Valley, the roads of these two formations had parted. But this estrangement was one of distance only, though their actions were coordinated for the achievement of the same object. Now, when these

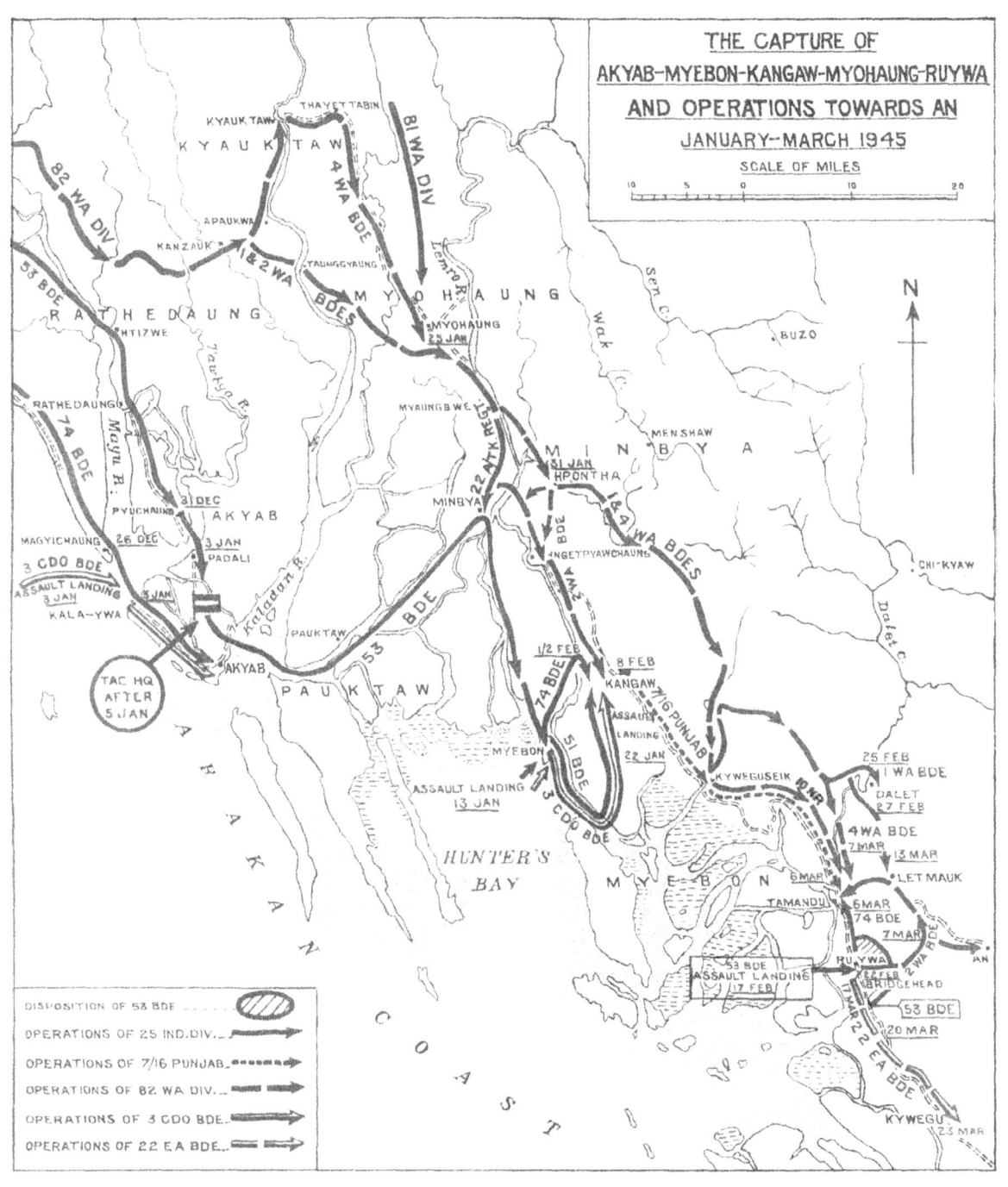

divisions were once again drawing nearer to each other, the closest co-operation was again re-established. At the beginning of February 1945 while the Kangaw battle was at its height, the African Division had advanced from Myohaung (capital of northern Arakan) and had reached Hpontha, which lies some twenty miles north of Kangaw. The division commander of the West African Division had then divided his forces. While the 2nd West African Brigade had driven south on to the Kangaw block, the divisional commander led the remainder of his division into the hills along the line of the Taywe chaung. In doing so he had a double object; firstly, to make for Kyweguseik in order to intercept the Japanese forces then withdrawing from Kangaw, and secondly, to endeavour to find a route across the mountains to Dalet, with a view to a further advance on An.

The village of An lies at the western end of the most northern pass across the Arakan Yomas over which the Japanese had only recently completed a new motor road into the Irrawaddy valley. Its capture would deny this escape route to any Japanese troops remaining west of the Mayu range. The 2nd West African Brigade, as already recorded, had made good progress and, coming under the command of the 25th Indian Division, had completed its part in the final expulsion of the Japanese forces from Kangaw. The drive on Kyweguseik by the rest of the West African Division only achieved a partial success, as the Africans found the approaches to this village resolutely held, and the ground was such that it favoured the defenders. Leaving, therefore, a detachment only to watch the Japanese and with orders to press on when opportunity offered, the 82nd West African Division Commander had turned the remainder of his force towards Dalet and An.

The commander of the XV Indian Corps had received fresh instructions for the operations of the Corps up to the onset of the monsoon in late April 1945. These instructions included the clearance of the Japanese from the whole of the coastal strip as far south as Taungup, Sandoway and Gwa as well as the continuation of operations to contain the Japanese forces in the An area, for as long as it was profitable. It was appreciated by the Allied High Command that the Japanese would make a very determined stand on two passes— the northern pass running through the mountains from An to Minbu in the Irrawaddy valley, being defended by the *54th Japanese Division* (less *121st Regiment*), and the southern pass from Taungup to Prome, being held by the *121st Regiment*. It was also appreciated that even a very small determined force would be able to defend either of these passes with considerable chance of success. The terrain of the country of these areas presented great difficulties, and was at the same time highly suitable for a protracted defence. On the other hand, the difficulties inherent in maintaining strong Allied offensive forces in either of these areas were going to present a substantial problem. It was also known that Sandoway and Gwa were being held by detachments of the Japanese *55th Division*.

One of the captured Japanese officers had given the information that the Japanese were prepared for a suicidal defence and that they were determined to defend the An and Taungup passes to the last drop of their blood. Neither of the passes had an all-weather road, hence a great deal would depend upon the speed with which it would be possible for the Allies to occupy the western end of the passes; at the same time, it was also appreciated that the coming of the monsoon would make maintenance problems well-nigh insurmountable. Even more dangerous was the possibility of committing a force to offensive operations in either of the passes before the onset of the monsoon, which, if it broke before the objectives were attained, would inevitably pin down parts of the corps for the whole monsoon period.

At the beginning of February 1945, therefore, two main essentials had to be borne in mind by the Allied High Command. Firstly, the gradual phasing out of the 25th and 26th Indian Divisions, 3rd Commando Brigade and the bulk of the 50th Tank Brigade, with such other corps troops as could be spared; this was with a view to easing the problem of maintenance. Secondly, the continuation of the offensive to contain the Japanese on the western side of the Yomas at An and Taungup and, later, to carry out the final clearance of Arakan from Sandoway down to Gwa.

XV Indian Corps Dispositions—

 (a) The whole of the 26th Indian Division was situated at Ramree island.
 (b) 3rd Commando Brigade and 25th Indian Division (less 51st Indian Infantry Brigade) were disposed in the Kangaw area and on the Myebon peninsula. The 51st Indian Infantry Brigade was in the process of being returned to Akyab island for concentration, before finally being sent to India.
 (c) 82nd West African Division—2nd West African Brigade had arrived at Kangaw and had passed under the Command of the 25th Indian Division on 9 February 1945. The 1st and 4th West African Brigades were en route from Hpontha to An; they were in contact with the Japanese who were endeavouring to withdraw eastwards in order to join the An pass garrison.

Joint Force Commanders' plan—

After completing the defeat of the Japanese in the Kangaw area the XV Indian Corps was given the following tasks:—

- (a) To provide a small pursuit force which would follow the Japanese vigorously on to Kyweguseik and completely defeat them in that area in conjunction with the operations of the 82nd West African Division. This pursuit force was eventually to approach Tamandu from the north; this pincer movement was expected to result in trapping a large body of the Japanese force which was known to be at Tamandu.
- (b) Having completed the defeat of the Japanese at Kyweguseik the 25th Indian Division was then to maintain a firm base in that area in order to facilitate the operations of the 82nd West African Division against the Japanese forces in the Dalet-An area.
- (c) In addition to the above two tasks, the Corps was also to carry out an assault landing and to establish a bridgehead on the mainland, west of An. D day for this was to be 16 February 1945. The 2nd West African Brigade was to pass through this bridgehead and take part in the battle of An under the orders of the Commander of the 82nd West African Division.

On completion of the An battle, the 25th Indian Division was required to find, temporarily, a back-stop of a brigade group in the An area which would help and enable the 82nd West African Division to advance towards Taungup. The remainder of the 25th Indian Division was then to be withdrawn to Akyab as soon as it could be spared. One troop of 19th Lancers was to remain under the command of the 25th Indian Division for this operation.

Apart from the above tasks, the XV Indian Corps was allotted further tasks as follows:—

- (1) The corps was to capture and maintain the Ruywa bridgehead and to send out reconnaissance parties to gain information about the Japanese and their lines of communication in that area. It was also to make the track to An fit for jeep traffic.
- (2) The corps was to exploit from the rear bridge-head to capture Tamandu as rapidly as possible so that the Field Maintenance Area (F.M.A.) could be established there. This F.M.A. was expected to be ready by 1 March 1945, the date on which the 82nd West African Division was to come off air supply.
- (3) The 2nd West African Brigade, as already mentioned, was to pass through the Ruywa bridgehead and reverting

under the command of the 82nd West African Division was to advance on An. For the purpose of maintaining the troops operating in the An area, a F.M.A. had also to be established in the Ruywa bridgehead. This F.M.A. was later to be moved to Tamandu when it had been captured. On establishing the F.M.A. at Tamandu, the F.M.A.s at Kangaw and Myebon were to be closed.

While advancing along the mainland, the XV Indian Corps was to leave a small detachment to contain the Japanese left behind in the Kangaw area; the corps was also to supply a minimum force necessary to assist 5 N.A.R. in capturing Kyweguseik.

The 26th Indian Division was given the following roles in this operation:

(a) To establish a base on the mainland between Kywegu and Lamu with a view to passing the 22nd East African Brigade; the latter was to attempt to destroy the *2nd Battalion, 111th Regiment* in the Kywegu area and then exploit towards An.

(b) To Capture and consolidate a suitable ground in the Taungup area which could be turned into a firm base to be held during the monsoon. This would also have involved the destruction of that part of the Japanese *54th Division* which was then holding the Taungup area in general.

(c) To contain as far as possible the majority of the *55th Japanese Division* in the area, south and south-east of Taungup, in order to prevent the latter from moving against the Fourteenth Army's advance.

D day for the operation mentioned in para (a) was to be as early as possible but not later than 14 March 1945. The 26th Indian Division was further ordered to be prepared to hand over its firm base in the Taungup aera to the 82nd West African Division, by 15 April 1945. This was to enable the former to be withdrawn to India in order to train for future operations.

XV Indian Corps plan

The 25th Indian Division was to establish a bridgehead in the area of Ruywa with the object of passing through a force which would be directed towards An. In view of this object the divisional commander decided to carry out the operation as follows:—

(1) On D – 1, the 3rd Commando Brigade would establish gun positions in order to cover the intended bridgehead in areas 8607 and 8405.

(2) An assault landing by the 53rd Indian Infantry Brigade Group, would be mounted from Myebon, in the area north of Ruywa, to seize a beach-head. The Brigade Group

would be landed in two trips on available craft and landing completed by D–1. It would then hold the Ruywa bridgehead as a firm base for future operations.

(3) The 2nd West African Brigade would then be ferried across from Kangaw to the bridgehead and would subsequently advance to An by the track Ruywa-An. This ferrying across was to commence on D—2. The track from Ruywa[1] to An was a winding one through the hills and was almost indefinable. The country was mountainous and thickly covered with forest and the track was obviously to be a most difficult line of communication. Arrangements, however, had been made in advance to improve this track, immediately after it had fallen into Allied hands. As will be remembered a Forward Maintenance Area had also been planned at Ruywa to supply the advancing 2nd West African Brigade, with the help of mules or jeep along this almost indefinable line of communication. 93 Field Company was detailed to work in the Ruywa bridgehead. It had been given the task of improving this track, constructing roads in the Ruywa area for tanks and wheels and also of developing its water supply.

(4) As soon as the 2nd West African Brigade had passed through the Ruywa bridgehead, the 74th Indian Infantry Brigade, with under command one troop of 19th Lancers and supported by 8 Field Regiment, was to land and concentrate in this bridgehead. The brigade was then to exploit northwards up the coast with the intention of attacking and capturing Tamandu.[2]

In addition, the 25th Indian Division was expected and ordered to provide a small pursuit force, to follow the success at Kangaw and advance rapidly southwards down the road, through the village of Kwaguseik. This pursuit force was eventually to approach Tamandu from the north, and this was expected to result in trapping a

---

[1] The village of Ruywa, lying 23 miles west of An, is technically on the coast but actually is several miles from the sea. From Myebon it is approachable only by a network of tidal chaungs which is nearly 45 miles in distance.

[2] The road from Tamandu to Kywegu in the south was, on the average, about 14 feet wide and was generally suitable for all wheeled traffic. The chaungs on the road where there were no bridges were also fordable. The road from Tamandu to An was jeepable throughout and could be made suitable for trucks. It had, however, a rough surface and there were many steep gradients. The Ruywa-An road was a good narrow jeepable track. The village of Tamandu lay three miles east of the Japanese Inland Waterways Transport base of Kantaunggyi. It was planned by the XV Indian Corps to shift the F.M.A. from Ruywa to Tamandu village after the latter had been captured. This village also provided reasonable port facilities and there existed a reasonable motorable track which led up to An. It was along this road that the supplies to the 82nd West African Division would be sent in the future.

large body of the Japanese force that was known to be in the Tamandu area.

(5) The 4th Indian Infantry Brigade of the 26th Indian Division, supported by Royal Navalcraft and the Royal Air Force, had to assault the Letpan and Mai Chaung area on 13 March 1945. Preliminary landings were to be made on 12 March and the operation was known as Operation 'Turret'.

This brigade, having established a beach-head in the Letpan area, would advance south along the axis Lamu-Sabyin to the general line of the Tanlive Chaung. This move would facilitate the southward advance of the 82nd West African Division and would also pin down the Japanese *55th Division* in the area south of Taungup.

(6) The 1st and 4th West African Brigades would be directed towards An to advance with all possible speed, eliminating any Japanese parties that they might meet on the way. These two brigades were to be maintained by air and would be the only formations of the XV Indian Corps supplied by this means.

Such a method of maintenance would allow these brigades freedom of movement in a part of country which was considered to be very difficult. It was intended that the brigades should avoid making a frontal assault on An from the west. They should move round by the north, where there was possibility of attacking, from a flank, the strong defensive positions that the Japanese were known to have prepared in the hills, which guarded the end of the pass, immediately east of the town. It was fully realised by the Allies that, in this position, the Japanese had every prospect of fighting a successful defensive action and would be most difficult to eject.

The village of An itself possessed no natural defences of value and was, therefore, not expected to prove very troublesome. Hence the proposed approach, by crossing the An chaung several miles north of An and going behind Lamaw Taung, avoided this frontal attack and had consequently every prospect of success, provided that the attacking force could be well supplied and maintained. This maintenance was entirely dependent on the continuance of air supply which had been decided upon for these two West African Brigades. Thus, any chance of the Japanese fighting a successful defensive action at An was lessened by this move of the Allies.

Plan of the assault landing

The assault landing had to be made by the 53rd Indian Infantry Brigade and the area chosen for the landing was named OBOE. This area was further subdivided into two areas:—

    I. OBOE GREEN—in area 923050.
    II. OBOE RED—in area 920060.

The overall intention was for 9 York and Lancaster to seize and hold a bridgehead north of Ruywa, at all costs. Through this bridgehead the remainder of the 53rd Indian Infantry Brigade had then to pass. D day for this assault was fixed on 16th February 1945, and H hour was to be 1030 hours.

After landing, the beach-head was to be rapidly cleared and secured up to the area of a point on the road at 930063; and before sunset on D day, 9 Yorks and Lancasters had also to establish small reconnaissance patrols on the two islands at 915050 and 905053.

The actual operation was planned to take place in six phases:—

    Phase *1*.—Move of assault troops to embarkation point.
    Phase *2*.—Embarkation and onward move to assault head.
    Phase *3*.—The actual assault landing by 9 Y & L.
        (*a*) Landing on beach OBOE GREEN.
            I. A company less one platoon, having landed on the right of this area was to proceed at maximum speed to intermediate objectives.
            II. D company was to land to the left of the area and was then to give covering fire to A company's advance for approximately five minutes.
        (*b*) Landing on beach OBOE RED.
            I. C company was to land on the right portion of the area and thereafter proceed at top speed to intermediate objectives.
            II. B company was to land on the left half of the area and then give covering fire to C company's advance for approximately five minutes.
    Phase *4*.—In this phase the assault troops had to consolidate various areas beyond the beach-head.
    Phase *5*.—Extension of bridgehead and final consolidations. 17/5 Mahratta Light Infantry having landed in two waves at H+65 and H+90 was to pass through and occupy the high ground to the east of the beaches. This high ground dominated the village of Ruywa. These features on relief by 17/5 M.L.I. would thereby release two platoons of D company

(9 Y & L) who would subsequently rejoin their parent unit.

Phase 6.—Subsequent operations.

    (a) On D+1, 4/18 Royal Garhwal Rifles was to land and clear the Ruywa area.

    (b) On D+3 day, the 2nd West African Brigade was to start arriving at Ruywa.

An intensive fire plan was laid down to help the landing of the assault troops. Shelling and strafing of the area at 9210 was to take place from H−10 to H+20 and an artillery barrage was also to be put down in the Dokekan area from H−20 to H+20.

The planning in general may, therefore, be outlined as follows:—

The 53rd Indian Infantry Brigade was to secure a beach-head in the area of Ruywa. Through this bridge-head the 2nd West African Division was to pass and then move via the track from Ruywa going east to capture the communication centre and Japanese base at the village of An, while another West African Brigade moving by way of the coast road from Kyweguseik was to put in a thrust and attack the area from the north-west. 9 Yorks and Lancasters was to make the initial landing on the beaches on 16 February and secure a beachhead in the area of 9205. Through this area, 17/5 Mahratta Light Infantry was to pass through to secure the high ground, to the east and south-east of the landing place. On 17 February, 4/18 Royal Garhwal Rifles was to consolidate the area of Ruywa and open the road for the West African Brigade's advance.

Operations on the mainland

It will be remembered that the task of the Commando Brigade was to clear the islands, west of the Sektaw river, and then, establish and reconnoitre a suitable area from which Allied guns could support the initial landing. Their task, therefore, began on 10 February 1945, when a small commando raiding party was despatched to destroy a Japanese chaung-watching observation post, reported by locals to be situated at Laungdarit, a small island about ten miles south of Myebon. The post was located and surprised and two Japanese were killed, but the rest made good their escape into the jungles. Later, other Commando patrols visited Kantaunggyi and the villages to its south and found them clear of Japanese troops. They also selected a suitable gun area on a flat island on the west bank of the Sektaw river, where there was also a limited amount of fresh water.

The work of the Commandos was now complete. Their fighting at Myebon and Kangaw had earned warm praise from all ranks of the 25th Indian Division and it was with real regret that the Indians said good-bye to this fine British formation. In a letter to the General

Officer Commanding of the 25th Indian Division, the Commander of the 3rd Commando Brigade reciprocated the feeling thus:—"It has been a very great honour for us to serve in the 25th Indian Division; whatever we have been able to achieve was only made possible by the enormous help given by the staff and all units with whom we came in contact. Every man in this brigade has learnt to admire the Indian soldier and we hope that one day we may serve under your command again."

It had always been an important feature of the plan for these operations to ensure that artillery was established in action before the landing was made; in the interest of secrecy, however, the 25th Indian Division Commander had ruled that this must not take place before the night preceding the assault. On the night of 15 February, therefore, two batteries of 25 pounders of 27 Field Regiment R.A. and a troop of medium guns were established with immense labour on CHARTER HOUSE, the "gun island" which was selected by the Commando patrol; accordingly these batteries were already in action by the time that the 53rd Indian Infantry Brigade arrived. This "gun island" lay some ten miles north-west of Ruywa and about seven miles due west of Dalet chaung and was heavily screened by mangrove trees.

In order to deceive the Japanese and thereby divert their attention from Ruywa, a deception plan had also been decided upon. According to this the Joint Force Commander decided to "turn the heat" on Tamandu with the double object of inflicting punishment and holding the Japanese attention to that area. To the end, a combined naval, air and artillery operation was mounted under the CRA of 25 Indian Division (Brigadier A.J. Dawell, DSO, MBE). The naval force comprised three sloops, H.M.S. *Flamingo*, H.M.I.S. *Narbada* and H.M.I.S. *Kistna*, and a number of motor launches manned by Indian, British and South African crews. Air support was from fighter-bombers of 224 Group R.A.F., and 27 Field Regiment R.A. produced two troops of 25 pounders mounted on Z craft. A series of targets was engaged in the vicinity of Tamandu and the Dalet crossing, both by day and night. The bombardment lasted four days and some 600 rounds were fired. Subsequently, it was very evident that as a deception measure it had fully achieved its object. Moreover, minor raids along the coast by the Commando had also helped in confusing the Japanese.

Appreciation of Japanese dispositions

It would be well to consider the dispositions of the Japanese troops facing the XV Indian Corps when the Allied assault was about to begin. Intelligence reports had intimated that Lieut.-General Katamura Shihachi, who was previously the General Officer

Commanding of the Japanese *54th Division*, had recently been appointed the General Officer Commanding of the Japanese *Fifteenth Army*. He was succeeded by Major-General Miyazaki Shigesaburo, who was previously the General Officer Commanding of the *31st Division Infantry Group*. Previous to his commanding the *31st Division Infantry Group*, General Miyazaki had commanded the *26th Brigade of the 13th Japanese Division* in Central China and had been the Japanese Military Attache at Canton, when the "China Incident" had broken out. He was about 53 years of age and possessed a slight knowledge of the English language.

At this time, evidence was rather scanty on which to base a concrete estimate of the strength of the units of the *55th Japanese Division*; it was, however, considered that they were likely to be much below establishment. At the end of the monsoon of 1944, *54th Division* had probably been very little below its establishment, but the battle that developed after that period and the casualties that this division suffered, had had a very great effect in reducing the strength of many of its units. In *111th Regiment*, the brunt of the 800 to 900 casualties had been borne by the *1st* and *3rd Battalions*; these could, therefore, be expected to be less than half their strength. The *2nd Battalion* was not known to have been engaged as yet and was, therefore, considered to be a full battalion. Generally speaking, therefore, the Allies appreciated that the strength of *111th Regiment* could be taken to equal rather less than two battalions.

Up to 30 January 1945, it was considered that the *154th Regiment* had sustained between 1100 and 1200 casualties; once again these had been borne by the *1st* and *3rd Battalions*, which implied that together they amounted to a little more than half a battalion. The *2nd Battalion* of this regiment was still on detached duty in the Mandalay area, but a draft of 50 had been indentified by means of captured documents, as having recently arrived at Regimental Headquarters.

The third regiment of the *54th Division—the 121st Regiment—* had seen the least amount of fighting and was not, therefore, greatly under strength. The *54th Reconnaissance Regiment* was also quite probably more or less complete, apart from the *2nd Squadron*, which was believed to have been practically wiped out at Myebon.

It was, therefore, appreciated that the strength of the *Japanese 54th Division* in Arakan, at the end of January 1945, would be equivalent to about six battalions. At the same time, the Japanese intention appeared to be to hold the An pass with this division less the *121st Regiment*; the latter was to defend the Taungup pass with the *1st and 3rd Battalions* and as much of the *2nd Battalion* as could be extricated from Ramree island.

The Assault

At 1030 hours on 16 February, the two leading battalions of the 53rd Indian Infantry Brigade touched down on their selected beaches. Their arrival exactly on time was in itself a major achievement, for several craft had been grounded along the route owing to difficulties in navigation. Also, since different routes were taken by each type of craft, it spoke much for the naval planning that almost all of them arrived to play their appointed part. The success of the naval plan earned the admiration of the troops taking part and was the key to the success of the operation. 9 Y & L made an unopposed assault landing on the beaches in accordance with the plan laid down. The concealed battery at "Gun Island" gave useful support to the assault troops when the Japanese artillery opened fire, thereby enabling them to quickly secure the main road, opposite the selected beach. The assault was supported[3] by naval guns, 25 pounders and air strafing, and a bridgehead about two miles in radius was quickly established after meeting with a token resistance. The Yorks and Lancasters were immediately followed by 17/5 Mahratta Light Infantry which passed through and, with the dash typical of their race, made its way to the summit of the various commanding hills, which were its objective.

The landings were made in heavy mud and through mangrove swamps on the beach which was so narrow that only two landing craft could be beached at one time. Although the chaungs in South Arakan proved to be more treacherous and narrow than those in the north, the assault troops found the mud and water, which had to be traversed, less of an obstacle than had been expected. Also, as the landing at that point came as a complete surprise to the Japanese, the assault troops were more or less unopposed except for long range artillery.

On 17 February, the remainder of the Brigade Group also landed; and except for small parties of Japanese, moving down the road, no opposition was encountered. One company from 17/5 Mahratta Light Infantry moved south along the road to Ruywa, and, although harassed by a small party of Japanese, it found this village to be unoccupied. Consequently the company seized the western end of the mountain track, leading towards An. On the same day 4/18 Royal Garhwal Rifles had also proceeded towards Ruywa area with the object of consolidating the village as well as the dominating features, east and south of it.

On the morning of 18 February a Japanese 3-ton lorry containing a party of about 12 men drove at great speed into the Indian Lines, from the south. It was fired at and halted by a combined Mahratta

---

[3] Hurricanes and Thunderbolts of 224 R.A.F. Group and the sloops of *"Flamingo"*, *"Cauvery"* and *"Narbada"* were in action.

and Garhwal ambush. D company of 17/5 Mahratta Light Infantry had punctured the tyres of this vehicle and of the 12 men that were in it two were Captains from the *54th Division Artillery Regiment*. One was killed but the other was captured, unharmed but very dazed. His interrogation showed that he was a member of the advanced party of his Regimental Headquarters which was moving from Kywegu to Tamandu. It appeared that complete surprise had been gained by the Allies in this assault and that the Japanese High Command was still unware of the fact that the landing had taken place. Apparently, the Japanese expected the Allied thrust furter north at Tamandu and not at Ruywa.

On 19 February the Japanese became a little more active. Apparently it had taken the Japanese three days before they reacted to this Allied landing. Two guns were brought down to the Me Chaung by the Japanese and thereafter they started bombardment of OBOE RED beach. Their fire was accurate and intense and soon movement by day on the beach became almost impossible.

On the night of 19/20 February, the Japanese launched a strong attack on the most northernly locality of the beach-head. This was a hill feature called ALPS, which, like all others in the area, was covered with thick bamboo. The approaches were either up steep slopes, or along a saddle, joining it with an adjacent hill to the east. ALPS was held at this time by a company of 17/5 Mahratta Light Infantry. The attacking force consisted of a company of Japanese who had originally been bound for Taungup from Tamandu. Apparently their orders were to destroy this Allied position *en route*. After hand-to-hand fighting the attackers were repulsed and broke contact, leaving their commander dead on the position. Three nights later, the Japanese again assaulted the same feature. Determined attacks persisted all night, and savage hand-to-hand fighting took place. Once more they obtained no success and again left the body of another commander on the scene of action.

On 20 February Japanese fire on OBOE RED beach became unbearable; a second beach was, therefore, reconnoitred and brought into use. This beach, named ROGER GREEN, was close to Ruywa village and possessed a good exit. But it was approached by a different and very much longer chaung route from the naval anchorage, and was only workable for three hours on either side of high water. It was not, however, under Japanese observation and was, therefore, never shelled throughout the period that it was in use.

Meanwhile, good progress was being made in the transportation of the 2nd West African Brigade from Kangaw. The 1st Battalion Group of this brigade had landed on 18 February and the rest of the brigade had followed during the next four to five days. By 22 February, the whole of the 2nd West African Brigade was beginning to pass through the 53rd Indian Infantry Brigade. The track had been made passable for wheels for a distance of nearly three miles and a troop of 25 pounders from 27 Field Regiment was moved forward to the road-head to support the advance.

By 25 February, forward elements of the 2nd West African Brigade had advanced about four miles to the east of Ruywa village. On the same day, the 74th Indian Infantry Brigade had landed on the beaches and had established the brigade headquarters at Ruywa (938059).

At this time the General Officer Commanding the 25th Indian Division had to go back to Myebon in order to attend a vital planning conference. There it was decided that the 82nd West African Division should continue the advance towards An, supplied entirely by air until such time as supply by road from Tamandu became possible. On the other hand, the 26th Indian Division operating from Kyaukpyu was to establish, as soon as possible a brigade group on the mainland at Letpan, which lies about 35 miles south-east of Ruywa, with a view to a drive down the coast to Taungup. The tasks of the 25th Indian Division were defined as follows:—

1. To maintain the Ruywa bridgehead and support the advance of the 2nd West African Brigade with artillery and engineers.
2. To exploit north from Ruywa and capture Tamandu.
3. To build up a F.M.A. in Ruywa to maintain all the troops in that area; subsequently to move this F.M.A. to Tamandu when the latter had been captured.
4. To close down the F.M.As at Kangaw and Myebon and thereafter withdraw the 51st Indian Infantry Brigade to Akyab by 1 March 1945.

General Wood thereupon decided that the 51st Indian Infantry Brigade should conclude the Kangaw battle and the pursuit to Kyweguseik, and that the Brigade commander should assume responsibility for the complete evacuation of the area. The 74th Indian Infantry Brigade less 19/10 Baluch was ordered to concentrate back in Myebon, preparatory to a move forward to Ruywa. 14/10 Baluch together with 7/16 Punjab, after concluding the Kyweguseik operation, were to be ferried direct from Kangaw to Ruywa. Finally, the divisional headquarters, with certain divisional troops were to be transported to Ruywa, as soon as craft were available.

This extensive regrouping, all of which had to be conducted by water, threw a tremendous strain on naval and inland water transport resources. However, every move was completed according to plan. The forward elements of the 74th Indian Infantry Brigade were landed on the beaches on 25 February and they established their brigade headquarters at Ruywa (938059); by 25 February the whole brigade was established in the northern part of the Ruywa beachhead and a day later, 7/16 Punjab also arrived.

The situation at this stage, therefore, ten days after the landing, was that the 25th Indian Division less the 51st Indian Brigade Group was concentrated at Ruywa with the 74th Indian Infantry Brigade feeling its way north for the bridgehead towards the Me Chaung. Local reports had indicated that all stores and a number of troops were being withdrawn by the Japanese from Tamandu, but with troops coming down from the Kangaw area it was estimated that there would still be about two Japanese battalions to oppose the 74th Brigade's advance.

The 2nd West African Brigade had struck out towards An and had reached a point on a track, about 4 miles east of Ruywa village. Here, however, the track stopped and all hopes of supplying the brigade forward by road were gone. Further progress could only be made by swinging north along the Kawchong to the Tamandu-An road and then by advancing east along it towards An. The plan of this brigade was, therefore, modified accordingly, although it meant that there would be no western arm to the pincer drive.

The 53rd Indian Infantry Brigade was patrolling extensively, east and south from its area, and several small clashes had occurred between its troops and the Japanese. By now it had become apparent that the remnants of the force, which had been driven off the ALPS by the Mahratta Regiment, were now forming a screen to block any attempt by the Allies, to swing north-east and thus by-pass Tamandu. Patrols of 9 Yorks and Lancasters operating south of Mawhun, however, reported that the Japanese had no offensive intentions from that area and had been content with mining the road and holding a road-block in order to delay any advance in that direction.

By 28 February, 14/10 Baluch of the 74th Indian Infantry Brigade had reached the village of Dokekan, which lay about halfway to Tamandu. Up to now there had been no organized Japanese resistance and the 74th Indian Infantry Brigade reached the southern bank of the Me Chaung. In this sector the Japanese later made a number of heavy counter-attacks and confused fighting remained in progress till 4 March 1945, the date on which Japanese resistance faded away.

Change of Plan

The original plan for the capture of Tamandu was to contain the Japanese wherever they were met, and to by-pass any strong opposition and either squeeze out the Japanese or surround them. Such an operation was likely to be economical, but would have proved a lengthy undertaking. A series of administrative changes, however, demanded a more rapid seizure of Tamandu to enable the overall plan of the XV Indian Corps to go ahead as arranged.

It had always been the intention that the 82nd West African Division was to be supplied by air during its advance along the mountain tracks between Delet and An. The successes won by the Fourteenth Army, however, in Central Burma called for a change in these plans. The need for their rapid exploitation called for all available air resources. It was decided by the Commander-in-Chief ALFSEA, to reduce the XV Indian Corps supply lift of 130 tons a day to 30 tons a day, which later was further reduced to 15 tons a day. It was also notified that supply aircraft supporting the XV Indian Corps advance would be transferred to the Fourteenth Army front in about ten days' time. The General Officer Commanding the 82nd West African Division was, therefore, compelled to change his line of advance in order that his brigades could be supplied by water and road. The corps commander ordered this brigade to cross the Delet Chaung and make for Letmauk on the Tamandu-An road. From here they were to link up with the 2nd West African Brigade, which was now approaching this road from the south, and there-after, the whole division was to launch a frontal assault upon An. Therefore, it became of paramount importance that Tamandu should be captured and that the F.M.A. in that area should be in working order by the time the 82nd West African Division reached the road at Letmauk. Accordingly, the corps commander ordered that Tamandu must be captured by 4 March 1945, *i.e.* within six days of the 47th Indian Infantry Brigade's having concentrated north of Ruywa.

Operations against Tamandu

The plan of the 74th Indian Infantry Brigade commander was to contain any Japanese holding the long ridge east of the road and immediately north of the Ruywa beach-head, ford the Me Chaung at low water, secure and repair the bridge which had been destroyed there in order to prevent the Japanese coming south, and subsequently to continue with all speed to pinch out Tamandu by capturing the SNOWDON (911161) hill, which dominated the village and ferry. Having done so the brigade commander intended to mop up the Tamandu area and exploit north-east through the hills, up to a distance of two miles, to an unnamed village on the south bank of the Delet Chaung. This village, later known as WETHERBY, appeared from air photographs to be an ideal place for an F.M.A.; it had at one time been used by the Japanese for the same purpose.

During the first two days of March 1945, 3/2 Gurkha Rifles increased the pressure on several small features between ALPS and the Me Chaung; but despite Allied artillery concentrations the

Japanese refused to move unless a full scale assault was initiated This there was no time to do, nor was it worth while in view of the small number of Japanese troops that were opposing them. 14/10 Baluch, therefore, passed through the 3/2 Gurkha Rifles' left flank and pushed on against scattered opposition to secure the southern bank of the Me Chaung. Here, a small "suicide" party of Japanese was discovered to be dug in on hill 898 (936101) from which perfect observation of the Chaung crossing was available. 14/10 Baluch contained this position while 6 Oxf Bucks moved forward and reconnaissance of the river was carried out on the evening of 2 March.

A stroke of good fortune favoured the operation. Low water was due shortly before dawn of 3 March and as it was the time of the spring tides an exceptionally low ebb could be predicted. Plans were, therefore, made for a crossing on the west or down stream side of the bridge and not at the recognised ford, which was situated higher up. At the same time, as a deception measure, 14/10 Baluch was told to make a feint crossing in the vicinity of the ford. In the event, this diversion on the part of the Baluch Regiment proved highly successful, as the Japanese directed all their fire on to this area, while the real crossing by 6 Oxf Bucks proceeded, almost unmolested. The Japanese were taken by surprise and quickly abandoned their post which was covering the site of the bridge.

This was a noteworthy performance, as it involved wading a deep muddy chaung in the dark against dug-in positions on the far bank. The skill and dash of the Light Infantry averted a situation where set-piece attacks would have been necessary against a position well suited to defence.

As soon as it was light on 3 March, 6 Oxf Bucks, supported by a troop of 19th Lancers, began exploiting northward along the road and overran more Japanese defended localities, some containing 37 mm guns. 14/10 Baluch, on the other hand, remained to protect the crossing place but later sent two of their companies north of the river.

Meanwhile, 3/2 Gurkha Rifles and 7/16 Punjab, which were now under the command of the 74th Indian Infantry Brigade, had begun to cross the Me Chaung. In this area the 25th Indian Divisional Engineers had been extremely busy; by nightfall of 3 March they not only had spanned the gaps in the bridge by a suspension trackway, but had also done a lot of work on either side of the ferry which was about 200 yards up-stream. The Japanese throughout this period had watched all this work in progress from hill 898, but beyond a few very small attacks, mostly by jitter parties at night, they had made no serious attempt to stop it.

By 4 March, 6 Oxf Bucks had pushed farther and with the aid of the tanks had reached their appointed objectives; 3/2 Gurkha

Rifles and 7/16 Punjab then passed through the positions of this British battalion. The Gurkha Regiment struck north-east into the hills and occupied the feature called SNOWDON. 7/16 Punjab, on the other hand, met with some opposition and fought a sharp but successful engagement in the vicinity of the road junction, south of Tamandu. Subsequently, the Punjab Regiment exploited northwards to the village, which was found derelict and deserted, and thence to the southern terminal of the ferry over the Delet Chaung.

It was late in the evening of 4 March, when the Gurkhas captured SNOWDON, and before consolidation was complete or reserve ammunition brought forward, a fierce Japanese attack forced A company of 3/2 Gurkha Rifles, situated on SNOWDON EAST (912164), to give ground, after which the Japanese occupied this feature. Next morning, B company of the Gurkha Battalion, after an artillery concentration, launched a counter-attack to recapture the lost ground. Furious hand-to-hand fighting ensued but finally SNOWDON EAST was re-taken. During this engagement Rifleman Bhan Bhagta Gurung was awarded the Victoria Cross for his conspicuous gallantry—the fourth V.C. gained by the 25th Indian Divisional Group in four months.

The An road from Tamandu ran in a north-easternly direction over the ridge, of which SNOWDON formed a part. The Japanese still held the top of the pass on features named WHISTLE (911167) and STRONG (909169), which dominated the road. Further west, a third feature named PIG was also in their hands. The 7/16th Punjab was, therefore, ordered to attack and occupy these positions from the west. On 5 March, this battalion attacked PIG at the point of the bayonet. As it was a silent attack from an unexpected angle, the Japanese were taken completely by surprise and retired from the hill. On the evening of the same day the battalion was ordered by the brigade commander to capture WHISTLE and STRONG and at the same time to retain its hold on Tamandu area as well as the feature PIG. It was decided that this attack would be put in from the south along the crest of the ridge, using the Gurkha positions on SNOWDON as a firm base. The attack across very difficult country was resisted furiously, and two companies had to be employed before WHISTLE was captured. Casualties of 7/16 Punjab were heavy, including both the company commanders and all the platoon commanders, but a final assault led by the havildar-major, overran the summit. Thereafter, an attack was immediately mounted on STRONG, but in spite of the most determined efforts, the Punjab Regiment could not progress along the knife-edge ridges in the face of concentrated artillery and LMG fire. The battalion suffered over a hundred casualties in the day's fighting.

While the 74th Indian Infantry Brigade was making this advance the West African Division had once again occasion to change its plan. The crossing of the Dalet Chaung had proved difficult owing to the Japanese opposition in strength and as time was getting short the divisional commander decided that he could decrease the strain on air supply, which was shortly to cease, by bringing the 4th West African Brigade down to the Tamandu ferry along the northern bank of the river where there was not so much opposition. He then decided to pass 5 Nigerian Regiment, through the 74th Indian Infantry Brigade positions, so that the former could join up with the 1st West African Brigade at Letmauk, which was the original objective. 5 Nigerian Regiment and 102 Light Regiment of this West African Division, which had been on detachment at Kyweguseik, were the first to arrive. A naval ferry service was organised and the decision was taken that these two units after crossing the Chaung should come under the command of the 74th Indian Infantry Brigade until such time as the rest of the 4th West African Brigade could come forward. The leading African troops were met at the ferry by the 25th Indian Division Commander.

The scene again reverts to the 7/16 Punjab front. It had been realised that the capture of the feature STRONG was vital to the accomplishment of the 25th Indian Division's task. A second attack was, therefore, planned; this time by a pincer movement simultaneously from the west as well as from the east. In view of the heavy casualties which were sustained up to date by this battalion, it had been decided not to continue the assault against this feature without a very heavy preliminary bombardment. 8 and 9 March were accordingly devoted to the continuous artillery concentrations by 25 pounder and 5.5" medium guns. Fighter patrols had also been vigorously active during this period as far as the bombardment safety line allowed.

On 10 March 1945, it was considered that STRONG must be almost untenable by now and therefore ready for capture by the Indian troops. A second attempt was thereupon made by D company of 7/16 Punjab, reinforced by two platoons, to get on to the feature. While this company advanced on the feature from the west, another company of 14/10 Baluch passed round the east side of SNOWDON and swung into STRONG from the south-east. Nevertheless, in spite of the most determined efforts by these troops to get on to the objective from different directions, all their attempts at infiltrating on to the feature failed completely. Even after such a heavy bombardment, one medium machine-gun, one 3.7 mm gun and six light guns were pinpointed by the attacking forces. The Japanese had most skilfully sited these weapons in bunkers connected to deep dug-outs burrowed out of the rock. It is worth while mentioning that the feature STRONG was surrounded on three sides by a road, which wound round its upper slopes; all attempts by the attackers to cross this strip were heavily opposed by the Japanese, in spite of the liberal use of 3" mortars, smoke bombs and smoke grenades.

By this time, 5 Nigerian Regiment had crossed the river and, under the command of the 74th Indian Infantry Brigade, had advanced south of SNOWDON and commenced an outflanking movement to cut the road north-east of WETHERBY. This move was partially successful, but a small party of Japanese troops prevented the physical occupation of the road. The remainder of the 4th West African Brigade had also reached the area by then and a second battalion followed the route which had been taken by 5 Nigerian Regiment. The third battalion made a new crossing of the Dalet Chaung and landed on the south bank of the river in the hills, just east of WETHERBY. Their landing was unopposed except for Japanese anti-tank gun-fire from the village which delayed the crossing of the administrative units until evening.

Orders were now received from the commander of the XV Indian Corps that the 25th Indian Division should withdraw to Akyab by the end of March 1945. The 22nd East African Brigade from Kyaukpyu was to relieve the 53rd Indian Infantry Brigade at Ruywa as early as possible. But until the F.M.A. at Tamandu was firmly established and the whole of that area had been cleared and made safe for the 82nd West African Division's advance, the 74th Indian Infantry Brigade must remain in the area. The 25th Indian Division headquarters were to move with the 53rd Indian Infantry Brigade; thereafter the command of the 74th Indian Infantry Brigade Group would pass to the 82nd West African Division.

Meanwhile, medium artillery was helping 8 Field Regiment in carrying out excellent practice shoots on STRONG. As time was now getting short it was clear that this feature would have to be captured by a direct assault on 11 March 1945, regardless of casualties. A and D companies of 7/16 Punjab along with two companies of 14/10 Baluch under command, were detailed for this task. A comprehensive fire plan was arranged, including intense bombing by thunderbolts and Mitchells. On 10 March 1945, the plan was worked out in great detail. Forming-up places were arranged and marked and timings were worked out to the last minute in relation to distances. Morale was very high and all ranks were determined to succeed in capturing this fortress which had defied them so vigorously.

But on the day appointed for the attack, a dawn patrol of 7/16 Punjab reported that there was no Japanese movement on STRONG.

In view of this information this patrol was immediately followed by a company which occupied the position without any opposition. It appeared that the Japanese had withdrawn from this feature during the previous night and had thus ended the bitter and prolonged fight for it. The bodies of 187 Japanese were counted on and around the position, and two field and three anti-tank guns were captured. It was fitting that the final action of the 25th Indian Division should have been fought by 7/16 Punjab. This splendid battalion had been employed in a reserve role throughout the offensive, and as such had participated in the crisis of the fighting with all three brigades of the division, and suffered more than any other battalion. It was estimated that the Japanese had suffered 400 to 500 casualties since the advance from Ruywa began, while the 25th Indian Division's losses were over 40 killed and 200 wounded.

The victory of the 25th Indian Division over the surrounding heights resulted in the capture of Tamandu village and on 13 March 1945, 14/10 Baluch headquarters established itself in this area. By 15 March, the 74th Indian Infantry Brigade was out of contact with the Japanese while the 4th West African Brigade was pursuing them eastward towards An. As soon as the Tamandu area had been cleared of the Japanese, 63 Indian Field Company had begun to work on the establishment of an F.M.A. in WETHERBY village and it also began to improve the track behind the advance of the West African Division. The F.M.A. at Ruywa was closed and transported to the new area. At the same time almost all the 25th Indian Division transport passed under the command of the 82nd West African Division, in order to assist the latter in their maintenance by road.

Thereafter, the evacuation of the 25th Indian Division to Akyab proceeded according to plan. The task of the 74th Indian Infantry Brigade was also accomplished and it followed the remainder of the division not many days later. For the first time in 12 months, therefore, the 25th Indian Division found itself no longer in contact with the Japanese. The Corps Commander, General Christison, issued a warm congratulatory Special Order of the Day on the departure of this division, in which he stated: "You have to your credit the successful accomplishment of perhaps the most difficult combined operations any British force has ever attempted. You have inflicted 8,300 casualties on the Japanese and taken 37 guns."

The Final Stages

On 13 March 1945, while the 1st West African Brigade was still manoeuvring to reach the Tamandu-An road, the 4th Indian Infantry Brigade of the 26th Indian Division crossed over from Ramree island and landed in no less than five places on the banks of the Me Chaung, due west of the village of Letpan. This final landing on the Arakan coast was once again designed to cut the Japanese main road communications, in the rear of its forward troops; this was yet another step nearer to Taungup and the western entrance to the last pass in the Irrawaddy valley. Letpan was nearly 36 miles south of Ruywa and still about 20 miles from the most southernly position that the 53rd Indian Infantry Brigade patrols had yet occupied.

The plan of this new landing, once the road had been cut and the surrounding high ground occupied, was for one battalion of the 4th Indian Infantry Brigade to exploit in the direction of Kywegu and join up with the troops, advancing south from Ruywa; the remaining two battalions of the 4th Indian Infantry Brigade were then to exploit south down the road through Sabyin towards Taungup. The 22nd East African Brigade was to be ferried across from Ramree island, and, after being put ashore at Ruywa, was to advance south down the road, with the object of relieving the 53rd Indian Infantry Brigade.

On 15 March 1945, 2/13 Frontier Force Rifles established a road-block south of Letpan to prevent the escape of five Japanese tankettes. At the same time, exploitation to the south was also proceeding very fast; very slight opposition was being met and the leading companies of 2/7 Rajput had reached Pada, about 3 miles south of Lamu. The advance of this battalion was supported by tanks of the 146th Regiment Royal Armoured Corps (Duke of Wellington's), and two Japanese tankettes manned by British personnel. In one of the minor actions during this advance, Lt. Claude Raymond of the Royal Engineers was awarded the Victoria Cross for his gallantry.

On 17 March, the 22nd East African Brigade was concentrated at Ruywa and had assumed command of all operations in that area. Meanwhile, progress of the 4th Indian Infantry Brigade, south of Letpan, had become so rapid that forward troops were being maintained through Lamu instead of Letpan. By 19 March, 2/13 Frontier Force Rifles had pushed the Japanese out of Sabyin, and was continuing to press south with vigour. During the next few days Allied advance maintained its momentum in all directions, being opposed by very minor resistance. By 22 March, the Japanese resistance at Zani had also been overcome and a further advance of six miles brought 2/7 Rajput to the north bank of the Tanlwe Chaung, which was only nine miles from Taungup.

The 22nd East African Brigade was finding little or no opposition in the path of its advance and its forward troops arrived on the north bank of the An chaung at Kwegu on 23 March. On the same day three companies of 2/7 Rajput supported by tanks of the 146th Regiment, Royal Armoured Corps, crossed the Tanlwe Chaung which the Japanese unsuccessfully attempted to oppose. Being thus threatened with an outflanking movement the Japanese withdrew after fighting a rearguard action. On 24 March, 1/18 Royal Garhwal Rifles passed through 2/7 Rajput and penetrated 2 miles further south of the town. By this time leading companies of the 1st Battalion King's African Rifles had crossed the An Chaung at Kyewa and were also pushing on towards the south.

By 30 March, leading troops of the 22nd East African Brigade had arrived in Letpan and the 4th Indian Infantry Brigade had begun to reorganise its dispositions for the final attack on Taungup town. 1/18 Royal Garhwal Rifles had successfully attacked and cleared Point 462, while 2/13 Frontier Force Rifles was firmly astride the road near Yabyo, about 4 miles north of Taungup.

The end of the campaign.

At this stage of the operations the Allied High Command decided to relieve the whole of the 26th Indian Division and return it to India as soon as possible. The 36th and 71st Indian Infantry Brigades of this division were still on Ramree Island and were no longer engaged in active operations. It was, therefore, only necessary to relieve the 4th Indian Infantry Brigade outside Taungup so that the 26th Indian Division could be concentrated, prior to its withdrawal. By the beginning of April 1945, the 26th Indian Division was already out of contact with the Japanese; on the main land, in addition to the 4th Indian Infantry Brigade, there remained the whole of the 2nd West African Division which was still disposed between Tamandu and An and the 22nd East African Brigade, under the command of the former, which was rapidly catching up with the 4th Indian Infantry Brigade from the north. On the Tamandu-An road, the situation had greatly improved; the road from Tamandu to Letmauk had been opened, where the 1st West African Brigade was in contact with the Japanese.

The rapid advance of the XXXIII Indian Corps necessitated a change of plan on the XV Indian Corps front. The former's leading troops had come appreciably close to Minbu, at the eastern end of the An-Minbu Pass. This move by the XXXIII Indian Corps made the Japanese realise that there was every prospect of their being taken in the rear and therefore a rapid withdrawal on their part, while there was still time, would be their most prudent course. On the other hand, it was clearly the responsibility of the XV Indian Corps to do all it could in its power to prevent the escape of this Japanese garrison. Any possibility of the Allies working a column round and behind An to block the way of the Japanese was no longer feasible, owing to maintenance difficulties. The most practical way, therefore, of ensuring that the Japanese remained employed in the An area was the maintenance of an offensive force before An, the activities of which would keep the maximum number of Japanese facing west. Meanwhile no real attempt to drive them from their positions was to be made.

The 1st West African Brigade was therefore selected for this task. The Japanese appeared remarkably sensitive to the presence of this force and the Allied ruse was wholly successful. While this brigade manoeuvred back and forth between An and Letmauk, the Japanese persisted in keeping a close contact and grimly opposed its various feints and moves. This new operation on the An road made available the 2nd and 4th West African Brigades for movement elsewhere. Consequently, the 2nd West African Brigade was at once ordered to march south along the coast road, to relieve the 4th Indian Infantry Brigade. The 4th West African Brigade was concentrated at Tamandu; it was given orders that as soon as possible it too was to proceed to Taungup.

While the 4th Indian Infantry Brigade continued its vigorous patrolling in the Taungup area, the 22nd East African Brigade was building up in support, on the Tanlwe Chaung. On 3 April, the 2nd Battalion of the Green Howards captured hill 370, some 3 miles north of Taungup, after a very successful air strike. On 4 April, the 22nd East African Brigade units began to move east along both banks of the Tanlwe Chaung with a view to getting behind the Japanese main positions in the Taungup area. On 5 April, however, the Japanese launched a determined counter-attack on hill 370; after a lot of confused fighting the Allied troops were obliged to withdraw. But later in the day the Allies put in two counter-attacks against this feature; the first was unsuccessful but in the second the hill was recaptured.

On 15 April 1945, patrols of the 4th Indian Infantry Brigade entered Taungup town and reconnoitred as far as two miles to its south. By 17 April, the relief of this brigade by the 2nd West African Brigade was completed, and on the same day 2/7 Rajput and 2/13 Frontier Force Rifles sailed for Ramree island; 1/18 Royal Garhwal Rifles had already been relieved on 11 April by the 6th Battalion of the Nigeria Regiment.

On 28 April 1945, the 4th West African Brigade was in actual occupation of Taungup town after having cleared that area of Japanese resistance. On this day also the 22nd West African Division and the 22nd East African Brigade passed directly under the command of the Headquarters, Allied Land Forces, South-East Asia. During the rest of April and the early part of May 1945, the 82nd West African Division kept pressing hard on the withdrawing

Garhwali Soldier by the side of a Japanese dummy tank made of bamboo, found in 25th Indian Division beach-head area at Ruywa.

Wire mesh and cocoanut mattings used as road over mangrove swamp for transporting heavy equipment from beach-head to forward areas.

Japanese forces in order to keep them facing west. At the same time they kept pushing south from Taungup and on 4 May 1945 occupied Sandoway. On 15 May 1945, Allied forces reached Gwa, thus claiming to have cleared Arakan of the Japanese forces for good.

APPENDICES

APPENDIX 1

ORDER OF BATTLE—14 INDIAN DIVISION

October 1942

Formation and Unit	Location	Remarks
HEADQUARTERS		
H.Q. 14 Ind. Div.	Comilla Area.	
H.Q. 14 Ind. Div. R.A.	Comilla Area.	
H.Q. 14 Ind. Div. Eng.	Comilla Area.	
H.Q. 14 Ind. Div. R.I.A.S.C.	Comilla Area.	
H.Q. 14 Ind. Div. Def. and Emp. Pl.	Comilla Area.	
H.Q. 14 Ind. Div. Ord. Wkshops.	Comilla Area.	
ARTILLERY		
H.Q. 130 Fd. Regt.	Mynamatti.	
314 Bty.	Comilla Area.	
315 Bty.	Fenny Area.	
404 Bty.	Dauratgang.	
H.Q. Fd. Regt.		
Bty.		
Bty.		
Bty.		
H.Q. 23 Mtn. Regt.	Chittagong Area.	
3 Bty.	Chittagong Area.	
8 Bty.	Fenny Area.	
17 Bty.	Fenny Area.	
2 J. & K. Bty.	Chittagong Area.	
ENGINEERS		
26 Ind. Fd. Coy.	Fenny Area.	One Sec. 26 Ind. Div.
73 Ind. Fd. Coy.	Chittagong Area.	
74 Ind. Fd. Coy.	Chittagong.	
306 Ind. Fd. Pk. Coy.	Maynamatti.	
SIGNALS		
14 Ind. Div. Sigs.	Comilla.	
130 Fd. Regt. R.A. Sig. Sec.	Maynamatti.	

Formation and Unit	Location	Remarks
Fd. Regt. Sig. Sec.		
23 Ind. Mtn. Regt. Sig. Sec.	Chittagong Area.	
47 Ind. Inf. Bde. Sig. Sec.	Fenny Area.	
55 Ind. Inf. Bde. Sig. Sec.	Chittagong.	
125 Ind. Inf. Bde. Sig. Sec.	Chittagong Area.	

INFANTRY

H.Q. 47 Ind. Inf. Bde. & Def. Pl.	Fenny Area.	
1 Innisks.	Fenny Area.	
1 Rajput	Fenny Area.	
5/8 Punjab ...	Fenny Area.	
H.Q. 55 Ind. Inf. Bde. & Def. Pl.	Chittagong.	
2/1 Punjab	Chittagong.	
8 Raj. Rif.	Chittagong.	
1 Dogra	Chittagong.	
H.Q. 123 Ind. Inf. Bde. & Def. Pl.	Chittagong Area.	
10 L.F.	Chittagong Area.	
8 Baluch.	Chittagong Area.	
1/15 Punjab	Chittagong Area.	

M. G. BN.

9 Jat.	Comilla.	

RIASC

14 Ind. Div. H.Q. Tpt. Sec.	Mynamatti.	
9 Ind. Mule Coy.	Dohazari.	
30 Ind. Div. Mule Coy.	Dohazari.	
30 Ind. Mule Coy.	Dohazari.	
15 Ind. Mule Coy.	Chittagong.	
44 Ind. Mule Coy.	Chittagong.	
48 Ind. Mule Coy. (less one Tp.)	Chittagong.	
58 Ind. Mule Coy.	Maynamatti.	
194 Ind. Sup. Pers. Sec. (Indept.)	Chittagong.	
68 Ind. S.I.S.	Ambala.	
69 Ind. S.I.S.	Chittagong.	
3 Ind. Fd. Amb. Tp.	Rawalpindi.	
16 Ind. Fd. Amb. Tp.	Bareilly.	

MEDICAL

41 Ind. Fd. Amb.	Fenny Area.	
45 Ind. Fd. Amb.	Chittagong.	

Formation and Unit	Location	Remarks
60 Ind. Fd. Amb.	Secunderabad.	
28 Ind. Fd. Hyg. Sec.	Maynamatti.	
VETERINARY		
8 Ind. Mob. Vet. Sec. (Mech.)	Comilla.	
ORDNANCE		
54 Ind. Ord. Mob. Wkshop. Coy.	Maynamatti.	
Ind. Ord. Mob. Wkshop. Coy.		
47 Ind. Inf. Bde. Ord. Wkshop. Sec. …	Fenny Area.	
49 Ind. Inf. Bde. Ord. Wkshop. Sec.	Chittagong Area.	123 Ind. Inf. Wkshop Sec. at Ranchi.
55 Ind. Inf. Bde. Ord. Wkshop. Sec.	Chittagong.	
14 Ind. Div. Ord. Rec. Coy. (HQ. & six Secs.)	Comilla Area.	Two secs. with 26 Ind. Div.
POSTAL		
52 Ind. Fd. P.O.	Fenny Area.	
67 Ind. Fd. P.O.	Comilla Area.	
80 Ind. Fd. P.O.	Chittagong Area.	
119 Ind. Fd. P.O.	Chittagong.	
PROVOST		
14 Ind. Div. Pro. Unit	Maynamatti.	
INTELLIGENCE		
14 Ind. Div. F.S.S. Sec.	Comilla Area.	

APPENDIX 2

ORDER OF BATTLE—14 INDIAN DIVISION

March 1943

Formation and Unit	Location	Remarks
HEADQUARTERS		
H.Q. 14 Ind. Div.		
H.Q. 14 Ind. Div. R.A.		
H.Q. 14 Ind. Div. Eng.	Arakan.	
H.Q. 14 Ind. Div. R.I.A.S.C.		
H.Q. 14 Ind. Div. Def. & Emp. Pl.		
H.Q. 14 Ind. Div. Ord. Wkshops.		
ARTILLERY		
H.Q. 130 Fd. Regt. & L.A.D.		
315 Bty.		
316 Bty.		
494 Bty.		
H.Q. 23 Ind. Mtn. + Regt.		
3 Bty.		
8 Bty.	Arakan.	
17 Bty.		
31 (Jammu) Bty.		
H.Q. 44 Lt. A.A. Regt.		
75 Bty.		
91 Bty.		
234 Bty.		
ENGINEERS		
26 Ind. Fd. Coy.		
73 Ind. Fd. Coy.	Arakan.	
74 Ind. Fd. Coy.		
306 Ind. Fd. Pk. Coy.		
SIGNALS		
14 Ind. Div. Sigs. (Less Bde. Sig. Sec.)		
130 Fd. Regt. R.A. Sig. Sec.		
23 Ind. Mtn. Regt. Sig. Sec.	Arakan.	
44 Lt. A.A. Regt. Sig. Sec.		
47 Ind. Inf. Bde. Sig. Sec.		
55 Ind. Inf. Bde. Sig. Sec.		
123 Ind. Inf. Bde. Sig. Sec.		

Formation and Unit	Location	Remarks
INFANTRY		
H.Q. 47 Ind. Inf. Bde. Def. Pl.		
1 Innisks.		
1 Rajput		
5/8 Punjab		
HQ. 55 Ind. Inf. Bde. & Def. Pl.		
2/1 Punjab	Arakan.	
8 Raj. Rif.		
1 Dogra		
H.Q. 123 Ind. Inf. Bde. & Def. Pl.		
10 L.F.		
8 Baluch.		
1/15 Punjab.		
M. G. Bn.		
9 Jat	Arakan.	
RIASC		
14 Ind. Div. H.Q. Tpt. Sec.	Arakan.	
15 Ind. Mule Coy.		
44 Ind. Mule Coy		
48 Ind. Mule Coy. (Less one Tp.)	Arakan.	
58 Ind. Mule Coy.		
41 Ind. G.P. Tpt. Coy.	Arakan.	
75 Ind. G.P. Tpt. Coy.	Arakan.	
318 Ind. G.P. Tpt. Coy.	Arakan.	
65 Ind. S.I.S.		
68 Ind. S.I.S.		
100 Ind. S.I.S.		
111 Ind. +S.I.S.		
15 Ind. Fd. Amb. Tp. (Cl. I) less Camel Sec.	Arakan.	
16 Ind. Fd. Amb. Tp. (Cl. I) less Camel Sec.		
Ind. Fd. Amb. Tp. (Cl. I) less Camel Sec.		To be allotted.
MEDICAL		
41 Ind. Fd. Amb.		
45 Ind. Fd. Amb.	Arakan.	
60 Ind. Fd. Amb.		
28 Ind. Fd. Hyg. Sec.	Arakan.	
VETERINARY		
8 Ind. Mob. Vet. Sec. (Mech.)	Arakan.	

Formation and Unit	Location	Remarks

ORDNANCE

44 Lt. A.A. Regt. Wkshop. Sec.	Arakan.	
54 Ind. Ord. Mob. Wkshop. Coy.	Arakan.	
82 Ind. Ord. Mob. Wkshop. Coy.	Dohazari.	
47 Ind. Ord. Wkshop. Sec.	Arakan.	
55 Ind. Ord. Wkshop. Sec.	Comilla Area.	
14 Ind. Ord. Rec. Coy.	Arakan.	

POSTAL

52 Ind. Fd. P.O.	Arakan.	
67 Ind. Fd. P.O.	Arakan.	
80 Ind. Fd. P.O.	Arakan.	
119 Ind. Fd. P.O.	Arakan.	

PROVOST

14 Ind. Div. Pro. Unit	Arakan.	

INTELLIGENCE

14 Ind. Div. F.S.S. Sec.	Karachi.	

NON-DIVISIONAL TROOPS ALLOTTED TO 14 INDIAN DIVISION

HEADQUARTERS

7 Ind. A.I.L. Sec.	Arakan.	
22 Air Support Control		

ENGINEERS

113 Ind. C.R.E. Works	Arakan.	
8 Ind. Eng. Bn. (less two Coys.)		
10 Ind. Eng. Bn.		
17 Ind. Eng. Bn.	Arakan.	
9 Ind. Br. Sec.		
11 Ind. Br. Sec.		
336 Ind. Fsty. Coy.	Chittagong.	
22 Ind. A.W. Coy.	Arakan.	

SURVEY

One sec. 6 Ind. Fd. Svy. Coy.	Arakan.	

Formation and Unit	Location	Remarks
TRANSPORTATION		
H.Q. 4 I.W.T. Opg. Gp.	Chittagong Area.	
250 Ind. I.W.T. Opg. Coy.		
257 Ind. I.W.T. Opg. Coy. (Country)		
258 Ind. I.W.T. Opg. Coy. (Craft)	Arakan.	
Det. 247 Ind. I.W.T. Wkshop. Coy.		
Sec. 141 Ind. Tn. Stores Coy.	Chittagong.	
INFANTRY		
1 Tripura Rif. (H.Q. & two Coys. less two pls.)	Arakan.	
One Coy. 14 F.F.R.	Cox's Bazaar.	
RIASC		
9 Ind. Mule Coy.		
19 Ind. Mule Coy.		
28 Ind. Mule Coy.	Arakan.	
30 Ind. Mule Coy.		To be returned subsequently to 30 Ind. Lt. Div.
60 Ind. Mule Coy.		
Jaipur Pony. Coy.		
H.Q. 4 M.T. Regt.	Dohazari.	
107 Ind. G.P. Tpt. Coy.	,,	
308 Ind. G.P. Tpt. Coy.	Chittagong.	
20 Ind. M.A. Sec.	Arakan.	
155 Ind. Sup. Pers. Sec.		
248 Ind. Sup. Pers. Sec.		
249 Ind. Sup. Pers. Sec.		
318 Ind. Sup. Sec.		
335 Ind. Sup. Sec.		
152 Sub-Sec. 21 Ind. Fd. Bky. Sec.		
222 Sub-Sec. 31 Ind. Fd. Bky. Sec.		
223 Sub-Sec. 31 Ind. Fd. Bky. Sec.		
258 Sub-Sec. 40 Ind. Fd. Butchery Sec.		
259 Sub-Sec. 40 Ind. Fd. Butchery Sec.		
37 Ind. R.H. Sup. Det.		
17 Ind. L.P.S.	,,	
46 Ind. Cattle Stock Sec.	,,	

Formation and Unit	Location	Remarks
MEDICAL		
Sec. 928 M.A.C.	Comilla Area.	
63 Ind. Fd. Amb.	Arakan.	To return subsequently to 39 Ind. Div.
15 Ind. C.C.S.		
43 I.S.S. (Comb.)		
44 " "		
46 " "		
50 " "		
18 Ind. Anti. Mal. Unit ...		
16 Ind. Mob. X-Ray Unit		
1 Ind. Bearer Coy.		⎫ To return subsequently to 39 Ind. Div.
2 Ind. Bearer Coy.		⎬
6 Ind. Mob. Surg. Unit ...		⎭
38 Ind. Dent. Unit (B.T.)		
ORDNANCE		
12 Ind. Ord. Salvage Unit	Arakan.	
32 " " "		
36 " " "		
Ind. Ord. Offrs. Shop	Chittagong.	
LABOUR		
17 Ind. Aux. Pnr. Bn. (less two Coys.)	Arakan.	
One Coy. 15 Ind. Aux. Pnr. Bn.	Cox's Bazaar.	
42 Ind. Aux. Pnr. Bn.	Arakan.	
55 " " "		
VETERINARY		
23 Ind. Adv. Fd. Vet. Hosp.	Arakan.	
24 Ind. Adv. Fd. Vet. Hosp.	Mynamatti.	
9 Ind. Mob. Vet. Sec. (Mech.)	Arakan.	
REMOUNTS		
6 Ind. Adv. Remount Dep.	Arakan.	
13 Ind. Fd. Remount Sec.		
MISCELLANEOUS		
60 Ind. Rest Camp	Chittagong.	
63 Ind. Rest Camp ...	Arakan.	
228 Ind. Mess Unit (B.O's) ...	"	⎫ With 113 Ind. C.R.E. Works.
84 Ind. Mess Unit (W.O's)	"	⎬
2000 Flotilla	Chittagong.	H.Q. Arakan.
Arakan "V" Force	Arakan.	
Tripura "V" Force	"	

APPENDIX 3

ORDER OF BATTLE—26 INDIAN DIVISION

(Temporarily under Operational Command of XV Indian Corps)

May 1943

Formation and Unit	Location	Remarks

HEADQUARTERS

H.Q. 26 Ind. Div. Def. & Emp. Pt.		
H.Q. 26 Ind. Div. R.A.		
H.Q. 26 Ind. Div. Eng.	Arakan.	
H.Q. 26 Ind. Div. R.I.A.S.C.		
H.Q. 26 Ind. Div. Ord. Wkshop.		

ARTILLERY

160 Fd. Regt.	Arakan.	
584 Bty.		
585 „		
586 „		
Fd. Regt.		To be allotted.
H.Q. 23 Ind. Mtn. Regt.	Arakan.	
3 Bty.		
8 do.		
17 do.		
30 (Jammu Bty.)		
H.Q. 44 Lt. A.A. Regt. & L.A.D.		
75 Bty.		
90 do.		
239 do.		

ENGINEERS

28 Ind. Fd. Coy.	Arakan.	
72 Ind. Fd. Coy.	Chittagong.	
98 Ind. Fd. Coy.	Arakan.	En route.
328 Ind. Fd. Pk. Coy.		

SIGNALS

26 Ind. Div. Sigs.	Arakan.	
160 Fd. Regt. Sig. Sec.		

Formation and Unit	Location	Remarks
Ind. Fd. Regt. Sig. Sec. 23 Ind. Mtn. Regt. Sig. Sec. 44 Lt. A.A. Regt. Sig. Sec. 4 Ind. Inf. Bde. Sig. Sec. 36 Ind. Inf. Bde. Sig. Sec. 71 Ind. Inf. Bde. Sig. Sec.	Arakan.	To be allotted.

INFANTRY

H.Q. 4 Ind. Inf. Bde. & Def. Pl. 8/8 Punjab 6 Sikh 3/9 G.R. *H.Q. 36 Ind. Inf. Bde. & Def. Pl.* 1 N. Staffs 8 F.F. Rif. 5/16 Punjab *H.Q. 71 Ind. Inf. Bde. & Def. Pl.* 1 Lincoln 7/15 Punjab 9/15 Punjab	Arakan.	

RIASC

107 Ind. G.P. Tpt. Coy.	Dohazari.	6 Ind. Ord. Wk-shop. attd.
166 Ind. G.P. Tpt. Coy.	Arakan.	16 Ind. Ord. Wk-shop. attd.
318 Ind. G.P. Tpt. Coy.		
51 Ind. Mule Coy. 44 Ind. Mule Coy. 48 Ind. Mule Coy. 58 Ind. Mule Coy.	Arakan.	
16 Ind. Comp. Sec. 17 " " " 18 " " " 19 " " " 11 Ind. Fd. Amb. Tp. 16 Ind. Fd. Amb. Tp.	Arakan.	
Ind. Fd. Amb. Tp.		To be allotted.

MEDICAL

1 Ind. Fd. Amb. 46 Ind. Fd. Amb. 48 Ind. Fd. Amb. 27 Ind. Fd. Hyg. Sec.	Arakan.	

Formation and Unit	Location	Remarks

VETERINARY

8 Ind. Mob. Vet. Sec. (Mech.)	Arakan.	

ORDNANCE

44 Lt. A.A. Regt. Wkshop. Sec. ...	Tumbru Ghat.	
One Sec. 8 Ind. Ord. Mob. Wkshop. Coy.	Cox's Bazaar.	
54 Ind. Ord. Mob. Wkshop. Coy.	Arakan.	
4 Ind. Ord. Wkshop. Sec.		
36 Ind. Ord. Wkshop. Sec.		
71 Ind. Ord. Wkshop. Sec.		
Ind. Ord. Rec. Coy.		To be allotted.

PROVOST

26 Ind. Div. Pro. Unit	Arakan.	

POSTAL

2 Ind. Fd. P.O.	Arakan.	
20 Ind. Fd. P.O.		
68 Ind. Fd. P.O.		
131 Ind. Fd. P.O.		

INTELLIGENCE

601 Ind. F.S.S. Sec.	Arakan.	

NON-DIVISIONAL TROOPS ALLOTTED TO 26 INDIAN DIVISION

HEADQUARTERS

22 Air Support Control	Arakan.	

ENGINEERS

113 Ind. C.R.E. Works	Cox's Bazaar.	
917 Ind. Wks. Sec.		
918 Ind. Wks. Sec.		
19 Ind. Eng. Bn.	Ukhia.	
7 Ind. Br. Sec.	Arakan.	
22 Ind. A.W. Coy.	Ukhia.	
1 Sec. 350 Ind. B.D. Coy. ...	Arakan.	

Formation and Unit	Location	Remarks
Transportation		
H.Q. 4 I.W.T. Opg. Gp.	Chittagong.	
250 Ind. I.W.T. Opg. Coy.	Chittagong Area.	
257 " " (Country Craft) ...	Arakan.	
258 Ind. I.W.T. Opg. Gp. (Country Craft) ...		
Det. 247 Ind. I.W.T. Wkshop. Coy. ...	Cox's Bazaar.	
Sec. 141 Ind. Tn. Stores Coy.	Chittagong.	
234 Ind. Port. Opg. Coy. ...		
Infantry		
12 F.F.R. M.G. Bn.	Chittagong.	
R.I.A.S.C.		
9 Ind. Mule Coy.		
19 " "	Arakan.	
28 " "		
H.Q. 4 Ind. M.T. Regt.	Idgaon.	
75 Ind. G.P. Tpt. Coy.	Arakan.	
308 Ind. G.P. Tpt. Coy. ...	Ramu Area.	
20 Ind. M.A. Sec.	Dohazari	
35 "	Nawapara.	
45 " "	Arakan.	For Ranchi.
155 Ind. Sup. Pers. Sec.	Cox's Bazaar.	
318 Ind. Sup. Sec.	Ukhia.	
335 Ind. Sup. Sec.	Arakan.	
343 Ind. Sup. Sec. ...		
152 Sub-Sec. 21 Ind. Fd. Bky. Sec. ...		
222 Sub-Sec. 31 Ind. Fd. Bky. Sec. ...		
223 Sub-Sec. 31 Ind. Fd. Bky. Sec. ...		
258 Sub-Sec. 40 Ind. Fd. Butchery Sec. ...		
259 Sub-Sec. 40 Ind. Fd. Butchery Sec.		
37 Ind. R.H. Sup. Det.	"	
40 "	Cox's Bazaar.	En route.
41 " "	Tumbru.	
17 Ind. L.P.S.	Arakan.	
46 Ind. Cattle Stock Sec.		
Medical		
Sec. 928 M.A.C.	Comilla Area.	
72 I.G.H. (Comb.)	Cox's Bazaar.	

Formation and Unit	Location	Remarks
63 Ind. Fd. Amb.	Arakan.	To return subsequently to 39 Ind. Lt. Div.
8 Ind. C.C.S.	Arakan.	
46 I.S.S. (Comb.)	,,	
50 ,, ,,	,,	
18 Ind. Anti. Mal. Unit ...	Cox's Bazaar.	
23 Ind. Anti. Mal. Unit	,,	
16 Ind. Mob. X-R. U.	Arakan.	
1 Ind. Bearer Coy.		
6 Ind. Mob. Surg. Unit ...		
7 Ind. Mob. Surg. Unit ...	,,	
38 Ind. Dent. Unit (B.T.)	Chittagong.	
8 Fd. Transfusion Unit	Arakan.	

ORDNANCE

12 Ind. Ord. Salvage Unit	Cox's Bazaar.	
32	Mymensingh.	
36	,,	For Ramkrishnapore.
37	Arakan.	
38 ,, ,, ,,	,,	
103 Ind. Ord. Offrs. Shop	Chittagong.	
103 Ind. Ord. Mob. Wkshop Coy.		For 4 Corps.

INTELLIGENCE

565 Ind. F.S.S. Sec.	Cox's Bazaar.	

LABOUR

17 Ind. Aux. Pnr. Bn. (less two Coys.)	Arakan.	
One Coy. 15 Ind. Aux. Pnr. Bn.	Cox's Bazaar.	
48 Ind. Aux. Pnr. Bn.	Arakan.	

VETERINARY

23 Ind. Adv. Fd. Vet. Hosp.	Ukhia.	
9 Ind. Mob. Vet. Sec. (Mech.)	Arakan.	

Formation and Unit	Location	Remarks
REMOUNTS		
23 Ind. Adv. Remount Dep. ...	Ukhia.	
13 Ind. Fd. Remount Sec.		
POSTAL		
167 Ind. Fd. P.O.	Cox's Bazaar.	
168	Ramu.	
MISCELLANEOUS		
64 Ind. Rest Camp	Cox's Bazaar.	En route.
63 Ind. Rest Camp ...		
228 Ind. Mess Unit (B.O.'s)		} With 113 Ind. C.R.E. Works.
84 Ind. Mess Unit (W.O's)	"	
Arakan "V" Force	Arakan.	
Tripura "V" Force		
11 Ind. Canteen B.I.D.		

APPENDIX 4

XV INDIAN CORPS LOCATION STATEMENT AND ORDER OF BATTLE

As at 0800 hrs. 17 December 43.

H.Q. 15 INDIAN CORPS & CORPS TROOPS

Formation or Unit	Location	Map Ref.	Remarks
HEADQUARTERS			
H.Q. 15 Ind. Corps	Dhechuapalong North	PG 0502	
H.Q. 15 Ind. Corps R.A.	"		
H.Q. 15 Ind. Corps C.B. Staff			No. 4 C.B. Team
H.Q. 15 Ind. Corps R.E.			
22 A.A.S.C.			
I.A.C.			
3 Gwalior L. & Sig. Sec.	Piska		Ranchi Area.
ARTILLERY			
H.Q. 6 Med. Regt. R.A. & Sig. Sec.	Beach Rd.	PM 025950	
18 Med. Bty.	Beach Road	PM 025950	
245 Med. Bty.	" "		
H.Q. 36 Lt. A.A. Regt. R.A. & Sig. Sec.	Cox's Bazaar		

APPENDIX 4

Formation or Unit	Location	Map Ref.	Remarks
97 Lt. A.A. Bty.	Cox's Bazaar		
128 Lt. A.A. Bty.	Sonapara		
266 Lt. A.A. Bty.	Ramu	PL 9997	
H.Q. 8 (Belfast) Hy. A.A. Regt. R.A. & Sig. Sec.	Cox's Bazaar	PG 0711	
21 Hy. A.A. Bty.	"		
22 Hy. A.A. Bty.	Bawli Bazaar		
23 Hy. A.A. Bty.	Kawapara	PM 1384	
No. 2 Gp. 2 Survey Regt.	Kaluiakhot	PM 060025	
H.Q. 5 (Mahratta) A. Tk. Regt. I.A. & Sig. Sec.	Barambe		Ranchi Area.
17 A. Tk. Bty.	"		
18 A. Tk. Bty.	"		"
19 A. Tk. Bty.	"		"
20 A. Tk. Bty.	"		
10 Ind. Lt. A.A. Bty.	Chiringa	PG 0554	
No. 2 Ind. Mob. Met. Sec.	Sabaigon South	PM 305657	att. 5 Ind. Div.

ENGINEERS

Formation or Unit	Location	Map Ref.	Remarks
H.Q. 15 Ind. Corps. Tps. Engrs.	Rumkhapalong South	PM 061945	
73 Ind. Fd. Coy.	Bawli North	PM 259696	
483 Ind. Fd. Coy.	"	PM 2570	
Malerkotla Fd. Coy.	"	PM 254701	
403 Ind. Fd. Pk. Coy.	Rumkhapalong	PM 062945	
11 Ind. Br. Sec.	Rumkhapalong South	PM 061994	
853 Ind. Hy. Br. Coy.	Rumkhapalong	PM 047991	det. only.

Formation or Unit	Location	Map Ref.	Remarks
337 Ind. Forestry Coy.	Uhalapalong	PM 133926	
H.Q. 456 Ind. Fwd. Airfield Engrs.	Ramu	PG 058174	under adm. control.
81 Ind. Fd. Coy.	Rumkhapalong	PM 047965	
365 Ind. Fd. Coy.	Ramu	PG 053174	
11 Ind. Engr. Bn.	Samadar Bazaar	PF 965136	
I.W.T.			
290 Special Purpose Coy. I.W.T.	Chittagong		
SIGNALS			
15 Ind. Corps Sigs.	Dhechuapalong North	PG 0502	
207 Ind. Tech. Maint. Sec.	"	"	
204 Ind. Line Sec.	Bawli North	PM 268700	
220 Ind. Line Sec.	Dhechuapalong North	PG 0502	
224 Ind. Line Maint. Sec.	"	"	
226 Ind. Lt. W/T. Sec.	Bawli North	PM 268700	
82 Opg. Sec.	Dhechuapalong North	PG 0502	
219 Ind. Opg. Sec.	"	"	
223 Ind. Opg. Sec.	Garretts Garden	PM 330698	
101 D.R. Sec.	Dhechuapalong North	PG 0502	
69 Med. W/T. Sec.	"	"	
207 Ind. Med. W/T. Sec.	"	"	
225 Ind. Med. W/T. Sec.	"	"	
208 Ind. Stores Sec.	"	"	
115 S.W.S.	"	"	att.
203 S.W.S.	Dhechuapalong North	PG 0502	att.

APPENDIX 4 325

Formation or Unit	Location	Map Ref.	Remarks
INFANTRY			
5 Jat	Mowdok	PG 6129	under Comd. 81 (W.A.) Div.
M.G. Bn. F.F.R.	Mynamatti		
1 Bihar	Lungleh	RT 0827	from 404 L. of C. Area.
79 Ind. Inf. Coy.	Dhechuapalong North	PG 0502	Corps H.Q. Def. Coy.
85 Inf Coy. F.F.R.			u/c. 290 (S.P.) Coy. I.W.T.
"V" FORCE			
H.Q. 7 V. Ops.	Taung Bazaar	PM 4960	
H.Q. 8 V. Ops.	Muallianpui	RT 4223	u/c. 26 Ind. Div.
RIASC			
20 Ind. M.A. Sec.	Dakhin Khuniapalong	PG 0202	
45 Ind. M.A. Sec.	"		
54 Ind. M.A. Sec.	Cox's Bazaar		
8 Ind. Mule Coy.	Garretts Garden	PM 3369	att. 7 Ind. Div.
18 Ind. Mule Coy.	"	"	
33 Ind. Mule Coy.	"	"	
39 Ind. Mule Coy.	"	"	
50 Ind. Mule Coy.	"		
81 Ind. Mule Coy.	Chiringa	PG 0554	
JAIPUR PONY Coy.	Garretts Garden	PM 3369	

Formation or Unit	Location	Map Ref.	Remarks
46 Ind. Comp. Issue Sec.	Briasco Br.	PM 3160	
52 Ind. Comp. Issue Sec.	Ultakhali	PG 0220	
54 Ind. Comp. Issue Sec.	Ukhia	PM 0891	

MEDICAL

Formation or Unit	Location	Map Ref.	Remarks
42 Ind. Sub Depot Medical Stores	Dhoapalong	PM 0298	
43 Ind. Sub Depot Medical Stores	Bawli North	PM 2569	
1 Ind. Bearer Coy.	Cox's Bazaar		att. 7 Ind. Div.
2 Ind. Bearer Coy.	Garretts Garden	PM 331699	u/c. 404 L. of C. Area.
37 I.S.S. (Comb.)	Cox's Bazaar		
42 I.S.S. (Comb.)	Tumbru	PM 1586	
46 I.S.S. (Comb.)	"	"	
50 I.S.S. (Comb.)	Chiringa	PG 0554	
55 Ind. Fd. Hyg. Sec.	Dhoapalong	PM 0298	
38 Ind. Anti Mal. Unit	Tumbru	PM 1586	
51 Ind. Anti Mal. Unit	Laung Chaung	PM 4353	att. 7 Ind. Div.
15 Ind. Mob. X-Ray Unit	Cox's Bazaar		u/c. 404 L. of C. Area.
16 Ind. Mob. X-Ray Unit	Dhoapalong	PM 0298	
80 Ind. Mob. X-Ray Unit	Bawli North	PM 2790	
81 Ind. Mob. X-Ray Unit	"	" 2790	
7 Ind. Mob. Surg. Unit	Badana Sampanhead	PM 489597	att. 7 Ind. Div.
8 Ind. Mob. Surg. Unit	Dhoapalong	PM 0298	
12 Ind. Mob. Surg. Unit	"	PM 0298	
28 Fd. Transfusion Unit			

APPENDIX 4

Formation or Unit	Location	Map Ref.	Remarks
18 Ind. Dental Mech. Unit	Cox's Bazaar		u/c. 404 L. of C. area.
8 Ind. C.C.S.	Dhoapalong	PM 0298	
15 Ind. C.C.S.	Bawli North	PM 2790	
25 Ind. C.C.S.	Dhoapalong	PM 0298	
HOSPITAL CRAFT			
Flat Pennar	Tumbru Ghat	PM 1482	
Six Creek Vessels			
ORDNANCE			
54 Ind. Ord. Fd. Pk.	Ramu	PG 0513	
12 Ind. Salvage Unit	Ukhia	PM 0891	for 5 Ind. Div.
30 Ind. Salvage Unit	Goppe Bazaar	PM 4270	att. 7 Ind. Div.
37 Ind. Salvage Unit	Bawli South	PM 2969	
38 Ind. Salvage Unit	Dhechuapalong North	PG 0502	
200 Ind. Mob. Cinema Unit	Chittagong		
28 Ind. Mob. Cinema Unit	Sabaigon South	PM 305657	att. 5 Ind. Div.
30 Ind. Mob. Cinema Unit			
MEDICAL			
80 Ind. Mob. Wkshop. Coy.	M 78 Rd. Ramu-Ukhia		
103 Ind. Mob. Wkshop. Coy.	Chittagong		
3 Gwalior L.A.D. (Type E)	Piska	PG 065101	Ranchi Area.
36 Lt. A.A. Wkshop. Sec.	Cox's Bazaar		
8 (Belfast) Hy. A.A. Wkshop Sec.	Ramu	PG 060165	

Formation or Unit	Location	Map Ref.	Remarks
REMOUNT			
6 Ind. Adv. Fd. Remount Depot	Ukhia	PM 0891	
41 Ind. Adv. Fd. Remount Depot	Mynamatti	PM 0891	
13 Ind. Fd. Remount Sec.	Ukhia		
19 Ind. Fd. Remount Sec.	"		
21 Ind. Fd. Remount Sec.	Mynamatti		
VETERINARY			
7 Ind. Adv. Fd. Vet. Hosp.	Rumkhapalong	PM 0694	
23 Ind. Adv. Fd. Vet. Hosp.	Ukhia	PM 0891	
9 Ind. Mob. Vet. Sec.	Bawli North	PM 2690	
INTELLIGENCE			
566 Ind. F.S. Sec.	Dhechuapalong North	PG 0502	
POSTAL			
51 Ind. F.P.O.	Dhechuapalong North	PG 0502	att. 18 A.B.P.O.
135 Ind. F.P.O.	Chittagong	PM 2869	
153 Ind. F.P.O.	Bawli South		
PROVOST			
15 Ind. Corps Pro. Unit	Dhechuapalong North	PG 0502	

APPENDIX 4

Formation or Unit	Location	Map Ref.	Remarks
	36 Ind. Inf. Bde. Gp. (from 26 Ind. Div.).		
H.Q. 36 Ind. Inf. Bde	Shalimar Camp Cox's Bazaar		
72 Ind. Fd. Coy.			
14 F.F.R.			
8 F.F. Rif.			
5/16 Punjab			
44 Ind. Mule Coy.			
16 Ind. Fd. Amb. Tp. Cl. I			
16 Ind. Comp. Issue Sec.			
41 Ind. G.P. Tpt. Coy.			
1 Ind. Fd. Amb.			
	5 INDIAN DIVISION		
HEADQUARTERS			
Main H.Q. 5 Ind. Div.	Chota Maunghnama	PM 343549	
Rear H.Q. 5 Ind. Div.		PM 344555	
H.Q. 5 Ind. Div. R.A.	Chota Maunghnama	PM 343549	
H.Q. 5 Ind. Div. R.E.	"	"	
H.Q. 5 Ind. Div. R.I.A.S.C.		PM 344555	
H.Q. 5 Ind. Div. I.E.M.E.			
ARTILLERY			
H.Q. 4 Fd. Regt. R.A. L.A.D. & Sig. Sec.	Kyunbouk	PM 232736	
7 Fd. Bty.			
14/66 Fd. Bty.			

Formation or Unit	Location	Map Ref.	Remarks
522 Fd. Bty.	Wabyin	PM 363496	
H.Q. 28 Jungle Fd. Regt. R.A. L.A.D. & Sig. Sec.	"	PM 3649	
1 Fd. Bty. (3.7 How.)	Cox's Bazaar		
5/57 Fd. Bty. (3.7 How.)	Wabyin	PM 3649	en route Wabyin.
3 Fd. Bty. (3" Mortar)	Bawli North	PM 2671	
H.Q. 56 A.A./A. Tk. Regt. R.A.	Briasco Br.	PM 3358	
163 A.A. Bty.	Bawli North	PM 2671	
164 A.A. Bty.	Nhila	PM 1962	
221 A. Tk. Bty.	Taungbro	PM 1484	
222 A. Tk. Bty.	Briasco Br.	PM 334584	
H.Q. 24 Ind. Mtn. Regt. & Sig. Sec.	Chittagong		en route Briasco Br.
2 Ind. Mtn. Bty.	Briasco Br.	PM 3358	
11 Ind. Mtn. Bty.	Chittagong		en route Briasco Br.
12 Ind. Mtn. Bty.	Taung Bazaar	PM 4960	
20 Ind. Mtn. Bty.			
Engineers			
2 Ind. Fd. Coy.	Ngangyaung	PM 316612	
20 Ind. Fd. Coy.	Maunghnama	PM 342555	
74 Ind. Fd. Coy.	Wabyin	PM 368499	
44 Ind. Fd. Pk. Coy.	Kyaukchaung	PM 349523	
1 Ind. Br. Sec.	Bawli North	PM 244715	
Signals			
Main 5 Ind. Div. Sigs	Chota Maunghnama	PM 343549	less R.A. & Inf. Bde. Sig. Secs.
Rear 5 Ind. Div. Sigs.	"	PM 305657	

APPENDIX 4

Formation or Unit	Location	Map Ref.	Remarks
INFANTRY			
3/2 Punjab (less four coys.)	Sabaigon South	PM 306649	Div. H.Q. Bn.
One coy. 3/2 Punjab	Chota Maunghnama	PM 343549	
H.Q. 9 Ind. Inf. Bde. & Sig. Sec.	Bawli North	PM 245718	
2 W. Yorks			
3 Jat			
3/14 Punjab			
One coy. 3/2 Punjab			
H.Q. 123 Ind. Inf. Bde. & Sig. Sec.	Ngakyedauk Pass (West End)	PM 373492	
2 Suffolk	Wabyin	PM 358498	
2/1 Punjab	Zeganbyin	PM 359468	
1 Dogra		PM 398463	
One coy. 3/2 Punjab	Ngakyedauk Pass	PM 373492	
H.Q. 161 Ind. Inf. Bde. & Sig. Sec.	Balukhali	PM 335574	
4 R.W.K.	Maunghnama	PM 338561	
1/1 Punjab	Bawli North	PM 250706	
4 Rajput	Nhila	PM 2062	
One coy. 3/2 Punjab	Balukhali	PM 335574	
RIASC			
23 Ind. Mule Coy.	Ngakyedauk Pass	PM 365505	
60 Ind. Mule Coy			
74 Ind. Mule Coy.	Ngakyedauk Pass	PM 4251	Under Comd. 7 Ind. Div.
82 Ind. Mule Coy.	Bawli North	PM 251712	

Formation or Unit	Location	Map Ref.	Remarks
5 Ind. Fd. Amb. Tp. Cl. I	Bawli North	PM 2472	
22 Ind. Fd. Amb. Tp. Cl. I	Balukhali	PM 335572	
23 Ind. Fd. Amb. Tp. Cl. I	Wabyin	PM 3550	
7 Ind. Comp. Issue Sec.	Kyauk Chaung	PM 3452	
60 Ind. Comp. Issue Sec.	"	PM 3453	
61 Ind. Comp. Issue Sec.			
62 Ind. Comp. Issue Sec.			Under Comd. 15 Ind. Corps for L. of C. duties.
238 Ind. G.P. Tpt. Coy.			
239 Ind. G.P. Tpt. Coy.			
240 Ind. G.P. Tpt. Coy.			

MEDICAL

Formation or Unit	Location	Map Ref.	Remarks
10 Ind. Fd. Amb.	Maunghnama	PM 342551	
45 Ind. Fd. Amb.	Nawapara	PM 135834	
75 Ind. Fd. Amb.	Sabaigon South	PM 305657	
7 Ind. Fd. Hyg. Sec.			

VETERINARY

Formation or Unit	Location	Map Ref.	Remarks
2 Ind. Mob. Vet. Sec.	Wabyin	PM 364504	

MEDICAL

Formation or Unit	Location	Map Ref.	Remarks
112 Ind. Mob. Wkshop. Coy.	Kyunbouk	PM 2375	
113 Ind. Mob. Wkshop. Coy.	m. 92 rd. Ukhia-Tumbru		
5 Ind. Rec. Coy.	Kyunbouk	PM 2375	
9 Ind. L.A.D. (Type E)			
125 Ind. L.A.D. (Type E)	Ngangyaung	PM 315615	
161 Ind. L.A.D. (Type E)	Kyunbouk	PM 2375	

APPENDIX 4

Formation or Unit	Location	Map Ref.	Remarks
POSTAL			
21 Ind. F.P.O.	Bawli North	PM 245718	
22 Ind. F.P.O.	Balukhali	PM 335574	
23 Ind. F.P.O.	Sabaigon South	PM 305657	
169 Ind. F.P.O.	Ngakyedauk Pass	PM 373492	
PROVOST			
5 Ind. Div. Pro. Unit	Sabaigon South	PM 305657	
INTELLIGENCE			
565 F.S. Sec.	Sabaigon South	PM 306637	
	7 INDIAN DIVISION		
HEADQUARTERS			
Main H.Q. 7 Ind. Div.	Laung Chaung	PM 438534	
Rear H.Q. 7 Ind. Div.	"	"	
H.Q. 7 Ind. Div. R.A.	Ngakyedauk Pass	PM 369500	
H.Q. 7 Ind. Div. R.E.	"	"	
H.Q. 7 Ind. Div. R.I.A.S.C.	Ramu	PG 0515	
H.Q. 7 Ind. Div. I.E.M.E.			
ARTILLERY			
H.Q. 135 F. Regt. R.A. L.A.D. & Sig. Sec.	Wabyin	PM 358509	Under Comd. 5 Ind. Div.
347 Fd. Bty.			

THE ARAKAN OPERATIONS

Formation or Unit	Location	Map Ref.	Remarks
384 Fd. Bty.	Wabyin	PM 358509	
500 Fd. Bty.	"		
H.Q. 139 Jungle Fd. Regt. R.A. L.A.D. & Sig. Sec.	Ngakyedauk Pass (East End)	PM 421516	
362 Fd. Bty.	"	PM 429519	
364 Fd. Bty.	"	PM 432514	
503 Fd. Bty.	Ngakyedauk Pass (East End)	PM 419506	
H.Q. 24 A.A./A. Tk. Regt. R.A.	Kutupalong	PM 1188	U/c. 5 Ind. Div.
86 A.A. Bty.	Wabyin	PM 352524	
491 A.A. Bty.	Nawapara	PM 1388	
205 A. Tk. Bty.	Elephant Point	PL 9884	
284 A. Tk. Bty.	Monakhali	PM 070715	
H.Q. 15 Ind. Mtn. Regt. & Sig. Sec.	Awlanbyin	PM 464524	
5 Mtn. Bty.		PM 455517	
19 Mtn. Bty.		PM 458519	
23 Mtn. Bty.		PM 486520	
Bikaner Bijey Mtn. Bty.		PM 484527	

ENGINEERS

Formation or Unit	Location	Map Ref.	Remarks
62 Ind. Fd. Coy.	Ngakyedauk Pass	PM 385515	
77 Ind. Fd. Coy.	"	PM 369501	
421 Ind. Fd. Coy.	Awlanbyin	PM 460525	
303 Ind. Fd. Pk. Coy.	Garretts Garden Rd.	PM 3369	
17 Ind. Br. Sec.	Tumbru	PM 1382	

SIGNALS

Formation or Unit	Location	Map Ref.	Remarks
7 Ind. Div. Sigs.	Laung Chaung	PM 438534	

APPENDIX 4

Formation or Unit	Location	Map Ref.	Remarks
INFANTRY			
1 Sikh (less four Coys.)	Goppe Bazaar	PM 4370	Div. H.Q. Bn.
One Coy. 1 Sikh	Laung Chaung	PM 4353	
H.Q. 33 Ind. Inf. Bde. & Sig. Sec.	Awlanbyin	PM 468523	
1 Queens	"	PM 4851	
4/15 Punjab	"	PM 4950	
4/1 G.R.	"	PM 465496	
One Coy. 1 Sikh	"	PM 4652	
H.Q. 89 Ind. Inf. Bde. & Sig. Sec.	Ngakyedauk Pass (East End)	PM 423512	
2 K.O.S.B.	"	PM 432499	
7/2 Punjab	"	PM 419523	
4/8 G.R.	"	PM 413474	
One Coy. 1 Sikh	"	PM 4251	
H.Q. 114 Ind. Inf. Bde. & Sig. Sec.	Bogyiyaung	PM 508573	
1 S.O.M. L.I.	Taung Bazaar	PM 4960	
4/14 Punjab	Bogyiyaung	PM 524583	
4/5 R.G.R.	"	PM 533534	
One Coy. 1 Sikh	Lepanywa	PM 5760	
RIASC			
20 Ind. Mule Coy.	Bawli South	PM 3068	
57 Ind. Mule Coy.	Taung Bazaar	PM 4960	
68 Ind. Mule Coy.	Awlanbyin	PM 4652	
65 Ind. Mule Coy.	Ngakyedauk Pass (West End)	PM 3750	
13 Ind. Fd. Amb. Tp. Cl. I	Badana Sampanhead	PM 1859	
14 Ind. Fd. Amb. Tp. Cl. I	Goppe Bazaar	PM 4370	

Formation or Unit	Location	Map Ref.	Remarks
15 Ind. Fd. Amb. Tp. Cl. I	Ngakyedauk Pass (East End)	PM 4251	
29 Ind. Comp. Issue Sec.	Taung Bazaar	PM 4960	
30 Ind. Comp. Issue Sec.	Bawli South	PM 3068	
31 Ind. Comp. Issue Sec.	Badana Sampanhead	PM 4859	
32 Ind. Comp. Issue Sec.	Ngakyedauk Pass (West End)	PM 3750	
60 Ind. G.P. Tpt. Coy.	Bawli South	PM 3068	
61 Ind. G.P. Tpt. Coy.	Ramu	PG 0420	
130 Ind. G.P. Tpt. Coy.	Kutupalong	PM 1188	
Medical			
44 Ind. Fd. Amb.	Goppe Bazaar	PM 4370	
54 Ind. Fd. Amb.	Badana Sampanhead	PM 482595	
66 Ind. Fd. Amb. …	Ngakyedauk Pass (West End)	PM 3750	
32 Ind. Fd. Hyg. Sec.	Laung Chaung	PM 4353	
Veterinary			
7 Ind. Mob. Vet. Sec.	Badana Sampanhead	PM 480600	
Medical			
6 Ind. Mob. Wkshop. Coy.	M 92 Rd. Ukhia-Tumbru	PM 0891	
39 Ind. Mob. Wkshop. Coy.	Ultakhali	PG 0220	
7 Ind. Rec. Coy. …	M 77 Rd. Ramu-Ukhia		
H.Q. 7 Ind. Div. Wkshops.	M 77 Rd. Ramu-Ukhia		
33 Ind. L.A.D. (Type E)	Link Rd.	PG 0202	
89 Ind. L.A.D. (Type E)			
114 Ind. L.A.D. (Type E)			

Formation or Unit	Location	Map Ref.	Remarks
POSTAL			
38 Ind. F.P.O.	Ngakyedauk Pass (West End)	PM 3750	
39 Ind. F.P.O.	Bogyiyaung	PM 5058	
79 Ind. F.P.O.	Awlanbyin	PM 4652	
94 Ind. F.P.O.	Ngakyedauk Pass (East End)	PM 4251	
PROVOST			
7 Ind. Div. Pro. Unit	Ngakyedauk Pass (West End)	PM 3750	
INTELLIGENCE			
568 F.S. Sec.	Laung Chaung	PM 4353	
No. 1 Pl. B.I.C.			

APPENDIX 5

XV INDIAN CORPS ORDER OF BATTLE

March 1944

Formation or Unit	Remarks
H.Q. 15 INDIAN CORPS & CORPS TROOPS	
HEADQUARTERS	
Main H.Q. 15 Ind. Corps.	
Rear H.Q. 15 Ind. Corps	
H.Q. 15 Ind. Corps R.A.	
22 A. Air S.C.	
R.A.C./I.A.C.	
25 D. Gp.	
3 Gwalior L., Sig. Sec. and L.A.D.(E.)	Horsed wing under comd. 7 Ind. Div.
81 (W.A.) Div. Recce. Regt.	under comd. 5 Ind. Div.
ARTILLERY	
1 Med. Regt. R.A.	
6 Med. Regt. R.A., Sig. Sec. and L.A.D. ...	en route.
18 Med. Bty.	
245 Med. Bty.	
36 L.A.A. Regt. R.A., Sig. Sec. and Wksp. Sec.	
97 L.A.A. Bty.	
128 L.A.A. Bty.	
266 L.A.A. Bty.	
8 (Belfast) H.A.A. Regt. R.A., Sig. Sec. and Wksp. Sec. ...	
21 H.A.A. Bty.	
22 H.A.A. Bty.	
23 H.A.A. Bty.	
44/2 Svy. Regt. R.A. ...	
7 Ind. Fd. Regt. I.A. and Sig. Sec. ...	
16 Bty.	
17 Bty.	
18 Bty.	
5 Mahratta A. Tk. Regt. I.A. and Sig. Det.	
17 A. Tk. Bty.	pass to under comd. 404 L of C. Area on arr. —approx. mid. Mar.
18 A. Tk. Bty.	
19 A. Tk. Bty.	
20 A. Tk. Bty.	

Formation or Unit	Remarks
No. 2 Ind. Mob. Met. Sec.	
No. 2 C.B. Team	with H.Q. R.A. 5 Div.
No. 4 C.B. Team	with H.Q. R.A. 7 Div.
No. 7 C.B. Team ...	⎫
H.Q. G.H.Q.(I) C.B. Pool	⎬ not yet arr.
656 Air. O.P. Sqn.	⎭

ENGINEERS

H.Q. 15 Ind. C. Tps. Engrs.	
72 Ind. Fd. Coy.	
483 Ind. Fd. Coy. ...	⎫ temp. under comd. 5 Ind.
MALERKOTLA Fd. Coy.	⎭ Div.
403 Ind. Fd. Pk. Coy.	
11 Ind. Br. Sec.	
24 Ind. Engr. Bn.	
23 Ind. Engr. Bn.	
853 Ind. Hy. Br. Coy. ...	
H.Q. 456 Fwd. Airfield Engrs.	
81 Ind. Fd. Coy.	
365 Ind. Fd. Coy.	
11 Ind. Engr. Bn. ...	
H.Q. 654 Ind. Mech. Exc. Coy.	under comd. C.R.E. 673 Mech. Exc. Gp.
713 Ind. Mech. Exc. Sec.	
714 Ind. Mech. Exc. Sec.	
45 Bomb. Disposal Sec.	

I.W.T.

290 I.W.T. (S.P.) Coy.

SIGNALS

15 Ind. Corps. Sigs, comprising—	
207 Tech. Maint. Sec.	
204 Ind. Line Sec.	
205 Ind. Line Sec.	
220 Ind. Line Sec.	att. to Sigs. 5 & 7 Div.
224 Ind. Line Maint. Sec.	
226 Ind. Lt. W.T. Sec.	
207 Ind. Med. W.T. Sec.	
101 D.R. Sec.	
201 Ind. D.R. Sec.	
82 Opg. Sec.	
219 Ind. Opg. Sec.	
323 Ind. Opg. Sec.	
225 Ind. Med. W.T. Sec.	
69 Med. W.T. Sec.	
C.M.A. Sec.	
114 Hy. W.T. Sec.	att. from Sigs. 14 Army.
Det. 228 Hy. W.T. Sec.	att. from Sigs. G.H.Q.(I).

Formation or Unit	Remarks
Det. 233 Med. W.T. Sec.	att. from 5 Ind. L. of C. sigs.
208 Ind. Store Sec.	
115 S.W.S.	} army tps. att. sigs. 15 Ind. Corps for adm. only.
203 S.W.S.	

INFANTRY

M.G. Bn. F.F.R.	bn. less mtr. pls. under comd. 5 div.
79 Ind. Inf. Coy. (8 Punjab)	corps H.Q. def. & emp. coy. att. for escort duties for ops. with 290 (S.P.) coy.
One pl. 25 G.R. ...	
85 Ind. Inf. Coy. (12 F.F.R.)	

"V" FORCE

H.Q. 7 V. Ops.	} det. under comd. 81 (W.A.) Div.
H.Q. 8 V. Ops.	

RIASC

20 M.A.S.	
45 M.A.S.	
53 M.A.S. ...	
8 Ind. Mule Coy.	under comd. 7 Div.
18 Ind. Mule Coy.	
33 Ind. Mule Coy.	
39 Ind. Mule Coy.	
59 Ind. Mule Coy.	under comd. 7 Div.
81 Ind. A.T. Coy.	
Jaipur Pony. Coy.	
46 Ind. C.I.S.	
52 Ind. C.I.S.	
54 Ind. C.I.S.	

MEDICAL

8 Ind. C.C.S.	
15 Ind. C.C.S.	
23 Ind. C.C.S.	
25 Ind. C.C.S.	
55 Ind. Fd. Hyg. Sec.	with Corps H.Q.
71 Ind. Fd. Amb.	
6 Ind. Mob. Surg. Unit	not yet arr.
7 Ind. Mob. Surg. Unit	being relieved.
8 Ind. Mob. Surg. Unit	with 54 Fd. Amb. 7 Div.
11 Ind. Mob. Surg. Unit	
12 Ind. Mob. Surg. Unit	with 66 Fd. Amb. 7 Div.
15 Ind. Mob. Surg. Unit	

Formation or Unit	Remarks
15 Ind. Mob. X-Ray Unit	
16 Ind. Mob. X-Ray Unit	with 8 Ind. C.C.S.
80 Ind. Mob. X-Ray Unit	with 25 Ind. C.C.S.
81 Ind. Mob. X-Ray Unit	
1 Ind. Bearer Coy.	with 5 Div.
2 Ind. Bearer Coy.	with 7 Div.
203 Mob. Dental Unit	with 15 Ind. C.C.S.
10 Ind. Dental Unit	not yet arr.
48 Ind. Dental Unit	
37 I.S.S.(C.)	
42 I.S.S.(C.)	
46 I.S.S.(C.)	
50 I.S.S.(C.)	
8 Fd. Transfusion Unit	in Sp. 5 Div.
28 Fd. Transfusion Unit	in Sp. 7 Div.
42 Ind. Sub Depot Med. Stores	
43 Ind. Sub Depot Med. Stores	

ARMY UNITS

18 A.M.U.	att. 5 Div.
30 A.M.U.	not yet arr.
51 A.M.U.	temp. under comd. 15 Ind. Corps.
H.Q. 15 Ind. Corps Ord. Fd. Pk. Corps and Army Tps. Sub Pk.	
5 Ind. Div. Sub Pk.	att. 5 Ind. Div.
7 Ind. Div. Sub Pk.	att. 7 Ind. Div.
12 Ind. Sal. Unit	att. 5 Ind. Div.
30 Ind. Sal. Unit	
37 Ind. Sal. Unit	att. 7 Ind. Div.
38 Ind. Sal. Unit	
20 Ind. Mob. Cinema Unit	att 15 Ind. Corps Sigs.
30 Ind. Mob. Cinema Unit	att. 5 Ind. Div.
31 Ind. Mob. Cinema Unit	for 7 Ind. Div.
9 Ind. Mob. Laundry Unit	
10 Ind. Mob. Laundry Unit	

MEDICAL

72 Ind. Mob. Wksp. Coy.
80 Ind. Mob. Wksp. Coy.
103 Ind. Mob. Wksp. Coy.
335 L. of C. Rec. Coy.
340 L. of C. Rec. Coy.

VETERINARY

3 Ind. Mob. Vet. Sec.

Formation or Unit	Remarks

INTELLIGENCE

566 Ind. F.S. Sec. — Corps H.Q.
691 Ind. F.S. Sec. — en route.
2 Mob. C.S.D.I.C.
C.L.O. B.I.C.
50 Observation Sqn.
55 Observation Sqn.
5 F.I.C.
202 Ind. Fd. Broadcasting Unit
204 Ind. Fd. Broadcasting Unit

POSTAL

51 Ind. F.P.O. — temp. att. 404 Area.
135 Ind. F.P.O.
153 Ind. F.P.O.

PROVOST

15 Ind. Corps Pro. Unit

LABOUR

H.Q. 23 Ind. Pnr. Gp., comprising
    1278 Ind. Pnr. Coy.
    1526 Ind. Pnr. Coy.
    1529 Ind. Pnr. Coy. — under 456 Fwd. Airfield Engrs.

    1548 Ind. Pnr. Coy.
    1550 Ind. Pnr. Coy.
    1551 Ind. Pnr. Coy.
    1552 Ind. Pnr. Coy.
    1553 Ind. Pnr. Coy.

MISCELLANEOUS

4 Graves Registration Unit

25 INDIAN DIVISION

HEADQUARTERS

H.Q. 25 Ind. Div.
H.Q. 25 Ind. Div. R.A.
H.Q. 25 Ind. Div. R.E.
H.Q. 25 Ind. Div. R.I.A.S.C.
H.Q. 25 Ind. Div. I.E.M.E.

DIV. RECCE. REGT.

Jodhpur Sardar Risala & L.A.D. (B.)

ARTILLERY

27 Jungle Fd. Regt. & L.A.D. (B.) &
    Sig. Sec.

Formation or Unit	Remarks

    21 Bty.
    24 Bty.
    37/47 Bty.
115 Fd. Regt. R.A. & Sig. Sec.
    239 Bty.
    240 Bty.
    480 Bty.
8 Ind. Fd. Regt. & Sig. Sec.
    11 Bty.
    12 Bty.
    13 Bty.
7 Ind. A. Tk. Regt.
    25 Bty.
    26 Bty.
    27 Bty.
    39 Bty.

ENGINEERS

63 Ind. Fd. Coy.
93 Ind. Fd. Coy.
425 Ind. Fd. Coy.
325 Ind. Fd. Pk. Coy.

SIGNALS

25 Ind. Div. Sigs. (less Bde. Sig. Secs.)

INFANTRY

8 Hybad. (Div. H.Q. Bn.)
H.Q. 51 Ind. Inf. Bde. & Sig. Sec.
    8 Y. & L.
    17 Mahrattas
    16 Baluch.
H.Q. 53 Ind. Inf. Bde. & Sig. Sec.
    9 Y. & L.
    2/2 Punjab
    4 R. Garh. Rig.
H.Q. 74 Ind. Inf. Bde. & Sig. Sec.
    6 Oxf. Bucks.
    14 Baluch.
    3/2 G.R.

RIASC

68 Ind. G.P. Tpt. Coy. & Wksp. Sec.
81 Ind. G.P. Tpt. Coy.
101 Ind. G.P. Tpt. Coy.   "
33 Ind. Comp. Issue Sec.
34
35
36

Formation or Unit	Remarks

MEDICAL

55 Ind. Fd. Amb.
58 Ind. Fd. Amb.
61 Ind. Fd. Amb.
30 Ind. Fd. Hyg. Sec.

IEME

76 Ind. Mob. Wksp. Coy.
77 Ind. Mob. Wksp. Coy.
78 Ind. Mob. Wksp. Coy.
51 Ind. L.A.D. Type E
53 Ind. L.A.D. Type E
74 Ind. L.A.D. Type E
25 Ind. Rec. Coy.

POSTAL

75 Ind. Fd. P.O.
126 Ind. Fd. P.O.
121 Ind. Fd. P.O.
128 Ind. Fd. P.O.

PROVOST

25 Ind. Div. Pro. Unit

INTELLIGENCE

606 Ind. F.S. Sec.

7 INDIAN DIVISION

HEADQUARTERS

Main H.Q. 7 Ind. Div.
Rear H.Q. 7 Ind. Div.
H.Q. 7 Ind. Div. R.A.
H.Q. 7 Ind. Div. R.E.
H.Q. 7 Ind. Div. R.I.A.S.C.
H.Q. 7 Ind. Div. I.E.M.E.

ARTILLERY

136 Fd. Regt. R.A. Sig. Sec. and L.A.D.
    347 Fd. Bty.
    348 Fd. Bty.
    500 Fd. Bty.
139 (J.) Fd. Regt. R.A. Sig. Sec. and L.A.D.
    362 Fd. Bty.
    364 Fd. Bty.
    503 Fd. Bty.

Formation or Unit	Remarks

24 A.A./A. Tk. Regt. R.A., Sig. Sec.
   and L.A.D.
      86 A.A. Bty.
      491 A.A. Bty.
      265 A. Tk. Bty.
      284 A. Tk. Bty.
25 Ind. Mtn. Regt. I.A. and Sig. Sec.
      5 Mtn. Bty.
      19 Mtn. Bty.
      23 Mtn. Bty.

ENGINEERS

62 Ind. Fd. Coy.
77 Ind. Fd. Coy.
421 Ind. Fd. Coy.
303 Ind. Fd. Pk. Coy.
17 Ind. Br. Sec.

SIGNALS

Main 7 Ind. Div. Sigs.
Rear 7 Ind. Div. Sigs.

INFANTRY

1 Sikh
H.Q. 33 Ind. Inf. Bde., Sig. Sec. and
   L.A.D.
      1 Queen
      4/15 Punjab
      4/1 G.R.
H.Q. 89 Ind. Inf. Bde., Sig. Sec. and
   L.A.D.
      2 K.O.S.B.
      7/2 Punjab
      4/8 G.R.
H.Q. 114 Ind. Inf. Bde., Sig. Sec. and
   L.A.D.
      1 Sqn. L.I.
      4/14 Punjab
      4/5 R.G.R.

RIASC

60 Ind. G.P. Tpt. Coy.
61 Ind. G.P. Tpt. Coy.
130 Ind. G.P. Tpt. Coy.
29 Ind. C.I.S.
30 Ind. C.I.S.
31 Ind. C.I.S.
32 Ind. C.I.S.
20 Ind. Mule Coy.

Formation or Unit	Remarks

57 Ind. Mule Coy.
63 Ind. Mule Coy.
65 Ind. Mule Coy.
13 Ind. Fd. Amb. Tp. Cl. I.
14 Ind. Fd. Amb. Tp. Cl. I.
15 Ind. Fd. Amb. Tp. Cl. I.

MEDICAL

44 Ind. Fd. Amb.
54 Ind. Fd. Amb.
66 Ind. Fd. Amb.
32 Ind. Fd. Hyg. Sec.

IEME

6 Ind. Mob. Wksp. Coy.
39 Ind. Mob. Wksp. Coy.
7 Ind. Rec.

VETERINARY

7 Ind. Mob. Vet. Sec.

POSTAL

37 Ind. F.P.O.
39 Ind. F.P.O.
79 Ind. F.P.O.
94 Ind. F.P.O.

PROVOST

7 Ind. Div. Pro. Unit

INTELLIGENCE

668 Ind. F.S. Sec.
1 Pl. B.I.C.

26 INDIAN DIVISION

HEADQUARTERS

Main H.Q. 26 Ind. Div.
Rear H.Q. 26 Ind. Div.
H.Q. 26 Ind. Div. R.A.
H.Q. 26 Ind. Div. R.E.
H.Q. 26 Ind. Div. R.I.A.S.C.
H.Q. 26 Ind. Div. I.E.M.E.

Formation or Unit	Remarks

ARTILLERY

160 (J.) Fd. Regt. R.A., Sig. Sec. and L.A.D.
    584 Bty. (Mtr.)
    585 Bty. (3.7 How.)
    586 Bty. (3.7 How.)
        } 3.7 How. Bty. only with Regt.

30 Mtn. Regt. I.A. and Sig. Sec.
    27 Mtn. Bty.
    32 Mtn. Bty.
    33 Mtn. Bty.
    34 Mtn. Bty.

ENGINEERS

28 Ind. Fd. Coy.
72 Ind. Fd. Coy.
98 Ind. Fd. Coy.
328 Ind. Fd. Pk. Coy.
7 Ind. Br. Sec.
    } remaining C.T.G. location.

SIGNALS

Main 26 Ind. Div. Sigs.
Rear 26 Ind. Div. Sigs.

INFANTRY

5/9 Jat
H.Q. 4 Ind. Inf. Bde., Sig. Sec. and L.A.D.
    1 Wilts
    2 Rajput
    2 F.F. Rif.
H.Q. 36 Ind. Inf. Bde., Sig. Sec. and L.A.D.
    8 F.F. Rif.
    5/16 Punjab
    1/8 G.R.
H.Q. 71 Ind. Inf. Bde., Sig. Sec. and L.A.D.
    1 Lincs.
    5/1 Punjab
    1/18 R. Garh. Rif.   Temp. under comd. 5 Ind. Div.

RIASC

41 Ind. G.P. Tpt. Coy.
75 Ind. G.P. Tpt. Coy.
166 Ind. G.P. Tpt. Coy.
16 Ind. C.I.S.
17 Ind. C.I.S.
18 Ind. C.I.S.

Formation or Unit	Remarks

19 Ind. C.I.S.
44 Ind. Mule Coy.
48 Ind. Mule Coy.
51 Ind. Mule Coy.
58 Ind. Mule Coy.
11 Ind. Fd. Amb. Tp. Cl. I.
16 Ind. Fd. Amb. Tp. Cl. I.
21 Ind. Fd. Amb. Tp. Cl. I.

MEDICAL

1 Ind. Fd. Amb.
46 Ind. Fd. Amb.
48 Ind. Fd. Amb.
27 Ind. Fd. Hyg. Sec.

IEME

54 Ind. Mob. Wksp. Coy.
65 Ind. Mob. Wksp. Coy.
26 Ind. Rec. Coy.

VETERINARY

8 Ind. Mob. Vet. Sec.

POSTAL

2 Ind. F.P.O.
20 Ind. F.P.O.
68 Ind. F.P.O.
131 Ind. F.P.O.

PROVOST

26 Ind. Div. Pro. Unit

INTELLIGENCE

601 Ind. F.S. Sec.

36 INDIAN DIVISION

(Troops forward of Calcutta)

HEADQUARTERS

H.Q. 36 Ind. Div. and Def. Pl.
H.Q. 36 Ind. Div. R.A.C.
H.Q. 36 Ind. Div. R.A. (incl. Sig. Sec.)
H.Q. 36 Ind. Div. R.E.
H.Q. 36 Ind. Div. R.I.A.S.C.

Formation or Unit	Remarks

ROYAL ARMOURED CORPS

C. Sqn. 149 Regt. R.A.C. (Shermans) and L.A.D.

ARTILLERY

130 Assault Fd. Regt. R.A., Sig. Sec. and L.A.D.
    315 Fd. Bty. (25 pr.)
    455 Lt. Bty. (3.7 How.)
    494 Lt. Bty. (3.7 How.)
178 Assault Fd. Regt. R.A., Sig. Sec. and L.A.D.
    366 Lt. Bty.
    516 Ed. Bty. (25 pdr.)
3 Met. Det.

SIGNALS

26 Ind. Div. Sig. (   )

INFANTRY

D. Coy. 2 Manch. (M.Gs.)

R.A.S.C./R.I.A.S.C.

90 Ind. G.P. Tpt. Coy. and Wksp. det.
56 Ind. C.I.S.
Det. 38 Div. Tps. Coy. R.A.S.C. (D.U.K.Ws.)
436 G. Tpt. Coy. R.A.S.C. (D.U.K.Ws.)

IEME

Det. 102 Ind. Mob. Wksp. Coy.

MEDICAL

22 C.C.S. (Brit.) with Ind. increament
27 Ind. Fd. Transfusion Unit
13 Ind. Mob. Surg. Unit

POSTAL

77 Ind. F.P.O.

PROVOST

36 Ind. Div. Sig. Unit (less two secs.)

INTELLIGENCE

29 F.S. Sec.

Formation or Unit	Remarks

29 Indep. Bde. G.P.

H.Q. 29 Indep. Bde. Gp. (Def. Pl. and Sig. Sec.)
236 Fd. Coy. R.E.
1 R.S.F.
2 R.W.F.
2 E. Lan. R.
2 S. Lan. R.
91 Ind. G.P. Tpt. Coy. and Wksp. Det.
55 Ind. C.I.S.
154 Fd. Amb.
29 Indep. Bde. Wksp. Sec. and L.A.D.
29 Indep. Bde. F.P.O.
1 Pro. Sec.
579 Ind. F.S. Sec.

72 Ind. Inf. Bde. Gp.

H.Q. 72 Ind. Inf. Bde. Gp., Def. Pl. and Sig. Sec. ⎫
30 Fd. Coy. I.E.
6 S.W.B.
10 Glosters
9 R. Sussex
169 Ind. Gp. Tpt. Coy. and Wksp. Sec.
21 Ind. C.I.S. ⎬ Army res.
69 Ind. Fd. Amb.
72 Ind. Inf. Bde. Wksp. Sec. and L.A.D.
148 Ind. F.P.O.
2 Pro. Sec.
577 Ind. F.S. Sec. ⎭

81 (WEST AFRICAN) DIVISION

(Troops operating with XV Indian Corps)

Headquarters

Main H.Q. 81 (W.A.) Div. and Def. Pl.
6 Lt. Bty. R.A.
1 A.R./A. Tk. Regt. and L.A.D.
81 (W.A.) Div. Sigs.
16 Pro. Sec.
6 F.S. Sec.
81 (W.A.) Div. Tps. Coy. Comp. Pl.

Formation or Unit	Remarks

1 (W.A.) Fd. Bchy.
26 M.A.C.
5 Pl. B.I.C.
Air Sup. L. Sec.

5 (W.A.) Bde. Gp.

H.Q. 5 (W.A.) Bde., Def. Pl., Sig. Sec., and L.A.D.
5 Lt. Bty. R.A.
5 G.C.R.
7 G.C.R.
8 G.C.R.
5 (W.A.) Bde. Pro. Sec.
3 Aux. Gp.
5 Fd. Coy.
4 Svy. Sec.
5 (W.A.) Bde. Gp. Coy. Comp. pl.
4 (W.A.) Fd. Bchy.
5 Fd. Amb.
5 Fd. Hyg. Sec.

6 (W.A.) Bde. Gp.

H.Q. 6 (W.A.), Bde., Def. Pl., Sig. Sec. and L.A.D.
3 Lt. Bty. R.A.
4 N.R.
1 Sa. L.R.
1 Gamb. R.
6 (W.A.) Bde. Pro. Sec.
4 Aux. Gp.
6 Fd. Coy.
3 Svy. Sec.
6 (W.A.) Bde. Gp. Coy. Comp. pl.
8 (W.A.) Fd. Bchy.
6 Fd. Amb.
6 Fd. Hyg. Sec.

APPENDIX 6

UNITS OF THE 15th INDIAN CORPS AND THEIR COMMANDERS
Under Seac

I. **15TH INDIAN CORPS**

Lt. Genl. Sir A. R. P. Christison, Bt., K.B.E., C.B., D.S.O., M.C.	16 Nov. 43-30 Sept. 45.

II. **25TH INDIAN DIVISION**

1. Maj.-Genl. H. L. Davies, C.B., C.B.E., D.S.O., M.C.	16 Nov. 43-11 Aug. 44.
2. Maj.-Genl. G. N. Wood, C.B.E., D.S.O., M.C.	14 Oct. 44-24 Feb. 46.

51 Indian Infantry Brigade

1. Brig. T. H. Angus, D.S.O., M.C.	16 Nov. 43-6 Nov. 44.
2. Brig. R. A. Hutton, D.S.O., O.B.E.	6 Nov. 44-21 Sep. 45.

53 Indian Infantry Brigade

1. Brig. G. A. P. Coldstream, D.S.O.	6 Mar. 44-5 Aug. 44.
2. Brig. A. G. O'C. Scott, O.B.E.	5 Aug. 44-28 Dec. 44.
3. Brig. B. C. H. Gerty, D.S.O.	29 Dec. 44-2 Dec. 45.

74 Indian Infantry Brigade

1. Brig. J. E. Hirst, D.S.O.	16 Nov. 43-31 Mar. 45.
2. Brig. J. C. W. Cargill, O.B.E.	31 Mar. 46-31 May 46.

III. **26 INDIAN DIVISION**

1. Maj.-Genl. C. E. N. Lomax, C.B., C.B.E., D.S.O., M.C.	16 Nov. 43-20 Mar. 45.
2. Maj.-Genl. H. M. Chambers, C.B.E.	1 Apr. 45-30 Jan. 46.

4 Indian Infantry Brigade

1. Brig. A. W. Lowther, C.B.E. D.S.O.	16 Nov. 43-19 Jan. 45.
2. Brig. J. F. R. Forman, D.S.O.	19 Jan. 45-29 Feb. 46.

36 Indian Infantry Brigade

1. Brig. (later Maj.-Genl.) L. G. Thomas, C.B.E., D.S.O., M.C.	16 Nov. 43-1 Apr. 45.
2. Brig. K. S. Thimaya	1 Apr. 45-1 Sep. 45.
3. Brig. G. L. Roberts, O.B.E.	1 Sep. 45-11 Dec. 45.
4. Brig. J. A. Mellsop	12 Dec. 45-31 May 46.

71 Indian Infantry Brigade

1. Brig. G. G. C. Bull, D.S.O., O.B.E.	16 Nov. 43-28 Jan. 44.
2. Brig. R. C. Cotterell-Hill, D.S.O., O.B.E., M.C.	28 Jan. 44-1 Mar. 45.
3. Brig. (later Maj.-Genl.) H. M. Chambers, C.B.E.	1 Mar. 45-22 Mar. 45.
4. Brig. H. P. L. Hutchinson	22 Mar. 45-31 May 46.

APPENDIX 6

IV.   **81 WEST AFRICAN DIVISION**
1. Maj.-Genl. C. G. Woolner, C.B., M.C.   16 Nov. 43-14 Aug. 44.
2. Maj.-Genl. F. J. Loftus-Tottenham, D.S.O.   24 Aug. 44-28 Mar. 46.

5 West African Brigade
1. Brig. N. H. Collins   16 Nov. 43-16 Sep. 44.
2. Brig. P. J. Jeffreys, D.S.O., O.B.E. ...   16 Sep. 44-28 Mar. 46.

6 West African Brigade
1. Brig. J. W. A. Hayes, D.S.O.   16 Nov. 43-13 Mar. 44.
2. Brig. R. N. Cartwright   26 Mar. 44-1 July 44.
3. Brig. A. A. Crook, D.S.O.   6 Aug. 44-31 May 46.

V.   **82 WEST AFRICAN DIVISION**
1. Maj.-Genl. G. Mc. I. I. S. Bruce, O.B.E., M.C.   16 Nov. 43-9 Feb. 45.
2. Maj.-Genl. H. C. Stockwell, C.B.E., D.S.O.   9 Feb. 45-22 May 45.
3. Maj. Genl. C. R. A. Swynnerton, D.S.O.   23 May 45-13 July 45.
4. Maj.-Genl. H. C. Stockwell, C.B.E., D.S.O.   14 July 45-28 May 46.

1 West African Brigade
1. Brig. (later Maj.-Genl.) C. R. A. Swynnerton, D.S.O.   16 Nov. 43-22 May 45.
2. Brig. F. W. Clowes ...   23 May 45-13 July 45.
3. Brig. (later Maj.-Genl.) C. R. A. Swynnerton, D.S.O.   14 July 45-28 May 46.

2 West African Brigade
1. Brig. E. W. D. Western, D.S.O.   16 Nov. 43-23 Mar. 45.
2. Brig. A. T. Wilson-Brand   23 Mar. 45-5 Aug. 45.
3. Brig. F. W. Clowes   5 Aug. 45-28 Apr. 46.

4 West African Brigade
1. Brig. H. Gibbons, M.C. ...   16 Nov. 43-20 Oct. 44.
2. Brig. A. H. G. Ricketts, D.S.O., O.B.E.   20 Oct. 44-14 Aug. 45.
3. Brig. N. C. Stockwell ...   14 Aug. 45-4 Dec. 45.
4. Brig. A. H. G. Ricketts, D.S.O., O.B.E.   5 Dec. 45-31 May 46.

VI.   **50 INDIAN TANK BRIGADE**
1. Brig. G. H. N. Todd, M.C.   16 Mar. 44-28 June 45.
2. Brig. R. O. Critchley   28 June 45-31 May 46.

VII.   **3RD COMMANDO BRIGADE**
1. Brig. W. I. Nonweiler   7 Dec. 43-26 Nov. 44.
2. Brig. P. G. Young   27 Nov. 44-18 Dec. 44.
3. Brig. C. R. Hardy, D.S.O.   19 Dec. 44-29 Apr. 46.

VIII.   **22ND EAST AFRICAN BRIGADE**
1. Brig. R. F. Johnstone   1 June 44-19 May 46.

APPENDIX 7

Personal narrative of the BIRD feature operations
April 1944

by

Major F. W. MacD. Quigley, 8 Hyderabad.

The objective

The feature in Sq. 4235 immediately south of Pt. 904 (in the Maungdaw Hills), consists of two pimples connected by a track, which look from its contour appearance, like two poached eggs.

Day 1-10 April 1944

My Company—'D'—was ordered up from 25 Indian Division Headquarters where it had been employed as Division Defence Coy., to join the remainder of the Battalion, now under 51 Indian Infantry Brigade, with Battalion Headquarters in the nullah running north-east of Kanbyin (Sq. 4036).

On arrival I received orders to lead a composite force consisting of 'C' and 'D' Companies with a Gunner Observation Post under Major Buxton, Royal Artillery, and to attack and take the above feature. The approach march was to be made during the night of 10/11 April, and the assault at first light on 11 April. The route indicated was to work through the jungle by nullah and elephant track in a direction north-west to south-east so as to arrive on the primary objective (the first poached egg) at 428352. The capture of the primary objective was the task laid down for my Company—'D'—after which 'C' Company, would pass through 'D' Company on to the other pimple, 426354. The known and more obvious line of approach to our objective, viz., the nullah running east to west from the feature towards Myaukingyaung (4135), was for these reasons to be avoided, and so it was hoped surprise would be achieved.

The plan was of the simplest. 'C' Company was to lead the approach march, laying down a telephone line, and seize a suitable position in the vicinity of the 'BIRD' feature as a starting line for 'D' Company's assault.

The route had not been previously reconnaissanced and was unfamiliar, but our primary objective, the 'BIRD' itself, denuded of all vegetation, would, in the clear moonlight, stand out as prominently as, to use the Commanding Officer's expression, 'the breasts of the Queen of Sheba'. Such information as was available about the enemy suggested that the 'BIRD' had been used as an Observation Post and very thinly held. An air report was to the effect that on the previous evening a long convoy of enemy casualties had been seen moving away from behind the high range due east. Concealed in position on this high range, which directly overlooked the feature, was an enemy gun believed to be of about 75 mm. calibre. It was believed that both Pt. 904 (Sq. 4236) and the high range were held in some strength by the enemy. A half Company of Mahrattas were in position on the western face of Pt. 904, but were so situated that they would not be able to support the attack if necessary.

From these factors it was deduced therefore that much opposition in the final assault might not be expected provided surprise was achieved by a silent march. Once in position, the Gunner Observation Post could quickly put down a protective screen of fire all round the feature, for the whole area had been previously registered. There was to be no artillery support to our approach march; the whole operation was to be carried out in silence.

The enterprise savoured of being extremely adventurous and our liabilities were unpredictable. I had taken part in similar shows in Scouts on the North West Frontier, where we repeatedly demonstrated that these apparently foolhardy operations often produced most excellent results accompanied by very few casualties. But there, we were familiar with every fold in the ground, the psychological outlook of the hostile tribesmen, and our liabilities opposed against an enemy armed with only the rifle were infinitely smaller. Protectively, one's mind refused to consider too closely these aspects of the forthcoming operation.

Day 1—Phase 1.

Before dark I moved the force down to the 'cow' area (Sq. 4135) and from an Observation Post on Pt. 176 was able to make a more detailed reconnaissance. Platoon and Section Commanders were shown the objective. Some private anxiety was occasioned by the appearance of the feature's most western aspect, a steep precipice of sandy shale which would be extremely difficult to negotiate if that should prove the only feasible route on to the feature itself. It was hoped that an easier approach might be discovered.

'D' Company was physically tired from a long day, but morale was good. Their complete ignorance of the country, and the nature of the fighting on this front were all favourable factors in a psychological sense, for it is undoubtedly true that 'fools tread where angels fear to!' Their physical tiredness provided a mental apathy towards anticipated danger and induced a sense of calmness of mind. We dropped our packs here, cutting down our carrying weights to personal arms and equipment.

Day 2—Phase 2

Operations began at 1830 hours. Major Horsfall with a signal group and telephone wire moved his Company—'C'. They disappeared silently into the scrub. At 1930 hours he phoned me that he had exhausted his drum of wire: so using the line as a guide, I marched off the remainder of the force well closed up and joined him in a nullah with the remaining wire. The march continued. The jungle was dense in places; the brilliant moonlight filtered in patches of light and shade through the tree tops, the objective being concealed from view, for long intervals. At about midnight, the weather changed—the moon was obscured by massing clouds: we found ourselves on a wooded spur too far west of the objective. A heavy downpour of rain descended on us accompanied by a cold wind. It was a little dispiriting. Buxton and I passed our rum flasks around. I noted that the wind was blowing strong towards us, which meant that the sounds of our approach would be concealed from the enemy. It appeared that God was on our side. Buxton went off on a little reconnaissance of his own and discovered a deep nullah pointing in the right direction. I joined him and we continued the march. Buxton's nullah was a very important discovery:

it was eventually to lead us right up to a spur running on to our objective. We continued the march.

Day 2—Phase 2 Contd.—11 April 1944

At about 0300 hours we found ourselves on a man-made path running along a wooded spur up to the objective, now clearly distinguishable. We hoped that we were not so obvious to the enemy. This path was a most fortuitous discovery and removed anxiety with regard to the assault—the ground would be negotiable, and provide good footholds.

At 0400 hours we came to a suitable line approximately 100 yards below the feature. We were all closed up on the pathway and if the enemy had been alert he could have inflicted heavy casualties. Buxton told me he had fire laid on a signal, which he could bring down if we should encounter opposition. I left Horsfall in position and passed through with the Company—16 Platoon leading. As soon as we got on to the feature he was to pass through on to the other 'poached egg' 200 yards to the south.

We reached the base of the pimple at 0430 hours and fanned out for the final 'pinch'—16 Platoon right, 17 Platoon left, Company Headquarters and 18 Platoon close up. There was a pause, silence except for whispered words of command and men moving through the scrub. The 'BIRD' was ominously silent. Immediately above us with numerous slit trenches cut into its face, it looked like a main gun turret of a battleship.

I was aware of a tremendous sense of physical weariness, of an extraordinary mental detachment, though at any moment the trenches above us might vomit forth fire. One felt that at this moment one's body which would now walk towards physical destruction was a quite separate entity to the spirit. The spirit itself was almost a spectator of this fantastic procedure.

Day 2—Phase 3—The Assault

Someone found his voice and shouted. Everyone shouted. The silence was broken by yells, screams, and the shattering detonations of exploding grenades and small arms fire. The men rushed forward in a splendid hysteria. I saw them right on top of the crest pouring Bren and Tommy Gun fire into the slit trenches, when something terrible happened. There was a thin wailing whine and a crash. A shell landed in the midst of them. One after another they came down smashing into my men. In their blood-red glare I saw a man with arms flung wide. I saw a man bunched up into a ball blown from the position, go slithering and bouncing down the precipitous western slope. There were wild cries: I flung myself flat on my face and prayed wordlessly. The darkness around was full of flying metal. Tracer rounds streaked through the darkness. Then the shelling suddenly stopped. Horsfall's Company was with us. 'Horsy' was splendid—a lion in aggressiveness, he shouted and beckoned them on. 'C' Coy. spread out and followed him on to the second objective. Buxton was with me. Horsy's men were closing on their position, shooting from the hip. Buxton suggested that I should reinforce them, which I refused, for actually they encountered no opposition. The other feature, like the 'BIRD' itself, was unoccupied. A young Sepoy discovered the solitary occupant of the 'BIRD', and emptied a Bren gun into him as he lay in his slit trench. It was a Japanese soldier, a Superior Private by his badges of rank. I found him later spreadeagled across his reconnaissances reaching for a hand grenade. We collected his documents.

As the light increased we could see our own dead and wounded—8 men dead and 17 wounded seriously—they lay like cut corn all over the summit. Jemedar Khem Singh and a Sepoy lay in a slit trench. The VCO's head was blown off. There was something vaguely obscene about his smashed truncated body. Again a screen asserted itself over the more sensitive perceptions of the mind. In astonishment at one's own apparent callousness we found ourselves regarding these smashed men without emotion or feeling. We were absolutely physically exhausted and mentally bemused. In a drugged stupor I surveyed the scene. Buxton suggested that we apply First Aid. I sent some men to tie up the mangled bodies with their First Aid bandages. The big wounds required several dressings. We gave them a little water. I left a man with each wounded and dying man. There was nothing else I could do. We had no morphia to dull their agony. *Why don't we carry morphia in action?* There was no doctor. They lay out there in the grilling sun, for there was no shade, until they were evacuated at 1630 hours that day. Several of them died.

We settled down in the trenches. Many of them were filled with putrefying dead, the terrible stench of which mingled with the sickly odour of cordite. This was the most befouled place in the world. Some dead Mahrattas blackened and bloated, covered with crawling flies, lay outside the position. Pieces of blood-soaked clothing and equipment bestrewed the area.

We did not feel like conquering heroes. Our tails were not up. We could not at that moment have withstood a determined counter-attack. Fortunately one did not immediately occur as we had anticipated.

The men had been through Hell. They were destined to become even better acquainted with Hell in the sleepless harassed hours which followed, when the enemy shelled us with field pieces at a few hundred yards range. Shot us up with 5 inch mortar in broad daylight, grenaded us at night, prowled around in the darkness, making animal noises, shouting fire orders, massing for attacks which they could not make; for our guns came down in a screen of fire all around the position.

APPENDIX 8

The Japanese in the Field

Morale

In the period between December 1941 and April 1944 when the yellow tide rolled over Malaya and Burma to the frontiers of India, the morale of the Japanese army was extremely high. This was not confined to the armed forces, but was also the case with civilians. A high ranking official of a (then) neutral country, writing from Tokyo in the middle of 1943, said: "I wish with all my heart that I could report that these hardships are weakening the civilian's morale, but I cannot. His will for war and victory is as hot as ever".

This was the spirit instilled into the Japanese soldier from early childhood and throughout his training.

"When I received my mobilization orders, I had already sacrificed my life for my country . . You must not expect me to return alive." This sentence is quoted from a letter which was found on the body of a dead conscript. It is by no means exceptional and indicates a fanatical conception of service which found expression in a disregard for personal safety and a readiness to fight to the last man and the last round. The morale from which such feelings of self-sacrifice sprang, was based on an attitude of mind assiduously cultivated from a very early age.

Japanese morale training instilled a strong religious belief: "Comrades who have fallen!" reads what was almost the last entry in a soldier's diary, "Soon we shall be fighting our last fight to avenge you, and all of us together, singing a battle song, will march to Kudan." (Kudan is a Shrine near Tokyo dedicated to the war dead).

The second pillar of Japanese morale was deep personal devotion to the Emperor. The army belonged to the Emperor and its mission was his divine will.

Finally, the Japanese believed that they were a chosen people, a superior race. By a different process they had reached that stage of fanatical self-confidence which the Nazis reached in 1939. "We are a superior race with a divine mission. We are invincible." These were the foundations upon which Germans and Japanese alike built their morale, and the initial military successes which both these countries achieved against their ill-prepared enemies gave ample credence to the lie of invincibility.

Japanese confidence in their legendary superiority, based as it was to a large extent on myths, was, however, rudely shaken by a series of defeats. In 1944 there was a definite change in their attitude; and although the Japanese troops in Burma still fought with courage and determination, sometimes against much superior forces, their diaries contained far less heroics than in the years before. In 1944 they launched two offensives which, they were told, were to bring them down into the plains of Bengal and Assam. Both their offensives failed and as a result many soldiers lost that fanatical enthusiasm for the war which they had in the past. The stories of dying for the Emperor had paled and the decline in morale had been sufficiently general to call for the writing of special directives on the subject. In an order of the day captured in Arakan in April 1944, the G.O.C. of a Japanese Divisional Infantry Group said:

"The general condition of the infantry group does not admit optimism. To win the battle we must develop to the utmost the spirit of Yamato. (Symbolic of the conquering destiny of Japan). To indulge in thoughts that we cannot win because our weapons are inferior is already to have lost the battle. As for the throwing away and careless abandoning of arms—these things must on no account happen. To abandon or throw away weapons bearing the Imperial crest is the height of humiliation, and represents a collapse of morale."

Further, an extract from a special order issued by the commander of the *33rd Divisional Infantry Group* in the Imphal area in Burma on 2 June 44 reads:

" . Still, should by any chance any delinquencies occur amongst you, I am considering what exceptional measures I shall have to take against the offenders .. In short, a commander must not hesitate to stain his sword with the blood of his own troops if it is to uphold the honour of his unit."

Generally speaking, however, there was no very serious decline in Japanese morale in Burma. The victory there was won partly by good generalship and partly by good fighting; but it was also contributed to largely by the immoderate confidence of the Japanese. So sure were they of capturing the British supply dumps in Imphal and Manipur Road in their offensive in 1944, that they dispensed with their own lines of communication. Thus they destroyed their own army; and thus the same confidence which had brought them 'strings of victories' in the past led them at last to irretrievable disaster.

Tactical Characteristics and the Principles of War

Japanese tactics in general were based on deception and rapid manoeuvre. They often went to extremes to create false impressions. One gets the impression that the perfect solution to a tactical problem was a neatly performed stratagem, followed by an encirclement or a flanking attack driven home with the bayonet. This allowed the commanders to demonstrate their ability and the men to show their courage and ferocity in hand-to-hand fighting. Their plans were a mixture of military artistry and vain glorious audacity. Bull-dog tenacity in carrying out a mission, even to annihilation, very frequently gave a most erroneous impression of Japanese strength, and often resulted in small Japanese forces overcoming larger ones, as their units were not rendered ineffective until they were nearly all casualties.

Offensive Action is described in one of the training pamphlets as a principle which gives moral superiority and tends to confer the initiative and, with it, liberty of action. A famous British general once simplified it thus: "The object of every soldier will be to kill Germans"; and this was very near to the Japanese interpretation, for the latter applied the principle of offensive action not only to their attacks but also to situations in which their defeat was a foregone conclusion.

Japanese soldiers from the highest to the lowest were thoroughly imbued with the spirit of offence. The almost instinctive reaction of any Japanese Commander in a new, expected or difficult situation was to seek some way of assuming the offensive.

It must, however, be borne in mind that the characteristic Japanese method of attack often resulted in a tactical defensive. This was the outflanking march and blocking of the enemy's line of communication, accompanied possibly by small frontal attacks, first to hold and secondly to encourage withdrawal. The method was to get round the enemy, on to his Lines of Communication and make strong defences on them; the enemy, after being harassed by small frontal attacks, jitter columns and the fear of being cut off, would then attempt to withdraw and be "impaled", as it were, on the defences of the road-blocks. The manoeuvre was not a flank *attack* but an outflanking movement to seize *defensive* positions which the enemy in his turn must attack. Generally, direct assault was used only when absolutely necessary, as for instance in ordinary counter-attack. *Surprise* was achieved in both strategy and tactics and ruses such as the use of disguise and of the language of the enemy, were extensively employed. A fifth column was also used extensively in the early stages of the war. Nevertheless, the principal Japanese method of securing surprise lay in the use they made of country generally regarded as impassable. This, together with the conduct of operations sometimes in foul weather enabled them to place at a disadvantage an enemy more sensitive to ground and climate.

Mobility was one of the most important factors in achieving surprise. The ability to exploit to the full the exceptional marching powers of the troops—they were capable of covering thirty or more miles per day—was closely allied with the ability to feed them. Thus, by choosing a circuitous path through difficult country, the Japanese were frequently able to cut the line of retreat of a force based on a road. If the chances of living on the country were small, forward troops with their own animal transport might carry up to a month's supplies. The Japanese soldier had been trained to carry up to 58 lb. which is what Napoleon's troops carried on their march to Moscow. Lest either of these loads be considered exceptional, we should not forget the British troops in the Peninsula who carried about 60 lb., and those at Mons in 1914 who carried only a few pounds less.

It must be noted, however, that the Japanese soldier did not habitually carry a heavy load of rations and equipment, for he prefers to fight as lightly equipped as possible; but the point worthy of note is that if several days' mobility could be achieved only at the price of carrying a load of rations on his back, the Japanese soldier was prepared to carry it.

About the mobility of British troops the Japanese stated: "Although the English Army has some mechanical mobility, in general it does not have much manoeuvrability."

Maintenance of the objective was strongly marked in Japanese operations. Once battle was joined the Japanese pursued their object with the greatest energy and the last ounce of strength, and their indifference to consequences tended to give them a distinct advantage in actions of the "slogging match" type when both sides were approaching exhaustion.

On the other hand, maintenance of the objective was often carried out to a pitch where lack of flexibility became disastrous.

In the Japanese Arakan offensive of February 1944, the Japanese forces were committed to a large enveloping movement intended to annihilate at least two British divisions. The plan, for which a hard and fast time-table had been provided, went drastically wrong soon after first contact, but as days went by it became increasingly clear that no new orders had been issued by higher command. Similarly, in Manipur in April-June 44, the fiction that Imphal could still be captured was maintained by the Japanese 15 Army long after the necessity for a revision of the object should have been clear. The result was the wearing down of the available forces in a series of fruitless attacks to the point where a costly withdrawal could not be avoided.

In their interpretation of the principle of *concentration* the Japanese differed widely from western and particularly German methods in both the assembling and the handling of forces for an operation. The characteristic form of attack mentioned in the para on "Offensive Action" above implied dispersion and involved advance on distant objectives with a number of columns not mutually supporting. Of the initial orders for the Manipur offensive in March 1944, not one mentioned assault on any of the main objectives. To isolate and then encourage the enemy to withdraw was the first object. The destruction of the enemy would come about by the disorganization inherent in some measure in any hasty withdrawal.

In committing forces for the attainment of a main object the Japanese observed the principle of *concentration* in that they held nothing back which could be used, committing even specialist troops in infantry roles. The consequence was that the commander found himself without reserves to influence the further course of the operation. Both in attack and defence reserves in the true sense of the term were conspicuously absent in Japanese practice. Similarly, reinforcements were commonly committed to battle piecemeal, as they arrived.

Economy of force.—By their toughness in defence and their willingness to accept risks and if necessary to leave forces to fight and die unsupported in Sectors not considered vital, the Japanese were able to achieve remarkable success. They were enabled thus to concentrate for their principal effort a high proportion of the total forces. A case in point was the way in which 18 (Jap) Division in the Hukawng and Mogaung valleys was sacrificed to the interests of the Manipur offensive in the spring and summer of 1944.

On the other hand, at all levels ambitious objects were regularly attempted with a strength which in Western armies would be regarded as inadequate. Japanese tactical instructions constantly reiterated that by manoeuvre and especially by superior morale small forces could overcome larger ones. The effect of this tactical doctrine was a tendency to attempt to gain objects out of all proportion to the forces in hand. The striking successes obtained early in the war in East-Asia by small forces against ill-trained or demoralised troops probably helped to confirm this Japanese doctrine.

Security.—The general impression is that the Japanese were less than normally attentive to security. Their deep and often thorough patrolling was often carried out in the interests of offensive action and not of Security; for the security of their own flanks and rear the Japanese tended rather to rely on retention of the initiative. In minor tactics inattention to security was noticeable, and parties on the move or in camp were often unduly liable to surprise.

Training.—In peace the Japanese trained for war. In war they trained for important operations. The severity of their training is worthy of note, and the following extracts from reports by officers who were attached to the Japanese Army before the Second World War give some indication of the thoroughness of their preparations:—

"The autumn manoeuvres of the Guards Division took place in the first half of November in the mountainous region round the semi-active volcano Mount Asama about a hundred miles north-west of Tokyo."

"The weather was extremely severe, the temperature well below freezing point in the day time and considerably colder at night, with snow, rain and high wind... According to the plan of the directing staff, a defensive position should have been occupied the following evening. but owing to the ice and snow the mountain roads had become dangerous for horses and vehicles so that part of the scheme was called off and the division marched on to the starting area for the next phase, whilst that part which was to form the skeleton enemy marched back over the Torii Pass to their billeting area, arriving at about six that evening, surprisingly fresh, considering they had marched some seventy miles in forty-eight hours under very trying conditions..."

Another report:

"The march to camp, a distance of twenty-six miles, was done under company arrangements, after the whole Regiment had left barracks together... On arrival at camp, after an average of eleven hours on the road, all companies carried out P.T. or rifle exercises before the evening meal. The companies of the battalion to which I was attached had breakfast at 4.30 a.m., lunch at 12.30 p.m. and supper at 5.30 p.m."

A third report:

"A full pack and three ammunition pouches were carried on all training .." (This was in 1938. The full weight of equipment carried was approximately 58 lb.).

When war came this tempo was intensified:

"August 25, 1942. Got up at 0300 hours for landing practice. 0400 hours landed and took up battle positions. 0600 hours the first fight ended near swamps. Have breakfast. From about 0800 hours do second attack and defence exercises and then some sea bathing. Return to ship. From 1500 hours cleaning of arms and equipment. How busy we are bathing every day fully equipped. Since formation of unit only 3 hours of sleep per day."

The troops which attacked Malaya were trained in French Indo-China carrying full equipment, *i.e.* 58 lb. Subsequently they advanced down the peninsula carrying the absolute minimum. The practice of making troops carrying more in training than in actual operation is an old one dating back to the time of the Roman legions.

Operations were fully rehearsed. Rehearsals included intensive training under conditions closely approximating those under which they would be required to operate.

Bibliography

This volume is based primarily on official records possessed by the C.I.S. Historical Section. Of these the most important are the war diaries of the various units which took part in the campaigns in Arakan. The Historical Section has an almost complete set of these diaries, particularly of the Indian forces. Though lacking in perspective owing to the nearness of events described, these diaries form the best source of information concerning the operational details and the tactical situation as it developed from day to day.

In addition, there are a number of 'appreciations' written during the course of the war by military officers and men at the top. The contents of these appreciations must have formed the basis for strategy in Arakan and Burma and a study of these is therefore not only valuable but essential.

The 'despatches' written by the different commanders soon after the completion of operations form another useful source for an understanding not only of higher policy but also of the administrative and logistical difficulties inherent in the conduct of a modern military campaign. It is not possible to give a complete list of all the diaries, appreciations and despatches consulted in the writing of this narrative but some of these are listed below.

Translations of interrogations of Japanese prisoners, and captured documents, some of the latter containing Japanese accounts meant for their own Government, are another very useful source of information. These also provide material for checking up certain facts and clearing up some obscure points, which would not otherwise be clear during the operations, on account of the inadequate intelligence system of the Allies. The reports by Japanese Generals and the answers to interrogations are generally very brief, but they are probably the only evidence of Japanese overall conduct of the war in Burma and their processes of reasoning and methods of working. Their intrinsic value is thus very great.

Since ample documentary sources of a primary nature were available, much use has not been made of the secondary published sources or accounts, except perhaps for describing Allied strategy and diplomacy at the highest level. However, a list of these secondary sources which have been consulted is also given below. It will be seen that there are no books dealing exclusively with the fighting in Arakan, but many books on Burma have some chapters or paragraphs about Arakan also. Some of these have also been included in the list.

War Diaries

War Diaries of all units that took part in the Arakan Campaigns, and particularly of the following:—

11th Army Group; Alfsea; Fourteenth Army; XV Indian Corps; 5th Indian Division; 7th Indian Division; 14th Indian Division; 25th Indian Division; 26th Indian Division; and their Brigades; 81st West African Division; 83rd West African Division; 3rd British Commando Brigade; 50th Indian Tank Brigade; 22nd East African Brigade Group; and their subordinate units. Also diaries of administrative units such as Medical, Ordnance, RIASC, Engineers, Signals, etc. These are too numerous to be given in detail.

PLANS AND APPRECIATION, ETC.

Appreciations *Assam/Burma front, 1942-43.*
Strategical Air Plan for defeat of Japan, 1 September 1943 to 5 January 1944.
Plans for *Amphibious Operations.*
Joint Planning Staff's papers particularly Nos 47, 60 and 100.
Outline plan for the *Capture of Akyab.*
HQ Eastern Army *Outline Plan for Operations, 1943-44.*

DESPATCHES, REPORTS, ETC.

Mountbatten's Despatch, *Report to the Combined Chiefs of Staff by the Supreme Allied Commander, South-East Asia.*

Despatch by Vice-Admiral Sir Arthur J. Power on *Naval Operations in Ramree Island Area, 19 January to 22 February 1954.*

Report by Field Marshal Sir Archibald Wavell on *Preparations for the Defence of India after the fall of Rangoon, March-December 1942.*

Despatch by Field Marshal Sir Archibald Wavell, *Operations in India Command, 1 January to 20 June 1943.*

Despatch by Field Marshal Sir Claude J. E. Auchinleck on *Operations in the Indo-Burma Theatre based on India, 21 June 1943 to 15 November 1943.*

Report from India Command by General Sir Claude Auchinleck, 16 November 1943 to 31 May 1944.

Report from India Command by General Sir Claude Auchinleck, 1 June to 31 December 1944.

Report from India Command by Field Marshal Sir Claude Auchinleck, 1 January to 31 December 1945.

Secretary of State's Political Despatch on *the Reorganisation of Commands in India and South-East Asia, 15 November 1943.*

Despatch by A.C.M. Sir Richard Pierse, *Air Operations of the RAF India Command, 1 January 1943 to 30 June 1943.*

Despatch by Air Chief Marshal Sir Richard Pierse on *Development of Air Forces in India and Air Operations for the period 21 June 1943 to 15 November 1943.*

Despatch by General Sir George Giffard C-in-C, 11th Army Group, *Operations in Burma and North-East India, 16 November 1943 to 22 June 1944.*

Despatch by Air Chief Marshal Sir Richard Pierse, *Operations of Air Command South-East Asia, 21 June to 15 November 1943.*

Despatch by Air Chief Marshal Sir Richard Pierse, *Operations of Air Command South-East Asia, 16 November 1943 to 31 May 1944.*

Despatch by Air Chief Marshal Sir Keith Park, *Operations of Air Command South-East Asia, 1 June 1944 to 2 May 1945.*

Despatch by Lieut.-General Stratemeyer, USAAF, *Air Operations in Eastern Air Command S.E.A., 15 December 1943 to 31 May 1944.*

Despatch by Air Vice-Marshal the Earl of Bandon, *Operation of 224 Group RAF, primarily in support of the Arakan Campaign, 15 October 1944 to 15 May 1945.*

Despatch by Air Commodore S. F. Vincent, covering *Operations of 221 Group during the Manipur Campaign, 1 March 1944 to 31 July 1944.*

Despatch by Air Commodore S. F. Vincent, covering *Operations of 221 Group during the first phase of advance into Burma, 1st August 1944 to 31 March 1945.*

XV Indian Corps Despatch, *History of the Arakan Campaign.*

Report on *Operations, December 1943 to February 1944* by Research Directorate of the 11th Army Group.

Despatch by SACSEA for period 1943-45, *General Naval Survey of SEAC.*

OTHER OFFICIAL DOCUMENTS

HQ Notes on *The Interpretation of Japanese military installations in Burma.*

The Japanese Campaign in Arakan, December 1943 to February 1944 (MID).

Japanese Campaign in Arakan 1942-43 (MID).

Japanese operations in Burma, August 1943 to August 1945 (Intelligence Division HQ SACSEA).

A brief History of 22 (EA) Inf Bde during operation in Burma, July 1944 to November 1945.

Weekly review of *Operations in SEAC.*

Joint Planning Staff Papers (Secret) regarding *Akyab and Andamans.*

UNIT HISTORIES (MANUSCRIPT)

History of the 5th Indian Division.

History of the 7th Indian Division and manuscript histories of other divisions involved.

JAPANESE ACCOUNTS, DOCUMENTS AND ANSWERS TO INTERROGATIONS

Japanese Methods (Interrogation reports—relevant numbers).

The Japanese Accounts of their operations in Burma, December 1941 to August 1945. Edited and issued by HQ 12th Army.

History of 33 Japanese Division.

Short History of Japanese 55 Division.

Report of the Conference between British and Japanese Commanders in Burma held at HQ Burma Command on 12 February 1946.

Discussions with Japanese Generals—interesting points on Burma Operations.

R.A.F. Questionnaire.

Questions concerning Japanese Air Force (with answers).

Short History of 54 Japanese Division.

Japanese Intelligence Organisation at HQ Burma Area Army.

Interrogation of Vice-Admiral Tanaka, Raizo.

A Japanese Officer's Account of *RAF attacks.*

Interrogation of General Kimura, Hyotaro—G.O.C., Burma Area Army.

Interrogation Report on Rear Admiral Chudo (SEATIC).

Interrogation Reports on other Japanese Officers.

Memorandum by Rear Admiral Chudo on *The Causes of Japanese Defeat.*

Personalities—Military Careers of some High Ranking Japanese officers.

Translations of Miscellaneous Japanese documents.

The Kohima Battle, April-June 1944.

Official Report on *Japanese Operations in Burma* being Field Marshal Teruchi's account.

SECONDARY SOURCES

The Military side of Japanese life, Capt. M. D. Kennedy, 1924.
Some aspects of Japan and Her Defence Forces, Capt. M. D. Kennedy, 1928.
Japan must fight Britain, Ishimaru, 1936.
Races of Burma. Handbooks for the Indian Army, compiled under the orders of the Government of India by Major C. M. Enriquez, 1933.
Far East in Ferment, Guenther Stein, 1936.
War Moves East, Strategicus.
Japan's Emergence as a Modern State, E. Herbert Norman, 1940.
Japan and the Modern World, Sir John Pratt, 1942.
A Million Died, a story of War in the Far East, Alfred Wagg, 1943, (relevant portions).
Kessing's *Contemporary Archives*.
Behind the Japanese Mask, The Right Hon. Sir Robert Craigie, GCMG, CB, His Majesty's Ambassador to Japan (1937-42), 1945.
Through Japanese Barbed Wire, G. Priestwood, 1944.
"Speaking Generally" Broadcasts, Orders and Addresses in time of war, General Sir Archibald Wavell, C-in-C India (1941-43), 1946.
Japanese Offensive in Burma.
Gazetteer of Arakan.
Gazetteer of Assam.
The Military Viceroy (Wavell), Burbidge.
Wavell, Kiernan.
The Fighting Fifth.
The Last Viceroy (Mountbatten), R. Murphy.
Ball of Fire (the Fifth Indian Division in the Second World War), Anthony Brett-James, 1951.
Manipur 1944—A documentary Record, Auchinleck.
Burma, Ma Mya Sein.
Burma Pamphlets, (relevant numbers).
Japan and the Modern World, Sir John Pratt.
The Strategy of the South-East Asia Campaign. A lecture given by Admiral the Viscount Mountbatten of Burma to the Royal United Service Institution.
Monsoon Victory, Gerald Hanley.
A Traveller's War, Alaric Jacob.
With the 14th Army, D. F. Karaka.
A Record of the War (relevant volumes), Philip Graves.
The Campaign in Burma, Frank Owen.
The War in Burma, Roy McKelvie.

INDEX

Ajmer Regt. 2nd Bn., 273.
Akyab, 55, 65-6, 111-2, 182, 188, 265, 282, Recapture of, 213-21.
Alethangyaw, 25.
Allied Air-craft,
    P-47s, 218.
    Hurri Bombers, 218, 219, 247.
    Spitfires, 218.
    P-38s, 218.
    B-25s, 218.
    Beaufighters, 219.
    Mitchells, 219.
    Thunderbolts, 219.
Amir H.M.I.S., 269.
Angus, Brigadier T.H., DSO., 148.
Animal Transport Coy. 18th, 190.
    39th, 189.
Anti-tank Battery 205th, 128.
    284th, 126.
Anti-tank Regt. 22nd, 196, 228.
    24th, 125.
Apaukwa, 34, 139, 212.
Appreciation by Director of Military Operations in GHQ, India, (28 March 1942), 14.
Arakan,
    Occupation of by the British, 4; Topography of, 6-10; Land and its People, 1-10; Planning for the offensive in, 11-22; Indian Lines of Communications in, 23-4; Japanese Lines of Communications in, 24-5; Monsoon Operation in, 89; Allies resume offensive in, 139-62; Operations during Monsoon in, 164-78; Post-monsoon operations in, 179-94; Operation 'ROMULUS' in, 195-212; Operation 'TALON' in, 213-21; Operation BLOCKADE in,
Archibald Campbell, Sir, 4, 5.
Army Commanders, 1, 5, 234.
Atet Nanra, 72-5, 87.
A.W.D. 76 Ind. Inf. W/Shop Company, 189-90.
Baluch Regt., 8/10th, 34, 68, 79.
    14/10th, 151-2, 158-9, 161, 164, 169, 172, 174-5, 189, 240, 243, 257-60, 297, 299, 301-3.
    16/10th, 148, 150, 160, 164, 168, 174-5, 191, 199-200, 202, 209, 248-53.
Bangona, Capture of, 113, 114.
Basu, Capt. S.N., 129.
Batarai, 60, 63.
Bawli Bazar, 27-9, 89, 91, 142, 148, 161, 167.
Bhan Bhagta Gurung, Rifleman, 300.
Bhandari Ram Sepoy, 200.
Bison Force, 173.

Bolster Force, 165-6, 168-9, 173-4.
Bombay Burma Trading Corporation, 5.
Bombay Grenadiers 4th, 193, 255.
Bose Brigade (of I.N.A.), 165-6, 182.
Brasdley, Wing Comdr., Chief Civil Affairs Officer for Arakan, 221.
Briggs, Major-General H.R., D.S.O., Comdr. 5th Indian Div., 101, 145.
British Brigade Group 6th, 22, 32-3, 56, 66, 71, 73-80, 82, 84, 90, 91.
British Div. 2nd, 103.
    5th, 14.
Buchanan Captain, R.A.N., 190.
Buthidaung, 26, 30, 33, 51, 84, 87, 103, 105, 111, 115, 118-9, 122, 142-4, 146, 161, 182, 186, 190-1, 193, 205, 207, Operations in, 25-35; Initial advance to, 25; Occupied by Japanese, 27-8; Bombing of, 28, 31; Japanese withdrawal from, 32.
Cavalry, 45 I.A.C., 194, 206.
Cavendish, Brigadier, 76.
Cheduba Island, Operations in, 273.
Chittagong, 32, 93, 265, Defence of, 25-6.
Christison, Lieut-General A.F.P., CB., MC., 96, 98-9, 106, 108-9, 138, 213.
Churchill, Sir Winston., Prime Minister of England, suggests a combined operation across the Bay of Bengal, 19.
Claude Raymond, 304.
Coldstream Brig. G.A.P., 148.
Commando Brigade 3rd, 197, 201, 215, 217-9, 230-3, 236, 243, 246, 283, 285, 287, 291-2.
Conference
    Between Col. Tanahashi, Comdg. Japan's *112th Regt.* and Chief of Staff *55th Div.* (20-3-43), 75.
Corps XV HQ, 79.
Cox's Bazar, 27-9, 32, 84, 91-3, 96, 141, 161, 214.
Curtis, Brigadier A.C., DSO, MC, Commander, Mayforce, 56.
Daingbon Village, Attack on, 247.
Davies, Major-General H.L., 148, 185.
Dawell, Brig. A.J. DSO, MBE, 292.
Divisional Anti-tank Regt., 210.
Divisional Reconnaissance Regt., 210, 212.
Dogra 1/17th, 40-1, 43-4, 47-8, 70, 82, 108.
Dohazari, 34, 84.
Doi Force, 115.
Donald, Lt.-Colonel, 29.
Donbaik, 44, 52, 61, 71, 87, 186, 203; Fighting at, 35-40; Further attack on, 45; Japanese defence of, 62; Final attack on, 65-6.

Dragoons Regimental Group (Tanks), 107-8, 123-5, 128, 130-1, 137, 142, 160.
Drake, Wing Comr. D.F.C., R.A.F., 234.
Durham Light Infantry 2nd, 81.
Earl of Bandon, Air-Vice Marshal, 213.
East African Brigade Group, 22nd, 180, 182, 191, 208, 232, 274, 278, 281, 287, 302, 304-6.
Eastern Army, Issues an Operational Instruction (17 Oct. 1942), 21, 25.
Engineer Battalion H.Q., 125.
Field Ambulance 66th, 123.
Field Company Indian Engineers 93rd, 172, 288.
   425th, 172.
Field Regiment 13th, 82.
   130th, 36, 77, 81, 142.
   136th, 126, 142.
   139th, 142.
Field Regt. R.A. 8th, 161, 189, 261, 320.
   27th, 190-1, 238, 247, 261, 291-2, 295.
   160th, 271, 275-7.
Field Security Section 606th, 189-90.
Flamingo, H.M.S., 269, 292.
Force Wellington, 264, 273.
Foul Point, 32-4, 65-6, 160, 182, 189-90, 203, 207-9, 216, 218.
Frontier Force Regt. 14/12th, 33.
Frontier Force Rifles 2/13th, 153, 278, 281, 304-6.
   8/13th, 83, 273-4.
Giffard, General Sir George, 101, 119.
Goppe Bazar, 28, 31-2, 89, 91, 94, 142, 167, 176, 187-8.
G.P.T. Company 68th, R.I.A.S.C., 189.
Green Howards, 2nd Bn., 306.
Gurkha Rifles 1/8th, 153-5.
   3/2nd, 160, 165-6, 169-70, 172, 189, 240-1, 298-9.
   3/9th, 81.
   4/1st, 106, 126, 145.
   4/5th, 94, 100, 104, 120-1.
   4/8th, 85, 101, 104, 122-3, 142.
Gwalior Lancers, 104.
Hardy, Brig. C.R., 234-5.
Hgerty, Brig. B.C., D.S.O., Commander 53 Ind. Inf. Bde., 223.
Hill, Capt. D., D.S.O., Royal Navy, 234.
Hirst, Brig., J.E., D.S.O., 148, 189, 202.
Hoey, Major, 135.
Hold Force, 210-2.
'Hook' Operation, 104, 120.
Hoshi Detachment, 68.
Htizwe, 34, 57-8, 65-6, 182, Attack on, 69, 207.
Hunt Brigadier, 66.
Hutton, Brig. R.A., 191, 202, 249, 251.
Hyderabad 8/19th, 150-1, 159, 164, 168, 170, 191, 198-9, 202, 208-9, 220, 248-50, 254, 258, 260.
I.A.C. 19 Lancers, 193.
I.A.C. 45 Cavalry, 193.
I.C.P. R.I.A.S.C., 35th, 189-91.
Independent Bde. Group 20th, 18.

Indian Anti-tank Regt. 7th, 190, 201, 261.
Indian Bearer Coy. No. 1, 261.
Indian Corps IV, 146-7.
   XV, 15, 20, 91, 96, 99, 102-3, 105, 108, 113-4, 116, 119-20, 124, 132-3, 139, 140-1, 145-6, 149, 151, 160-1, 164-6, 168, 174, 176-7, 179-80, 192-3, 205, 211, 213-4, 217-8, 220-1, 228, 232, 234, 243, 248, 281, 283, 285-7, 289, 292, 298, 305.
   XXXIII, 305.
Indian Division 5th, 96, 98-9, 100-3, 105-9, 110, 117-9, 130-1, 133-5, 141, 145-8, 158.
   7th, 26, 93, 95-6, 98-9, 100-1, 103, 105, 108-9, 110, 114, 117-9, 121, 123-5, 128-31, 133-5, 140, 142-3, 145-9, 161.
   14th, 15, 20, 22, 26-9, 31-5, 47, 50, 52, 56, 60, 65-6, 71, 73, 75, 77-8.
   25th, 146-51, 158-62, 164-5, 168-9, 173-4, 180-2, 184-9, 192-4, 197-8, 200-1, 208, 216-8, 231-2, 234, 240, 259, 262, 282-8, 291, 295, 297, 299, 300-3.
   26th, 15, 20, 56, 79, 84, 89-91, 93-4, 119, 133, 135, 142, 145, 147-9, 152, 161, 166-7, 176, 180-2, 194, 198, 215, 231-2, 264, 271, 281, 283, 285, 287, 289, 296, 303, 305.
   36th, 119, 142, 149.
Indian Divisional Artillery 25th, 247.
Indian Field Ambulance 56th, 191.
   58th, 190, 261.
   61st, 189, 261.
Indian Field Company 4/25th, 190.
   63rd, 191, 199, 237, 303.
   93rd, 189.
   425th, 204-5.
Indian Field Regt. 5th, 161.
   7th, 107, 126, 142.
Indian Infantry Brigade 4th, 56-7, 72-3, 78-84, 90-2, 134-5, 152-3, 167, 176-7, 231, 264, 270, 274, 278, 288, 303-6.
   9th, 99, 106, 108, 121, 145.
   14th, 84, 90-91.
   23rd, 84, 90-91.
   29th, 141.
   33rd, 96, 100-1, 103, 105, 125-6, 128-9, 130, 137, 142.
   36th, 80, 82, 89, 92, 134, 146, 151, 161, 192, 216, 231, 264-5, 273-4, 278, 280, 305.
   47th, 26, 31, 33, 35-6, 39, 47, 56, 71-5, 77, 79-80, 82, 298.
   49th, 26.
   51st, 147-50, 159, 161, 164, 168, 175, 185-6, 188, 191, 193-4, 197-8, 200-2, 208-9, 222, 232, 243, 246, 248-9, 251, 254-6, 258-9, 261, 285, 296-7.
   53rd, 148, 150-2, 158-9, 161, 164, 175, 185, 188, 190, 193, 197, 201-3, 205-8, 216-7, 222, 225, 213-2, 234,

243, 247, 258, 287, 290-2, 294-5, 297, 302, 304.
71st, 47, 56-7, 72, 79-82, 89, 92, 133, 167, 215, 231, 264, 265-6, 270, 274, 279, 280-1, 305.
55th, 26, 31, 33, 39, 41, 45-7, 56, 62, 65-6, 69-70, 79-80, 82-3, 86, 89-91, 96.
74th, 148, 150, 159, 161, 165--6, 168, 175, 186, 188, 190-1, 194, 197-8, 200-1, 203, 207-8, 216-8, 220, 225, 232, 235, 240-2, 243-4, 257, 278, 288, 295-9, 300, 313.
88th, 26, 31.
89th, 94-6, 100, 105-6, 119, 121, 123, 128, 130, 142-3.
114th, 93-6, 101-3, 107-8, 120-1, 125-6, 134, 137, 144.
123rd, 26-9, 30-1, 33-5, 44-5, 47-8, 56, 66, 79, 82, 99, 102-3, 107, 134, 145, 148.
161st, 99, 101, 107, 145.
Indian Mountain Regt., 34, 104, 120, 120, 126, 190.
Indian Mule Company 18th, 131.
Indian National Army, 110, 131, 165, 188.
Indian Tank Brigade 50th, 180, 193, 283, 285.
Indin, 186.
Indin-Sinoh area, Fighting in, 74-81.
Infantry Regt. 213th, 40.
Irwin, Lt-General N.M.S., C.B., D.S.O., M.C., General Officer Commanding Eastern Army, 22, 72.
Inniskillings 1st, 33, 36, 38, 44, 46-8.
Japan, counter-attacks in Arakan, 51-5; advances northwards, 56-64.
Japan's Lines of Communication in Arakan, 23.
Japan's moves and countermoves, 86.
Japanese forces in Arakan, 51-5.
  Ancillary Troops, 111, 116.
  Cavalry Regt. 55th, 69, 111-2, 115-6, 165, 182.
  Division 2nd, 165.
    33rd, 64, 72.
    54th, 140, 188, 225, 227, 284, 287, 293, 295.
    55th, 54, 58, 61, 64, 68, 72, 74, 108, 110-1, 121, 175, 192, 230, 285, 287, 289, 293.
  Divisional Infantry Group, 113, 115, 128.
  Division Signals 55th, 59, 116.
  Doi Force, 115-7, 122, 125, 128, 130, 135.
  Independent Anti-tank Battalion, 116.
  Infantry Regt. 213th, 25, 51-2, 54, 57-9, 60, 63, 67, 69, 70, 74-5, 78, 86, 111, 116.
  Jungle Battery 503, 126.
  Jungle Field Regt. 27th, 150.
  Kawashima Force, 115.
  Kubo Force, 111, 113, 115, 117, 121, 125, 131, 133-4.
  Medical Unit, 116.
  Medium Artillery Regt., 111, 116.
  Mountain Artillery, 55th, 59, 67-8, 111-2, 116.
  Ordnance Unit, 116.
  Platoon, Machine Gun Company No. 1, 113.
  Regiment 11th, 111, 113, 115-6, 216, 222, 227, 230, 293.
    112th, 52-4, 57-9, 60-1, 63, 67-70, 74-5, 77-8, 85-6, 111-2, 114-6, 121-2, 124, 129, 141.
    121st, 265, 284, 293.
    143rd, 53-4, 60, 62, 74, 77-8, 85-8, 109, 111, 113-6, 121-2, 133, 165, 182, 207.
    144th, 111, 113, 115-6, 222, 227, 230, 287, 293.
    154th, 227, 230, 255, 293.
    214th, 62, 88.
  Regiment Reconnaissance 54th, 230, 241, 293.
  River Crossing Materials Company 10th, 116.
  Sakurai Volunteer Platoon, 112, 140-1.
  Tanahashi Regiment 58th, 116-8, 120-1.
  Task Force, 176.
  Transport Regiment 55th, 115-6.
  Veterinary Unit, 116.
  Yoshida Force, 116.
Jat Regiment, 3rd, 145-6.
  9th, 33, 36, 46, 176.
Joint Planning Staff, Examines the possibility of recapturing Burma (May 1942), 15-6; Prepares another Plan for Operations in Burma (July 1942), 17-8.
Jumna H.M.I.S., 235.
Kaladan Detachment, 68-9.
Kaladan River, 8, 10, 26, 34, 57, 61, 68, 73, 48-5, 88, 138-40, 161, 167, 175, 177, 181, 183-4, 193, 209, 216-7, 222, 224, 283, Japanese offensive from, 66.
Kalapanzin river, 31, 34, 108, 111, 113, 115, 161, 175, 182, 185-8, 190-1.
Kanetoshi Unit, 114, 116.
Kangaw Battle, 243-62, 283-5, 291, 296-7.
Katamura Shihachi, Lt-General, G.O.C. Japanese 15th Army, 292.
Kawashima, Colonel, Japanese 55th Division Cavalry Regiment, 112.
Kawashima Force, 115.
King's African Rifles 1st, 305.
King's Own Scottish Borderers 2nd, 95, 100, 105-6, 122-3, 144.
Kistna H.M.I.S., 269, 292.
Knowland, Lieut., G.A., 256.
Koba, Major-General, (Japanese), 188, 230-1.
Kobayashi, Lt-Colonel Japanese Artillery Unit, 116.
Kodingauk, 36.
Koga, Lt-General, Commander Japanese 55th Division, 57.
Kyaukit, 146; Battle at, 144.

Kyaukpyu township, 263-71, 278, 281-2, 296.
Kyauktaw, 62, 139; Attack on, 69.
Kyeyebyin, Battle at 225-7.
Kwazon, 206-7.
Labawa, 195.
Lambaguna, 35.
Lancers 19th, 191, 193-4, 205, 241, 248, 255, 258, 286, 288, 299.
Lancashire Fusiliers 10th, 35, 44-5, 48, 66, 82.
Lees, Squadron Leader, D.T., R.A.F., 235.
Leese, General Sir Oliver, Bt., KCB, CBE, DSO, 213.
Light Anti-Aircraft Battery 86th, 126.
    491st, 128.
Light Anti-Aircraft Regiment, 124th, 128.
Lincolnshire Regiment, 1st, 48, 82, 93, 134, 266-73, 275-6, 278-80.
Llyod, General W.L., Comdg. 14th Indian Division, 72.
Lomax, Major-General C.E.N., OBE, DSO, MC, 72, 79-80.
Mahrattas 5th, 138.
    17th, 150-1, 159, 161, 165, 170, 172, 190, 204.
Mahratta Light Infantry 17/5th, 207, 209, 228, 258, 291, 294-5.
Mandalay, 283.
Marine Force, 264.
Martin, Rear Admiral B.C.S., 213.
Martin Force, 273.
Matsu Force, 188, 217, 222, 230, 243-4, 255, 257, 259.
Maungdaw, 26-7, 30-1, 33, 51, 82, 89, 93, 102-3, 105, 110-1, 113-4, 119, 141, 160, 162, 164, 169, 180, 185; Operations in, 26-35; Initial advance to, 26; Occupied by Japanese, 27-8; Bombing of, 28; Japanese withdrawal from 32; Final withdrawal and evacuation of, 83-8.
Mayforce, 89.
Mayu River, 10, 26-7, 30, 34-5, 51, 65-6, 81, 88, 98, 108, 118, 181-2, 184, 186, 194, 198, 216.
Mayu Range, Operations in, 72-4, 197.
Me Chaung, 297-8.
Medium Regt. 1st, 142.
    6th, 105, 107, 128, 142, 189, 247.
Messervy, General F.W. Comdr., 7th Indian Division, 124, 126.
Minbya, Occupation of, 228.
Miyazaki Shigesaburo, Maj-General Comdg. Japanese 31st Division Infantry Group, 293.
Mountain Regiment, 24th, 128.
    30th, 196, 210.
Mountbatten, Admiral Lord Louis (Earl), Supreme Allied Commander, South-East Asia, 96, 117, 179.
Mowdok, 195.
Mrawchaung, 69-70.
Mule Company, 63rd, 126.
Murayama, Colonel, Comdr., Japanese Field Engrs., 255-6.

Myebon, 247, 261, 291, 296, Landing at, 230-42.
Myinbu, 78.
Myohaung, 2; Fall of, 212, 227, 252, 284.
Naf River, 26, 160, Origin of, 8.
Nand Singh Naik, V.C., 143.
Napier, H.M.A.S., 235, 237, 269.
Narbada, H.M.I.S., 235, 237, 247, 292.
Naval Bombardment Force, 265.
Nigeria Regiment, 4th, 195-6.
    5th, 301-2.
Nott, Capt. M.H. St.L., R.I.N., 235.
Oxf Bucks, 148, 152, 160, 165-6, 169, 174, 189, 202-3, 221, 240, 243, 257-8, 299.
O'Carrol Scott, Brig., A.G., 190.
Pagoda Hill, Capture of, 139.
Paladin, H.M.S., 281.
Paletwa, 34, 195-7.
Parkash Singh, Havildar, V.C., 38-9.
Pathfinder H.M.S., 271-3, 281.
Phoebe, H. M. S., 235, 240, 269.
Pi-Chaung area, 195, 211.
Pioneer Company 1st, 126.
Punjab Regiment,
    1/1st, 108, 145
    2/1st, 40-1, 43-4, 46-7, 65-6, 70, 82, 102.
    5/1st, 266-9, 270-3, 275, 278-9, 280-1.
    2/2nd, 158-9, 161, 164, 169, 191, 200, 202, 208, 249, 250-4.
    3/2nd, 102.
    7/2nd, 95, 100, 104, 106, 122, 123, 126, 144.
    2/8th, 77, 82.
    5/8th, 33-4, 38, 46, 71.
    8/8th, 81.
    4/14th, 94, 101, 104, 120, 122, 144.
    1/15th, 26-8, 44-5, 48, 66, 82.
    4/15th, 100, 103, 125-6, 137, 142, 144.
    7/15th, 82.
    9/15th, 48, 82.
    7/16th, 138, 140, 189-91, 209, 222-3, 225-7, 231-2, 234, 256, 258-60, 296-7, 299-303.
Queens 1st, 103, 125, 137, 142, 144.
Queen Elizabeth H.M.S., 269.
R.A.C. 146 Regiment, 193-4, 215, 276.
R.A.F. 224 Group, 213, 283, 292.
Rajput Regiment,
    1/7th, 30, 34, 36, 38-9, 47.
    2/7th, 152-4, 156-8, 176, 264, 270, 278-9, 304-6.
    4/7th, 107, 145.
Ramree Island, 293, 305; Invasion of, 263-81.
Rapid H.M.S., 269.
Rathedaung, 46, 52, 54, 56, 60-1, 65, 74; Bombing at, 26, 32-6; Attack on, 44; Japanese resistance at, 51; Defence of, 57; Japanese offensive from, 56.
Razabil Village, 31, 106, 110, 114, 141, 145-6, 148, 161, 170, 186, 192, 200-1.
Read, Rear Admiral, A.A., CB., 218.

Reconnaissance Regiment 81st, 196, 212.
Royal Armoured Corps Regiment 146th, 40, 264, 304.
Royal Berks, 1st, 73-4, 76, 82.
Royal Scotts, 1st, 76, 82.
Royal Engineers, 199, 272, 275, 278.
Royal Garhwal Rifles.
  1/18th, 266-7, 269-72, 274-7, 280-1, 305-6.
  4/18th, 159, 161, 164, 169, 176-7, 190, 205-9, 220, 222, 224, 227-8, 258, 291, 294.
Royal Marine Commandos, 234.
Royal Welch Fusiliers, 82.
Royal West Kents, 145.
Ruywa, 292, 295-6.
Sakurai, Detached Force (Japanese), 165, 230.
Sakurai, Major General, Comdg. Japanese 55th Division Infantry Group, 112, 116, 128, 130, 165, 176, 188.
Sakurai Volunteer Platoon (Japanese), 112.
Saugan Chaung, 36.
Scott, Brig., A.G.O'C., O.B.E., 202.
Sen, Colonel, L.P., 202.
Sher Shah, L/Nk., 226.
Sierra Leone Regiment, 1st, 195.
Sikhs, 1/11th, 126, 137, 142-5.
  6/11th, 82.
Sinoh, 115, Attack on, 74-81.
Sinohbyin, Attack on, 128.
Slim, General Sir William, CB, CBE, DSO, MC, Comdr. Fourteenth Army, 80-1, 84, 95, 96, 119, 137. Issues Operation Instruction, 92.
Somerset Light Infantry, 94, 100, 104, 120.
Soutcol Force, 34.
South-East Asia Command, 96, 98, 116.
Special Service Brigade 3rd, 159, 181, 198, 215, 230.
Strategic Air Command, 107.
Suffolks 2nd, 108.
Tactical Air Force, Third, 105.
Tamandu, 297, 306, Operations against, 298.
Tanahashi, Colonel, Comdr. Japanese 112th Regiment, 57, 60-1, 63, 68, 74-6, 78, 128-30, 134. Appreciation of the Situation by, 58.
Tanahashi Detachment (Japanese), 58, 116-8, 120-1, 123-5, 129-30, 133-5, 137, 161.
Taung Bazar, 28, 30-4, 68, 84, 91, 94, 117, 121, 124, 161, 188, 192, 194, 206, 210.

Taunghlamah Village, 44, 45.
Taungup, 53, 305-6.
Thibaw, King, 5.
Thimayya, Major, K.S., 159, 202, 208.
Thorat, Lieut-Colonel, S.P.P., 202.
Treaty of Yandabo between General Campbell and Ba-gyi-daw (February 1826), 5.
Tripforce, 34.
Tripura Rifles, 1st, 167.
Ukhia, 28, 40.
Umrao Singh, Havildar, 30 Mtn. Regt., 210.
Usman, Major, M., 200.
"V" Force, 189-90, 200.
Wavell, General Sir Archibald, P.
  C-in-C in India, 11; Appreciation of the situation by, 12, 30; Despatch to the British War Cabinet by, 13; Comments on the Joint Planning Staff Plan (May and July 1942), 16-7; Issues Operation Instruction (17 Sept. 1942), 19-20.
West African Brigade,
  1st, 192-4, 201, 204-6, 211, 227-8, 259, 283, 288, 301, 303, 305-6.
  2nd, 192-4, 200, 204-5, 207, 257, 259, 284, 286, 289, 291, 295, 297-8, 305-6.
  4th, 192-4, 200, 206-7, 210, 212, 259, 283, 285, 289, 301-3, 306.
  5th, 195-7, 221.
  6th, 195-6, 209-11.
West African Division,
  81st, 96, 98, 102-3, 107-8, 117, 138-40, 142, 149, 161, 167, 177, 180-5, 192-5, 209-12, 217, 224-5, 227, 230, 232, 251, 281.
  82nd, 180-2, 185, 188, 190, 192-4, 197, 201, 203, 205-7, 210, 227, 230, 232, 243-4, 254, 257, 259, 283, 285-7, 289, 296, 298, 302-3, 306.
West Hill, 45.
West Yorks, 102, 107, 128-31.
Wiltshire Regiment, 153.
Wood, Major General, G.N., OBE, MC, 185, 218, 234, 259, 296.
Yagi, Colonel, (Japanese), 230.
Yamaguchi, Lieutenant (Japanese) 67.
York & Lancaster, 161, 164, 168, 174, 185, 190, 198-201, 205-7, 223-4, 258, 290-1, 294, 297.
Yoshida Force, 116, 148.
Zadidaung, Battle at, 144.

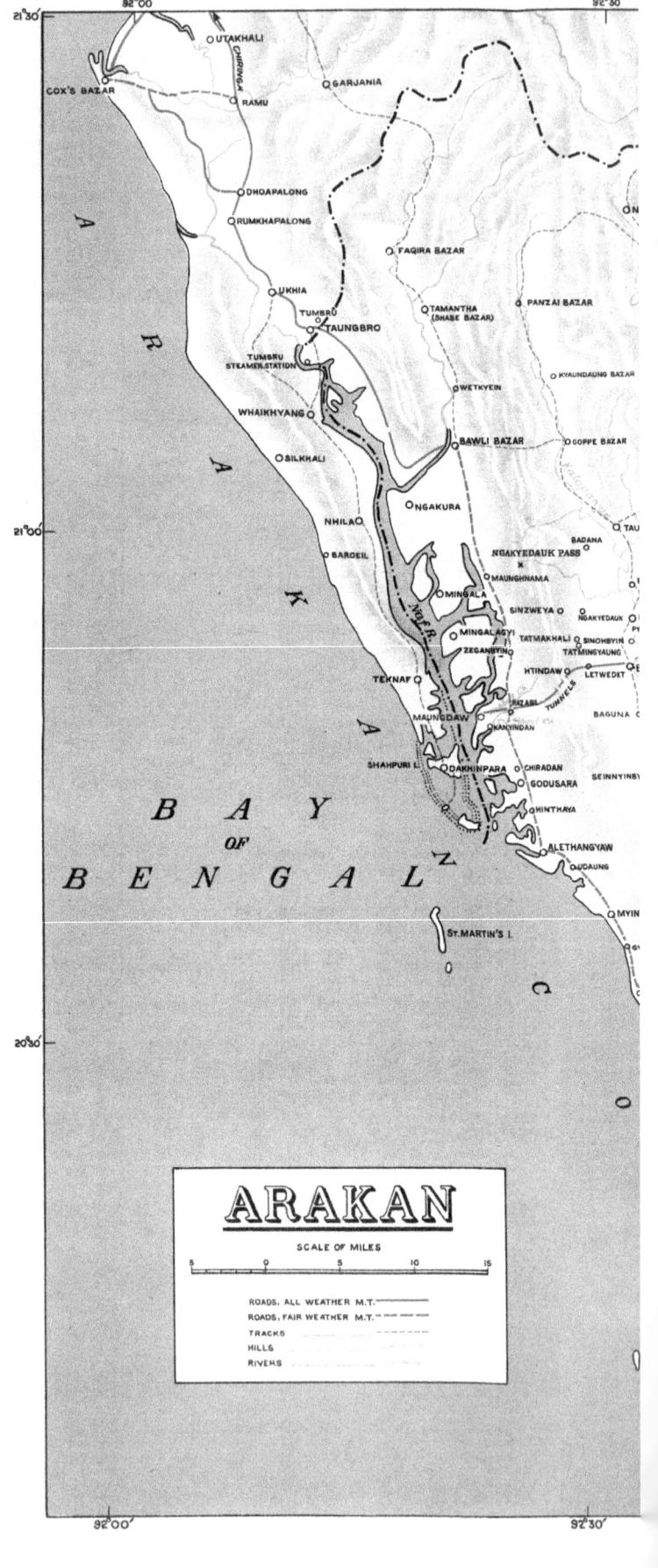

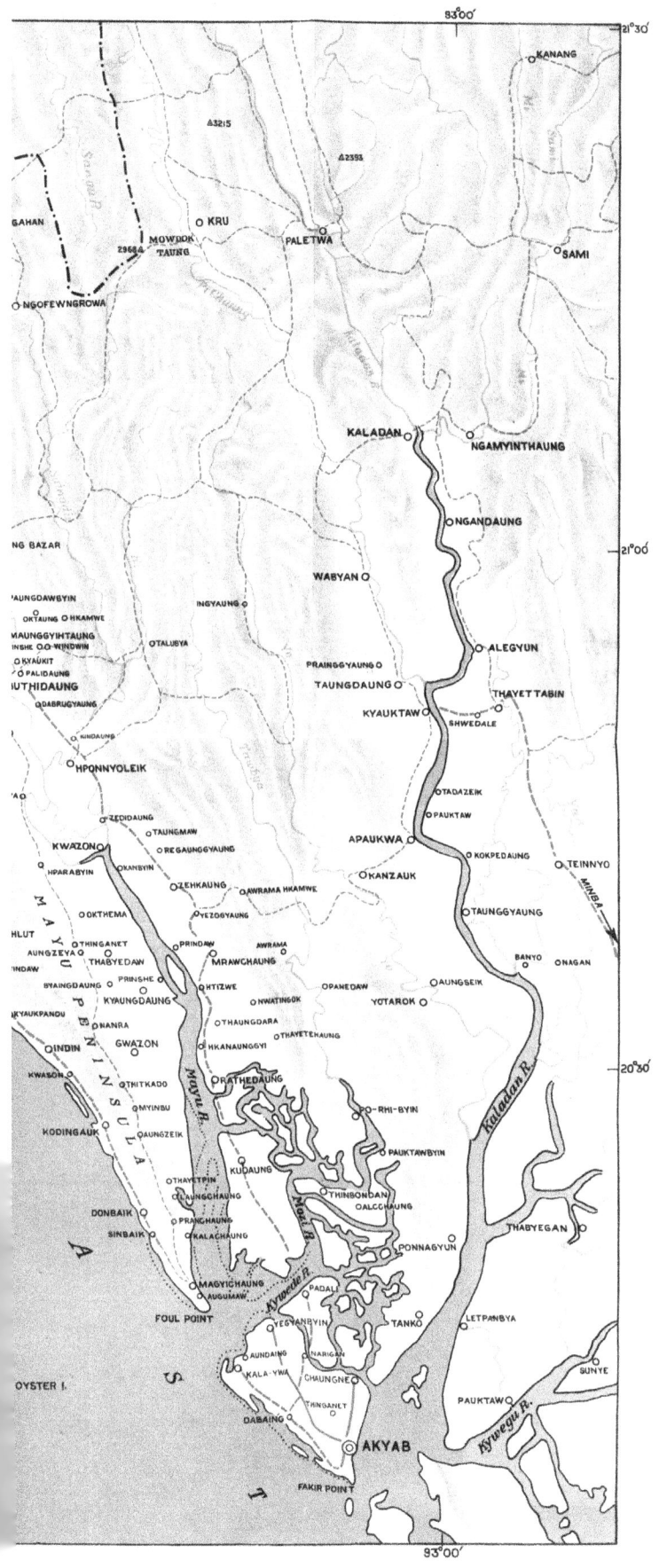

INDIAN DIVISIONS WON A FINE REPUTATION IN WORLD WAR TWO

Field Marshal Auchinleck, Commander-in-Chief of the British Indian Army from 1942, asserted that the British "*couldn't have come through both wars (World War I and II) if they hadn't had the British Indian Army*". British Prime Minister Winston Churchill also paid tribute to "*the unsurpassed bravery of Indian soldiers and officers*".

Between 1945 and 1947, the Director of Public Relations, War Department, Government of India, published a series of short publications covering the individual histories of the WWII Indian Divisions. They followed a consistent format, having between 44 and 48 pages within illustrated soft card covers. They have an average of 50 monochrome photographic illustrations, and each has a full colour centrespread depicting a scene from the Division's wartime operations (drawn by official war artists). They were printed at various presses in Bombay and New Delhi, and each contains at least one map.

As condensed histories they are useful – particularly those which relate to Divisions for which no other record was ever produced.

The British Indian Army during World War II began the war, in 1939, numbering just under 200,000 men. By the end of the war, it had become the largest volunteer army in history, rising to over 2.5 million men in August 1945. Serving in divisions of infantry, armour and a fledgling airborne force, they fought on three continents: in Africa, Europe and Asia.

This Army fought in Ethiopia against the Italian Army, in Egypt, Libya, Tunisia and Algeria against both the Italian and German Army and, after the Italian surrender, against the German Army in Italy. However, the bulk of the British Indian Army was committed to fighting the Japanese Army, first during the British defeats in Malaya and the retreat from Burma to the Indian border; later, after resting and refitting for the victorious advance back into Burma, as part of the largest British Empire army ever formed. These campaigns cost the lives of over 87,000 Indian service- men, while another 34,354 were wounded, and 67,340 became prisoners of war. Their valour was recognised with the award of some 4,000 decorations, and 18 members of the British Indian Army were awarded the Victoria Cross or the George Cross.

RED EAGLES
The Story of the 4th Indian Division
9781474537520

During the Second World War, the 4th Indian Division was in the vanguard of nine campaigns in the Mediterranean theatre, Egypt, Eritrea, Syria, Tunisia, Italy and Greece. The 4th Division captured 150,000 prisoners and suffered 25,000 casualties, more than the strength of a whole division. It won over 1,000 honours and awards, which included four Victoria Crosses and three George Crosses. Field Marshal Lord Wavell wrote: "The fame of this Division will surely go down as one of the greatest fighting formations in military history."

THE FIGHTING FIFTH
History of the 5th Indian Division
9781474537513

As described in much greater detail in Anthony Brett James's book 'The Ball of Fire', the division saw active service in East Africa, North Africa and Burma.

GOLDEN ARROW
The Story of the 7th Indian Division
9781474537506

The role of this division is also duplicated by a much larger work: the book by Brig. M. R. Roberts. However, this booklet gives a good account of Kohima and Imphal and the crossing of the Irrawaddy. In 1945, the division was flown into Siam, so becoming the first Allied formation to re-enter South East Asia.

BLACK CAT DIVISION
17th Indian Division
9781474537483

This formation was committed to Burma from the early days when the British were in full flight from the invading Japanese. It remained in Burma right through to the end, when the starving remnants of the Japanese Army were making their own desperate retreat.

ONE MORE RIVER
The Story of the 8th Indian Division
Biferno, Trigno, Sangro, Moro, Rapido, Arno, Senio, Santerno, Po, Adige

9781474537490

The 8th Indian Division started its overseas service in the Middle East in the garrisoning of Iraq and then the invasion of Persia to secure the oil fields of the area for the Allies, before moving to Italy in 1943. Landing at Taranto, it pushed up the length of the peninsula in a series of major battles: breaking the Sangro Line, forcing the Rapido and turning the defences at Cassino, breaking the stubborn German resistance at Monte Grande and, finally, forcing the Po River. It won four VCs, 26 DSOs and 149 MCs along the way. During the war the 8th Indian Division sustained casualties totalling 2,012 dead, 8,189 wounded and 749 missing.

TIGER HEAD
The Story of the 26th Indian Division
Arakan, Ragoon

9781474537452

This is a history of the division said later by the Japanese to have been the opponent which they most feared. The 26th held the Allied monsoon line in the Arakan during two such seasons, repulsing every attack launched against it. Later it made a series of leap-frog landings down the coast to clinch the issue in the Arakan. It was the first division to enter Ragoon, invading the city from the sea.

THE TWENTY THIRD INDIAN DIVISION
"The Fighting Cock Division"
Burma, Malaya, Java

9781474537469

The Fighting Cock Division is well recorded in the book by Doulton. This book gives coverage of the heavy fighting at the Kohima Battle, the capture of Tamu, the reoccupation of Malaya in August 1945, and then its strange role on the island of Java – concurrently disarming the Japanese garrison, fighting the insurgent Indonesian nationalists, and caring for 65,000 former internees pending the arrival of a new Dutch administration.

A HAPPY FAMILY
The Story of the Twentieth Indian Division,
9781474537476

One of the few Indian divisions in the 14th Army trained specifically for the war in Burma. Raised in Bangalore in 1942, it commenced active operations in late 1943 and served from Imphal through to the end. It established the 14th Army's first brigade-head across the Chindwin and its second such brigade-head across the Irrawaddy. Its final task was to round up the Japanese in French Indochina.

TEHERAN TO TRIESTE
The Story of the Tenth Indian Division
9781783317028

This History deals with the 10th Indian Div's exploits in Iraq (under Maj Gen "Bill" Slim) its role in the Libyan battles leading up to El Alamein, the following two years of garrison duties in Cyprus and Syria, and finally, its fighting services in the Italian campaign (from Ortona onwards).

THE STORY OF THE 25th INDIAN DIVSION
The Arakan Campaign
9781783317585

Formed in Southern India in August 1942 for defence of that area in case of Japanese invasion, the "Ace of Spades" Division had its baptism of fire in Arakan in February 1944. It served throughout the remainder of that campaign the climax being the battle of Tamandu. Its victorious fight for the Kangaw roadblock was considered by many to have been the fiercest battle of the entire Burma war, while its liberation of Akyab was the first convincing proof to the rest of the world that the tide had turned against the Japanese.

DAGGER DIVISION
The Story of the 19th Indian Division
9781783317035

Raised in the late 1941, the 19th was the first "standard" Indian Division. Its troops were the first to breach the Japanese defence line in Burma and to raise the flag at Fort Dufferin. It crossed the Chindwin in November 1944, driving on to Mandalay and Ragoon during seven months of continuous fighting. The 19th's exploits are graphically described also in John Masters' personal memoir, *The Road Past Mandalay*.

www.ingramcontent.com/pod-product-compliance
Lightning Source LLC
Chambersburg PA
CBHW060417300426
44111CB00018B/2877